Created Equal

A History of the United States

Fifth Edition

Volume 2

Since 1865

Jacqueline Jones
University of Texas at Austin

Peter H. Wood
Duke University

Thomas Borstelmann
University of Nebraska

Elaine Tyler May
University of Minnesota

Vicki L. Ruiz
University of California, Irvine

PEARSON

Boston   Columbus   Indianapolis   New York City   San Francisco
m   Cape Town   Dubai   London   Madrid   Milan   Munich   Paris   Montréal   Toronto   Delhi
Mexico City   São Paulo   Sydney   Hong Kong   Seoul   Singapore   Taipei   Tokyo

Editor in Chief: Dickson Musslewhite
Executive Editor: Ed Parsons
Editorial Program Manager: Deb Hartwell
Director of Marketing: Brandy Dawson
Executive Marketing Manager: Wendy Albert
Production Managing Editor: Denise Forlow
Production Project Manager: Manuel Echevarria
Senior Operations Supervisor: Mary Fischer
Operations Specialist: Mary Ann Gloriande
Art Director: Maria Lange
Cover Design: Maria Lange

Cover: Awaiting examination, Ellis Island, 1907, Library of Congress LC-B201-5202-13
Digital Media Editor: Michael Halas
Digital Media Project Manager: Elizabeth Roden Hall
Content and Editorial Development: Ohlinger Publishing Services
Full-Service Project Management and Composition: SPi Global
Printer/Binder: RR Donnelley/Kendallville
Cover Printer: RR Donnelley/Kendallville
Text Font: 9.5/13 Palatino LT Pro Roman

Acknowledgments of third party content appear on pages 757–758, which constitute an extension of this copyright page.

Library of Congress Cataloging-in-Publication Data

Names: Jones, Jacqueline, 1948- author.
Title: Created equal : a history of the United States / Jacqueline Jones,
    University of Texas at Austin, Peter H. Wood, Duke University, Thomas
    Borstelmann, University of Nebraska, Elaine Tyler May, University of
    Minnesota, Vicki L. Ruiz, University of California, Irvine.
Description: Fifth edition. | Boston : Pearson, 2017. | Includes index.
Identifiers: LCCN 2015044008 | ISBN 9780134101972
Subjects: LCSH: United States—History. | United States—Social conditions. |
    United States—Politics and government. | Cultural pluralism—United
    States—History. | Minorities—United States—History. | Cultural
    pluralism—United States—History—Sources. | Minorities—United
    States—History—Sources.
Classification: LCC E178 .J767 2017 | DDC 973—dc23
LC record available at http://lccn.loc.gov/2015044008

10 9 8 7 6 5 4 3 2 1

Volume 1
ISBN 10: 0-13-410198-7
ISBN 13: 978-0-13-410198-9

Volume 2
ISBN 10: 0-13-410199-5
ISBN 13: 978-0-13-410199-6

Volume 1 à la carte:
ISBN 10: 0-13-432380-7
ISBN 13: 978-0-13-432380-0

Volume 2 à la carte:
ISBN 10: 0-13-432381-5
ISBN 13: 978-0-13-432381-7

Brief Contents

Contents

19 Visions of the Modern Nation: The Progressive Era, 1900–1912   472

20 War and Revolution, 1912–1920   494

21 All That Jazz: The 1920s   515

Preface

The fifth edition of *Created Equal* has a greatly strengthened focus on its overarching **theme of contested equality.** This emphasis on one theme renders the text a strikingly **more effective pedagogical tool.** Students will be more engaged and will appreciate the chance to think critically about the ongoing struggles over equal rights and the shifting boundaries of inclusion and acceptance. Amid all the new challenges of the twenty-first century, this unifying theme feels more relevant than ever.

> We hold these truths to be self-evident: That all men are created equal; that they are endowed by their Creator with certain unalienable rights; that among these are Life, Liberty, and the pursuit of Happiness.

Ever since the Continental Congress approved the Declaration of Independence on July 4, 1776, the noble sentiments expressed therein have inspired people in the United States and around the world. The Founding Fathers conceived of the new nation in what we today would consider narrow terms—as a political community of white men of property. Gradually, as the generations have unfolded, diverse racial and ethnic groups, as well as women of all backgrounds, have cited the Declaration in their struggles to achieve a more inclusive definition of American citizenship. American history is the story of various groups of men and women, all "created equal" in their common humanity, claiming an American identity for themselves.

In fact, the fabric of American history is distinguished by many major threads—territorial growth and expansion, the rise of the middle class, generations of technological innovation and economic development, and ongoing U.S. engagement with the wider world. *Created Equal* incorporates these traditional narratives into a new and fresh interpretation of American history, one that includes the stories of diverse groups of people, explores expanding notions of American identity, and employs a rich mix of history and analysis—in service of six principal outcomes:

- to demonstrate knowledge of the key events, people, institutions, and chronology of a diverse American nation [*Basic History*]

- to recognize the cultural, economic, diplomatic, and military relations between the United States and the rest of the world [*Global Context*]

- to distinguish the role of individuals—the famous and not-so-famous—in shaping American history [*Human Agency*]

- to engage with the contested meanings of equality over the course of American history [*Contested Equality*]

- to critically analyze primary and secondary sources—such as maps, documents, images, and graphs—across a variety of formats (text, images, videos, music) [*Historical Sources*]

- to make arguments based on historical fact and evidence of various kinds [*Historical Argument*]

New to This Edition
REVEL™

Educational technology designed for the way today's students read, think, and learn

When students are engaged deeply, they learn more effectively and perform better in their courses. This simple fact inspired the creation of REVEL: an immersive learning experience designed for the way today's students read, think, and learn. Built in collaboration with educators and students nationwide, REVEL is the newest, fully digital way to deliver respected Pearson content. REVEL enlivens course content with media interactives and assessments—integrated directly within the authors' narrative—that provide opportunities for students to read about and practice course material in tandem. This immersive educational technology boosts student engagement, which leads to better understanding of concepts and improved performance throughout the course. **Learn more about REVEL** at http://www.pearsonhighered.com/revel/.

Rather than simply offering opportunities to read about and study U.S. history, REVEL facilitates deep, engaging interactions with the concepts that matter most. By providing opportunities to improve skills in analyzing and interpreting primary and secondary sources of historical evidence, for example, REVEL engages students directly and immediately, which leads to a better understanding of course material. A wealth of student and instructor resources and interactive materials can be found within REVEL. Some of our favorites are mentioned in the paragraphs that follow.

- **Interactive Maps**

  Custom-built interactive maps, with locator insets, contextual hotspots, animated routes, chronological layers, and panning and zooming functionality, provide students with multiple ways of engaging with map visualizations.

- *Before You Begin/After You Finish* **Videos**

  Sixty short videos—positioned at the start and at the close of each chapter—capture the essential concepts and perspectives of *Created Equal.* The perfect tools for previewing and reviewing chapter content, our *Before* and *After* videos were developed and produced to help the *Created Equal* audience find its way into and through the full sweep of American history, from its earliest roots, which stretch back in time far before the settlement at St. Augustine, to the present day.

- **Integrated Writing Opportunities**

  To help students reason more logically and write more clearly, each chapter offers three varieties of writing prompts. *Journal prompts,* all of which tie in neatly to chapter imagery, are designed to elicit free-form topic-specific responses to questions that address matters of economic, cultural, and political power. *Shared Writing prompts* focus on issues of human agency. By encouraging students to share their viewpoints and respond to the viewpoints of others, the Shared Writing prompts in *Created Equal* are meant to let students see how their ideas about the distinguishing roles of individuals in shaping American history overlap. Finally, each chapter includes an *Essay prompt* from Pearson's Writing Space, where instructors can assign both automatic-graded and instructor-graded prompts.

- **Embedded Primary Source Documents**

  A curated collection of primary source documents accompanies each chapter, more than 150 documents in all.

* * * * *

For more information about all of the tools and resources in REVEL and access to your own REVEL account for *Created Equal,* Fifth Edition, go to http://www.pearsonhighered.com/REVEL/.

Signature Content, Revised and Updated

Welcome to the new, sleeker design of *Created Equal,* where a signature mix of content, graphics, storytelling, and exploration, combined with the interactive qualities of REVEL, provides a rich, immersive, clear-eyed view of U.S. history along with learning experiences designed to engage a diverse readership and improve critical thinking.

- **Improved Structure and Design**

  With the aim of providing students and instructors with a clear and accessible reading experience, the structure and design of the content in *Created Equal* has been reformulated with fewer distractions and clearer subheadings.

- **Chapter Introductory Vignettes**

  Chapter introductory vignettes provide brief firsthand accounts of individuals whose personal journeys share common ground with the themes of equality that characterize American history. Their journeys, often made more difficult, complicated, or exhausting by the struggle to achieve an inclusive definition of American citizenship, are the stories that *Created Equal* was specifically designed to tell.

- **Photographs, Figures, and Maps**

  Photographs, figures, and maps are bigger, more visually interesting, and instructive. Their captioning has been revised and reformatted to encourage students to look these illustrations with a critical eye and to answer, with reasoned opinion, questions that address their multiple layers of meaning. Where appropriate, new photos and new maps have been added and figures have been revised to accommodate new data.

- **Interpreting History Essays**

  Interpreting History essays are guided historical inquiries into primary sources that directly engage students with the singular voices of America's past. Every chapter features a full-page Interpreting History essay that relates the content of each chapter to the unique perspective of a particular person from a particular place and time.

- **Focus Questions and Chapter Reviews**

  Focus questions, which highlight important issues and themes in each chapter's main sections, are reconsidered in question-and-answer format in end-of-chapter reviews.

- **Timelines**

  Timelines reinforce the essential events in the narrative and clarify the chronology of the period.

- **Glossaries of Key Terms**

  A consolidated list of key terms has been added to the end of each chapter.

- **New Content and Data**

  Statistics on trade, income, population, and religious affiliation have been updated to reflect the latest data. Chapter 30, having undergone a particularly comprehensive review, has been revised to include new discussions of marriage equality, *Obergefell v. Hodges* (2015), ISIS, and the reopening of diplomatic relations with Cuba.

Key Supplements and Customer Support

Supplements for Instructors

Instructor's Resource Center. www.pearsonhighered.com/irc. This website provides instructors with additional text-specific resources that can be downloaded for classroom use. Resources include the Instructor's Resource Manual,

PowerPoint presentations, and the test item file. Register online for access to the resources for *Created Equal.*

Instructor's Manual. Available at the Instructor's Resource Center for download, www.pearsonhighered.com/irc, the Instructor's Manual contains detailed chapter overviews, including REVEL interactive content in each chapter, activities, resources, and discussion questions.

Test Item File. Available at the Instructor's Resource Center for download, www.pearsonhighered.com/irc, the Test Item File contains more than 2,000 multiple choice, true-false, and essay test questions.

PowerPoint Presentations. Strong PowerPoint presentations make lectures more engaging for students. Available at the Instructor's Resource Center for download, www.pearsonhighered.com/irc, the PowerPoints contain chapter outlines and full-color images of maps and art.

MyTest Test Bank. Available at www.pearsonmytest.com, MyTest is a powerful assessment generation program that helps instructors easily create and print quizzes and exams. Questions and tests can be authored online, allowing instructors ultimate flexibility and the ability to efficiently manage assessments anytime, anywhere! Instructors can easily access existing questions and edit, create, and store using simple drag-and-drop and Word-like controls.

Supplements for Students

CourseSmart. www.coursesmart.com. CourseSmart eTextbooks offer the same content as the printed text in a convenient online format—with highlighting, online search, and printing capabilities. You'll save 60 percent **over the list price** of the traditional book.

Books a la Carte. These editions feature the exact same content as the traditional printed text in a convenient, three-hole-punched, loose-leaf version at a discounted price—allowing you to take only what you need to class. You'll save 35 percent **over the net price** of the traditional book.

Library of American Biography Series. www.pearsonhighered.com/educator/series/Library-of-American-Biography/10493.page. Pearson's renowned series of biographies spotlighting figures who had a significant impact on American history. Included in the series are Edmund Morgan's *The Puritan Dilemma: The Story of John Winthrop*, B. Davis Edmond's *Tecumseh and the Quest for Indian Leadership*, J. William T. Young's *Eleanor Roosevelt: A Personal and Public Life*, and John R.M. Wilson's *Jackie Robinson and the American Dilemma*.

Prentice Hall American History Atlas. This full-color historical atlas designed especially for college students is a valuable reference tool and visual guide to American history. This atlas includes maps covering the scope of American history from the lives of the Native Americans to the 1900s. Produced by a renowned cartographic firm and a team of respected historians, it will enhance any American history survey course.

ISBN: 0321004868; ISBN-13: 9780321004864

About the Authors

Jacqueline Jones was born in Christiana, Delaware, a small town of 400 people in the northern part of the state. The local public school was desegregated in 1955, when she was a third grader. That event sparked her interest in American history. She received her undergraduate education at the University of Delaware and her Ph.D. in history at the University of Wisconsin, Madison. Her scholarly interests have evolved over time, focusing on American labor and women's, African American, and southern history. She teaches American history at the University of Texas at Austin, where she is the Mastin Gentry White Professor of Southern History and the Walter Prescott Webb Chair in History and Ideas. Dr. Jones is the author of several books. In 2001, she published a memoir that recounts her childhood in Christiana: *Creek Walking: Growing Up in Delaware in the 1950s*. Her most recent book is titled *A Dreadful Deceit: The Myth of Race from the Colonial Era to Obama's America* (2013). She is currently working on a biography of the radical labor agitator Lucy Parsons (1851–1942).

Peter H. Wood was born in St. Louis and recalls visiting the courthouse where the *Dred Scott* case originated. Emeritus professor of history at Duke University, he studied at Harvard and attended Oxford as a Rhodes Scholar. In 1974, he published the pioneering book *Black Majority*, concerning slavery in colonial South Carolina. He recently earned the Eugene Asher Distinguished Teaching Award of the American Historical Association. Topics of his articles range from the French explorer LaSalle to Gerald Ford's pardon of Richard Nixon. He has written a short overview of early African Americans, entitled *Strange New Land*, and he has published three books about the famous American painter Winslow Homer. Wood, who now lives in Longmont, Colorado, has served on the boards of the Highlander Center and Harvard University. His varied interests include archaeology, documentary film, and growing gourds. He keeps a baseball bat used by Ted Williams beside his desk.

Thomas ("Tim") Borstelmann grew up in North Carolina. His formal education came at Durham Academy, Phillips Exeter Academy, Stanford University (A.B., 1980), and Duke University (M.A., 1986; Ph.D., 1990). An avid cyclist, runner, swimmer, and skier, he taught history at Cornell University from 1991 to 2003, when he moved to the University of Nebraska-Lincoln to become the first E. N. and Katherine Thompson Distinguished Professor of Modern World History. Dr. Borstelmann's first book, *Apartheid's Reluctant Uncle: The United States and Southern Africa in the Early Cold War* (1993), won the Stuart L. Bernath Book Prize of the Society for Historians of Foreign Relations. His second book, *The Cold War and the Color Line: American Race Relations in the Global Arena*, appeared in 2001. He has won major teaching awards at both Cornell and Nebraska, and his most recent book is *The 1970s: A New Global History from Civil Rights to Economic Inequality* (2012). In 2015 he served as president of the Society for Historians of American Foreign Relations.

Elaine Tyler May developed a passion for American history in college when she spent her junior year in Japan. As an American student in Asia, she yearned for a deeper understanding of America's past and its place in the world. She returned home to study history at UCLA, where she earned her B.A., M.A., and Ph.D. She has taught at the University of Minnesota since 1978. Her widely acclaimed *Homeward Bound: American Families in the Cold War Era* was the first study to link the baby boom and suburbia to the politics of the Cold War. The *Chronicle of Higher Education* featured *Barren in the Promised Land: Childless Americans and the Pursuit of Happiness* as a pioneering study of the history of reproduction. Her most recent book is *America and the Pill: A History of Promise, Peril and Liberation*. Professor May served as president of the American Studies Association in 1996 and president of the Organization of American Historians in 2010.

Vicki L. Ruiz grew up in Florida. For her, history remains a grand adventure, one that she began at the kitchen table, listening to the Colorado stories of her mother and grandmother. The first in her family to receive an advanced degree, she graduated from Gulf Coast Community College and Florida State University, then went on to earn a Ph.D. in history at Stanford in 1982. She is the author of *Cannery Women, Cannery Lives* and *From Out of the Shadows: Mexican Women in 20th-Century America*. She and Virginia Sánchez Korrol have co-edited *Latinas in the United States: A Historical Encyclopedia*. She has participated in student mentorship projects, summer institutes for teachers, and public humanities programs. A fellow of the Society of American Historians, Dr. Ruiz was inducted into the American Academy of Arts and Sciences in 2012. Past president of the Organization of American Historians (2006), she is currently President of the American Historical Association, the flagship organization for historians across all fields with over 14,000 members. Since 2001, she has taught history and Chicano/Latino studies at the University of California, Irvine. The mother of two grown sons, she is married to Victor Becerra, an urban planner and community activist.

Acknowledgments

As authors, we could not have completed this project without the loving support of our families. We wish to thank Jeffrey Abramson, Lil Fenn, Lynn Borstelmann, Lary May, and Victor Becerra for their interest, forbearance, and encouragement over the course of several editions. Our own children have been a source of inspiration, as have our many students, past and present. We are grateful to scores of colleagues and friends who have helped shape this book, both directly and indirectly, in more ways than they know. Along the way, Matt Basso, Chad Cover, Robert Heinrich, Ryan Johnson, Deirdre Lannon, Jeff Manuel, Rob McGreevey, Eben Miller, Sharon Park, Andrea Sachs, Jason Stahl, Mary Strunk, Melissa Williams, and Patrick Wilz provided useful research and administrative assistance; their help was invaluable. Rob Heinrich is deserving of special thanks for his close read of the manuscript and proofs and research assistance. Louis Balizet provided careful reading of several chapter drafts.

We are grateful that Judy O'Neill, of Ohlinger Publishing Services, has been especially diligent and supportive at each stage in preparing this new edition.

Our friends at Pearson have continued their generous support and assistance for our efforts. We thank all the creative people associated with Pearson (and there are many) who have had a hand in bringing this book to life.

Chapter 15
Consolidating a Triumphant Union, 1865–1877

CHILDREN AT SCHOOL, CHARLESTON, SOUTH CAROLINA An illustration in *Harper's Weekly*, from December 15, 1866, shows African American pupils in a schoolroom in Charleston, South Carolina. After the Civil War, many southern black communities created, or enlarged and solidified, their own institutions, including schools and churches. At the same time, these communities pressed for full and equal citizenship rights.

The Library of Congress [LC-USZ62-117666]

Was there a conflict between freedpeople's goals of cultural and economic autonomy on the one hand and integration into the body politic on the other? Why or why not?

 ## Contents and Focus Questions

15.2 Claiming Territory for the Union
What human and environmental forces impeded the Republican goal of western expansion?

15.3 The Republican Vision and Its Limits
What were some of the inconsistencies in, and unanticipated consequences of, Republican notions of equality and federal power?

Why did a procession of black children through the streets of Savannah, Georgia, in January 1865 cause so much excitement?

The day of jubilee had come at last! In late December 1864, African American men, women, and children rejoiced when the troops of Union General William Tecumseh Sherman liberated the city. Savannah's black community immediately formed its own school system under the sponsorship of a new group, the Savannah Education Association (SEA). On the morning of January 10, 1865, just two weeks after Sherman's forces entered the city, several hundred black children gathered at the First African Baptist Church. From there they processed in a group to the Old Bryant Slave Mart where, surrounded by the trappings of slavery—whips, handcuffs, bills of receipt—they commenced their studies as free children.

The old slave market was just one of several schools opened by the SEA, which aimed to provide elementary schooling for 1,000 children. By late March, the group's leaders were hoping to receive aid from the U.S. Bureau of Refugees, Freedmen, and Abandoned Lands, a government agency created earlier that month to ease the transition between slavery and freedom for more than 3.5 million black people. Many southern blacks believed that a hallmark of freedom was the freedom to learn to read and write.

*   *   *   *   *

During the months and years immediately after the war, a major conflict raged between supporters of African American rights and supporters of southern white privilege. Republican congressmen hoped to *reconstruct* the South by enabling African Americans to own land and to become full citizens. Southern freedpeople sought to free themselves from white employers, landlords, and clergy, and to establish control over their own workplaces, families, and churches. In contrast, President Andrew Johnson appeared bent on *restoring* the antebellum power relations that made southern blacks dependent on white landowners.

After the war, the U.S. government sought to weld the whole nation into one political and economic unit. On the Plains and in the Northwest, Indians resisted white efforts to force them to abandon their nomadic way of life and take up sedentary farming. At the same time, the Civil War hardened the positions of the two major parties. The Republicans remained in favor of a strong national government and promoted a robust partnership between private enterprise and the federal government. The Democrats tended to support states' rights, which included regulating relations between employers and employees, whites and blacks.

Reconstruction era
The twelve years after the Civil War when the U.S. government took steps to integrate the eleven states of the Confederacy back into the Union.

The postwar years, now called the **Reconstruction era**, saw a spirited, often bitter, national debate about the meaning of equality as that concept applied to the rights of African Americans, women, workers, and Indians. Many whites argued that "equality" was not an absolute condition but, rather, a matter of degree; for example, just because freedmen were no longer slaves, should they be able to vote, sit on juries, or run for office? Women were not slaves, but should they be allowed to hold property and vote? The ongoing debate over these questions suggested that the military defeat of the South had only begun the process of consolidating the Union, North and South, East and West.

15.1 The Struggle over the South

How did various groups of Northerners and Southerners differ in their vision of the postwar South?

The Civil War had a devastating impact on the South in physical, social, and economic terms. Estimates of fatalities among southern soldiers amounted to 260,000 men, as many as 33 percent of the total who marched off to war. The region had lost an estimated

$2 billion in investments in slaves; modest homesteads and grand plantations alike lay in ruins; and gardens, orchards, and cotton fields were barren. More than 3 million former slaves eagerly embraced freedom, but the vast majority lacked the land, cash, and credit necessary to build family homesteads for themselves. Hoping to achieve social and economic self-determination, African American men and women traveled great distances, usually on foot, in efforts to locate loved ones and reunite families that had been separated during slavery. At the same time, landowning whites considered black people primarily as a source of agricultural labor; these whites resisted the idea that freedpeople should be granted citizenship rights.

In the North, Republican lawmakers disagreed among themselves how best to punish the defeated but defiant rebels. President Abraham Lincoln had indicated early that after the war the government should bring the South back into the Union quickly and painlessly. His successor wanted to see members of the southern planter elite humiliated, but resisted the notion that freedpeople should become independent of white landowners. In Congress, moderate and radical Republicans argued about how far the government should go in ensuring the former slaves' freedom. Nevertheless, most white Republicans agreed among themselves that black people should return to tilling the soil on plantations owned by their former masters.

During this period, the question of "equality" was a complicated one. Some whites, Northerners and Southerners, argued that the former slaves were completely equal to white people now that they were free. These whites believed that freedom from slavery did not necessarily mean that black people should be able to vote, hold office, or send their children to taxpayer-supported schools. Radical Republicans and blacks in general held that the federal government should guarantee certain basic rights that would provide freedpeople with a measure of economic opportunity, and some went further to suggest that meaningful economic opportunity would require a program of land re-distribution from former Confederates to former slaves. For their part, black people resisted a return to the gang system of labor, which seemed too close to the system of bondage they hoped to leave behind. Yet few whites, regardless of political loyalties, supported the notion of "social equality," which they defined as the ability of whites and blacks to become close friends on equal terms or to marry each other. A contest over the meaning of "equality" and "rights" shaped the postbellum (postwar) years in both the North and the South.

15.1.1 Wartime Preludes to Postwar Policies

Wartime experiments with African American free labor in Union-occupied areas foreshadowed bitter postwar debates. As early as November 1861, Union forces had occupied the Sea Islands off Port Royal Sound in South Carolina. In response, wealthy cotton planters fled to the mainland. Over the next few months, three groups of northern civilians landed on the Sea Islands with the intention of guiding blacks in the transition from slave to free labor. Teachers arrived intent on creating schools, and missionaries hoped to start churches. A third group, representing Boston investors, had also settled on the Sea Islands to assess economic opportunities; by early 1862, they decided to institute a system of wage labor that would reestablish a staple crop economy and funnel cotton directly into northern textile mills. The freed slaves, however, preferred to grow crops for their families to eat rather than cotton to sell, relying on a system of barter and trade among networks of extended families. Their goal was to break free of white landlords, suppliers, and cotton merchants.

Meanwhile, in southern Louisiana, the Union capture of New Orleans in the spring of 1862 enabled northern military officials to implement their own free (that is, non-slave) labor system. General Nathaniel Banks proclaimed that U.S. troops should forcibly relocate blacks to plantations "where they belong"; there they would continue to work for their former owners in the sugar and cotton fields, but now for wages supposedly negotiated annually. The Union army would compel blacks to work if they resisted doing so. In defiance of these orders, however, some blacks went on strike for higher wages, and others refused to work at all. Moreover, not all Union military men relished the prospect of forcing blacks to work on the plantations where they had been enslaved. Thus, federal policies returning blacks to plantations remained contested even within the ranks of the army itself.

The Lincoln administration had no hard-and-fast policy to guide congressional lawmakers looking toward the postwar period. In December 1863, the president outlined his Ten Percent Plan. This plan would allow former Confederate states to form new state governments once 10 percent of the men who had voted in the 1860 presidential election had pledged allegiance to the Union and renounced slavery. Congress instead passed the Wade-Davis Bill, which would have required a majority of southern voters in any state to take a loyalty oath affirming their allegiance to the United States. By refusing to sign the bill before Congress adjourned, Lincoln vetoed the measure (through a **pocket veto**). However, the president approved the creation of the **Freedmen's Bureau** in March 1865. The bureau was responsible for coordinating relief efforts on behalf of blacks and poor whites loyal to the Union, for sponsoring schools, and for implementing a labor contract system on southern plantations. At the time of his assassination, Lincoln seemed to be leaning toward giving the right to vote to southern black men.

pocket veto

An indirect veto of a legislative bill made when an executive (such as a president or governor) simply leaves the bill unsigned, so that it dies after the adjournment of the legislature.

Freedmen's Bureau

Federal agency created by Congress in March 1865 and disbanded in 1869. Its purposes were to provide relief for Southerners who had remained loyal to the Union during the Civil War, to support black elementary schools, and to oversee annual labor contracts between landowners and field hands.

FREEDMEN'S BUREAU, BEAUFORT, SOUTH CAROLINA Freedmen's Bureau agents distributed rations to former slaves and southern whites who had remained loyal to the Union. Agents also sponsored schools, legalized marriages formed under slavery, arbitrated domestic disputes, and oversaw labor contracts between workers and landowners. The bureau faced many challenges; it was chronically understaffed, and many freedpeople lived on isolated plantations, far from the scrutiny of bureau agents. But by 1869 the bureau had ceased to exist.

Historical/Corbis

Can you speculate about the way this building was used before and during the war? How do you think southern whites reacted to the various roles and responsibilities of bureau agents?

15.1.2 Presidential Reconstruction, 1865–1867

When Andrew Johnson, the seventeenth president of the United States, assumed office in April 1865 after Lincoln's death, he brought his own agenda for the defeated South. Throughout his political career, Johnson had seen himself as a champion of poor white farmers in opposition to the wealthy planter class. A man of modest background, he had been elected U.S. senator from Tennessee in 1857. He alone among southern senators remained in Congress and loyal to the Union after 1861. Lincoln first appointed Johnson military governor of Tennessee when that state was captured by the Union in 1862 and then tapped him as his running mate for the election of 1864.

Soon after he assumed the presidency, Johnson disappointed congressional Republicans who hoped that he would serve as a champion of the freedpeople. The new president had no interest in black equality. He welcomed back into the Union those states reorganized under Lincoln's Ten Percent Plan. He advocated denying the vote to wealthy Confederates, though he would allow individuals to come to the White House to beg the president for special pardons. Johnson also outlined a fairly lenient plan for readmitting the other rebel states into the Union. Poor whites would have the right to vote, but they must convene special state conventions that would renounce secession and accept the Thirteenth Amendment abolishing slavery. Further, they must repudiate all Confederate debts. The president opposed granting the vote to former slaves; he believed that they should continue to toil as field workers for white landowners.

Johnson failed to anticipate the speed and vigor with which former Confederate leaders would move to reassert their political authority. In addition, he did not gauge accurately the resentment of congressional Republicans, who thought his policies toward the defeated South were too forgiving. The southern states that took advantage of Johnson's reunification policies passed so-called **Black Codes**. These state laws were an ill-disguised attempt to institute a system of near-slavery. They aimed to penalize "vagrant" blacks, defined as those who did not work in the fields for whites, and to deny blacks the right to vote, serve on juries, or in some cases even own land. The Black Code of Mississippi restricted the rights of a freedperson to "keep or carry firearms," ammunition, and knives and to "quit the service of his or her employer before the expiration of his or her term of service without good cause." The vagueness of this last provision threatened any blacks who happened not to be working under the supervision of whites at any given moment. People arrested under the Black Codes faced imprisonment or forced labor.

Black Codes
Southern state laws passed after the Civil War to limit the rights and actions of newly liberated African Americans.

At the end of the Civil War, congressional Republicans were divided by their commitment (or lack thereof) to various forms of black equality. Radicals wanted to use strong federal measures to advance black people's civil rights and economic independence. In contrast, moderates were more concerned with the free market and private property rights; they took a hands-off approach regarding former slaves. But members of both groups reacted with outrage to the Black Codes. Moreover, when the legislators returned to the Capitol in December 1865, they were in for a shock: among their new colleagues were four former Confederate generals, five colonels, and other high-ranking members of the Confederate elite, including former Vice President Alexander Stephens, now under indictment for treason. All of these rebels were duly elected senators and representatives from southern states. In a special session called for December 4, a joint committee of fifteen lawmakers (six senators and nine members of the House) voted to bar these men from Congress.

By January 1865, both houses of Congress had approved the Thirteenth Amendment to the Constitution, abolishing slavery. The necessary three-fourths of the states ratified the measure by the end of the year. However, President Johnson was becoming more openly defiant of his congressional foes who favored aggressive federal protection of black civil rights. He vetoed two crucial pieces of legislation: an extension and expansion of the Freedmen's Bureau and the Civil Rights Bill of 1866. This latter measure was an unprecedented piece of legislation. It called on the federal government—for the first time in history—to protect individual rights against the willful indifference of the states (as manifested, for example, in the Black Codes). Congress managed to override both vetoes by the summer of 1866.

In June of that year, Congress passed the Fourteenth Amendment. This amendment guaranteed the former slaves citizenship rights, punished states that denied citizens the right to vote, declared the former rebels ineligible for federal and state office, and voided Confederate debts. This amendment was the first to use gender-specific language, guarding against denying the vote "to any of the male inhabitants" of any state.

Even before the war ended, certain groups of Northerners had moved south, and the flow increased in 1865. Black and white teachers volunteered to teach the former slaves to read and write. Some Northerners journeyed south to invest in land and become planters in the staple crop economy. White southern critics called all these migrant **carpetbaggers**. This derisive term suggested that the Northerners hastily packed their belongings in rough bags made of carpet scraps and then rushed south to take advantage of the region's devastation and confusion. To many freedpeople, whether they worked for a carpetbagger or a Southerner, laboring in the cotton fields was but a continuation of slavery.

Some former southern (white) Whigs, who had been reluctant secessionists, now found common ground with northern Republicans who supported government subsidies for railroads, banking institutions, and public improvements. This group consisted of some members of the humbled planter class as well as men of more modest means. Southern Democrats, who sneered at any alliances with the North, scornfully labeled these whites **scakawags** (the term referred to a scrawny, useless type of horse on the Scottish island of Scalloway).

Soon after the war's end, southern white vigilantes launched a campaign of violence and intimidation against freedpeople who dared to resist the demands of white planters and other employers. Calling itself the Ku Klux Klan, a group of Tennessee war veterans soon became a white supremacist terrorist organization and spread to other states. In May 1866, violence initiated by white terrorists against blacks in Memphis, Tennessee, left forty-six freedpeople and two whites dead, and in July, a riot in New Orleans claimed the lives of thirty-four blacks and three of their white allies. These bloody encounters demonstrated the lengths to which ex-Confederates would go to reassert their authority and defy the federal government.

Back in Washington, Johnson vetoed the Fourteenth Amendment, traveling around the country and urging the states not to ratify it. He argued that policies related to black suffrage should be decided by the states. The time had come for reconciliation between the North and South, maintained the president. (The amendment would not be adopted until 1868.) Johnson's opposition to the amendment revealed how thoroughly questions of black equality had become enmeshed in postbellum politics. Those questions did not necessarily reveal a partisan divide, however; the views of Johnson and other conservative Republicans were similar to those of southern Democrats in many respects.

Congressional Republicans fought back. In the election of November 1866, they won a two-thirds majority in both houses of Congress. These numbers allowed them to claim a mandate from their constituents and to override any future vetoes by the president. Moderates and radicals together prepared to bypass Johnson to shape their own Reconstruction policies.

carpetbaggers
A negative term applied by Southerners to Northerners who moved to the South after the Civil War to pursue political or economic opportunities.

scakawags
A negative term applied by southern Democrats after the Civil War to any white Southerners who allied with the Republican party.

15.1.3 The Postbellum South's Labor Problem

While policymakers maneuvered in Washington, black people throughout the postbellum South aspired to labor for themselves and gain independence from white overseers and landowners. Yet white landowners persisted in regarding blacks as field hands who must be coerced into working. With the creation of the Freedmen's Bureau in 1865, Congress intended to form an agency that would mediate between these two groups. Bureau agents encouraged workers and employers to sign annual labor contracts designed to eliminate the last vestiges of the slave system. All over the South, freed men, women, and children would contract with an employer on January 1 of each year. They would agree to work for either a monthly wage, an annual share of the crop, or some combination of the two.

According to the Freedmen's Bureau, the benefits of the annual labor contract system were clear. Employers would have an incentive to treat their workers fairly—to offer a decent wage and refrain from physical punishment. Disgruntled workers could leave at the end of the year to work for a more reasonable landowner. In the postbellum South, however, labor relations were shaped not by federal decree but by a process of negotiation that pitted white landowners against blacks who possessed little but their own labor.

For instance, blacks along the Georgia and South Carolina coast were determined to cultivate the land on which their forebears had lived and died. They urged General Sherman to confiscate the land owned by rebels in the area. In response, in early 1865, Sherman issued Field Order Number 15, mandating that the Sea Islands and the coastal region south of Charleston be divided into parcels of 40 acres for individual freed families. He also decreed that the army might lend mules to these families to help them begin planting. Given the provisions of this order, many freed families came to expect that the federal government would grant them "forty acres and a mule."

As a result of Sherman's order, 20,000 former slaves proceeded to cultivate the property once owned by Confederates. Within a few months of the war's end, however, the War Department bowed to pressure from white landowners and revoked the order. The War Department also provided military protection for whites to return and occupy their former lands. In response, a group of black men calling themselves Commissioners from Edisto Island (one of the Sea Islands) met in committee to protest to the Freedmen's Bureau what they considered a betrayal. Writing from the area in January 1866, one Freedmen's Bureau official noted that the new policy must be upheld but regretted that it had brought the freedpeople into "collision" with "U.S. forces."

The Commissioners from Edisto Island, together with black people all over the South, recognized the hollowness of their freedom—the limits to their "equality"—without the ability to own land. Lacking cash or credit, they had few options but to return to the cotton fields, now as sharecroppers. Lacking literacy skills, they could not aspire to many of the better jobs that whites held. The Freedmen's Bureau, the chief government agency that was supposed to ensure a measure of fairness in white landowners' relations with black workers, was short-lived.

During its brief life (1865 to 1869), the Freedmen's Bureau compiled a mixed record. The individual agents represented a broad range of backgrounds, temperaments, and political ideas. Some were former abolitionists who considered northern-style free labor to be "the noblest principle on earth." These men tried to ensure safe and fair working arrangements for black men, women, and children. In contrast, some agents had little patience with the freedpeople's drive for self-sufficiency. Some bureau offices became havens for blacks seeking redress against abusive or fraudulent labor practices, but other offices had little impact on the postwar political and economic landscape. For agents without means of transportation (a reliable horse), plantations scattered throughout the vast rural South remained outside their control. Because white landowners crafted the wording and specific provisions of labor contracts, the bureau agents who enforced such agreements often served the interests of employers rather than laborers.

The outlines of sharecropping, a system that defined southern cotton production until well into the twentieth century, were visible just a few years after the Civil War. Poor families, black and white, contracted annually with landlords, who advanced them supplies, such as crop seed, mules, plows, food, and clothing. Fathers directed the labor

Interpreting History

M. C. Fulton: An Appeal of a Georgia Planter to a Freedmen's Bureau Officer (1866)

"Poor white women have to work—so should all poor people—or else stealing must be legalized."

In April 1866, M. C. Fulton, a white planter living near Thomson, Georgia, wrote to Brigadier General Davis Tillson, the head of the Freedmen's Bureau in Georgia, appealing for help in getting black women back to work in the fields in time for spring cotton planting.

Dear Sir—Allow me to call your attention to the fact that most of the Freedwomen who have husbands are not at work—never having made any contract at all—their husbands are at work, while they are as nearly as idle as it is possible for them to be, pretending to spin—knit or something that really amounts to nothing for their husbands have to buy them clothing. . . .

Now these women have always been used to working out & it would be far better for them to go to work for reasonable wages & their rations—both in regard to health & in furtherance of their family wellbeing. . . . It is impossible for one man to do this [work] & maintain his wife in idleness without stealing more or less of their support, whereas if their wives (where they are able) were at work for rations & fair wages—which they can all get; the family could live in some comfort and more happily—besides their labor is a very important percent of the labor of the South. . . .

Now & then there is a woman who is not able to work in the field—or has 3 or 4 children at work & can afford to live on her childrens labor—with that of her husband—Even in such a case it would be better she should be at work—Generally however most of them should be in the field—Could not this matter be referred to your agents[?] They are generally clever men and would do right. I would suggest that you give this matter your

SHARECROPPERS AT WORK After the Civil War, many rural southern blacks, such as those shown here, continued to toil in cotton fields owned by whites. As sharecroppers, these workers made very little in cash wages, and even when they did accumulate some money, many learned that whites would not sell them land.

Library of Congress Prints and Photographs Division [LC-USZ62-45067]

What were the limits of Reconstruction as a federal program designed to assist freed slaves to become truly free?

favorable consideration & if you can do so to use your influence to make these idle women go to work. You would do them & the country a service besides gaining favor & the good opinion of the people generally.

I beg you will not consider this matter lightly for it is a very great evil & one that the Bureau ought to correct—if they wish the Freedmen & women to do well. . . . I am very respectfully your ob[edien]t servant

M. C. Fulton

Fulton added a postscript:

These idle women are bad examples to those at work & they are often mischief makers—having no employment their brain becomes more or less the Devil's workshop as is always the case with idle people—black or white. . . .

Such people are generally a nuisance—& ought to be reformed if possible or forced to work for a support. . . . Poor white women have to work—so should all poor people—or else stealing must be legalized—or tolerated for it is the twin sister of idleness. . . .

Questions for Discussion

1. How does Fulton define "idleness"? Why does he believe that women who stay home and care for their families are not really working?

2. Is Fulton making a race-based or a class-based argument in his appeal to Tillson? Explain.

3. Does Fulton have good reason for assuming—or hoping—that Tillson will be responsive to this letter?

SOURCE: M. C. Fulton to Brig. Gen. Davis Tillson, 17 April 1866, Unregistered Letters.

of their children in the fields. At the end of the year, many families remained indebted to their employer and, thus, entitled to nothing and obliged to work another year in the hope of repaying the debt. If a sharecropper's demeanor or work habits displeased the landlord, the family faced eviction.

Single women with small children were especially vulnerable to the whims of landlords in the postbellum period. Near Greensboro, North Carolina, for example, planter Presley George Sr. settled accounts with his field worker Polly at the end of 1865. For her year's expenses, Polly was charged a total $69 for corn, cloth, thread, and board for a child who did not work. By George's calculations, Polly had earned exactly $69 for the labor she and her three children (two sons and a daughter) performed in the course of the year, leaving her no cash of her own. Under these harsh conditions, freedpeople looked to each other for support and strength.

15.1.4 Building Free Communities

Independence in the workplace was not the only concern of freedpeople. Soon after the war's end, southern blacks set about organizing themselves as an effective political force and as free communities devoted to the social and educational welfare of their own people. Differences among blacks based on income, jobs, culture, and skin color at times inhibited institution-building. Some black communities found themselves divided by class, with blacks who had been free before the war (including many literate and skilled light-skinned men) assuming leadership over illiterate field hands. In New Orleans, a combination of factors contributed to class divisions among people of African heritage. During the antebellum period, light-skinned free people of color, many of whom spoke French, were much more likely to possess property and a formal education than were enslaved people, who were dark-skinned English speakers. After the Civil War, the more privileged group pressed for public accommodations laws, which would open the city's theaters, opera, and expensive restaurants to all blacks for the first time. However, black churches and social organizations remained segregated according to class. Few black people expected that the end of slavery would usher in a time and place where all blacks would be equal to one another in terms of their wealth or material condition.

For the most part, postbellum black communities united around the principle that freedom from slavery should also mean full citizenship rights: the ability to vote, own land, and educate their children. These rights must be enforced by federal firepower: "a military occupation will be absolutely necessary," declared the blacks of Norfolk, "to protect the white Union men of the South, as well as ourselves." Freedpeople in some states allied themselves with white yeomen who had long resented the political power of the great planters and now saw an opportunity to use state governments as agents of democratization and economic reform.

Networks of freedpeople formed self-help organizations. Like the sponsors of the Savannah Education Association, blacks throughout the South formed committees to raise funds and hire teachers for neighborhood schools. Small Georgia towns, such as Cuthbert, Albany, Cave Spring, and Thomasville, with populations no greater than a few hundred, raised up to $70 per month and contributed as much as $350 each for the construction of school buildings. Funds came from the proceeds of fairs, bazaars, and bake sales; subscriptions raised by local school boards; and tuition fees. In the cash-starved postbellum South, these amounts represented a great personal and group sacrifice for the cause of education.

All over the South, black families charted their own course. They elected to take in orphans and elderly kin, pool resources with neighbors, and arrange for mothers to stay home with their children. These choices challenged the power of former slaveholders and the influence of Freedmen's Bureau agents and northern missionaries and teachers. At the same time, in seeking to attend to their families and to provide for themselves, southern blacks resembled members of other mid-nineteenth-century laboring classes who valued family ties over the demands of employers and landlords.

Tangible signs of the new emerging black communities infuriated most southern whites. A schoolhouse run by blacks proved threatening in a society where most white children had little opportunity to receive an education. Black communities were also quick to form their own churches, rather than continue to occupy an inferior place in white churches. Other sights proved equally unsettling: on a main street in Charleston, an armed black soldier marching proudly or a black woman wearing a fashionable hat and veil, the kind favored by white women of the planter class. These developments help to account for the speed with which whites organized themselves in the Klan and various other vigilante groups, aiming to preserve "the supremacy of the white race in this Republic."

15.1.5 Congressional Reconstruction: The Radicals' Plan

The rise of armed white supremacist groups in the South helped spur congressional Republicans to action. On March 2, 1867, Congress seized the initiative. A coalition led by two radicals, Senator Charles Sumner of Massachusetts and Congressman Thaddeus Stevens of Pennsylvania, prodded Congress to pass the **Reconstruction Act of 1867**. The purpose of this measure was to purge the South of disloyalty once and for all. The act stripped thousands of former Confederates of voting rights. The former Confederate states would not be readmitted to the Union until they had ratified the Fourteenth Amendment and written new constitutions that guaranteed black men the right to vote. The South (with the exception of Tennessee, which had ratified the Fourteenth Amendment in 1866) was divided into five military districts. Federal troops were stationed throughout the region. These troops were charged with protecting Union personnel and supporters in the South and with restoring order in the midst of regional political and economic upheaval. In essence, the radicals' plan yoked southern states' readmission to the Union with a pledge to protect the political equality of blacks.

Congress passed two additional acts specifically intended to secure congressional power over the president. The intent of the Tenure of Office Act was to prevent the president from dismissing Secretary of War Edwin Stanton, a supporter of the radicals. The other measure, the Command of the Army Act, required the president to seek approval for all military orders from General Ulysses S. Grant, the army's senior officer. Grant also was a supporter of the Republicans. Both of these acts probably violated the separation of powers doctrine as put forth in the Constitution. Together, they would soon precipitate a national crisis

During the Reconstruction period, approximately 2,000 black men of the emerging southern Republican party served as local elected officials, sheriffs, justices of the peace, tax collectors, and city councilors. Many of these leaders were of mixed ancestry, and many had been free before the war. They came in disproportionate numbers from the ranks of literate men, such as clergy, teachers, and skilled artisans. In Alabama, Florida, Louisiana, Mississippi, and South Carolina, black men constituted a majority of the voting public. Throughout the South, 600 black men won election to state legislatures. However, nowhere did blacks control a state government, although they did predominate in South Carolina's lower House. Sixteen black Southerners were elected to the U.S. Congress during Reconstruction. Most of those elected to Congress in the years immediately after the war were freeborn. However, among the nine men elected for the first time after 1872, six were former slaves. All of these politicians exemplified the desire among southern blacks to become active, engaged citizens.

Newly reconstructed southern state legislatures provided for public school systems, fairer taxation methods, bargaining rights of plantation laborers, racially

Reconstruction Act of 1867
An act that prevented the former Confederate states from entering the Union until they had ratified the Fourteenth Amendment and written new constitutions that guaranteed black men the right to vote. It also divided the South (with the exception of Tennessee, which had ratified the Fourteenth Amendment) into five military districts and stationed federal troops throughout the region.

Map 15.1 RADICAL RECONSTRUCTION

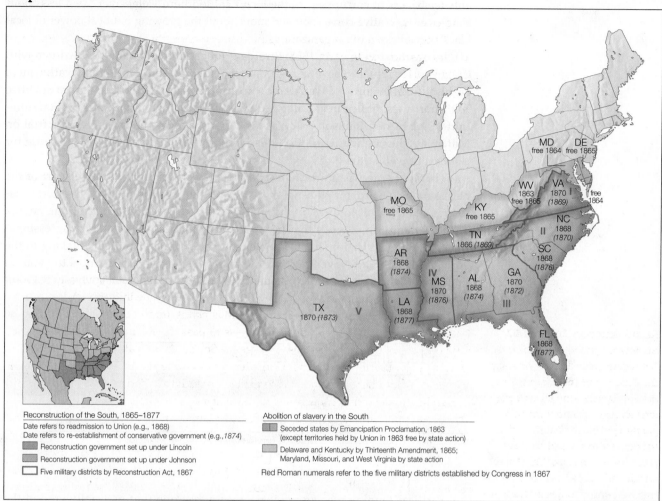

Reconstruction of the South, 1865–1877

Date refers to readmission to Union (e.g., 1868)
Date refers to re-establishment of conservative government (e.g.,*1874*)

Reconstruction government set up under Lincoln

Reconstruction government set up under Johnson

Five military districts by Reconstruction Act, 1867

Abolition of slavery in the South

Seceded states by Emancipation Proclamation, 1863
(except territories held by Union in 1863 free by state action)

Delaware and Kentucky by Thirteenth Amendment, 1865;
Maryland, Missouri, and West Virginia by state action

Red Roman numerals refer to the five military districts established by Congress in 1867

Four of the former Confederate states, Louisiana, Arkansas, Tennessee, and Virginia, were reorganized under President Lincoln's Ten Percent Plan in 1864. Neither this plan nor the proposals of Lincoln's successor, Andrew Johnson, provided for the enfranchisement of former slaves. In 1867 Congress established five military districts in the South and demanded that newly reconstituted state governments implement universal manhood suffrage. By 1870, all of the former Confederate states had rejoined the Union, and by 1877, all of those states had installed conservative (i.e., Democratic) governments.

integrated transportation systems and accommodations, and public works projects, especially railroads. These measures reflected the priorities among Republicans— to pass legislation that would, first, promote economic development and, second, yield a rough equality of economic opportunity among workers regardless of status or skin color. Enjoying a public education and some modest measure of job security should not be advantages for a favored few, black and white, Republicans argued. Some Democrats, hoping to appeal to poor white constituents on the one hand or to railroad interests on the other, at times joined with Republicans to pass certain measures.

Nevertheless, the legislative coalitions forged between Northerners and Southerners, blacks and whites, were uneasy and, in many cases, less than productive. Southern Democrats (and later, historians sympathetic to them) claimed that Reconstruction governments were uniquely corrupt, with some carpetbaggers, scalawags, and freedpeople vying for **kickbacks** from railroad and construction magnates. In fact, whenever state legislatures sought to promote business interests, they opened the door to the bribery

kickbacks

Money paid illegally in return for favors (for example, to a politician by a person or business that has received government contracts).

of public officials. In this respect, northern as well as southern politicians were vulnerable to charges of corruption. In the long run, southern Democrats cared less about charges of legislative corruption and more about the growing political power of local black Republican party organizations.

In Washington in early 1868, President Johnson forced a final showdown with Congress. He replaced several high military officials with more conservative men. He also fired Secretary of War Stanton, in apparent violation of the Tenure of Office Act. Shortly thereafter, in February, a newly composed House Reconstruction Committee impeached Johnson for ignoring the act, and the Senate began his trial on March 30. The president and Congress were locked in an extraordinary battle for political power.

The final vote was thirty-five senators against Johnson, one vote short of the necessary two-thirds of all senators' votes needed for conviction. Nineteen senators voted to acquit Johnson of the charges. Nevertheless, to win acquittal, he had had to promise moderates that he would not stand in the way of congressional plans for Reconstruction. Johnson essentially withdrew from policymaking in the spring of 1868. That November, with Republicans urging Northerners to "vote as you shot" (that is, to cast ballots against the former Confederates), Ulysses S. Grant was elected president.

Table 15.1 THE ELECTION OF 1868

Candidate	Political Party	Popular Vote (%)	Electoral Vote
Ulysses S. Grant	Republican	52.7	214
Horatio Seymour	Democratic	47.3	80

SOURCE: Historical Election Results, Electoral College, National Archives and Records Administration

Political reunion was an uneven process, but one that gradually eroded the newly won rights of former slaves in many southern states. By the end of 1868, Arkansas, North Carolina, South Carolina, Louisiana, Tennessee, Alabama, and Florida had met congressional conditions for readmission to the Union, and two years later, Mississippi, Virginia, Georgia, and Texas followed. The Fifteenth Amendment, passed by Congress in 1869 and ratified by the necessary number of states a year later, granted all black men the right to vote. However, in some states, such as Louisiana, reunification gave Democrats license to engage in wholesale election fraud and violence toward freed men and women. In 1870–1871, a congressional inquiry into the Klan exposed pervasive and grisly assaults on Republican schoolteachers, preachers, and prospective voters, black and white. The Klan also targeted men and women who refused to work like slaves in the fields. In April 1871, Congress passed the Ku Klux Klan Act, which punished conspiracies intended to deny rights to citizens. But Klan violence and intimidation had already taken their toll on Republican voting strength.

15.2 Claiming Territory for the Union

What human and environmental forces impeded the Republican goal of western expansion?

While blacks and whites, Northerners and Southerners clashed over power in the South, poet Walt Whitman celebrated the "manly and courageous instincts" that propelled a brave, adventurous people westward. Whitman hailed the march across the prairies and over the mountains as a cavalcade of progress. He and other Americans believed that the postbellum migration fulfilled a mission of national regeneration begun by the Civil War. Kansas's population grew by 240 percent in the 1860s, Nebraska's by 355 percent.

To unite the entire country together as a single economic and political unit was the Republican ideal. The railroads in particular served as vehicles of national integration. When the Central Pacific and Union Pacific met at Promontory Point, Utah, in 1869, the hammering of the spike that joined the two railroads produced a telegraphic signal received simultaneously on both coasts, setting off a national celebration.

Meanwhile, regular units of U.S. cavalry, including two regiments of blacks, were launching attacks on Indians on the Plains, in the Northwest, and in the Southwest. Between 1865 and 1890, U.S. military forces conducted a dozen separate campaigns against western Indian peoples and met Indian warriors in battle or attacked Indian settlements in more than 1,000 engagements.

In contrast to African Americans, who adamantly demanded their rights as American citizens, defiant western Indians battled a government to which they owed no allegiance. Indians did not lobby for the right to vote, sit on juries, or run for office; the notion of "equality" with whites meant little to them. They preferred to live apart from white society and to manage their own affairs rather than to push for political integration into the United States.

15.2.1 Federal Military Campaigns Against Western Indians

In 1871 the U.S. government renounced the practice of seeking treaties with various Indian groups. This change in policy opened the way for a more aggressive effort to subdue Native populations. It also hastened the expansion of the reservation system, an effort begun in the antebellum period to confine specific Indian groups to specific territories.

On the Plains, clashes between Indians and U.S. soldiers persisted after the Civil War. In 1867 at Medicine Lodge Creek in southern Kansas, the United States signed a treaty with an alliance of Comanche, Kiowa, Cheyenne, Arapaho, and Plains Apache. This treaty could not long withstand the provocation posed by the railroad, as Indians continued to attack the surveyors, supply caravans, and military escorts that preceded the railroad work crews. The year before, the Seventh U.S. Cavalry, under the command of Lieutenant Colonel George Custer, had been formed to ward off Indian attacks on the Union Pacific, snaking its way across the central Plains westward from Kansas and Nebraska. In November 1868, Custer destroyed a Cheyenne settlement on the Washita River, in present-day Oklahoma. Custer's men murdered women and children, burned tipis, and destroyed 800 horses.

The Apache managed to elude General George Crook until 1875. Crook employed some of these Apache to track down the war chief Geronimo of the Chiricahua. Like many other Indian leaders, Geronimo offered both religious and military guidance to his people. He believed that a spirit would protect him from the white man's bullets and from the arrows of Indians in league with government troops. Yet Geronimo was tricked into an initial surrender in 1877 and was held in irons for several months before gaining his release and challenging authorities for another nine years.

In 1874 Custer took his cavalry into the Black Hills of the Dakotas. Supposedly, the 1868 Treaty of Fort Laramie had rendered this land off-limits to whites. Custer's mission was to offer protection for the surveyors of the Northern Pacific Railroad and to force Indians onto reservations as stipulated in the 1868 treaty. However, the officer lost no time trumpeting the fact that Indian lands were filled with gold. This report prompted a rush to the Black Hills, lands sacred to the Sioux. Within two years, 15,000 gold miners had illegally descended on Indian lands to seek their fortunes. The federal government proposed buying the land, but leaders of the Sioux, including Red Cloud, Spotted Tail, and Sitting Bull, spurned the offer.

RAILROAD TAXIDERMIST'S BUF-FALO TROPHY HEADS With this 1870 photograph, the Kansas Pacific Railroad advertised the opportunity for western travelers to shoot buffalo from the comfort and safety of their railroad car. The company's official taxidermist shows off his handiwork. Railroad expansion facilitated the exploitation of natural resources while promoting tourism.

Art Resource, NY

What groups of people might have been eager to take advantage of the buffalo-hunting services offered by the Kansas Pacific Railroad?

During the morning of June 25, 1876, Custer and his force of 264 soldiers attacked a Sun Dance gathering of 2,500 Sioux and Cheyenne on the banks of the Little Big Horn River in Montana. Custer foolishly launched his attack without adequate backup, and he and his men were easily overwhelmed and killed by Indian warriors, led by the Oglala Sioux Crazy Horse and others. Reacting to this defeat, U.S. military officials reduced the Lakota and Cheyenne to wardship status, ending their autonomy.

Indians throughout the West maintained their distinctive ways of life during these turbulent times. Horse holdings, so crucial for hunting, trading, and fighting, varied from group to group, with the Crow wealthy in relation to their Central Plains neighbors the Oglala and the Arikara. Plains peoples engaged in a lively trading system. They exchanged horses and their trappings (bridles and blankets) for eastern goods such as kettles, guns, and ammunition. Despite their differences in economy, these groups held similar religious beliefs about an all-powerful life force that governed the natural world. People, plants, and animals were all part of the same order.

15.2.2 The Postwar Western Labor Problem

In 1865 the owners of the Central Pacific Railroad seemed poised for one of the great engineering feats of the nineteenth century. In the race eastward from California, they would construct trestles spanning vast chasms and roadbeds traversing mountains and deserts. Government officials in Washington were eager to subsidize the railroad. What the owners lacked was a dependable labor force. The Irish workers who began the line in California struck for higher wages in compensation for brutal, dangerous work. These immigrants dropped their shovels and hammers at the first word of a gold strike nearby—or far away. As a result, in 1866 the Central Pacific had decided to tap into a vast labor source by importing thousands of Chinese men from their native Guangdong province.

The Chinese labored to extend the railroad tracks eastward from Sacramento, California, up to ten miles a day in the desert, only a few feet a day in the rugged Sierra Nevada Mountains. In nerve-wracking feats of skill, they lowered themselves in woven

CHINESE IMMIGRANT RAILROAD LABORERS, SECRET TOWN, CALIFORNIA Chinese construction workers labor on the Central Pacific Railroad, around 1868. Many Chinese immigrants toiled as indentured laborers, indebted to Chinese merchant creditors who paid for their passage to California. Isolated in all-male work camps, crews of railroad workers retained their traditional dress, language, and diet. After the completion of the Transcontinental Railroad in 1869, some immigrants returned to China, and others dispersed to small towns and cities throughout the West.

Picture History/Newscom

From this photo, can you speculate about the engineering challenges faced by builders of western railroads?

baskets to implant nitroglycerine explosives in canyon walls. Chinese laborers toiled through snowstorms and blistering heat to blast tunnels and cut passes through granite mountains. With the final linking of the railroad in Utah in 1869, many Chinese sought work elsewhere in the West.

Signed in 1868, the Burlingame Treaty, named for Anson Burlingame, an American envoy to China, had supposedly guaranteed government protection for Chinese immigrants as visitors, traders, or permanent residents. Most immigrants were men. (Six out of ten California Chinese women were listed in the 1870 census as prostitutes, most the victims of their compatriots.) Yet the treaty did not inhibit U.S. employers, landlords, and government officials from discriminating against the Chinese.

By 1870, 40,000 Chinese lived in California and represented fully one-quarter of the state's wage earners. They found work in the cigar, woolen-goods, and boot and shoe factories of San Francisco; in the gold mining towns, now as laundry operators rather than as miners as they had before the Civil War; and in the fields as agricultural laborers. White workers began to cry unfair competition against this Asian group that was becoming increasingly integrated into the region's economy.

As a group, Chinese men differed from California Indians, who remained trapped in the traditional agricultural economy of unskilled labor. Whites appropriated Indian land and forced many men, women, and children to work as wage earners for large landowners. Deprived of their familiar hunting and gathering lands, and wracked by disease and starvation, California Indians had suffered a drastic decline in their numbers by 1870, from 100,000 to 30,000 in twenty years.

15.2.3 Land Use in an Expanding Nation

The Union's triumph in 1865 prompted new conflicts and deepened long-standing ones over the use of the land in a rich, sprawling country. In the South, staple crop planters began to share political power with an emerging elite, men who owned railroads and textile mills. Despairing of ever achieving antebellum levels of labor efficiency, some landowners turned to mining the earth and the forests for saleable commodities. These products, obtained through extraction, included phosphate (used in producing fertilizer), timber, coal, and turpentine. Labor in extractive industries complemented labor in the plantation economy. Sharecroppers alternated between tilling cotton fields in the spring and harvesting the crop in the fall, while seeking employment in sawmills and coal mines in the winter and summer.

As European Americans settled in the West and Southwest, they displaced natives who had been living there for generations. For example, the U.S. court system determined who could legally claim property. Western courts also decided whether natural resources such as water, land, timber, and fish and game constituted property that could be owned by private interests. In the Southwest, European American settlers, including army soldiers who had come to fight Indians and then stayed, continued to place Hispanic land titles at risk. Citing prewar precedents, American courts favored the claims of recent squatters over those of long-standing residents. In 1869, with the death of her husband (who had served as a general in the Union army), Maria Amparo Ruiz de Burton saw the large ranch they had worked together near San Diego slip out of her control. The first Spanish-speaking woman to be published in English in the United States, de Burton was a member of the Hispanic elite. Nevertheless, she had little political power. California judges backed the squatters who occupied the ranch.

As they controlled more land and assumed public office, some European Americans in the Southwest exploited their political connections and economic power. In the 1870s, the so-called Santa Fe Ring wrested more than 80 percent of the original Spanish grants of land from Hispanic landholders in New Mexico. An alliance of European American lawyers, businesspeople, and politicians, the Santa Fe Ring defrauded families and kin groups of their land titles and speculated in property to make a profit. Whereas many ordinary Hispanic settlers saw land—with its crops, pasture, fuel, building materials, and game—as a source of livelihood, groups such as the Santa Fe Ring saw land primarily as a commodity to be bought and sold.

Seemingly overnight, boom towns sprang up wherever minerals or timber beckoned: southern Arizona and the Rocky Mountains west of Denver, Virginia City in western Nevada, the Idaho–Montana region, and the Black Hills of South Dakota. In all these places, increasing numbers of workers operated sophisticated kinds of machinery, such as rock crushers. When the vein was exhausted or the forests depleted, the towns went bust.

Railroads facilitated not only the mining of minerals but also the growth of the cattle-ranching industry. Rail connections between the Midwest and East made it profitable for Texas ranchers to pay cowboys to drive their herds of long-horned steers to Abilene, Ellsworth, Wichita, or Dodge City, Kansas, for shipment to stockyards in Chicago or St. Louis. Cattle drives were huge; an estimated 10 million animals were herded north from Texas alone between 1865 and 1890. They offered employment to all kinds of men with sufficient skills and endurance. Among the cowhands were African American horsebreakers and gunmen and Mexicans skilled in the use of the *reata* (lasso). Blacks made up about 25 percent and Hispanos about 15 percent of all cowboy outfits.

Table 15.2 ESTIMATES OF RAILROAD CROSSTIES USED AND ACRES OF FOREST CLEARED, 1870–1910

Year	Miles of Track	Ties Renewed Annually (millions)	Ties Used on New Construction (millions)	Total Ties Annually (millions)	Acres of Forest Cleared (thousands)
1870	60,000	21	18	39	195
1880	107,000	37	21	58	290
1890	200,000	70	19	89	445
1900	259,000			91	455
1910	357,000			124	620

SOURCE: Michael Williams, *Americans and Their Forests* (Cambridge: Cambridge University Press, 1989), 352.

In knitting regional economies together, federal land policies were crucial to the Republican vision of a developing nation. The Mineral Act of 1866 granted title to millions of acres of mineral-rich land to mining companies, a gift from the federal government to private interests. The Timber Culture Act of 1873 allotted 160 acres to individuals in selected western states if they agreed to plant one-fourth of the acreage with trees. Four years later, the Desert Land Act provided cheap land if buyers irrigated at least part of their parcels.

The exploitation of western resources raised many legal questions: Must ranchers pay for the prairies their cattle grazed on and the trails they followed to market? How could one "own" a stampeding buffalo herd or a flowing river? What was the point of holding title to a piece of property if only the timber, oil, water, or minerals (but not the soil) were of value? The Apex Mining Act of 1872 sought to address some of these issues. This law legalized traditional mining practices in the West by validating titles approved by local courts. According to the law, a person who could locate the apex of a vein (its point closest to the surface) could lay claim to the entire vein beneath the surface. The measure contributed to the wholesale destruction of certain parts of the western landscape as mining companies blasted their way through mountains and left piles of rocks in their wake. It also spurred thousands of lawsuits as claimants argued over what constituted an apex or a vein.

It was during this period that a young Scottish-born naturalist named John Muir began to explore the magnificent canyons and mountains of California. He contrasted nature's majesty with the artificial landscape created by and for humans. In the wilderness, there is nothing "truly dead or dull, or any trace of what in manufactories is called rubbish or waste," he wrote; "everything is perfectly clean and pure and full of divine lessons."

Muir was gratified by the creation of the National Park system during the postwar period. Painters and geologists were among the first Easterners to appreciate the spectacular vistas of the western landscape. In 1864 Congress set aside a small area within California's Yosemite Valley for public recreation and enjoyment. Soon after the war, railroad promoters forged an alliance with government officials in an effort to block commercial development of particularly beautiful pockets of land. Northern Pacific Railway financier Jay Cooke lobbied hard for the government to create a 2-million-acre park in what is today the northwest corner of Wyoming. As a result, in March 1872, Congress established Yellowstone National Park. Tourism would continue to serve as a key component of the western economy.

Muir and others portrayed the Yosemite and Yellowstone valleys as wildernesses, empty of human activity. In fact, both areas had long provided hunting and foraging grounds for Native peoples. Yellowstone had been occupied by the people now called the Shoshone since the fifteenth century. This group, together with the Bannock, Crow, and Blackfoot, tried to retain access to Yellowstone's meadows, rivers, and forests after it became a national park. However, U.S. policymakers and military officials persisted in their efforts to mark off territory for specific commercial purposes, while Indians were confined to reservations.

15.2.4 Buying Territory for the Union

Before the war, Republicans had opposed any federal expansionist schemes that they feared might benefit slaveholders. However, after 1865 and the outlawing of slavery, some Republican lawmakers and administration officials advocated the acquisition of additional territory. Secretary of State William Seward led the way in 1867 by purchasing Alaska from Russia. For $7.2 million (about 2 cents an acre), the United States gained 591,004 square miles of land. Within the territory were diverse indigenous groups—Eskimo, Aleut, Tlingit, Tsimshian, Athabaskan, and Haida—and a small number of native Russians. Though derided at the time as "Seward's icebox," Alaska yielded enough fish, timber, minerals, oil, and water power in the years to come to prove that the original purchase price was a tremendous bargain.

The impulse that prompted administration support for the Alaska purchase also spawned other plans for territorial acquisitions. In 1870 some Republicans joined with Democrats in calling for the annexation of the Dominican Republic. These congressmen argued that the tiny Caribbean country would make a fine naval base, provide investment opportunities for American businesspeople, and offer a refuge for southern freedpeople. The abolitionist Frederick Douglass argued in favor of annexation as a way for the United States to establish a foothold in the Caribbean and thereby "strike a blow at slavery wherever it may exist in the tropics"—especially in the Spanish colony of Cuba.

However, influential Senator Charles Sumner warned against a takeover without considering the will of the Dominican people, who were currently involved in their own civil war. Some congressmen, in a prelude to foreign policy debates of the 1890s, suggested that the dark-skinned Dominican people were unequal to whites in intelligence and ambition and were therefore incapable of appreciating the blessings of American citizenship. In 1871 an annexation treaty failed to win Senate approval.

In facilitating western expansion, Republicans upheld the ideal that prosperity would come to all people who worked hard. Indians were not part of the Republican vision of western prosperity. But other groups also questioned the Republican vision as it affected their own interests.

15.3 The Republican Vision and Its Limits

What were some of the inconsistencies in, and unanticipated consequences of, Republican notions of equality and federal power?

After the Civil War, victorious Republicans envisioned a nation united in the pursuit of prosperity. All citizens would be free to follow their individual economic self-interest and to enjoy the fruits of honest toil. In contrast, some increasingly vocal and well-organized groups saw the expansion of legal rights, and giving black men the right to vote in particular, as only initial, tentative steps on the path to an all-inclusive citizenship. Women, industrial workers, farmers, and African Americans made up overlapping constituencies pressing for equal political rights and economic opportunity. Together they challenged the mainstream Republican view that defeat of the rebels and destruction of slavery were sufficient to guarantee prosperity for everyone.

Partnerships between government and business also produced unanticipated consequences for Republicans committed to what they believed was the collective good. Some politicians and business leaders saw these partnerships as opportunities for private gain. Consequently, private greed and public corruption accompanied postwar economic growth. Thus, Republican leaders faced challenges from two very different sources: people agitating for civil rights and people hoping to reap personal gain from political activities.

15.3.1 Postbellum Origins of the Women's Suffrage Movement

After the Civil War, the nation's middle class, which had its origins in the antebellum period, continued to grow. Dedicated to self-improvement and filled with a sense of moral authority, many middle-class Americans (especially Protestants) felt a deep cultural connection to their counterparts in England. Indeed, the United States produced its own "Victorians," so called for the self-conscious middle class that emerged in the England of Queen Victoria during her reign from 1837 to 1901.

At the heart of the Victorian sensibility was the ideal of domesticity: a harmonious family living in a well-appointed home, guided by a pious mother and supported by a father successful in business. Famous Protestant clergyman Henry Ward Beecher and his wife were outspoken proponents of this domestic ideal. According to Eunice Beecher, women had no "higher, nobler, more divine mission than in the conscientious endeavor to create a *true home*."

Yet the traumatic events of the Civil War only intensified the desire among a growing group of American women to participate fully in the nation's political life. They wanted to extend their moral influence outside the narrow and exclusive sphere of the home. Many women believed that they deserved the vote and that the time was right to demand it.

In 1866 veteran reformers Elizabeth Cady Stanton, Susan B. Anthony, and Lucy Stone founded the Equal Rights Association to link the rights of white women and African Americans. Nevertheless, in 1867, Kansas voters defeated a referendum proposing suffrage for both blacks and white women. This disappointment convinced some former abolitionists that the two causes should be separated—that women should wait patiently until the rights of African American men were firmly secured. Frederick Douglass declined an invitation to a women's suffrage convention in Washington, D.C., in 1868. He explained, "I am now devoting myself to a cause [if] not more sacred, certainly more urgent, because it is one of life and death to the long enslaved people of this country, and that is: negro suffrage." But African American activist and former slave Sojourner Truth warned, "There is a great stir about colored men getting their rights, but not a word about the colored women; and if colored men get their rights, and not colored women get theirs, there will be a bad time about it."

In 1869 two factions of women parted ways and formed separate organizations devoted to women's rights. The more radical wing, including Cady Stanton and Anthony, bitterly denounced the Fifteenth Amendment because it gave the vote to black men only. They helped to found the National Woman Suffrage Association (NWSA), which argued for a renewed commitment to the original Declaration of Sentiments passed in Seneca Falls, New York, two decades earlier. They favored married women's property rights, liberalization of divorce laws, opening colleges and trade schools to women, and a new federal amendment to allow women to vote. Lucy Stone and her husband, Henry Blackwell, founded the rival American Woman Suffrage Association (AWSA). This group downplayed the larger struggle for women's rights and focused on the suffrage question exclusively. Its members supported the Fifteenth Amendment and retained ties to the Republican party. The AWSA focused on state-by-state campaigns for women's suffrage.

In 1871 the NWSA welcomed the daring, flamboyant Victoria Woodhull as a vocal supporter, only to renounce her a few years later. Woodhull's political agenda ranged from free love and dietary reform to legalized prostitution, working men's rights, and women's suffrage. (In the nineteenth century, free love advocates denounced what they called a sexual double standard, one that glorified female chastity while tolerating male promiscuity.) In 1872 one of Woodhull's critics successfully challenged her. Woodhull spent a month in jail as a result of the zealous prosecution by vice reformer Anthony Comstock, a clergyman who objected to her public discussions and writings on sexuality. Comstock assumed the role of an outspoken crusader against vice. A federal law passed in 1873, and named after him, equated information related to birth control with pornography, banning this and other "obscene material" from the mails.

Susan B. Anthony used the 1872 presidential election as a test case for women's suffrage. She attempted to vote and was arrested, tried, and convicted as a result. By this time, most women suffragists, and most members of the NWSA for that matter, had become convinced that they should focus on the vote exclusively; they therefore accepted the AWSA's policy on this issue. In the coming years, they would avoid other related causes with which they might have allied themselves, including black civil rights and labor reform.

15.3.2 Workers' Organizations

Many Americans benefited from the economic changes of the postwar era. Railroading, mining, and heavy industry helped fuel the national economy and in the process boosted the growth of the urban managerial class. In the Midwest, many landowning farmers prospered when they responded to an expanding demand for grain and other staple crops. In Wisconsin, wheat farmers cleared forests, drained swamps, diverted rivers, and profited from the booming world market in grain. Yet the economic developments that allowed factory managers and owners of large wheat farms to make a comfortable living for themselves did not necessarily benefit agricultural and manufacturing wage-workers.

Indeed, during this period growing numbers of working people, in the countryside and in the cities, became caught up in a cycle of indebtedness. In the upcountry South (above the fall line, or Piedmont), formerly self-sufficient family farmers sought loans from banks to repair their war-damaged homesteads. To qualify for these loans, the farmer had to plant cotton as a staple crop, to the neglect of corn and other foodstuffs. Many sharecroppers, black and white, received payment in the form of credit only; for these families, the end-of-the-year reckoning yielded little more than rapidly accumulating debts. Midwestern farmers increasingly relied on bank loans to purchase expensive threshing and harvesting machinery.

Several organizations founded within five years of the war's end offered laborers an alternative vision to the Republicans' brand of individualism and nationalism. In 1867 Oliver H. Kelley, a former Minnesota farmer now working in a Washington office, organized the National Grange of the Patrons of Husbandry, popularly known as the **Grange**. This movement sought to address a new, complex marketplace increasingly dominated by railroads, banks, and grain elevator operators. The Grange encouraged farmers to form cooperatives that would market their crops and to challenge discriminatory railroad rates that favored big business.

Founded in Baltimore in 1866, the National Labor Union (NLU) consisted of a collection of craft unions and claimed as many as 600,000 members at its peak in the early 1870s. The group welcomed farmers as well as factory workers and promoted legislation for an eight-hour workday and the arbitration of industrial disputes.

In 1873 a nationwide depression threw thousands out of work and worsened the plight of debtors. Businesspeople in agriculture, mining, the railroad industry, and manufacturing had overexpanded their operations. The free-wheeling loan practices of major banks had contributed to this situation. The inability of these businesspeople to repay their loans led to the failure of major banks. With the contraction of credit, thousands of small businesses went bankrupt. The NLU did not survive the crisis.

However, by this time, a new organization had appeared to champion the cause of the laboring classes in opposition to lords of finance. Founded in 1869 by Uriah Stephens and other Philadelphia tailors, the Knights of Labor eventually aimed to unite industrial and rural workers, the self-employed and the wage earner, blacks and whites, and men and women. The Knights were committed to private property and to the independence of the farmer, the entrepreneur, and the industrial worker. The group banned from its ranks "nonproducers," such as liquor sellers, bankers, professional gamblers, stockbrokers, and lawyers.

This period of depression also laid the foundation for the Greenback Labor party, organized in 1878. Within three years after the end of the Civil War, the Treasury had withdrawn from circulation $100 million in wartime paper currency ("greenbacks"). With less money in circulation, debtors found it more difficult to repay their loans. The government also ceased coining silver dollars in 1873, despite the discovery of rich silver lodes in the West. To add insult to injury, the Resumption Act (1875) called for the government to continue to withdraw paper greenbacks. Thus, hard money became dearer, and debtors became more desperate. In 1878 the new Greenback Labor party managed to win 1 million votes and elect fourteen candidates to Congress. The party laid the foundation for the Populist party that emerged in the 1890s.

Grange

An organization founded by Oliver H. Kelley in 1867 to represent the interests of farmers by pressing for agricultural cooperatives, an end to railroad freight discrimination against small farmers, and other initiatives. Its full name was National Grange of the Patrons of Husbandry.

Several factors made coalition building among these American workers difficult. One was the nation's increasingly multicultural workforce. Unions, such as the typographers, were notorious for excluding women and African Americans, a fact publicized by both Frederick Douglass and Susan B. Anthony, to no avail. In 1869 shoe factory workers (members of the Knights of St. Crispin) went on strike in North Adams, Massachusetts. They were soon shocked to see seventy-five Chinese strikebreakers arrive by train from California. Their employer praised the new arrivals for their "rare industry." The shoemakers' strike collapsed quickly after the appearance of what the workers called this "Mongolian battery." Employers would continue to manipulate and divide the laboring classes through the use of ethnic, religious, and racial prejudices.

15.3.3 Political Corruption and the Decline of Republican Idealism

Out of the new partnership between politics and business emerged an extensive system of bribes and kickbacks. Greedy politicians of both parties challenged the Republicans' high-minded idealism.

In the early 1870s, the *New York Times* exposed the schemes of William M. "Boss" Tweed. Tweed headed Tammany Hall, a New York City political organization that courted labor unions and contributed liberally to Catholic schools and charities. Tammany Hall politicians routinely used bribery and extortion to fix elections and bilk taxpayers of millions of dollars. One plasterer employed on a city project received $138,000 in "payment" for two days' work. After the *Times* exposé, Tweed was prosecuted and convicted. His downfall attested to the growing influence of newspaper reporters.

Another piece of investigative journalism rocked the political world in 1872. In 1867 major stockholders of the Union Pacific Railroad had formed a new corporation, called the Crédit Mobilier, to build railroads. Heads of powerful congressional committees received shares of stock in the new company. These gifts of stock were bribes to secure the legislators' support for public land grants favorable to the new corporation. The *New York Sun* exposed a number of the chief beneficiaries in the fall of 1872, findings confirmed by congressional investigation. Among the disgraced politicians was Grant's vice president, Schuyler Colfax.

The 1872 presidential election pitted incumbent Grant against the Democratic challenger, *New York Tribune* editor Horace Greeley. Many Republicans, disillusioned with congressional corruption and eager to press forward with civil service reform, endorsed the Democratic candidate. Greeley and his Republican allies decried the patronage (or "spoils") system by which politicians rewarded their supporters with government jobs. Nevertheless, Grant won the election.

Table 15.3 THE ELECTION OF 1872

Candidate	Political Party	Popular Vote (%)	Electoral Vote
Ulysses S. Grant	Republican	55.6	286
Horace Greeley	Democratic, Liberal Republican	43.9	66

SOURCE: Historical Election Results, Electoral College, National Archives and Records Administration

By 1872, after four bloody years of war and seven squandered years of postwar opportunity, the federal government seemed prepared to hand the South back to unrepentant rebels. The North showed what one House Republican called "a general apathy among the people concerning the war and the negro." The **Civil Rights Act of 1875** guaranteed blacks equal access to public accommodations and transportation. Yet this act represented the final, half-hearted gesture of radical Republicanism. The Supreme Court declared the measure unconstitutional in 1883 on the grounds that the

Civil Rights Act of 1875
Congressional legislation that guaranteed black people access to public accommodations and transportation; the Supreme Court declared the measure unconstitutional in 1883.

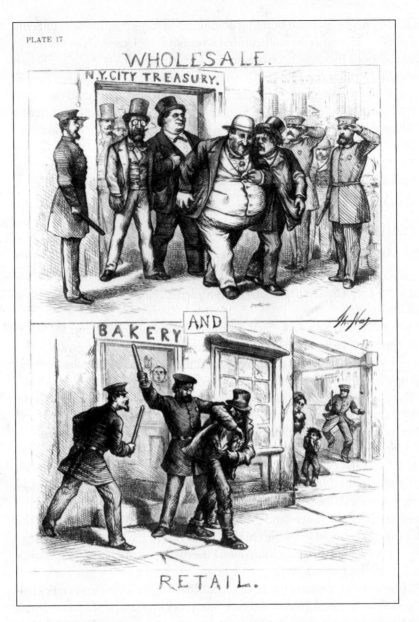

CORRUPTION AT TAMMANY HALL In 1871 Thomas Nast drew a series of cartoons exposing the corruption of New York City Democratic boss William M. Tweed and his political organization, Tammany Hall. In this drawing, published in *Harper's Weekly* in 1871, Nast depicts Tweed and his cronies engaging in a "wholesale" looting of the New York City treasury with the assistance of compliant police officers. Those same officers stand ready to crack down on the impoverished father who robs a bakery to feed his family. By portraying Tweed as an enemy of the poor, Nash ignored the fact that the political boss gained a large following among immigrant voters.

Thomas Nast/Library of Congress Prints and Photographs Division

What message was Nast trying to convey about the nature of urban political machines and the corruption they spawned?

government could protect only political and not social rights. White Southerners reasserted their control over the region's political economy.

The presidential election of 1876 intensified public cynicism about deal making in high places. A dispute over election returns led to what came to be known as the Compromise of 1877. In the popular vote, Democrat Samuel J. Tilden outpolled Republican Rutherford B. Hayes, a former Ohio governor. However, when the electoral votes were counted, the Democrat had only 184, one short of the necessary number. Nineteen of the twenty votes in dispute came from Louisiana, South Carolina, and Florida, and these three states submitted two new sets of returns, one from each of the two main parties. A specially appointed congressional electoral commission, the Committee of Fifteen, was charged with resolving the dispute. It divided along partisan lines. The eight Republicans outvoted the seven Democrats to accept the Republican set of returns from Florida.

To break the logjam, the Democrats agreed that Hayes could assume office in return for the withdrawal of all remaining federal troops from the South. The Republicans tacitly agreed that their work there was finished and that blacks in the region should fend for themselves. Hayes declined to enforce the Civil Rights Act of 1875. White Southerners were free to uphold the principle of states' rights that had been traditionally invoked to deny blacks their rights in the region. Thus the Civil War failed to solve one of the most pressing issues of the day—the relation between federal and state power in protecting the rights of individuals.

Table 15.4 THE ELECTION OF 1876

Candidate	Political Party	Popular Vote (%)	Electoral Vote
Rutherford B. Hayes	Republican	48.0	185
Samuel J. Tilden	Democratic	51.0	184

SOURCE: Historical Election Results, Electoral College, National Archives and Records Administration

Conclusion

During the dozen or so years after the Civil War, both northern Republicans and southern Democrats registered a series of spectacular wins and crushing losses. Though humiliated by the Union victory, southern white supremacists eventually won for themselves the freedom to control their own local and state governments. As landlords, sheriffs, and merchants, these men defied the postwar federal amendments to the Constitution and deprived African Americans of basic citizenship rights. By the end of Reconstruction, northern Republicans had conceded local power to their former enemies. Even an aggressive nationalism, it turned out, could accept traditional southern hierarchies: white over nonwhite, rich over poor.

Yet the Civil War was not only a fight between whites. During the conflict, black people had served as combatants in the struggle for freedom. They saw the war in different terms than did northern white Republicans and southern white Democrats. After the war, blacks pursued full citizenship rights while attempting to maintain institutional and cultural autonomy from white people regardless of political affiliation. In their quest, freed men and women met with mixed success. Black men gained the (formal) right to vote. Yet white Republicans, both in Congress and in southern state legislatures, proved to be disappointing allies to blacks who found themselves, increasingly, at the mercy of white vigilantes and other terrorist groups. During the Reconstruction period, blacks consolidated their families, established their own churches, and sought to work on their own terms in the fields. Yet lacking money and credit, they found it difficult to buy land and in the process achieve true independence from white landowners, bankers, and politicians.

At the end of Reconstruction, Republicans remained in firm control of national economic policy. The white South had secured its right to conduct its own political affairs, but the Republican vision of economic growth and development had become the law of the land. This vision was a guiding principle of historic national and, increasingly, international significance. Economic innovation in particular proved to be a force of great unifying power, stronger even than all the federal military forces deployed during and after the Civil War.

Chapter Review

15.1 The Struggle over the South

How did various groups of Northerners and Southerners differ in their vision of the postwar South?

Congressional Republicans united in opposition to President Johnson's conciliatory approach toward the South. They pushed for basic civil rights and a measure, at least, of economic independence for African Americans. White Southerners opposed black rights and sought to maintain their control over African American labor. Black Southerners, on the other hand, desired land ownership and freedom from white supervision. They set about reuniting their families, providing for themselves, and organizing themselves as an effective political force.

15.2 Claiming Territory for the Union

What human and environmental forces impeded the Republican goal of western expansion?

Republicans had to clear western land of the Indians who lived there and who fought to maintain their distinctive ways of life. Republicans also wanted to subsidize railroads to aid westward expansion, and owners, who lacked a dependable labor force, solved this problem by exploiting the labor of Chinese immigrants. Traversing mountains and canyons required the use of sophisticated engineering techniques. To manage the land and natural resources, Republicans passed legislation favorable to expansion, such as the Apex Mining Act of 1872.

15.3 The Republican Vision and Its Limits

What were some of the inconsistencies in, and unanticipated consequences of, Republican notions of equality and federal power?

Most Republicans believed that the defeat of the Confederacy and the destruction of slavery were sufficient to guarantee prosperity for everyone. Women, industrial workers, farmers, and African Americans, however, challenged this notion and pressed for equal political rights and economic opportunity. Partnerships between government and business produced unanticipated consequences, as private greed and public corruption accompanied economic growth.

Timeline

1865	Freedmen's Bureau is formed
	Thirteenth Amendment abolishing slavery is ratified
1868	Johnson is impeached and acquitted
	Fourteenth Amendment protecting civil rights is ratified
1869	Transcontinental Railroad is completed
	National Woman Suffrage Association and American Woman Suffrage Association are formed
1870	Fifteenth Amendment enfranchising black men is ratified
1873	Panic of 1873
1876	Battle of Little Big Horn
1877	Compromise of 1877

Glossary

Reconstruction era The twelve years after the Civil War when the U.S. government took steps to integrate the eleven states of the Confederacy back into the Union.

pocket veto An indirect veto of a legislative bill made when an executive (such as a president or governor) simply leaves the bill unsigned, so that it dies after the adjournment of the legislature.

Freedmen's Bureau Federal agency created by Congress in March 1865 and disbanded in 1869. Its purposes were to provide relief for Southerners who had remained loyal to the Union during the Civil War, to support black elementary schools, and to oversee annual labor contracts between landowners and field hands.

Black Codes Southern state laws passed after the Civil War to limit the rights and actions of newly liberated African Americans.

carpetbaggers A negative term applied by Southerners to Northerners who moved to the South after the Civil War to pursue political or economic opportunities.

scakawags A negative term applied by southern Democrats after the Civil War to any white Southerners who allied with the Republican party.

Reconstruction Act of 1867 An act that prevented the former Confederate states from entering the Union until they had ratified the Fourteenth Amendment and written new constitutions that guaranteed black men the right to vote. It also divided the South (with the exception of Tennessee, which had ratified the Fourteenth Amendment) into five military districts and stationed federal troops throughout the region.

kickbacks Money paid illegally in return for favors (for example, to a politician by a person or business that has received government contracts).

Grange An organization founded by Oliver H. Kelley in 1867 to represent the interests of farmers by pressing for agricultural cooperatives, an end to railroad freight discrimination against small farmers, and other initiatives. Its full name was National Grange of the Patrons of Husbandry.

Civil Rights Act of 1875 Congressional legislation that guaranteed black people access to public accommodations and transportation; the Supreme Court declared the measure unconstitutional in 1883.

Chapter 16
Standardizing the Nation: Innovations in Technology, Business, and Culture, 1877–1890

RAILROAD PROPERTY DESTRUCTION, JULY 1877 The "Great Labor Uprising" of July 1877 was the first national strike in U.S. history. As railroad lines proliferated, owners slashed wages in a bid to remain competitive. Railroad workers in some cities destroyed trains, tracks, and other equipment. Spreading eventually to fourteen states, the conflict claimed the lives of more than a hundred people and resulted in the loss of millions of dollars' worth of private property.

Carnegie Library of Pittsburgh

How might railroad workers have disputed the definition of "progress" advanced by Andrew Carnegie and other industrialists?

Contents and Focus Questions

Who in late nineteenth-century America could boast the most impressive "rags-to-riches" life story?

Andrew Carnegie eventually became the richest man in the world, but he began life in modest circumstances. He was born in Scotland in 1835, the son of a skilled weaver. His parents and younger brother eventually moved to Pittsburgh, Pennsylvania, where Andrew took a series of jobs to help support the family: bobbin boy in a textile mill, tender of a steam boiler in a factory, clerk and then messenger in a telegraph office.

By the time he was eighteen, Andrew Carnegie was the personal assistant to the head of the Pennsylvania Railroad. It was in this job that he learned a great deal about running a gigantic business efficiently and profitably. Carnegie also invested in oil and railroads. In 1872, he visited England and gained firsthand information about the production of steel—a lighter, stronger material than iron. Three years later, he opened his own steel plant in Pittsburgh and proceeded to buy rival steel mills.

Earning $25 million a year by the early 1890s, he nonetheless believed that "The amassing of wealth is one of the worst species of idolatry." During the course of his career, Carnegie gave away 90 percent of his fortune, founding the Carnegie Endowment for International Peace, as well as many public libraries around the country.

It was significant that Carnegie spent his formative years in business learning about railroads. The railroad industry was both a great centralizer and a great standardizer. Trains ran on schedules that were set by a central office, and those schedules relied on definitions of actual time that were standard throughout the nation. Moreover, trains broke down regional boundaries by transporting goods all over the country. For the first time, trains carried brand-name goods to a national market.

Providers of goods and services celebrated a "standard" American viewed as white, native born, middle class, heterosexual, and Protestant. Yet the energy and vitality associated with American popular culture served as a magnet for people all over the world. Beginning in the 1880s, eastern European immigrants streamed to the United States. They were eager to partake of the country's plentiful jobs, material prosperity, and democratic openness.

*   *   *   *   *

Few Americans amassed the fabulous fortunes of rich industrialists like Carnegie, yet most people aspired to a better life, even in modest terms. Proprietors, managers, and office workers filled the ranks of the comfortable middle class, men and women freed from the danger and drudgery of manual labor. Enjoying steady work and cash salaries, middleclass employees such as clerical workers and business managers began to move their families out of the city. At the same time, urban areas were becoming increasingly befouled by smokestacks and congested with new factories and workshops where large numbers of newcomers—men, women, and children—toiled. Well into the twentieth century, the nation still showed the ethnic and cultural diversity that was shaped by patterns of immigration during the late nineteenth century.

16.1 The New Shape of Business

What were the challenges faced by large business owners and managers who sought to mass produce and mass market their goods?

In 1882, prospectors discovered gold in the creeks of Idaho's Coeur d'Alene region (in Indian Territory, about 90 miles east of Spokane, Washington). Multiethnic boomtowns mushroomed in the region. The Northern Pacific Railway promoted settlement, and the primitive techniques that had been used in surface mining soon yielded to far more efficient hydraulic methods of extraction (a process in which powerful water hoses wash the soil away to expose gold deposits).

The mining industry in the region soon emerged as a big business. In 1885, an unemployed carpenter named Noah S. Kellogg set in motion a dramatic chain of events. Kellogg discovered a lode containing not only gold but also zinc and lead. In short order, he sold his mines to a Portland businessman, who paid a whopping $650,000 for them. A group of eastern and California investors, and finally several large corporations, soon controlled major interests in the mines. By the mid-twentieth century, mining companies had dug more than a billion dollars' worth of metal out of Noah Kellogg's original stake.

Crucial to the process of innovation were engineers, who mastered the technical aspects of construction and design. Many American engineers were trained in Germany, but others attended such schools as the Massachusetts Institute of Technology (MIT) or Cornell University, in New York state, both of which introduced electrical engineering into their curricula in 1882. American engineers, such as those who worked in Mexico under the auspices of mining companies and the railroads, served as the vanguard of American capitalism throughout the world.

By 1877, the emergence of a national rail system signaled the rise of big business. The railroad industry produced America's first business bureaucracies, employing gigantic workforces to maintain, schedule, operate, and staff trains that traversed 93,000 miles of track. In 1890, the Pennsylvania Railroad was the nation's largest employer, with 110,000 workers on its payroll. The personnel in charge of coordinating these vast operations were among the country's first professional, salaried managers.

No matter what industry they were in, advocates of standardized industrial processes and mass marketing hoped to break down regional barriers and create an integrated national economy. Whether they specialized in railroads or shoes, wheat or steel, business owners and managers who possessed the necessary resources and resourcefulness pursued similar goals: to mine, grow, manufacture, or process large quantities of goods and then market them as widely, cheaply, and quickly as possible. Business put a premium on technological innovation, on the efficient use of workers, and on the reduction of uncertainties that accompanied a competitive workplace. Manufacturers of mass-produced goods relied on new technologies, and aimed to make a profit by meeting—or creating—a large, national demand for their products. At the same time, these manufacturers also believed that they were benefitting the nation by raising the standard of living among all Americans regardless of where they lived. These guiding principles, formulated during the late 1870s and 1880s, laid the foundations of economic progress in late nineteenth-century America.

16.1.1 New Systems and Machines—and Their Price

The free enterprise system thrived on innovation. Indeed, during the 1880s, new machines, new technical processes, new engineering feats, and new forms of factory organization fueled the growth and efficiency of U.S. businesses. Many devices that became staples of American life appeared during this period. Alexander Graham Bell invented the telephone in 1876. Thomas A. Edison patented the phonograph in

1878 and developed the electric light in 1879. Cash registers, stock tickers, and type-writers soon became indispensable tools for American businesses. Beginning in the 1880s, railroad cars installed steam heat and electric lights, boosting the comfort of passengers.

During these years, more and more businesses perfected the so-called American system of manufacturing, which dated back half a century and relied on the mass production of interchangeable parts. Factory workers made large numbers of a particular part, each part exactly the same size and shape. This system enabled manufacturers to assemble products more cheaply and efficiently, to repair products easily with new parts, and to redesign products quickly. The engineers who designed the modern bicycle (which has wheels of equal size) used the American system to make their product affordable to almost anyone who wanted one. The bicycle craze of the late nineteenth century resulted from the novelty and cheapness of this new form of transportation and recreation, one enjoyed by males and females of all ages. Production techniques used to make bicycles were later adapted to the manufacture of automobiles.

New technical processes also facilitated the manufacture and marketing of foods and other consumer goods. Distributors developed pressure-sealed cans, which enabled them to market agricultural products in far-flung parts of the country. Innovative techniques for sheet metal stamping and electric resistance welding transformed a variety of industries. By 1880, 90 percent of American steel was made by the Bessemer process, which injected air into molten iron to yield steel.

The agriculture business benefited from engineering innovations as well, which often reached across national boundaries. As just one example, the first modern irrigation systems in the Southwest were constructed by Native Americans and mestizos (people of both indigenous and Spanish ancestry). And in the 1870s, Japan began importing American farm implements and inviting U.S. engineers to construct dams and canals for new steam- and water-powered gristmills and sawmills. Technology was a universal language, one that many peoples around the globe sought to master.

Long active in territorial exploration and land surveying, the federal government continued to assume a leading role in applied science. In 1879, the U.S. Geological Survey (USGS) was formed, charged with compiling and centralizing data describing the natural landscape, an effort that had originated in 1804 with the Lewis and Clark expedition. In the 1880s, the federal government also began to systematize and disseminate information useful to farmers through the U.S. Department of Agriculture. In 1881, for example, the department's Entomology Bureau began to combine current research on insects with practical techniques for pest control.

Like factory machines, new agricultural machinery benefited consumers, but the need for hired hands gradually evaporated. Early in the nineteenth century, producing an acre of wheat took fifty-six hours of labor; in 1880, that number dropped to twenty hours. One agricultural worker in Ohio observed, "Of one thing we are convinced, that while improved machinery is gathering our large crops, making our boots and shoes, doing the work of our carpenters, stone sawyers, and builders, thousands of able, willing men are going from place to place seeking employment, and finding none. The question naturally arises, is improved machinery a blessing or a curse?"

This worker's concerns illustrated a central tension of the new standardized economy: while the large producers sought to cut costs by innovating and mechanizing in order to make their products cheaper, such measures often came at the price of jobs for laboring men and women. Progress, then, could mean a higher standard of living for many, but it could also lead to high rates of unemployment among the most vulnerable manual laborers.

Map 16.1 AGRICULTURAL REGIONS OF THE MIDWEST AND NORTHEAST

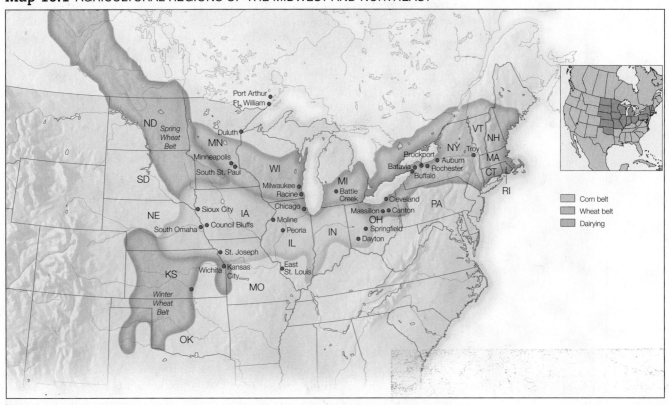

By 1890, several midwestern cities served as shipping centers, getting wheat and corn to the growing metropolitan areas of the Northeast and Mid-Atlantic. Farmers complained that the railroads gave discounts to large shippers, such as Standard Oil, and discriminated against small producers.

16.1.2 Alterations in the Natural Environment

Innovation altered the natural landscape and hastened the depletion of certain natural resources. By the mid-1870s, Texas had new steam-powered lumber mills equipped with saw rigs that could produce up to 30,000 board feet a day. This capacity made Texas lumbering a big business, especially when it was combined with infusions of capital and the expansion of railroad lines into the piney woods region, along the eastern edge of the state. Texas lumber mills were poised to benefit from the exhaustion of the great forests of the eastern and Great Lakes states.

In the Chesapeake Bay, dredge boats were becoming more efficient in harvesting oysters, and shellfish reserves began to decline. In the mid-1880s, oyster harvesters took a record 15 million bushels from the bay; the shellfish simply could not replenish themselves. New means of commercial fishing also reduced supplies of salmon in the Northwest.

In 1884, in California, a federal court issued a permanent injunction against hydraulic mining because it contributed to soil erosion and water pollution. Hydraulic mining had washed an estimated 12 billion tons of earth into San Francisco Bay, raising the floor of the bay several feet. At the same time, mercury flowing into nearby streams from gold mines in the San Jose hills was poisoning fish in the bay, creating pollution that would be felt well into the twentieth century. Similar cases of industrial pollution despoiled other parts of the country. In the absence of any laws to restrain them, Chicago meatpackers befouled the Chicago River with the byproducts of sausage, glue, and fertilizer.

By stimulating manufacturing and extractive enterprises alike, the railroads powered these great environmental transformations, for better or worse. Since buffalo herds

SHOOTING BUFFALO FROM A MOVING TRAIN An 1871 drawing suggests the role of the railroad in decimating buffalo populations in the West. Travelling from Ellis, Kansas, to Kit Carson, Colorado, this Kansas-Pacific train mows down the animals that get in its way, while passengers practice their marksmanship from the cars. Following the wholesale slaughter of buffalo, settlers earned money by gathering the skeletons. "The bones are shipped East by the carloads," reported the *Dodge City Times*, "where they are ground and used for fertilizing and manufactured into numerous useful articles."

North Wind Picture Archives/Alamy

In addition to the railroad, what other forms of U.S. technology severely limited the hunting practices, and forever transformed the cultures, of Great Plains Native groups?

impeded rail travel, railroads promoted the shooting of buffalo from trains, a "sport" that almost eradicated the species. By the mid-1880s, the great herds had disappeared, victims of ecological change (the incursion of horses into grazing areas), disease (brucellosis spread by domestic livestock), and commercial enterprise. Sioux leader Black Elk decried the slaughter and the heaps of bones left to rot in the sun.

16.1.3 Innovations in Financing and Organizing Business

As agents of economic development and cultural change, the railroads knew no peer. As private enterprises, however, they faced the same challenges that all big businesses ultimately must address. The proliferation of independent lines and the high fixed costs associated with the industry made profits slim and competition intense. As a result, railroad companies began to come together in informal pools to share equipment and set prices industrywide. In the 1880s, these pools gave way to consolidation, a process by which several companies merged into one large company. Moreover, like other large businesses, including oil and steel, the railroads sought to slash wages in order to decrease their cost of doing business. This decision had profound consequences for workers, who in some cases reacted violently.

In these years, U.S. businesses grew larger and more quickly than their western European counterparts. This difference stemmed in large part from America's astonishing population growth and its rich natural resources. Equally significant, the United States possessed a social and legal culture favorable to big business. The absence of an entrenched, conservative elite, along with the spread of state and national laws that protected private property, stimulated the entrepreneurial spirit. The U.S. government refrained from owning industries, although it heavily subsidized the railroad industry. It taxed business lightly and did not tax individual incomes at all until 1913. Finally, American bankers such as J. P. Morgan aggressively promoted growth through their lending practices and bond sales.

Several large enterprises began to conquer not just local but also national markets. Examples include Bell Telephone (founded in Boston), the Kroger grocery business (Cincinnati), Marshall Field department store (Chicago), and Boston Fruit Company. In the South, Midwest, and West, investors rushed to finance gigantic mining operations and agribusinesses, such as the 1.5 million acres devoted to rice cultivation in southeastern Louisiana and bonanza wheat farms (as large as 38,000 acres) in the Red River Valley of North Dakota.

Owners of these enterprises devised new forms of business organization that helped their companies grow and survive in a dynamic economy. By combining, or integrating, their operations, manufacturers created large businesses called **trusts** to cut costs and monopolize an entire industry in the process. Unable to withstand the ruthless competition that favored larger enterprises, smaller companies folded. The two icons of American big business in the 1880s—Andrew Carnegie in steel and John D. Rockefeller in petroleum—proved master innovators in both the managerial and technical aspects of business.

trust
A combination of firms or corporations created for the purpose of reducing competition and controlling prices throughout an industry.

Within a year of opening the Edgar Thomson Steelworks, Carnegie was producing steel at half the prevailing market price. He excelled at vertical integration, in which a single firm controls all aspects of production and distribution. Carnegie employed laborers in the Lake Superior region to mine the raw material, and he owned the ships and railroads that brought the ore to the mills in Pittsburgh and then transported the manufactured steel to customers.

Another form of business consolidation was horizontal integration, in which a number of companies producing the same product merge to reduce competition and control prices. In 1882, John D. Rockefeller, a former bookkeeper, horizontally integrated the petroleum industry by forming Standard Oil Trust. Stockholders in small companies turned over their shares to Standard Oil, which then coordinated operations and eliminated competition from other smaller firms. Standard Oil also practiced vertical integration. Soon Rockefeller had positioned himself to buy out his rivals—or ruin them. Trusts placed a premium on efficient production, but they also worked to the disadvantage of consumers, who were hostage to high prices within industries that lacked competition.

16.1.4 Immigrants: New Labor Supplies for a New Economy

To operate efficiently, expanding industries needed expanding supplies of workers to grow crops, extract raw materials, and produce manufactured goods. Many of these workers came from abroad. The year 1880 marked the leading edge of a new wave of immigration to the United States. Over the next ten years, 5.2 million newcomers entered the country, almost twice the previous decade's level of 2.8 million.

In the mid-nineteenth century, most immigrants hailed from western Europe and the British Isles—from Germany, Scandinavia, England, and Ireland. Between 1880 and 1890, Germans, Scandinavians, and the English kept coming, but they were joined by numerous Italians, Russians, and Poles. In fact, these last three groups predominated among newcomers for the next thirty-five years, their arrival rates peaking between

1890 and 1910. At the same time, immigrants from Asia, especially from China, were making their way to the Kingdom of Hawaii, which was annexed by the United States in 1898. Between 1852 and 1887, 26,000 Chinese arrived on the islands. Almost 40 percent of all immigrants to the United States during this period were known as "birds of passage," men who were recruited by American employers and who, after earning some money, migrated back to their native land.

In some cases, domestic politics affected patterns of foreign immigration to the continental United States. For example, on the West Coast, the Chinese faced intense hostility from native-born white men who feared that "coolies" (Chinese immigrants) would depress their wages and take their jobs. Passed in 1882, the **Chinese Exclusion Act** aimed to stem the flow of Chinese immigration to the United States.

Many of the new European immigrants sought to escape oppressive economic and political conditions in Europe, even as they hoped to make a new life for themselves and their families in the United States. Russian Jews fled discrimination and violent **anti-semitism** in the form of pogroms, organized massacres conducted by their Christian neighbors and Russian authorities. Southern Italians, mostly landless farmers, suffered from a combination of declining agricultural prices and high birth rates. Impoverished Poles chafed under cultural restrictions imposed by Germany and Russia. Hungarians, Greeks, Portuguese, and Armenians, among other groups, also participated in this great migration; members of these groups, too, were seeking political freedom and economic opportunity.

Immigrants replenished America's sense of itself as a haven for the downtrodden, a place where opportunity beckoned to hard-working and ambitious people. "The New Colossus," written by American poet Emma Lazarus in 1883, pays tribute to the "huddled masses yearning to breathe free"—people from all over the world who sought refuge in the United States. The words of her poem are inscribed on the Statue of Liberty at the entrance to New York Harbor.

The story of Rosa Cassettari, a young woman who emigrated from northern Italy to the United States in 1884, suggests the challenges that faced many newcomers during this period. Rosa's husband, Santino, had preceded her to America. He had settled in an iron-mining camp in Missouri. Leaving her son with relatives, Rosa received the assurances of friends and relatives: "You will get smart in America. And in America you will not be so poor."

Life in the Missouri iron camp proved harsh—nothing like what Rosa had expected. Her husband, who was much older than she, neglected her; he preferred the company of prostitutes in the town. The iron was almost depleted, and some workers and their wives had moved on to a new mine in Michigan. Rosa's days centered on caring for her new baby and cooking for thirteen of the miners.

Despite these realities, within a couple of years, Rosa grew used to America and considered herself an American. She returned briefly to her hometown in Italy but expressed impatience with the rigid social etiquette that separated the rich from the poor. She also yearned for the hearty meals that had become her staple in the iron camp. Back in Missouri, she mustered enough courage to leave Santino, traveling to Chicago and making a new life for herself in the Italian *colonia* (community) there. She eventually married another Italian man (the two had fallen in love in Missouri) and found work as a cleaning woman at Chicago Commons, a social settlement house.

Specific groups of immigrants often gravitated toward particular kinds of jobs. For example, many Poles found work in the vast steel plants of Pittsburgh, and Russian Jews went into the garment industry and street-peddling trade in New York City. California fruit orchards and vegetable farms employed numerous Japanese immigrants. Cuban immigrants rolled cigars in Florida. In Hawaii, the Chinese and Japanese labored in the sugar fields; after they had accumulated a little money, they became rice farmers and shopkeepers. In Boston and New York City, second-generation Irish took advantage of their prominent place in the Democratic party to become public school teachers, firefighters, and police officers.

Chinese Exclusion Act
Legislation passed by Congress in 1882 to deny any additional Chinese laborers entry into the country while allowing some Chinese merchants and students to immigrate.

anti-semitism
Prejudice against Jews.

Map 16.2 POPULATION OF FOREIGN BORN, BY REGION, 1880

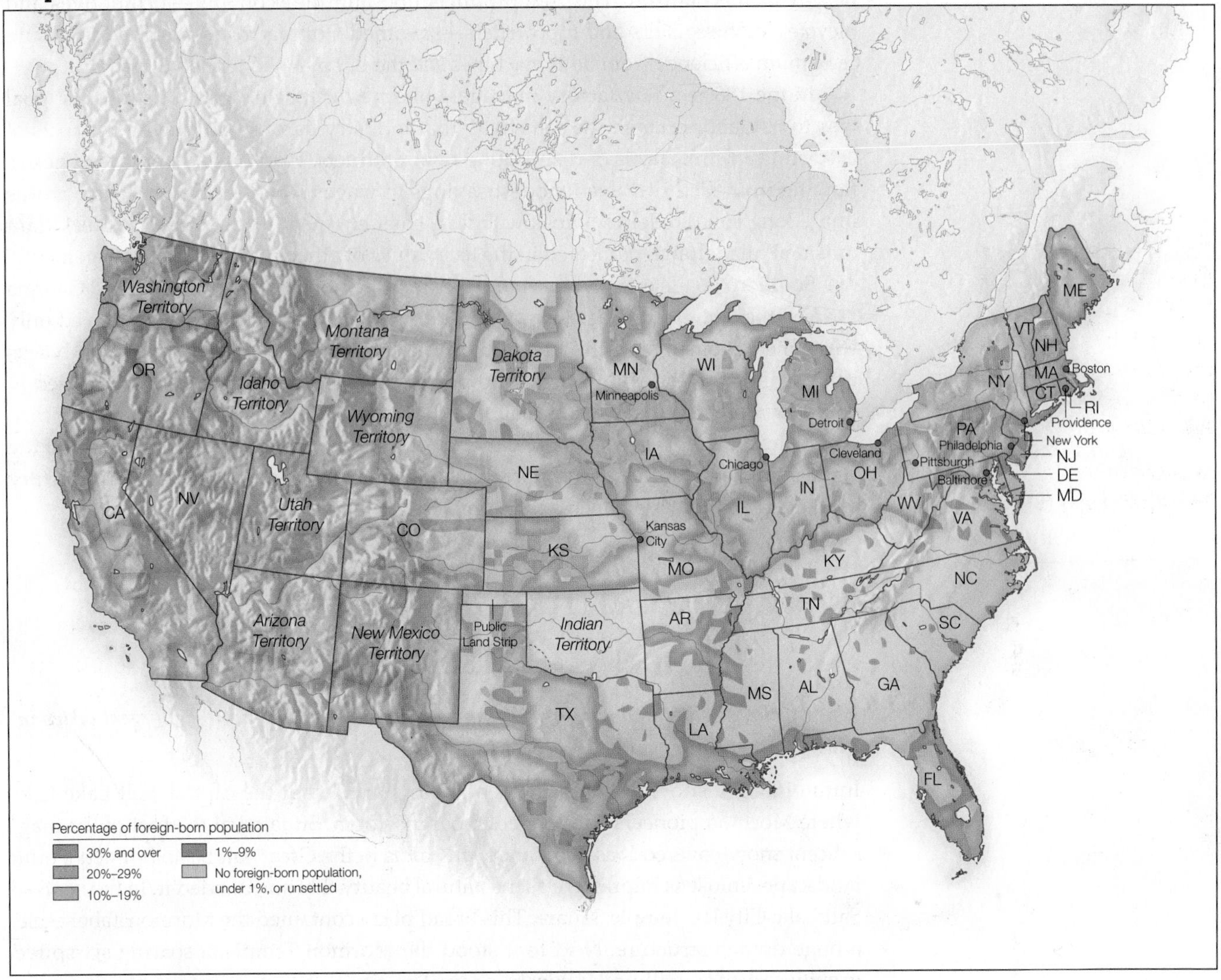

After the Civil War, large numbers of immigrants settled in northeastern cities. In addition, the upper Midwest and parts of the western mining frontier drew many newcomers from western Europe. The area along the country's southwestern border was home to immigrants from Mexico. Cuban cigar makers established thriving communities in southern Florida.

The experience of Kinji Ushijima (later known as George Shima) graphically illustrates the power of immigrant niches. Shima arrived in California in 1887 and, like many other Japanese immigrants, found work as a potato picker in the San Joaquin Valley. Soon, Shima moved up to become a labor contractor, securing Japanese laborers for the valley's white farmers. With the money he made, he bought 15 acres of land and began his own potato farm. Eventually, he built a large potato business by expanding his holdings, reclaiming swampland, and investing in a fleet of boats to ship his crops up the coast to San Francisco. Taking advantage of a Japanese niche, Shima prospered through a combination of good luck and hard work.

16.1.5 Efficient Machines, Efficient People

Unlike George Shima, most immigrant workers did not become business owners. By the late nineteenth century, the typical industrial employee labored within an immense, multistory brick structure and operated a machine powered by water or steam. Smoky, smelly kerosene lamps gave way to early forms of electric lighting, first arc and then incandescent light bulbs. Long-standing industries, such as textiles and shoes, were now fully mechanized. The new products flooding the economy—locomotives and bicycles, cash registers and typewriters—streamed from factories designed to ensure maximum efficiency from both machines *and* the people who tended them.

In the 1880s, a few factory managers hired efficiency experts. The experts' goal was to cut labor costs in the same way that industry barons had shaved the costs of extracting raw materials or distributing final products. With huge quantities of goods flowing from factories, even modest savings in wages could mean significant profits in the long run. Frederick Winslow Taylor, chief engineer for the Midvale Steel Plant outside Philadelphia, pioneered in the techniques of efficient "scientific management."

Southern textile mill owners in the Piedmont region of South Carolina and Georgia devised their own strategies for shaping a compliant workforce. They employed only white men, women, and children as machine operators, but threatened to hire blacks if the whites protested low wages and poor working conditions. Poor whites lived in company housing, their children attended company schools, and they received cash wages. In contrast, blacks remained in the countryside, impoverished and without the right to vote. In the cities of the North as well as the textile villages of the South, factory workers remained exclusively white until well into the twentieth century.

16.2 The Birth of a National Urban Culture

What technological and managerial innovations shaped the nation's largest cities in the late nineteenth century?

In the 1880s, visitors to the territory of Utah marveled at the capital, Salt Lake City, where Mormon pioneers had made the desert bloom. Situated at the foot of the magnificent snow-covered Wasatch Range, this oasis in the Great Salt Basin boasted a built landscape almost as impressive as the natural beauty that surrounded it. In the heart of Salt Lake City lay Temple Square. This broad plaza contained the Mormon Tabernacle, a huge domed structure. Next to it stood the Mormon Temple, a soaring six-spired granite cathedral still under construction. The city had the advantage of rail service (Promontory Point, where the Transcontinental Railroad was joined, was not far away). Mines in nearby Bingham Canyon yielded rich lodes of silver, and large local smelters refined copper ores. Irrigation systems made the city self-sufficient in the production of foodstuffs. A settlement inspired by religious faith, Salt Lake City was at the same time thoroughly modern.

Not only Salt Lake City but also other cities around the country began to assume monumental proportions. In New York, the 1880s marked the completion of Central Park and the Brooklyn Bridge and the arrival of the Statue of Liberty from France. Chicago, rebuilding after a disastrous fire in 1871, became a sprawling rail hub dotted with yards for western cattle, northern timber, and the trains that hauled them. In 1885, Chicago also became the location for a major architectural breakthrough by engineer William LeBaron Jenney. He designed the ten-story Home Insurance Building, the world's first metal-frame skyscraper. The steel skeleton weighed only one-third as much as the thick stone walls needed to support a similar masonry building, and the design left room for numerous windows. Urban architecture would never be the same again.

Cities represented American notions of progress and prosperity; they were places where innovation, consumer culture, and new forms of entertainment grew and flourished. From 1875 to 1900, American cities developed increasingly sophisticated systems of communications and transportation. Streetlights, transportation networks, and sewer lines provided basic services to swelling populations of immigrants and rural in-migrants. Cities also represented a new cultural diversity in American life. At

BROOKLYN BRIDGE Admirers hailed New York City's Brooklyn Bridge as the eighth wonder of the world when it was completed in 1883. With a central span of 1,595 feet, it became the largest suspension bridge in the world and a familiar icon of America's increasingly urbanized landscape. Built over fourteen years, the bridge links Brooklyn to Manhattan across the East River, using steel suspension cables that are nearly 16 inches thick. Its total cost was about $18 million.

Three Lions/Getty Images

How did public improvements, such as bridges and railroads, promote the idea of equality of economic opportunity, and prosperity, for all Americans?

times uneasily, they accommodated immigrants from around the world. San Francisco's Chinatown formed a "city within a city" as hostile European Americans sought to circumscribe its residents. These growing cities required larger local governments to manage the services necessary for daily life. Politics, prejudice, and technology came together to shape the urban landscape.

16.2.1 Economic Sources of Urban Growth

Northeastern and mid-Atlantic cities emerged as centers of concentrated manufacturing activity. Yet, with the aid of eastern capital, western cities also flourished. New York's Wall Street and Boston's State Street, home to the nation's largest investment bankers, financed the Main Streets of the Midwest and West. Some urban areas prospered through milling, mining, or other enterprises, such as lumber and flour milling in Minneapolis and ore smelting in Denver. Others focused on manufacturing to serve a growing western population. Chicago was rivaled only by New York in terms of its industrial economy and the vast territory that it supplied with raw materials, processed food, and manufactured goods. Salt Lake City produced goods for the so-called Mormon Corridor of settlements that stretched west from the city to southern California. By the 1880s, San Francisco had a commercial reach that encompassed much of the West as well as Hawaii and Alaska.

No trend supported urban growth more than the arrival of newcomers from abroad. To stoke its furnaces, mill its lumber, and slaughter its cattle, Chicago relied on immigrants from Ireland, Slovakia, Germany, Poland, and Bohemia. The three cities with the highest percentage of foreign-born residents in 1880 were San Francisco (45 percent), Chicago (42 percent), and New York (40 percent). Yet all large cities also attracted migrants from America's own countryside, as native-born men and women fled the hardships of life on the farm. Moreover, the use of increasingly efficient agricultural machines meant that rural workers had fewer job opportunities. Most of the in-migrants from rural areas to the cities were young women; they included Yankee girls from the hardscrabble homesteads of New England, daughters of Swedish immigrants in Minnesota, and native-born farm tenants in Indiana.

Rural folk sought the steady work and wages afforded by jobs in the city, but they were also drawn to the excitement that had become the hallmark of the urban scene. They moved off the countryside in an effort to share in the material prosperity represented by the city. The nation's largest urban centers thus beckoned to all with expanding economic and leisure-time opportunities, while rural folk saw their own opportunities swiftly declining. In the early nineteenth century, Thomas Jefferson had located the heart of America in its sturdy yeoman farmers. By the late nineteenth century, that heart had shifted to the city.

16.2.2 Building the Cities

The American city was emerging as a technological marvel. Through a combination of money and engineering skill, cities managed to provide an adequate water supply for private and commercial purposes, move large numbers of people and goods efficiently, get rid of waste materials, and illuminate thoroughfares at night. Professionals, such as landscape contractors, construction architects, and civil engineers, designed the parks, bridges, public libraries, and museums that made cities so attractive.

Cities grew upward and outward as a result of developments in mass production and technology. Elevators extended living and office spaces upward. The invention of the electric streetcar in 1888 permitted cities to spread out. Soon, residential suburbs cropped up many miles from urban commercial cores. Wealthy and middle-class urban residents followed the streetcar lines out of the city, hoping to find a green refuge from the grime and noise of downtown while maintaining a manageable commute to work.

As cities expanded, the challenges associated with providing services also grew more complex and expensive. A polluted water supply, for example, meant epidemics of diphtheria and cholera, so city taxpayers demanded waterworks that delivered drinkable water through intricate systems of dams, pumps, reservoirs, and pipes. Chicago had long pumped its sewage into Lake Michigan, the source of its drinking water. In the 1880s, the city financed the building of a canal and the reversal of the flow of the Chicago River. These changes sent the city's sewage away from Lake Michigan and westward into the Mississippi River instead. Begun in 1889, the 28-mile Chicago Sanitary and Ship Canal was completed seven years later. One awed observer marveled at the "powerful machinery for digging and hoisting, steam shovels, excavators, inclines, conveyors, derricks, cantilevers, cableways, channelers, steam drills, pumps, etc." The cost: $54 million.

16.2.3 Local Government Gets Bigger

These new systems of services, combined with the mushrooming immigrant neighborhoods, changed both the quality and the quantity of urban problems. Zoning issues—who could build what, where, and when—became flashpoints for conflict as the interests of homeowners, developers, storekeepers, and municipal engineers collided. Urban political leaders struggled to improve the city's public works while meeting the needs of multiple ethnic groups. Governing a city was an expensive, full-time enterprise and one that had the potential to be very lucrative to businesspeople and politicians alike.

Although New York's "Boss" Tweed had been convicted on charges of corruption in the early 1870s, the infamous Tammany Hall gang carried on his legacy. The Democratic officials associated with this social and political organization perfected a system of kickbacks linked to municipal construction projects. Under this system, contractors paid politicians for city construction contracts. For example, a New York City courthouse that was supposed to cost a quarter of a million dollars ended up costing taxpayers fifty-two times that amount, or twice as much as the United States paid Russia for Alaska! In the 1880s, secretive networks of corruption linking law enforcement personnel, city officials, and construction contractors flourished in many cities. These webs, or "machines," characterized urban life for decades to come.

Urban machines existed to secure jobs for their loyal supporters and line the pockets of those at the highest levels of power. Deal-making blurred the lines between private enterprise and public service as everyone from mayors to local ward organizers benefited from the modernization of the American city. In the process, urban bosses ensured that the streets were paved, tenement buildings erected, sewer lines laid, and trolley tracks extended. But taxpayers footed the bill, which included outrageous amounts of money for bribes and kickbacks.

Local officials went out of their way to support the provision of illegal services, such as prostitution and gambling, demanded by their constituents. Corrupt politicians, judges, and police extorted "hush money" from brothels, gambling parlors, and unlicensed taverns. Urban bosses also had a vested interest in sponsoring new money-making venues for professional sports and supporting other forms of commercialized leisure activity. Baseball parks, boxing rings, and race tracks yielded huge sums in the form of kickbacks from contractors. Once built, stadiums and boxing rings generated profits indefinitely as fans filled the stands.

Despite the outcry of reformers, who condemned corrupt urban bosses, these local politicians gained favor among their constituents when they provided needed goods and services, especially among the poor. The boss who provoked the wrath of "good government" men and women also won the loyalty of immigrants whom he helped by providing jobs, food, clothing, loans, and proper burials for loved ones. For the boss, charity was good politics.

16.3 Thrills, Chills, and Toothpaste: The Emergence of Consumer Culture

What were the social and economic consequences of the new consumer culture?

On a hot summer day in 1890, a young mother named Emily Scanlon, with her three-year-old daughter in tow, paid the five-cent admission fee to a popular ride called the Toboggan Slide at the Brandywine Springs Amusement Park near Wilmington, Delaware. The two of them ascended a stairwell to the top of the three-story-high structure and then stepped into a car that ran on a wooden trough. When the attendant released the brakes, the car descended, pulled by gravity. It moved slowly at first, then picked up speed around a curve. Suddenly, Emily Scanlon stood up in the car (perhaps to retrieve her hat, which had blown off), and she and her daughter were thrown from the car. Mrs. Scanlon died instantly of a broken neck, but the youngster survived. Significantly, the tragedy did not provoke a shutdown of the ride or the installation of safety measures. Instead, park managers simply posted a sign that read, "Passengers must keep their seats." Patrons continued to enjoy the thrills of the toboggan.

Brandywine Springs boasted an ornate gateway that proclaimed "Let All Who Enter Here Leave Care Behind." In cities around the country, amusement parks brought men and women, girls and boys together to enjoy merry-go-rounds, prizefights, and circus sideshows. By 1880, railroads and steamships were transporting crowds out of Manhattan to Coney Island, where working-class people mingled with the self-proclaimed "respectable" middle classes. In this way, amusement parks represented the democratization of commercial leisure, appealing to men and women, young and old, rich and poor. Shows and spectacles aimed to ensure that all spectators were equally enthralled.

Late in the century, Americans of all kinds began to sample a new realm of sensual experience—one of physical daring, material luxury, and visual fantasy—either as participants or as observers. Central to this emerging consumer culture was mass advertising, a form of appeal that sought to instill in consumers the desire for things that were new and visually attractive. Colorful spectacles of all kinds—whether in the form of a department store window or a well-publicized athletic event—became an integral part of American life.

16.3.1 Shows and Sports as Spectacles

Public officials, college administrators, and ambitious entrepreneurs alike discovered that Americans craved new and stimulating forms of entertainment and were willing to pay for them. Athletic events began to draw large crowds, revealing their potential as big business. Traveling circus and road shows promoted new products and services by charming their audiences with exotic performances. Though modest by today's standards, such spectacles found a ready market in the United States and other countries.

In the quarter-century after Reconstruction, three major sports began to attract large national audiences. Organized baseball had existed since 1846, when the Knickerbocker Base Ball Club of New York met the New York Nine in Hoboken, New Jersey. (The score was 23 to 1, in favor of the Nine.) The National Baseball League, consisting of eight professional teams, was founded in 1876, the American League in 1900. In the 1880s, several new regulations—those governing the overhand pitch, foul balls, and swingless strikes—helped to standardize the game.

Also in the 1880s, Walter Camp, a former Yale University football player, introduced rules—for instance, the system of downs and the center snap to the quarterback—that made that sport quicker and more competitive. Camp was also behind the selection of the first "All America" team (1889) to stimulate fan interest. By this time, towns, high schools, and colleges were fielding football teams.

Likewise, boxing emerged as a national, regulated sport. John L. Sullivan, an American, won renown as the world's bare-knuckled champion in 1882, even as more and more fighters had started wearing gloves. Sullivan then joined a traveling theatrical group and demonstrated gloved boxing to enthusiastic crowds all over the country. In 1889, Sullivan defeated an opponent in a 75-round match, the last heavyweight, bare-knuckled championship.

Performances based on skills of all kinds gained national audiences, as the career of William "Buffalo Bill" Cody reveals. Born in Iowa in 1846, Cody parlayed his early years as a Pony Express postal rider, cavalry scout, Indian fighter, and buffalo hunter into a form of mass entertainment. In his "Buffalo Bill Combination" show, cowboy and Indian actors performed skits depicting dramatic events in western history (from a European American point of view, at least).

In 1882, Cody produced "Buffalo Bill's Wild West," a traveling road show that featured sharpshooter Annie Oakley, cowboy musicians, and Sioux warriors performing authentic Native American dances. Sioux leader Sitting Bull (Tatanka Iyotake), long an admirer of Annie Oakley (he called her "Little Sure Shot"), joined the show in 1885. Like other Indians who worked for Cody, Sitting Bull took advantage of the opportunity to escape the confines of the reservation (in his case, Standing Rock in North Dakota). As a member of the "Wild West" troupe, he also enjoyed decent food and accommodations.

"BUFFALO BILL" CODY AND SITTING BULL "Buffalo Bill" Cody and Sitting Bull pose for a promotional photo for the 1885 season of the "Wild West." Cody refrained from calling the production a "show," maintaining that it demonstrated frontier skills and recreated historical encounters (such as Custer's Last Stand and stagecoach robberies). The "Wild West" toured Canada and Europe and inspired many imitators.

Library of Congress Prints and Photographs Division [LC-USZ62-107167]

How did the "Wild West" and other forms of modestly priced entertainment promote the idea of equality among Americans regardless of their ethnicity, income, age, and political affiliation?

At a time when whites were denigrating Indian culture, Sitting Bull affirmed that culture by demonstrating his shooting and riding skills. However, white audiences jeered him—they saw him as less an entertainer and more an enemy warrior—and he left after just a year. By the 1890s, Cody was playing to audiences in Europe as well as the United States, dramatizing a West that was fast disappearing.

16.3.2 Mass Merchandising as Spectacle

In the cities of the late nineteenth century, the act of shopping for goods, especially luxury goods, became an adventure in itself. A new piece of the cityscape, the department store, welcomed customers into a world of luxury and abundance, a place of color, light, and glamour. These "palaces of consumption" showcased a variety of technological innovations. In Marshall Field's "Grand Emporium" (Chicago), Wanamaker's (Philadelphia), and Lord & Taylor (New York), shoppers glided from story to story on escalators and in elevators. Warmed by central heating, they browsed display cases, racks, and tables laden with enticing goods and illuminated by arc lighting. Their money streamed into cash registers or to a central clerk through cash conveyors.

Thus, department stores not only offered a dazzling array of goods but also made shopping an exciting experience. Middle-class women in particular had the leisure time and the cash to indulge in day-long shopping excursions. In 1880, a New Yorker could arrive at Macy's by taking the Sixth Avenue elevated train and spend the morning exploring any number of specialized departments: ribbons, women's and children's muslin underwear, toys, candy, books, men's furnishings, china and glassware, and so on. Fatigued at noon, she might visit the lunchroom to partake of a modest meal and then devote the rest of her day to examining the colored dress silks, a new department established the year before.

REFUGIO AMADOR AND DAUGHTERS, LAS CRUCES, NEW MEXICO Refugio Amador and her five daughters, Emilia, Maria, Clotilde, Julieta, and Corina, were members of an elite Hispanic family in Las Cruces, New Mexico. Her husband, Martin Amador, was a prominent politician, merchant, hotel owner, and freighter. A subcontractor for the U.S. government, he supplied military troops in the area. The family shopped by mail-order catalogue from Bloomingdale's Department Store in New York City.

Fine Art Museums/Corbis

How did mass merchandisers such as department stores represent the ideal of consumption as a great democratizing force for all Americans?

The department store was an exclusively urban phenomenon, but mass merchandising reached far beyond cities. The material riches of American society became accessible to rural people through the mail-order catalogue. This marketing device was pioneered in 1872 by the Chicago company Montgomery Ward, the official supply house for the Farmers' Grange. On homesteads throughout the Midwest, family members gathered to pore over the thousands of items displayed in "The Great Wish Book." The company's motto? "Satisfaction guaranteed or your money back." Farm wives delighted in the latest Parisian fashions, their husbands pondered the intricacies of McCormick threshing machinery, and the children studied the newest line of toys and fishing rods. Late in the decade, a competitor appeared on the scene in the form of the Sears, Roebuck Catalogue.

The mass production needed to satisfy eager customers depended on mass advertising, an enterprise still in its infancy in the 1880s. Yet some of the principles that would shape the future of this business were in place even at this early date. For instance, soon after the Civil War, the makers of Sozodont dentifrice (toothpaste) plastered the name of their product all over weekly religious magazines and more mainstream publications, such as *Harper's* and *Scribner's*. They labeled the natural landscape as well. Indeed, the word *Sozodont* on Maiden's Rock in Red Wing, Minnesota, was so large that steamboat passengers on the Mississippi River three miles away could plainly read it.

16.4 Defending the New Industrial Order

What arguments were offered by defenders of the new industrial order, including politicians, business owners, and influential writers and thinkers?

By the late 1870s, as consumer culture expanded, intense conflict over fundamental issues all but evaporated from national politics. Although ethnic and cultural loyalties continued to inflame local and state elections, Republicans and Democrats at the national level disagreed about little except the tariff. Adhering to tradition, Republicans favored a higher tariff that would benefit domestic businesses by making imported goods more expensive. In contrast, Democrats argued that a higher tariff, and resulting higher prices for goods produced in the United States, would harm consumers. Members of the Republican party called themselves the Grand Army of the Republic; they waved the "**bloody shirt**"—that is, reminded voters that many of their Democratic opponents, especially those in the South, had supported secession a generation before. Still, the two major parties openly shared a similar goal: to win as many jobs as possible for their respective supporters. Politics served as a vehicle for patronage and favors rather than as a conduit for ideas and alternative visions of the nation's future.

Many politicians also shared a belief in the idea of **laissez-faire** (a French phrase meaning to leave alone, referring to the absence of government interference in the economy). Laissez-faire was actually a flexible concept, invoked to justify government indifference in some areas but government intervention in others. Indeed, politicians tended to favor laissez-faire in social matters more than in the economy. Thus, support for manufacturers and railroads in the form of tariff protection and land grants, for example, was justified.

At the same time, however, Congress, the president, and the Supreme Court were reluctant to enact bold measures to redress the growing gap between rich and poor. In fact, certain clergy, businesspeople, and university professors sought to explain and defend the inequality between the captains of industry and the masses of ill-paid laborers. They argued that the system of industrial capitalism was desirable because it was "natural."

bloody shirt
A partisan rallying cry used to stir up or revive sectional or party animosity after the American Civil War; for example, post–Civil War Republicans "waved the bloody shirt," associating some Democrats with a treasonous acceptance of secession during the war, while opponents had spilled their blood for the Union.

laissez-faire
A belief in little or no government interference in the economy.

One view of this period was provided by Mark Twain (Samuel Clemens) and Charles Dudley Warner in *The Gilded Age* (1873). Their book satirized the trend toward corruption in public affairs and the wild financial speculation that produced both poverty and great wealth. The growth of large businesses that received economic and political support from government officials served to enrich employers, investors, and politicians at the expense of workers and farmers. The term *Gilded Age* became synonymous with the excess and extravagance on the part of politicians and businessmen alike during the last quarter of the nineteenth century.

16.4.1 The Contradictory Politics of Laissez-Faire

In 1880, the undistinguished President Rutherford B. Hayes chose not to run for office again. That summer the Republicans nominated James A. Garfield of Ohio, a former mule driver who had become a Civil War general. To counter the "bloody-shirt" effect, Democrats put forth their own former Union general: Winfield S. Hancock, who had been wounded at Gettysburg. Garfield won the popular vote by a narrow margin but overwhelmed Hancock in the electoral college.

Table 16.1 THE ELECTION OF 1880

Candidate	Political Party	Popular Vote (%)	Electoral Vote
James A. Garfield	Republican	48.5	214
Winfield S. Hancock	Democratic	48.1	155
James B. Weaver	Greenback-Labor	3.4	—

SOURCE: Historical Election Results, Electoral College, National Archives and Records Administration

Garfield's arrival in the White House set off a race for patronage jobs among loyal Republicans. Indeed, besieged by office-seekers, the new president remarked, "My God! What is there in this place that a man should ever want to get into it?" Then on July 2, 1881, Charles J. Guiteau, who had unsuccessfully sought the position of U.S. consul in Paris, shot Garfield in a Washington, D.C., train station. Garfield languished for a few months, finally dying on September 19.

Vice President Chester A. Arthur, a former New York politician, assumed the reins of government. Arthur's administration supported certain forms of government intervention in society, or "social engineering." Arthur and others believed that laissez-faire policies had their limits; strong measures were needed to counter what they and other conservatives considered immoral personal behavior. In 1882, Congress passed the **Edmunds Act**. Targeting Mormons, the act outlawed polygamy (the practice of having more than one wife at a time), took the right to vote away from the law's offenders, and sent a five-member commission to Utah to oversee local elections.

That same year, Congress responded to pressure from West Coast European American politicians, the San Francisco Workingmen's party in particular, and approved the Chinese Exclusion Act. The act became the first piece of legislation to bar a particular national group from entering the United States. Most Chinese immigrants took jobs that native-born whites shunned. Moreover, unemployment among California white manufacturing workers in the 1870s was caused not by Chinese competitors, but by the flood of cheap eastern-made goods carried into the state by the Transcontinental Railroad. As eastern goods entered California, manufacturers in the West laid off workers and closed factories. The Chinese thus became scapegoats for groups hit hard by larger economic changes.

In 1883, the Supreme Court set back the cause of blacks' civil rights by declaring the Civil Rights Act of 1875 unconstitutional. The five cases involved in the Court's decision focused on exclusions of blacks from hotels, railroad cars, and theaters. The Court held that state governments could not discriminate on the basis of race

Edmunds Act

Congressional legislation passed in 1882 and aimed at Utah Mormons; it outlawed polygamy, stripped polygamists of the right to vote, and provided for a five-member commission to oversee Utah's elections.

but that private individuals could do so. This decision put an official stamp of approval on racist practices of employers, hotels, restaurants, and other providers of jobs and services.

Arthur surprised his critics by embracing the cause of **civil service reform**. This movement sought to inject professional standards into public service and rid the country of the worst excesses of the corrupt "spoils system," where political victors put loyal supporters into public jobs regardless of their qualifications. In response to Garfield's assassination by Guiteau, the disappointed patronage-seeker, Congress passed the **Pendleton Act** (1883). This measure established a merit system for federal job applicants and created the Civil Service Commission, which administered competitive examinations to candidates in certain classifications.

In 1884, Arthur fell ill (he would die shortly), and the Republicans nominated James G. Blaine of Maine as their candidate for the presidency. Blaine, who had benefited from corrupt deals in the past, offended the sensibilities of a group of reform-minded Republicans, who called themselves Mugwumps. (The term reportedly had its roots in an Indian word that meant "holier than thou.") As a result, Blaine was bested in the national election by the former mayor of Buffalo, Grover Cleveland, who became the first Democratic president in twenty-eight years.

civil service reform
Measures designed to eliminate the spoils system in government hiring, in favor of maintaining professional standards in public service.

Pendleton Act
Congressional legislation passed in 1883; established a merit system for federal job applicants and created the Civil Service Commission, which administered competitive examinations to candidates in certain job classifications.

Table 16.2 THE ELECTION OF 1884

Candidate	Political Party	Popular Vote (%)	Electoral Vote
Grover Cleveland	Democratic	48.5	219
James G. Blaine	Republican	48.2	182

SOURCE: Historical Election Results, Electoral College, National Archives and Records Administration

Throughout the 1880s, Congress and the chief executive applied the laissez-faire principle selectively—for example, to the status of Indians. Like other critics of federal Indian policy, writer Helen Hunt Jackson in her 1881 book *A Century of Dishonor* called for applying the "protection of the law to the Indian's rights of property." Moved to act, Congress passed the Dawes General Allotment (Severalty) Act in 1887. The new act was intended to improve the economic condition of Indians by eliminating common ownership of tribal lands in favor of a system of private property. The law distributed plots of land to individual Indians who renounced traditional customs. The law also encouraged these landowners to become sedentary farmers and to adopt "other habits of civilized life." In the end, however, the act amounted to little more than a land-grab on the part of whites; between 1887 and 1900, Indian-held lands decreased from 138 million acres to 78 million acres.

By the 1880s, local citizens, through the Grange and their elected public officials, were calling for the states to restrict the monopolistic practices of the railroads, which routinely gave shipping discounts to large corporations. Nevertheless, in *Wabash v. Illinois* (1886), the Supreme Court invalidated a state law regulating railroads, ruling that only Congress, and not the states, could control interstate transportation. The next year, Congress passed the Interstate Commerce Act of 1887. This legislation mandated that the railroads charge all shippers the same rates and refrain from giving rebates to their largest customers. The act also established the Interstate Commerce Commission to oversee and stabilize the railroad industry. Congress thus acknowledged that the public interest demanded some form of business regulation, although enforcement of the act was less than vigorous.

Cleveland invoked laissez-faire principles in 1887 when he vetoed legislation that would have provided seeds for hard-pressed farmers in Texas. As the president put it, "Though the people support the government, the government should not support the people." Cleveland also favored lower tariff rates, but most Americans favored government protection of domestic manufacturing in the form of higher tariffs. The Republicans exploited Cleveland's unpopular views on this issue in the 1888 campaign, nominating Benjamin Harrison, grandson of President William Henry ("Tippecanoe") Harrison. The younger Harrison defeated his rival in the electoral college but not in the popular vote.

The principle of government laissez-faire was of little use in addressing a central paradox of the late nineteenth century: the free enterprise system was being undermined by the very forms of business organization it had spawned and nourished. Trusts and combinations were inherently hostile to competition. In 1890, Congress passed a piece of landmark legislation, the **Sherman Anti-Trust Act**, designed to outlaw trusts and large business combinations of all kinds.

Sherman Anti-Trust Act
Congressional legislation passed in 1890 outlawing trusts and large business combinations.

Table 16.3 THE ELECTION OF 1888

Candidate	Political Party	Popular Vote (%)	Electoral Vote
Benjamin Harrison	Republican	47.9	233
Grover Cleveland	Democratic	48.6	168
Clinton B. Fisk	Prohibition	2.2	—
Anson J. Streeter	Union Labor	1.3	—

SOURCE: Historical Election Results, Electoral College, National Archives and Records Administration

16.4.2 Social Darwinism and the "Natural" State of Society

In the late nineteenth century, human-made devices and engineering feats helped create a new social order, one marked by a few very wealthy industrialists, a growing middle class, and an increasingly diverse workforce of ill-paid field and factory hands. Brazenly borrowing from the theories of Charles Darwin, a British naturalist who had pioneered the study of evolution, some prominent clergy, businesspeople, journalists, and university professors sought to defend this new order as God-ordained or "natural." These observers drew parallels between Darwin's theory of "survival of the fittest" and the workings of modern society. (In his book *On the Origin of Species*, Darwin had discussed the study of animals, not people or societies.) In the United States, Social Darwinists warned that "unnatural" forms of intervention—specifically, labor unions or social welfare legislation—were misguided, dangerous, and ultimately doomed to failure. In essence, Social Darwinists distorted a compelling scientific theory, misusing it to justify exploitation of the poor and laboring classes.

The ideology of **Social Darwinism** evolved in response to class conflict and other forms of social turbulence in the 1870s and 1880s. Famed Brooklyn minister Henry Ward Beecher cited what he called "the great laws of political economy" to preach the virtues of poverty ("it was fit that man should eat the bread of affliction") and the evils of labor unions. Beecher and like-minded thinkers agreed that the government had the right and the obligation to come to the rescue of private companies threatened by angry workers or consumers. These observers also made a distinction between public subsidies to railroads and tariff protection for domestic manufacturers on one hand and public intervention on behalf of workers on the other.

Social Darwinism
A late-nineteenth-century variation on the theories of British naturalist Charles Darwin, promoting the idea that only the "fittest" individuals will, or deserve to, survive (i.e., the idea that society operates on principles of evolutionary biology).

Yale sociologist William Graham Sumner declared that society was like a living organism. For the species to remain healthy, individuals must prosper or decline according to their inherent characteristics. "Society, therefore, does not need any care or supervision," Sumner wrote in his 1883 treatise *What the Social Classes Owe to Each Other*. These views rationalized not only the hierarchies of the workplace but also the triumph of "Anglo Saxons" on the North American continent and beyond. Editors of

GILDED AGE INEQUALITY Although Social Darwinists argued that the increasing inequality of the Gilded Age was the "natural" result of the "fittest" Americans triumphing over the weak, many Americans criticized laissez-faire capitalism and the rise of big business. This *Puck* cartoon features prominent businessmen Cyrus Field, Jay Gould, Cornelius Vanderbilt, and Russell Sage riding atop the struggling masses—workers in the cloth, linen, iron, lumber, paper, and leather industries.

Everett Collection Inc/Alamy

How does the artist characterize the relationship between the wealthy and the laboring classes? In what ways does the cartoon critique the ideology of Social Darwinism?

the *New York Times* interpreted Darwin's ideas as suggesting that "the red man will be driven out, and the white man will take possession. This is not justice, but it is destiny." In his book *Our Country* (1885), the Reverend Josiah Strong also drew on the ideas of Social Darwinism to claim that just as the fittest plants and animals endure in the natural kingdom, so "civilized" whites would eventually displace "barbarous," dark-skinned peoples, whether on the High Plains of South Dakota or on the savannas of Africa.

Not all Americans studied or debated the theories of Charles Darwin, of course. Nevertheless, middle-class opinion-makers, many of them Victorian Protestants, believed that their own religious and cultural values remained superior to those of other groups of people, at home and abroad. The United States was becoming increasingly diverse in both economic and ethnic terms. At the same time, white, prosperous, native-born Protestants contended that they set the standards for the rest of the nation. These standards revolved around the middle-class domestic ideal, with its rigidly proscribed gender roles, devotion to personal achievement (for men at least), and commitment to moral suasion (that is, regulating a person's behavior by appealing to his or her conscience). Agents of the Victorian middle class included schoolteachers, clergy, magazine editors, business leaders, and other well-educated people able and willing to influence the beliefs and behavior of others.

Interpreting History

Andrew Carnegie: On the "Gospel of Wealth" (1889)

"It is a waste of time to criticize the inevitable."

In an article titled "Wealth," published in the North American Review *in 1889, steel manufacturer Andrew Carnegie defended the amassing of large fortunes on the part of a few. He hailed this trend as a sign of progress.*

The conditions of human life have not only been changed, but revolutionized, within the past few hundred years. In the former days there was little difference between the dwelling, dress, food, and environment of the chief and those of his retainers. The Indians are to-day where civilized man then was. When visiting the Sioux, I was led to the wigwam of the chief. It was just like the others in external appearance, and even within the difference was trifling between it and those of the poorest of his braves. The contrast between the palace of the millionaire and the cottage of the laborer with us to-day measures the change which has come with civilization.

This change, however, is not to be deplored, but welcomed as highly beneficial. It is well, nay, essential for the progress of the race, that the houses of some should be homes for all that is highest and best in literature and the arts, and for all the refinements of civilization, rather than that none should be so. Much better this great irregularity than universal squalor. . . . Whether the change be for good or ill, it is upon us, beyond our power to alter, and therefore to be accepted and made the best of. It is a waste of time to criticize the inevitable.

Carnegie believed that wealthy people had the responsibility to give away their money before they died, although he had distinct ideas about to whom—or to what—such money should be given. He elaborated on what came to be called the "gospel of wealth":

There remains, then, only one mode of using great fortunes; but in this we have the true antidote for the temporary

CARTOON ILLUSTRATION OF ANDREW CARNEGIE This *Judge* cartoon depicts Andrew Carnegie dispersing his fortune. Many of his donations were used for the establishment of public libraries, a worthy cause according to Carnegie's "gospel of wealth."

Fotosearch/Getty Images

Carnegie believed that a society was "civilized" to the degree that the gap between rich and poor was wide and growing. Why did admirers claim, however, that his philanthropic projects—especially schools and libraries—actually promoted equality?

unequal distribution of wealth, the reconciliation of the rich and the poor—a reign of harmony—another ideal, differing indeed, from that of the Communist in requiring only the further evolution of existing conditions, not the total overthrow of our civilization. . . . Under its sway we shall have an ideal state, in which the surplus wealth of the few will become, in the best sense, the property of the many, because it is administered for the common good, and this wealth, passing through the hands of the few, can be made a much more potent force for the elevation of our race than if it had been distributed in small sums to the people themselves. Even the poorest can be made to see this, and to agree that the great sums gathered by some of their fellow-citizens and spent for public purposes, from which the masses reap the principal benefit, are more valuable to them than if scattered through the course of many years in trifling amounts.

In 1901 Carnegie sold his steel company to banker J. P. Morgan for $480 million. By the time of his death, Carnegie had given away an estimated $350 million to a variety of causes and institutions.

Questions for Discussion

1. How does Carnegie link extremes of wealth and poverty with progress?

2. Why did Carnegie focus his philanthropic energies on building public libraries?

3. Why would Carnegie have rejected as impractical and unreasonable the argument that he should have paid his workers higher wages rather than distributing his profits to charity?

SOURCE: Andrew Carnegie, "Wealth," *North American Review* (1889).

Conclusion

Some historians suggest that the great captains of industry were the chief representatives of widely held values in late-nineteenth-century America. Men such as Carnegie and Rockefeller had the vision and personal ambition necessary to build large corporate enterprises. They became fabulously wealthy by providing the United States with the ingredients necessary to an economic revolution: steel, oil, and other materials. Their ideology of unbridled individualism encouraged many people to aspire to entrepreneurial independence: the tailor's hope that he would someday own his own store, the waiter's dream of opening his own restaurant. The explosion of economic activity during this period—a second American industrial revolution—widened the middle class and lent credence to the notion of widespread upward mobility, modest though it was in most cases.

Nevertheless, a case can be made that engineers were the true representatives of the age. As designers of railroad routes, gravity-defying skyscrapers, and new systems of shop-floor management, they oversaw the technical aspects of economic growth and development. Engineers melded science with mass production to yield a form of capitalism that thrived on consumers' deepest desires and anxieties. In the process, a new, complex national culture emerged.

This culture valued innovation, newness, fashion, change, and sensory stimulation. Advertisers sought to convince consumers that they should buy products that were up to date. Customers all over the country desired to experience thrilling and novel theatrical spectacles and athletic contests. "Desires" replaced more traditional "needs" when Americans of all ages contemplated buying clothes and household furnishings. Yet this culture also embraced impulses that were conservative, promoting the idea that white, Protestant, native-born Americans set the standard against which other Americans were judged, and often found wanting. Still, many native-born Americans and immigrants to the United States found this vital consumer culture enormously appealing.

At the same time, the effort to homogenize and standardize American cultural impulses was not without complications. Throughout the nation, various groups rejected standardization in favor of local tradition or new forms of collective action. Thus, politicians and the Social Darwinists were forced to defend their outlook on life. Some of their critics advanced the idea that society was not a living organism at all. Rather, it was like a machine, a creation of people who had the ability—and the duty—to repair or adjust it. Around the country, in fact, the standardizers met with stiff resistance.

Chapter Review

16.1   The New Shape of Business

What were the challenges faced by large business owners and managers who sought to mass produce and mass market their goods?

Large business owners wanted to eliminate competition, to market and distribute their products to far-flung parts of the country, and to control labor costs. They formed larger organizations known as pools or trusts; utilized technological innovations in transportation, production, and distribution; and sought lower-paid, efficient, and compliant workers.

16.2   The Birth of a National Urban Culture

What technological and managerial innovations shaped the nation's largest cities in the late nineteenth century?

Urban planners and engineers developed sophisticated transportation networks, supplied water for commercial and private purposes, built skyscrapers, designed parks and bridges, and created ways of getting rid of waste. Local governments expanded, and political machines provided goods and services to residents in exchange for votes.

16.3   Thrills, Chills, and Toothpaste: The Emergence of Consumer Culture

What were the social and economic consequences of the new consumer culture?

The new consumer culture was big business. Athletic events, traveling circuses, and department stores stimulated the rise of mass advertising. Although commercialized leisure brought different groups together in the same physical space, it also promoted the idea that white, native-born Protestants set the standards of consumption and behavior.

16.4   Defending the New Industrial Order

What arguments were offered by defenders of the new industrial order, including politicians, business owners, and influential writers and thinkers?

Politicians selectively invoked the concept of laissez-faire to justify government indifference in some areas but government intervention in others. Certain businesspeople, writers, and thinkers defended social inequality by arguing that the system of industrial capitalism was "natural" and that people would, and did, prosper or fail according to their inherent characteristics.

Timeline

1877	"Great Labor Uprising" of railroad employees and other workers
1878	Thomas Edison patents the phonograph
	San Francisco Workingmen's party stages anti-Chinese protests
1879	First telephone line connects two American cities (Boston and Lowell, Massachusetts)
1880	New York City streets lit by electricity
1882	Standard Oil Trust is created
	Chinese Exclusion Act
1883	Pendleton Act (civil service reform)
1887	Interstate Commerce Act creates Interstate Commerce Commission
1889	First All-American football team, consisting of players from Yale, Harvard, and Princeton

Glossary

trust A combination of firms or corporations created for the purpose of reducing competition and controlling prices throughout an industry.

Chinese Exclusion Act Legislation passed by Congress in 1882 to deny any additional Chinese laborers entry into the country while allowing some Chinese merchants and students to immigrate.

anti-semitism Prejudice against Jews.

bloody shirt A partisan rallying cry used to stir up or revive sectional or party animosity after the American Civil War; for example, post–Civil War Republicans "waved the bloody shirt," associating some Democrats with a treasonous acceptance of secession during the war, while opponents had spilled their blood for the Union.

laissez-faire A belief in little or no government interference in the economy.

Edmunds Act Congressional legislation passed in 1882 and aimed at Utah Mormons; it outlawed polygamy, stripped polygamists of the right to vote, and provided for a five-member commission to oversee Utah's elections.

civil service reform Measures designed to eliminate the spoils system in government hiring, in favor of maintaining professional standards in public service.

Pendleton Act Congressional legislation passed in 1883; established a merit system for federal job applicants and created the Civil Service Commission, which administered competitive examinations to candidates in certain job classifications.

Sherman Anti-Trust Act Congressional legislation passed in 1890 outlawing trusts and large business combinations.

Social Darwinism A late-nineteenth-century variation on the theories of British naturalist Charles Darwin, promoting the idea that only the "fittest" individuals will, or deserve to, survive (i.e., the idea that society operates on principles of evolutionary biology).

Chapter 17
Challenges to Government and Corporate Power, 1877–1890

WOMEN OF THE KNIGHTS OF LABOR Women delegates at the national meeting of the Knights of Labor in 1886 pose for a group portrait. Women workers, like their black counterparts, belonged to segregated auxiliaries of local all-male unions. The Knights prided themselves on their inclusive approach to labor organizing. Their approach differed from that of most other national unions, such as the American Federation of Labor, which organized mostly white male skilled workers.

Library of Congress Prints and Photographs Division [LC-USZ62-12485]

What barriers did the Knights of Labor face, both within and outside their organization, in their efforts to build a labor movement based on the equality of all workers?

Contents and Focus Questions

17.1 Resistance to Legal and Military Authority
What were the various protest strategies used by different groups of people who faced discrimination, and at times violence, from employers, government officials, vigilantes, and the U.S. military?

17.2 Revolt in the Workplace
What technological and structural changes in the workplace prompted farmers and workers to organize between 1877 and 1890?

17.3 Crosscurrents of Reform
How did social reformers differ from labor radicals in their assumptions about the need for, and the means of, social change?

Who were the mysterious nightriders who attacked the property of ranchers and railroad owners in northern New Mexico in 1889 and 1890? What were their motives?

In the spring of 1889, men in San Miguel County, northern New Mexico Territory, armed themselves, donned masks, and rode out on horseback to attack those whom they considered their enemies. As members of a secret organization called *las Gorras Blancas* (the White Caps), they banded together to destroy the fences of local cattle ranchers. They also burned bridges, haystacks, and piles of lumber, cut telegraph wires, and took axes to electric light poles and railroad ties belonging to the Atchison, Topeka, and Santa Fe Railroad. Their membership overlapped with that of the **Knights of Labor**, a national labor union that boasted twenty local assemblies in San Miguel County, east of Santa Fe. On the night of March 11, 1890, *las Gorras Blancas* nailed copies of their platform to buildings; the document declared, "Our purpose is to protect the rights and interests of the people in general; especially those of the helpless classes."

These nightriders consisted mainly of Spanish-speaking natives of the area who were desperately, and violently, struggling to preserve a traditional way of life that was rapidly disappearing. Fenced lands prevented the area's Hispanic settlers from grazing their stock herds in the customary open-range manner. The fence cutters and the railroad tie burners believed they were upholding American principles of justice and fair play by warring against the sheep and cattle ranchers, lawyers, speculators, commercial lumberers, and railroads that were all transforming the local landscape and economy.

*   *   *   *   *

Las Gorras Blancas represented a unique response to local conditions. But it was also part of a growing, nationwide movement against the standard imposed by industrialization and capitalism. Around the country, a wide variety of individuals and organizations emerged in the late 1870s and the 1880s to challenge employers, landlords, and military and government officials. Members of these latter groups responded with a challenge of their own: business, they proclaimed, must be allowed to develop fully and freely without "unnatural" intervention in the form of regulatory legislation or grassroots rebellions such as that of *las Gorras Blancas*.

It is difficult to generalize about those who contested the emerging order. Even their names could be misleading. In the early 1890s, another group called "White Caps," this one in Mississippi, consisted of whites who terrorized black landowners and sharecroppers. And the Knights of Labor shaped its program in accordance with local issues. In San Miguel County, for example, the issue was land—who controlled it and for what purposes. In Washington, D.C., the concern of the Knights was the welfare of workers in the building trades. The Richmond, Virginia, Knights pioneered interracial organizing, living up to the group's motto, "an injury to one is an injury to all." In contrast, the San Francisco Knights spearheaded the move to bar Chinese laborers from the United States and to limit job opportunities for those who remained. Indeed, groups that challenged the authority of government and large business interests often disagreed among themselves about goals and strategies for change.

Knights of Labor
A secret fraternal order founded in 1869. Terence V. Powderly was the most influential leader of the Knights, which sponsored local labor-organizing drives among all kinds of workers, black and white and skilled and unskilled. Their motto was "an injury to one is an injury to all."

17.1 Resistance to Legal and Military Authority

What were the various protest strategies used by different groups of people who faced discrimination, and at times violence, from employers, government officials, vigilantes, and the U.S. military?

America's march toward national economic centralization and integration was not steady. In the workplace, and in the courts, European Americans pressed their advantage, but these efforts met with stiff resistance from a variety of aggrieved groups. Members of these groups rightly believed they had much to lose from so-called progress. European Americans repeatedly used the notion of "racial" difference as a justification for depriving darker-skinned peoples of their claims to land, jobs, and education. For example, California lawmakers approved legislation that discriminated against the Chinese as workers and as parents of school-aged children. In an effort to seek redress, some Chinese took their claims to court. These immigrants saw the English language and the American legal system as resources as they pressed for their own claims to equality and fair play under the law.

In a similar vein, prejudice against African Americans assumed the form of discriminatory legislation and random violence. Blacks chafed under restrictions intended to bar them from good jobs and from associating with white people on an equal basis. Varieties of black resistance to white authority included migration out of the South to the West, creation of community institutions, and violent retaliation.

For their part, during the late 1880s, the Plains Indians responded to encroaching railroads, settlers, and military regiments by embracing a movement of spiritual regeneration. On the Plains, whites, and especially U.S. military officers, perceived this movement as more dangerous than an armed uprising, and they reacted accordingly.

17.1.1 Chinese Lawsuits in California

Some white people believed that they would only prosper to the extent that they could deny certain groups—immigrants, African Americans—equality of opportunity. Throughout California, for example, unemployed whites agitated for the violent expulsion of Chinese from jobs. (Most of these immigrants received two-thirds the wages of their white counterparts for the same work.) Opposition to the Chinese hardened in the 1880s. In San Francisco, the Knights of Labor and the Workingmen's party of California helped to engineer the passage of the **Chinese Exclusion Act**, approved by Congress in 1882. This measure denied any additional Chinese laborers entry into the country while allowing some Chinese merchants and students to immigrate. In railroad towns and mining camps, vigilantes looted and burned Chinese communities, in some cases murdering or expelling their inhabitants. In 1885, in Rock Springs, Wyoming, white workers massacred twenty-eight Chinese and drove hundreds out of town in the wake of an announcement by Union Pacific officials that the railroad would begin hiring the lower-paid immigrants. Cheered on by others, a mob burned the Chinese section of town to the ground.

Whites held that the Chinese, with their distinctive customs, would never fit into American life. Nevertheless, early on the Chinese demonstrated an understanding and appreciation of American political and legal processes. Beginning in Gold Rush days, Chinese immigrants had taken their grievances to court. In 1862, in San Francisco, Ling Sing protested the $2.50 personal tax levied on Chinese miners. The California Supreme Court agreed (in *Ling Sing v. Washburn*) that the group could not be singled out for special taxes. In the 1870s, Chinese merchants used the provisions of the Civil Rights Act to challenge state and local laws that forbade them from holding certain jobs, living in white neighborhoods, and testifying in court.

Chinese Exclusion Act
Legislation passed by Congress in 1882 to deny any additional Chinese laborers entry into the country while allowing some Chinese merchants and students to immigrate.

In San Francisco in 1885, laundry operator Yick Wo was convicted under an 1880 municipal law prohibiting the construction of wooden laundries without a license. A native of China, Yick Wo had arrived in the United States in 1861. By the time of his arrest, he had operated a legal laundry for twenty-two years. When he applied for a license, the board of supervisors turned him down, just as the board had denied licenses to all Chinese laundry operators who applied. In 1885, his lawyers petitioned the California Supreme Court, which upheld Yick Wo's arrest. The lawyers continued their appeal to the U.S. Supreme Court, maintaining that the board of supervisors intended to bar Chinese from independent laundry work altogether. In *Yick Wo v. Hopkins* (1886), the Supreme Court reversed the state court's decision. The higher court held that the San Francisco laundry-licensing board had engaged in the discriminatory *application* of a law that on the surface was nondiscriminatory.

Still, many cases challenging discriminatory laws never made it to the nation's highest court. And state and local courts in general often refused to acknowledge that Chinese immigrants had any civil rights at all. (Chinese immigrants were not granted citizenship until World War II, although their children born in this country qualified as citizens.) In 1885, the California Supreme Court heard the case *Tape v. Hurley*, brought by Joseph and Mary Tape on behalf of their daughter Mamie. Joseph Tape was a Chinese immigrant with some standing in the San Francisco Chinese community. Mary Tape had been raised in a Shanghai orphanage and had come to the United States with missionaries when she was eleven years old. She grew up to speak English fluently and dressed as a European American. Their daughter Mamie was quite westernized as well.

Even so, Mamie Tape was barred from the city's public school system. The school board claimed that Mamie's presence in the classroom would be "very mentally and morally detrimental" to her classmates. The Tapes sued the city and won, but the school board retaliated by creating a separate school for children of Asian descent within Chinatown. Mary Tape wrote an angry letter to the board: "Dear Sirs, Will you please to tell me! Is it a disgrace to be Born a Chinese? Didn't God make us all!!! What right! have you to bar my children out of the school?" In the end, the Tapes decided to enroll their two children in the segregated school. Yet their legal protest kept alive the ideal of equality under the law.

17.1.2 Blacks in the "New South"

Similar problems plagued African Americans in what Atlanta journalist Henry Grady hailed as the "**New South**." The former Confederate states, he claimed, were now forward looking, prepared to embrace industrialization and promote the reconciliation of blacks and whites. According to the journalist, it was time for the South to march forward and join with a larger, modernizing America.

Grady's speech about the "New South" provided a label that stuck. Yet he doubtless spoke too soon and in terms too grandiose. True, he could point with pride to some dramatic industrial developments in the South. Soon after James Bonsack invented a cigarette-rolling machine in 1880, James Buchanan Duke pioneered the production of machine-made cigarettes. In 1884, Duke's Durham, North Carolina, company was selling 400,000 of them each day. The southern textile labor force more than doubled between 1880 and 1890. And by the mid-1880s, with the backing of the Tennessee Coal, Iron, and Railway Company, the city of Birmingham, Alabama, specialized in pig iron production.

Factory and professional work in towns and cities offered new opportunities in the South as industry developed. However, these jobs were dominated by white men. Low-paid heavy labor, primarily in rural areas, continued to be the primary source of work for black men. The hardest and lowest-paid jobs, such as digging ore out of a hill in northern Alabama or constructing a railroad through the swamps of Florida, often went to convicts whom private employers had leased from the state. Most of these

New South

A term coined by Atlanta journalist Henry Grady in 1886 to suggest that the former Confederate states were now willing to embrace industrialization and modernization.

AH QUIN, AH SUE, AND FAMILY Some Chinese made a prosperous life for themselves in the United States. This photo shows Ah Sue, her husband, Ah Quin, and their twelve children. Ah Sue found refuge in the San Francisco Chinese Mission Home in 1879. Two years later, she and Ah Quin celebrated their Christian wedding in the Mission Home. Ah Quin rose from the position of cook to become a successful railroad contractor and merchant in San Diego.

Library of Congress Prints and Photographs Division [LC-USZ62-75205]

In what ways did the Quin family differ from the vast majority of Chinese immigrants who came to the West Coast during the late nineteenth century?

"convict lease" workers were black men who had been arrested on minor charges and then bound out when they could not pay their fines or court costs. In Mississippi, a black man could be picked up for "some trifling misdemeanor," in the words of one observer, fined $500, and compelled to work off the fine (at a rate of 5 cents a day) for a local planter. With an almost unlimited supply of such workers, employers had little incentive to ease the brutal living and working conditions endured by these convicts.

Patterns of migration within and outside the South reveal blacks' efforts to resist discrimination. Some blacks fled the countryside and settled in southern cities, where good jobs were still limited but personal freedom was greater. Gradually, a new black elite arose. These physicians, lawyers, insurance agents, and undertakers reached out to an exclusively black clientele. They also nourished a sense of community. Black men and women continued to sustain their own institutions, such as schools, lodges, benevolent societies, burial organizations, and churches.

Despite Henry Grady's pronouncements, clearly the South had not abandoned its historical legacy of white supremacist ideologies. In fact, in the late 1880s, white Democrats feared the assertiveness of the new black elite. According to whites, this generation of men and women born as free persons and not as slaves must be "put in their place," quite literally. As a result, new state and local laws mandated separate water fountains for blacks and whites, restricted blacks to separate railroad cars and other forms of public transportation, and excluded them altogether from city parks and other public spaces. Long-standing customs barring black people from white-owned theaters, restaurants, and hotels now carried the weight of law. There were two separate school systems, one white and well funded, one black and starved of cash. Legal discrimination against blacks came to be called **Jim Crow**, a set of laws akin to twentieth-century South Africa's system of apartheid mandating the strict segregation (in public) of groups labeled according to their heritage or the color of their skin.

Jim Crow
The name given to the set of legal institutions that ensured the segregation of nonwhite people in the South.

Because of the economic and political restrictions imposed upon them, many black men and women had to make do with many fewer opportunities than those enjoyed by their white counterparts. In Savannah, Georgia, for example, well-educated black men who aspired to positions of political influence remained active in community organizations such as the Baptist and Methodist churches, and the Masons, a fraternal order. For decent jobs, many of them relied on patronage positions with the local federal custom house or post office (positions available to them only if a Republican president was in the White House). Small business owners such as butchers and grocers catered to members of their own community. Yet black men and women deeply resented the unequal public education reserved for black children, the separate streetcars reserved for black riders, and the poll tax and other means of disfranchisement that kept potential black voters powerless.

Black leaders throughout the country tried to keep a national spotlight on the legal and violent manifestations of the Jim Crow system. A rising tide of lynching engulfed the South, cresting in the 1890s, but white officials did little or nothing to halt it. Black men, women, and children were all vulnerable to the fury of the white lynch mob—on the most flimsy pretext. Blacks throughout the segregated South rightly feared that they would be targeted if they spoke out against lynching. Yet northern blacks did not hesitate to highlight the hypocrisy of the federal government, which turned a blind eye toward this practice. Frances Ellen Watkins Harper, an educator and writer living in Philadelphia, issued the following challenge to an audience of white club women: "A government which has the power to tax a man in peace, draft him in war, should have the power to defend his life in the hour of peril." Harper condemned "the government which can protect and defend its citizens from wrong and outrage and does not."

17.1.3 Jim Crow in the West

Racial segregation was not limited to the South. The U.S. military enforced its own set of Jim Crow regulations. In 1869, Congress created the 24th and 25th Infantries (Colored), composed of African American soldiers. White officers were appointed to lead these segregated units. Consequently, black men who aspired to positions of military leadership found their way blocked. Some white officers, such as George Custer, refused to command black troops at all.

Military officials assigned black soldiers to the West, where they became known as buffalo soldiers. (The origins of the term are unclear. It may refer to the buffalo robes worn by many of the soldiers or to Plains Indians' respect for the black men's skills on horseback.) Many of these men were proud to wear a U.S. soldier's uniform, an emblem of their newly won citizenship rights. They helped to construct new roads and forts, protect wagon trains of settlers, and patrol the border between the United States and Mexico. They were an integral part of campaigns to subdue the Cheyenne, Comanche, Sioux, Ute, Kiowa, and Apache. They were among the soldiers deployed to quash strikes among workers (silver miners in Idaho, for example) and to fight forest fires in the Northwest.

Often the buffalo soldiers encountered hostility from local townspeople, who resented their patronage of local establishments. In 1881, black Tenth Cavalry troops stationed at Fort Concho near San Angelo, Texas, reacted angrily when a local white man killed a black soldier in a saloon. Another soldier had died at the hands of a local white within the previous two weeks. In the absence of justice for the murderers, the soldiers blanketed San Angelo with handbills. Signed "U.S. soldiers," the message read, "If we do not receive justice and fair play . . . someone will suffer, if not the guilty, the innocent. It has gone far enough." When some of the soldiers attacked one of the men they believed guilty, the Texas Rangers entered the town to restore order. The army transferred the black companies out of the area and disciplined the leaders of the protest.

Once they were mustered out of the army, some black soldiers decided to settle permanently in the West. There they joined thousands of black migrants who were fleeing the Jim Crow South. In the late 1870s, 20,000 blacks from Tennessee, Mississippi, and Louisiana, called "Exodusters," migrated into western Kansas. The migrants cited the South's convict lease system, poor schools, and pervasive violence and intimidation as reasons for their flight. Some of these migrants established all-black towns in Kansas, Colorado, Nebraska, and New Mexico. Though generally small and poor, such towns provided places for blacks to live in safety and on their own terms.

17.1.4 The Ghost Dance on the High Plains

In contrast to African Americans and Chinese immigrants, for the most part Indians did not aspire to full civil rights within the United States. Rather, most Native groups maintained as their goal independence from whites—that is, group sovereignty within the boundaries of the nation. Some of these groups sought "equality" not with whites, but with their ancestors who had lived free from white interference, free to hunt and live on the Plains according to their own traditions.

Their lands and way of life threatened by whites, western Indians sought desperately to revitalize their culture and protect themselves. In 1889, an Indian named Wovoka offered the Plains Indians a mystical vision of the future, a vision that promised a return to the beloved past. A leader of the Paiute in Nevada, Wovoka preached what came to be called the **Ghost Dance**, part religion and part resistance movement. In 1889, a solar eclipse occurred while Wovoka was wracked by fever, and he claimed that the conjunction of the two events enabled him to glimpse the afterworld. The Indians could usher in a new day of peace, Wovoka proclaimed, and this new day would be a time free of disease and armed conflict. The buffalo would return, he promised, and the Indian men and women who had died would come back to replenish depleted villages.

Many of the Indians who performed the Ghost Dance fell into a trance-like state, bringing inspiration to impoverished and disheartened reservation communities. However, as the ritual spread across the Plains, U.S. military officials grew anxious. In November 1890, E. B. Reynolds, a Special U.S. Indian Agent, described to his superiors in Washington the strange, seemingly dangerous behavior that had gripped the Indians on Pine Ridge Reservation in South Dakota: "The religious excitement aggravated by almost starvation is bearing fruits in this state of insubordination; Indians say they had better die fighting than to die a slow death of starvation, and as the new religion promises their return to earth, at the coming of the millennium, they have no fear of death."

As tensions between whites and Indians mounted, Sitting Bull emerged as a spiritual and political leader. After leading his followers into Canada, Sitting Bull returned to the United States in 1881 and later performed briefly with Buffalo Bill Cody in the "Wild West" show. He surrendered at Fort Buford, Dakota Territory, where he was held prisoner for two years. His brief stint as a performer in Buffalo Bill Cody's "Wild West" show left him disgusted with the ways of white people.

Ghost Dance
A dance performed as part of a mystical vision of the future, a time free of disease and armed conflict, as offered by an Indian named Wovoka in 1889. Many of the Plains Indians who performed the dance fell into a trance-like state.

Sitting Bull offered a pointed critique of the sedentary, materialistic way of life promoted by whites:

> White men like to dig in the ground for their food. My people prefer to hunt the buffalo as their fathers did. White men like to stay in one place. My people want to move their tepees here and there to the different hunting grounds. The life of white men is slavery. They are prisoners in towns or farms. The life my people want is a life of freedom. I have seen nothing that a white man has, houses or railways or clothing or food, that is as good as the right to move in open country, and live in our own fashion.

Sitting Bull rejected white notions of "progress" in favor of his people's traditions. In mid-December 1890, military officials ordered Indian police to arrest Sitting Bull at his cabin on the Standing Rock Reservation in South Dakota. Alarmed by what they perceived as rising Indian militancy, white settlers in Nebraska and South Dakota pressured the government to rid the area of the "savages . . . armed to the teeth," men who were "traitors, anarchists, and assassins." While arresting Sitting Bull, his Indian captors killed him.

A week later, on December 28 and 29, soldiers of the Seventh Cavalry under Colonel James Forsyth attacked Indians at **Wounded Knee Creek**, South Dakota. Estimates of the number of Indians killed range from 150 to 250. More than sixty women and

Wounded Knee Creek
The site of a massacre of 150–250 South Dakota Indians by U. S. troops in 1890. This was the last violent encounter between Plains Indians and U. S. Cavalry forces.

Map 17.1 INDIAN LANDS LOST, 1850–1890

Indian cessions 1850–1890
- Indian lands ceded before 1850
- Indian lands ceded 1850–1890 with dates of "Treaties"
- Indian lands seized without any formal "Treaty" cession
- Modern state boundaries

Between 1850 and 1890, many "treaties" signed by Indian groups and the U.S. government provided that Indians turn over land in exchange for cash payments. Yet U.S. military forces seized a large portion of western Indian lands by force, without signing any treaty agreements at all. By 1890, many Indians lived on reservations, apart from European American society.

children were among those slain as they fled the oncoming troops. The massacre at Wounded Knee proved the last major violent encounter between Plains Indians and U.S. cavalry forces. By this time, many Indians throughout the Midwest lived on reservations and engaged in farming. Government agents, eager to create independent farmers, instructed Indian men in the use of the plow. But plowing became a collective effort, as bands would work together until their task was done. Thus, some Indian groups attempted to maintain customs of collective endeavor in opposition to the European Americans' glorification of ambition and individualism.

Nevertheless, Chinese immigrants, southern African Americans, and Plains Indians were not the only groups to feel aggrieved at the hands of private and public interests. In some cases, native-born white American men and women also protested against what they perceived to be unfair policies and practices on the part of business and the federal government.

17.2 Revolt in the Workplace

What technological and structural changes in the workplace prompted farmers and workers to organize between 1877 and 1890?

During the late nineteenth century, workers launched different kinds of challenges against the system of industrial capitalism, which, many charged, enriched a few industrialists and bankers at the expense of the vast majority of laboring people. Workers joined together in unions, and in many cases, they fought the violence of private company security forces with violence of their own. Some men and women destroyed the machinery that threatened to replace them in the workplace. By the early 1890s, critics of the new industrial and agribusiness order—a system driven by technological innovation—had come together in the form of a new political group, the People's party, or **Populists**. This organization aimed to bring together urban and rural, male and female, agricultural and industrial workers to protest the hardships suffered by laborers of all kinds and to demand that the federal government take strong action in rectifying social ills.

Nevertheless, in workplace conflicts, the lines were not always strictly drawn between employees and employers. For example, the late nineteenth-century laboring classes never achieved the level of unity called for by the Populists. White workers often expressed intense hostility toward their African American and Chinese counterparts. Within small towns, shopkeepers and landlords at times showed solidarity with striking workers; in these cases, community ties were stronger than class differences. Also, despite their critique of big business, workers often embraced the emerging consumer culture. In fact, many of them fought for shorter work days and higher wages so that they could enjoy their share of the material blessings of American life—in department stores, movie theaters, and amusement parks. In the end, Populism was primarily a rural movement composed of small farmers, sharecroppers, and wage hands.

Populists

Agrarian reformers who formed the Populist, or People's party, a major (third) political party that emerged mostly in the Midwest and South in the late 1880s to address the needs of workers and farmers in opposition to government monetary policies and big business. The party faltered after its presidential candidate, William Jennings Bryan, lost in the 1896 election.

17.2.1 Trouble on the Farm

In the late summer of 1878, the combined effects of the recent national economic depression and the loss of jobs to labor-saving technology catalyzed a rash of machine breaking throughout rural Ohio. In the Midwest, displaced farmhands burned the reapers, mowers, and threshers of their former employers. Some wealthy farmers responded by abandoning their machinery and rehiring their farmhands. Technology, one noted, "ought to be dispensed with in times like these." By contrast, critics charged the machine-breakers with "short-sighted madness." The protests revealed that even family farming had become a business. Now farmers needed to secure bank loans, invest in new machinery, and worry about the price of crops in the world market. These changes had profoundly altered labor relations between farm workers and farmers and between farmers and their creditors.

On the Northern Plains, farmers endured extremes of weather and the anxiety of uncertain harvests. In the mid-1880s, the plight of Plains farmers worsened when a series of natural disasters highlighted their vulnerability to the elements. Drought and declining wheat prices drove half the population of western Kansas and Nebraska back east to Iowa and Illinois between 1888 and 1892. Meanwhile, the bitterly cold winter of 1886–1887 decimated cattle herds throughout the region.

These problems contributed to a radical turn in farmers' politics. In the 1880s, a national movement emerged and tapped into a wellspring of anger and discontent in farming regions throughout the nation. The Southern Alliance in Louisiana, Texas, and Arkansas pressed for an expanded currency, taxation reform, and government ownership of transportation and communication lines. Its members tended to ally with the Democratic party. The Northern Alliance from the Plains states also focused on the expansion of the currency supply—specifically, the coinage of silver—but advocated the formation of a third political party to advance its interests. Both of these large regional groups found adherents in the mountain West. There, miners and farmers joined together to protest the monopolistic powers of the railroads, privately owned water companies, and silver mining interests. These monopolies drove up consumer prices and depressed workers' wages.

Most Alliance men and women farmed modest parcels of land. As small producers, they felt powerless to influence the businesspeople and politicians who affected their

WINDMILL ON A NEBRASKA FAMILY FARM A Nebraska farm family poses proudly with their new windmill, around 1890. Such devices powered water pumps that reached deep into the earth. Though expensive, windmills were necessities for drought-stricken farmers on the Plains, especially during the harsh years of the mid-1880s to the mid-1890s.

Library of Congress Prints and Photographs Division [LC-DIG-ppmsca-08371]

How might a modest farm family hope to pay for an expensive piece of machinery like a windmill?

livelihoods and their life possibilities. Members of the Alliance also presented themselves as the last line of defense for the noble yeoman in the face of the corrupting influences of modern corporate capitalism. In rural Alabama, where the Farmers' Alliance had links with local schools and churches, the group's newspapers railed against the "filthy city," a "wicked place" of vice, crime, and dissipation. Farm folk thus distanced themselves from the "New South Creed," which promoted materialism and industrialization.

Yet most rural organizations had little hope of forestalling the kind of "progress" that promoted commercial development. For example, in northern New Mexico Territory, *las Gorras Blancas* had only mixed success in their campaign against the railroads, ranchers, and land speculators. For a time the group managed to discourage new European Americans from settling the area, and they prevented the railroads from buying more rail ties in the region. Yet nightriders could not stem the tide of land loss throughout the Southwest. The Court of Private Land Claims, established in 1891 by the U. S. government, resolved land disputes between Hispanic and European American claimants. Of the more than 35 million acres of land in dispute in the early 1890s, Hispanic claimants received little more than 2 million acres—barely one-twentieth of the land they held in common.

Local rural and agricultural groups more successfully pressed their interests when they forged alliances across regions and between urban residents and farmers. Although the Farmers' Alliance identified itself primarily with agricultural interests, it made some notable forays into coalition-building as well. In 1899, the northern and southern groups attempted to combine with the Colored Farmers' Alliance, whose members were outspoken in the claim that modest farmers in general would not enjoy equality of opportunity until the barriers between blacks and whites were eliminated. Together, these groups claimed more than 4 million members. They also sought to join with the Knights of Labor and thus bring all members of the "producing classes" together. By representing the financial interests of all farmers and highlighting the vulnerabilities of debtors, the organization foreshadowed the wider national appeal of the Populist party in the 1890s.

17.2.2 Militancy in the Factories and Mines

The new economy wrought profound hardship on members of the urban laboring classes as well as on small farmers. Many industrial workers faced layoffs and wage cuts during the depressions of the 1870s and 1880s. The great railroad strikes of 1877 (see Chapter 16) foreshadowed an era of bitter industrial conflict. Because no laws regulated private industry, employers could impose ten- to fifteen-hour workdays, six days a week. Industrial accidents were all too common, and most industries lacked safety precautions. Steelworkers labored in excessive heat, and miners and textile mill employees alike contracted respiratory diseases. With windows closed and machines speeded up, new forms of technology created new risks for workers. The Chicago meatpackers, who wielded gigantic cleavers in subfreezing lockers, and the California wheat harvesters, who operated complex mechanical binders and threshers, were among those confronting danger on the job.

In 1884, the Massachusetts Bureau of Statistics of Labor issued a report outlining the occupational hazards for working women in the city of Boston. In button-making establishments, female workers often got their fingers caught under punch-and-die machines. Employers provided a surgeon to dress an employee's wounds the first three times she was injured; thereafter, she had to pay for her own medical care. Women operated heavy power machinery in the garment industry and exposed themselves to dangerous chemicals and processing materials in paper-box making, fish packing, and candy manufacturing.

Some women workers, especially those who monopolized certain kinds of jobs, organized and struck for higher wages. Three thousand Atlanta washerwomen launched such an effort in 1881 but failed to get their demands met. Most women found it difficult to win the respect not only of employers but also of male unionists. Leonora Barry, an organizer for the Knights of Labor, sought to change that. Barry visited mills and factories around the country. At each stop, she highlighted women's unique difficulties and condemned the "selfishness of their brothers in toil" who resented women's intrusion into the workplace. Barry was reacting to men such as Edward O'Donnell, a prominent labor official who claimed that wage-earning women threatened the role of men as family breadwinners.

For both men and women workers, the influx of 5.25 million new immigrants in the 1880s stiffened job competition at worksites throughout the country. To make matters worse, vast outlays of capital needed to mechanize and organize manufacturing plants placed pressure on employers to economize. Many of them did so by cutting wages. Like the family farmer who could no longer claim the status of the independent yeoman, industrial workers depended on employers and consumers for their physical well-being and very survival.

Not until 1935 would American workers have the right to organize and bargain collectively with their employers. Until then, laborers who saw strength in numbers and expressed an interest in a union could be summarily fired, blacklisted (their names circulated to other employers), and harassed by private security forces. The Pinkerton National Detective Agency, founded in 1850 by a Scottish immigrant named Allan Pinkerton, initially found eager clients among the railroads. The Pinkertons, as they were called, served as industrial spies and policemen during some of the most bitter and violent strikes of the late nineteenth century.

The Knights of Labor, a secret fraternal order founded in 1869, came under the leadership of Terence V. Powderly a decade later. With this Irish American at the helm (he was called Grand Master Workman), the labor union made impressive gains in the 1880s. In appealing to many different kinds of workers around the country, the Knights blended a critique of the late nineteenth-century wage system with a belief in the dignity of labor and a call for collective action. According to the Knights, business monopolies and corrupt politicians everywhere shared a common interest in exploiting the labor of ordinary men and women. The Knights advocated a return to the time when workers controlled their own labor and received a just price for the products they made. "We declare an inevitable and irresistible conflict between the wage system of labor and republican system of government," the Knights proclaimed. By "republican system," the Knights meant a society governed by workers and small farmers.

In condemning the concentration of wealth in the hands of a few, the Knights drew on the ideas of popular social critics of the day. In New York City, Henry George, an economist and land reformer, achieved national prominence with his book *Progress and Poverty* (1879), in which he advocated a single tax on property as a means of distributing wealth more equally. In his popular novel titled *Looking Backward* (1888), journalist-turned-novelist Edward Bellamy envisioned a "cooperative commonwealth" in the year 2000, a socialist paradise in which poverty and greed had disappeared and men and women of all classes enjoyed material comfort and harmonious relations with their neighbors. George and Bellamy were not only social critics; they were critics who made explicit arguments for economic equality.

Between 1885 and 1886, the Knights undertook the difficult task of organizing black workers. Many blacks remained suspicious of white-led unions, and for good reason. Historically, the white labor movement had conceived itself as a way to exclude black men and women from stable, well-paying jobs. Throughout the South, segregation was the norm within biracial unionism. Whites, whether New Orleans dockworkers, Birmingham District coal miners, or lumber workers in East Texas and Louisiana, insisted on separate locals from blacks. Yet African Americans did not necessarily acquiesce to this arrangement.

In 1886, workers around the country began to mobilize on behalf of the eight-hour day. "Eight hours to constitute a day's work" was their slogan. The issue had broad appeal, but the growing diversity of the labor force made unity difficult. In 1880, between 78 and 87 percent of all workers in San Francisco, St. Louis, Cleveland, New York, Detroit,

Milwaukee, and Chicago were either immigrants or the children of immigrants. In many places, the laboring classes remained vulnerable to divisive social and cultural animosities. The diversity of ethnic groups, coupled with the fact that many newcomers from Europe adopted racist ideas to become "Americans," drove wedges between workers.

17.2.3 The Haymarket Bombing

The year 1886 marked the end of an era dominated by the Knights of Labor as the organization experienced the difficulties of overcoming its members' diverse crafts, racial loyalties, and political allegiances. Industrialists dug in their heels and, with the aid of hired detectives, took union leaders to court on charges of sabotage, assault, conspiracy, and murder.

On May 1, 1886, 350,000 workers in 11,562 business establishments went out on a one-day strike as part of the eight-hour workday movement. In Chicago, home to militant labor **anarchists,** 40,000 workers participated in the strike. Among the Chicago leaders was Albert Parsons. A descendant of New England Puritans and a printer by trade, Parsons had lived in Waco, Texas, where he met his future wife, Lucy, the daughter of an enslaved woman. In 1873, the Parsonses moved to Chicago to avoid Texas laws against "race mixing," which prohibited interracial marriage. There Albert joined the International Typographical Union, and Lucy took up dressmaking. They were counted among the most famous and feared radicals in the city.

anarchists
Persons who reject all forms of government as inherently oppressive and undesirable.

On May 4, 1886, things took a bloody turn. Strikers called a rally in Chicago's Haymarket Square to protest the murder of two McCormick Reaper strikers the day before. During the rally, a bomb went off, killing a police officer and wounding seven others, who later died. Although the identity of the culprit was never discovered, eight anarchists, including Albert Parsons, were arrested, tried, and sentenced to death for conspiring to provoke violence in what came to be called the Haymarket bombing. Though Parsons and several of the others had not been present when the bomb exploded, he and three other detainees were hanged in November 1887.

The Haymarket hangings demoralized the labor movement nationwide. Now associated in the minds of the middle class with wild-eyed bomb throwers, the Knights saw their ranks plummet from 700,000 in 1886 to 100,000 by 1890. With the demise of the Knights of Labor, the American Federation of Labor (AFL) emerged to become the most powerful national labor movement. Samuel Gompers, an English immigrant cigar maker, had founded the new group in 1886 partly in response to the Knights' attempts to usurp the Cigar Makers' International Union with a socialist-dominated local. The AFL garnered the allegiance of skilled trade workers (most of them white men) and promoted basic goals such as better wages and working conditions.

Yet the radical labor tradition persisted. Meeting in Paris in 1889, a congress of world socialist parties voted to set aside May 1, 1890, as a day of worldwide celebrations in support of labor and demonstrations in favor of the eight-hour workday. (May 1 became an international labor day, celebrated annually.) In the United States, the United Mine Workers (founded in 1890) and the American Railway Union (1893) followed the radical labor-organizing principles of the Knights of Labor long after the AFL attained its ascendancy.

17.3 Crosscurrents of Reform

How did social reformers differ from labor radicals in their assumptions about the need for, and the means of, social change?

In the 1880s, a young Danish-born journalist named Jacob Riis prowled New York's East Side slum district in search of stories for the *New York Tribune* and the Associated Press bureau. In this part of the city, more than 37,000 tenement buildings housed more than 1 million people in inhuman living conditions. In 1890, Riis published a collection of

Interpreting History

Albert Parsons: A Plea for Anarchy (1886)

"Anarchy is the perfection of personal liberty."

On August 30, 1886, the New York Herald *published an essay by convicted Haymarket defendant Albert R. Parsons. In it, Parsons defends his views on anarchism. His theories on the inevitable clash between workers and capitalists echo the arguments of Karl Marx, the German political theorist. Marx predicted that the capitalist system would inevitably self-destruct and that the working classes would rise to rule the world.*

So much is written and said nowadays about socialism or anarchism, that a few words on the subject from one who holds to these doctrines may be of interest to the readers of your great newspaper.

Anarchy is the perfection of personal liberty or self-government. It is the free play of nature's law. . . . It is the negation of force or the domination of man by man. In the place of the law maker it puts the law discoverer and for the driver, or dictator, or ruler, it gives free play to the natural leader. It leaves man free to be happy or miserable, to be rich or poor, to be mean or good. The natural law is self-operating, self-enacting, and cannot be repealed, amended or evaded without incurring a self-imposed penalty. . . .

The capitalist system originated in the forcible seizure of natural opportunities and rights by a few, and converting these things into special privileges, which have since become vested rights formally entrenched behind the bulwarks of statute law and government.

And what of the laborer who for twelve or more hours weaves, spins, bores, turns, builds, shovels, breaks stones, carries loads, and so on? Does his twelve hours weaving, spinning, boring, turning, building, shoveling, etc. represent the active expression or energy of his life? On the contrary, life begins for him exactly where this activity, this labor of his ceases—viz: at his meals, in his tenement house, in his bed. His twelve hours work represents for him as a weaver, builder, spinner, etc., only so much earnings as will furnish him his meals, clothes, and rent. . . . The wage slaves are "free" to compete with each other for the opportunity to serve capital and capitalists to compete with each other in monopolizing the laborer's products.

Parsons argues that it is only a matter of time before the capitalist system "will collapse, will fall of its own weight, and fall because of its own weakness." He asserts that the fall of capitalism will usher in a new era of socialism, a system in which all property is held in common and workers can govern themselves. He concludes:

To quarrel with socialism is silly and vain. To do so is to quarrel with history; to denounce the logic of events; to smother the aspirations of liberty. Mental freedom, political

ALBERT PARSONS, ANARCHIST Albert Parsons believed that ordinary people's "aspirations of liberty" would inevitably produce a system whereby workers owned the means of production. To quarrel with this prediction, he thought, "is silly and vain."
Courtesy of the Chicago History Museum [ICHi-03695]

What factors prevented Parsons's prediction—that workers would come to own the means of production—from coming true?

freedom, industrial freedom—do not these follow in the line of progress? Are they not the association of the inevitable?

Ten days after this essay was published, Albert Parsons and the other Haymarket defendants were found guilty and sentenced to be hanged. Four of them, including Parsons, were executed on November 11, 1887. The true identity of the bomb-thrower remains a mystery to this day.

Questions for Discussion

1. What is the significance of Parsons's claim that the triumph of socialism is "inevitable" and "natural"?

2. What was Parsons's anarchist critique of capitalism?

3. Bring Parsons and Andrew Carnegie into conversation with each other about the "inevitable" future of the United States.

4. Why did many Americans identify anarchists with violence?

SOURCE: *New York Herald*, August 30, 1886.

his own photographs, along with explanatory notes, under the title *How the Other Half Lives*. His book galvanized the public in support of slum clearance and housing codes. *How the Other Half Lives* is a powerful indictment of greedy landlords, indifferent city officials, and rapacious sweatshop owners.

During the last decades of the nineteenth century, reformers adopted a range of causes. Some, like Riis, focused on the plight of the urban poor. Others challenged the Indian reservation system, which, they charged, left Indians poor and dependent on the federal government. Settlement house workers aimed to improve the lives of immigrant families. Middle-class women sought to protect and empower women by aiding abused or vulnerable wives and mothers, promoting temperance in alcohol use, and supporting women's suffrage. Many reformers participated in a transatlantic community of ideas, learning about reform strategies and institutions from their European counterparts.

Certain kinds of social reformers were less interested in promoting economic equality than in fostering what they considered moral behavior among the people they aimed to help. In addition, although some urban reformers professed to favor the full integration of various ethnic groups into American life, at times they could hardly help but look down on the "objects" of their benevolence. *How the Other Half Lives*, for all its sympathetic portrayals of the poor, reinforces negative ethnic stereotypes of many immigrants. Some of the people whom reformers hoped to help rejected part of their benefactors'

THE OTHER HALF, ON THE LOWER EAST SIDE, MANHATTAN Jacob Riis titled this photograph "Street Arabs in Sleeping Quarters [Areaway, Mulberry St.]." Riis's photos, collected in his book *How the Other Half Lives*, exposed the poverty and wretched living conditions endured by many immigrants in New York's Lower East Side. In certain cases, Riis carefully positioned his subjects before photographing them. It is doubtful that these little boys were sleeping while the photographer noisily set up his equipment a few feet away.

The Museum of the City of New York / Art Resource, NY

What emotions is Riis attempting to inspire in the viewers of photographs like "Street Arabs"?

package of values—Protestantism, for example—while accepting forms of concrete aid, such as shelter from abusive husbands. Thus, the history of late nineteenth-century reform reveals the value and goals of not just middle-class Americans but of a wide variety of other social groups as well.

17.3.1 The Goal of Indian Assimilation

In the mid-nineteenth century, many European Americans, including government officials, believed that the reservation system was a much-needed reform to protect western Indians. Whites reasoned that reservation Indians would remain separate from the rest of American society, to the benefit of everyone. Indians could preserve their own culture, and they would remain safe from the attacks of both homesteaders and U.S. Army troops. By segregating this group, European Americans were free to settle on rich farmlands, mine for gold and silver, and take advantage of timber resources in the West.

By the 1870s, the harsh reality of the reservation system had prompted a group composed of both Native Americans and European Americans to call for reform. The reformers pointed out that many western Indians had previously roamed the Plains in search of buffalo and other sources of food, clothing, and shelter. Confining whole tribes to reservations meant that they lost not only their traditional means of feeding and housing themselves but their entire way of life. Reservation lands were often unsuitable for farming, leaving the residents to depend on supplies of food, blankets, and clothing provided by the federal government. Kept apart from the rest of American society, denied the rights of citizenship such as education and the vote, many Indians fell victim to self-destructive behavior, including alcoholism and suicide.

Convinced that the reservation system was a failure, in 1879 reformers began to call for the assimilation of Native Americans into American life. This cause was promoted by some Indians as well as Protestant missionaries. In 1879, Ponca chief Standing Bear toured the East Coast, speaking before large, receptive audiences in Boston, New York, Philadelphia, and Washington.

Standing Bear's appeal helped to galvanize eastern reformers. The campaign for Indian assimilation bore a marked resemblance to the antislavery crusade before the Civil War. Both movements focused on the wrongs perpetrated by the U.S. government (slavery and the Indian reservation system). Both argued that the group in question deserved full citizenship rights. And both promoted the ideal of group self-sufficiency: blacks and Indians tilling the soil, embracing mainstream Christianity, and learning trades.

Beginning in 1883, advocates of Indian assimilation sponsored annual conferences at Lake Mohonk, New York, to plot strategy for the coming year. These conferences brought together scholars, clergy, reformers, and politicians, all of whom considered their cause as part of the tradition of Protestant missionary outreach work. The reformers believed that the values of white middle-class Protestants provided the best guide for Indians seeking to rid themselves of the hated reservation system. Advocates of assimilation also received support from people who simply wanted the Plains Indians removed from their land to make way for European American settlers.

Out of these conflicting impulses—one on behalf of the Indians' welfare, the other in support of the destruction of Indians' claims to large tracts of land—came two major initiatives that would shape federal Indian policy in the years to come. The first was the Indian boarding school movement, begun in 1879 with the founding of a school near Carlisle, Pennsylvania. The purpose of the movement was to convert Indian children to Christianity and to force them to abandon their Native culture and learn literacy skills. The second was the Dawes Severalty Act of 1887, allowing reservation land to be divided into separate farms for individual Native American families. However, ambitious land speculators and corrupt government officials sought to enrich themselves

HAMPTON INSTITUTE PAGEANT, HAMPTON, VIRGINIA Susan LaFlesche was the first Indian woman to become a physician in the United States. Together with her sisters Marguerite and Lucy, Susan attended Hampton Institute in Virginia, a vocational school for African Americans and Indians. This photo, taken around 1885, shows Hampton students performing in a pageant at the school. Susan, center, and the woman on the right represented "Indians of the Past." The other students represented "Indians of the Present." Hampton's mission was to prepare its students for farming and the skilled trades.

Hampton University Museum

In focusing on kinds of agricultural and manufacturing work that were becoming increasingly mechanized in the larger society, was the Hampton Institute doing a good job of preparing its students for employment in the emerging economy? What were the opportunities available to graduates of Hampton and other similar vocational schools?

from the provisions of the act, which allowed the sell-off of Indian lands to white buyers.

17.3.2 Transatlantic Networks of Reform

During this period, American reformers derived ideas and inspiration from their European counterparts. This transatlantic exchange of ideas was greatly facilitated by improvements in sea transportation. During the 1870s and 1880s, ocean travel became cheaper and safer as well as more efficient and comfortable. In 1890, a tourist embarking from New York could cross the Atlantic in just ten days for about $30 (the price of a bicycle) on a well-appointed steamship.

Contacts between European and American scholars, students, artists, clergy, writers, and reformers enriched the intellectual life of the United States and bolstered the reform impulse. American women's rights supporters conferred with their counterparts in London. American college students attended classes at German universities. Out of

Social Gospel
A reform movement around the end of the twentieth century that stressed the responsibility of religious organizations to remedy a wide range of social ills related to urban life.

social settlement house
An institution (most but not all were located in cities) that offered various services to local impoverished populations, usually immigrants, as a means of assimilating them. Many settlement houses also served as meeting places for intellectuals, policy-makers, writers, and labor leaders who debated the relative worth of various kinds of social reform.

these contacts emerged the **Social Gospel**, a moral reform movement that stressed the responsibility of Christians to address the ills of modern urban life.

An idealistic graduate of Rockford (Illinois) Female Seminary, Jane Addams journeyed to Europe for the first time in 1883. The sight of large numbers of poor people in London's East End made a lasting impression on her. In 1888, she went again to England and visited Toynbee Hall, a social settlement founded to alleviate the problems of the laboring classes. Back in Chicago, she and her friend and former classmate Ellen Gates Starr decided to open a settlement house of their own in 1889. Called Hull House, it was located in the Nineteenth Ward, home to 5,000 Greek, Russian, Italian, and German immigrants.

Hull House was a favorite meeting place for Chicago reformers of all kinds. Addams herself embraced a variety of strategies in order to promote what she considered a more just society. Concerned about the public-health hazards of trash-strewn streets and back alleys, she lobbied for better garbage pick-up and disposal in her neighborhood. As a result, the mayor appointed her as the local garbage inspector. She campaigned against child labor and in favor of workers' freedom to negotiate with their employers for better wages and working conditions. She believed that immigrants should preserve certain ethnic traditions related to crafts and food ways, on the theory that "Americanization" did not demand uniformity among all its citizens.

A **social settlement house**—so-called because its goal was to help immigrants with the transition of settling in the United States—provided a variety of services for immigrants, including English language classes, neighborhood health clinics, after-school programs for children, and instruction in personal hygiene and infant care. In 1891, six settlements were in operation. By 1900, the number stood at 200.

17.3.3 Women Reformers: "Beginning to Burst the Bonds"

Like the Indian assimilation movement, women's reform work in general during this period had a strong missionary strain. In San Francisco, the Occidental Branch of the Women's Foreign Missionary Society enlisted the aid of well-to-do women in sponsoring a rescue home for Chinese prostitutes. Without the protection of traditional kin ties, these immigrants remained vulnerable to sexual and physical abuse. The rescue home enabled the young women to escape the men who exploited them and, in some cases, to reenter society, now as married women, factory wage-earners, or small merchants.

In Salt Lake City, a group of women challenged the Mormon practice of plural marriage. In 1886, their Industrial Christian Home Association received a subsidy from Congress to provide shelter for "women who renounce polygamy and their children of a tender age." That same year, some Denver women founded the Colorado Cottage Home, a rescue home for pregnant girls and women.

The Woman's Christian Temperance Union (WCTU) is an apt example of the missionary impulse behind late nineteenth-century reform. Though best known for its antialcohol crusade, the WCTU also sponsored homes for unwed mothers and day and night nurseries for the children of working women. It also stressed the need for women's "purity," claiming that women and children were the chief victims of men's alcohol consumption. But the group went further to denounce women's victimization at the hands of men in general.

By the 1870s, the issue of women's suffrage had captured the attention of men and women throughout the country. The issue had special resonance in the West for several reasons. When European American women overcame the hardships associated with the challenge of settling the trans-Mississippi West, they considered themselves worthy of having an equal voice in the polling booth. Reflecting on her hard life as a settler in Circle Valley, Utah, Mrs. L. L. Dalton wrote in 1876 that she was "proud and thankful" to see women "beginning to burst the bonds of iron handed custom" and asserting their "co-heirship" with fathers, brothers, and husbands. Abigail Scott Duniway, who sympathized with the plight of overworked and often lonely farm wives, published a women's rights journal, *New Northwest*, in Portland, Oregon, from 1871 to 1887.

Western politics pitted cattle ranchers against farmers, and religious and cultural groups against each other. These conflicts prompted the men of various groups to seek allies wherever they could find them—within their own households if necessary. The territorial legislature of Wyoming granted women the right to vote in 1869. Utah Territory followed suit in 1870, and Washington Territory in 1883. The states of Wyoming (in 1890), Colorado (in 1893), and Utah and Idaho (both in 1896) approved suffrage for women.

FRANCES WILLARD, PRESIDENT, WOMAN'S CHRISTIAN TEMPERANCE UNION Frances Willard (1839–1898) grew up on a farm in Wisconsin Territory. She served as the first dean of women at Northwestern University in Illinois. In the mid-1870s, she decided to devote her life to the cause of temperance. From 1879 until her death, she was president of the Woman's Christian Temperance Union. Willard developed what she called a "Do-Everything policy." Under her leadership, the WCTU addressed a range of issues, including women's suffrage and workers' rights.

Library of Congress Prints and Photographs Division [LC-USZ61-790]

Why did Frances Willard consider the fight for temperance a women's rights issue?

Conclusion

In the 1870s and 1880s, the Americans who challenged the power of government and big business represented a wide spectrum of ideologies, tactics, and goals. Some resisted violently. Others formed new institutions such as settlement houses, reform associations, or political parties. Some people hoping to effect social change used the language of evangelical Protestantism, echoing the reform activities of persons who called for the abolition of slavery before the Civil War. Others collected data and interviewed specific groups of workers, women, or immigrants in an effort, first, to expose the conditions under which these groups lived and labored and, second, to propose specific legislation to remedy those conditions. Plains Indians embraced religious mysticism in a failed attempt to halt the incursion of European Americans into their ancient hunting grounds. Thus, powerful groups encountered much resistance from people opposed to their narrow idea of progress—the idea that bigger factories, more efficient farm machinery, and a nationwide network of railroad lines would bring prosperity to all Americans.

As Americans began to think more broadly about their own society, they began to think more broadly about their place in the world. Some men and women hoped to apply the principles of moral and civic reform to other countries west of the United States. The 1880s thus laid the foundations not only for a transatlantic republic of cultural exchange, but also for a trans-Pacific empire of missionary work and trade. In the process, a new ideology of expansionism emerged, one that blended elements of economic gain, national security, and Christian missionary outreach to peoples in far-off lands.

Chapter Review

17.1 Resistance to Legal and Military Authority

What were the various protest strategies used by different groups of people who faced discrimination, and at times violence, from employers, government officials, vigilantes, and the U.S. military?

Chinese immigrants in California took their claims to equality and fair play under the law to court. African Americans resisted white authority by migrating out of the South to the West and creating new community institutions. The Plains Indians turned to a movement of spiritual regeneration, the Ghost Dance.

17.2 Revolt in the Workplace

What technological and structural changes in the workplace prompted farmers and workers to organize between 1877 and 1890?

Farmers faced losing their jobs to new technology such as reapers, mowers, and threshers. Family farms had to secure bank loans, invest in new machinery, and worry about world market prices. Urban workers suffered layoffs and wage cuts. They also endured occupational hazards stemming from new and dangerous forms of technology.

17.3 Crosscurrents of Reform

How did social reformers differ from labor radicals in their assumptions about the need for, and the means of, social change?

Many middle-class reformers were less interested in promoting economic equality than in fostering what they considered to be moral behavior among the people they aimed to help. These reformers believed that social problems could be cured through reshaping individuals, forming new institutions, and changing laws, rather than through radical change or protest.

Timeline

1878	San Francisco Workingmen's party stages anti-Chinese protests
1882	Chinese Exclusion Act
1886	Accused Haymarket bombers tried and convicted
1888	Edward Bellamy, *Looking Backward*
	National Farmers' Alliance is founded

1890	Wyoming admitted to the Union, first state to enfranchise women
	National American Woman Suffrage Association is formed
	Wounded Knee Massacre

Glossary

Knights of Labor A secret fraternal order founded in 1869. Terence V. Powderly was the most influential leader of the Knights, which sponsored local labor-organizing drives among all kinds of workers, black and white and skilled and unskilled. Their motto was "an injury to one is an injury to all."

Chinese Exclusion Act Legislation passed by Congress in 1882 to deny any additional Chinese laborers entry into the country while allowing some Chinese merchants and students to immigrate.

New South A term coined by Atlanta journalist Henry Grady in 1886 to suggest that the former Confederate states were now willing to embrace industrialization and modernization.

Jim Crow The name given to the set of legal institutions that ensured the segregation of nonwhite people in the South.

Ghost Dance A dance perfor[med] . . . vision of the future, a time [. . .] conflict, as offered by an Indi[an . . .] Many of the Plains Indians w[. . .] into a trance-like state.

Wounded Knee Creek The sit[e . . .] South Dakota Indians by U. S. [. . .]

last violent encounter between Plains Indians and U. S. Cavalry forces.

Populists Agrarian reformers who formed the Populist, or People's party, a major (third) political party that emerged mostly in the Midwest and South in the late 1880s to address the needs of workers and farmers in opposition to government monetary policies and big business. The party faltered after its presidential candidate, William Jennings Bryan, lost in the 1896 election.

anarchists Persons who reject all forms of government as inherently oppressive and undesirable.

Social Gospel A reform movement around the end of the twentieth century that stressed the responsibility of religious organizations to remedy a wide range of social ills related to urban life.

[settlement] house An institution (most but not all [. . .] cities) that offered various services to [. . .]d populations, usually immigrants, as a [. . . assimila]ting them. Many settlement houses also [. . . meetin]g places for intellectuals, policy-makers, [. . .] leaders who debated the relative worth [. . .] of social reform.

Chapter 18
Political and Cultural Conflict in a Decade of Depression and War: The 1890s

APACHE STUDENTS AT BOARDING SCHOOL, CARLISLE, PENNSYLVANIA

This group of Chiricahua Apache students arrived at the Carlisle Indian boarding school in 1890. Government-sponsored Indian education included dressing them in European American clothing and cutting their hair. One of Luther Standing Bear's classmates protested, "If I am to learn the ways of the white people, I can do it just as well with my hair on."

The Huntington Library, San Marino, California/The Huntington Library, Art Collections, and Botanical Gardens; The Huntington Library, San Marino, California/The Huntington Library, Art Collections, and Botanical Gardens

Why did Carlisle Indian boarding school officials believe that certain clothing and hairstyles were a significant marker of "Americanness"?

Contents and Focus Questions

How Americanized could a young man of Lakota Sioux origin become? In the early 1890s, Luther Standing Bear found himself suspended between two worlds. Born in 1868 in South Dakota, he had learned to hunt buffalo in the traditional manner of the western Sioux. In 1879, he bowed to the wishes of his father, who sent him to attend the new federal Indian boarding school in Carlisle, Pennsylvania. Once at the school, he discovered that he was to become an "imitation of a white man"—and quickly.

Called Ota Kte, or Plenty Kill, at home, now he was required to pick a new first name from among those listed on a classroom blackboard. He chose Luther. His teachers took away his blanket and moccasins and gave him a coat, trousers, and vest to wear. They forbade him to speak his native language, and they cut his long hair. They encouraged him to embrace Christianity. In 1885, he returned to South Dakota, where he taught Sioux children near the place of his birth, now the Rosebud Indian Reservation.

In December 1890, U.S. military officials attacked and killed 150 to 200 Indians at Wounded Knee, South Dakota, near Luther Standing Bear's home. The young man moved with his family to the nearby Pine Ridge Reservation, and he began work as a shopkeeper and postal clerk. In the late 1890s, he served as an interpreter for Buffalo Bill's "Wild West" show during its tour in London. By 1912, he had become an American citizen and settled in California. There he began an acting career in the new motion picture industry, and appeared in some of the first movie westerns. He also began speaking out against the "government prison" known as the reservation.

*   *   *   *   *

In the 1890s, Luther Standing Bear's journey took place amid economic depression, civil strife, and war. Throughout the decade, workers and employers showed that the United States was not immune to the bloody class conflict that had long plagued Europe. Some scholars lamented the closing of the western frontier, prompting fears that America's unique dynamic of growth and social improvement had come to an end. Native-born whites began to seize upon new categories of racial difference to draw distinctions among various groups in the United States and around the world. In contrast to Americans who tried to define rigid racial and nationalistic boundaries, others, such as a new political party called the Populists, sought avenues of connections among different groups.

Faced with declining consumer demand at home, politicians and businesspeople joined forces to expand American markets abroad. America's expansionist ventures would reveal a blend of economic and military interests and missionary outreach, particularly in Cuba and the Philippines. These ventures abroad would pit the enduring ideal of democracy against the emerging reality of **imperialism**, the notion that stronger powers had the right and even the obligation to assume control over the politics and natural resources of weaker peoples.

imperialism
The policy of extending a nation's authority by territorial acquisition (through negotiation or conquest) or by the establishment of political or economic control over other nations.

18.1 Frontiers at Home, Lost and Found

How did fears about a closing western frontier affect American political, social, and cultural life in the 1890s?

In 1893, historian Frederick Jackson Turner proposed a new way of thinking about American history. According to Turner, the process of settling the West had shaped all of American history. He argued that during the colonial period, the rigors of taming the land had transformed English colonists into more resourceful, more democratic people—in other words, into Americans. With each successive wave of western settlement, American society renewed itself. In his view, the West served as a safety valve, a place of opportunity that beckoned people out of crowded eastern cities. Turner suggested that the United States could guarantee equality of opportunity for all as long as people had access to the land—and a fresh start in life—out west. However, he noted, an 1890 Census Report had concluded that the frontier—the unsettled area of the western part of the country—had recently disappeared. "And now," Turner concluded, "four centuries from the discovery of America, at the end of a hundred years of life under the Constitution, the frontier has gone, and with its going has closed the first period in American history."

Turner's thesis promoted the idea of American "exceptionalism": the idea that its individualism and democratic values made the United States unique among the nations of the world. Yet, in his celebration of the sturdy frontiersman, Turner ignored the bloody legacy of western settlement and its devastating effects on Spanish-speaking and Native peoples.

Nevertheless, at the end of the nineteenth century, Turner and others were asking questions. Did America need to conquer new lands and "tame" certain peoples to preserve its distinctive character? Now that the frontier had disappeared, what was to prevent the United States from becoming more like Europe? These concerns led to efforts to assimilate and Americanize certain groups of people and to tighten systems of legal discrimination against others. In addition, some Americans turned their attention to "interior" frontiers of psychology, art, and spirituality. These issues also inspired some Americans to advocate extending the nation's military might and political authority beyond U.S. territorial boundaries. In the view of imperialists, if the American frontier at home was closing, the American frontier abroad should expand.

18.1.1 Claiming and Managing the Land

With a dwindling amount of land available for cultivation, grazing, and mining, the politics of rural development entered a new phase. In the early 1890s, the last great parcel of Indian land was opened to European American farmers. Congress established the Territory of Oklahoma in 1890. Three years later, the Cherokee Outlet in the north-central part of the territory, combined with Tonkawa and Pawnee reservations, was thrown open to settlers and oil developers. On September 16, 1893, 100,000 people claimed 6.5 million newly opened acres in a single day. The "sooners," people who rushed to claim the land, gave Oklahoma its nickname. The "Sooner State" was admitted to the Union in 1907.

Congress took other steps to manage western lands during the 1890s. The Court of Private Land Claims (1891) oversaw land disputes in New Mexico, Colorado, and Arizona. This court favored recent European American claimants over the Hispanic settlers who had received title to the lands from either Spain or Mexico generations earlier.

Land courts were only one example of an expanded federal role in the settlement of the West and management of the land. During the 1890s, the federal government continued to provide information and services for farmers through the U.S. Department of Agriculture. Policymakers argued over the proper balance between conserving

Map 18.1 INDIAN RESERVATIONS, 1900

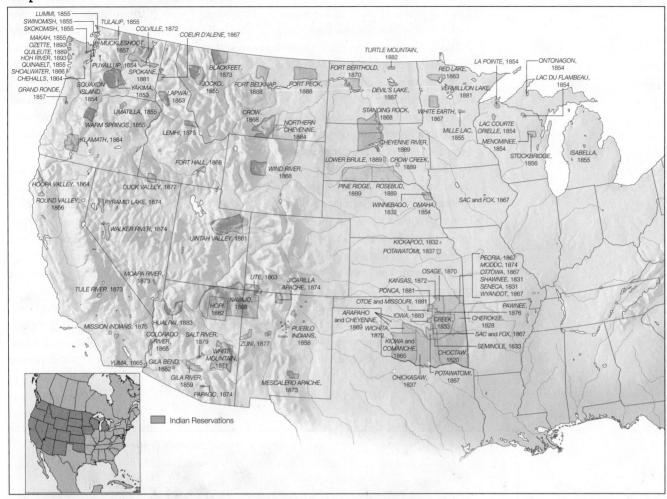

Indian Reservations

The Dawes Act, passed by Congress in 1887, intended to abandon the reservation system and integrate Indians into mainstream American society. Nevertheless, many reservations remained intact. As a group, Indians lived apart from European Americans. By the early twentieth century, the Indian as a "vanishing race" had become a familiar theme in novels and films. Yet Indian activists continued to press the cause of their people: to preserve Native cultures and, at the same time, protest persistent poverty.

natural resources for use by farmers, loggers, and oilmen and preserving the beauty of unspoiled panoramas for the enjoyment of all. In 1890, Congress established a national park in California's spectacular Yosemite Valley, where the Yosemite Indians had lived for hundreds of years. The 1891 Forest Reserve Act set aside forest reserves in the public domain (the vast tracts of land still owned by the federal government). Logging companies were allowed to exploit these areas for timber.

With his appointment as chief of the Division of Forestry in 1898, Gifford Pinchot sought to bring the issue of natural resource conservation to national attention. He believed that a managed forest could provide lumber and then renew itself. By contrast, John Muir and others argued that uninhabited regions should be preserved in their natural state, unmarred by dams, mines, or logging operations. In 1892, Muir founded the Sierra Club, a group devoted to preserving wilderness. In 1899, both Muir and the Northern Pacific Railroad lobbied successfully for two new national parks, Mount Rainier in Washington and Glacier in Montana, highlighting the ongoing significance of railroad tourism. "Rusticating," or hiking and enjoying the beauty of nature, became a popular pastime for many Americans in the 1890s.

18.1.2 The Tyranny of Racial Categories

The supposed closing of the western frontier, and with it the disappearance of the "safety valve" for restless Easterners, highlighted urban America's increasing class and cultural diversity. In an effort to categorize social groups, many national opinion makers claimed that people should be distinguished from one another by their inborn, "natural" characteristics, ranging from skin color to facial bone structure and intelligence. Supposedly, these differences defined specific racial categories, such as Caucasoid, Mongoloid, and Negroid. Late nineteenth-century scientific racists ranked "superior" and "inferior" races on an elaborate hierarchy encompassing all groups, native and foreign born. In fact, so-called racial differences between groups were cultural differences.

Numerous individuals and groups promoted and perpetuated theories of "racial" difference that directly challenged the ideal of equality among all Americans. Social theorists and other scholars gave such ideas the stamp of "scientific" approval. Politicians used these ideas to disenfranchise black men in the South. Supreme Court justices enshrined prejudicial views in law. White terrorists advanced the idea of black "inferiority" to justify mob violence against black men and women. Regardless of its source, the idea of "race" divided Americans and rationalized discriminatory treatment of specific groups.

Several factors account for this renewed obsession with the idea of race in the 1890s. European and American efforts to colonize and explore the far reaches of the globe brought whites face to face with darker-skinned peoples, whom scholars in the new discipline of anthropology studied and classified. The "New Immigration" from eastern Europe raised concerns about conferring citizenship on non-Anglos, such as Russian

KLAN INTIMIDATION This 1892 political cartoon, titled "The Political Pinkertons," portrays Ku Klux Klan members and poor whites as vigilantes bent on preventing southern black men from voting. The artist compares these vigilantes to the Pinkertons, the private security forces hired by employers to intimidate workers who went on strike.

The New York Public Library/Art Resource, NY

Why does the artist of "The Political Pinkertons" depict a cannon in this drawing?

Jews, Poles, and Italians. Persistent violence along the U.S.–Mexican border, combined with the resistance of Indians and African Americans to the authority of white people, alarmed local and federal officials. Theories of "racial difference" were used to justify attempts to subordinate these groups, by violence if necessary.

In the South, the doctrine of white supremacy had disastrous consequences for African Americans. Beginning with Mississippi in 1890, over the next twenty years, white Democrats in all states in the South met in state constitutional conventions and imposed restrictions on the voting rights of African American men, including literacy requirements and poll taxes (fees that people had to pay to vote).

In 1896, the Supreme Court put its stamp of approval on segregated schools, trains, and streetcars in its *Plessy v. Ferguson* opinion. By a seven-to-one majority, the Supreme Court ruled that such Jim Crow laws did "not necessarily imply the inferiority of either race." Justice John Marshall Harlan dissented from the majority view, pointing out the obvious: "The white race deems itself to be the dominant race," a view that conflicted with the "colorblind" U.S. Constitution.

Plessy v. Ferguson
The 1896 case in which the Supreme Court decided that states could segregate public accommodations by race.

Between 1882 and 1901, more than 100 people, most of them black men, were lynched every year in the United States; the year 1892 set a record of 230 deaths. In the South, lynch mobs targeted black men and women who refused to subordinate themselves to whites. Many black men victimized by lynch mobs were falsely accused of raping white women. Black Memphis newspaper editor Ida B. Wells charged that accusations of rape were merely a pretext for the murder of black men. The white Southerner, wrote Wells, "had never gotten over his resentment that the Negro was no longer his plaything, his servant, and his source of income." Death threats forced the editor to move north.

Yet even in the South, racial definitions were never as clear-cut or self-evident as racists, scientific or otherwise, claimed. For example, Italians and Jews occupied a middle ground between black and white, as class issues intermingled with racial categories. In 1891, in New Orleans, the lynching of a group of eleven Italian prisoners accused of conspiring to murder the city's chief of police met with no public outcry. Instead, a local newspaper condemned the "lawless passions" and "the cutthroat practices" that it claimed were characteristic of all Italian immigrants. However, the Italian government protested loudly against the incident. Armed conflict between the two nations was averted only when the United States agreed to compensate the victims' families.

At the same time, Jewish shopkeepers and merchants in the South gained a conditional entry into the ranks of "whites." In Natchez, Mississippi, the small but prosperous Jewish community owned forty-five businesses, about a third of all in the town. However, living in an overwhelmingly Protestant region of the country, many southern Jews found themselves barred from local social organizations.

18.1.3 New Roles for Schools

Between 1890 and 1899, nearly 3.7 million immigrants entered the United States, fewer than 1.4 million of them English speakers from the United Kingdom and Ireland; nearly 2.3 million were non-English speakers from Germany, Italy, Austria-Hungary, and Russia. During this period, public displays of patriotism became increasingly characteristic of American life. The recitation of the Pledge of Allegiance was introduced into public classrooms and courtrooms in the 1890s.

Many Americans saw formal education as a great equalizer of social groups, and many younger immigrants and the children of immigrants eagerly embraced American schooling as a means of upward mobility. However, schools did not always fulfill their promise as agents of equal opportunity for all. Increasingly, schools separated and grouped children according to their culture, religion, and class as well as skin color.

Many of the schools established by reformers and missionaries focused not on classical education but on teaching practical trades to students. At the Carlisle Indian

POWHATAN FAMILY PORTRAIT A middle-class Powhatan Indian family in Virginia poses for the camera, around 1900. Since the seventeenth century, the Powhatan had intermarried with the Nanticoke of Delaware, as well as with African Americans of the mid-Atlantic region.

National Anthropological Archives, Smithsonian Institute

How did communities of color defy the efforts of scientists and others to rigidly categorize people according to race? Can you identify the "race" of this family?

school, boys learned to make harnesses, tin pots and pans, wagons, and carriages, among other products, many of which were sold to local residents to raise money for the school. Girls took in laundry and ironed, also part of the school's money-making effort. The goal of such activities was to enable the pupils to become self-supporting upon graduation.

The school as a vehicle for vocational instruction also found support in the North among philanthropists concerned about the education of black children in the South. A generation after the Civil War, the persistent poverty of many rural blacks in the South convinced reformers in the North that this group of Americans should be educated for a distinct form of second-class citizenship. Philanthropists, such as Julius Rosenwald of Chicago, upheld the notion of segregated public education. They created new institutions, or modified existing ones, to stress the trades and "domestic arts" at the expense of such subjects as philosophy, mathematics, and foreign languages.

This emphasis on **vocational training** provoked varied reactions from African American leaders. Born a slave in 1858, Booker T. Washington had labored in a West Virginia coal mine before attending Hampton Normal (teacher-training) and Agricultural Institute in Virginia. In 1881, he assumed the leadership of Tuskegee Institute, an Alabama school for blacks founded on the Hampton model. Speaking at the Cotton States Exposition, a fair held in Atlanta in 1895, Washington urged blacks to "Cast down your buckets where you are"—in other words, to remain in the South and to concentrate on acquiring manual skills that would bring a measure of self-sufficiency to black families and communities. In the same address, Washington proposed that blacks refrain from agitating for civil rights, such as the vote. In return, whites should refrain from attacking innocent men, women, and children. Ignoring this last part of the speech, whites hailed Washington's "Atlanta Compromise" proposal as one that endorsed segregation and second-class citizenship for blacks.

Challenging Washington's message, scholar-activist W. E. B. Du Bois ridiculed the notion that blacks should be content to become maids, bootblacks, and sharecroppers. Similarly, in 1896 John Hope, a young professor at Roger Williams University in Nashville, Tennessee, and future president of Morehouse College and later Atlanta University, renounced Washington's apparent accommodationist stance: "If we are not striving for equality, in heaven's name for what are we living?" he demanded. "Rise, Brothers! Come let us possess this land. Never say, 'Leave well enough alone.'" Du Bois, Hope, and other black leaders were outspoken and defiant in their view that blacks must strive for full equality with whites in every realm of American life—political, economic, and social. To them, the vocational education advocated by Washington was a sure guarantee of continued inequality between blacks and whites.

Some immigrant groups, responding specifically to the Protestant agenda of most public school systems, preferred to sponsor their own schools. In many urban areas, Roman Catholic nuns founded and staffed parochial (parish) schools that appealed to certain immigrant communities. By 1900, Catholics constituted the largest single denomination in the country, with 9 million members from diverse backgrounds.

New forms of schooling reinforced class and cultural distinctions. No longer dependent on the income their children might earn in the workplace, late nineteenth-century urban middle-class families could allow their sons and daughters to prolong their schooling. High school came to be considered a logical extension of public schooling. Between 1890 and 1900, the number of students graduating from high school doubled, from 43,731 to 94,883.

The spread of private institutions of higher education reflected the wealth of a new industrial owner class and new forms of socialization for young people of privilege. Increasingly, educational institutions were becoming agents of inequality, separating the rich from poor as well as whites from blacks. Philanthropists founded and funded private colleges and universities that remained out of the reach of most American youth. In 1891, Central Pacific Railroad builder Leland Stanford founded Stanford University in California in honor of his recently deceased son. The previous year, Standard Oil's John D. Rockefeller established the University of Chicago.

College life was becoming associated with a particular stage of personal development, a stage marked not only by academic endeavors, but also by uniquely American group activities, such as playing with or cheering for the school football team. The game of basketball was invented in 1891, and soon after, many colleges formed teams that played the new sport. But not everyone viewed these developments as positive. An 1893 editorial in the *Nation* decried "the inordinate attention given to athletics in college" and suggested that "debt, drink, and debauchery" were the natural consequence.

vocational training
Instruction, usually in manual or skilled trades, to prepare a student for future gainful employment.

18.1.4 Connections Between Consciousness and Behavior

In the 1890s, some scholars and writers proposed that, although America's geographic frontier was closed, the "interior" frontier (of the human will and imagination) might still attract the curious. In Vienna, professor-physician Sigmund Freud pioneered the study of the human unconscious, the mysterious realm of thought and feeling that lies hidden beneath the mundane activities of everyday life. Freud's *The Interpretation of Dreams* (1900) suggested that dreams reveal the dreamer's unconscious desires and that these desires shape routine behavior. In the United States, the new discipline of psychology owed much to the work of Harvard University professor William James. In his *Principles of Psychology* (1890), James described the human brain as an organism constantly adjusting itself to its environment; people's surroundings profoundly influence their behavior, he argued.

Novelist Stephen Crane combined an unflinching look at reality—a blood-soaked Civil War battlefield or the slums of New York City—with a sensitive probing of human psychology. In *The Red Badge of Courage* (1894), Crane explores the fears and self-delusions of a Union soldier, basing his account on firsthand descriptions of the fighting a generation before. By stripping the story of all ideology—Union soldiers are hardly distinguishable from Confederate soldiers, and political issues are never mentioned—Crane suggests that the real war was that of the combatants battling their own private demons.

Kate Chopin's novel *The Awakening* (1899) prompted outrage among critics. They objected to the sympathetic portrayal of the wealthy married heroine, Edna Pontellier, who anguishes over her inability to reconcile her artistic, free-spirited temperament with her roles of wife and mother. At the end of the story, set in New Orleans, she chooses to commit suicide rather than submit to a life of convention. The novel focuses on Edna's reaction to the expectations other people have of her and on her gradual awakening to the idea that she must live life—or die—on her own terms.

Religious leaders also explored the uncharted territory of the mind. In the late nineteenth century, the Church of Christ, Scientist, founded by Mary Baker Eddy in 1879, prospered and grew. Eddy held that physical illness was a sign of sin and that such illness could be healed by Christian faith and prayer. In 1892, she reorganized her Christian Science faith around a mother church in Boston. Through branch churches, the American-born sect spread to more than sixty countries throughout the world.

18.2 The Search for Domestic Political Alliances

What coalitions and institutions were created and strengthened in an effort to unite diverse groups in common purpose?

In the 1890s, groups of Americans seemed to be estranged from each other as they rarely had been before. A few were enjoying the fruits of astonishing wealth, building for themselves magnificent, multimillion-dollar "summer cottages" reminiscent of glittering European palaces. In 1899, University of Chicago sociologist Thorstein Veblen coined the term **conspicuous consumption** to describe the expensive tastes of the ostentatious rich. Meanwhile, working men and women toiled long hours under dangerous conditions—when they had jobs. In 1895, the average worker was unemployed for three months of the year. Categories of race pitted various groups, native born and immigrant, against one another. Self-styled sophisticated city folk derided the **hayseeds** on the farm.

conspicuous consumption
A term coined by the American social theorist Thorstein Veblen to describe the behavior of wealthy persons who flaunt their status through their purchase of fine clothes, large houses, fancy cars, and other highly visible material goods.

hayseeds
A derogatory term applied to rural people deemed uneducated and naive (in contrast to self-proclaimed sophisticated city dwellers).

Still, the prosperous middle class hoped that certain unifying forces would connect different classes and ethnic groups. Businessmen, lawyers, and other professionals placed their faith in public schools, such cultural institutions as public museums and libraries, and the desire for a more comfortable life to instill "American" values in newcomers and the poor. The 1890s also witnessed some remarkable alliances between groups of people who had never before found common ground. The Populist party had a profound impact on the nation's political landscape in the 1890s. And women, through their local and national organizations, helped to blend domestic concerns with politics, offering a new model of civic involvement. In sum, many individuals believed that the government and voluntary associations had a critical role to play in ensuring equality of opportunity among all Americans, regardless of their gender or background.

18.2.1 Class Conflict

Congress passed the Pension Act of 1890 to provide pensions for all disabled men who had served in the Union army during the Civil War. To pay for the pensions, Congress imposed a high tariff (named the McKinley Tariff after Representative William McKinley of Ohio) on a wide variety of imported goods. The northeastern states, dependent on domestic manufacturing, traditionally supported a high tariff. Western states supported the McKinley Tariff in return for the Sherman Silver Purchase Act of 1890, under which the federal government promised to buy a total of 4.5 million ounces of silver each month and to issue banknotes for that amount redeemable in gold or silver. As a result, Westerners benefited from the infusion of federal cash used to purchase silver mined in the West.

But the pairing of a high tariff with the purchase of silver produced explosive political and economic results. The tax on imported manufactured goods hurt consumers,

Map 18.2 MANUFACTURING IN THE UNITED STATES, 1900

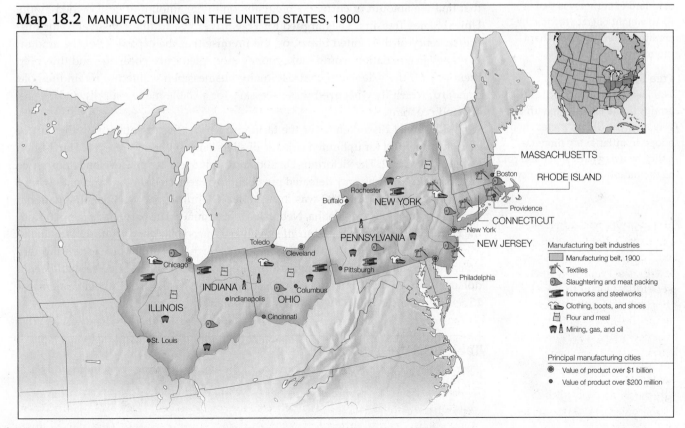

During the late nineteenth century, most manufacturing took place in the northeastern United States. Exceptions included flour milling in Minneapolis, the growing textile industry in the southern Piedmont, and the emergence of steel production in Birmingham, Alabama.

and when wages did not keep pace with prices, workers revolted. In 1892, steel magnate Andrew Carnegie and his company chairman Henry Clay Frick initiated a drastic wage cut at the Carnegie Steel Company's Homestead plant, near Pittsburgh. Workers struck in June. They armed themselves with rifles and dynamite and engaged in a pitched battle with some 300 detectives from the Pinkerton agency, men hired by Frick to break the strike. (Homestead town officials had refused Frick's request to subdue the strikers.) Ten people died, and sixty were wounded. In response to the violence, the governor of Pennsylvania mobilized the state's National Guard. The troops escorted strikebreakers to work. The company cut its workforce by 25 percent and reduced the wages of the strikebreakers. The steelworkers' union lay in ruins. Frick gloated, "Our victory is now complete and most gratifying."

Around the same time, gold, copper, and silver miners in the West faced daunting barriers to labor organization from within and outside their ranks. Protestants harbored suspicions of Roman Catholics. Ancient hatreds prevented the Irish from cooperating with the English. European Americans disdained Mexicans and the Chinese. However, the workers in Idaho's Coeur d'Alene mines managed to overcome these animosities and strike for union recognition. In March 1892, mine owners in the region formed a "protective association" and slashed wages. When workers walked off the job, the owners imported strikebreakers from other areas of the West. The strikers retaliated by blowing up a mine with dynamite. Fifteen hundred state and federal troops arrived on the scene, and the resulting clash left seven miners dead. The troops confined 300 striking miners in bullpens, where they remained for several weeks before their trials. In this case, too, the strikers met with defeat. However, out of this conflict came a new organization, founded in Butte, Montana, in 1893: the Western Federation of Miners.

By the 1890s, the **gold standard** had come under attack from debtors, including many farmers in the South and Midwest. They objected to the "hard money" policy that tied the amount of currency in circulation to the amount of gold owned by the United States Treasury. They argued for **Free Silver**, the addition of silver to the official currency of the United States, on the premise that the expansion of the amount of money in circulation would make money more plentiful—cheaper—and thus help them pay off their debts. In contrast, many businessmen wanted to retain the gold standard, which they believed was necessary for a stable money supply and, hence, a sound economy.

Widespread discontent over the tariff and simmering resentment on the part of debtors clamoring for unlimited coinage of silver helped unseat President Harrison in the election of 1892. The victorious Democratic candidate, Grover Cleveland, took office once more in 1893 (the only defeated president to be reelected). A new and noteworthy player in the election of 1892 was the People's (Populist) party, whose first national convention took place in Omaha, Nebraska, that summer. The party had emerged from the Farmers' Alliances that had so effectively organized black and white farmers in the Midwest and in the South in the 1880s. In the 1890s, the plight of western farmers reflected the state of American agriculture in general. The price of wheat had been a dollar a bushel in 1870, but it was only 35 cents twenty years later. Dakota farmers lost 15 cents on every bushel of wheat they sent to market.

gold standard

A monetary system in which the standard of currency is tied to a fixed weight of gold; favored by creditors who support a "hard money" policy.

Free Silver

The idea, popular among some groups in the late nineteenth century, that the United States should adopt an inflationary monetary policy by using both silver and gold as the nation's official currency.

Table 18.1 THE ELECTION OF 1892

Candidate	Political Party	Popular Vote (%)	Electoral Vote
Grover Cleveland	Democratic	46.1	277
Benjamin Harrison	Republican	43.0	145
James B. Weaver	Populist	8.5	22
John Bidwell	Prohibition	2.2	—

SOURCE: Historical Election Results, Electoral College, National Archives and Records Administration

The Populist party platform endorsed at the Omaha convention supported "free and unlimited coinage of silver and gold at the present legal ratio of sixteen to one"; a graduated income tax; government ownership of railroad, telegraph, and telephone companies; and an end to land speculation. The delegates condemned government subsidies to private corporations and called for the direct election of U.S. senators. The Populists' 1892 platform also included resolutions sympathizing "with the efforts of organized workmen to shorten the hours of labor" to an eight-hour workday (many workers were forced to toil twelve to fourteen hours daily) and expressing solidarity with the (now considerably weakened) Knights of Labor in their struggles against "tyrannical" employers. Compared to the Republicans and Democrats, then, the Populists built their political platform around various forms of inequality in the United States—inequality between landowner and tenant or sharecropper, between white and black, between factory owner and employee, between the rich and privileged and the poor and vulnerable.

The Populists gained strength when a national economic depression hit in 1893. This dramatic downturn stemmed from several causes. As debtors clamored for "free silver," foreign investors in the United States became nervous, and European bankers began to call in their loans. A bubble of overbuilding and land speculation burst.

The effects of the depression were widespread. Within six months, 8,000 businesses failed. As many as 20 percent of all workers lost their jobs. In 1894, Jacob S. Coxey, an Ohio quarry owner, dubbed himself a "general" and mobilized 5,000 men to march to Washington, D.C. There, in April, **"Coxey's Army"** protested the failure of the federal government to provide relief, now that the country was in the midst of the worst depression ever. However, on April 30, Washington police arrested Coxey and his followers for walking on the grass of the U.S. Capitol, ending the first mass march to descend upon the District of Columbia to protest policies of the federal government.

Coxey's Army
A mass protest march, numbering an estimated 5,000 persons, organized by Ohioan Jacob Coxey, who led his followers to Washington, D. C., to demand that the federal government enact relief measures in response to the depression that began in 1893.

Also in 1894, Eugene V. Debs, head of the American Railway Union (ARU), inspired the union's 150,000 members to protest conditions at the Pullman Palace Car Company. Employees in the company town of Pullman, near Chicago, felt squeezed when Pullman cut their wages by one-third but left intact the rents on their company-owned houses. The resulting strike crippled railroads from Chicago to California. President Cleveland declared that he could not stand by while the strikers interfered with the delivery of the U.S. mail. The president sent troops to quell the uprising, crushing the strike. For the first time, a federal court issued an injunction to force workers to go back to their jobs. Debs and other ARU leaders defied the order and went to jail.

To workers all over the country, the response to the Pullman strike signaled a troublesome alliance between government and big business, two powerful forces that the poor and the unemployed could not hope to counter. Judicial decisions confirmed the belief of many farmers and workers that all branches of the federal government were conspiring to favor the rich at the expense of the poor. In 1895, the Supreme Court rendered two opinions that favored big business and the wealthiest Americans. In *United States v. E. C. Knight*, the Court ruled that the Sherman Anti-Trust Act of 1890 applied only to interstate commerce and not to manufacturers. The Court had decided in favor of the subject of the suit, the sugar trust that controlled 98 percent of the industry. In *Pollock v. Farmers' Loan and Trust Company*, the Court struck down a modest federal income tax (2 percent on incomes over $4,000 per year). These decisions helped set the stage for the showdown between the Populists and the two major parties in 1896.

18.2.2 Rise and Demise of the Populists

In 1896, the Republicans nominated Congressman William McKinley of Ohio, whose name had graced the widely unpopular tariff bill of 1890. The Democrats turned their back on Cleveland, regarded as a pariah by members of his own party for his ties to big business and his high-handed tactics against the Pullman strikers. Without an obvious presidential candidate at their convention in Chicago in July, the Democrats seemed at loose ends. Then, out of the audience, a young man rose to address the 15,000 delegates. William Jennings Bryan, a 36-year-old Populist from Nebraska, electrified the assembly with his passionate denunciation of arrogant industrialists and indifferent politicians. The country must abandon the gold standard once and for all, he thundered: "You shall not press down upon the brow of labor this crown of thorns, you shall not crucify mankind upon a cross of gold." One awestruck listener, an alternate member of the Nebraska delegation, later said of Bryan's "Cross of Gold" speech, "There are no words in our language to picture the effect it produced upon the vast multitude which heard it." The next day, the Democrats chose Bryan as their candidate for president.

By nominating this eloquent upstart, the Democrats took on the Populist cause of free silver. Conservative Democrats bolted the party or sat out the election. Meeting in their own convention later in the summer, the Populists also chose Bryan as their candidate for president.

In the general election, McKinley received much support from his friend and political supporter Marcus (Mark) Hanna. A wealthy iron magnate and chair of the Republican National Committee, Hanna coordinated an effort to raise large sums of money for the Republicans ($16 million in total, compared with the Democrats' $1 million). Hanna charged that Bryan as president would mean disaster for businessmen, bankers, and other creditors, who would now be at the mercy of working people, small farmers, and other debtors. McKinley triumphed in November, and, as a national force, the People's party rapidly disintegrated after the election of 1896.

Table 18.2 THE ELECTION OF 1896

Candidate	Political Party	Popular Vote (%)	Electoral Vote
William McKinley	Republican	51.1	271
William J. Bryan	Democratic/Populist	45.5	176

SOURCE: Historical Election Results, Electoral College, National Archives and Records Administration

Yet, as a political movement encompassing disparate elements, the Populists left a mixed legacy. In some areas of the country, the party yielded some remarkable, if short-lived, interracial coalitions. In North Carolina, Republican–Populist fusion captured the state legislature in 1894 and the governorship in 1896. Throughout the South, however, the black population was growing—from 4.5 million on the eve of the Civil War to a total of 10 million people in 1890. Frightened by this development, white Democrats in the South campaigned to disfranchise black men, beginning in the 1890s. Landless blacks and whites would find no common political ground again until the 1930s.

18.2.3 Barriers to a U.S. Workers' Political Movement

In the 1890s, workers in Europe were forging new political parties to represent their interests and, in some cases, to press a bold socialist agenda, in the forum of national politics. Although late nineteenth-century America showed dramatic evidence of bitter class conflict, it produced no viable workers' party or socialist movement. Why? The answer is not simple. Together, farmers and members of the industrial laboring classes aspired to self-sufficiency, a life free of debt that released their wives and children from unremitting toil and provided some measure of material comfort. Nevertheless, both groups found it difficult to ally with each other. The large influx of immigrants meant that competition for even low-paying jobs remained fierce among wage-earning men and women.

Employers manipulated racial, ethnic, and religious prejudices among workers to keep them estranged. White Protestant workers seized on ethnic and religious distinctions to win for themselves advantages in the workplace. Their unions excluded certain minority and ethnic groups altogether. Even somewhat egalitarian unions fell prey to prejudice. In addition, skilled workers, taking pride in their craft and its traditions, distanced themselves from those who tended machines.

Many American workers, regardless of ethnicity, religion, or industry, continued to aspire to own their own land or business. They resisted casting their lot permanently with unions or other working-class organizations, and instead believed that individuals should strive for self-sufficiency. These workers had less interest in equality among the classes and racial groups and more interest in bettering their own personal condition. High rates of geographic mobility also prevented workers from committing themselves to a particular union in a particular place. And the power of antistrike forces proved daunting. Private security agencies, such as the Pinkertons, as well as state-deployed National Guard troops, backed up the authority of employers, judges, mayors, and governors.

18.2.4 Challenges to Traditional Gender Roles

In the 1890s, the women's suffrage, club, missionary, and social settlement movements emerged as significant political forces. In 1890, the two major national women's suffrage associations, the National Woman Suffrage Association and the American Woman Suffrage Association, merged to form the National American Woman Suffrage Association (NAWSA). Elizabeth Cady Stanton served as the new group's first president for two years. But the suffrage movement exhibited contradictory impulses. On one hand, it brought together supporters from around the country and also yielded striking examples of international cooperation.

On the other hand, white suffragists often distanced themselves from poor people, African Americans, and the laboring classes within their own country. Many NAWSA leaders accepted basic forms of inequality that separated native-born from immigrant, Protestant from Catholic, white from black. These leaders, then, offered a vision of society that stressed the equality among men and women of the so-called "respectable classes," rather than the equality of all men and all women.

Identifying themselves primarily as wives and mothers, some women entered the political realm through local women's clubs. They believed that personal intellectual development and group political activity would benefit both their own families and society in general. In the 1880s, the typical club focused on self-improvement through reading history and literature. By the 1890s, many clubs had embraced political activism. They lobbied local politicians for improvements in education and social welfare and raised money for hospitals and playgrounds. The General Federation of Women's Clubs (GFWC), founded in 1892, united 100,000 women in 500 affiliate clubs throughout the nation.

Yet the GFWC specifically excluded African American clubs. Black women formed their own national federation, the National Association of Colored Women (NACW), in 1896. Through club work, they spoke out against lynch mobs and segregationists and worked to improve their local communities. In some areas of the country, black and white women did make common cause—to further the goals of temperance, for example—although white women embraced these alliances uneasily.

In the West, Protestant-sponsored "mission homes" ministered to women in need. The San Francisco Presbyterian Chinese Mission Home offered a safe haven for Chinese women fleeing abuse and exploitation. Eastern women supported not only the San Francisco mission but also shelters for unwed mothers and abused girls in other cities, in the name of virtuous womanhood.

Social settlements were unique institutions, founded and staffed by well-educated women, many of whom had attended elite women's colleges. The daily operations of the settlement house reflected the priorities of its founders, who often brought activists, public health officials, journalists, and laboring men and women together around

**ELECTION CAMPAIGN CARD,
1896** In 1896, Charles H. Epps, the
city sergeant of Richmond, Virginia,
ran for reelection. He distributed election campaign cards to prospective
voters. The cards suggest the masculine nature of politics at this time.
Epps's card doubled as a scorecard for
the city's professional baseball team
and carried advertisements for a local
whiskey manufacturer and liquor and
tobacco store.

Virginia Historical Society/Bridgeman Art
Library

*What was the presumed link between
the products advertised and the
athletic team sponsored on Epps's
election campaign card?*

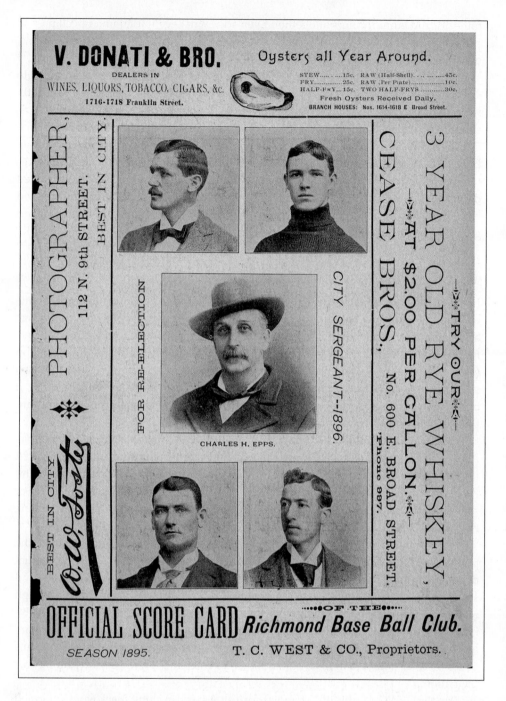

the dinner table to discuss problems of the poor. Settlement house workers hoped to
instill in poor women the values of domesticity and pride in American citizenship. By
1900, more than 200 social settlement houses were helping to acculturate immigrants
by offering classes in a variety of subjects, including English, health, and personal
hygiene.

Although often associated with immigrants in the largest cities, settlement houses
reached diverse populations. In the late 1890s, a coalition of the Kentucky Federation
of Women's Clubs and other organizations sponsored several teachers who organized
a summer settlement called Camp Cedar Grove in the eastern part of the state. This
venture provided the foundation for the Hindman Settlement School. The school, still in
existence, initially aimed to acculturate mountain people to middle-class ways in dress,
eating habits, and manners and to preserve traditional mountain music and crafts.

Sensitive to the prejudices of their clients and their neighbors, most early settlements failed to reach out to African Americans. This policy stimulated the

development of black-led settlements, such as the Phyllis Wheatley Settlement in Minneapolis and the Neighborhood Union in Atlanta. Founded by Lugenia Burns Hope in 1908, the Neighborhood Union aimed "to bring about a better understanding between the races, but also to advance the rights of black people."

Some women challenged traditional gender relations that relegated women to dependence on men. Emma Goldman, a Russian immigrant and self-proclaimed anarchist, paired the sexual liberation of women with the rights of workers to live a decent life. A radical by any measure, Goldman was, nevertheless, not alone in rejecting the idea that marriage should always be permanent. Between 1890 and 1900, the divorce rate increased from one out of every seventeen new marriages to one out of twelve. More and more couples, middle class and working class, native born and immigrant, were seeking means to dissolve marriages that had failed.

Charlotte Perkins Gilman was among the most prolific and well-known critics of the conventional division of labor in the home. She proclaimed that women, no longer content to remain dependent on men, must take their rightful place within the economy, working as equals with their brothers and husbands. Gilman proposed that housework be divided into its specialized tasks to be performed by professionals. This system would free women from the unpaid, mind-numbing task of combined "cook-nurse-laundress-chambermaid-housekeeper-waitress-governor." In her critique of gender conventions, Gilman anticipated the feminist movement of the 1960s.

Men also pondered the effects of industrializing society on their own roles. As assistant secretary of the U.S. Navy in the late 1890s, Theodore Roosevelt worried that, in this age of machines, young men lacked the opportunities for "the strenuous life" their grandfathers had enjoyed. He argued that unapologetic masculine bravado provided the key to American strength and rejuvenation on both a national and personal level. In his multivolume history *The Winning of the West* (1889–1896), Roosevelt extolled America's relentless march to the Pacific: "The rude, fierce settler who drives the savage from the land lays all civilized mankind under a debt to him." Imperialism at home and abroad, he declared, was a "race-important work," one that should claim the energies of men as politicians and soldiers. These views helped to propel the United States into the realms of imperialism and international conflict.

18.3 American Imperialism

How did different groups define and, in some cases, further American interests abroad?

In the 1890s, the United States began to extend its political reach and economic dominance to other parts of the world. Americans looked beyond their borders and saw exotic peoples who represented a variety of opportunities—as consumers of American goods, producers of goods Americans wanted to buy, and objects of American benevolence. This view represented an extension of the reform impulse at home, and served to promote inequalities based on social, and especially "racial," difference. Few advocates of American expansion abroad argued that foreign peoples were equal to U.S. citizens in culture or intelligence; rather, these advocates justified expansion by arguing that the inferiority of these peoples demanded that Americans instruct, convert, and exert political control over them.

The country's mighty industrial manufacturing sector demanded new markets and a wider consumer base. The depression of 1893, in particular, raised fears that manufacturers would have to contend with surpluses of goods that Americans could not afford to buy. American businesspeople and State Department officials established a partnership that combined private economic self-interest with national military considerations. Some molders of public opinion used the new languages of race and masculine virility to justify an "Anglo-Saxon" mission of conquest of "childlike" peoples. Meanwhile, European countries were carving up Africa and making economic inroads into China. Many Americans believed their own country should join the "race" for riches and "march" to glory as part of the international competition to exploit the natural resources and trade potential of weaker countries.

18.3.1 Cultural Encounters with the Exotic

In early October 1897, 30,000 spectators paid their 25-cent fee to enter New York's Excursion Wharf and observe the novel cargo of the recently arrived steamship *Hope*. Arctic explorer Robert Peary had returned from Greenland, bringing with him six Greenland Eskimo and a 37.5-ton meteorite dislodged from the Cape York region. The American public hailed the intrepid explorer Peary as a hero. The American Museum of Natural History put the Eskimo on display, and New Yorkers regarded their odd clothing, language, and eating habits with intense curiosity.

During the late nineteenth century, Americans were fascinated by artifacts and images dealing with faraway places, especially Africa, the Middle East, and Asia. This impulse, revealed in high art as well as popular culture, stereotyped darker-skinned, non-Christian peoples as primitive, sensual, and inscrutable. Chicago's Columbian Exposition of 1893 featured exhibits depicting harems, spice merchants, and turbaned warriors and performances of "hootchy kootchy dancers," scantily clothed young women writhing to the music of exotic instruments.

Throughout the late nineteenth century, photographers took pictures of Middle Eastern nomads and African villagers. American artists traveled abroad to render romantic scenes of deserts, ancient ruins, and mysterious peoples in oils and in watercolors. These cultural tendencies could be used to sell products and entertainment. The glassmaker-jeweler Tiffany and Co. evoked Islamic art in its tea services and silver patterns. Tobacco companies marketed mass-produced cigarettes with "Oriental" brand names: "Fatima," "Omar," and "Camel." Thus, a fascination with the exotic encompassed a wide range of impulses in American life and letters, bringing together explorers, scientists, artists, and advertising agents.

18.3.2 Initial Imperialist Ventures

The opening of Asia to American trade, combined with the military challenges posed by the major European imperial powers, stimulated the growth of the U.S. Navy in the 1880s. In his book *The Influence of Sea Power upon History, 1660–1783* (1890), Captain Alfred Thayer Mahan contended that if the United States aspired to be a world power, it must control the seas.

Seeking way stations for its ships, the United States negotiated control over both Pearl Harbor in Hawaii and the harbor at Pago Pago in Samoa in 1887. Three years later, Secretary of State James G. Blaine hosted the first Pan-American Conference in Washington, D.C., a gathering of representatives from nineteen independent Latin American republics.

In 1895, the United States signaled to Great Britain that it was prepared to go to war to bar Europeans from colonizing or intervening in the Americas, a policy outlined in the Monroe Doctrine more than seventy years before. Britain had persisted in its long-standing claims to the jungle boundary between its colony of British Guiana and the country of Venezuela on the north coast of South America. President Cleveland made clear his intention to enforce the Monroe Doctrine. Britain, sensitive to other threats posed by European imperial powers to the far-flung British empire, backed down. Thereafter, Britain began to concentrate on strengthening its diplomatic ties with the United States.

GREENLAND ESKIMO MINIK The Greenland Eskimo Minik is shown here soon after his arrival in New York City in 1897, when he was seven years old. Minik was devastated by the death of his widowed father, Qisuk; the two were among six Eskimos brought to New York by Arctic explorer Robert E. Peary. Later in his life, Minik spoke of his father to a newspaper reporter, saying, "He was dearer to me than anything else in the world, especially when we were brought to New York, strangers in a strange land."

Courtesy Dept. of Library Services/American Museum of Natural History

What is the significance of the fact that the American Museum of Natural History put Minik and other Eskimos brought to New York on display?

Meanwhile, in the Pacific, the Hawaiian Islands seemed to pose both a threat and an opportunity for American interests. Located 2,000 miles from the California coast, Hawaii had a population of 150,000 in 1890. In 1875, sugar planters and merchants, many of whom were related to missionaries, had negotiated a treaty with the United States that let them ship the crop to the United States duty-free. Production of Hawaiian sugar increased from fewer than 10,000 tons in 1870 to 300,000 tons by 1900.

By this time, Chinese, Koreans, Filipinos, Puerto Ricans, Japanese, and Portuguese had made their way to the Hawaiian Islands. These groups formed the bulk of the plantation labor force, for disease had decimated the native population. In the fields and in their barracks, immigrant contract workers followed a disciplined regimen under the supervision of mounted, whip-wielding overseers called *lunas*. Indeed, these laborers' workday bore a marked resemblance to that of sharecroppers on the largest cotton plantations of the U.S. South.

The McKinley Tariff of 1890 raised duties on imports of the islands' sugar. This tariff served to overturn the 1875 pro-planter treaty, causing planters (mostly Americans) to panic about their livelihood. They received no support from the islands' native leader, Queen Liliuokalani, who believed foreigners should be barred from running the country. In 1893, the planters, backed by American marines, launched a successful revolt that deposed the queen. They then called for the United States to annex the islands as a territory. Upon investigation, President Cleveland discovered that native Hawaiians opposed annexation and so refused to agree to the move. His refusal incurred the wrath of American imperialists, who claimed that the "Hawaiian pear" had been "ripe for the plucking."

18.3.3 The Spanish-American-Cuban-Filipino War of 1898

Those seeking to expand American influence also looked just south of Florida. In the Caribbean, Cuban nationalists staged an uprising against the island's Spanish colonial authorities in 1895. Native *insurrectos* under the leadership of José Martí burned crops of sugar cane and attacked passenger trains. American companies with large investments in the Cuban sugar industry (a total of about $50 million) were outraged at the destruction of their property; they had no sympathy for the *insurrectos*. Yet the arrival of Spanish military officials, who herded the rebels into barbed-wire concentration camps, inflamed public opinion in the United States. By 1897, both businesspeople and humanitarians urged President McKinley to intervene in Cuba.

Two major American newspaper publishers, William R. Hearst and Joseph Pulitzer, highlighted Spanish atrocities against Cubans. On February 9, 1898, Hearst published a letter written by the Spanish minister in Washington, D.C., Dupuy de Lôme, in which de Lôme denounced President McKinley as a spineless politician. Six days later, the American battleship *Maine*, which had been sent to Havana harbor to evacuate Americans should the need arise, exploded and sank. Two hundred sixty officers and men were killed. Subsequent investigations concluded that the heat from one of the coal bins had ignited an adjacent powder magazine. But the Hearst papers implied that the Spanish were responsible for the blast. Attempting to expand their readership, the Hearst and Pulitzer newspapers engaged in **yellow journalism**: sensational news reporting that blurred the line between fact and fiction, spontaneous reality and staged theater.

McKinley responded to American businesspeople who feared for their interests in Cuba and to other Americans who decried Spain's brutality toward the *insurrectos*. On April 11, 1898, McKinley called on Congress to declare war against Spain. To war supporters, much was at stake: the large American sugar investment, trade with the island, and American power and influence in the Western Hemisphere. Congress responded

yellow journalism
Newspaper articles, images, and editorials that exploit, distort, or exaggerate the news in order to inflame public opinion.

EXPLOSION OF THE BATTLESHIP MAINE The battleship *Maine* exploded and sank in Havana Harbor on February 15, 1898. Outraged by the (false) claims of "yellow" journalists who charged that Spain was responsible for the disaster, Americans prepared for war. They considered native Cubans and Filipinos not as equals in the fight against Spain but rather as victims who needed American protection.

Glasshouse Images/Alamy

How did the War of 1898 reveal a variety of interests that shaped America's foreign policies during the late nineteenth century and beyond?

to McKinley's message by adopting the Teller Amendment, which declared that the United States would guarantee Cuba its independence once the Spanish were driven from the island. America went to war on April 29.

McKinley hoped to hobble the Spanish navy by making a preemptive attack on the fleet in the Spanish colony of the Philippines. Commodore George Dewey, stationed with the American Asiatic Squadron in Hong Kong, was dispatched with his ships to Manila Bay, where on May 1, 1898, his force of four battleships sank all ten rickety Spanish vessels, killing 400, with only a few minor American casualties. Dewey waited in the harbor until American reinforcements arrived in August. Then, with the help of Filipino nationalists led by Emilio Aguinaldo, U.S. forces overran Manila on August 13.

Meanwhile, congressional Republicans had found the necessary votes to annex Hawaii. They claimed that the United States needed the Pacific islands to secure a refueling way station for Dewey's troops. McKinley signed the congressional resolution on July 7, 1898. Hawaiian residents were granted citizenship rights, and the islands became an official U.S. territory in 1900.

Earlier in the summer of 1898, halfway around the globe, 17,000 American troops had traveled to Tampa, Florida, in preparation for their incursion into Cuba. Among them were the Rough Riders, volunteers organized by Lieutenant Colonel Theodore Roosevelt, who had resigned his post as assistant secretary of the navy to serve as an officer. The troops landed near Santiago, Cuba, in late June. On July 1, Roosevelt and

Map 18.3a THE SPANISH-AMERICAN-CUBAN-FILIPINO WAR OF 1898 (PACIFIC THEATER)

This map, and its companion on the following page, shows the major battles and troop movements in the War of 1898. The United States sought to eliminate Spanish control of the Philippines and Cuba. Broader U.S. motives included fear for the property rights of American sugar companies in Cuba and a desire for strategic bases in the Pacific theater.

his men engaged an unprepared Spanish force of about 2,000 men at El Caney and San Juan Hill. The Rough Riders charged up nearby Kettle Hill (they were on foot, not on horses) and into American legend. They received crucial backup support from two African American regiments that day. By late July, American warships had destroyed the Spanish fleet in Santiago Bay. According to Secretary of State John Hay, it had been "a splendid little war," just 113 days long. Battles claimed 385 American lives (although many times that number died from disease).

Map 18.3b THE SPANISH-AMERICAN-CUBAN-FILIPINO WAR OF 1898 (CARIBBEAN THEATER)

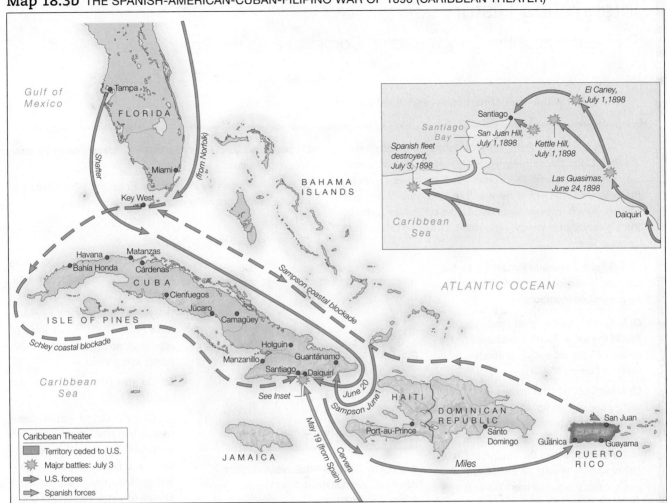

18.3.4 Critics of Imperialism

Theodore Roosevelt seemed to personify the late nineteenth-century idea of American manifest destiny: the notion that the core of the nation's history was a militant mission to expand its territorial reach. However, not all Americans agreed with Roosevelt. New York financier Mark Hanna called him a "madman" and "that damned cowboy." Writer Mark Twain believed him "clearly insane" and "insanest upon war and its supreme glories." Twain and other prominent people founded the Anti-Imperialist League in 1898 in an attempt to stem the rising tide of militarism.

It is difficult to generalize about the politics of anti-imperialists during this period. Some critics of imperialism advocated a hands-off policy toward other nations in the belief that all peoples were entitled to self-determination. In contrast, other anti-imperialists such as Social Darwinists used arguments about racial hierarchies to justify their opposition to expansion.

In the summer of 1900, the Democrats and Republicans prepared for the upcoming presidential election. Receiving the Democratic nomination once again, William Jennings Bryan was eager to press the outdated cause of free silver. He also condemned the American presence in the Philippines, although this issue, too, was rapidly losing the attention of the electorate. At the Republican convention, Roosevelt's supporters managed to win for him the slot as McKinley's running mate. That fall, the former Rough Rider waged an exuberant campaign. Accompanied by a retinue of gun-toting cowboys, he wrapped the Republicans in the American flag. When McKinley swept to

Interpreting History

Proceedings of the Congressional Committee on the Philippines (1900)

"But is that within the ordinary rules of civilized warfare?"

In January 1900, Congress established the Committee on the Philippines. Senator Henry Cabot Lodge of Massachusetts was appointed chair. The committee's task was to review the American conduct of the war. The testimony of two U.S. officers, which follows, foreshadows the difficulties faced by the United States in fighting a guerrilla war in Vietnam six decades later.

Brigadier General Robert P. Hughes testified in response to questions posed by committee members:

Q: In burning towns, what would you do? Would the entire town be destroyed by fire or would only offending portions of the town be burned?

Gen. Hughes: I do not know that we ever had a case of burning what you would call a town in this country; but probably a *barrio* or a *sitio;* probably a half dozen houses, native shacks, where the *insurrectos* [rebels] would go in and be concealed, and if they caught a detachment passing they would kill some of them.

Q: What did I understand you to say would be the consequence of that?

Gen. Hughes: They usually burned the village.

Q: All of the houses in the village?

Gen. Hughes: Yes, every one of them.

Q: What would become of the inhabitants?

Gen. Hughes: That was their lookout. . . . The destruction was as a punishment.

Q: The punishment in that case would fall, not upon the men, who would go elsewhere, but mainly upon the women and little children.

Gen. Hughes: The women and children are part of the family, and where you wish to inflict a punishment you can punish the man probably worse in that way than in any other.

Q: But is that within the ordinary rules of civilized warfare? Of course you could exterminate the family, which would be still worse punishment.

Gen. Hughes: These people are not civilized.

BATTLING A PHILIPPINE INSURGENCY
After the United States defeated Spanish forces in the Philippines in 1898, American soldiers faced a new enemy—Filipino insurgents who resisted American rule.

Hulton Archive/Getty Images

Discuss the scene in the photograph above, of insurgents hiding from U.S. troops in dense jungle interiors, from the point of view of pro-imperialists on the one hand and critics of American foreign policy on the other. What did the United States gain by its colonial ventures in the 1890s? What did it lose?

Sergeant Charles S. Riley also testified in response to the committee's questions:

Q: During your service there [in the Philippine Islands] did you witness what is generally known as the water cure?

A: I did.

Q: When and where?

A: On November 27, 1900, in the town of Igbaras, Iloilo Province, Panay Island.

Riley described to the committee a Filipino man, 40–45 years of age, stripped to the waist, with his hands tied behind him.

Q: Do you remember who had charge of him?

A: Captain Glenn stood there beside him and one or two men were tying him. . . . He was then taken and placed under the tank, and the faucet was opened and a stream of water was forced down or allowed to run down his throat; his throat was held so he could not prevent swallowing the water, so that he had to allow the water to run into his stomach. . . . When he was filled with water it was forced out of him by pressing a foot on his stomach or else with their hands. . . .

Q: What had been his crime?

A: Information had been obtained from a native source as to his being an insurgent officer. After the treatment he admitted that he held the rank of captain in the insurgent army—an active captain. . . .

Q: His offense was treachery to the American cause?

A: Yes, sir.

Questions for Discussion

1. In what ways did the Filipino insurrection challenge the conventions of what congressional committee members called "civilized warfare"?

2. How did General Hughes justify the destruction of whole villages as part of the U.S. effort to suppress the insurrectionists?

3. What are the arguments for and against the practice of torture as a means of extracting information from enemy combatants?

4. Do you think that some Americans might have approved the harsh interrogation techniques used against Filipinos primarily because the latter group belonged to a darker-skinned race? Why or why not?

5. Contrast U.S. postwar actions in Cuba and the Philippines with the rhetoric of "reform" and "equality" at home at the same time.

SOURCE: Proceedings of the Congressional Committee on the Philippines, in Harvey Graff, ed., *American Imperialism and the Philippine Insurrection* (Boston: Little, Brown and Company, 1969), 64–79.

reelection in the fall, few Americans could have anticipated how central Roosevelt's vision would become to the country over the next two decades.

As Americans greeted the twentieth century, they might have marveled at the dramatic changes that had occurred in their country over the last 100 years. In 1800, the United States was home to 5.3 million people who lived in 16 states. One hundred years later, the country included 45 states and boasted a population of 76 million people. Many workplaces, fields as well as factories, were dominated by machines and the people who tended them. The economy was shifting toward the mass production of consumer goods.

In 1900, the United States exerted control over the land and peoples of Alaska, the Hawaiian and Samoan Islands, the Philippines, Guam, Puerto Rico, and Cuba. These holdings, notable for their strategic significance, illustrated the growing willingness of the United States to extend its influence and economic reach—by armed force if necessary—to the far corners of the earth. The new drive for worldwide economic and political power ran counter to America's revolutionary heritage, with its values of democracy and self-determination.

Platt Amendment

A measure (1901) stipulating the conditions for the withdrawal of U.S. troops from Cuba at the end of the War of 1898. Ensured continued U.S. involvement in Cuban affairs, and affirmed U.S. claims to certain parts of the island, including Guantánamo Bay Naval Base.

Conclusion

On August 12, 1898, Spain signed an armistice and later in the year ceded its claim to remnants of its empire, including Cuba and Puerto Rico in the Caribbean and the island of Guam in the Pacific. The United States forced Cuba to incorporate into its constitution (written in 1901) the so-called **Platt Amendment**, which guaranteed continuing U.S. influence over the country, including the stationing of American troops at a naval station on Guantánamo Bay. Meeting with Spanish negotiators in Paris, the United States agreed to pay $20 million for the Philippines.

But Filipino rebels were not about to bow to a new colonial power. Over the next two years, the United States committed 100,000 troops to subdue the rebels, using tactics that foreshadowed the U.S. war in Vietnam 70 years later. Hunting down guerrillas hiding in the jungle, American soldiers torched villages and crops. They forced water down the throats of suspected rebel leaders—a form of torture known as the "water cure" then and "waterboarding" today—in an effort to extract information. Four thousand Americans and 20,000 Filipinos died in combat. As many as 600,000 Filipino civilians succumbed to disease and starvation.

Ownership of the Philippine Islands gave the United States a foothold in Asia. In 1894–1895, Japan had waged a successful war against China, and European traders rushed in to China to monopolize local markets and establish their own spheres of influence. Secretary of State John Hay issued a communication called the Open Door note in the summer of 1899; in it, he urged imperial powers to respect the trading interests of all nations. In 1900, the Boxer Uprising in China prompted cooperation among Western powers. The Boxers, radical Chinese nationalists, killed 200 foreign missionaries and other whites in an effort to purge China of outsiders. Together, the Germans, Japanese, British, French, and Americans sent 18,000 troops to quell the revolt. The United States and European nations continued to compete for the China market well into the twentieth century.

Chapter Review

18.1 Frontiers at Home, Lost and Found

How did fears about a closing western frontier affect American political, social, and cultural life in the 1890s?
Some Americans advocated conquering new lands and "taming" foreign peoples in order to preserve what they viewed as the nation's distinctive character. Fears of the closing frontier led to a hardening of racial ideologies; the spread of formal schooling; and new writing and scholarship that probed the "interior" frontier of the human will and imagination.

18.2 The Search for Domestic Political Alliances

What coalitions and institutions were created and strengthened in an effort to unite diverse groups in common purpose?
Businessmen, lawyers, and other professionals looked toward public institutions such as schools and libraries to instill "American" values in newcomers and among the poor. The Populist party united workers who wanted to reshape the workplace, the government, and the economy. Women formed suffrage organizations and clubs that blended domestic concerns with politics.

18.3 American Imperialism

How did different groups define and, in some cases, further American interests abroad?
Americans viewed the nation's interests abroad as having economic and cultural components. Some believed that colonizing new lands would create new consumer markets for American goods, as well as protect American military and economic interests around the globe. Reformers viewed dark-skinned peoples especially as inferior objects of American benevolence.

Timeline

1890	National American Woman Suffrage Association is formed
1891	Populist party formed
1892	Steelworkers strike at Carnegie's Homestead plant near Pittsburgh
1893	Worst nationwide economic depression to date
1894	Coxey's Army marches on Washington, D.C. Pullman workers strike
1896	Supreme Court decides *Plessy v. Ferguson*, upholding segregation
1898	United States annexes Hawaii
	United States defeats Spain in Spanish-American-Cuban-Filipino War
1899	Emilio Aguinaldo leads Filipino revolt against 100,000 U.S. forces

Glossary

imperialism The policy of extending a nation's authority by territorial acquisition (through negotiation or conquest) or by the establishment of political or economic control over other nations.

Plessy v. Ferguson The 1896 case in which the Supreme Court decided that states could segregate public accommodations by race.

vocational training Instruction, usually in manual or skilled trades, to prepare a student for future gainful employment.

conspicuous consumption A term coined by the American social theorist Thorstein Veblen to describe the behavior of wealthy persons who flaunt their status through their purchase of fine clothes, large houses, fancy cars, and other highly visible material goods.

hayseeds A derogatory term applied to rural people deemed uneducated and naive (in contrast to self-proclaimed sophisticated city dwellers).

gold standard A monetary system in which the standard of currency is tied to a fixed weight of gold; favored by creditors who support a "hard money" policy.

Free Silver The idea, popular among some groups in the late nineteenth century, that the United States should adopt an inflationary monetary policy by using both silver and gold as the nation's official currency.

Coxey's Army A mass protest march, numbering an estimated 5,000 persons, organized by Ohioan Jacob Coxey, who led his followers to Washington, D. C., to demand that the federal government enact relief measures in response to the depression that began in 1893.

yellow journalism Newspaper articles, images, and editorials that exploit, distort, or exaggerate the news in order to inflame public opinion.

Platt Amendment A measure (1901) stipulating the conditions for the withdrawal of U.S. troops from Cuba at the end of the War of 1898. Ensured continued U.S. involvement in Cuban affairs, and affirmed U.S. claims to certain parts of the island, including Guantánamo Bay Naval Base.

Chapter 19
Visions of the Modern Nation: The Progressive Era, 1900–1912

SISTER IRENE FITZGIBBON AND "FLOCK" Sister Irene Fitzgibbon, who founded the New York Foundling Hospital in 1869, is pictured here with some of her young charges in the late nineteenth century. As the numbers of orphans increased, the Sisters of Charity began to send children to approved Catholic homes in parishes in the West. The trains carrying youngsters west to waiting families came to be known as "orphan trains."

Schomburg Center, NYPL/Art Resource, NY

What does the photograph of the New York Foundling Hospital suggest about the conditions of care for the children in the orphanage? Why would the effort to place children into Catholic families in Clifton and Morenci in 1904 create such a storm of resistance?

Contents and Focus Questions

Why would residents of a Southwestern town disrupt the adoption of children coming from New York? An incident in 1904 reveals the ethnic, class, and religious tensions that prevailed along the nation's southern border.

A train carrying Irish orphans from a Roman Catholic **foundling home** in New York chugged westward to deliver its small passengers to waiting Catholic families in Clifton and Morenci in the Arizona territory. Reform-minded church officials at the New York orphanage hoped to provide a better life to their young charges. They had screened the families carefully to be certain that the couples who would adopt these children were devout churchgoing Catholics, industrious workers, and respectable members of the community. The local parish priest approved these couples, and on the appointed day, they waited eagerly as the orphans, dressed in their best clothes, departed from the train. But when the Anglo-Protestant residents of the town discovered that Mexican Catholic foster parents claimed these fair-skinned children, they were outraged.

That night, the Anglo women gathered to mobilize their husbands into a vigilante posse. In the middle of the night, during a driving rainstorm, the men went to the homes of the Mexican couples and kidnapped the children at gunpoint. The next day, the children were distributed to the vigilantes' wives and other Anglo foster parents. Although the Catholic foundling home that had placed the children with the Mexican couples fought a lengthy legal battle to regain custody of the children, the Anglos managed to keep the orphans. The Arizona Supreme Court validated the kidnapping in the name of the best interests of the children, and the U.S. Supreme Court let the ruling stand.

The struggle over the orphans reflected tensions and divisions in the region along lines of class as well as race. In the early twentieth century, large numbers of Mexicans migrated to the Southwest, looking for work. The year before the arrival of the orphans, Mexican mine workers had struck for better wages and working conditions against the Anglo owners of the Arizona Copper Company. The owners put down the strike, and the conflict left bitter feelings on both sides. The vigilante kidnapping of the orphans was, in part, retaliation against the Mexican workers who had organized the strike the previous year.

*   *   *   *   *

During this period, the nation began to emerge as something profoundly different from what it had been in the past. With the influx of immigrants, industry expanded and cities grew. The dramatic changes taking place, from industry and technology down to the most intimate levels of life, sparked equally dramatic efforts to control them. People from all parties participated in the wide range of reform efforts known as **Progressivism**.

Progressive Era reformers did not always agree. Some Americans pushed vigorously for greater equality; others, such as the Anglo-Americans who took the orphans away from Mexican families, worked just as hard to maintain prevailing hierarchies. The tensions among these visions of the nation shaped the politics of the era.

foundling home
A residence for orphaned children.

Progressivism
A belief in the potential for progress through social reform that found expression in the Progressive Era, when political leaders and urban reformers sought to solve local and national problems through political and civic means.

19.1 Expanding National Power

In what ways did Theodore Roosevelt promote Progressive reform?

Along with flourishing radical and reform movements at the grassroots, the Progressive Era gave rise to a reformist impulse at the national level. The person who most fully embodied the national Progressive movement was Theodore Roosevelt, president from 1901 to 1908. Roosevelt used his power to regulate big business, intervene in labor disputes, control the uses of the natural environment, and extend the reach of the nation across the world. His hand-picked successor in the White House, William Howard Taft, followed mostly similar policies.

19.1.1 Theodore Roosevelt: The Rough Rider as President

Roosevelt rose to prominence in the Republican party in the 1880s and held several important political posts, including assistant secretary of the Navy (1897–1898) and governor of New York (1899–1900). In 1900, Roosevelt became vice president; in September 1901, President McKinley was assassinated, and at age 42 Roosevelt became the youngest person ever to occupy the Oval Office.

Roosevelt was a strong proponent of American military and commercial presence in the world. He expanded the power of the federal government both at home and abroad and used the bully pulpit of the presidency to exert moral leadership. Using the Sherman Anti-Trust Act of 1890, which gave the federal government the power to break up monopolies, Roosevelt earned the title of trust-buster. But it was not his intention to weaken big business. In fact, he believed that a strong country needed large, powerful industries, and he hoped to regulate them to keep big business strong.

Table 19.1 THE ELECTION OF 1900

Candidate	Political Party	Popular Vote (%)	Electoral Vote
William McKinley	Republican	51.7	292
William Jennings Bryan	Democratic-Populist	45.5	155

SOURCE: Historical Election Results, Electoral College, National Archives and Records Administration

Roosevelt's efforts to strengthen the state and foster American nationalism extended to his attitudes toward immigrants. He believed that discrimination against loyal newcomers harmed democracy: "It is a base outrage to oppose a man because of his religion or birthplace." He was proud of appointing a cabinet in which "Catholic and Protestant and Jew sat side by side." But Roosevelt did not believe in cultural pluralism, that is, the idea that the United States could include citizens who retained their ethnic heritage. Rather, Roosevelt promoted the idea of a melting pot that would blend all diverse cultures into a unique American "race." Although Roosevelt was a firm believer in Anglo-Saxon superiority, he was also the first president to invite an African American leader, Booker T. Washington, to the White House.

19.1.2 Protecting and Preserving the Natural World

Industrial smoke had long been a problem in both European and American cities, and Progressive Era reformers established organizations to fight air pollution. At the same time, mining and other industries were depleting natural resources while destroying the natural beauty of the land. More than any previous president, Roosevelt used the federal government to manage the natural world. Although his actions did not please everyone, Roosevelt's environmental efforts were among his most enduring legacies.

Roosevelt advocated both preservation and conservation. His preservation policies doubled the number of national parks, created sixteen national monuments, and established fifty-one wildlife refuges. At the same time, he shared the view of **conservationists** that timberlands, areas for livestock grazing, water, and minerals needed federal government management. Roosevelt transferred 125 million acres of public land into the forest reserves to prevent the depletion of timber and he set aside land for dam sites, oil and coal reserves, and grazing. But these measures did not benefit all citizens equally. John Muir and the Sierra Club campaigned to protect the beautiful Hetch Hetchy Valley in Yosemite National Park, but Congress passed the Raker Act in 1913, allowing the city of San Francisco to build a dam and flood the valley. The struggle pitted those who loved the natural wilderness against city dwellers who wanted the water. Residents of the Owens Valley in eastern California also protested the building of an aqueduct that diverted water they needed to the Los Angeles area. Dams, reservoirs, and aqueducts brought water and electricity to arid regions, allowing such cities as Las Vegas and Los Angeles to flourish in environments that would otherwise be unable to support large populations. People who lived in those expanding cities benefitted, at the expense of others who faced withered landscapes, flooded valleys, and parched farmlands as their water flowed elsewhere.

conservationists
Advocates of conserving and protecting the natural world through the use of renewable natural resources.

19.1.3 Expanding National Power Abroad

While government projects at home shaped the landscape, national leaders forged a new role for the nation in the world. The turn of the twentieth century marked the high point of European and American imperial expansion, bringing 75 percent of the world's land under the control of Europeans or their descendants. Roosevelt hoped to strengthen the federal government at home, develop the nation's military and commercial might, and extend American power abroad. To further these ends, he sent troops to China as part of the international expedition to crush the nationalist Boxer Uprising in 1900. He also proposed the construction of a canal across the Isthmus of Panama, which Congress approved in 1902. But Panama was still a province of Colombia, and Roosevelt was unhappy with the Colombian government's negotiating position regarding an American canal project. So he aided Panamanian nationalists who seceded from Colombia in 1903. In return, the U.S. president got his canal deal with a newly independent Panama.

In 1904, Roosevelt further increased the authority of the United States to intervene in the affairs of nations in the Western Hemisphere through what came to be known as the Roosevelt Corollary to the Monroe Doctrine of 1823. Fearing political uprisings that might threaten American commercial interests, Roosevelt asserted that "chronic wrongdoing" might require the intervention by "some civilized nation" in the affairs of another. "In the Western Hemisphere," he concluded, this may force the "United States . . . to the exercise of an international police power." The Roosevelt Corollary justified later interventions in the Dominican Republic, Cuba, Nicaragua, Mexico, and Haiti. While the Monroe Doctrine had told Europeans to stay out of the hemisphere, the Roosevelt Corollary declared that the United States would intervene where it wanted to.

Table 19.2 THE ELECTION OF 1904

Candidate	Political Party	Popular Vote (%)	Electoral Vote
Theodore Roosevelt	Republican	57.9	336
Alton B. Parker	Democratic	37.6	155
Eugene V. Debs	Socialist	3.0	—

SOURCE: Historical Election Results, Electoral College, National Archives and Records Administration

The bloody U.S. war against Filipino nationalists that began in 1899 lasted four years before the Americans crushed the revolt and established firm colonial rule in the Philippines. William Howard Taft became the colony's first governor-general in 1901. Taft developed a public works program that included roads, bridges, and schools.

He also transferred government functions to Filipinos who cooperated with American colonial powers. Although the United States promised to grant Philippine independence, that promise was deferred until 1946.

19.1.4 William Howard Taft: The One-Term Progressive

When Roosevelt declined to run for reelection in 1908, the Republicans selected Roosevelt's hand-picked successor, William Howard Taft. Taft was a loyal ally who worked closely with Roosevelt on foreign and domestic policies. Roosevelt assumed that Taft, after his victory in the general election, would fulfill Roosevelt's reform agenda.

Table 19.3 THE ELECTION OF 1908

Candidate	Political Party	Popular Vote (%)	Electoral Vote
William H. Taft	Republican	51.6	321
William Jennings Bryan	Democratic-Populist	43.1	162
Eugene V. Debs	Socialist	2.8	—

SOURCE: Historical Election Results, Electoral College, National Archives and Records Administration

"Dollar Diplomacy"
President William Howard Taft coined the term to refer to a policy that encouraged economic investment in foreign countries.

Taft's respect for the separation of powers spelled out in the U.S. Constitution made him dubious about some of Roosevelt's extensions of the powers of the presidency. Nevertheless, Taft initiated far more antitrust suits than Roosevelt had during his presidency. Despite similar political inclinations, Roosevelt's support for his protégé cooled. Although Roosevelt counted major business leaders among his own advisors, he was displeased when Taft appointed corporate lawyers rather than activist reformers to his cabinet. Taft departed from Roosevelt's foreign policy as well. In contrast to Roosevelt, who emphasized military might, Taft claimed that "**Dollar Diplomacy**"—substituting ballots for bullets—was the best way for the United States to exert influence in the world.

When Taft signed the higher Payne-Aldrich Tariff in 1909, he disappointed progressive Republicans and aligned himself with the conservative old guard of the party, who were critical of Roosevelt. The breach between Taft and the Progressives widened when Taft's secretary of the interior, Richard A. Ballinger, opened up for commercial development 1 million acres of land that Roosevelt had placed under federal protection. In a further affront to conservationists, Gifford Pinchot, still head of the National Forest Service, discovered that Ballinger had sold Alaskan coal deposits to corporate moguls J. P. Morgan and David Guggenheim. When Taft defended Ballinger, Pinchot leaked the news to the press and called for a congressional investigation. Taft subsequently fired Pinchot, but Roosevelt publicly supported Pinchot and signaled his break from Taft.

New Nationalism
Theodore Roosevelt's plan for a far-reaching expansion of the federal government to stabilize the economy and institute social reforms.

Roosevelt returned from hunting in Africa to enter the political spotlight again. He toured the country in 1910, describing his plan for a "**New Nationalism**," a far-reaching expansion of the federal government to stabilize the economy and institute social reforms. When the Republican party's old guard managed to renominate Taft at the Republican National Convention, Roosevelt and his supporters withdrew from the Republican party and formed the Progressive party. Roosevelt boasted, "I am as strong as a bull moose," inspiring his followers to call themselves the **Bull Moosers**. Their reformist platform called for extensive controls on corporations, minimum wage laws, child labor laws, a graduated income tax, and women's suffrage.

Bull Moosers
Supporters of Theodore Roosevelt in the 1912 presidential election when he broke from the Republican party and ran as a third-party candidate on the ticket of the Progressive (or Bull Moose) party.

In contrast to Roosevelt's "New Nationalism," Democratic candidate Woodrow Wilson was reluctant to vest so much power in the government. He called his own approach the "New Freedom," believing that the government should dismantle the trusts and then revert to limited powers. The Republican vote split between Taft and Roosevelt, and the victory went to Wilson. Wilson took office amid an overwhelming popular mandate for reform.

Table 19.4 THE ELECTION OF 1912

Candidate	Political Party	Popular Vote (%)	Electoral Vote
Woodrow Wilson	Democratic	41.9	435
Theodore Roosevelt	Progressive	27.4	88
William H. Taft	Republican	23.2	8
Eugene V. Debs	Socialist	6.0	—

SOURCE: Historical Election Results, Electoral College, National Archives and Records Administration

19.2 Immigration: Visions of a Better Life

Where did immigrants settle, and what conditions did they encounter?

As political alliances shifted, the nation itself changed in profound ways. Between 1900 and 1910, nearly 9 million immigrants entered the United States, the largest number for any single decade in the nation's history until the 1990s (see Figure 19.1). They came particularly from southern and eastern Europe, as well as Mexico and Asia.

Figure 19.1 NUMBER OF IMMIGRANTS ENTERING THE UNITED STATES, 1821–2009.

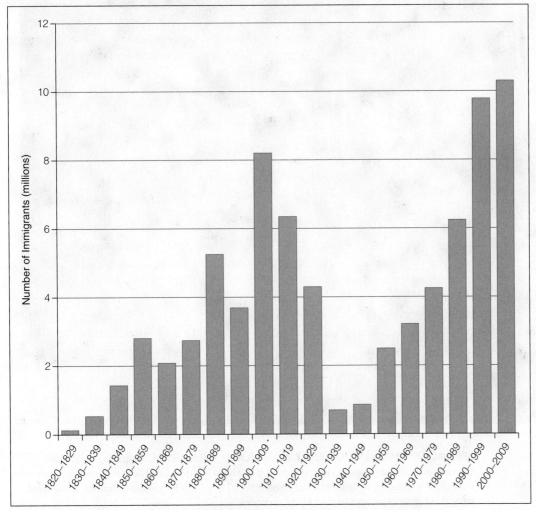

The number of immigrants entering the United States spiked in the first decade of the twentieth century and then dropped drastically as a result of the immigration restriction laws passed by Congress in the 1920s. Immigration increased again as laws changed after World War II, allowing new immigrant groups to enter.

SOURCE: U.S. Department of Homeland Security, *2013 Yearbook of Immigration Statistics*, August 2014, table 2.

The United States was one of several potential destinations for these courageous and hopeful sojourners. It was particularly appealing because of its often exaggerated, but nonetheless real, opportunities for jobs and economic advancement, its official commitment to freedom of religion and political thought, and its reputation as a nation that welcomed newcomers from abroad.

On arrival, many found that the "promised land" was not the paradise they expected. They faced crowded living conditions in urban tenements, jobs in sweatshops and factories with long hours, low wages, and miserable working conditions, and a hostile reception. Many Americans—including some whose own parents or grandparents had come to the United States as immigrants—looked down on the newcomers as "racially inferior" and morally suspect, feared competition for jobs, and worried that the masses of poor foreigners in their midst would become a burden on taxpayers and public institutions. The Statue of Liberty may have held up the torch of welcome, but many citizens, from union halls to legislative chambers, had little sympathy for their plight and wanted the newcomers to leave.

Some reformers tried to improve conditions for the newcomers. One such reformer was Upton Sinclair, a writer and political activist who joined the expanding Socialist

ARRIVAL OF IMMIGRANT FAMILY AT ELLIS ISLAND At Ellis Island, this immigrant family received identification tags, indicating that they had been examined and declared healthy. Those who were ill, or youngsters without relatives to meet them, were sent to quarantine houses. Some were refused entry and sent back to their home countries.

SZ Photo/Scherl/DIZ Muenchen GmbH, Sueddeutsche Zeitung Photo/Alamy

What do the faces of the immigrants in the photograph above suggest about their journey? Do they appear scared or humiliated by the inspection, or do they look proud, dignified, and optimistic about their arrival in their new country?

party in 1902. Four years later, at the age of twenty-eight, he published *The Jungle*, an exposé of the brutal exploitation of immigrant workers in the meat packing industry. The novel tells the story of Jurgis Rudkus, a Lithuanian immigrant who works in one of Chicago's meat packing plants. The book describes the squalid working conditions Jurgis endured in the plant, where filth, rats, and even workers' body parts ended up in the packages of ground meat. Sinclair hoped his descriptions of the appalling conditions would lead to improvements for laborers in the meat packing plants and turn the nation toward socialism.

The Jungle had a powerful impact, but the effect was not what Sinclair had hoped. Rather than spark interest in socialism, or even improved wages and working conditions, the novel aroused consumer indignation and led to the passage of the Pure Food and Drug Act (1906) and the Meat Inspection Act, which prohibited adulterated or fraudulently labeled food and drugs from interstate commerce. Sinclair later wrote with regret, "I aimed at the public's heart and by accident hit the stomach."

Sinclair had a vision of a nation where immigrants as well as native-born workers labored in dignity with good wages and working conditions in industries kept in check by government ownership. Most of his readers, however, had a different vision: of an affluent nation where consumers could count on the quality of the products they purchased, without concern about the workers who produced those products. The Pure Food and Drug Act and Meat Inspection Act satisfied consumers and industry leaders, but left Sinclair's primary concern—immigrants who suffered under miserable working conditions in the plants—largely unchanged.

Facing such harsh circumstances, many immigrants decided to leave. One-third of immigrants to the United States returned to their home countries. Known as "**birds of passage**," some came for only a few years and returned to their native lands, including nearly 90 percent of migrants from the Balkans. Other groups, especially those who faced severe hardships in the lands of their birth, were more likely to make the United States their permanent home. Only 11 percent of the Irish and 5 percent of the Jews returned between 1908 and 1923.

"birds of passage"
A term applied to immigrants who came to the United States for a brief period of time, and then returned to their home countries.

19.2.1 The Heartland: Land of Newcomers

At the dawn of the twentieth century, it was not the coastal cities, with their visible immigrant ghettos, but the settlements in the upper Midwest, along with the lower Southwest, where the greatest concentration of foreign-born residents lived. The Southwest remained home to large numbers of Mexicans and Mexican Americans, many of whose families had lived in the area when it was still a part of Mexico.

Farther north, in the growing towns and cities of the Midwest, newcomers from central Europe and Italy joined the earlier settlers from Germany and Scandinavia to form farming and mining communities on the rich soil and abundant mineral deposits of the region.

In the 1890s, the upper Midwest was sparsely settled. As a result of the Dawes Act of 1887, which divided tribal lands into individual parcels, much of the land originally held by Indians had been divided and sold. Most of the Indians who were native to that region were removed to reservations. The iron-rich areas near Lake Superior, previously the hunting, fishing, and gathering areas of the Native Americans, were now inhabited by lumberjacks who cut the forests. Mining companies discovered the iron deposits and began recruiting workers, first from northern Europe and then, after 1900, from southern and eastern Europe. By 1910, the iron range was home to 35 European immigrant groups. Gradually, these cohesive working-class communities, like others elsewhere, developed their own brand of ethnic Americanism, complete with elaborate Fourth of July celebrations and other festivities that expressed both their distinctive ethnic identities and their allegiance to their adopted country.

19.2.2 Asian Immigration and the Impact of Exclusion

Asians continued to face the most severe restrictions on immigration. The Chinese Exclusion Act of 1882, which prohibited most Chinese from immigrating to the United States, was renewed and extended in 1902. As a result, the mostly bachelor Chinese community in the United States declined by nearly half between 1890 and 1920. Many died or returned to China, reducing the numbers from more than 107,000 to about 61,000. The sex ratio remained severely unbalanced, with about fourteen men for every woman.

During the exclusion era, certain categories of Chinese immigrants were allowed entry. Wives of Chinese men already in the United States could enter, as could teachers, students, and merchants. More than 20,000 Chinese arrived during the first decade of the new century. One such emigrant was Sieh King King, an eighteen-year-old student. In 1902, at a political meeting, she addressed a packed hall in San Francisco's Chinatown. The *San Francisco Chronicle* reported that "she boldly condemned the slave girl system, raged at the horrors of foot-binding [a traditional Chinese practice in which girls' feet were tightly bound to keep them small] and, with all the vehemence of aroused youth, declared that men and women were equal and should enjoy the privileges of equals." Sieh King King expressed ideas that were not only emerging among urban radicals in the United States but also reflected political movements in their home countries.

Individual Chinese could immigrate if they had family members in the United States. As a result, American-born Chinese frequently traveled back and forth, claiming on their return that they left a child in China and requesting permission for their

AFTER THE EARTHQUAKE, CHINATOWN, SAN FRANCISCO An earthquake devastated San Francisco on April 18, 1906. Here a Chinese immigrant watches as the city goes up in flames. Chinatown was destroyed, along with much of the downtown.

Library of Congress Prints and Photographs Division [LC-USZ61-531]

Why would it be particularly difficult for Chinese immigrants to recover from the San Francisco earthquake of 1906?

offspring to emigrate. In this way, they created space holders for imaginary kin, allowing other Chinese to enter the country. The American authorities knew of this system of "paper sons" and "paper fathers" and tried to stop the practice with elaborate and lengthy investigations that could last a year or more while hopeful Chinese immigrants waited as virtual prisoners in wretched conditions on Angel Island, the immigrant gateway in San Francisco Bay. Those who were fortunate enough to enter the country still faced hardships and suffered disproportionately when misfortune struck. In 1906, the San Francisco Earthquake devastated much of the city and destroyed Chinatown.

In the 1880s, there were only about 3,000 Japanese immigrants in mainland United States. Japanese immigrants could still enter the country, and nearly 300,000 did so between 1890 and 1920, when opportunities for higher-paying jobs in Hawaii and California offered an alternative to the economic crisis they faced in Japan. As in many countries around the world, marriages in Japan generally were arranged by families, and some men returned to Japan to meet and marry their brides. But cost and distance often prevented those meetings. Some women came to the United States as "picture

Map 19.1 AREAS EXCLUDED FROM IMMIGRATION TO THE UNITED STATES, 1882–1952

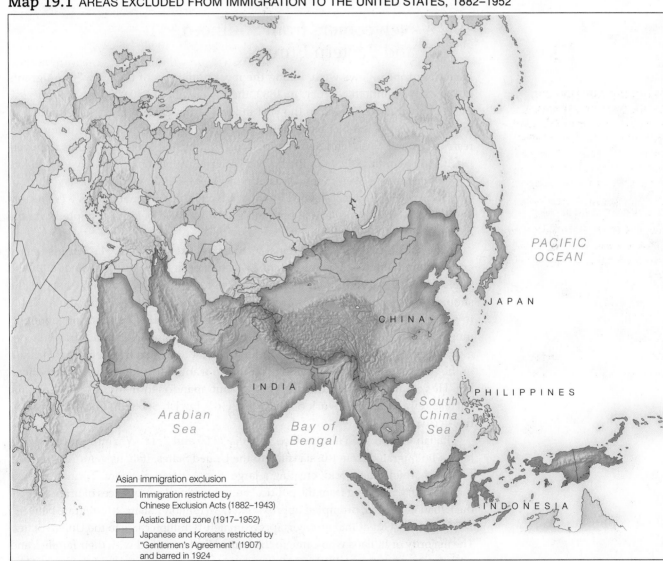

Asian immigration exclusion
- Immigration restricted by Chinese Exclusion Acts (1882–1943)
- Asiatic barred zone (1917–1952)
- Japanese and Koreans restricted by "Gentlemen's Agreement" (1907) and barred in 1924

In 1882, the United States barred Chinese immigrants from entering the country; Japanese and Koreans were barred in 1924. In 1917, the exclusion was extended to people from India, Indonesia, and the Arabian Peninsula. Those laws remained in effect until 1943 and 1952, respectively.

brides" after an exchange of photographs. Although some were disappointed with their often much older husbands, most accepted their fate as they would have accepted an arranged marriage in Japan. Others were delighted with the opportunity for adventure and life in the new land. As one picture bride explained, many of the people from her village had already gone to the United States, and she wanted to go, too: "I didn't care what the man looked like."

Although the Japanese comprised less than 1 percent of California's population, they faced intense nativist hostility. The Japanese in California protested against the discrimination they faced, and in one case, they successfully turned a local case of school segregation into an international incident. In response to the segregation of Japanese children in San Francisco, the Japanese government expressed its extreme displeasure. Hoping to avoid a confrontation with Japan—a significant military power that had just won a war with Russia—President Theodore Roosevelt interceded and convinced the San Francisco school board to rescind its segregation order. This incident led to the "Gentlemen's Agreement" of 1907, in which the Japanese government agreed to limit the number of immigrants to the United States. The numbers of immigrants from Japan dwindled, and Japanese immigrants instead began to settle in Brazil.

19.2.3 Newcomers from Southern and Eastern Europe

Eastern European Jews were among the most numerous of the "new" immigrants in the early twentieth century. In 1880, there were about 250,000 Jews in America; by 1920, there were 4 million, the vast majority from eastern Europe. A number of factors motivated Jews to leave their small towns, or *shtetls.* Economic turmoil and restrictions on Jewish land ownership, trade, and business left many Jews impoverished. Anti-Semitic policies in Russia and eastern Europe confined many Jews to live in restricted areas. Even more devastating was anti-Semitic violence in the form of riots, or *pogroms*, in which Jewish towns were attacked and many Jews were beaten and killed. Many young Jewish boys emigrated to avoid being conscripted into the czar's army.

One such immigrant was young Morris Bass. At age twelve, he left his family and ventured alone across the Atlantic. A butcher in New York's crowded Jewish ghetto quickly offered him a job and a place to sleep on a straw mat behind the shop. Like many others, Morris prospered modestly. After a few years, he was able to strike out on his own as a pushcart peddler. Eventually, he sent home enough money to bring his parents and siblings to America. Some Jewish immirants struggled to retain the faith and practices of Jewish orthodoxy that had defined their lives in the *shtetl.* But Morris was among those who wanted to assimilate into American life. He retained Jewish cultural practices but abandoned many religious rituals, such as refraining from work on Saturdays (the Jewish Sabbath) and wearing distinctive clothes.

Italian immigration also peaked between 1900 and 1914. While 90 percent of the Jews who migrated from Russia came to the United States, Italians ventured to many countries around the world, creating a large global Italian diaspora. Turmoil in their home country, resulting from the political and economic consequences of unification of the Italian peninsula, prompted approximately 13 million Italians to emigrate between 1870 and 1920. Out of that number, approximately 3 million came to the United States. The majority of Italians who came to the United States arrived with their families and settled permanently, establishing strong communities and mutual aid societies. Most Italians were committed Roman Catholics, and they preserved their rituals, festivals, and faith in the new country.

Interpreting History

Defining Whiteness in *John Svan v. the United States* (1908)

> "the Finns in very remote times were of Mongol origin"

Naturalization laws pertaining to immigrants in the early twentieth century were based on racial categories. Asian immigrants, classified racially as "Mongolians," were not allowed to apply for U.S. citizenship. Naturalization was available only to aliens being free white persons and "to aliens of African nativity and to persons of African descent." Because racial theories were imprecise and fluid, and racial identities were not linked to nationality, immigrants occasionally challenged their racial classification to claim that they were "white." John Svan, who was Finnish, petitioned in federal court to contest the labeling of Finns as Mongolians, claiming he was white and, therefore, allowed to apply for U.S. citizenship. The petition demonstrates the acceptance of racial definitions based on phenotype—particularly skin color—as well as the imprecise nature of those definitions. In the case of John Svan v. the United States Government, *the court granted Svan's petition, legally changing his racial identity from Mongolian to white and reclassifying Finns as white people. Here is the court's 1908 memorandum, which allowed Svan to become a citizen:*

John Svan was born in Finland and calls himself a Finn. . . . According to ethnologists, the Finns in very remote times were of Mongol origin; but the various groupings of the human race into families is arbitrary and, as respects any particular people, is not permanent but is subject to change and modification through the influences of climate, employment, intermarriage and other causes. There are indications that central and western Europe was at one time overrun by the Finns; some of their stock remained, but their racial characteristics were entirely lost in their remote descendants,

"WHITENESS" DEFINED These Finnish men living in Minnesota were among those whose racial classification was changed from "Mongolian" to "white" as the result of one Finnish immigrant's petition. Along with the Jews, Italians, Irish, and other immigrant groups now considered "white," Finns were classified as non-white until the laws and customs changed.

Fotosearch/Getty Images

Racial categories were fluid and imprecise, but whiteness conferred status and privileges. What new privileges were Finns in Minnesota now likely to claim as a result of the decision in **Svan v. United States**?

who now are in no danger of being classed as Mongols. The Osmanlis, said to be of Mongol extraction, are now among the purest and best types of the Caucasian race. Changes are constantly going on and those occurring in the lapse of a few hundred years with any people may be very great.

The chief physical characteristics of the Mongolians are as follows: They are short of stature, with little hair on their body or face; they have yellow-brown skins, black eyes, black hair, short, flat noses, and oblique eyes. In actual experience we sometimes, though rarely, see natives of Finland whose eyes are slightly oblique. We sometimes see them with sparse beards and sometimes with flat noses; but Finns with a yellow or brown or yellow-brown skin or with black eyes or black hair would be an unusual sight. They are almost universally of light skin, blue or gray eyes, and light hair. No people of foreign births applying in this section of the country for the full rights of citizenship are lighter-skinned than those born in Finland. In stature they are quite up to the average. Confessedly, Finland has often been overrun with Teutons and by other branches of the human family, who, with their descendants, have remained within her borders and are now called Finns. They are in the main indistinguishable in their physical characteristics from those of purer Finnish blood. Intermarriages have been frequent over a very long period of time. If the Finns were originally Mongols, modifying influences have continued until they are now among the whitest people in Europe. It would, therefore, require a most exhaustive tracing of family history to determine whether any particular individual born in Finland had or had not a remote

Mongol ancestry. This, of course, cannot be done and was not intended. The question is not whether a person had or had not such ancestry, but whether he is now a "white person" within the meaning of that term as usually understood. This is the practical construction which has uniformly been placed upon the law. . . . Under such law Finns have always been admitted to citizenship, and there is no occasion now to change the construction.

The applicant is without doubt a white person within the true intent and meaning of such law.

The objections, therefore, in my opinion should be overruled and it will be so ordered.

Questions for Discussion

1. According to the court, what might cause changes in the "groupings of the human race into families" over time?

2. How does the court's opinion reflect prevailing attitudes toward race during the Progressive Era?

3. How did the court explain the transformation of Finns from the classification as "Mongols" to becoming "among the whitest people in Europe"?

SOURCE: William Alexander Cant, Memorandum, in *John Svan v. United States*, U.S. District Court for the District of Minnesota, Duluth, issued Jan 17, 1908.

19.3 Work, Science, and Leisure

How did scientific and technological advances improve the lives of ordinary Americans and, at the same time, lead to abuses that benefitted some at the expense of others?

As the nineteenth century gave way to the twentieth, working women and men could increasingly expect to be employed in industry rather than farms, in large organizations rather than small shops, and in enterprises that relied more on efficiency than craftsmanship. Towering skyscrapers began to dot the urban landscape, symbolic of the triumph of commerce and corporate power. Science and technology reigned, changing the nature of work as well as the fruits of production. Professional organizations of educators, social workers, physicians, and scientists emerged, while experts with academic credentials became leaders of many public institutions. It seemed as though science could solve virtually any problem. Although social problems like poverty persisted, advances in medical science contributed to improved public health.

This more urban society developed new forms of leisure and entertainment. The film industry emerged in Hollywood, a suburb of Los Angeles. Amusement parks and nightclubs provided new venues for greater intimacy between unmarried men and women. And American art and literature began to emphasize the vitality and diversity in the nation's cities.

19.3.1 The Uses and Abuses of Science

Breakthroughs in science and medicine led to improvements in public health. Reformers exposed the dangers of potions and remedies sold by street vendors, as standards for medications improved. But crowding and lack of sanitation still fostered the spread of disease, especially among the poor. Lack of access to clean water was one of the major causes of disease, along with crowding, lack of medical care, and other chronic problems of poverty. Improved public sanitation alleviated the problem considerably in the early years of the twentieth century, reducing the incidence of typhoid fever by 70 percent. Among those who contributed to better conditions were community nurses. In 1900, the New York Charity Organization Society hired Jessie Sleet Scales, the first African American public health nurse, to address problems related to tuberculosis. Scales and other public health professionals implemented sanitation standards and provided care for poor communities, helping to control the spread of disease. Public sanitation remained a problem, however, especially in crowded cities.

Reflecting an impulse to blame social problems on allegedly flawed individuals or groups was the eugenics movement, which advocated scientific breeding to improve the nation's racial stock. Drawing on theories of white racial superiority and unscientific notions of genetic inheritance, eugenicists believed that character traits were inherited, including tendencies toward criminality, sexual immorality, and lack of discipline leading to poverty. Eugenicists claimed that social problems resulted from the high birthrate of immigrants and others they considered to be racially inferior to educated middle-class Anglo-Saxon Americans.

President Theodore Roosevelt was an outspoken advocate of eugenics reform. Alarmed by the dramatic decline in the birthrate of native-born Americans and the tendency of some college-educated women to remain single and childless, he feared that the immigrants, with their much higher birthrate, would overrun the nation. Roosevelt called upon Anglo-Saxon women to prevent what he called **race suicide**, much as male citizens had an obligation to defend the country if called to military duty.

Some eugenics crusaders proposed compulsory sterilization of those they deemed unfit for parenthood. Indiana enacted a eugenic sterilization law in 1907 and other states soon followed. These laws gave legal sanction to the surgical sterilization of thousands of men and even greater numbers of women whom government and medical officials deemed "feebleminded." The criteria were vague at best; often sexual impropriety or out-of-wedlock pregnancy landed young women—generally poor and often foreign-born—in institutions for the feebleminded, where the operations took place. The Supreme Court upheld compulsory sterilization laws in the 1920s. Increasingly, women of color were targeted, and the practice continued well into the 1980s.

race suicide
A fear articulated by Theodore Roosevelt and others that the low birthrate of Anglo-Saxon Americans, along with the high birthrate of immigrants from southern and eastern Europe and elsewhere, would result in a population in which "inferior" peoples would outnumber the "American racial stock."

19.3.2 Scientific Management and Mass Production

Scientific ideas also took hold in the nation's industries. In 1911, Frederick Winslow Taylor wrote *The Principles of Scientific Management*, a guide to increased industrial efficiency. While working in the Midvale Steel Works near Philadelphia, Taylor developed a system to improve mass production in factories to make more goods more quickly. Taylor's principles included analysis of each job to determine the precise motions and tools needed to maximize each worker's productivity, detailed instructions for workers, and wage scales with incentives to motivate workers to achieve high production goals. Over the next decades, industrial managers all over the country drew on Taylor's studies. Business leaders rushed to embrace Taylor's principles, and Taylor himself became a pioneering management consultant.

Henry Ford was among the most successful industrialists to employ Taylor's techniques. Born in 1863 on a farm near Dearborn, Michigan, the mechanically inclined Ford became an apprentice in a Detroit machine shop in 1879. Although he did not invent the automobile—the first motor cars were manufactured in Germany—he developed design and production methods that brought the cost of an automobile within the reach of the average worker. Experimenting with the new internal combustion engine in the 1890s, he built his first automobile in 1896. In 1903, Ford established the Ford Motor Company and began a profitable business. He introduced the popular and relatively inexpensive, mass-produced Model T automobile in 1908, which sold for $850. In 1913, Ford introduced the **assembly line**, a production system in which each worker performed one task repeatedly as each automobile in the process of construction moved along a conveyor. Assembly-line manufacturing increased production while cutting costs. In 1914, Ford increased his workers' wages to $5 per day at a time when industrial laborers averaged only $11 per week. By 1916, the price of the Model T dropped to $360. In this sense, Ford was a pioneer not only in production but also in consumption. While his business practices enabled his workers to also become consumers, his motives were to maintain a stable work force and sell more cars. He was adamantly opposed to labor unions, and was well known for his anti-Semitic views, which he expressed in many publications. Ford also maintained friendships with Nazi supporters in the United States and Germany. Ironically, the Jews whom he so vehemently despised, like Henry Ford himself, helped to usher in the **mass consumption society** that would characterize twentieth-century America.

assembly line
A form of industrial production popularized by the Ford Motor Company in which workers perform one task repeatedly as the products they are jointly assembling move along a conveyor.

mass consumption society
The term refers to a shift in the early twentieth century from a society focused on frugality and production to one that embraced and celebrated consumer goods and leisure pursuits.

19.3.3 New Amusements

As Americans increasingly moved from rural to urban areas, and from farms to factories, new institutions of leisure emerged in the growing cities. Consumer culture was the flip side of business culture in the early twentieth century. One of the great ironies of American history in the twentieth century is that its popular culture—which more than anything else identifies the United States to the rest of the world—was largely a creation of immigrants and people of color. During the very years when these groups faced intense discrimination, they developed the cultural products that came to define America.

The movie industry is a case in point. In 1888, Thomas Edison invented the kinetoscope, the early motion picture camera. The pragmatic Edison thought that his new device might be used in education and industry and did not see much commercial potential for the gadget. Not until the early twentieth century did the moving picture begin to reach a wide audience. Moviemakers left the East Coast and moved to the West, taking advantage of the even climate, cheap land, and nonunion labor. Within a few years, the moviemakers, mostly Jewish immigrants, established the film industry. Hollywood emerged as a major center of American popular culture, sending its products across the nation and abroad.

The first motion picture audiences were in the working-class neighborhoods of the growing cities. In New York alone, by 1910, there were 1,000 small storefront theaters and fun houses known as penny arcades where there had been none twenty years earlier. The number of saloons also increased from 7,000 to 9,000, while the Coney Island amusement park drew thousands to its shimmering lights and thrilling rides. During these same years, the sounds of African American music began attracting audiences among immigrants and native-born whites, as youths from all ethnic groups flocked to dance halls. Glamorous nightclubs, known as cabarets, also began to appear, offering dining, dancing, music, and entertainment to the wealthy.

19.3.4 Sex O'Clock in America

The sexual mores and behavior of Americans seemed to be changing so dramatically that one observer announced that "sex o'clock" had struck. Indeed, the codes of the past were challenged at every turn. Among the middle class, unchaperoned dating began to replace the previous system of a man "coming to call" at the home of a woman he hoped to court.

Immigrants often brought traditional courtship patterns to the new world and extended them into the next generation. One Italian man described his thwarted efforts to woo his fiancée in private. When he visited her home, "She sat on one side of the table, and I at the other. They afraid I touch." Finally, less than a month before their wedding, he got permission to take her to the theater. But the family was unwilling to let them go alone. "We came to the aisles of the theater. My mother-in-law go first, my fiancée next, my little sister, my father in law. I was the last one. I had two in between. . . . I was next to the old man." He tried to steal a kiss a few days before the wedding, but his fiancée rebuffed him: "No, not yet."

In spite of efforts by their elders, native-born as well as immigrant youth challenged the sexual codes of the past. Increasing sexual intimacy between unmarried men and women reflected heightened expectations for sexual satisfaction—for women as well as men. These years also witnessed a rise in the proportion of brides who were pregnant at marriage, from a low of 10 percent in the mid-nineteenth century to 23 percent by 1910. Artists challenged sexual mores as well. Theodore Dreiser's 1900 novel *Sister Carrie* narrates the story of an independent young woman who uses her sexuality to advance her ambition. Because of the novel's scandalous content, Dreiser's publisher did not promote the book, although it was revived and republished in later years.

THE CAFÉ FRANCIS, BY GEORGE LUKS, c. 1906 *The Café Francis*, by George Luks, around 1906.
Luks was one of many artists who celebrated urban street life, popular culture, and diverse working-
class subjects. His art exuded the vitality of urban life and conveyed a gritty reality without moral condemnation. The raw and sensual depictions of city entertainments stirred controversy among art critics
at the time. Contemptuous critics referred to them as the "Ashcan School," a label they embraced.

The Cafe Francis, 1906 (oil on canvas), Luks, George (1867-1933)/© Butler Institute of American Art, Youngstown,
OH, USA/Museum Purchase 1960/The Bridgeman Art Library

What emotions are evoked in **The Café Francis,** *by George Luks? Are the subjects depicted as*
immoral and impoverished, or gracious and dignified?

Marriage increasingly held the promise not only of love, intimacy, and mutual obligation, as it had in the nineteenth century, but of sexual fulfillment and shared leisure
pursuits. However, some women did not marry but instead formed lifelong attachments
to other women. Rarely identified as lesbian, but often described as **Boston marriages**,
these unions signified long-term emotional bonds between women who lived together.
Meanwhile, lesbians, as well as gay men, gained greater visibility in the cities. They
frequented bars and clubs in such places as Greenwich Village and Harlem, hoping to
avoid the attention of police, who were likely to arrest them for indecent conduct.

Boston marriages
Unions of two women based on
long-term emotional bonds in
which the women live together as
if married to each other.

19.4 Reformers and Radicals

Who were the reformers and radicals, and what strategies did they use to promote
their visions of society?

Progressivism responded to these changes with two distinct impulses. On the one hand,
many Anglo-Saxon Protestants tried to impose order on a rapidly changing nation.
They hoped to stem the tide of immigration, bolster rapidly eroding sexual codes, and

quell the movements for social change. On the other hand, women's rights activists, workers, and African Americans struggled to achieve the rights and privileges available to white men of property and standing. The tensions between these two very different approaches to reform shaped the politics of the era.

19.4.1 Muckraking, Moral Reform, and Vice Crusades

muckrakers
The name given to a group of investigative journalists in the early twentieth century whose exposés often challenged corporate and government power.

In the early twentieth century, a group of investigative journalists, the **muckrakers**, began to expose the ills of industrial life. Their best-known works illuminated corruption in business and politics. Ida Tarbell wrote a powerful exposé of the ruthless business practices of John D. Rockefeller, who transformed the Standard Oil Company into a monopoly. Lincoln Steffens unearthed scandals in city and state politics.

Child labor was another concern of reformers. Children worked in fields and factories across the country, picking cotton in Texas, mining coal in West Virginia, working in the textile mills of North Carolina, and sewing buttons in urban sweatshops. Children of immigrants and rural migrants often assisted parents on farms or in shops, their labor an accepted part of the household economy. But the jobs available to children in urban industries often were dangerous and unhealthy, characterized by long hours, low pay, and miserable working conditions. Reformers attempted to improve children's working conditions and to establish age limits so that children could attend school and spend time in healthful recreation rather than in grim sweatshops and factories. Ultimately, child labor activists succeeded in passing legislation at the state level that restricted child labor, although these efforts were more successful in northern states than in the South.

Protective legislation for women was also controversial. Reformers campaigned for laws that would establish minimum wages, maximum hours, regulations against night work, and restrictions on heavy lifting. When they were unable to secure such safety measures for all workers, they argued that women needed special protections because of their physical frailty and their role as future mothers. Women's rights activists disagreed over these measures. Some argued that they were necessary to protect women from exploitation and dangerous working conditions. Others claimed that women should be treated the same as men, arguing that protective legislation implied that women needed special care and were not suited for particular kinds of work. The Supreme Court affirmed the ten-hour working day for women—and the principle of protective legislation—in its landmark 1908 decision *Muller v. Oregon*.

One noted reformer was Helen Keller, whose work on behalf of the blind called attention to the needs of the disabled. Keller lost her sight and hearing from an illness at the age of nineteen months and learned to communicate through Braille and sign language, which she mastered through touch, with the help of her extraordinary teacher, Anne Sullivan. Keller went on to study at schools for the deaf and graduated with honors from Radcliffe College in 1904. A passionate socialist and advocate of women's rights along with other movements for equality, Keller wrote several books and, with the assistance of interpreters, lectured widely all over the world.

Most Progressive reformers were prosperous American-born Anglo-Saxon Protestants. Along with their efforts to improve living and working conditions and alleviate the suffering of the poor, they also hoped to eradicate vice from their society. Vice crusaders in most of the nation's large cities tried to eliminate prostitution and to patrol dance halls, movie theaters, and saloons. Vice crusading culminated in the passage of the Mann Act in 1910, which made it illegal to transport women across state lines for "immoral purposes."

19.4.2 Women's Suffrage

The movement for women's rights, including the effort to gain the vote, was more than half a century old by 1900. But the movement gained momentum at the dawn of the twentieth century. A new generation of women's rights leaders came together in

INJURED CHILD LABORER HARRY McSHANE, CINCINNATI, OHIO This photo, taken in August 1908, shows sixteen-year-old Harry McShane on the first day he was able to stand on his feet after an accident in the Cincinnati, Ohio, Spring factory where he had been working for more than two years. Three months before this photo was taken, he was caught on the belt of a machine, which pulled off his left arm near his shoulder, and broke his right leg through his kneecap. Harry's father said that his employers paid no attention to the boy either at the hospital or at home, and he received no compensation for his injuries.

Lewis Wickes Hine, 1874-1940/Library of Congress Prints and Photographs Division [LC-DIG-nclc-01313]

What does the photograph of Harry McShane suggest about child labor, the dangers of the industrial work force, and the prospects for injured workers?

the suffrage movement. The militancy of the suffrage movement in England inspired American activists to develop new tactics and international alliances. These activists achieved legislative success when several western states granted women the right to vote: Washington in 1910, California in 1911, and three more states in 1912. Eventually, the movement united around the goal of enacting a federal amendment.

The suffrage movement, for all its radicalism, was largely a movement of white middle-class women. White suffrage leaders feared that any alliance with women of color would alienate southern voters whom they needed for ratification of the Nineteenth Amendment. They also hoped to win over to their cause racist and nativist critics in the North who feared that granting the vote to women would enfranchise "undesirable" voters, specifically immigrant and minority women. The suffrage movement also gained the support of conservatives who believed that women would vote for conservative causes such as prohibition and immigration restriction.

Many minority women, such as Hispana activist Adelina Otero Warren, supported the suffrage movement, even though white leaders kept their distance and refused to embrace the antiracist campaigns of their nonwhite sisters. The African American anti-lynching activist Ida B. Wells (also known by her married name as Ida B. Wells-Barnett) supported women's suffrage but was unable to convince the white women's rights leaders to denounce lynching. Ultimately, the passage of the Nineteenth Amendment resulted from a combination of factors, including radical activism, strong support of a wide range of reformers, and an alliance with conservative, racist, and anti-immigrant forces.

19.4.3 Radical Politics and the Labor Movement

Progressive reformers believed that American capitalist democracy was a fundamentally sound system that simply needed to be fixed to achieve its full promise. Radicals of the era, by contrast, believed that the system itself was flawed and needed to be fundamentally transformed. Emma Goldman, a Russian Jewish immigrant, was one of many radical activists who gained both fame and notoriety for her outspoken support of radical causes.

Clara Lemlich was another Jewish immigrant who arrived in America filled with a passion for the rights of workers. "I am a working girl," she declared in her native Yiddish, "one of those striking against intolerable conditions." Still in her teens, the petite young woman took the podium on the night of November 22, 1909, before thousands of striking workers in New York and roused them with stirring words. The next morning, 15,000 garment workers went on strike, demanding a 52-hour workweek, overtime pay, and union recognition. Soon the number of strikers swelled to more than 20,000. Observers at the time were astonished to see lively, fashionably dressed young women filling the picket lines. Ninety percent of the striking workers were Jewish and Italian immigrants.

The strike ended when the striking workers overwhelmingly rejected an offer of better wages and working conditions that did not include recognition of their union. Calling the strikers "socialists," their more moderate allies broke from the union and left the young female workers vulnerable to the power of the company owners. The coalition of support fell apart, and most of the strikers eventually went back to work.

Less than two years later, a fire broke out in the top floors of the Triangle Shirtwaist Company, one of the centers of the 1919 strike. Scraps of material piled everywhere created a fire trap, quickly spreading the flames into a raging inferno. Eight hundred workers, most of them young Jewish and Italian women, were trapped in the conflagration because company officials had locked interior doors to prevent the women from taking breaks outside.

The flames tore through the building in less than half an hour, leaving 146 young women dead. The factory owners were charged with manslaughter, but their attorney argued that the building was in full compliance with safety laws, so they were acquitted of all wrongdoing. But compliance with the laws did not ensure safety for the workers. No laws at the time required adequate fire escapes or fire drills. Just a few months before the fire, the building had been inspected and declared "fireproof." The brutal working conditions that led to the Triangle Shirtwaist fire prevailed all over the country and mobilized workers in a wide range of industries.

Socialism was never as strong in the United States as it was in Europe, but it did gain strength at the turn of the century. Socialists promoted labor unions and the rights of women and formed their own political party. Socialist leader Eugene V. Debs, who had gained national fame for his role in the 1894 railroad strike, became the spokesperson and leader of the Socialist party. Between 1900 and 1920, he was the party's candidate for president, gaining nearly a million votes, or 6 percent of the electorate, in the 1912 election. Although the socialists never gathered a large enough following to win national elections, they elected hundreds of candidates to local office.

The Industrial Workers of the World (IWW), also known as the **Wobblies**, offered another possibility for labor radicalism. It was organized in 1905 by socialists and labor militants. The IWW included women, blacks, immigrants, and unskilled and migratory laborers, workers generally shunned by the American Federation of Labor (AFL). The Wobblies organized workers in the mines of the Rocky Mountain states, in the lumber camps of the Pacific Northwest and the South, and in the eastern textile and steel mills. IWW membership reached about 3 million people, although no more than 150,000 were members at any one time.

Wobblies

Members of the Industrial Workers of the World (IWW), a radical labor union formed in 1905.

19.4.4 Resistance to Racism

The Progressive Era was anything but progressive for nonwhite Americans. Although there were notable exceptions, such as Jane Addams, many white Protestant reformers were either indifferent to racial minorities or actively hostile to them. Moreover, most blacks lived in the rural South, not in northern cities where Progressives were most active. Lynching continued into the twentieth century, with nearly 100 lynchings per year between 1900 and 1910. African Americans were the primary targets of lynch mobs, although other minorities were also vulnerable. Between 1850 and 1930, 597 Mexicans died at the hands of vigilante mobs, half of them in Texas.

Black leaders spoke out against lynching and other forms of racial injustice. Ida B. Wells-Barnett, who had launched an international crusade against lynching in the 1890s, worked to establish local and national networks of black women's clubs. Although she was unable to persuade white suffrage leaders to support the cause of racial justice, she worked closely with Jane Addams to prevent the establishment of segregated schools in Chicago.

A number of other black leaders came to prominence in the first decade of the twentieth century. In 1905, scholar and civil rights leader W. E. B. Du Bois joined with other black leaders to form the Niagara Movement, which called for an end to segregation and discrimination in unions, the courts, and public accommodations, as well as for equal economic and educational opportunity. In 1909, prominent African Americans joined with white Progressive allies to establish the National Association for the Advancement of Colored People (NAACP). The new organization adopted the platform of the Niagara Movement, and Du Bois became the editor of its journal, *The Crisis.*

Conclusion

When Woodrow Wilson entered the White House in 1913, the nation looked and behaved differently than it had at the turn of the century. Millions of immigrants from Europe, Asia, and Mexico had arrived in the United States and settled in towns and cities across the nation. Growing urban areas with new amusements and increasingly diverse populations emerged as centers of a national mass culture. New developments in science and technology brought the automobile and the motion picture to American consumers. At the same time, industrial production contributed to environmental damage, pollution, and dangerous working conditions.

Progressive reformers and labor activists mounted efforts to curb the ill effects of urban industrial society. Faith in science and expertise gave rise to pervasive optimism that social problems could be solved. Muckrakers exposed corruption, women's rights activists pushed for the vote, and African American leaders organized for civil rights and against lynching. In the West and Southwest, Mexicans and Asians challenged discriminatory laws and labor practices. At the same time, moralists and vice crusaders sought to tame what they considered dangerous challenges to the social order.

These years also witnessed a major expansion of national power. Presidents Roosevelt and Taft strengthened the role of the federal government through new efforts to regulate big business and by extending America's military and economic presence abroad. By 1912, most Americans supported a strong reform agenda. But within a few years, the nation became embroiled in a major world war that would challenge the inherent optimism of Progressivism, signaling the end of an era.

Chapter Review

19.1 Expanding National Power

In what ways did Theodore Roosevelt promote Progressive reform?

Theodore Roosevelt strengthened the executive branch of government in order to promote a number of reforms. He expanded the power of the federal government both at home and abroad. Although his successor, William Howard Taft, was not as enthusiastic about expanding the power of the presidency, he continued to promote many of Roosevelt's reform measures.

19.2 Immigration: Visions of a Better Life

Where did immigrants settle, and what conditions did they encounter?

In the first decade of the twentieth century, nearly 9 million immigrants entered the United States. They brought with them their dreams of a better life. Although one-third of all immigrants eventually returned to their home countries, those who stayed built new lives and contributed to the economic, social, and cultural development of the nation.

19.3 Work, Science, and Leisure

How did scientific and technological advances improve the lives of ordinary Americans and, at the same time, lead to abuses that benefitted some at the expense of others?

Science and technology reigned in the early years of the twentieth century. The growth of industries, the construction of towering skyscrapers, and advancements in medicine and public health generated a widespread faith in the ability of experts to solve the nation's problems. Entertainment also flourished with the help of new technologies, particularly the motion picture industry.

19.4 Reformers and Radicals

Who were the reformers and radicals, and what strategies did they use to promote their visions of society?

Progressive reformers sought to improve working and living conditions through policies regulating work safety and child labor and to expand democratic participation by extending the vote to women. Others had more conservative goals, such as restricting immigration. Radicals, by contrast, believed that the system of capitalist democracy was fundamentally flawed and needed to be transformed.

Timeline

1901	McKinley is assassinated; Vice President Theodore Roosevelt becomes president
1905	Industrial Workers of the World founded
1906	San Francisco earthquake
1907	"Gentlemen's Agreement" with Japan
1908	*Muller v. Oregon* limits maximum hours for working women
1909	National Association for the Advancement of Colored People (NAACP) founded
1911	Triangle Shirtwaist Company fire, New York City
1912	Theodore Roosevelt helps form Progressive party
	Woodrow Wilson elected president

Glossary

foundling home A residence for orphaned children.

Progressivism A belief in the potential for progress through social reform that found expression in the Progressive Era, when political leaders and urban reformers sought to solve local and national problems through political and civic means.

conservationists Advocates of conserving and protecting the natural world through the use of renewable natural resources.

"Dollar Diplomacy" President William Howard Taft coined the term to refer to a policy that encouraged economic investment in foreign countries.

New Nationalism Theodore Roosevelt's plan for a far-reaching expansion of the federal government to stabilize the economy and institute social reforms.

Bull Moosers Supporters of Theodore Roosevelt in the 1912 presidential election when he broke from the Republican party and ran as a third-party candidate on the ticket of the Progressive (or Bull Moose) party.

"birds of passage" A term applied to immigrants who came to the United States for a brief period of time, and then returned to their home countries.

race suicide A fear articulated by Theodore Roosevelt and others that the low birthrate of Anglo-Saxon Americans, along with the high birthrate of immigrants from southern and eastern Europe and elsewhere, would result in a population in which "inferior" peoples would outnumber the "American racial stock."

assembly line A form of industrial production popularized by the Ford Motor Company in which workers perform one task repeatedly as the products they are jointly assembling move along a conveyor.

mass consumption society The term refers to a shift in the early twentieth century from a society focused on frugality and production to one that embraced and celebrated consumer goods and leisure pursuits.

Boston marriages Unions of two women based on long-term emotional bonds in which the women live together as if married to each other.

muckrakers The name given to a group of investigative journalists in the early twentieth century whose exposés often challenged corporate and government power.

Wobblies Members of the Industrial Workers of the World (IWW), a radical labor union formed in 1905.

The authors argue that between 1900-1912 society promoted social reforms in order for the suppressed groups such as immigrant can live comfortable lives.

The progressives promote social reform. Such as better working conditions.

Chapter 20
War and Revolution, 1912–1920

W. E. B. DU BOIS The son of a Haitian immigrant, W. E. B. Du Bois (1868–1963) was the first African American to earn a PhD at Harvard University. Du Bois became a distinguished historian and sociologist, as well as one of the nation's most influential voices on racial issues.

Everett Collection Inc/Alamy

How might Du Bois's family background have helped shape his understanding of national and world politics?

Contents and Focus Questions

How would the terrible costs and sacrifices of America's first overseas war impact the loyalty and unity of its people?

"This is the crisis of the world," wrote prominent African American scholar and activist W. E. B. Du Bois in his July 1918 editorial in *The Crisis*, as desperate armies struggled on the battlefields of Europe and the outcome of World War I hung in the balance. Du Bois served as editor of this influential NAACP journal, the circulation of which soared from 1,000 in its first year of publication in 1910 to over 100,000 by 1918. Arguing that the threat of imperial German power "spells death to the aspirations of Negroes and all darker races for equality, freedom and democracy," Du Bois concluded, "Let us, while this war lasts, forget our special grievances and close our ranks with our own white fellow citizens and the allied nations that are fighting for democracy." Black Americans joined Americans of every European ancestry in taking up arms to serve their country, even as they did so in segregated units.

World War I, as Du Bois understood, would touch every continent abroad and would reshape American life and politics at home. The decade of the 1910s opened with rising optimism about solving the real problems of an increasingly urban, industrial, and immigrant society. From 1910 to 1914, Progressive reformers made headway in ameliorating some of the worst aspects of modern industrial life.

But international developments then turned American attentions abroad. Traumatic revolutions swept through Mexico, China, and Russia, and the conflagration of the Great War—World War I, as it became known later—consumed all of Europe from 1914 to 1918 and eventually drew in the United States. The fresh troops and impressive equipment of the American Expeditionary Force helped turn the tide of a very close struggle and defeat Germany and its Central Power allies.

What President Woodrow Wilson called the war "to make the world safe for democracy" encouraged people of color, both in the vast European-ruled colonies of Asia and Africa and in the segregated United States, to claim a place of greater equality. But at home the war also created pressures for conformity. Sending American soldiers to fight and die on the battlefields of northern France in 1917–1918 stirred up intolerance for dissent. The perils and costs of war stimulated a backlash against further immigration and against socialists and other leftist reformers.

*   *   *   *   *

World War I marked the end of the Progressive era. The United States ultimately emerged with great prestige and new power in world affairs, but the Versailles Treaty of 1919 failed to create a lasting structure for world peace.

20.1 A World and a Nation in Upheaval

What were the greatest challenges to the existing international and domestic order in the 1910s?

American politics in the 1910s and the U.S. involvement in World War I must be understood within the context of change and uncertainty in the international system. While world affairs were still dominated by the wealthy nations of western Europe and North America, the first wave of the great revolutions of the twentieth century was beginning to wash away much of the old order. Tensions also sharpened within the United States over traditional hierarchies of color, gender, and class. The struggle between Progressive reform and conservative reaction pervaded public life in the United States and much of the rest of the world in this era.

20.1.1 The Apex of European Conquest

On the eve of World War I, three-quarters of the world's population lived under the rule of Europeans or their descendants. Exploration of the most remote parts of the globe filled in the last blank spaces on world maps, including the North (1909) and South (1911) poles. The granting of statehood to Arizona and New Mexico in 1912 completed the forty-eight mainland states.

Technological innovations in transportation and communication tied the world more closely together. Just as the Suez Canal (1870) and the trans-Siberian railroad (1904) linked Europe more directly to Asia, the Panama Canal (1914) cut in half the travel time by water between the East and West coasts of the United States. Cables laid on the floor of the Atlantic Ocean in 1914 inaugurated telephone service between Europe and the United States.

The competition that arose from the expansion of European power sowed the seeds of World War I. Germany, France, Britain, Italy, and Russia raced each other for new colonies and greater influence across Africa and Asia. The central rivalry emerged between a newly unified Germany (1871) and traditionally dominant Britain. Anticipating trouble, each of the major European powers sought allies to bolster its position. Britain, France, and Russia formed an alliance that became known as the **Entente** or sometimes the Allies. Germany and Austria-Hungary established their own alliance, known as the Central Powers. Italy remained neutral when war broke out, finally joining the Entente a year into the conflict.

Entente
The alliance of Britain, France, and Russia, later joined by Italy and the United States, during World War I.

The United States emerged as a global power in this same period around the turn of the century. Fifteen years after it seized overseas colonies in 1898, the country's economic growth was stunning. In 1913, U.S. consumption of energy from coal and oil equaled that of Britain, Germany, France, Russia, and Austria-Hungary combined. The United States also brought a different history to the world stage. It had been born in 1776 in the first successful revolution by colonies against a European empire. Americans had long understood themselves as a people who opposed empires and supported self-government. The events of 1898 contradicted this legacy, and Americans remained ambivalent about their country's imperial venture. The U.S. Congress in 1916 promised eventual independence to the Philippines and granted U.S. citizenship to residents of Puerto Rico in 1917.

20.1.2 Confronting Revolutions in Asia, Europe, and the Americas

As nationalist movements in China, Russia, and Mexico overturned weak central governments controlled by foreign investors, American economic and security interests seemed to be at stake on three continents. In Asia, the Chinese deeply resented exclusive foreign enclaves that dominated their nation's coastal region and exempted foreigners from the constraints of Chinese laws. In 1911, nationalist revolutionaries inspired by Sun

Yat-sen, a Hawaiian-educated Christian democratic reformer, overthrew the corrupt Qing dynasty that had proven unable to resist western incursions.

The American desire for an open door into China's trade—a door that no other powerful nation could close at will—conflicted with the rising imperial power of the region: Japan. The Tokyo government, which had annexed Korea in 1910, responded to the outbreak of World War I by seizing the valuable German-held Shantung Peninsula in northeastern China. In its Twenty-One Demands to China, issued in January 1915, Japan made clear its plans to dominate the development of the Chinese economy. The American relationship with both China and Japan was undercut at home by continued discrimination and violence against immigrants from Asia.

Revolutionary struggles with implications for America also threatened the monarchs who ruled eastern Europe. For Russians, defeat at the hands of Japan in 1905 helped precipitate a thwarted revolution followed by two years of political turmoil. The czar survived to rule another decade, and thousands of political reformers—unionists, anarchists, and socialists—joined a growing wave of immigration from Russia and elsewhere to the United States. The wave crested in 1914 at 1.2 million people, most of them from east or south of the Alps. That same year, the assassination of the heir to the Austro-Hungarian throne by a Serbian nationalist in Sarajevo provided the spark that ignited the Great War.

Before World War I, the most important region of the world for the United States was Latin America, especially Central America, Mexico, and the Caribbean islands. This area guarded the nation's strategic southern flank, and American citizens and corporations invested more money in Latin America than in any other region of the world. American anxieties about stability to the south centered on Mexico. "Land for the landless and Mexico for the Mexicans" became the slogan of revolutionaries there between 1910 and 1920. U.S. stakes in the Mexican revolution were high. American investors

Map 20.1 U.S. INTERESTS AND INTERVENTIONS IN THE CARIBBEAN REGION, 1898–1939

By its size, wealth, and military power, the United States dominated the Caribbean region to its south. American capitalists invested heavily in Mexico, Central America, and the Caribbean islands, and U.S. troops often intervened to protect those investments. Puerto Rico (by acquisition from Spain) and the Panama Canal Zone (by lease from Panama) became particularly important territories ruled by the United States.

owned 43 percent of all Mexico's wealth (other foreigners owned another 25 percent), and more than half of the country's trade flowed north to the United States. Moreover, by 1921, Mexico was the world's second largest exporter of oil. Washington feared the spread of radical political ideas northward as almost a million Mexicans crossed their northern border during the revolutionary decade, tripling the number of Americans with recent roots south of the Rio Grande.

Many came through El Paso, the "Ellis Island" for immigrants from the south. Fleeing poverty and violence, they found both discrimination and employment. Most immigrants sought unskilled positions, but members of Mexico's professional class—teachers, architects, and lawyers—also came north, for political asylum. The new arrivals joined Mexican Americans who had lived in the region since it was part of Mexico. They had not crossed the border; in 1848, the border had crossed them.

Wilson sought unsuccessfully to reestablish in Mexico a political order respectful of the rights of foreign property owners. Wilson twice sent U.S. troops into Mexico, at Veracruz in April 1914 to block a German arms shipment and then in pursuit of Francisco ("Pancho") Villa and his army after their 1916 assault on Columbus, New Mexico. The American forces under General John J. Pershing withdrew in early 1917 as the president prepared to enter the much larger war in Europe. Land redistribution and national control of the country's abundant mineral wealth, particularly oil, were written into Mexico's new constitution passed a few days later, and the revolutionary upheaval ended by 1920.

20.1.3 Social Conflicts at Home

Just as social upheaval threatened monarchies and international investors abroad, less privileged Americans contested traditional lines of hierarchy and inequality in the United States. Americans of all colors applauded the spectacular successes of Native American athlete Jim Thorpe at the 1912 Olympic Games in Sweden. In 1916, Wilson appointed Louis Brandeis as the first Jewish justice of the Supreme Court, but that same year, anxieties about the future of white supremacy found a voice in the popular new book of a reactionary New York intellectual named Madison Grant. *The Passing of the Great Race*, a bigoted sociology tract, identified Jesus as "Nordic" to distance the central figure of the Christian faith from the many new Jewish immigrants in America.

The Wilson administration's "New Freedom" slogan did not apply to African Americans, who faced continuing discrimination in employment and housing. The president filled his cabinet with white Southerners who segregated the few federal agencies that had employed blacks. When Wilson took office, African Americans continued to be murdered publicly by vigilante mobs across the South at a rate of more than one person per week. But the president ignored requests from the recently formed NAACP for an anti-lynching law.

Women of all colors lived under particular burdens of discrimination. Their uniquely intimate relationships—as daughters, wives, mothers—with those who did not treat them as equals complicated their efforts at reform. So did their dilemma about women's roles in society: some sought full legal equality with men, and others wanted special protections for women on the grounds that they were fundamentally different from men.

American women's long struggle to vote came to a head in this decade. By 1912, a growing number of European nations and nine American states, all in the West, had granted the franchise to citizens of both sexes. The moderate National American Women Suffrage Association under the leadership of Carrie Chapman Catt worked within the political system, building an alliance with President Wilson after he endorsed **women's suffrage** in 1916 and supporting the U.S. entry into World War I the following year. Alice Paul and other militants formed the National Women's Party and opposed the war effort as inherently undemocratic because half the adult population could not vote. In 1918, suffragist organizers helped elect a more sympathetic Congress that passed the Nineteenth

women's suffrage
The right of women citizens to vote, and the movement to win that right.

Amendment, ending sex discrimination in voting two years later. The Nineteenth Amendment marked the single largest increase in political equality in American history.

Most adult Americans were workers, and they continued to find themselves in frequent conflict with their employers. Industrial capitalism's efficiency produced great material wealth, but 60 percent of it belonged to the top 2 percent of the population, whereas the bottom two-thirds of Americans owned only 2 percent of the wealth. The anticapitalist aspirations of the Socialist party and the Industrial Workers of the World frightened both industrialists and the more conservative labor leaders of the American Federation of Labor, especially when the western-based IWW led two major strikes in the East, one a success in Lawrence, Massachusetts, in 1912 and the other a failure in Paterson, New Jersey, in 1913. The campaign against a wage cut at the vast Lawrence textile factory was especially impressive in uniting 20,000 workers of 40 different national backgrounds.

Some business owners sought to undercut union campaigns by providing better working conditions and even company-run "unions." These carrots of concession were accompanied by the stick of force. Bolstered by sympathetic federal courts and state governors, companies usually refused to negotiate with workers who went on strike. This pattern reached a violent climax on Easter night in 1914 outside Ludlow, Colorado, in a mining camp owned by John D. Rockefeller Jr.'s Colorado Fuel and Iron Company. State militia and company guards broke a strike there with torches and machine guns, burning the miners' tent colony and killing two women and eleven children.

ON THE PICKET LINE AT THE WHITE HOUSE In February 1917, as the United States broke relations with Germany and began preparing to enter World War I, supporters of women's suffrage continued to picket on the sidewalk outside the White House. College women joined the effort to ensure that winning liberty at home would go hand in hand with fighting for democracy abroad.

Library of Congress Prints and Photographs Division [LC-USZ62-31799]

Note the great diversity on the picket line in the photograph above, which represents women from small, elite eastern colleges, women from large, public universities in the Midwest, and a woman from Stanford—a then-new private university in California. Would noncollegiate women have also supported the effort for political equality for female citizens? How might men have felt about the campaign for women's suffrage?

Such brutality by owners against workers appalled most Americans. The Wilson administration slowly began supporting the right of laborers to organize for collective bargaining with their employers. Wilson's strong backing from Samuel Gompers and the AFL in the 1912 election initiated the modern alliance between labor and the Democratic party.

20.2 American Neutrality and Domestic Reform

What were Americans' priorities from 1914 to 1917?

Most Americans had roots of some kind in Europe and had long defined themselves in relation to life on "the continent." But they also considered themselves part of the New World that was separate from the Old World of kings, castles, and rigid social classes. When Europe stepped off the precipice in August 1914 into a war larger than any previously fought or imagined, few Americans wanted any part of it. Make "no entangling alliances," George Washington had urged his fellow citizens. Europeans must stay out of our hemisphere, the Monroe Doctrine had declared. Faithful to this tradition, Americans focused on domestic political reforms and on an economy revived by European demands for war-related goods, which created new jobs in industry that lured many black Southerners north. But international ties proved too important to the well-being of Americans for the country to remain indefinitely on the sidelines of World War I.

20.2.1 "The One Great Nation at Peace"

The alliance system pulled all the great powers of Europe into the war that began between Serbia and Austria-Hungary. Following traditional U.S. policy, Wilson urged Americans to remain neutral "in fact as well as in name" to promote an eventual "peace without victory." Neutrality was profitable. Wilson stoutly defended the rights of neutrals to trade with belligerents, the same principle that had led the United States into the War of 1812 against England. After the recession of 1913–1914, war-related demand from abroad for American farm and factory products jump-started the economy. In the course of World War I, American bankers extended $10 billion in loans to the Allies (primarily Britain and France), and the United States changed from a debtor nation to the world's largest creditor.

The nature of the fighting in Europe further bolstered the American determination to avoid being drawn into the conflict. Industrialized warfare brought fiendish new ways to kill human beings, including machine guns and poison gas. Gone were the days of bold maneuvers and dashing cavalry charges; now was the time of trench warfare, with its unrelenting misery, terror, and helplessness. Eight and a half million young men lost their lives and at least another 16 million were wounded, devastating an entire generation of European society. Between 6 and 13 million civilians also died as a result of the fighting, and an international outbreak of influenza in 1918 killed another 20 million around the world.

In the United States, neutrality also made political sense. Immigrants from every part of Europe lived and voted in the United States, so Americans had blood ties to all the belligerents. Commercial and political elites tended to identify with Britain and France, as did many other Americans. But among two of the largest groups of Americans, those with roots in Germany and Ireland, many took a different view. Few Irish Americans equated England with the cause of democracy after centuries of British rule in Ireland. Native-born white Americans were already concerned with preserving unity in their increasingly diverse society. Allowing in the hatreds from Europe's battlefields would only exacerbate the ethnic and class tensions that worried social reformers and many politicians, including President Wilson.

20.2.2 Reform Priorities at Home

Americans traditionally considered powerful government to be the primary threat to individual liberty, but the rise of mammoth corporations at the start of the twentieth century altered that calculation. Competition was disappearing, particularly in critical sectors of the economy such as oil production and railroads. Laissez-faire policies, by which federal agencies encouraged economic expansion, seemed no longer adequate. Only government, argued Progressive reformers in both major parties, could balance the new might of the largest companies. This meant modest regulation of some aspects of the marketplace. Wilson's first term also encouraged such democratic reforms as the ratification of the Seventeenth Amendment for the direct popular election of U.S. senators (1913), previously chosen by state legislatures.

Three areas topped the Wilson administration's reform agenda: taxes, the money system, and monopolies. The Underwood-Simmons Tariff of 1913 cut duties—taxes—on imported goods by almost one-half, helping American consumers and promoting freer trade. The Sixteenth Amendment (1913) allowed a federal income tax, which the 1916 Revenue Act put into effect. This was a progressive tax, one that took a larger percentage of the income of the rich than of the poor. The legislation also levied higher taxes on corporate profits and created the first federal estate tax on inheritances.

Congress moved to regulate the money system in another new way as well. The absence of a centrally managed money system had long contributed to the exaggerated boom-and-bust cycles in the American economy. The Federal Reserve Act of 1913 created a system of 12 Federal Reserve Banks to control the amount of currency in circulation, increasing it in deflationary times and decreasing it when inflation threatened. The system aimed to abolish depressions and prevent bank closures. It did not fully succeed, as the years after 1929 showed, but the Federal Reserve System did stabilize the American banking industry and helped position the dollar to become the central global currency.

No issue so dominated American politics between 1913 and 1915 as the tension between huge new corporations and the nation's antimonopoly tradition. The size and market share of companies such as U.S. Steel, American Tobacco, and DuPont (chemicals) inhibited competition. Congress created the Federal Trade Commission (1914) to investigate business practices that unfairly prevented competition. The Clayton Antitrust Act of 1914 supplemented the 1890 Sherman Antitrust Act by outlawing specific unfair business practices such as local price cutting and granting rebates to undermine competitors.

Another kind of legislation focused on preserving natural landscapes. An increasingly urban, industrial society looked to its most beautiful rural places for solace. Local and state governments set aside parklands throughout the Progressive Era. Wilson followed in Roosevelt's conservationist footsteps by creating the National Park Service in 1916 to provide unified management of such new national treasures as Glacier National Park in Montana (1910), Rocky Mountain National Park in Colorado (1915), Lassen Volcanic National Park in California (1916), and Acadia National Park in Maine (1919).

20.2.3 The Great Migration

The Progressive Era of roughly 1900–1920 was anything but progressive from the viewpoint of many African Americans. White mob violence reached its apex in these years, with hundreds of lynchings and dozens of race riots. Most blacks lived in the South, where segregation and discrimination trapped the majority in poverty. Many therefore seized the unprecedented opportunity offered by the outbreak of the Great War. War-related orders created huge needs for workers in northern factories, at the same time that the war also closed the spigot of European immigration, drying up the standard source of new labor. Along with other cities, Chicago and Detroit became centers of the **Great Migration** of more than half a million African Americans out of Dixie during the war years.

Great Migration
The movement of African Americans out of the South to northern cities, which accelerated during World War I.

Black Southerners still found plenty of discrimination in the urban North. But the large black communities of Philadelphia, Cleveland, and New York offered far greater independence than the rural South they left behind. African Americans could vote, earn higher wages, send their children to better schools, and even sit where they wanted on streetcars. One woman newly arrived in Chicago was stunned the first time she boarded a trolley and saw black people sitting next to whites. "I just held my breath, for I thought any minute they would start something. Then I saw nobody notices it, and I just thought this is a real place for Negroes."

When war in Europe shut off most Atlantic immigration in 1914, it opened the door to newcomers who did not have to cross the submarine-infested ocean. Blacks who boarded trains for the North were joined by a similar number of white Southerners leaving rural poverty to look for jobs. A small stream of French Canadians found work in New England factories. A much larger stream of Mexicans and Mexican Americans flowed to jobs across the American Southwest and Midwest. World War I and the Mexican Revolution increased their numbers sharply, with the growing cities of Los Angeles, San Antonio, and El Paso remaining particular magnets for new immigrants. The number of Mexican Americans in Los Angeles soared from 6,000 in 1910 to nearly 100,000 in 1930.

THE GREAT MIGRATION NORTH A migrant family from the South arriving in Chicago, c. 1916.
Southerners of all colors, like Europeans, were drawn by the lure of better jobs to the industrial cities
of the American Northeast and Midwest. With immigration from Europe slowed to a trickle by the
onset of World War I, white and black Southerners moved north.

Chicago History Museum/Getty Images

How might international migration and domestic migration be connected to each other, then and now?

20.2.4 Limits to American Neutrality

Meanwhile, the fighting in Europe did not diminish, and a steady undertow of interests and inclinations pulled against American neutrality. Most Americans who paid
attention to events abroad favored the Allies over the Central Powers. The diversity
of Americans' ethnic roots across Europe, Africa, Asia, and Latin America could not
mask fundamental cultural and linguistic connections to England, the one-time "mother
country." President Wilson deeply admired British political values and institutions, and
most influential newspaper editors supported the British cause. Even Americans critical
of the British Empire did not want to see the European continent under the autocratic
rule of German Kaiser Wilhelm II.

Concrete economic interests also tied the United States to the Allied side. During
three years of neutrality (1914–1917), American bankers lent 85 times as much to the
Entente nations as to the Central Powers ($2.3 billion versus $27 million), and agricultural and industrial workers earned decent wages in filling Allied war orders.

Certain powerful Americans, concentrated on the East Coast, tried from the start
to prepare the country for entering the war. They emphasized that the U.S. military
was much smaller than the forces of European states because of Americans' traditional
aversion to large standing armies. Republicans such as Theodore Roosevelt and former
Secretary of State Elihu Root led the war preparedness movement.

Progressives split over the war. More radical reformers opposed joining it as a matter of principle. "Let the capitalists do their own fighting and furnish their own corpses," Socialist Eugene Debs wrote in 1914, "and there will never be another war on the face of the earth." They feared, presciently, that going to war would take the wind out of the sails of domestic reform.

Most Progressives followed President Wilson's leadership, opposing U.S. involvement in Europe at first but gradually shifting to support it. The president squeaked by conservative Republican nominee Charles Evans Hughes in the 1916 election, winning a second term in the White House. "He kept us out of war," his supporters declared, but Wilson himself was less optimistic. He knew where German submarine warfare might lead: "Any little German lieutenant can put us into the war at any time by some calculated outrage."

Table 20.1 THE ELECTION OF 1916

Candidate	Political Party	Popular Vote (%)	Electoral Vote
Woodrow Wilson	Democratic	49.4	277
Charles E. Hughes	Republican	46.2	254
A. L. Benson	Socialist	3.2	—

SOURCE: Historical Election Results, Electoral College, National Archives and Records Administration

20.3 The United States Goes to War

How did fighting in World War I change the United States?

Wilson won reelection as a liberal reformer and a man of peace, only to go to war within six months. On April 2, 1917, the president asked Congress for a declaration of war against Germany "to make the world safe for democracy." Congress agreed by a large majority, and four days later, the United States entered the Great War. The government limited anti-war criticism in an effort to ensure unity. Mobilization went slowly; it took almost a year before American soldiers in large numbers saw combat in the trenches of northern France. But American foodstuffs and munitions arrived more quickly, as did American naval ships protecting cargo vessels bound for England. The U.S. entry into the war ultimately provided the narrow margin of victory against the Central Powers.

20.3.1 The Logic of Belligerency

Wilson's insistence on the traditional rights of neutral nations to trade with belligerents clashed with both German and British efforts to prevent trade destined for their enemy. The German use of the new submarines, or **U-boats** (from the German *Unterseeboote*), against superior British surface ships pulled Americans into the war. Submarines were extremely vulnerable when not submerged. Before firing on a merchant or passenger ship that might be armed or carrying contraband (war materials), they refused to surface and warn civilian passengers—as required under international law—to evacuate on lifeboats. With Britain arming merchant ships and stowing munitions in the holds of passenger ships, U-boats were the key element in the German campaign to weaken the enemy. The British navy, in turn, seized American goods bound for Germany. But Britain's blockade of the German coastline and neutral ports nearby did not endanger civilians in the same way. "One deals with life; the other with property," Secretary of State Robert Lansing explained.

The deaths of civilians without warning on the high seas shocked and angered the American public, especially the sinking of the magnificent British ocean liner *Lusitania* in May 1915, which killed 128 U.S. citizens and a thousand others. Hoping to keep the United States out of the war, the German government twice put its unrestricted

U-boats

German submarines in World War I that attacked civilian and officially neutral ships, helping bring the United States into the war.

CAUGHT IN NO MAN'S LAND, ON THE WESTERN FRONT The body of a soldier lies caught in barbed wire in the "no man's land" between opposing trenches on the western front. Technological advances in weaponry helped make the fighting in World War I vastly more destructive than in previous wars. The sheer scale of the slaughter stunned combatants and observers, both in Europe and America, and helped turn many in the postwar generation to deep skepticism regarding the use of military force.

American Stock Archive/Archive Photos/Getty Images

If the postwar pursuit of justice and peace in international relations seemed to some to require new forms of cooperation, such as the League of Nations (founded in 1919), how might World War I have inspired others, such as young Austrian corporal Adolf Hitler, to believe more fervently in the use of force to attain one's goals?

submarine warfare on hold. But by January 1917, the British blockade had reduced German food rations per person to less than half the prewar level. Facing imminent starvation, Berlin decided to take one last chance with unrestricted submarine warfare. The German government calculated that it could force a British and French surrender before enough American assistance arrived.

Preparing for war with the Americans, German Ambassador Arthur Zimmermann secretly offered German aid to the revolutionary Mexican government "to reconquer the lost territory in Texas, New Mexico, and Arizona" if it joined the Central Powers. Mexico declined, but the Zimmermann telegram leaked to the press on March 1 and outraged Americans. One last hindrance to joining the Allies disappeared with the revolution that same month in Russia, which replaced the monarchy with a social democratic government.

Still guarding American autonomy and wary of close identification with the French, British, and Russian empires, Wilson took the nation into war as an "Associated" power rather than a full-blown member of the Entente. The president believed that the United States, unique among the belligerents, sought only to defend principles rather than to acquire territory. "We have no quarrel with the German people" but only with the "Prussian autocracy" whose U-boats were engaged in "a warfare against mankind," Wilson declared in calling Americans to a great crusade in Europe.

20.3.2 Mobilizing the Home Front

Going to war entailed a complete reorientation of the American economy. For the U.S. Army and Navy to succeed abroad, mass production of war materials had to be centrally planned, and only the federal government could fulfill this role. The Wilson administration created several new agencies to manage the war effort at home. The Selective Service Act established local boards to draft young men into the military. The U.S. Railroad Administration took control of the nation's primary transportation system to solve railroad tie-ups caused by heavy demands for war materials. The War Industries Board supervised all war-related production, allowing large manufacturers to coordinate their schedules without fear of antitrust action. The War Labor Board resolved disputes between workers and employers. The Committee on Public Information had the task of inspiring and maintaining public support for Wilson's war policies.

The close cooperation between industry and government, combined with strong demand for American goods from the Allied governments, caused corporate earnings to soar. "We are all making more money out of this war than the average human being ought to," one steel company official admitted privately. And some of the war gains were spread around, for a collaborative effort entailed keeping workers productive and content. Taking a position unprecedented in the U.S. government, the War Labor Board promoted an eight-hour workday and the right of workers to form unions.

20.3.3 Ensuring Unity

The deaths of U.S. soldiers and sailors made support for the war an emotional issue, and a pattern of repressing dissent took hold that outlasted the war itself. Several states banned teaching the German language. Sauerkraut became "liberty cabbage," frankfurters became hot dogs, and many German Americans anglicized their names. Temperance reformers cited German beer drinking in their successful campaign for a constitutional prohibition of alcohol production. Congress approved the controversial **Eighteenth Amendment** in December 1917 as a way to save grain for the war effort, and the states ratified it in 1919. Anti-German sentiment led to sometimes deadly violence against Americans of German descent by the summer of 1918. Congress passed sharply restrictive immigration legislation in 1917 as anti-German feelings fed broader prewar fears of new immigrants. The **Espionage** (1917) and **Sedition** (1918) **Acts** banned written and verbal organizing against the war.

Most African Americans agreed with W. E. B. Du Bois's call to "close our ranks shoulder to shoulder" with white fellow citizens in support of the war effort, although anti-black violence escalated. The arrival of half a million black Southerners in northern cities increased competition for jobs and housing, causing resentment among many whites. Employers contributed to tensions by recruiting African Americans as strikebreakers and pitting them against white workers. Whites rioted in East St. Louis on July 1, 1917, causing at least 47 fatalities, most of them black. Black soldiers from the North at times rebelled against the Jim Crow restrictions they found on southern military bases.

20.3.4 The War in Europe

When the United States entered the war in Europe in 1917, crisis gripped the Allies. In the east, much of the war effort collapsed in the confusion of Russia's revolution against the czar. In the west, forty-nine divisions of the French army mutinied, refusing orders to make further suicidal advances. In the south, at Caporetto, Austro-Hungarian forces inflicted a disastrous defeat on the Italian army. It was not clear whether the Americans had joined soon enough to help stave off defeat.

Eighteenth Amendment
Allowed Congress to prohibit the production of alcoholic beverages, creating the period of Prohibition that lasted until 1933.

Espionage and Sedition Acts
Banned written and verbal dissent against U.S. participation in World War I, imperiling freedom of speech.

Map 20.2 WORLD WAR I IN EUROPE AND THE WESTERN FRONT, 1918

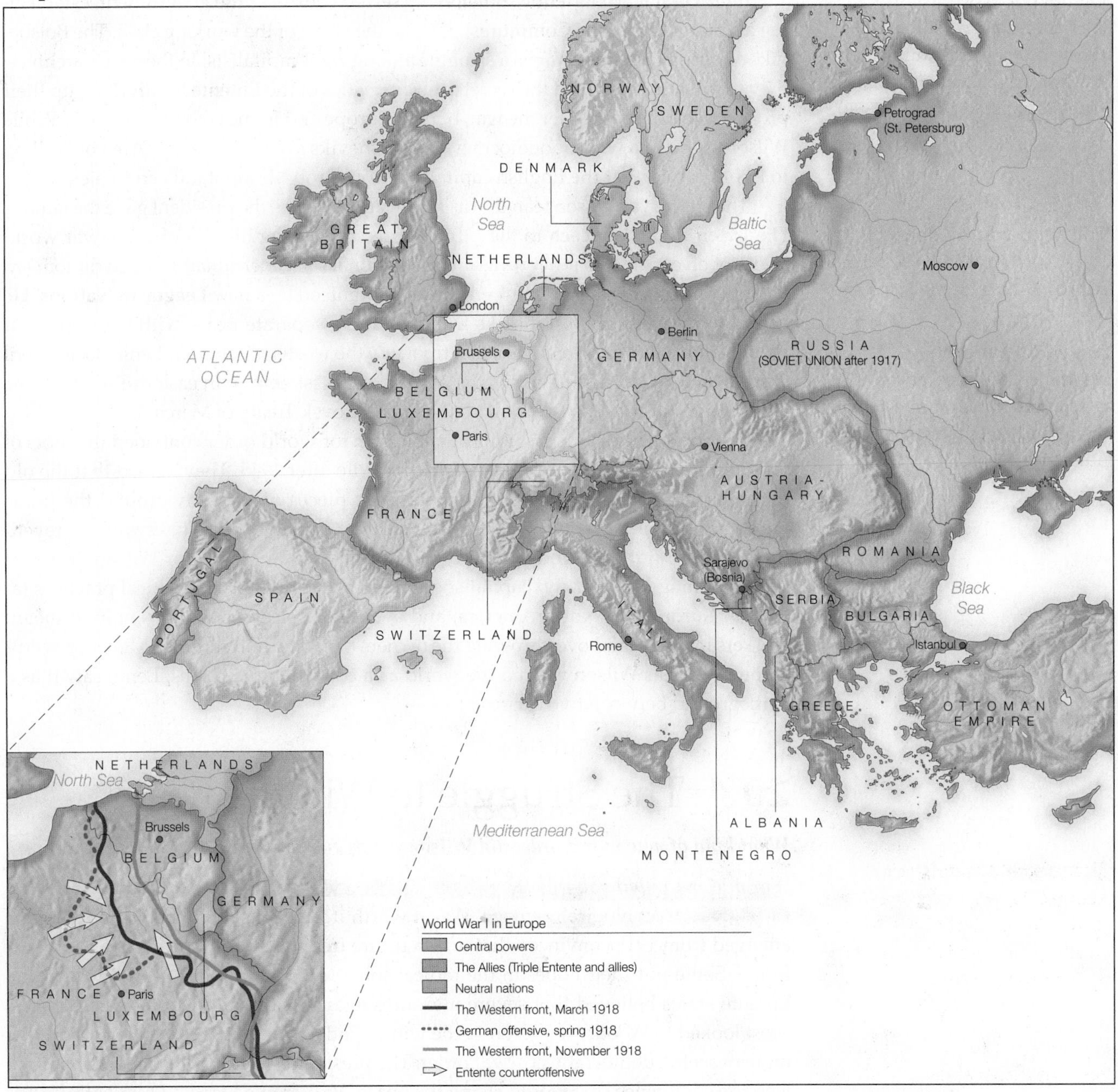

By the time U.S. troops arrived in force on the western front in northern France, the new Bolshevik (Communist) government of Russia had made peace with the Germans and withdrawn from the war. Germany now faced enemies only on one front—the western front—and moved all its troops there. In this dire situation for the French and British, American soldiers helped fill the gap in 1918.

No battle-ready American army waited at ports for immediate shipment to the trenches of northern France. U.S. commanders instead had to conscript and train nearly 5 million young men for an American Expeditionary Force (AEF) under General Pershing, while 16,000 young women volunteered for service overseas as nurses and Red Cross workers. Although the veteran French and British lines had to stand largely on their own against the final German spring offensive, American soldiers later engaged in fierce combat at Belleau Wood, Château-Thierry, and St. Mihiel, ultimately losing 114,000 men. As the only army growing stronger in 1918, the AEF contributed crucially to the fall offensive that convinced Germany to surrender on November 11.

Bolsheviks
The Communist revolutionaries who seized power in Russia in 1917 and established the Union of Soviet Socialist Republics (USSR).

"Fourteen Points" speech
Wilson's address to the world outlining U.S. aims for the postwar order.

League of Nations
Created by the Treaty of Versailles as a forum for peaceful resolution of international problems in the future.

Events in Russia provoked the greatest long-term concerns. In October 1917, Vladimir Lenin and his fellow **Bolsheviks** seized control of the government, establishing a dictatorship of the Communist party in the name of the working class. The Bolsheviks opposed the Great War as a struggle among rival capitalists. In the czar's archives, they found and published the secret prewar treaties of the Entente for dividing up their prospective conquests after the war, both in Europe and in the colonies overseas. While Wilson spoke of a war for democracy, the Bolsheviks asked Russians, "Are you willing to fight for this, that the English capitalists should rob Mesopotamia and Palestine?"

The answer, as Wilson feared, was no. In January 1918, the president gave the famous **"Fourteen Points" speech** to the U.S. Congress, outlining his aim of a postwar world built not on expansion and revenge but on national self-determination, open diplomacy, and freedom of commerce and travel, to be guaranteed by a new **League of Nations**. He hoped to dissuade the Bolsheviks from making a separate peace with Germany that would allow Germany to move all its troops to the western front. But Lenin, facing civil war at home, conceded huge swaths of the old czarist empire in eastern Europe to the Germans in order to gain peace with the Brest-Litovsk Treaty of March 3, 1918.

The competing visions of Wilson and Lenin for world order contained the roots of the Cold War that would dominate American life after 1945. They agreed that the old diplomacy of imperialist states competing for pieces of property around the globe would no longer work and that only the creation of democratic states would prevent further wars. But they understood democracy very differently. For Wilson, it meant self-governing nations with capitalist economies and republican political practices (at least in Europe and North America, and eventually elsewhere). For Lenin, it meant workers in every land overthrowing the owners of capital and setting up Soviet governments. Whereas Wilson viewed the world as a collection of nations, Lenin saw it as a battleground between two classes.

20.4 The Struggle to Win the Peace

What kind of new world order did Wilson want, and to what extent did he achieve it?

World War I killed roughly 20 million people and wrought immeasurable physical, social, and psychological damage. Was it worth it? Citizens of the belligerent nations emerged from 1918 convinced that only a future free of war could legitimate such suffering. Some put their hopes in the radical solution unfolding in Russia. Some in the Entente states believed that severe measures against Germany would ensure peace. Most looked to Woodrow Wilson in the winter and spring of 1919, with his vision of a more peaceful, democratic postwar order. The president sailed for Europe in January to lead the conference that would shape the peace. Vast crowds greeted him enthusiastically as he toured England, Italy, and France.

20.4.1 Peacemaking and the Versailles Treaty

War and revolution destroyed the four great empires of Russia, Germany, Austria-Hungary, and the Ottomans (based in modern Turkey). Meeting in Paris from January to June 1919, the "Big Three" of Wilson, French President Georges Clemenceau, and British Prime Minister David Lloyd George took on two major tasks to shape the postwar order. First, the three leaders redrew the map of eastern and central Europe and the Middle East to create new nation-states out of the vanished empires. Second, they had to decide what to do about a defeated Germany. The possible spread of revolution gave the negotiations a particular urgency. Anticolonial revolts broke out in India and China, and pro-Soviet workers' councils seized power briefly in Hungary and southern Germany. "We are running a race with Bolshevism," Wilson warned, "and the world is on fire."

Interpreting History

Addie W. Hunton and Kathryn M. Johnson: Two African American Women on Their Time Abroad During the Great War (1920)

> "the first full breath of freedom that had ever come into our limited experience"

Just as black American men served in the American Expeditionary Force in France in 1917–1918, black American women served in auxiliary organizations such as the Red Cross and the Young Men's and Women's Christian Associations (YMCA and YWCA), which worked to boost the soldiers' morale. They staffed canteens set up to provide social and educational support for American troops as an alternative to such entertainments as prostitution and gambling. Addie W. Hunton and Kathryn M. Johnson felt a particular calling to encourage African American soldiers, who suffered from discrimination and segregation even as they fought for democracy. As devout Christians, the two women believed they must model a life of service and compassion, even in the face of persecution. An account of their time in Europe published soon after they returned to the United States suggests some of the complications of a segregated society sending people abroad.

ENTERTAINING THE TROOPS, NEWARK, NEW JERSEY
American women supported the war effort in many ways, including working in munitions factories, buying war bonds, acting as single parents while husbands were away in the military, and volunteering as nurses for the armed forces in France. Here, African American women entertain black soldiers with music in a service club in Newark, New Jersey, 1918.

National Archives and Records Administration

If you had been a black American woman in 1918, how do you think you might have felt about the U.S. war effort?

Two Colored Women with the American Expeditionary Forces

The relationship between the colored soldiers, the colored welfare workers, and the French people was most cordial and friendly and grew in sympathy and understanding, as their associations brought about a closer acquaintance. It was rather an unusual as well as a most welcome experience to be able to go into places of public accommodation without having any hesitations or misgivings; to be at liberty to take a seat in a common carrier, without fear of inviting some humiliating experience; to go into a home and receive a greeting that carried with it a hospitality and kindliness of spirit that could not be questioned.

These things were at once noticeable upon the arrival of a stranger within the gates of this sister democracy, and the first ten days in France, though filled with duties and harassed with visits from German bombing planes, were nevertheless a delight, in that they furnished to some of us the first full breath of freedom that had ever come into our limited experience.

The first post of duty assigned to us was Brest. Upon arriving there we received our first experience with American prejudices, which had not only been carried across the seas, but had become a part of such an intricate propaganda, that the relationship between the colored soldier and the French people is more or less a story colored by a continued and subtle effort to inject this same prejudice into the heart of the hitherto unprejudiced Frenchman.

[An order posted by a white officer of a black battalion read:] "Enlisted men of this organization will not talk to or be in company with any white women, regardless of whether the women solicit their company or not."

[Another order read:] "There are two Y.M.C.A.'s, one near the camp, for white troops, and one in town, for the colored troops. All men will be instructed to patronize their own Y."

The Account Also Describes Segregation Imposed During the Return Voyage to the United States:

Quite a bit of unpleasantness was experienced on the boats coming home. . . . On [one] boat there were nineteen colored welfare workers; all the women were placed on a floor below the white women, and the entire colored party was placed in an obscure, poorly ventilated section of the dining-room, entirely separated from the other workers by a long table of Dutch civilians. The writer immediately protested; the reply was made that the southern white workers on board the ship would be insulted if the colored workers ate in the same section of the dining-room with them, and, at any rate, the colored people did not expect any such treatment as had been given them by the French.

Questions for Discussion

1. How did serving in France affect the ways African American men and women viewed their own country?

2. What might the impact of blacks' service in France have been on American society when they returned home after the war?

SOURCE: Addie W. Hunton and Kathryn M. Johnson, *Two Colored Women with the American Expeditionary Forces* (New York: Brooklyn Eagle Press, 1920), 28–30, 182–183, 186.

To put out the fire, the Big Three created a string of new nations running from Finland in the north to Yugoslavia in the south. Eastern Europeans were to be self-governing within the new political boundaries. How far would "self-determination" go? Secretary of State Lansing worried that the president's language of democracy was "loaded with dynamite." The world's nonwhite majority wondered whether it applied to them. The Big Three created the mandate system to provide for eventual self-determination for colonies after a period of tutelage under an established power, and they rejected Japan's proposal to include racial equality as a principle of the new League of Nations.

THE NEGOTIATORS AT VERSAILLES The major negotiating powers at Versailles in 1919 were represented by, left to right, British prime minister David Lloyd George, Italian prime minister Vittorio Orlando, French president Georges Clemenceau, and U.S. president Woodrow Wilson. Orlando walked out of the conference once it became clear that Italy would not receive the territories it demanded on the eastern shore of the Adriatic Sea. This left "the Big Three"—Wilson, Lloyd George, and Clemenceau—to hammer out the final decisions regarding the new map of eastern Europe and the extent and limits of national self-determination.

Classic Image/Alamy

At the conference that would shape the postwar peace, which compromises did Wilson make to mesh U.S. interests with British and French interests?

The German question predominated at the Paris conference. To create a long-term peaceful order in Europe, Wilson wanted lenient terms for Germany. But the French and British had lost much more in the war than the Americans, and they believed Germany must pay for that. To satisfy France and England, Germany had to admit guilt for causing the war and pay $33 billion in reparations, while losing much of its eastern territory to the new Polish and Czechoslovakian states. For Wilson, the League of Nations was the key: this new and unprecedented global organization would keep the peace by ensuring collective security for all nations.

Back home, most Republicans objected on principle to one key aspect of the Versailles Treaty (named for the estate of King Louis XIV, where it was signed): Article 10 of the League of Nations charter, guaranteeing ahead of time a collective response to defend any member's territory from attack. Treaty opponents were determined to preserve complete American autonomy, including freedom of action in Latin America. Henry Cabot Lodge Jr. of Massachusetts, the powerful Republican chair of the Senate Foreign Relations Committee, organized the two Senate votes rejecting American membership in the League. Hoping to stave off defeat for his idealistic plan, Wilson undertook an ill-advised national speaking tour to promote the League. His strenuous effort failed to win American participation in the League, and it ultimately broke his fragile health. Wilson suffered a stroke on October 2, 1919, that left him incapacitated for the rest of his presidency.

20.4.2 Waging Counterrevolution Abroad

Soon after Russia withdrew from the war, Britain, France, and the United States intervened in the civil war there between the Bolsheviks (the "Reds") and the various counterrevolutionary forces (the "Whites"). The initial military rationale in the summer of 1918 was to reopen the eastern front against Germany. The United States landed 7,000 troops in Vladivostok, on Russia's far Pacific coast. In conjunction with the British, another 5,000 U.S. soldiers went ashore at Archangel in northern Russia. They quickly became involved in fighting the Red Army. The Wilson administration meanwhile funneled money and military intelligence to leaders of the White forces.

The Bolsheviks rejected certain values cherished by most Americans: the sanctity of private property and contracts, political liberty, and religious freedom. They liberalized divorce laws and legalized abortion, challenging conservative American attitudes about the relationships between women and men. And they established the Comintern in 1919 to promote Communist revolutions around the world. Allied intervention in the Russian civil war failed to overthrow Lenin's government, and American troops pulled out in 1920.

20.4.3 The Red and Black Scares at Home

In the United States, industrial unrest provoked fears of a Soviet-style revolution at home. Four million American workers, one out of every five, went out on strike in 1919—the highest proportion of the workforce ever. They sought improved wages and working conditions as well as recognition of the right to collective bargaining. In Seattle, a walkout by shipyard workers mushroomed into a general strike that shut down most of the city for a week. In Pittsburgh, the AFL led a bitter strike against U.S. Steel in pursuit of union recognition. The United Mine Workers led walkouts by hundreds of thousands of coal miners, which evolved into open warfare between miners and coal companies in West Virginia over the next two years. In Boston, three-quarters of the police force went on strike to protest wages lower than those of common laborers. Between April and June, anarchists mailed or delivered bombs to thirty-six prominent public figures, including Attorney General A. Mitchell Palmer. All were defused except two.

Red Scare
Post–World War I repression of socialists, communists, and other left-wing radicals ("Reds").

Whereas many Americans sympathized with struggles for unionization, others viewed them as dangerous to private property and social order. They associated strikes with radical immigrants and anarchists and considered them "un-American." The **Red Scare** of 1919 associated reform and social justice movements of any kind with subversion. Attorney General Palmer directed the deportation to Russia of 249 foreign-born radicals aboard the *Buford* in December 1919, including prominent anarchist and feminist Emma Goldman. "Palmer raids" led to the arrest of thousands more within a month.

Violence against workers extended to African Americans after World War I. An upsurge in lynching included at least ten black veterans still in uniform and was not limited to the South. White mobs burned entire black communities to the ground, including Tulsa's Greenwood neighborhood in 1921 and the all-black town of Rosewood, Florida, in 1923. The Red Scare merged with the "Black Scare" in Phillips County, Arkansas, where black sharecroppers, many of them veterans, formed a union in 1919 to pursue equitable crop settlements from landlords. Fearing insurrection, local white leaders used 2,500 federal troops and white vigilantes to massacre more than 200 sharecroppers. But any inclination toward deference in the face of brutality was gone, and African Americans fought back fiercely against white marauders in deadly riots in Washington and Chicago in the summer of 1919.

STRIKERS, SEATTLE, WASHINGTON The Seattle General Strike Committee took on the responsibility of keeping essential services running in the city. In the photograph above, members issue groceries to union families in January 1919. The cooperation necessary among organized workers to keep a strike going offered a different model of community interaction than did the individualism often touted by wealthier Americans.

PEMCO Webster & Stevens Collection, Museum of History & Industry

Is the tension between individualism and communitarianism evident in other aspects of modern American life other than in labor and trade unionism?

Where was the president during this turmoil? Incapacitated by his stroke, he lay resting in his bed in Washington, the administration managed largely by his wife, Edith, and his secretary, Joseph Tumulty. In any case, Wilson's segregationist policies suggested that he would have been unlikely to provide effective leadership in bridging the nation's racial divides.

Conclusion

How much success could a varied generation of Progressive reformers claim by 1920? Women had won the vote with the Nineteenth Amendment. But daily life for Americans of darker hue continued to entail picking one's way through a maze of discrimination. Most union campaigns stalled by 1920, beaten back by the physical force and clever tactics of corporate employers and their government sympathizers. And when the Red Scare dissipated, Americans did not return to the reform spirit of Progressivism. Voter turnout in 1920 dipped below 50 percent for the first time in a century. Those who did vote that year gave the Republican party a sweeping victory and put Ohio Senator Warren G. Harding in the White House. His speeches may have been, as one rival said, "an army of pompous phrases moving over the landscape in search of an idea," but most of the nation sought calm after the upheavals of the previous decade.

American contributions to democracy abroad were similarly ambivalent. Whereas eastern Europeans named streets in their newly independent nations for President Wilson, few Latin Americans believed that U.S. invasions of Caribbean and Central American countries promoted self-government. Russians admired much about American society and the U.S. economy while resenting American troops in their land. Above all hung the problem of Germany, still the most potentially powerful single nation in Europe. The Versailles Treaty imposed harsh terms and embittered a generation of German people. "If I were a German, I think I should not sign it," Wilson admitted privately. The Weimar Republic that replaced the abdicated German Kaiser lasted through the 1920s. But the storms of the Great Depression after 1929 swamped Germany's republican experiment and gave rise to Adolf Hitler.

Chapter Review

20.1 A World and a Nation in Upheaval

What were the greatest challenges to the existing international and domestic order in the 1910s?
Major social revolutions unfolded in China, Russia, and Mexico. Through investments abroad or refugees coming to American shores, these events impacted the United States. At the same time, women, people of color, and workers in the United States organized to challenge many of the inequalities that limited their lives.

20.2 American Neutrality and Domestic Reform

What were Americans' priorities from 1914 to 1917?
Most Americans wanted to avoid being drawn into the Great War in Europe. They viewed their country as different from—and better than—the violence-prone sphere of the great European imperial powers. Instead, like Woodrow Wilson, they focused on improving society through Progressive reforms such as limiting monopolies and rationalizing the currency system.

20.3 The United States Goes to War

How did fighting in World War I change the United States?
In order to mobilize the economy for war, the U.S. government took on a much larger role in organizing the nation's highly productive economy. To ensure wartime unity, the government cracked down on dissent and limited immigration. U.S. soldiers and equipment helped the Entente defeat the Central Powers in Europe.

20.4 The Struggle to Win the Peace

What kind of new world order did Wilson want, and to what extent did he achieve it?
Faced with economic devastation in Europe and the threat of Communist revolution spreading out from Russia, Wilson helped establish new nations in eastern Europe. The harsh terms of the Versailles Treaty undercut his aim to reconcile Germany to its neighbors, and his domestic opponents kept the United States from joining the new League of Nations.

Timeline

1913	Federal Reserve Act	**1919**	Versailles Treaty ends World War I
1914	World War I breaks out in Europe		U.S. Senate rejects League of Nations
1915	Germans sink *Lusitania*	**1920**	Nineteenth Amendment (women's suffrage) ratified
1917	United States enters World War I		
	Russian Revolution		
1918	Spanish influenza epidemic kills 20 million worldwide		
	Wilson's "Fourteen Points" speech to Congress		

Glossary

Entente The alliance of Britain, France, and Russia, later joined by Italy and the United States, during World War I.

women's suffrage The right of women citizens to vote, and the movement to win that right.

Great Migration The movement of African Americans out of the South to northern cities, which accelerated during World War I.

U-boats German submarines in World War I that attacked civilian and officially neutral ships, helping bring the United States into the war.

Eighteenth Amendment Allowed Congress to prohibit the production of alcoholic beverages, creating the period of Prohibition that lasted until 1933.

Espionage and Sedition Acts Banned written and verbal dissent against U.S. participation in World War I, imperiling freedom of speech.

Bolsheviks The Communist revolutionaries who seized power in Russia in 1917 and established the Union of Soviet Socialist Republics (USSR).

"Fourteen Points" speech Wilson's address to the world outlining U.S. aims for the postwar order.

League of Nations Created by the Treaty of Versailles as a forum for peaceful resolution of international problems in the future.

Red Scare Post–World War I repression of socialists, communists, and other left-wing radicals ("Reds").

Chapter 21
All That Jazz:
The 1920s

BEACH POLICE, WASHINGTON, D.C. Col. Sherrell, Superintendent of Public Buildings and Grounds, issued an order that bathing suits at the Washington bathing beach must not be over six inches above the knee. In this 1922 photo, we see Bill Norton, the bathing beach policeman, measuring the distance between knee and garment on a "new woman" of the 1920s. The bathing suit she is wearing is similar to the one worn by the flapper whose husband divorced her for her flamboyant and sexy attire and behavior.

Library of Congress Prints and Photographs Division [LC-USZ62-99824]

What does the photograph of the women on the beach suggest about the tension, in the 1920s, between the revolution in manners and morals and the effort to maintain traditional notions of public behavior?

Contents and Focus Questions

Now that the Nineteenth Amendment granted women political equality, would social equality be granted as well? Could the "new woman" become an obedient wife?

A respectable Los Angeles barber confronted this question directly. He wooed and wed a flamboyant and sexually alluring "**flapper**," one of the young women of the 1910s and 1920s who broke from the time-honored conventions that had restricted women's public and private behavior. But then, he divorced her for the same reasons he married her. In 1920, he explained to the Court that although his wife held him in "high regard and esteem as her husband," there were "evidences of indiscretion" in her conduct. She wore a new bathing suit, "designed especially for the purpose of exhibiting to the public the shape and form of her body."

To his further humiliation, she had "a desire to sing and dance at cafés and restaurants for the entertainment of the public." When he complained about her "appetite for beer and whisky" and extravagant tastes for luxury, she replied that he was "not the only pebble on the beach, she had a millionaire 'guy' who would buy her all the clothes, automobiles, diamonds and booze that she wanted." The ultimate insult was her refusal to have any sexual intercourse, because she did not want any "dirty little brats around her." The judge was sympathetic, and granted the divorce.

This couple's difficulties represent a larger struggle as Americans shifted from the nineteenth-century producer economy, with its clearly defined gender roles and sexual mores, to the **consumer economy** of the twentieth century and to new amusements, changing sexual behavior, and "new women." With short, "bobbed" hair, knee-length dresses, and boyish styles unencumbered by layers of petticoats, flappers flirted, petted, and danced "wild" dances. Flappers sought the same freedoms that men enjoyed. In the process, they blurred the lines between "good girls" and "bad girls" that had previously defined proper female behavior.

New forms of popular entertainment became defining features of the nation itself. At a time when white, Anglo-Saxon, Protestant (WASP) men had control of nearly all government and business institutions, Jewish moviemakers and African American musicians were creating the culture that would soon represent the nation.

The great heroes of the 1920s were celebrities admired for their individual achievements. In 1927, Babe Ruth hit a record 60 home runs, and Charles Lindbergh became a national hero when he flew his small monoplane nonstop from New York to Paris. At age 19, Gertrude Ederle became the first woman to swim the English Channel, two hours faster than the six men who had preceded her. These heroes drew cheering crowds wherever they went.

*　　*　　*　　*　　*

Often characterized as the "roaring twenties" of giddy prosperity, these were also years of widespread poverty, especially in rural areas and urban ghettos. They reflected the extremes of radicalism and conservatism as well. Conservative politics at the national level prevailed throughout the decade. A Red Scare followed World War I targeting radical immigrants, and Prohibition

---

flapper
Young woman in the 1910s and 1920s who rebelled against the gender conventions of the era with respect to fashion and behavior.

consumer economy
An economic system in which most people work for wages, which they use to purchase manufactured goods and foodstuffs.

made alcohol consumption illegal until 1933. High-profile court cases revealed public ambivalence about the use of new scientific knowledge. The expansion of consumer credit weakened traditions of saving and frugality. For those with money to invest, Wall Street beckoned. The stock market rose to perilous heights, only to collapse at the end of the decade.

21.1 The Business of Politics and the Decline of Progressive Reform

What major developments signaled the end of the Progressive Era?

In 1924, President Calvin Coolidge declared, "The business of America is business." Despite its many critics, business reigned, with the support of national political leaders. After a recession following World War I, the U.S. economy grew steadily under Republican leadership. The Gross National Product (GNP) increased 5.5 percent annually, from $149 billion in 1922 to $227 billion in 1929. Official unemployment remained below 5 percent throughout the decade, and real wages rose 15 percent. These trends fueled the popularity of the conservative, business-friendly presidents of the 1920s. Economic interests also drove foreign policy during the decade. After World War I, with much of Europe in shambles, the United States made loans to foreign countries, becoming the world's leading creditor nation. International markets opened up for American-made products, leading to a tremendous expansion in foreign trade.

Reformers who had championed the causes of the marginalized and disadvantaged lost influence in the business-dominated 1920s. After achieving the vote, the women's rights movement splintered as younger women sought new freedoms not through politics but through a social and sexual revolution. Widespread hostility toward immigrants and various ethnic groups was at the root of the outlawing of liquor, new laws restricting immigration, and the rise of the Ku Klux Klan. But progressive political impulses did not entirely disappear, especially among African Americans, who continued to mobilize and organize for civil rights.

21.1.1 Women's Rights After the Struggle for Suffrage

One indication of the waning of progressive reform was the fragmentation of women's rights activism in the 1920s. The radical wing of the suffrage movement, the National Woman's Party (NWP), in 1923 launched a campaign for the **Equal Rights Amendment** (ERA), which declared simply: "Equality of rights under the law shall not be denied or abridged by the United States or by any state on account of sex."

Equal Rights Amendment (ERA) A proposed amendment to the U.S. Constitution that would have guaranteed equal rights for women.

The debate over the ERA in the 1920s reflected the fundamental divide that would permeate women's rights activism throughout the rest of the twentieth century. On one side were those who believed that women were fundamentally the same as men and deserved equal rights; on the other side were those who argued that women were different and deserved special privileges and protections. Many women's rights activists opposed the ERA because it would undercut efforts to gain special legislative protections for women based on their presumed physical weakness and their potential for childbearing, such as maximum hours, regulations against night work, and limitations on the weights they could lift. These women disapproved of the NWP and formed their own nonpartisan organization, the League of Women Voters, which promoted social and political reform.

Social changes as well as political developments affected women's lives. New expectations for marital happiness put pressure on couples to achieve domestic bliss. Marital breakdown still carried a heavy negative stigma, especially for women. Nevertheless, the divorce rate doubled between 1900 and 1920 and continued to rise throughout the 1920s, in part the result of women's increasing independence. As job opportunities for women increased, more women felt able to abandon unhappy marriages.

21.1.2 Prohibition: The Experiment That Failed

Another social movement that had its roots in progressive reform was the effort to ban liquor. Several diverse interests came together in the prohibition movement. Temperance crusaders in the Anti-Saloon League and the Women's Christian Temperance Union had long argued that women and children suffered when men spent their paychecks at the saloon and returned home drunk and violent. World War I prompted others to support a ban on the manufacture of liquor to save grain for the war effort. Anti-immigrant "drys" had political motives for promoting prohibition. They hoped to undercut immigrant and ethnic politicians who used local saloons to forge their constituencies and **political machines**. The "wets" included alienated intellectuals, Jazz Age rebels, and many city dwellers whose social lives revolved around neighborhood pubs, especially in Irish and German communities.

The Eighteenth Amendment, which prohibited the manufacture and sale of alcohol, went into effect in January 1920. However, enforcement was impossible. Federal agents had responsibility for enforcing the law, but their numbers were inadequate. To be effective, federal agents had to work closely with local law enforcement officials. In some urban areas, local officials refused to cooperate with federal agents. Americans who wanted to drink liquor found many ways to acquire it. Illegal "**speakeasies**" abounded where customers could buy drinks delivered by rumrunners who smuggled in liquor from Canada, Mexico, and the West Indies. Many people concocted their own "bathtub gin" or "moonshine whiskey," homemade brews using readily available ingredients and household equipment.

Prohibition was intended to cure society's ills. Instead, it provided vast opportunities for crime and profit. Organized crime received a major boost in the scramble to profit from illegal liquor. Chicago witnessed 550 gangland killings in the 1920s, with few arrests or convictions. By 1929, Chicago mob king Al Capone controlled a massive network of speakeasies that raked in $60 million annually.

Prohibition failed to live up to its promise. Although alcohol consumption declined by two-thirds within a year of the passage of the amendment, by 1929 the consumption of alcohol had climbed back up to 70 percent of its pre-Prohibition level.

21.1.3 Reactionary Impulses

The Red Scare after World War I (see Chapter 20) inaugurated a decade of hostility to political radicals and foreigners. Shoemaker Nicola Sacco and fish peddler Bartolomeo Vanzetti were both Italian **aliens** and self-proclaimed anarchists. In May 1920, the paymaster and guard of a South Braintree, Massachusetts, shoe company was robbed and murdered, and Sacco and Vanzetti were arrested and charged with the crime. Sacco testified that he was in Boston at the time, applying for a passport, and his alibi was corroborated. Both men proclaimed their innocence and insisted that they were on trial for their political beliefs rather than the crime itself. Their Italian accents and advocacy of anarchism in the courtroom did not help their case with many Americans suspicious of foreign radicals, including the judge presiding at their trial. Despite a weak case against them, Sacco and Vanzetti were convicted of first-degree murder and sentenced to death.

Lawyers for the two anarchists appealed the case several times to no avail. The convictions sparked outrage among Italian Americans, political radicals, labor activists, and liberal intellectuals who believed the two men were falsely convicted. The case soon generated mass demonstrations, appeals for clemency, and petitions from around the world. The governor of Massachusetts appointed a commission to review the case, but the commission concluded that there were no grounds for a new trial. Finally, on August 23, 1927, Sacco and Vanzetti were executed by electric chair.

political machines
Groups that effectively exercise control over a political party, usually at the local level and organized around precincts and patronage.

speakeasies
Establishments where alcohol was illegally sold during the Prohibition era.

aliens
Foreign-born residents of the United States who have not been naturalized as U.S. citizens.

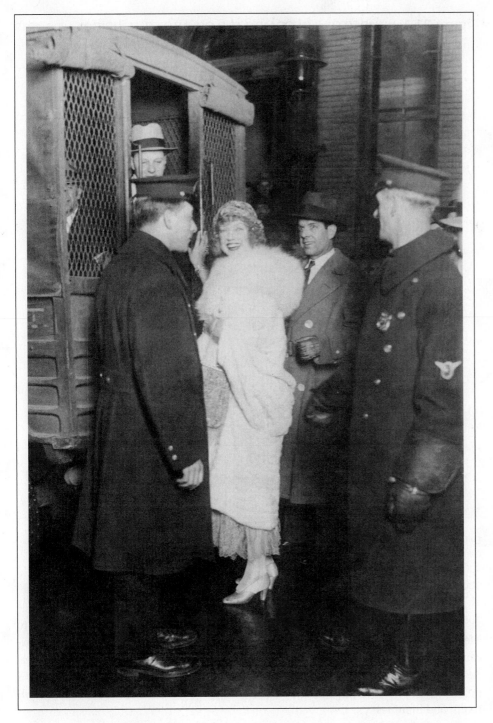

ARREST OF NIGHTCLUB HOSTESS MARY LOUISE GUINAN, NEW YORK CITY Speakeasy hostess Mary Louise Guinan appears unrepentant as she is arrested for selling alcohol during the Prohibition era. Law enforcement was futile because speakeasies that were raided and closed simply reopened in new locations.

Bettmann/Corbis

In the photograph above, what do Guinan's demeanor and expression suggest about her attitude toward law enforcement and her feeling about being arrested?

Sacco and Vanzetti's case underscored the anti-immigrant sentiment that prevailed in the 1920s. In 1924, Congress passed the Johnson-Reid Act, imposing a limit of 165,000 immigrants from countries outside the Western Hemisphere and using a quota system for each country based on the year 1890, a time when British, German, and Scandinavian immigrants dominated the foreign-born population. The Johnson-Reid Act limited entry every year to 2 percent of the total number of immigrants from each country who were present in 1890. This measure effectively barred Jews, Slavs, Greeks, Italians, and Poles because their numbers were so small in 1890. The 1924 law also reaffirmed the exclusion of Chinese immigrants and added Japanese and other Asians to the list, effectively closing the door to all migrants from Asia.

Figure 21.1 NUMBER OF IMMIGRANTS AND COUNTRIES OF ORIGIN, 1890–1919 AND 1920–1939

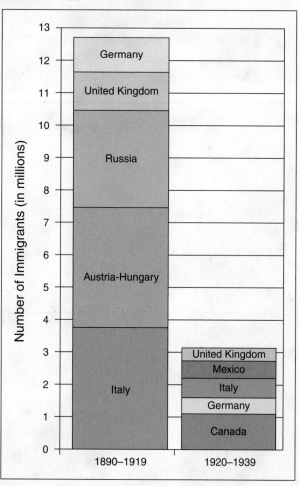

Before the immigration restriction laws passed in the 1920s, many immigrants came from Russia and southern and eastern Europe. After immigration restriction, most came from western Europe and Canada.

SOURCE: U.S. Department of Homeland Security, *2013 Yearbook of Immigration Statistics*, August 2014, table 2.

Agricultural interests in California and Texas lobbied to keep the door open to Mexicans because of the low-wage labor they provided. In the aftermath of the Mexican Revolution, many Mexicans hoped to find stability and jobs in the United States. Between 1910 and 1930, more than 1 million Mexicans, nearly one-tenth of Mexico's population, migrated to the United States, where they found work on farms, on railroads, and in mines.

One of the most reactionary developments of the 1920s was the revival of the Ku Klux Klan (KKK), which became the most powerful white supremacy group in the nation, remaining active throughout the twentieth century. The Klan used vigilante violence as well as political mobilizations not only to attack African Americans, their primary targets in the South following the Civil War, but also immigrants, Mexicans, Jews, Catholics, communists, feminists, and other radicals, as well as divorced or allegedly promiscuous women. Klan membership included laborers, business people, physicians, judges, social workers, and women who believed their homogeneous small-town Protestant culture was threatened by the evils of modern life, brought on by the presence and influence of morally suspect outsiders. The Klan wielded considerable power in the 1920s in certain states, particularly Texas, Oklahoma, Oregon, and Indiana.

21.1.4 Marcus Garvey and the Persistence of Civil Rights Activism

In the midst of a decade of reactionary policies toward outsiders and political activists, African Americans continued their struggle for civil rights. Jamaican-born black nationalist Marcus Garvey moved to Harlem in 1916 and opened a branch of his Universal Negro Improvement Association (UNIA). Garvey urged black people to establish their own nation-state in Africa: "Africa was peopled with a race of cultured black men, who were masters in art, science, and literature. . . . Africa shall be for the black peoples of the world." By the 1920s, the UNIA had nearly 1 million followers. In keeping with his belief in black-owned businesses, Garvey established the Black Star Line shipping company. But the business ran into problems. In 1922, Garvey was arrested and charged with mail fraud. Although the government lacked any concrete evidence against him, Garvey was convicted and sentenced to five years in prison, where he kept up his political activities. After his release, he was deported to Jamaica as an undesirable alien. Nevertheless, the momentum he sparked continued.

21.1.5 Warren G. Harding: The Politics of Scandal

Activists such as Garvey were operating in a conservative political environment, which was reflected in presidential elections throughout the decade. Warren G. Harding, a Republican U.S. senator from Ohio, won the 1920 presidential election by the biggest landslide since 1820. He established the conservative agenda that would last throughout the decade, supporting immigration restriction and opposing labor unions. After World War I, Harding distanced himself from Woodrow Wilson's peace settlement but promoted international treaties. In 1921 and 1922, Secretary of State Charles Evans Hughes achieved the first major disarmament accord, the Five-Power Treaty, signed by Japan, Britain, France, Italy, and the United States. The five nations agreed to scrap more than 2 million tons of warships in the first such pact of its kind. Hughes extended the power of the United States abroad through economic ties, encouraging banks to provide loans to war-ravaged Europe.

Table 21.1 THE ELECTION OF 1920

Candidate	Political Party	Popular Vote (%)	Electoral Vote
Warren G. Harding	Republican	60.4	404
James M. Cox	Democratic	34.2	127
Eugene V. Debs	Socialist	3.4	—

SOURCE: Historical Election Results, Electoral College, National Archives and Records Administration

But Harding's presidency was marred by scandal. He had built his political base by handing out favors and deals to his friends, and he continued to do so as president. His buddies used their offices for personal gain, while Harding caroused with them, drinking, despite Prohibition, and engaging in notorious extramarital affairs. The press initially ignored these abuses, but by 1923, the many scandals finally broke. Harding's cronies were exposed for selling government appointments and providing judicial pardons and police protection for bootleggers.

The most serious scandal of Harding's presidency involved the large government oil reserves at Teapot Dome, Wyoming, and Elk Hills, California. At the urging of Secretary of the Interior Albert Fall, Harding transferred control over the reserves from the U.S. Navy to the Department of the Interior. After accepting a bribe of nearly $400,000 from two oil tycoons, Harry F. Sinclair and Edward L. Doheny, Fall secretly issued leases to them without opening up the competition to other oil companies. Fall went to jail for a year as a result. The scandals reflected the political and economic excesses of the period. When he learned of the corruption in his close circle, Harding grew deeply worried. The stress may have been among the causes of the heart attack that killed him in 1923.

21.1.6 Calvin Coolidge: The Hands-Off President

Harding's vice president, Calvin Coolidge, took over the presidency. Sober and serious, this aloof New Englander was not vulnerable to scandal as Harding had been. Coolidge believed that the government should meddle as little as possible in national affairs. He took long naps every day and exerted little presidential leadership. Known mostly for his hostility to labor unions and his laissez-faire attitude toward business, he was a popular president during the complacent mid-1920s.

Not everyone was pleased with Coolidge's probusiness politics, and opposition mobilized for the 1924 election. Progressive Republicans formed a new Progressive party and nominated Robert M. La Follette of Wisconsin for president. The Progressive platform promoted conservation, higher taxes on the wealthy, replacing the electoral college with direct election of the president, and the abolition of child labor. Democrats deadlocked between Catholic candidate Alfred E. Smith, an urban politician from New York, and Protestant William G. McAdoo, who drew support in the South and West. On the 103rd ballot, delegates finally chose a compromise candidate, John W. Davis, a corporation lawyer. The Republicans nominated Coolidge, who claimed responsibility for the nation's prosperity and won easily, receiving more votes than the other two candidates combined.

Table 21.2 THE ELECTION OF 1924

Candidate	Political Party	Popular Vote (%)	Electoral Vote
Calvin Coolidge	Republican	54.0	382
John W. Davis	Democratic	28.8	136
Robert M. La Follette	Progressive	16.6	13

SOURCE: Historical Election Results, Electoral College, National Archives and Records Administration

21.1.7 Herbert Hoover: The Self-Made President

The 1928 election was a major turning point for the presence of ethnic minorities in politics. The Democrats broke tradition by selecting an Irish Roman Catholic, New York governor Alfred E. Smith, as their candidate. It was the first time a major party had nominated a Catholic for president. Coolidge decided not to run for reelection in 1928, and the Republican party selected Secretary of Commerce Herbert Hoover as its nominee. Prohibition—the Eighteenth Amendment banning the manufacture and sale of alcohol—figured prominently in the 1928 presidential campaign. Although the Democratic platform gave lukewarm support to the continuation of Prohibition, Smith made no secret of his support for repealing the Eighteenth Amendment. By contrast, Republican Herbert Hoover praised Prohibition as "a great social and economic experiment." The other major issue of the campaign was religion. Anti-Catholic sentiment was strong throughout the country, especially in the South, where Democrats either sat out the election or voted Republican. Smith's opponents attacked his Catholicism, charging that he was more loyal to the Vatican than to the United States.

Herbert Hoover epitomized the values of the self-made man. He was orphaned as a child and raised by relatives of modest means. After graduating from Stanford University, Hoover went into mining and rose to become a wealthy corporate leader. By age 40, he was already a millionaire. Hoover began his career in government during World War I, when he earned widespread admiration for handling the distribution of

Table 21.3 THE ELECTION OF 1928

Candidate	Political Party	Popular Vote (%)	Electoral Vote
Herbert Hoover	Republican	58.2	444
Alfred E. Smith	Democratic	40.9	87
Norman Thomas	Socialist	0.7	—

SOURCE: Historical Election Results, Electoral College, National Archives and Records Administration

food relief to European war refugees. He then served ably as secretary of commerce in the Harding and Coolidge administrations. Shortly after the election, President Hoover predicted, "We in America today are nearer to the final triumph over poverty than ever before in the history of any land." But less than a year into his presidency, his optimism, along with the nation's economy, came crashing down.

21.2 Hollywood and Harlem: National Cultures in Black and White

What developments in the arts and technology helped forge a national popular culture in the 1920s?

In 1920, for the first time, the majority of Americans lived in towns and cities with populations greater than 2,500. Although this shift often is considered a watershed in the transformation from rural to urban America, it is worth noting that because the census defined any town with more than 2,500 inhabitants as urban, the majority of Americans still lived in small and ethnically homogeneous towns. Many small-town Americans viewed big-city life with suspicion. They feared the decline of traditional Protestant American values of hard work, thrift, and discipline. Yet many were drawn to the new urban life.

Hollywood on the West Coast and Harlem on the East Coast became centers of cultural innovation. Eventually, the artistic productions of both centers attracted audiences of all racial, class, and regional backgrounds. Increasingly, as Americans moved from place to place, they encountered similar entertainments, music, arts, and consumer products. Movies, automobiles, radios, and advertising all fostered this emerging national culture.

Figure 21.2 URBAN AND RURAL POPULATION, 1890–1990

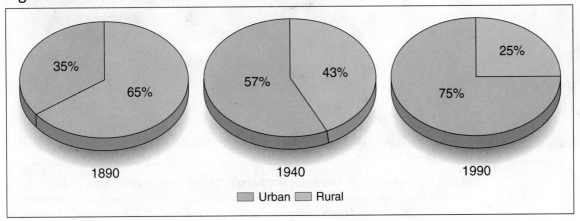

In the nineteenth century, the American population was primarily rural. During the twentieth century, the population became predominantly urban.

SOURCE: U.S. Bureau of the Census, "Selected Historical Decennial Census Population and Housing Counts," 1990 Census of Population and Housing, table 4.

21.2.1 Hollywood Comes of Age

As movie theaters spread into towns and cities across the country, Hollywood's messages began to reach a mass audience and forge a nationwide popular culture. Movie stars provided models for how to adopt new styles of manhood and womanhood. Douglas Fairbanks showed middle-class men how to break free from the humdrum of white-collar work into the world of leisure. His attire of sports clothes changed the way men dressed in their off-work hours. Female stars, such as Clara Bow, epitomized the flapper and taught female viewers how to be "naughty but nice."

Ironically, as the nation closed its doors to immigrants, foreigners on screen captivated the imagination of a native-born population drawn to the allure of the outsider. Movie stars like Greta Garbo from Sweden, Dolores del Rio, Lupe Velez, and Ramon Navarro from Mexico, and Rudolph Valentino from Italy drew audiences with their foreignness. And yet, because movies were silent until the late 1920s, their accented voices were not heard. Sound arrived in the late twenties, bringing their ethnic voices and dialects into the movies. For native-born Americans watching films in small towns and cities, sound movies brought the diverse voices of the cities into their communities. For immigrants, sound movies carried their familiar accents and allowed for identification with the stars on the screen.

RUDOLPH VALENTINO IN *THE FOUR HORSEMEN OF THE APOCALYPSE*, 1921 Rudolph Valentino dances the tango in this famous scene from the 1921 film *The Four Horsemen of the Apocalypse*. Films in the 1920s featured exotic locales with foreign stars such as the Italian-born Valentino. In keeping with the public's taste for grandeur, lavish movie palaces emerged in cities across the country.

Everett Collection Inc/Alamy; 515: Courtesy of the Everett Collection

What is "foreign" in the photographic still from **The Four Horsemen of the Apocalypse,** *and what is "American" about the scene?*

21.2.2 The Harlem Renaissance

While Hollywood in the 1920s developed on the West Coast, a flourishing center of African American culture emerged on the East Coast. The black arts movement known as the **Harlem Renaissance** drew on European as well as African and African American artistic traditions and gathered white as well as black intellectuals and artists. The young black poet Arna Bontemps was among the many artists drawn to Harlem. In 1924, he described Harlem as "a foretaste of paradise. A blue haze descended at night and with it strings of fairy lights on the broad avenues. From the window of a small room in an apartment on Fifth and 129th Street, I looked over the rooftops of Negrodom and tried to believe my eyes. What a city! What a world!"

Harlem Renaissance
A period in American history immediately following World War I (c. 1918–37) characterized by a surge of creativity in the literary, theatrical, musical, and visual arts among African Americans.

Harlem Renaissance writers claimed their identity as Americans while articulating the culture, aesthetics, and experiences of African Americans. The poet Langston Hughes challenged white America to accept African Americans in his 1925 poem "I, Too, Sing America." The poem asserted the full inclusion, as well as the beauty and strength, of black citizens, and their right to participate in the promise of America.

The music of black America was so prominent that it provided the decade with its most lasting moniker, the Jazz Age. Emanating from New Orleans, Chicago, and St. Louis, jazz was central to the black arts movement and the emerging national culture. With the help of the recording industry and radio, jazz and the blues began to reach a wide audience, primarily among blacks but increasingly among whites as well. Blues lyrics expressed themes of working-class protest and resistance to racism. Women who sang the blues, including Bessie Smith, Ma Rainey, and Ethel Waters, asserted their sexuality, their passion for men or for women, their resistance to male domination, their sorrows, and their strength.

21.2.3 Radios and Autos: Transforming Leisure and Connecting the Country

Radios brought the songs of these blues singers to American homes, transforming the way music was enjoyed. Americans became more inclined to listen to music on their Victrolas and radios than to make music themselves. Annual radio production increased from 190,000 in 1923 to almost 5 million in 1929. By the mid-1920s, sales of records surpassed those of sheet music; production and sales of pianos also dropped precipitously.

In addition to bringing jazz and other forms of popular music to the airwaves, radio played a major role in linking people across regions through shared information, advertising, and entertainment. The number of radio stations soared from 30 in 1922 to 556 the following year, and national broadcasts began to supersede local ones. Airwaves became so cluttered that by the mid-1920s, the federal government created the Federal Radio Commission to regulate and organize access. Meanwhile, American Telephone and Telegraph (AT&T) and the National Broadcasting Company (NBC) combined to form the first national network system, which gave programs and advertisers access to audiences across the country.

Automobiles also enabled Americans to make connections across regions. The automobile offered the possibility of commuting to work without relying on public transportation, encouraging the expansion of suburban communities. The number of passenger cars in the nation more than tripled during the twenties. The Federal Highways Act of 1916 had produced a network of roads all over the country, providing construction jobs and a slew of new roadside businesses, from restaurants to garages. Automobiles also stimulated the tourist industry; Florida, California, and Arizona became vacation destinations in this period.

**HARLEM RENAISSANCE POET
LANGSTON HUGHES** Poet Langston
Hughes was a major literary figure of
the Harlem Renaissance. In this 1925
portrait, modernist painter Winold
Reiss connects Hughes to the aesthetics of the modernist movement
then in vogue in the United States
and Europe. In his poetry, Hughes
expressed the hopes, dreams, and
sorrows of African Americans. Reiss,
an American artist born in Germany,
painted several prominent figures of
the Harlem Renaissance.

National Portrait Gallery, Smithsonian
Institution/Art Resource, NY

*What does the artist's portrait of
Langston Hughes convey about
the poet? How is the portraitist's
background as an immigrant and as a
modernist reflected in his work?*

planned obsolescence
A concept whereby producers
intend for their products to eventually become obsolete or outdated
and require replacement, thus
perpetuating a cycle of production
and consumption.

Automobile production also revolutionized the consumer industry. The pragmatic
Henry Ford built inexpensive, functional automobiles that he expected his workers to
be able to purchase and keep. But Ford faced serious competition from General Motors'
Alfred P. Sloan, Jr., who developed the concept of **planned obsolescence** and emphasized auto styling to encourage customers to trade in their old cars for newer and more
expensive models.

The automobile was part of a consumer society increasingly focused on leisure,
pleasure, and intimacy. Courtship patterns changed, and sexual activity increased as
young couples abandoned the front porch for the back seat. Women gained new freedom and autonomy when they, too, took the wheel. Moralists worried that the automobile would provide youth with too much independence and privacy. One juvenile court
judge announced that "the automobile has become a house of prostitution on wheels."

21.3 Science on Trial

*What did science contribute to American life in the 1920s, and where did scientific
ideas fall short?*

Although advances in technology and medicine improved the quality of life for many
Americans in the early twentieth century, scientific efforts to alter the natural world did
not always lead to expected social benefits. One case in point was the engineering project
to build levees along the Mississippi River to prevent flooding, which failed to hold and
caused devastating results. Scientific ideas were also tested in the nation's courtrooms.

Two major cases, the *Scopes* trial and the Supreme Court's decision in *Buck v. Bell*, subjected scientific ideas to judicial and cultural scrutiny. The questions raised in these cases continued to generate controversy and debate throughout the rest of the century.

21.3.1 The Great Flood of 1927

For half a century, the engineers of the Mississippi River Commission had adhered to a policy of building levees, assuming that strong barricades against the river's banks would prevent flooding. Presumably, the levees would allow the rich soil of the floodplains along the river to be settled and farmed rather than leaving the basins empty to provide places for the river to expand and contract with seasonal rains. But the levee policy proved to be a disastrous example of human efforts to master the natural contours of the land. In March 1927, the rains came, and the river rose. Public authorities and river experts assured those who watched and worried that the levees would hold. They were wrong. Torrential rains caused the river to rage across the levees and the land beyond, submerging 26,000 square miles of prime farmland across seven states. More than 900,000 people were forced from their homes. The flood caused more than $100 million in crop losses and $23 million in livestock deaths. Journalists at the time called it "America's greatest peacetime disaster."

Map 21.1 THE MISSISSIPPI RIVER FLOOD OF 1927

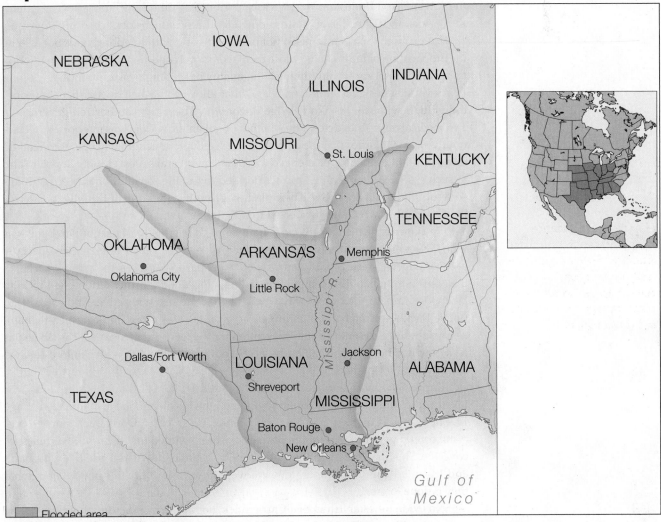

Flooded area

The Mississippi River flood in 1927 sent water across a huge area of the South, extending as far west as Texas, covering most of Louisiana, Arkansas, and Mississippi, and reaching north into Kansas, Illinois, and Indiana.

With the help of the Department of Commerce and the National Guard, the Red Cross set up 154 relief camps for flood victims. But the suffering, as well as the relief efforts, did not affect people equally. The camps were racially segregated. Refugees in the white camps were free to come and go and had more comfortable and generous accommodations and rations than those in the black camps. Armed guards patrolled the camps for black refugees and restricted people attempting to enter or leave. Black laborers had to register and give the names of their employers to receive any shelter or assistance.

Federal authorities, including Secretary of Commerce Herbert Hoover, refused to intervene in local camp management. As a result, southern whites were able to force black sharecroppers back to work on their plantations. Despite the prisonlike conditions, many African American refugees managed to escape and made their way north.

21.3.2 The Triumph of Eugenics: *Buck v. Bell*

Scientific ideas also contributed to theories about racial differences. Supposedly scientific theories of race bolstered claims that distinct, biologically based characteristics divided humans into superior and inferior races. These theories had no scientific merit and were later thoroughly discredited. But in the 1920s, many Americans, including large numbers of policymakers, believed in white racial superiority, and these dubious theories supported measures such as immigration restriction and eugenic sterilization laws. Eugenics was a pseudo-science based on notions of racial superiority. Eugenicists claimed that the Anglo-Saxon Protestant "race" was superior to all others, including Jews, southern Europeans, and Catholics, as well as nonwhites. Racial superiority, according to eugenic reformers, might be compromised not only by mixing with inferior groups but also by the propagation of individuals whose mental or moral condition rendered them inferior, and whose offspring would diminish the quality of the Anglo-Saxon "stock."

Several states enacted eugenic laws that allowed the state to sterilize "inferior" individuals without their knowledge or consent. These laws authorized government and medical officials to determine whether or not an individual was inferior, or "feebleminded," and to order that the person be sterilized. Opponents of eugenic sterilization, mostly Catholic activists, challenged these laws in several states. Hoping to put an end to such challenges, eugenic advocates decided to test the constitutionality of Virginia's compulsory sterilization law. Their plan was to bring the case all the way to the U.S. Supreme Court, which they expected to uphold the law.

Proponents of the law selected the case of Carrie Buck, in part because she was white. Eugenic advocates did not want race to be at the center of the case, especially because eugenic sterilization laws did not target particular races; they simply targeted the "feeble-minded." Feeblemindedness was a loosely defined criterion often used to label poor, immigrant, or minority women who were sexually active. At the age of 17, Carrie Buck, the daughter of an unmarried woman, was raped and became pregnant; as a result, she was sent to a state institution for the feebleminded. Buck was labeled as feebleminded because she had borne a child out of wedlock and was therefore deemed morally unfit for parenthood.

Carrie Buck was sterilized in 1927. The following year, Buck's sister Doris was taken to the Virginia Colony for Epileptics and the Feebleminded and sterilized at age 16. She was told that she had had an appendectomy. Later, Doris Buck married and tried to get pregnant. None of the physicians she consulted told her why she could not conceive. She finally learned the truth in 1979. "I broke down and cried. My husband and I wanted children desperately. We were crazy about them. I never knew what they'd done to me."

No evidence established that Carrie Buck, her mother, or her daughter was below normal intelligence. Buck's daughter died as a child, but her teachers described the girl as bright. In writing the majority opinion for the Supreme Court that upheld the law, Justice Oliver Wendell Holmes wrote, "Three generations of imbeciles are enough." Within the next few years, 30 states had compulsory sterilization laws, and the number of operations rose dramatically. In the 1930s, the Nazis in Germany modeled their sterilization policies on the California law. Finally, in the 1980s, a rare alliance of traditional Catholics and feminist activists succeeded in repealing compulsory sterilization laws.

21.3.3 Science, Religion, and the *Scopes* Trial

Populist leader and longtime reformer William Jennings Bryan was among those troubled by eugenics. In his last public crusade, Bryan opposed another scientific theory in a Dayton, Tennessee, courtroom in July 1925. Tennessee had recently outlawed the teaching of Charles Darwin's theory of evolution in the schools. A 24-year-old science teacher from the local high school, John Thomas Scopes, agreed to test the law. Using a state-approved textbook, Scopes taught a lesson on evolutionary theory. He was arrested and quickly indicted by a grand jury. Bryan agreed to represent the prosecution; famed Chicago criminal lawyer Clarence Darrow defended Scopes.

Bryan did not oppose science, but he objected to its misapplication. Darrow did not oppose religion. But he argued that religious fundamentalists—"creationists" who believed in the literal interpretation of the Bible—should not determine how science was taught in the schools. Reporters at the time, and since, cast the trial as a struggle between religion and science, with rural and small-town Americans on the side of creationism and secular urbanites supporting evolution. But the divide was not so clear-cut. Almost all advocates on both sides of the *Scopes* trial were Christians who disagreed over how to interpret the Bible. They were also believers in science; those opposed to the teaching of evolution considered it to be an unscientific theory.

The *Scopes* trial also contained elements of popular entertainment. Dubbed "the Monkey trial" because Darwin's theory of evolution demonstrated that humans evolved from an earlier primate form from which monkeys and chimpanzees also descended, the trial was one of the first national media events. The judge invited reporters from around the country, including broadcast journalists. The *Scopes* trial was the first jury trial broadcast on live radio. More than 900 spectators packed the courtroom, and hundreds more gathered in the streets, where a carnival atmosphere prevailed, complete with souvenir stands, food vendors, itinerant preachers, and hucksters, including numerous chimpanzees accompanied by their trainers.

The jury reached a guilty verdict in just nine minutes. Bryan technically won the case, but most reporters deemed the spectacle a victory for Darrow and the teaching of evolution. That assessment was premature. The Tennessee Supreme Court overturned the verdict on a technicality, robbing Darrow of his chance to take the case to the U.S. Supreme Court. Before the trial, most science textbooks included discussion of evolution; after the trial, material on evolution began to disappear. Laws against the teaching of evolution remained on the books until the U.S. Supreme Court overturned an Arkansas law in 1968.

The *Scopes* trial did not resolve the debate between creationists and evolutionists, a controversy that continued throughout the century. As late as 2000, the school officials in Kansas ruled that creationism and evolution were both unproven theories and that both could be taught in the schools.

21.4 Consumer Dreams and Nightmares

What were the positive and negative effects of the 1920s consumer culture?

Unlike religion and politics, the material prosperity of many in the Jazz Age seemed a unifying force. During the 1920s, spending on recreation nearly doubled. Faith in continuing prosperity promoted the extension of consumer credit to unprecedented heights. Previously, the only major item routinely purchased on credit was a house. But in the twenties, **installment buying** became the rage for a wide range of consumer goods,

installment buying
A system in which a consumer could make a down payment to purchase a product and then pay the remaining installments over time.

from autos and radios to household appliances. Consumer debt rose from $2.6 billion in 1919 to $7.1 billion in 1929. As one official in a midwestern loan company remarked, "People don't think anything nowadays of borrowing sums they'd never have thought of borrowing in the old days. They will assume an obligation for $2,000 today as calmly as they would have borrowed $300 or $400 in 1890." This habit of buying on credit boosted the standard of living for many but also left families in a precarious situation and vulnerable to the vagaries of the broader economy. Even more vulnerable were the large numbers of Americans living in poverty, especially in rural areas. The stock market crash and subsequent depression made that vulnerability vividly clear.

21.4.1 Marketing the Good Life

The vast array of consumer goods newly available in the 1920s encouraged those with money to spend it. Advertising fueled much of the new spending. As one contemporary reporter noted, "Advertising is to business what fertilizer is to a farm." According to advertisers, consumer goods promised health, beauty, success, and the means to eliminate personal and embarrassing flaws, such as bad breath or dandruff. Cigarette companies used advertising to promote smoking as a symbol of independence for women and as a means to achieve beauty. Clever advertising campaigns promised women that if they would "reach for a Lucky Strike" instead of a sweet, they would remain slim, healthy, and sexually appealing.

Advertising also fostered a vision of big business as a benevolent force, promoting individual happiness. In his 1925 best-seller *The Man That Nobody Knows*, advertising executive Bruce Barton portrayed Jesus as a businessman who gathered a group of twelve followers who believed in his enterprise and, through effective public relations and advertising, sold his product to the world. The consumer culture had its temples: movie palaces, department stores, and the 1920s innovation, the shopping center. Kansas City's elegant Country Club Plaza was the first shopping center in the nation.

A much less successful venture was the Florida land boom. Exaggerated promotions fed fantasies of a consumer paradise, sparking a frenzy of investment in Florida real estate. Developers rushed to construct roads and find new land on which to build, fueling a spree of speculative property purchasing. The boom peaked in 1925 and quickly collapsed. In 1926, a hurricane hit Miami, killing 130 people and causing millions of dollars of property damage. Human folly and nature's fury contributed to the Florida land boom and bust.

21.4.2 Writers and Critics

Some social critics claimed that consumerism fostered not only economic disasters such as the Florida land boom but also a stifling conformity. Sinclair Lewis was one of several novelists of the twenties whose books expressed biting criticism of the frantic pursuit of material gain and status. George Babbitt, the protagonist of Lewis's novel *Babbitt* (1922), struggles to become accepted and successful in his small town by conforming to the empty materialism and standardized opinions accepted and prized by his neighbors.

F. Scott Fitzgerald wrote not about small-town conformity, as Lewis did, but about the modern urban life that was its antithesis. Fitzgerald glamorized, criticized, and in many ways embodied the giddy nightlife and status seeking of the Jazz Age. Born in St. Paul, Minnesota, into a family of modest means, he grew up admiring and emulating the wealthy. He married glamorous flapper Zelda Sayre, daughter of a prominent Alabama judge, and together they embraced the dizzy, indulgent, free-spirited life of the decade. But Fitzgerald's novels, including *This Side of Paradise* (1920), *The Beautiful and the Damned* (1922), and *The Great Gatsby* (1925), criticized the era's obsessions with success, glamour, consumerism, advertising, and status. The Fitzgeralds, along with other writers who were critical of American superficiality and conformity, moved to

THE NEW BEAUTY OF
THE BLOWOUT-PROOF TIRE
IS DISTINCTIVE — ON ANY CAR — IN ANY COMPANY

The new General Dual-Balloon is unmistakably the tire of the year. The striking
beauty of the prismatic sidewall is an accomplishment in modern design. The added
smartness it gives to any car is only one of its many exclusive features. General is
The Blowout-Proof Tire and *no other manufacturer has been licensed to build it.* It
is patented and made only by General. With increasing speeds and summer heat
it is important that you have this blowout-proof protection now as well as the
skid-safe travel that General's low pressure will mean to you next fall. All of these
advantages cost so little when you total up General's almost unheard of big mileage.
THE GENERAL TIRE AND RUBBER COMPANY, AKRON, OHIO

NOTICE: IT WILL PAY YOU TO SEE THE GENERAL TIRE DEALER ABOUT THE SPECIAL CHANGE-OVER PLAN FOR OLD OR NEW CARS

The New
GENERAL
DUAL BALLOON
THE BLOWOUT-PROOF TIRE
80% MORE NON-SKID   40% LESS AIR

SELLING TIRES? In the 1920s, advertisers used sexualized images to sell all sorts of products. This
advertisement for automobile tires provides very little information about the product but evokes
images of fun and romance to capture consumers' attention.

Image Courtesy of The Advertising Archives

*What does the advertisement suggest about the lifestyle that General Tire is trying to promote with
its product?*

Paris. Eventually, the life Fitzgerald both lived and criticized caught up with him. By
the end of the decade, he—like the nation—was broken by excesses. In 1931, he came
home to Baltimore an alcoholic; Zelda was diagnosed with schizophrenia and spent the
rest of her life in mental institutions.

21.4.3 Poverty amid Plenty

Most Americans in the 1920s were neither investing in Florida real estate nor frequent-
ing expatriate American writer Gertrude Stein's Paris salon. Even so, they were not
immune to the desires and dreams that the consumer society sparked. The middle class

Map 21.2 AMERICANS ON THE MOVE, 1870s–1930s

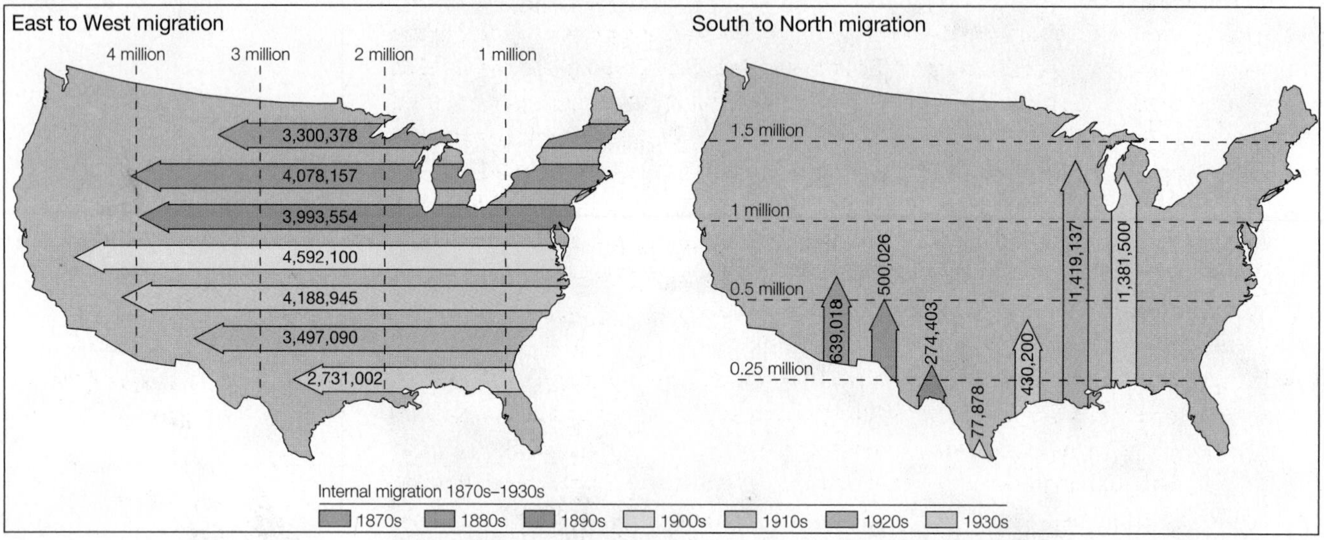

East to West migration

| 4 million | 3 million | 2 million | 1 million |

3,300,378
4,078,157
3,993,554
4,592,100
4,188,945
3,497,090
2,731,002

South to North migration

1.5 million
1 million
0.5 million
0.25 million

639,018
500,026
274,403
77,878
430,200
1,419,137
1,381,500

Internal migration 1870s–1930s

| 1870s | 1880s | 1890s | 1900s | 1910s | 1920s | 1930s |

Between the 1870s and the 1930s, millions of Americans moved around the country, mostly from East to West, but also from South to North.

SOURCE: U.S .Bureau of the Census, Historical Statistics of the United States: 1789 to 1945 (Washington, D.C.: U.S. Government Printing Office, 1949), 30–31.

and the more prosperous members of the working class enjoyed many of the comforts, amusements, and appliances that the booming economy made available. The poor, by contrast, struggled just to make ends meet. Throughout the twenties, the nation's poorest people continued to be the most mobile, moving in search of jobs, security, and a place they could settle and call home. Henry Crews, son of a white Georgia share-cropper, longed for "that single house where you were born, where you lived out your childhood . . . your anchor in the world." But he never had such a home. Like many other hardworking sharecroppers and factory workers, his family moved frequently in search of a better life, a dream that often proved elusive.

Sharecropping required hard work and careful planning to carve out a meager life, but many did so with pride. Ed Brown, a young black sharecropper, had no formal education but considered himself "pretty schemy." He worked on six different planta-tions, moving about in search of better circumstances or to escape from debt or threats of violence. Although he and his wife, Willie Mae, were never able to buy a place of their own, they did improve their circumstances over time. When they finally got out of debt and secured a bit of cash, they used it to adorn their meager cabin. In 1929, they bought an old Model T Ford. But finding it too costly to maintain, they swapped it for a cow and a butter churn and dasher, which provided more practical benefits. Meanwhile, Ed took odd jobs to earn extra money, while Willie Mae took care of the children, picked cotton, took in laundry, and, as Ed noted with appreciation, kept "things . . . lookin very pretty."

Industrial workers struggled throughout the decade, especially in a political cli-mate hostile to unions. With the crushing of labor radicalism in the Red Scare after World War I, union organizing and strikes declined. But workers continued to protest low wages and poor working conditions. In March 1929, young women textile workers in Elizabethton, a small town nestled in the Blue Ridge Mountains of eastern Tennessee, closed down the American Glanzstoff plant in protest against low wages, petty rules, and arrogant employers. Soon, the protest spread to textile mills across the region. At Glanzstoff, the strikers returned to work when the company promised better pay and agreed not to discriminate against union members. But the employers broke their prom-ises, so the women struck again. The governor sent in the National Guard, armed with machine guns. More than 1,000 people were arrested in confrontations with the troops.

21.4.4 The Stock Market Crash

Persistent poverty and labor struggles signaled that not everyone prospered during the "roaring twenties." But soon disaster hit the entire nation. The symbolic end of the 1920s arrived on "Black Tuesday," October 29, 1929, when the inflated and overextended stock market came crashing down. In one day, stocks fell in value $14 billion. By the end of the year, stock prices were down 50 percent; by 1932, they had dropped another 30 percent. In three years, $74 billion of the nation's wealth had vanished. The effect on the economy was catastrophic. Industrial production fell by half. More than 100,000 businesses went bankrupt. Banks failed at an alarming rate: more than 2,000 closed in 1931 alone. Unemployment rose to staggering levels, reaching 25 percent by 1932 and rarely dropping below 17 percent throughout the 1930s.

In keeping with the social policies that had prevailed throughout the 1920s, relief efforts were slim. No federal relief or welfare, no unemployment insurance, no Social Security, no job programs existed to help those who had lost their jobs, their savings, and their homes. Although many wealthy people lost their fortunes, which had been built on speculative investments, the poor suffered the most. People who lost their homes and farms moved into makeshift shelters in shantytowns, which they nicknamed **Hoovervilles** to mock the ineffectual efforts of President Herbert Hoover to respond to their plight.

Hoovervilles
Shantytowns, named for President Hoover and occupied largely by people who lost their homes and farms during the Great Depression.

The causes of the stock market crash and the decade-long depression that followed were complex and varied. Stock prices had risen dramatically, especially at the end of the 1920s. Speculators had been purchasing stocks on 10 percent margins, meaning they put down only 10 percent of the cost and borrowed the rest from brokers and banks. The popularity of installment buying in the consumer goods market had devastating effects when applied in this manner to the stock market. Investors expected to get rich quickly by selling their stocks at a higher price and paying back the loans from their huge profits. This system worked for a few years, encouraging investors with limited funds to make risky investments in the hope of gaining large fortunes. When the price of stocks spiraled out of control, far beyond their actual value, creditors demanded repayment of their loans, and investors were unable to pay their debts. The collapse was the worst of the twentieth century. Nothing of comparable magnitude occurred until 2008, when a similar combination of inflated stock and housing prices and irresponsible, unregulated business practices led to an economic catastrophe.

The collapse of the stock market alone would not necessarily have caused such a severe and prolonged depression. Poor decision making by financial and political leaders exacerbated underlying weaknesses in the economy. The Federal Reserve curtailed the amount of money in circulation and raised interest rates, making it more difficult for people to get loans and pay off their debts. These policies had profound worldwide implications and contributed to an international crisis. Banks in Germany and Austria, for example, depended on loans from the United States, and many went bankrupt, causing a ripple effect across Europe. The Hawley-Smoot Tariff of 1930 also contributed to the downward spiral. The new high tariff was intended to protect American commodities from competition from cheaper foreign goods. Foreign governments retaliated by raising their own tariffs to keep out American goods. These monetary and trade policies backfired, and the economic crisis spread throughout the western industrial world. Only the Soviet Union was spared the effects of the global economic crisis. As a communist state-run economy, it was largely immune from the collapse of worldwide capitalism.

Within the United States, the unequal distribution of wealth exacerbated the effects of the economic downturn. The nation may have looked prosperous, but most of the wealth was concentrated in the hands of a small number of people. If average Americans had been able to buy more cars, household appliances, and other products, those industries might have survived, and the economy might have recovered more quickly. Political leaders, and the business-oriented public policies they had promoted throughout the decade, left the country ill prepared to address the crisis and meet the needs of families deprived of their means of livelihood.

Interpreting History

F. Scott Fitzgerald: *The Great Gatsby* (1925)

"Gatsby believed in the green light, the orgastic future that year by year recedes before us."

F. Scott Fitzgerald's 1925 novel The Great Gatsby *expressed the longings of many Americans of the 1920s to partake of the glamorous life of the wealthy and live out their vision of the American dream. The story revolves around the desires of the newly wealthy Jay Gatsby to be accepted into the ranks of New York's elite. He is infatuated with Daisy Buchanan, who lives across the Sound from him in Long Island, a green light from her dock beckoning to him. In this passage from the final paragraphs of the book, the narrator, Nick Carraway, comments on the elusiveness of Gatsby's dream—the American dream. The poignant ending of the novel foreshadows the collapse of the overextended leisure and consumer culture of the 1920s that led to the Great Depression of the 1930s.*

I spent my Saturday nights in New York because those gleaming, dazzling parties of his were with me so vividly that I could still hear the music and the laughter, faint and incessant, from his garden, and the cars going up and down his drive. One night I did hear a material car there, and saw its lights stop at his front steps. But I didn't investigate. Probably it was some final guest who had been away at the ends of the earth and didn't know that the party was over.

On the last night, with my trunk packed and my car sold to the grocer, I went over and looked at that huge incoherent failure of a house once more. On the white steps an obscene word, scrawled by some boy with a piece of brick, stood out clearly in the moonlight, and I erased it, drawing my shoe raspingly along the stone. Then I wandered down to the beach and sprawled out on the sand.

Most of the big shore places were closed now and there were hardly any lights except the shadowy, moving glow of a ferryboat across the Sound. And as the moon rose higher the inessential houses began to melt away until gradually I became aware of the old island here that flowered once for Dutch sailors' eyes—a fresh, green breast of the new world.

JAZZ AGE ICONS F. SCOTT AND ZELDA FITZGERALD Pictured here on their honeymoon, writer F. Scott Fitzgerald and his flapper wife, Zelda, personified the glamorous literati of the Jazz Age.

Princeton University Library/Library of Congress Photographs and Prints Division LC-USZ62-111780

In his writing, how did Fitzgerald both romanticize and criticize the decadent consumerism of the aspiring and upwardly mobile middle class?

Its vanished trees, the trees that had made way for Gatsby's house, had once pandered in whispers to the last and greatest of all human dreams; for a transitory enchanted moment man must have held his breath in the presence of this continent, compelled into an aesthetic contemplation he neither understood nor desired, face to face for the last time in history with something commensurate to his capacity for wonder.

And as I sat there brooding on the old, unknown world, I thought of Gatsby's wonder when he first picked out the green light at the end of Daisy's dock. He had come a long way to this blue lawn, and his dream must have seemed so close that he could hardly fail to grasp it. He did not know that it was already behind him, somewhere back in that vast obscurity beyond the city, where the dark fields of the republic rolled on under the night.

Gatsby believed in the green light, the orgastic future that year by year recedes before us. It eluded us then, but that's no matter—tomorrow we will run faster, stretch out our arms farther. . . . And one fine morning—

So we beat on, boats against the current, borne back ceaselessly into the past.

Questions for Discussion

1. Why would Fitzgerald use the Dutch sailors of the colonial period as a point of reference in this passage?

2. Critics have often pointed to Fitzgerald's ambivalence about modern urban life as expressed in *The Great Gatsby*. Do you see any ambivalence in this passage?

3. In this passage, is Fitzgerald optimistic or pessimistic about the American dream?

Conclusion

The stock market collapse, and the prolonged depression that followed, revealed the flaws in the economic system that spurred the apparent prosperity of the 1920s. Beneath the visible affluence was the hidden poverty that prevailed throughout the decade. National leaders promoted business interests and paid little attention to social welfare, the environment, or the need to regulate the economy. By the end of the 1920s, it was clear that Prohibition was a dismal failure and that the federal government was ill equipped to enforce it.

Although political reform withered, cultural vitality flowered. Hollywood emerged as a major industry, and the Jazz Age reflected the widespread appeal of African American music. A black arts movement flourished, centered in Harlem, and writers—disenchanted with the status quo—gathered in Greenwich Village or moved to France. Across the country, a youth culture challenged the gender and sexual mores of the past. Consumer culture expanded as increasing numbers of families purchased cars, radios, and new fashions. Few who were involved in the private preoccupations of the decade could have foreseen the disaster ahead, when the stock market crashed and the Depression set in.

Chapter Review

21.1 The Business of Politics and the Decline of Progressive Reform

What major developments signaled the end of the Progressive Era?

The reform spirit waned during the 1920s, as business became the focus of politics. Hostility to radicals and immigrants led to new public policies. After women achieved the vote, the women's rights movement divided over goals and strategies. Yet some reform efforts remained vibrant, especially among African Americans, who continued to mobilize for civil rights.

21.2 Hollywood and Harlem: National Cultures in Black and White

What developments in the arts and technology helped forge a national popular culture in the 1920s?

Culture flourished in the 1920s, especially in Hollywood with the expansion of the motion picture industry and in New York with the flourishing of African American art, literature and jazz known as the Harlem Renaissance. Remarkably, these quintessential American arts—movies and jazz—were the creation of outsiders to the American mainstream: Jews and African Americans.

21.3 Science on Trial

What did science contribute to American life in the 1920s, and where did scientific ideas fall short?

Scientific and medical advances continued to improve life for many Americans, but not all scientific developments yielded social benefits. Levees built along the Mississippi River did not prevent massive flooding in 1927. The movement for human breeding, known as eugenics, led to many abuses. Science itself came on trial when the theory of evolution landed in court.

21.4 Consumer Dreams and Nightmares

What were the positive and negative effects of the 1920s consumer culture?

Consumerism reigned in the 1920s. Americans who could afford them—and even many who could not—purchased automobiles, radios, household appliances, and all sorts of goods. The expansion of consumer credit led many consumers to spend beyond their means. Meanwhile, many Americans, especially in rural areas, suffered extreme poverty in the midst of plenty.

Timeline

1920	Nineteenth Amendment (women's suffrage) ratified
1924	Johnson-Reid Act limits immigration
	Portable radio introduced
1925	*Scopes* trial, Dayton, Tennessee
1926	Gertrude Ederle is first woman to swim across the English Channel
1927	Charles Lindbergh flies nonstop from New York to Paris
	Sacco and Vanzetti executed
	Buck v. Bell upholds compulsory sterilization laws
1928	Hoover elected president
1929	Stock market crash

Glossary

flapper Young woman in the 1910s and 1920s who rebelled against the gender conventions of the era with respect to fashion and behavior.

consumer economy An economic system in which most people work for wages, which they use to purchase manufactured goods and foodstuffs.

Equal Rights Amendment (ERA) A proposed amendment to the U.S. Constitution that would have guaranteed equal rights for women.

political machines Groups that effectively exercise control over a political party, usually at the local level and organized around precincts and patronage.

speakeasies Establishments where alcohol was illegally sold during the Prohibition era.

aliens Foreign-born residents of the United States who have not been naturalized as U.S. citizens.

Harlem Renaissance A period in American history immediately following World War I (c. 1918–37) characterized by a surge of creativity in the literary, theatrical, musical, and visual arts among African Americans.

planned obsolescence A concept whereby producers intend for their products to eventually become obsolete or outdated and require replacement, thus perpetuating a cycle of production and consumption.

installment buying A system in which a consumer could make a down payment to purchase a product and then pay the remaining installments over time.

Hoovervilles Shantytowns, named for President Hoover and occupied largely by people who lost their homes and farms during the Great Depression.

Chapter 22
Hardship and Hope: The Great Depression of the 1930s

SOCIAL SATIRIST WILL ROGERS Will Rogers, Cherokee comic, movie star, and political activist, poses here with his cowboy gear, surrounded by admiring fans. Rogers was one of the most popular celebrities of the 1930s and a playful but pointed social critic.

Library of Congress Prints and Photographs Division [LC-DIG-ggbain-35961]

What were the conditions of the Great Depression that fueled the popularity of Will Rogers?

Contents and Focus Questions

During the Great Depression, why would a Native American become a popular national leader promoting the common good?

Will Rogers was a Cherokee, a comedian, a plainspoken critic of the nation's rich and powerful, a movie star, a journalist, and an adviser to President Franklin Delano Roosevelt (FDR). In contrast to earlier notions of the United States as an Anglo-Saxon country into which newcomers might assimilate, Rogers articulated a new Americanism that included ethnic minorities. The Great Depression tarnished the status of the business elite and opened up the political process to party realignments and new leaders. The popular culture expressed this new Americanism; Will Rogers was its most prominent voice.

The Great Depression gave rise to a cultural and political upheaval that helped propel Rogers to stardom and political influence. President Franklin Roosevelt coveted his support, and Rogers obliged by promoting the New Deal, the president's program for economic recovery. However, Rogers also pushed the president to the left by advocating such measures as taxing the rich and redistributing wealth. In 1932, Oklahoma nominated Rogers for president as the state's favorite son; three years later, California Democratic leaders urged him to run for the Senate. But in 1935, before any of these possibilities could come to fruition, Rogers died in a plane crash.

The response to Rogers's death illustrates his stature as a national leader and spokesperson for a new multicultural Americanism. Congress adjourned in his memory, President Roosevelt sent a well-publicized letter to Rogers's family, the governor of California proclaimed a day of mourning, flags flew at half staff, bells rang in Rogers's honor in more than 100 cities, and nearly 100,000 people filed by his coffin at Forest Lawn Cemetery. Radio stations across the country broadcast his memorial service from the Hollywood Bowl, presided over by a Protestant minister and a Catholic priest, while a Yiddish performer sang a Hebrew mourning chant. Across town, Mexican American citizen groups placed a wreath on Olvera Street that read "Nosotros Lamentamos la Muerte de Will Rogers" ("We Mourn the Death of Will Rogers"). An African American fraternal group in Los Angeles joined black performers from Rogers's films in a parade to honor the Cherokee movie star. In his hometown of Claremore, Oklahoma, Cherokee Indians performed a death dance in memory of their fallen kinsman.

*　　*　　*　　*　　*

This massive national grieving reveals not only Rogers's popularity, but also the culture of 1930s America. Shared economic hardship unleashed changes in society that opened the door for a politically radical Cherokee Indian to become one of the most popular figures of the Great Depression. The Great Depression also gave President Roosevelt the opportunity to draw together a new political coalition of immigrants and minorities that elected him to the presidency four times.

The New Deal, a package of remedies that President Roosevelt put together to address the problems of the Depression, provided relief to many Americans but did not eradicate poverty or end the crisis. Yet, as Americans drew around their radios to hear the president's **fireside chats**, and as they held onto their faith in the nation's promise despite its worst economic downturn, they helped forge a more inclusive culture.

fireside chats
The broadcasts by President Franklin Delano Roosevelt during which he spoke directly to American families, often gathered around a radio in their living rooms.

22.1 The Great Depression

What caused the Great Depression, and how did it affect ordinary Americans?

The Great Depression defined the 1930s in the United States. It shaped the political life of the nation, the public policies that resulted, and the cultural expressions that reflected the spirit of the people during a time of national crisis. Its effects permeated the lives of Americans from the mansions of the wealthy to the shanties of the poor and from the boardrooms to the bedrooms. The Depression drove thousands of farmers from the drought-stricken southern Great Plains to California. But the story is not simply one of despair and hardship. It is also one of strong communities, resourcefulness, and hope.

The Great Depression was a global economic catastrophe. Of the major world powers, only the Soviet Union—a communist society with state-directed labor, agriculture, and industry—was immune to the collapse of the capitalist system after 1929. The Soviet economy grew throughout the 1930s, and its relative health led many people in troubled capitalist systems to look to communism as an alternative. Socialism also gained many converts across Europe. The world's powerful nations all moved toward greater government intervention in their economies. England, France, and the United States used deficit spending to help stimulate the economy and instituted relief programs. Italy, Germany, and Japan also increased government intervention in the economy, but they used different strategies to address the crisis, particularly military spending. These varied responses to the Depression contributed to the conflicts and alliances that would eventually culminate in World War II.

22.1.1 Causes of the Crisis

The Great Depression of the 1930s was the worst economic depression in the twentieth century. But it was neither the first nor the last. A complex set of factors led to the collapse. Economists at the time, and since, have debated its cause, with no widely-shared explanation. **Capitalism**, the economic system that forms the basis of the American economy, has cycles of ups and downs. In the United States, prior to the 1930s, the government stepped in to regulate the economy primarily to protect economic competition. Progressive Era reforms prevented corporations from establishing monopolies, so that competition could flourish. In the free market economy, consumers would determine which companies would succeed, based on the quality of their products and services. Because the government did not determine the levels of industrial or agricultural productivity, and did not set the prices, the economy was subject to changing circumstances that led to times of prosperity and times of recession or, in the case of severe economic downturns, depression.

capitalism
The now almost worldwide economic system of private ownership of property and profit-seeking corporations.

Before the 1930s, the United States provided no **welfare state** benefits, such as medical care, relief from poverty, income for the unemployed, or old-age insurance. Without policies that would serve as a safety net for workers who lost their jobs, many wage earners and their families fell into poverty during economic downturns. In the Great Depression of the 1930s, the economic crisis was so severe that one-quarter of the nation's workers, nearly 14 million people, lost their jobs, leaving them and their families—40 million people in all—without any income or security. Many of these people had never known poverty before. Among the newly poor were thousands of middle-class Americans who now faced the loss of their homes and savings. For working-class and poor Americans, the impact of the Depression was devastating because they had little economic security to begin with.

welfare state
A nation in which the government provides a "safety net" of entitlements and benefits for citizens unable to economically provide for themselves.

For many Americans, the Depression really began in the 1920s. Food production and distribution stumbled along weakly throughout the 1920s, contributing to widespread rural poverty. During the 1920s, 1,200 big corporations absorbed more than 6,000 independent businesses. By 1929, 200 corporations controlled nearly half of all industry, which limited competition and made it difficult for new, smaller businesses to flourish.

Although the economy looked healthy on the surface, prosperity rested on an unsound foundation. Many people obtained consumer goods on credit, so when people lost their jobs, they could not pay their debts. Throughout the 1920s, the gap between the rich and poor increased. Nearly 80 percent of the nation's families had no savings at all. Americans with high annual incomes of $10,000 or more—2.3 percent of the people—held two-thirds of all savings. The concentration of wealth among the richest Americans during the 1920s contributed to the persistence of the crisis in the 1930s.

22.1.2 Surviving Hard Times

In human terms, the Depression of the 1930s dealt a devastating blow to large numbers of Americans: crushing poverty, hunger, humiliation, and loss of dignity and self-worth. Many felt a profound shame that they could no longer earn a living and support their families. The few jobs available often went to the young, strong, well-fed, and well-groomed. Thousands of citizens poured out their hearts in letters to the president, hoping that the government could provide some assistance. In 1934, an Oklahoma woman lamented, "The unemployed have been so long without food-clothes-shoes-medical care-dental care etc.—we look pretty bad—so when we ask for a job we dont' get it. And we look and feel a little worse each day—when we ask for food they call us bums—it isent our fault . . . no we are not bums."

Families provided the first line of defense against disaster, especially in the early days of the crisis. Many families adapted to hard times by abandoning time-honored gender roles. As men lost jobs, women went to work. Working women did not take jobs from men; rather, they held jobs defined as "traditional women's work" as secretaries, nurses, and waitresses. These jobs offered lower wages than most jobs held by men. A white woman working for wages earned, on average, 61 percent of a white man's wages; a black woman earned a mere 23 percent. Still, they provided at least a modicum of much-needed income.

Many parents struggled to provide for their families under difficult conditions, sometimes risking their health and safety to do so. Erminia Pablita Ruiz Mercer remembered when her father was injured while working in the beet fields in 1933. "He didn't want to live if he couldn't support his family," so he risked experimental back surgery and died on the operating table. Young Erminia then dropped out of school to work as "a doughnut girl" to support her mother and sisters.

22.1.3 Enduring Discrimination

For many poor families, hard times were nothing new. As one African American noted, "The Negro was born in depression. It only became official when it hit the white man." Throughout the 1930s, black Americans suffered the impact of economic hard times disproportionately. By 1932, black unemployment reached 50 percent. With local white authorities in charge of relief, impoverished southern blacks had few places to turn for assistance. African Americans also faced increasing violence; the number of lynchings rose from eight in 1932 to twenty in 1935.

hobos
Migrant workers or poor and homeless vagrants who traveled on trains from location to location, usually in search of employment.

Many poor people joined the growing ranks of **hobos**, riding the rails from town to town, looking for work. But poverty did not erase racial hierarchies or sexual codes, especially for nine young African Americans in 1931 who came to be known as the "Scottsboro Boys." The youths were riding the rails when they were arrested in Paint Rock, Alabama. Two white women on the train with them accused them of rape. Narrowly avoiding a lynching, they were taken to jail in Scottsboro. An all-white jury convicted them of rape, and they were sentenced to death. In November 1932, the U.S. Supreme Court ordered a new trial on the grounds that the defendants did not get a fair trial. But the new trial also resulted in convictions.

The case became a major rallying point for civil rights activists, liberals, and radicals throughout the 1930s. Support for the young men came from all over the world.

IN LINE FOR BREAD, LOUISVILLE, KENTUCKY In this 1937 photograph, "At the Time of the Louisville Flood," Margaret Bourke-White depicts the painful irony of poverty in the midst of affluence. Here, hungry Americans line up at a breadline in front of a billboard proclaiming American prosperity.

Margaret Bourke-White/Masters/Time Life Pictures/Getty Images

What does Bourke-White's breadline photograph say about race and class in 1930s America?

In 1935, the U.S. Supreme Court reversed the second set of convictions on the grounds that excluding blacks from the jury denied the defendants due process. Yet, in the next two years, five of the defendants were again tried and found guilty. Although none of the Scottsboro Boys was executed, they all spent long years in prison.

Mexican Americans also suffered disproportionately during the Depression. Many families could barely survive on the low wages paid to Mexican laborers. According to a 1933 study, working children's earnings constituted more than one-third of their families' total income. The work was often grueling. Julia Luna Mount recalled her first day at a Los Angeles cannery: "I didn't have money for gloves so I peeled chilies all day long by hand. After work, my hands were red, swollen, and I was on fire! On the streetcar going home, I could hardly hold on my hands hurt so much." Young Julia was lucky—her father saw her suffering and did not make her return to the cannery. But Carmen Bernal Escobar's father could not afford to be soft-hearted about work: "My father was a busboy and to keep the family going . . . in order to bring in a little more money . . . my mother, my grandmother, my mother's brother, my sister and I all worked together" at the cannery.

Those with cannery work, hard as it was, were among the fortunate. Many more Mexicans were deported. Between 1931 and 1934, more than 500,000 Mexicans and

Map 22.1 DUST AND DROUGHT, 1931–1939

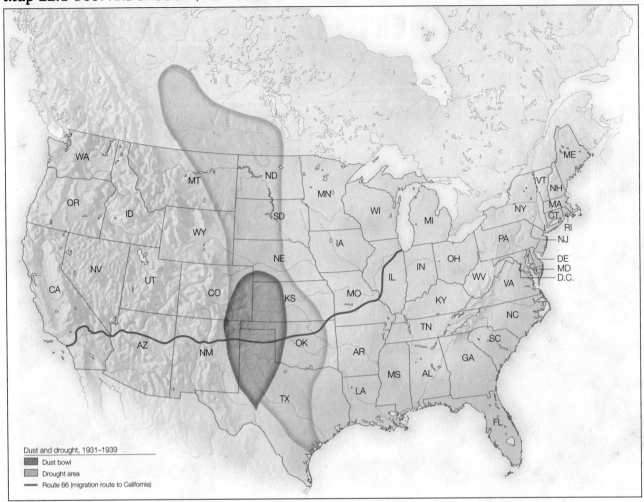

Drought cut a giant swath across the middle of America during the years of the Great Depression. The hardest hit region was the Dust Bowl area of Oklahoma, Texas, New Mexico, Colorado, and Kansas. Many people fled the afflicted areas, abandoning farms, piling their belongings into their cars, and driving along Route 66 to California. While many considered the dust and drought to be acts of nature, land overuse was a significant contributor to the loose and dry topsoil that caused storms of dust to cover the region.

Mexican Americans—approximately one-third of the Mexican population in the United States—were sent to Mexico. Most were children born in the United States. Throughout the century, the United States opened or closed its doors to Mexican immigrants depending on the need for their labor. They were deported during the Depression when unemployment was high, then recruited again during the labor shortage of World War II.

22.1.4 The Dust Bowl

Dust Bowl

The plains regions of Oklahoma, Texas, Colorado, New Mexico, and Kansas affected by severe drought in the 1930s.

Severe drought exacerbated the difficulties of farmers across Oklahoma, Texas, Kansas, Colorado, and New Mexico, an area that came to be known as the **Dust Bowl**. Farmers had used the land mainly for grazing until high grain prices during World War I enticed them to plow under millions of acres of natural grasslands to plant wheat. Plowing removed root systems from the soil, and years of little rainfall caused the land to dry up. By the middle of the decade, high winds picked up the loose topsoil, creating dust storms across the open plains. The ecological disaster, largely the result of farming strategies that depleted the soil, drove 60 percent of the population out of the region.

Migrant farm families fleeing the Dust Bowl came to symbolize the suffering wrought by the Depression. The photographs of Dorothea Lange, the songs of Woody

DUST BOWL STORM, CIMARRON COUNTY, OKLAHOMA An Oklahoma farmer and his sons try to find shelter from the storm of dust that blew across the plains in 1935. Severe drought after years of excessive plowing created dry loose topsoil that was picked up by high winds. More than half of the residents of the Dust Bowl moved out of the area as a result of the devastation.

Arthur Rothstein, 1915-1985/Library of Congress Prints and Photographs Division [LC-DIG-ppmsc-00241]

What historical and economic factors led to the excessive plowing that contributed to dust storms?

Guthrie, and the writings of John Steinbeck all immortalized their plight. Steinbeck's Pulitzer prize–winning novel *The Grapes of Wrath* (1939) and its film version have remained classics of American popular art. Writing in *The Nation* in 1936, Steinbeck described the Dust Bowl migrants streaming into California:

> Poverty-stricken after the destruction of their farms, their last reserves used up in making the trip, they have arrived so beaten and destitute that they have been willing at first to work under any conditions and for any wages offered. . . . They are not drawn from a peon class, but have either owned small farms or been farm hands in the early American sense, in which the "hand" is a member of the employing family. They have one fixed idea, and that is to acquire land and settle on it. . . . They are not easily intimidated. They are courageous, intelligent, and resourceful. Having gone through the horrors of the drought and with immense effort having escaped from it, they cannot be herded, attacked, starved, or frightened.

Thousands of **Okies** piled belongings on their cars and made their way to California in hopes of starting over. There they joined Mexican migrant farm workers, African American laborers, and others down on their luck, hoping for work.

Okie
Migrant from Oklahoma who left the state during the Dust Bowl period in search of work.

22.2 Presidential Responses to the Depression

How did Presidents Hoover and Roosevelt respond to the Great Depression?

Until the economic collapse, President Herbert Hoover's political achievements had earned wide admiration. He seemed the perfect embodiment of the spirit of the prosperous 1920s. But his ideas about politics and economics were ill suited to the crisis of the 1930s. Dissatisfaction with Hoover's response to the Depression gave Franklin Delano Roosevelt a landslide victory in the 1932 presidential election. Promising to take action to ease the nation's suffering, the optimistic Roosevelt sparked hope for an end to the crisis.

Table 22.1 THE ELECTION OF 1932

Candidate	Political Party	Popular Vote (%)	Electoral Vote
Franklin D. Roosevelt	Democratic	57.4	472
Herbert Hoover	Republican	39.7	59
Norman Thomas	Socialist	2.2	—

SOURCE: Historical Election Results, Electoral College, National Archives and Records Administration

22.2.1 Herbert Hoover: Failed Efforts

Had prosperity continued, Hoover might have left a legacy of presidential leadership to match his earlier achievements as a Progressive administrator of food relief in Europe.

Declaring that "excessive fortunes are a menace to true liberty," he favored steeply graduated inheritance and income taxes on the wealthy, with no tax burden on the poor. He believed that society had a responsibility to care for those in need and that the prosperous should bear much of the burden. After the stock market crash, Hoover increased spending for public works—programs in which the government created jobs for people who needed employment—to the unprecedented sum of $700 million. He established the Reconstruction Finance Corporation to make government credit available to banks and other financial institutions. Seeking to restore confidence in the economy, he strove for a balanced budget by raising taxes and cutting spending—a strategy that underestimated the depth of the Depression and made the situation worse.

As the Depression set in and brought widespread misery, Hoover fully expected that charitable organizations would step in and provide aid to the poor. He believed that government relief to the needy had demoralizing effects on people. Even when it was clear that the crisis was beyond the help of charitable groups, Hoover remained strongly opposed to direct relief for the poor. Private giving did increase to record levels; unfortunately, it was not sufficient.

Hoover's popularity reached its lowest ebb in 1932. A group of World War I veterans in Portland, Oregon, organized a march on Washington, D.C., called the Bonus March. The veterans were due to receive a bonus of $1,000 each in 1945. The group had asked to have their bonuses early, in 1932, to help ease their suffering during the Depression. Hoover refused, compelling more than 20,000 veterans to travel to Washington and petition Congress. The determined veterans set up a tent city and settled in with their families. When Hoover refused to meet with the protesters, the veterans began to leave. But some did not depart quickly enough, and a police officer began shooting at the unarmed demonstrators, killing one person.

Army Chief of Staff Douglas MacArthur stepped in and escalated the violence. His troops used tear gas and bayonets to prod the veterans and their families to vacate the area, then set fire to the tent city. The attack injured more than 100 people and killed one baby. The image of federal troops assaulting a group of peaceful veterans stunned the public. Although MacArthur had ordered the brutality, the public blamed Hoover. As most people saw it, Hoover had heartlessly spurned the veterans' legitimate request. By the time of the 1932 election, Hoover had lost most of his public support.

22.2.2 Franklin Delano Roosevelt: The Pragmatist

In contrast to Hoover, Franklin Delano Roosevelt was born into a family of wealth and privilege. Pampered as a child, he was educated at elite schools and colleges. In 1905, he married a distant cousin, Eleanor Roosevelt, the niece of President Theodore Roosevelt.

RARE PHOTOGRAPH OF ROOSEVELT IN WHEELCHAIR In this 1941 photograph, FDR is pictured with his dog Fala and Ruthie Bie, a friend's granddaughter, in Hyde Park, New York. This is one of only two known photographs of Roosevelt in his wheelchair. Careful to project an image of strength, vitality, and optimism, FDR avoided photos that would call attention to his physical disability. Yet many Americans found inspiration and hope knowing that their president, like the nation, could triumph over adversity.

Margaret Suckley/Krt/Newscom

What do the details in this photograph of the wheelchair-bound president reveal about FDR's personality and his life beyond public view?

Like Franklin, Eleanor came from a sheltered, upper-class background. But her early life, unlike his, was filled with sadness. Both her parents died when she was a young child, and at age ten, her grandmother left her in the care of a harsh governess. The young woman began to flourish when she went abroad to study. The rigorous education developed her strengths and confidence.

Franklin Roosevelt was elected to the New York State Senate in 1911, and in 1913, he became Assistant Secretary of the Navy. His political plans derailed suddenly in 1921 when he was stricken with polio and lost the use of his legs. The painful and incapacitating illness threw the normally ebullient young man into despair. The formerly athletic Roosevelt depended on braces, crutches, and a wheelchair to move around. But his extraordinary reserves of self-confidence and optimism helped to sustain him in the face of his paralysis.

FDR's bout with polio did nothing to dampen his political ambitions. He became governor of New York in 1928, following in the footsteps of his Republican cousin, Theodore Roosevelt. In his 1932 Democratic presidential campaign, FDR made few specific proposals, but promised the American people a "New Deal." Many Americans, facing dire circumstances in their own lives, identified with their disabled president, who overcame his own adversity to lead the nation in a time of crisis.

Interpreting History

Franklin Roosevelt: On Banking (Fireside Chat, March 12, 1933)

"Let us unite in banishing fear."

When the banks collapsed, President Franklin D. Roosevelt used the radio to speak candidly with the American people about the banking crisis and urge them to be calm and patient. A master of the media, President Roosevelt explained how the government would intervene in the crisis and protect citizens' savings. Here he demonstrates his ability to connect with Americans in their everyday struggles and fears and persuade them to trust his leadership—and the government—to work in their best interests.

I want to talk for a few minutes with the people of the United States about banking—with the comparatively few who understand the mechanics of banking but more particularly with the overwhelming majority who use banks for the making of deposits and the drawing of checks. I want to tell you what has been done in the last few days, why it was done, and what the next steps are going to be. . . .

First of all, let me state the simple fact that when you deposit money in a bank the bank does not put the money into a safe deposit vault. It invests your money in many different forms of credit—bonds, commercial paper, mortgages and many other kinds of loans. In other words, the bank puts your money to work to keep the wheels of industry and of agriculture turning around. A comparatively small part of the money you put into the bank is kept in currency—an amount which in normal times is wholly sufficient to cover the cash needs of the average citizen. . . .

What, then, happened during the last few days of February and the first few days of March? Because of undermined confidence on the part of the public, there was a general rush by a large portion of our population to turn bank deposits into currency or gold—a rush so great that the soundest banks could not get enough currency to meet the demand. The reason for this was that on the spur of the moment it was, of course, impossible to sell perfectly sound assets of a bank and convert them into cash except at panic prices far below their real value.

By the afternoon of March 3, scarcely a bank in the country was open to do business. . . .

It was then that I issued the proclamation providing for the nationwide bank holiday, and this was the first step in the Government's reconstruction of our financial and economic fabric. . . .

It is possible that when the banks resume, a very few people who have not recovered from their fear may again begin withdrawals. Let me make it clear that the banks will take care of all needs—and it is my belief that hoarding during the past week has become an exceedingly unfashionable pastime. It needs no prophet to tell you that when the people find that they can get their money—that they can get it when they want it for all legitimate purposes—the phantom of fear will soon be laid. People will again be glad to have their money where it will be safely taken care of and where they can use it conveniently at any time. I can assure you that it is safer to keep your money in a reopened bank than under the mattress. . . .

I hope you can see from this elemental recital of what your Government is doing that there is nothing complex, or radical, in the process. . . .

After all, there is an element in the readjustment of our financial system more important than currency, more important than gold, and that is the confidence of the people. Confidence and courage are the essentials of success in carrying out our plan. You people must have faith; you must not be stampeded by rumors or guesses. Let us unite in banishing fear. We have provided the machinery to restore our financial system; it is up to you to support and make it work.

It is your problem no less than it is mine. Together we cannot fail.

THE FIRESIDE CHAT George Segal's sculpture at the Franklin Delano Roosevelt Memorial in Washington, D.C., portrays an American listening with rapt attention to a "fireside chat." At a time of uncertainty and hardship, Roosevelt's reassuring words calmed the fears of an anxious nation.

Hisham Ibrahim/Photolibrary/Getty Images

Consider the way in which the figure in Segal's **Fireside Chat** *sits. Does the position of the sitter contribute any particular meaning to the sculpture or communicate anything about Roosevelt's particular political skills?*

Questions for Discussion

1. What rhetorical strategies did Roosevelt use in this speech to calm the fears of the American people?

2. What does this speech indicate about the role of the president and the government in responding to the economic crisis?

SOURCE: *The Public Papers and Addresses of Franklin D. Roosevelt* (New York: Random House, 1938), 2: 61-65.

22.2.3 "Nothing to Fear but Fear Itself"

In his inaugural address, Roosevelt endeavored to ease the nation's anxieties with reassuring words: "Let me assert my firm belief that the only thing we have to fear is fear itself—nameless, unreasoning, unjustified terror which paralyzes needed efforts to convert retreat into advance." Roosevelt launched his advance immediately. Panic had prompted many Americans to pull out their bank savings, causing many banks to fail. To stop the run on banks, FDR announced a "bank holiday," temporarily closing all the nation's banks. He could have nationalized the banking system, a move toward socialism that would likely have received widespread support. But Roosevelt favored government regulation, not government ownership. He proposed the Emergency Banking Bill, providing government support for private banks. Congress passed the bill instantly, to the applause of the bankers who helped draft it.

In the first of his "fireside chats" to millions of radio listeners, whom he addressed as "my friends," Roosevelt assured citizens that the reopened banks were sound. He used the medium of radio skillfully to explain his policies and to communicate comforting and reassuring messages that reached people in the intimate setting of their homes. The next day, bank deposits exceeded withdrawals as a result of the confidence he inspired.

22.3 The New Deal

What was the New Deal, and how did it develop over time?

The New Deal drew on Progressive Era reform impulses to extend the reach of the federal government to solve social problems. It provided assistance to many Americans suffering the effects of the Depression and established the welfare state that would last half a century. Based on pragmatism, experimentation, and shrewd political calculation, FDR's plan began with a flurry of activity in the first 100 days of his administration and developed into a more progressive agenda by 1935, often called the **Second New Deal**. New Deal programs countered capitalism's cyclical nature and offered a safety net for industrial workers. They legitimized labor unions and established a system of regulation and cooperation between industry and labor. These federal initiatives won Roosevelt a resounding reelection in 1936. Many New Deal programs failed, but those that succeeded created the foundation of the modern American state. The broad-based reform effort, however, did not end the Depression nor eradicate poverty.

Second New Deal
The agenda of policies and programs initiated by President Franklin Delano Roosevelt beginning in 1935 that was intended to improve the lot of American workers while simultaneously preserving the capitalist system.

22.3.1 The First Hundred Days

Roosevelt acted quickly and pragmatically. As one of his first acts, he encouraged Congress to repeal Prohibition. In 1933, the states quickly ratified the Twenty-First Amendment, repealing the Eighteenth. Repeal of Prohibition helped the economy by providing additional tax revenues from liquor sales, since they were once again legal, and a market for farmers' corn and wheat, which were used to produce liquor. Congress also created the Securities and Exchange Commission (SEC) to oversee the stock market and the Federal Deposit Insurance Corporation (FDIC) to reform the banking system and provide insurance for deposits.

One of FDR's most pressing challenges was to prop up prices for producers while keeping them low enough for consumers. Poverty in the midst of plenty was one of the Depression's cruelest ironies. Farmers could not afford to transport their goods to market and food rotted while millions of people went hungry. Through the Agricultural Adjustment Act, the government sought to prop up farm prices by limiting supply. It paid farmers to destroy livestock and take acreage out of production.

A MIGRANT FAMILY, SISKIYOU COUNTY, CALIFORNIA Dorothea Lange took photographs for the Farm Security Administration (FSA), documenting the lives of Depression-era migrants. This 1939 photo, "Mother and Children on the Road, Tulelake, Siskiyou County, California," is one of Lange's many portraits of impoverished families.

Dorothea Lange/Library of Congress Prints and Photographs Division [LC-USF34-T01-020993-E]

Why would Lange's photograph become one of the most important iconic images of life in America during the Great Depression? What about the demeanor and faces of the woman and her children creates an emotional response in the viewer?

Another challenge for Roosevelt and the federal government was to create jobs. Most Americans in need desperately wanted to work. They considered government relief a sign of failure and shame. Many citizens searched for ways to preserve their pride. One woman wrote to Eleanor Roosevelt asking to borrow money to avoid charity:

> Please Mrs. Roosevelt, I do not want charity, only a chance from someone who will trust me. . . . I am sending you two of my dearest possessions to keep as security, a ring my husband gave me before we were married, and a ring my mother used to wear. . . . If you will consider buying the baby clothes, please keep them (rings) until I send you the money you spent. It is very hard to face bearing a baby we cannot afford to have, and the fact that it is due to arrive soon, and still there is no money for the hospital or clothing, does not make it any easier. I have decided to stay home, keeping my 7 year old daughter from school to help with the smaller children. . . . The 7 year old one is a good willing little worker and somehow we must manage—but without charity.

In March 1933, Congress passed the Federal Emergency Relief Administration (FERA), which provided $500 million in grants to the states for aid to the needy. The program was headed by Harry Hopkins, an energetic and brash young reformer, who disbursed $2 million during his first two hours on the job. He then persuaded Roosevelt to launch a temporary job program, the Civil Works Administration (CWA). The CWA provided government-sponsored jobs for more than 4 million workers. But the program came under fire from conservatives, and FDR ended it a few months later.

In 1933, Roosevelt combined his interest in conservation with his goal of providing work for unemployed young men. The Civilian Conservation Corps (CCC) operated under the control of the Army. CCC workers lived in camps, wore uniforms, and conformed to military discipline. They planted millions of trees, built more than 30,000 wilderness shelters, stocked rivers and lakes with nearly 1 billion fish, and preserved historic sites. Their work revived depleted forests and provided flood control. By 1935, the CCC had employed more than 500,000 young men and kept them, in FDR's words, "off the city street corners."

Another measure that linked natural resources to the recovery effort was the Tennessee Valley Authority (TVA), an experiment in government-owned utilities that brought power to rural areas along the Tennessee River in seven states in western Appalachia—among the poorest areas in the nation. This far-reaching government-owned project offered a radical alternative to American capitalism. Under the TVA, the government built five dams, improved twenty others, and constructed power plants; it produced and sold electricity to farmers and facilitated the development of industry in the region. The TVA also provided flood control and became one of the largest and cheapest suppliers of power in the nation.

In addition to the dams built as part of the TVA, gigantic new dams provided electricity and irrigation in the arid West: Hoover Dam on the Colorado River outside Las Vegas, and the huge Grand Coulee Dam across the Columbia River in Washington State that provided electricity to much of the Northwest and irrigation for over half a million acres of land in the Columbia basin. The Golden Gate Bridge, another Depression-era project, spanned the entrance to San Francisco Bay. In 1930, construction began on the Empire State Building in New York City, the tallest building in the world up to that time.

The 1933 National Industrial Recovery Act (NIRA) became the centerpiece of the first New Deal. The NIRA established the National Recovery Administration (NRA) to oversee regulation of the economy. In his second "fireside chat," Roosevelt called the NRA "a partnership in planning" between business and government. The NRA enabled

Map 22.2 AREAS SERVED BY THE TENNESSEE VALLEY AUTHORITY

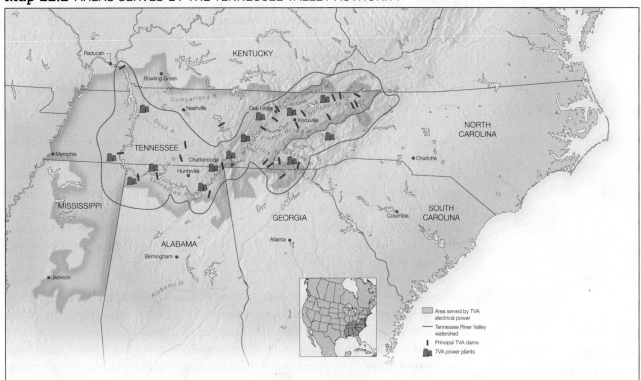

The Tennessee Valley Authority (TVA) brought electricity to a large area in western Appalachia, one of the poorest regions in the country. The government-owned project strengthened the economy and improved living conditions in the area. But the many dams, along with other TVA projects, disrupted natural ecosystems and had negative environmental consequences that were unforeseen at the time.

businesses in each sector of the economy to form trade associations and set their own standards for production, prices, and wages. Section 7(a) of the NIRA also guaranteed collective bargaining rights to workers, sparking new hope for union organizers.

FDR's first 100 days also included the creation of the Home Owners' Loan Corporation, providing refinancing of home mortgages at low rates. Because the plan helped stem the tide of foreclosures and guaranteed the repayment of loans, it pleased homeowners, banks, and real-estate interests. It helped FDR gain the support of a large segment of the middle class.

One of the boldest New Dealers was John Collier, whom Roosevelt appointed as Commissioner of Indian Affairs. Collier opposed the policy of land allotment that the Dawes Act of 1887 had enacted. Under allotment, Native American land holdings had dwindled from 130 million acres to 49 million acres—much of it desert. Collier rejected the assumption that Indians' survival depended on their assimilation into white culture. He altered the government boarding schools' curriculum to include bicultural and bilingual education and eliminated military dress and discipline.

Collier's ideas came to fruition in the 1934 Indian Reorganization Act, which recognized the autonomy of Indian tribes, did away with the allotment program, and appropriated funds to help Indians add to their land holdings. It also provided for job and professional training programs as well as a system of agricultural and industrial credit. In keeping with Collier's goal of Indian self-government, each tribe decided whether to accept the terms of the Indian Reorganization Act. In the end, 181 tribes voted to accept the law, while 77 opted out of it.

22.3.2 Protest and Pressure from the Left and the Right

Despite these accomplishments, challenges to Roosevelt's New Deal took many forms. Although FDR strove to help businesses survive and remain profitable during the Depression, many business leaders continued to oppose the New Deal, charging that FDR was a dictator and that his program amounted to socialism. At the same time, FDR faced criticism from the left. Many people believed that Roosevelt's policies did not go far enough to ease the suffering caused by the economic crisis. Some thought that New Deal policies aimed at bolstering capitalism were ill-advised, and that capitalism itself was the problem. Disenchantment with capitalism drew many Americans to the cause of socialism and swelled the ranks of the small Communist party.

By 1934 and 1935, much of the pressure on Roosevelt came from workers, whose hopes that the NIRA would guarantee collective bargaining rights were dashed by the intransigence of employers. In 1934, nearly 1.5 million workers participated in 1,800 strikes. Although most African Americans supported FDR and the Democratic party during the Depression, between 3,000 and 4,000 members of the black community of Birmingham, Alabama, joined the Communist party and related organizations during the 1930s. One successful effort at biracial organizing occurred in the Arkansas delta in 1934. The Southern Tenant Farmers' Union (STFU) brought together black and white tenants and sharecroppers to fight for better working conditions.

In addition to the communists, socialists, labor unions, and grassroots organizations that sprang up all over the country, a number of individuals proposed alternatives to Roosevelt's program and gained large followings. The most influential of these were Dr. Francis Townsend, Father Charles E. Coughlin, and Senator Huey P. Long. In 1934, Townsend, a retired physician and health commissioner from Long Beach, California, introduced an idea for a pension plan that sparked a nationwide grassroots movement. Townsend proposed a 2 percent national sales tax that would fund a pension of $200 a month for Americans over age 60. The **Townsend Plan** became hugely popular, especially among elderly Americans. In 1936, a national survey indicated that half of all Americans favored the plan. Though the plan was never implemented, the groundswell

Townsend Plan
A proposal by Dr. Francis Townsend in 1934 for a 2 percent national sales tax that would fund a guaranteed pension of $200 per month for Americans older than age 60.

of support that it generated probably hastened the development and passage of the old-age insurance system contained in the 1935 Social Security Act.

Coughlin also inspired a huge following. A Catholic priest, he served as pastor of a small church outside Detroit, Michigan. He began to broadcast his sermons on the radio, using his magnetic personality to address political as well as religious issues. Soon he became a media phenomenon, broadcasting through twenty-six radio stations to an audience estimated at 40 million. The "Radio Priest" called for a redistribution of wealth and attacked Wall Street, international bankers, and the evils of capitalism. But his message turned from social justice populism to right-wing bigotry. His virulent anti-Semitism and admiration for the fascist regimes of Adolf Hitler in Germany and Benito Mussolini in Italy drove away many of his followers. By 1940, Coughlin had ceased broadcasting and abandoned all political activities, under orders of the Catholic Church.

Huey P. Long was among the most powerful, and colorful, politicians of the era. He rose from modest origins to become a lawyer and a public service commissioner. In 1928, Long won the governorship of Louisiana. His progressive leadership inspired tremendous loyalty, especially among poor workers and farmers. He did more for the underprivileged people of Louisiana than any other governor. He expanded the state's infrastructure; developed social services; built roads, hospitals, and schools; and changed the tax code to place a greater burden on corporations and the wealthy. Unlike many other southern politicians, his public statements were free of racial slurs. But his ambition had no bounds, and he used any means to accumulate power.

In 1932, Long resigned the governorship and won election to the U.S. Senate. Soon, he gained a huge national following. Initially he supported FDR, but by 1933 he had broken with the president and forged his own political movement based on his Share-Our-Wealth Plan. Giving voice to many Americans' resentment toward "wealthy pluto-crats," Long advocated a radical redistribution of the nation's wealth. He called for new taxes on the wealthy and proposed to guarantee a minimum annual income of $2,500 for all those in need. As he put it, "How many men ever went to a barbecue and would let one man take off the table what was intended for nine-tenths of the people to eat? The only way you'll ever be able to feed the balance of the people is to make that man come back and bring back some of the grub he ain't got no business with." By 1935, he was planning to challenge FDR in the next presidential election. But he never had the chance. In September 1935, the son-in-law of one of his vanquished political opponents assassinated him.

Eleanor Roosevelt also pushed FDR to the left, particularly on the issue of civil rights. Although the president was reluctant to support an anti-lynching bill in Congress for fear of alienating Southern white voters, the First Lady campaigned vigorously against lynching. When the Daughters of the American Revolution (DAR) denied African American opera star Marian Anderson the right to perform at Constitution Hall in Washington, D.C., Eleanor promptly resigned from the DAR in protest and arranged for Anderson to perform at the Lincoln Memorial on Easter Sunday 1939, where a huge audience stood in the cold to hear her sing.

22.3.3 The Second New Deal

FDR was careful not to alienate southern Democrats by cultivating African American voters. However, he did reach out to industrial workers. In the spring of 1935, Congress passed the National Labor Relations Act, also known as the Wagner Act, which guaranteed collective bargaining and gave a huge boost to labor unions.

Also in 1935, Congress passed the Social Security Act, perhaps the most important and far-reaching of all New Deal programs. The act established a system of old-age pensions, unemployment insurance, and welfare benefits for dependent children and the disabled. The framework of the Social Security Administration shaped the welfare system for the remainder of the century. But the welfare state established by the Social

Table 22.2 KEY NEW DEAL LEGISLATION, 1933–1938

Year	Act or Agency	Key Provisions
1933	Emergency Banking Act	Reopened banks under government supervision
	Civilian Conservation Corps (CCC)	Employed young men in reforestation, flood control, road construction, and soil erosion control projects
	Federal Emergency Relief Act (FERA)	Provided federal funds for state and local relief efforts
	Agricultural Adjustment Act (AAA)	Granted farmers direct payments for reducing crop production; funds for payment provided by a processing tax, later declared unconstitutional
	Farm Mortgage Act	Provided funds to refinance farm mortgages
	Tennessee Valley Authority (TVA)	Constructed dams and power projects and developed the economy of a seven-state area in the Tennessee River Valley
	Home Owners' Loan Corporation	Provided funds for refinancing home mortgages of nonfarm homeowners
	National Industrial Recovery Act (NIRA)	Established a series of fair competition codes; created National Recovery Administration (NRA) to write, coordinate, and implement these codes; NIRA's Section 7(a) guaranteed labor's right to organize (act later declared unconstitutional)
	Public Works Administration (PWA)	Sought to increase employment and business activity by funding road construction, building construction, and other projects
	Federal Deposit Insurance Corporation (FDIC)	Insured individual bank deposits
	Civil Works Administration (CWA)	Provided federal jobs for the unemployed
1934	Securities and Exchange Act	Created Securities and Exchange Commission (SEC) to regulate trading practices in stocks and bonds according to federal laws
	Indian Reorganization Act	Restored ownership of tribal lands to Native Americans; provided funds for job training and a system of agricultural and industrial credit
	Federal Housing Administration (FHA)	Insured loans provided by banks for the building and repair of houses
1935	Works Progress Administration (WPA)	Employed more than 8 million people to repair roads, build bridges, and work on other projects
	National Youth Administration (NYA)	WPA program that provided job training for unemployed youths and part-time jobs for students in need
	Federal One	WPA program that provided financial assistance for writers, artists, musicians, and actors
	National Labor Relations Act (Wagner Act)	Recognized the right of employees to join labor unions and to bargain collectively, reinstating the provisions of NIRA's Section 7(a); created the National Labor Relations Board (NLRB) to enforce laws against unfair labor practices
	Social Security Act	Created a system of social insurance that included unemployment compensation and old-age survivors' insurance; paid for by a joint tax on employers and employees
1938	Fair Labor Standards Act	Established a minimum wage of 25 cents an hour and a standard work week of 44 hours for businesses engaged in interstate commerce

Security Act left out many of the most needy by establishing a two-track system of welfare. One track provided workers with unemployment insurance and support in their old age (the Social Security program). But Social Security did not cover domestics, seasonal or part-time workers, agricultural laborers, or housewives. The other track made matching funds available to states to provide relief for the needy, mostly dependent women and children with no means of support. Unlike Social Security, which was provided to all retired workers regardless of their circumstances, relief programs, which came to be known as "welfare," were administered according to need.

The architects of this welfare system included many women who had been active reformers, such as Eleanor Roosevelt. These advocates hoped to protect women and children from the destitution that almost certainly resulted if a male breadwinner lost his job, deserted his family, or died. The system presumed that a man ordinarily earned a **family wage** that let him support his wife and children and that women were necessarily economically dependent on men. Thus, a deeply entrenched gender system prevailed through the 1930s. As a result, some—though not all—male breadwinners received benefits like Social Security. Impoverished women and children, on the other hand, received public charity. These payments were usually meager, not enough to lift a woman and her children out of poverty.

Because there were no nationally established guidelines on how to distribute welfare funds, states could determine who received assistance. As a result, the Social

family wage
A level of income sufficient for an individual worker, usually a man, to support a spouse and family through a single salary.

Security Act did little to assist African Americans, especially in the South, where black women were deliberately excluded by local authorities who preferred to maintain a pool of cheap African American labor rather than to provide relief for black families.

In 1935, Congress allocated the huge sum of nearly $5 billion for the Emergency Relief Appropriation. Roosevelt used a significant portion of the money to expand his public works program. By executive order, he established the Works Progress Administration (WPA), which provided millions of jobs for the unemployed. The project mandated that WPA jobs would make a contribution to public life and would not compete with private business. The jobs included building streets, highways, bridges, and public buildings; restoring forests; clearing slums; and extending electricity to rural areas. The WPA National Youth Administration gave work to nearly 1 million students.

The most effective WPA program was Federal One, which provided financial support for writers, musicians, artists, and actors. The Federal Theater Project, under the direction of Hallie Flanagan, former head of Vassar College's Experimental Theater, became an arena for experimental community-based theater. The Federal Theater Project included sixteen black theater units. Federal One supported thousands of artists and brought the arts to a wide public audience through government-funded murals on public buildings, community-theater productions, local orchestras, and the like.

The New Deal did not reach everyone. New Deal programs were geared toward full-time industrial workers, most of whom were white men. Domestic workers, Mexican migrant laborers, black and white sharecroppers, Chinese and Japanese truck farmers—all were among those ineligible for Social Security, minimum wages and maximum hours, unemployment insurance, and other New Deal benefits. But the New Deal established the national welfare state and provided assistance and security to millions of working people along with disabled, dependent, and elderly Americans. Such sweeping programs also solidified Roosevelt's popularity among the poor, workers, and much of the middle class.

22.3.4 FDR's Second Term

In the 1936 campaign, FDR claimed that the election was a battle between "the millions who never had a chance" and "organized money." He boasted that the "forces of selfishness and of lust for power" had united against him: "They are unanimous in their *hate* for *me—and I welcome their hatred*." His strategy paid off. Roosevelt won the election by a landslide of more than 60 percent of the popular vote. His strongest support came from the lower ends of the socioeconomic scale. The election also swept Democrats into Congress, giving them a decisive majority in both the House and the Senate.

With such a powerful mandate, Roosevelt was well positioned to promote a new legislative program. As his first major effort, he took on the Supreme Court. Dominated by conservative justices, the Court had invalidated some major legislation of Roosevelt's first term, including the AAA and the NIRA. Roosevelt feared that the justices would unravel the New Deal by striking down its progressive elements. To shift the balance of power on the Court, he proposed a measure that would let the president appoint one new justice for every one on the Court who had at least ten years of service and who did not retire within six months after turning 70.

Emboldened by his landslide victory, FDR believed that he could persuade Congress and the nation to go along with any plan he put forward, but he was mistaken. Many viewed his "court packing" plan as a threat to the fundamental separation of powers and feared that it would set a dangerous precedent. Powerful Republicans in Congress forged an alliance with conservative Democrats, mostly from the South, to defeat the plan. This informal alliance dominated Congress for the following two decades. The Court blunder cost Roosevelt considerable political capital and empowered his opponents. In the end, his plan proved unnecessary anyway. The Court did not undercut the New Deal. Within the next few years, retirements allowed Roosevelt to appoint several new justices who tipped the balance in his favor.

Table 22.3 THE ELECTION OF 1936

Candidate	Political Party	Popular Vote (%)	Electoral Vote
Franklin D. Roosevelt	Democratic	60.8	523
Alfred M. Landon	Republican	36.5	8
William Levine	Union	1.9	—

SOURCE: Historical Election Results, Electoral College, National Archives and Records Administration

22.4 A New Political Culture

How did the Depression and the New Deal change the way Americans of different backgrounds thought of themselves and their fellow citizens?

FDR continued to face strong opposition from conservatives on the right and from radicals, communists, and socialists on the left. But his political fortunes benefited from the emergence of a new and more inclusive national culture. This new Americanism emanated from the working class and found expression in the labor movement, popular culture, and the political coalition that came together in the Democratic party. These nationalizing forces cut across lines of class and region and occasionally challenged hierarchies of gender and race.

22.4.1 The Labor Movement

The labor insurgency that erupted during the 1930s demonstrated the need for a new national labor movement. The American Federation of Labor (AFL), restricted to skilled workers, left out most of the nation's less skilled industrial laborers. John L. Lewis of the United Mine Workers (UMW) and Sidney Hillman of the Amalgamated Clothing Workers of America were among several union leaders from a number of industries—including mining, steel, rubber, and automobile—who left the AFL to form a new broad-based labor organization, the Congress of Industrial Organizations (CIO). Hillman and others argued that higher wages were good for the economy by enabling workers to purchase consumer goods, which would then benefit industry as well as workers. Lewis and Hillman played key roles in the CIO's growth into a national force, but the impetus came from the workers themselves.

The CIO's first major action came in 1936 in Akron, Ohio, where workers in the rubber industry organized a **sit-down strike**, a new strategy whereby laborers stopped work and simply sat down, shutting down production and occupying plants so that strikebreakers could not enter and take their jobs. Sit-down strikes became a prominent labor tactic during 1936 when forty-eight strikes broke out across the nation. The numbers shot up the following year to about 500 strikes that lasted more than one day.

The most powerful demonstration of workers' discontent came in the automobile industry, where speed-ups of the assembly line drove workers to rebellion. In 1936, a spontaneous strike erupted against General Motors in Atlanta; it soon spread to Kansas City, Missouri; Cleveland, Ohio; and the main plants at Flint, Michigan. Two weeks into the strike, workers clashed with police. Frank Murphy, Michigan's pro-labor governor, refused to use National Guard troops against the strikers, and Roosevelt declined to send in federal troops.

Women as well as men participated actively in the Flint strike. Twenty-three-year-old Genora Johnson Dollinger, wife of a striker and mother of two young sons, organized 500 women into the Women's Emergency Brigade, made up primarily of strikers' wives, sisters, and girlfriends. Wearing red berets and armbands, they ran soup kitchens and first-aid stations. They also entered the fray when necessary, as when they broke plant windows so that the company could not use tear gas effectively against the strikers inside.

sit-down strike
A strategy employed by workers agitating for better wages and working conditions in which they stop working and simply sit down, thus ceasing production and preventing strikebreakers from entering a facility to assume their jobs.

LABOR UNREST, MINNEAPOLIS, MINNESOTA Some strikes became violent, as did this one in 1934 when police battled striking teamsters armed with pipes on the streets of Minneapolis.

National Archives and Records Administration

What does this photograph of strikers at war with the police suggest about the passion and determination of the striking workers and about the police called in to quell the disturbance?

The sit-down strike at Flint lasted 44 days and forced General Motors to recognize the United Auto Workers (UAW), which was a CIO union. The strike scored a clear victory for the workers and boosted the CIO's stature as a national union of industrial workers. Membership in the UAW quadrupled in the next year. Bowing to the formidable power of the national union in the wake of the UAW success, U.S. Steel conceded to the CIO even without a strike, ending its policy of hiring nonunion workers and signing an agreement with the Steel Workers' Organizing Committee. The CIO brought together workers from all over the country. Most of its member unions were open to racial and ethnic minorities and women.

22.4.2 The New Deal Coalition

FDR's support of labor unions brought workers solidly into the Democratic fold. They joined a coalition that included voters who had never before belonged to the same party, particularly northern blacks and Southern whites. Although African Americans in the South were disenfranchised, blacks in the North had voted Republican for 60 years, loyal

FAMILY OF MEXICAN AMERICANS ON THE ROAD DURING THE DEPRESSION This Mexican American family took to the road as did thousands of others, searching for work and a better life. Some joined other families down on their luck in shanty towns. But nearly half a million were sent back to Mexico. High unemployment led to deportations of Mexicans and Mexican Americans whose labor was no longer needed. For those who stayed, life was difficult. Most New Deal programs did not reach Mexican American laborers because they worked on farms rather than in factories.

Dorothea Lange/Library of Congress Prints and Photographs Division [LC-USZ62-131733]

What does this photograph of Mexican American migrants, stopped on the roadside with tire trouble, reveal about the conditions of life facing this family?

to the party of Lincoln. In a dramatic shift, black voters in northern cities overwhelmingly backed FDR in 1936 and remained in the Democratic party for the rest of the century.

Other racial and ethnic minorities also joined the New Deal coalition. In 1939, Latinos organized their first national civil rights assembly, El Congreso de Pueblos de Habla Española (the Spanish-Speaking People's Congress), which opened with a congratulatory telegram from Eleanor Roosevelt. Immigrants from Europe and their children also became loyal Democratic voters.

In spite of this diverse coalition, many Americans remained bitterly opposed to FDR. On the left, socialists and communists criticized the New Deal for patching up capitalism rather than transforming the economic system. On the right, conservative business leaders despised Roosevelt for the constraints he placed on business and the intrusion of the government into the economy. Critics from the political right considered the New Deal akin to communism. In 1938, Congress created the House Un-American Activities Committee (HUAC), chaired by Martin Dies of Texas. Formed ostensibly to investigate American fascists and Nazis in the United States, the committee instead pursued liberal and leftist groups throughout World War II and the Cold War.

22.4.3 A New Americanism

The New Deal coalition reflected not only Roosevelt's popularity but also a new and more inclusive American identity. An expanding mass culture fostered this sensibility, spread largely through the national media. It is no accident that Franklin Roosevelt found his way into the homes and hearts of Americans through his "fireside chats" over the radio; his mastery of that technology made him the first media-savvy president. During the 1930s, 70 percent of all households owned a radio—more than the number that owned a telephone. The motion-picture industry also expanded into small towns across the country. Talking films brought vernacular speech and a variety of accents to diverse audiences who gathered in neighborhood theaters.

Movie plots portrayed the triumph of common people over the rich and powerful and celebrated love across class and ethnic lines. Although racial stereotypes persisted in motion pictures throughout the decade, notable exceptions, such as Will Rogers's films, featured strong minority characters. Popular movies also challenged traditional gender and class hierarchies. Female stars, such as Katharine Hepburn, Rosalind Russell, Bette Davis, and Mae West, portrayed feisty, independent women.

New sports celebrities also embodied the nation's diversity. Baseball star Joe DiMaggio, son of an Italian immigrant fisherman, became a national hero. African American boxer Joe Louis, the "Brown Bomber," who was born into a sharecropper family in Alabama, became heavyweight champion of the world at age 23. In 1938, when Louis fought German boxer Max Schmeling at Yankee Stadium, the fight attracted 70,000 fans and grossed more than $1 million. When the black fighter knocked out Schmeling in the first round, he seemed to strike a blow for America against Hitler's Nazi Germany.

A number of women also became heroes in the 1930s for their daring exploits, personal courage, and physical prowess. Athletes like tennis champion Helen Wills and Olympic track star and brilliant golfer "Babe" (Mildred) Didrikson (later Zaharias) greatly expanded the popularity of women's sports. Renowned aviator Amelia Earhart, the first woman to fly solo across the Atlantic, devoted her life to advancing both feminism and commercial aviation. When her plane disappeared during an attempted round-the-world flight in 1937, many of her admirers were so convinced of her invincibility that they refused to believe she had died. Even today, people still speculate about her fate.

Conclusion

Before the New Deal, people suffered the fluctuations of the market economy with no recourse beyond the assistance of kin, communities, and charities. Older Americans who could no longer work had no government-guaranteed pensions and often faced poverty in old age. Bank failures could wipe away life savings. Unemployment could mean starvation for a worker's family. In an effort to provide a safety net for citizens in these circumstances, the New Deal set in place a welfare state that established the principle of government responsibility for the well-being of vulnerable citizens. It provided Social Security for the elderly, unemployment compensation for workers who had lost their jobs, minimum standards for hours and wages, and economic aid to women and children who had no means of support. New Deal legislation also established national economic regulations and regulatory agencies as well as the right of workers to unionize and engage in collective bargaining. These government protections offered many Americans an unprecedented level of economic security.

Most New Deal policies protected factory workers in large companies. The safety net did not extend to many of the neediest Americans, including Mexican American migrant workers, African American and white sharecroppers, seasonal agricultural laborers, and domestic workers. FDR was reluctant to press for antilynching legislation for fear of alienating southern congressmen who still retained enormous power. Although FDR's conservative opponents accused him of socialist leanings, the New Deal actually rescued and shored up capitalism.

The New Deal, with both its limited reach and its extension of government programs, was the Roosevelt administration's response to a global economic crisis. With the exception of the communist Soviet Union, which had already abandoned capitalism, all industrialized nations responded to the Depression by increasing the role of the state in the economy. Italy, Germany, and Japan moved to fascism and the nearly total state direction of the economy, while Britain and France established welfare states that would become more fully developed after World War II. The U.S. system of social welfare was not as extensive and inclusive as those that emerged in some western European democracies. But it was part of a larger trend toward government intervention in the economy and greater protections for citizens.

Chapter Review

22.1   The Great Depression

What caused the Great Depression, and how did it affect ordinary Americans?

Although the country appeared prosperous in the 1920s, poverty was widespread. Many people bought consumer goods on credit and ended up with bills they could not pay. By the end of the 1920s, wealth was concentrated at the top. Ordinary Americans suffered from widespread unemployment and hardship throughout the 1930s.

22.2 Presidential Responses to the Depression

How did Presidents Hoover and Roosevelt respond to the Great Depression?

President Hoover increased government spending for public works, and he tried to balance the budget, raise taxes, and cut spending. However, his efforts were insufficient, and his strategy made conditions worse. President Roosevelt established several new programs that comprised the "New Deal" in an effort to address the crisis.

22.3 The New Deal

What was the New Deal, and how did it develop over time?

The New Deal was Roosevelt's wide-ranging program of government investment in jobs, assistance for Americans who were suffering, and establishment of the welfare state. His agenda became more progressive after 1935 with programs that provided a safety net for industrial workers.

22.4 A New Political Culture

How did the Depression and the New Deal change the way Americans of different backgrounds thought of themselves and their fellow citizens?

The Depression was a time of widespread hardship, yet common suffering of Americans all over the country led to a more inclusive national culture. This new sense of American identity cut across lines of class and region, and it even began to level hierarchies of ethnicity, race, and gender.

Timeline

1931	Nine young African Americans (the "Scottsboro Boys") arrested on charges of rape
1932	Black unemployment rate reaches 50 percent Bonus Army marches on Washington, D.C.
1933	Initial New Deal ("Hundred Days") legislation: AAA, FERA, CCC, TVA, NIRA
1934	Indian Reorganization Act
1935	Congress of Industrial Organizations (CIO) organized
1936	Hoover Dam on Colorado River completed, creating Lake Mead
1937	FDR's court-packing plan fails
1939	First meeting of El Congreso de Pueblos de Habla Española

Glossary

fireside chats The broadcasts by President Franklin Delano Roosevelt during which he spoke directly to American families, often gathered around a radio in their living rooms.

capitalism The now almost worldwide economic system of private ownership of property and profit-seeking corporations.

welfare state A nation in which the government provides a "safety net" of entitlements and benefits for citizens unable to economically provide for themselves.

hobos Migrant workers or poor and homeless vagrants who traveled on trains from location to location, usually in search of employment.

Dust Bowl The plains regions of Oklahoma, Texas, Colorado, New Mexico, and Kansas affected by severe drought in the 1930s.

Okie Migrant from Oklahoma who left the state during the Dust Bowl period in search of work.

Second New Deal The agenda of policies and programs initiated by President Franklin Delano Roosevelt beginning in 1935 that was intended to improve the lot of American workers while simultaneously preserving the capitalist system.

Townsend Plan A proposal by Dr. Francis Townsend in 1934 for a 2 percent national sales tax that would fund a guaranteed pension of $200 per month for Americans older than age 60.

family wage A level of income sufficient for an individual worker, usually a man, to support a spouse and family through a single salary.

sit-down strike A strategy employed by workers agitating for better wages and working conditions in which they stop working and simply sit down, thus ceasing production and preventing strikebreakers from entering a facility to assume their jobs.

Chapter 23
Global Conflict: World War II, 1937–1945

FRANZ STEINER, CAMP SURVIVOR In this photograph taken just after his release from Dachau, Franz Steiner simply stands and waits. Starved prison laborers were fed boiled potatoes to fatten them up before they were released so that their emaciated bodies would not be visible to the outside world. Later, as the war progressed, the Nazis no longer made any effort to keep up appearances.

Photograph courtesy of Elaine Tyler May

What do Steiner's facial expression, demeanor, and body language suggest about his emotions upon his release from Dachau?

Contents and Focus Questions

23.1 The United States Enters the War
Why were most Americans initially opposed to entering the war, and what changed their minds?

23.2 Total War
What were the major differences for the United States between the war in Europe and the war in the Pacific?

23.3 The Home Front
In what ways did World War II alter life for the Americans who remained at home?

23.4 The End of the War
What alternatives were available for ending the war in Europe and in the Pacific, and why did the United States choose the strategies it employed to end the war?

By what forces of history would an educated European Jew end up imprisoned, released, and wandering the globe until he ended up in the United States?

In 1938, Franz Steiner was a young man with a newly minted law degree. A talented artist and musician, he was well-educated and spoke several languages. But then everything changed when he was rounded up by the Nazis and taken from his home in Vienna, Austria, to the Dachau concentration camp. There he was imprisoned to provide slave labor for the Germans.

Dachau was not yet an official Nazi death camp in 1938, but imprisoned Jews who were weak or ill perished nonetheless. Franz was lucky: he was relatively healthy, and he had a sponsor in the United States who agreed to take him in. But the quota of Jews allowed to enter the United States was already filled for the year. In spite of the horror unfolding in Europe, American officials granted few exceptions to the immigration restrictions put into place in the 1920s.

With the doors to the United States closed, Franz secured a ticket on a French ship bound for Shanghai, China, an open city that required no entry visa. Because he had a ticket to leave, he was released from Dachau. After a year in Shanghai, Franz was finally allowed to enter the United States, where he became a citizen. But he remained worried about his parents and his brother. It was not until after the war that Franz learned that his parents had died in a death camp, along with millions of other Jews. His brother also died, trying to flee with some friends, but the Germans finally caught up with them and shot them all, dumping them in a makeshift grave.

* * * * *

The story of Franz Steiner and his family is one small piece of the global saga of disruption, dislocation, loss, suffering, death, and survival during World War II. The enormous scale of destruction was unlike that of any previous war. At least 55 million people died, including 25 million in the Soviet Union, 10 million in China, and 6 million in Poland. In the Holocaust, Nazi Germany's campaign of genocide, 6 million European Jews perished along with thousands of Romani (Gypsies), Poles, mentally and physically disabled people, homosexuals, and others deemed "racially inferior."

The war also had a tremendous impact on countries under colonial rule. Germany's bombardment of England and occupation of France, Holland, and Belgium weakened these countries' hold over their vast colonies. Japan's defeat of the American, British, Dutch, and French forces in Southeast Asia from 1940 to 1942 shocked the Western powers and ended white rule in the region, setting in motion a wave of decolonization in Asia and Africa after the war.

The United States was the only major combatant that did not suffer massive destruction on its home territory. Although the Soviet Union carried the largest burden of fighting the war and suffered the highest losses, millions of Americans also fought, and many died in the conflict.

Military service had a leveling effect on social relations, as soldiers came together from all classes and ethnic groups. The vast majority of the troops—more than 85 percent—were white men from a wide variety of backgrounds. Soldiers of color generally fought in segregated units, but their battlefield successes and sacrifices gave them a sense of belonging to the nation and fueled postwar movements for equality and civil rights.

23.1 The United States Enters the War

Why were most Americans initially opposed to entering the war, and what changed their minds?

During the 1930s, the rise of **fascism** and militarism in Italy, Germany, and Japan created a terrible dilemma for Americans. Disillusioned by World War I and preoccupied with the hardships of the Great Depression, they disagreed strongly about how to respond to overt aggression in Africa, Europe, and Asia. The ensuing "Great Debate" became a turning point in the nation's relationship with the outside world. Mobilizing for the enormous crusade of World War II gave rise to a unity of purpose that lasted throughout the war and into the postwar era.

fascism
A form of right-wing dictatorship exalting nation and race above the individual.

23.1.1 Fascist Aggression in Europe and Asia

In the 1930s, Depression-era Americans grappled with domestic problems and avoided entanglements abroad. But they found it difficult to ignore events in Europe and Asia. In Italy, Spain, and Germany, where a weak economy and high unemployment created political unrest, fascist leaders rose to power with strong popular support. These new leaders promised economic recovery through strengthening militaries and national expansion. They also encouraged intense nationalist sentiments, urging people to identify strongly with the state. Fascist governments were antidemocratic, antiparliamentary, and frequently antisemitic. These governments generally ruled by police surveillance, coercion, and terror.

Germany emerged as the most powerful fascist state in Europe. After its defeat in World War I and a severe economic depression in the 1920s, Adolf Hitler's National Socialist (Nazi) party won broad support in the weakened country. On January 30, 1933, Hitler became chancellor of Germany. Extolling fanatical nationalism and the racial superiority of "Aryan" Germans, Hitler blamed Jews for Germany's problems. He began a campaign of terror against Jews, homosexuals, suspected communists, and anyone else he saw as promoting "un-German" ideas. Hitler vowed to unite all German-speaking peoples into a new empire, the "Third Reich."

The fascist governments forged alliances to increase their power and launched campaigns of aggression and expansion. In 1935, Italy invaded Ethiopia, the sole independent African nation. The following year, Nazi troops occupied the Rhineland, in the western region of Germany, in violation of the Versailles agreement. Hitler and Mussolini signed the **Axis Pact**, and Japan forged an alliance with Germany. Soon after that, civil war erupted in Spain. Hitler and Mussolini extended aid to the fascist General Francisco Franco, who was trying to overthrow Spain's republican government.

Axis Pact
An alliance among Germany, Italy, and Japan during World War II.

Although Spanish republicans appealed to antifascist governments for help in the fight against Franco, only the Soviet Union came to their assistance. The United States maintained an official policy of neutrality, but many on the left, including large numbers of writers and intellectuals, championed the beleaguered Spanish government and denounced the fascists. Some joined Soviet-organized international forces to fight against Franco. The American volunteers were known as the Abraham Lincoln Brigades.

In the spring and summer of 1938, Hitler annexed Austria to the Third Reich and then demanded that the Sudetenland be turned over to Germany. After World War I, this German-speaking area had become part of the newly formed Czechoslovakia.

In September, the leaders of France and Britain met with Hitler in Munich and agreed to let him have the Sudetenland in return for his promise that he would seek no more territory. Soviet leader Josef Stalin feared that the anticommunist leaders of France and Britain were trying to turn Hitler's aggression toward the Soviet Union. To prevent that possibility, Stalin signed a nonaggression pact with Hitler. Eventually, Hitler broke all his promises. Throughout the war and after, the Munich meeting became the symbol of "appeasement," a warning that compromise with the enemy leads only to disaster.

In 1939, with the help of the Soviet Union and in violation of the Munich agreement, Germany invaded Poland, which fell quickly. At that point, Britain and France declared war on Germany. That same year, Madrid finally fell to Franco's forces.

By 1940, Hitler was sweeping through Europe, invading Denmark, Norway, Holland, Belgium, Luxembourg, and then France. In just six weeks, the Nazis had seized most of western Europe. Hitler then turned his forces on Great Britain. In the summer and fall of 1940, German raids on British air bases nearly destroyed the British Royal Air Force (RAF). Hitler ordered the bombing of London and other English cities, attacking civilians day and night in what came to be called the Battle of Britain.

In the Far East, events had taken an equally alarming turn. Nationalistic militarists gained control of the Japanese government in Tokyo and began a course of expansion. In 1931–1932, Japanese troops occupied the large Chinese province of Manchuria. Five years later, the Japanese launched a full-scale war against China. The United States extended aid to China and discontinued trade with Japan. In 1940, Japan joined Germany and Italy in the Axis alliance and invaded the French colony of Indochina.

23.1.2 The Great Debate over Intervention

In the mid-1930s, the overwhelming majority of Americans opposed intervention in foreign conflicts. Congress passed the Neutrality Acts of 1935, 1936, and 1937, outlawing arms sales or loans to nations at war and forbidding Americans from traveling on the ships of belligerent powers. When Japan invaded China in 1937, FDR refused to comply with the provisions of the latest Neutrality Act, on the technicality that neither combatant had officially declared war. By creatively interpreting the law, he was able to offer loans to the embattled Chinese. Roosevelt felt strongly that the United States should actively help to resist the Axis powers.

America First Committee

A group that opposed Roosevelt's efforts to intervene in World War II against the Axis powers.

The largest organization to oppose Roosevelt's effort was the **America First Committee**. With 450 chapters, the group claimed several hundred thousand members, including famed aviator Charles Lindbergh. Centered largely in the Midwest, the America Firsters included some active Nazi supporters. Nevertheless, in 1940, the popular FDR became the first president elected to a third term. Soon, public opinion began to shift. Americans were shocked when Hitler swiftly conquered much of Europe. News of the German occupation of France and the intense bombardment of England in the Battle of Britain bolstered FDR's efforts to take action. In his "Four Freedoms" speech to Congress in January 1941, FDR cited the freedoms he considered necessary for the postwar world—freedom of speech, of worship, from want, and from fear—and pledged his support for England against the Nazis. A few months later, Congress approved the Lend-Lease agreement to lend, rather than sell, munitions to the Allies.

Table 23.1 THE ELECTION OF 1940

Candidate	Political Party	Popular Vote (%)	Electoral Vote
Franklin D. Roosevelt	Democratic	54.8	449
Wendell L. Willkie	Republican	44.8	82

SOURCE: Historical Election Results, Electoral College, National Archives and Records Administration

When Hitler broke his promise to Stalin and attacked the Soviet Union in June 1941, FDR extended Lend-Lease to the Soviets. During the summer, FDR and British Prime Minister Winston Churchill met on a ship off the coast of Newfoundland to develop a joint declaration known as the Atlantic Charter. The two leaders announced that the United States and Britain sought no new territories, they recognized the right of all peoples to choose their own form of government, and they called for international **free trade** and navigation. Realizing the possible cost of losing colonies, Churchill retreated from the global implications of the charter, while Roosevelt walked a fine line between contradicting Churchill and supporting the idea of empire. Nevertheless, the charter emboldened anticolonial activists around the world.

free trade
International economic relations characterized by multinational investment and a reduction or elimination of tariffs.

23.1.3 The Attack on Pearl Harbor

For nearly a decade, tensions had been mounting between the United States and Japan as American leaders tried to contain Japan's expansion in Asia. Roosevelt assumed that a strong U.S. military presence in the Pacific would persuade Japan's premier, General Hideki Tojo, to avoid a confrontation with the United States. When Japan continued its aggression in Asia, FDR froze Japanese assets in the United States, putting trade with Japan under presidential control. This move, he hoped, would bring Japan to the bargaining table. Instead, on November 25, the Japanese dispatched aircraft carriers toward Hawaii.

Although U.S. intelligence sources had broken the codes with which the Japanese encrypted messages about their war plans, they did not realize that the Japanese intended to strike Hawaii. At 7:55 a.m. on December 7, Japanese planes swooped over Pearl Harbor and bombed the naval base. The assault caught the American forces completely off guard and destroyed most of the U.S. Pacific fleet. Only a few aircraft carriers that were out at sea survived. Two hours after the attack on Pearl Harbor, the Japanese also struck the main U.S. base at Clark Field in the Philippines, destroying half of the U.S. Air Force in the Far East.

THE ATTACK ON PEARL HARBOR On December 7, 1941, the Japanese launched a surprise attack on the U.S. naval base at Pearl Harbor, Hawaii. The attack brought the United States immediately into World War II and was the only time that the war came to American soil.

AFP/Getty ImagesNewscom

What does this photograph reveal about the nature of the attack on Pearl Harbor, and why would the day "live in infamy," as President Roosevelt told the nation? Why, also, were Japanese Americans the only U.S. citizens interned solely because of their ancestry?

When the smoke cleared, 2,323 American service personnel were dead. President Roosevelt somberly told millions of Americans gathered around their radios that the day of the attack would "live in infamy." Congress immediately declared war against Japan. Three days later, Germany and Italy declared war against the United States. Most former doubters about American intervention now joined the war effort.

23.1.4 Japanese American Relocation

The assault on Pearl Harbor sparked widespread rumors along the U.S. West Coast that Japanese and Japanese Americans living there planned to sabotage the war effort. Although no charges of criminal activity or treason were ever brought against any Japanese Americans, powerful white farming interests eager to eradicate Japanese American competition pushed for an evacuation.

Not everyone supported the internment idea. U.S. Attorney General Francis Biddle protested that there was "no reason" for a mass relocation. J. Edgar Hoover, director of the FBI, also opposed the plan, arguing that it reflected "hysteria and lack of judgment." Nevertheless, in February 1942, Roosevelt signed Executive Order 9066, which authorized the removal of 110,000 Japanese and Japanese Americans from the West Coast.

HIRANO FAMILY, COLORADO RIVER RELOCATION CENTER, POSTON, ARIZONA The family pictured here was among thousands of loyal citizens of Japanese ancestry removed from their homes on the West Coast and relocated to internment camps. Here, the Hirano family, George, Hisa, and Yasbei (left to right), pose at the Colorado River Relocation Center in Poston, Arizona. Hisa holds a photo of her son, an American soldier, who is off fighting the war. Even as Japanese American soldiers fought against racist foes abroad, the U.S. Supreme Court upheld the conviction of U.S.-born Fred Korematsu, who defied a relocation order requiring him to submit to a forced move away from his Oakland, California, home.

National Archives and Record Administration

What does this relocation center photograph indicate about the national identity and patriotism of the Hiranos and of other Japanese American families just like them?

Of those, 70,000 were *Nisei*, native-born American citizens. Families received at most a week's notice to evacuate their homes and move to prisonlike camps surrounded by barbed wire and guarded by armed soldiers. There were ten such camps in seven states, most of them located in arid, desolate spots in the West. At the camps, internees lived in makeshift wooden barracks, where entire families crowded into one room.

While the internment experience alienated some Japanese Americans, fully 33,000 joined the armed services—including 1,200 who enlisted from the internment camps—and proved their patriotism on the battlefield. In the Pacific, their knowledge of the Japanese language proved critical in translating intercepted Japanese military documents. They also served ably in Europe, suffering huge casualties. The Japanese Americans of the 442nd Regiment lost one-fourth of their soldiers in battles in North Africa and Italy. They suffered 800 casualties rescuing the Texan "Lost Battalion," 211 men surrounded by German troops in the Vosges Mountains of France. The U.S. government took its time acknowledging that the internment had been a grave injustice. The Supreme Court upheld the constitutionality of the policy, and Roosevelt would not rescind the evacuation order until after his reelection in 1944. The camps finally closed in 1945. All told, Japanese Americans lost property valued at $500 million. In 1988, Congress enacted legislation awarding restitution payments of $20,000 each to 60,000 surviving internees—a small gesture for American citizens whose only "crime" was their Japanese ancestry.

23.1.5 Foreign Nationals in the United States

Although Japanese Americans were the only U.S. citizens interned solely because of their ancestry, German and Italian nationals living in the United States were also subject to new regulations, and, in some cases, relocation and incarceration. The Smith Act of 1940 required all foreign-born residents to be registered and fingerprinted, and broadened the grounds for deportation.

Six hundred thousand Italians and 314,000 Germans living in the United States were subject to these requirements. Several hundred were deemed potentially dangerous and interned for the duration of the war. Approximately 10,000 Italian nationals were forced to relocate from their homes on the West Coast. A few hundred German and Italian immigrants who were naturalized U.S. citizens were also relocated from designated coastal areas.

23.1.6 Wartime Migrations

Even before the United States officially entered World War II, the conflict had begun to change the face of the nation. The sleepy town of Richmond, California, perched near the north end of San Francisco Bay, underwent a profound transformation when the nation stepped up war production. The town's mostly white population of 23,000 ballooned to 120,000 after industrialist Henry Kaiser constructed four shipyards there. The yards employed over 150,000 workers, more than one-fourth of them African American.

Many cities, however, were ill equipped to handle the influx of migrants. An estimated 60,000 African Americans moved into Chicago, causing an enormous housing crisis. Many newcomers lacked even a modicum of privacy as they crowded into basements and rooms rented from total strangers. Huge numbers of whites also came north, many leaving hardscrabble farms and hoping to prosper in booming war industries.

Wartime also saw new migration from abroad and a reversal of earlier immigration policies. Because of the alliance with China in the war against Japan, in 1943, Congress repealed the Chinese Exclusion Act, and migrants from China became eligible for citizenship for the first time. An executive agreement between the United States and Mexico created the ***bracero*** program, under which 300,000 Mexican laborers, mostly agricultural workers, came to rural areas like California's San Joaquin Valley. By the mid-1960s, nearly 5 million Mexicans had migrated north under the program.

braceros

Mexican nationals working in the United States in low-wage jobs as part of a temporary work program between 1942 and 1964. (The bracero program was established by an executive agreement between the presidents of Mexico and the United States, providing Mexican agricultural labor in the Southwest and the Pacific Northwest.)

23.2 Total War

What were the major differences for the United States between the war in Europe and the war in the Pacific?

World War II consisted of two wars: one centered in Europe and the other in the Pacific. Combatants in both conflicts engaged in total war—the targeting of civilian as well as military targets. Although hundreds of thousands of Americans died, those numbers were small compared to the millions of casualties in other countries involved in the war. Of all the combatants, only the United States escaped physical destruction on its own national soil (with the exception of Pearl Harbor). Coming out of the war physically unscathed, economically sound, and politically strong, the United States became the most prosperous and powerful nation in the world.

23.2.1 The Holocaust

While Americans who remained at home watched the fighting from afar, Europeans lived with war's horrors every day. None suffered this reality more intensely than the Jews. Hitler's war aims included conquering all of Europe and destroying European Jewry. Throughout the war, Nazi anti-Jewish policies escalated from persecution and officially sanctioned violence to imprisonment in concentration camps, slave labor, and ultimately Hitler's "Final Solution," genocide. Nazis developed increasingly efficient means of killing Jews. German firing squads shot large numbers of Jews after forcing them to dig their own graves. In the infamous Nazi death camps, guards herded prisoners into "shower rooms" that were actually gas chambers. The genocidal murder of 6 million Jews during World War II is known as the **Holocaust**.

Holocaust
The name given to the Nazi genocide against the Jews during World War II. Six million Jews were murdered.

American officials knew of the Nazi persecution of the Jews but did little to stop it. Throughout the 1930s, American Jewish groups pressured the Roosevelt administration to ease immigration laws to allow Jewish refugees to enter the country. But the United States raised the legal quota of Jewish immigrants only slightly.

When the Nazis began their policy of extermination in 1941, they tried to keep it a secret. U.S. State Department officials heard reports of the Holocaust but decided to keep the information quiet. Despite official silence, Rabbi Stephen S. Wise, a prominent American Jewish leader, heard the news and held a press conference in November 1942. But the American press, preoccupied with military events and reluctant to publish stories of atrocities without official verification, gave the Holocaust little coverage. Meanwhile, despite reports of Nazi genocide, the U.S. government turned away boatloads of Jewish refugees, sending them back to Germany to their deaths.

Nazi persecution of the Jews raised American sensitivity to racism but did little to diminish antisemitism within the United States. In fact, American hostility toward Jews reached new heights during World War II and exceeded the level of prejudice against any other group. In 1944, when asked to identify the greatest "menace" to the nation, 24 percent of Americans polled listed Jews—more than those who listed Germans, Japanese, radicals, Negroes, and foreigners. In Europe, American military strategists knew of the existence and location of Nazi death camps, but they chose not to try to bomb them or the railroad lines leading to the camps.

23.2.2 The War in Europe

The leaders of the Allied powers, including the United States, Britain, and the Soviet Union, had to develop a strategy to defeat the Axis powers. But the Allies did not always agree on how to conduct the war, and relations between the United States and the Soviet Union remained strained. Unable to fully overcome the hostility and suspicion that had marked their earlier encounters, leaders of both countries fought the war with postwar power considerations in mind.

Like the United States at Pearl Harbor, the Soviet Union suffered a shocking blow when Germany launched a surprise invasion in June 1941 in violation of the nonaggression pact Hitler had signed with Stalin in 1938. With the full might of the Nazi forces now concentrated against the Russians in eastern Europe, Soviet premier Joseph Stalin wanted the United States to open a second front in western Europe to divert the Nazis toward the west and relieve pressure on the Soviet Union. In May 1942, Roosevelt assured Stalin that the United States would support an Allied invasion across the English Channel into France. But the British prime minister, Winston Churchill, persuaded FDR to delay that dangerous maneuver and instead launch an invasion of French North Africa, which was controlled by the Nazi occupation forces in Vichy, France.

While the Allies turned their attention to North Africa, the Soviets singlehandedly forced the German army into retreat at Stalingrad, where fierce fighting lasted from August 1942 to January 1943. The Battle of Stalingrad was a major turning point in the war. Axis soldiers in North Africa also surrendered in May 1943. The following summer, the Allied forces overran the island of Sicily and moved into southern Italy. Italians overthrew Mussolini and opened communication with General Dwight D. Eisenhower, commander of the Allied forces in Europe. By 1944, the Allied forces reached Rome.

The long-awaited Allied invasion across the English Channel finally began on June 6, 1944, code named D-Day. At dawn, in the largest amphibious landing in history, more than 4,000 Allied ships descended on the French beaches at Normandy. As the troops splashed onto shore, they met a barrage of German fire. Many thousands died on the beach that day. Over the next ten days, more than 1 million soldiers landed at Normandy, along with 50,000 vehicles and more than 100,000 tons of supplies, opening the way for an advance into Nazi-occupied France.

In the months after D-Day, the western Allies liberated Paris and went on to defeat the Germans in Belgium at the Battle of the Bulge, sending the Nazis into full retreat. The Allied armies then crossed the Rhine River and headed for Berlin. Eisenhower stopped his troops at the Elbe River to let Soviet troops take Berlin. Eisenhower hoped that giving the Soviets the final triumph would ease postwar relations with the Soviet Union—but he also wanted to save American lives. Huge numbers of Soviet troops died in the siege of Berlin, but the war in Europe was nearly over. With the Soviets approaching his bunker in April 1945, Hitler committed suicide. Germany surrendered on May 7, 1945—V-E (Victory in Europe) Day. FDR himself had died suddenly of a cerebral hemorrhage on April 12, 1945.

[Handwritten margin note: The years leading to the end of the war the tensions between the USA and Soviet Union increased]

23.2.3 The War in the Pacific

As the conflict in Europe came to an end, the war in the Pacific continued to rage. Following the attack on Pearl Harbor, Japan continued its Pacific conquests. In April 1942, General Douglas MacArthur, driven from the Philippines to Australia, left 12,000 American and 64,000 Filipino soldiers to surrender to the Japanese on the Bataan peninsula and the island of Corregidor. On the infamous "Bataan Death March" to the prison at Camp O'Donnell, the Japanese beat, tortured, and shot the sick and starving troops. As many as 10,000 men died on the march.

Now in control of Indochina, Thailand, the Philippines, and the chain of islands from Sumatra to Guadalcanal, Japan's military leaders planned to destroy what remained of the U.S. fleet. But MacArthur marshaled his forces and achieved a major victory in the Battle of the Coral Sea in May 1942. U.S. intelligence sources discovered that the Japanese were planning a massive assault on Midway Island, a naval base key to Hawaii's defense. Under the command of Admiral Chester Nimitz, the United States launched a surprise air strike on June 4, 1942, sinking four Japanese carriers, destroying 322 planes, and virtually eliminating Japanese offensive capabilities. Two months later, Nimitz's forces landed at Guadalcanal in the Solomon Islands, subduing the Japanese in five months of brutal fighting. Having seized the offensive, U.S. troops

Map 23.1 WORLD WAR II IN EUROPE

Along the eastern front of the war in Europe, Soviet troops did the bulk of the Allied fighting in Europe and sustained the highest casualties. The Battle of Stalingrad, in which Soviet troops finally drove back the Nazis after months of brutal fighting, was a major turning point in the war. The long-awaited Allied invasion across the English Channel finally began on June 6, 1944. It remained to be seen if the four freedoms that Roosevelt articulated in 1941—freedom of speech, freedom of worship, freedom from want, and freedom from fear—would have a lasting place in the postwar world after the fighting had ended.

D-DAY LANDING, OMAHA BEACH A photograph taken on D-Day, June 6, 1944, as U.S. troops waded to shore from their landing craft and faced German artillery fire on Omaha Beach. This is a rare surviving photograph from the initial Normandy invasion because so many of the photographers, along with thousands of soldiers, died at the scene.

National Archives and Record Administration[NWDNS-26-G-2343]

What does the photograph of the D-Day landing indicate about the nature of warfare in World War II?

continued toward Japan. MacArthur's forces took New Guinea, and, by February 1944, Nimitz secured the Marshall Islands and the Marianas. Next came Saipan, Iwo Jima, and Okinawa in the spring of 1945.

Crucial to these victories were the sensitive radio communications of a special U.S. Marine unit of Navajo **code talkers**. Keith Little was one of the young Navajo men who volunteered for military service. Little and 400 other Navajo Marines became part of a special unit that developed an intricate code, based on the Navajo language, to transmit top-secret information without risk of decoding by the Japanese. Ironically, many of these men had been educated in government boarding schools that forbade them to speak their native language. Now that same government called upon them to use their language to help win the war. The Navajo language was particularly well suited to code because very few people besides the Navajo knew it. In a process code named "Magic," the all-Navajo 382nd Platoon of the U.S. Marine Corps encoded and decoded sensitive military information almost instantly and flawlessly. In two days

code talkers

Navajo Marines who developed a code based on the Navajo language to transmit secret information.

Map 23.2 WORLD WAR II IN THE PACIFIC

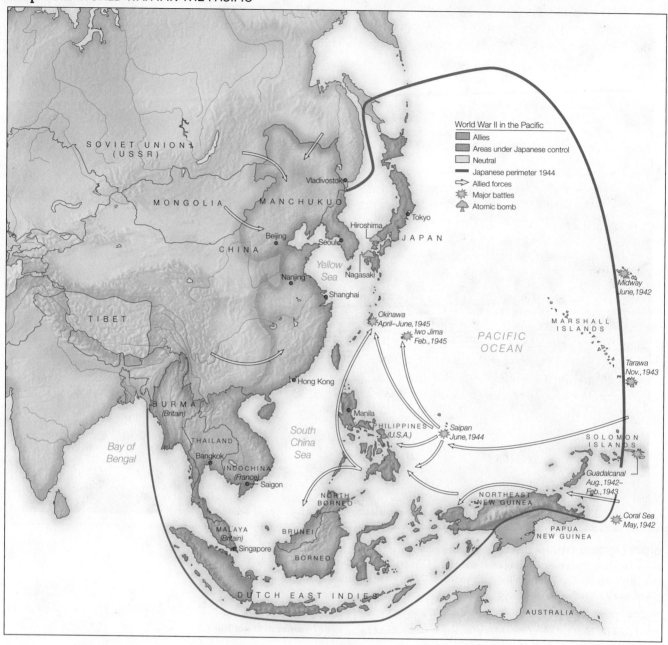

During World War II, the Japanese occupied vast territories in Asia and the Pacific. The Battle of Midway in 1942 was the first major victory for the United States in the Pacific and helped turn the tide of the war in favor of the Allies.

on the Pacific island of Iwo Jima, six code talkers transmitted more than 800 messages, working around the clock, without a single error. Signal Officer Major Howard Conner recalled, "Without the Navajos the Marines would never have taken Iwo Jima."

The war in the Pacific was particularly vicious. Racism on both sides fueled acts of extreme brutality. Japan's leaders believed that their racial superiority gave them a divine mission to conquer Asia. The Japanese tortured prisoners of war and civilians in their conquered lands. They tested biological weapons and conducted medical experiments on live subjects. Japanese troops forced Chinese and Korean women into sexual slavery, euphemistically calling them "comfort women."

Racial hostility also promoted American battlefield savagery. U.S. troops in the Pacific often killed the enemy instead of taking prisoners and desecrated the enemy dead with disrespect equal to that meted out by the Japanese on the bodies of their foes. War correspondent Ernie Pyle explained that "in Europe we felt that our enemies, horrible and deadly as they were, were still people. But . . . the Japanese were looked upon as something subhuman and repulsive, the way some people feel about cockroaches or mice."

23.3 The Home Front

In what ways did World War II alter life for the Americans who remained at home?

While war had the power to cause brutality on the battlefield, it also had the capacity to bring Americans from all regions and backgrounds together in shared service and sacrifice on the home front. Citizens made do with government-rationed basic staples, from food to gasoline. Automobile manufacturers stopped making cars and instead turned out tanks, jeeps, and other military vehicles. As able-bodied men left their jobs to fight the war, new work opportunities opened up for women as well as for disabled Americans. Cities and centers of war production brought together young women and men who found new opportunities for sexual experimentation, while gay men and lesbians discovered newly visible communities. The war raised expectations of women and minorities that they would achieve full inclusion in the American promise.

Many Americans hoped that the liberal spirit of the New Deal would endure during the war; others were eager for an end to what they perceived as Depression-era class conflict and hostility to business interests. To some extent, both sides got their wish. Full employment, the increasing strength of unions, and high taxes on the wealthy pleased New Deal liberals. Profit guarantees, freedom from antitrust actions, no-strike pledges, and low-cost imported labor gratified probusiness conservatives. And Roosevelt was elected to an unprecedented fourth term in 1944.

Table 23.2 THE ELECTION OF 1944

Candidate	Political Party	Popular Vote (%)	Electoral Vote
Franklin D. Roosevelt	Democratic	53.5	432
Thomas E. Dewey	Republican	46.0	99

SOURCE: Historical Election Results, Electoral College, National Archives and Records Administration

23.3.1 Propaganda and Building Morale

The United States, like all other major powers involved in the conflict, mounted a propaganda drive to promote support for the war effort. The Office of War Information (OWI) coordinated morale-boosting and censorship initiatives. Working in partnership with the motion picture industry and other media outlets, the OWI sponsored movies, radio programs, publications, and posters. These productions portrayed the war as a crusade to preserve the "American way of life" and encouraged American women and men to work in war industries, enlist in the armed forces, and purchase war bonds. Eric Johnston, head of the Motion Picture Producers' Association and FDR's business adviser, insisted that Hollywood remove class conflict from its films: "We'll have no more *Grapes of Wrath*, we'll have no more *Tobacco Roads*, we'll have no more films that deal with the seamy side of American life. We'll have no more films that treat the banker as a villain."

Within the United States, government censors made sure that no photographs showing badly wounded soldiers or mutilated bodies reached the public. Rarely, if ever, did those on the home front see the true extent of the war's destructiveness and brutality.

23.3.2 Home Front Workers, Rosie the Riveter, and Victory Girls

Wartime opened up new possibilities for jobs, income, and labor organizing, for women as well as for men, and for new groups of workers. Disabled workers entered jobs previously considered beyond their abilities, fulfilling their tasks with skill and competence. Norma Krajczar, a visually impaired teenager from North Carolina, served as a volunteer aircraft warden where her sensitive hearing gave her an advantage over sighted wardens in listening for approaching enemy planes. Deaf people streamed into Akron, Ohio, to work in the tire factories that became defense plants, making more money than they ever made before.

Along with new employment opportunities, workers' earnings rose nearly 70 percent. Income doubled for farmers and then doubled again. Labor union membership grew 50 percent, reaching an all-time high by the end of the war. Women and minorities joined unions in unprecedented numbers. Energetic labor organizers like Luisa Moreno and Dorothy Ray Healy organized Mexican and Russian Jewish workers at the California Sanitary Canning Company into a powerful CIO cannery union that achieved wage increases and union recognition.

World War II ushered in dramatic changes for American women. Wartime scarcities led to increased domestic labor as homemakers made do with rationed goods, mended clothing, collected and saved scraps and metals, and planted "victory gardens" to help feed their families. Employment opportunities for women also increased. As a result of the combined incentives of patriotism and good wages, many women took "men's jobs" while the men went off to fight.

Rosie the Riveter became the heroic symbol of the woman war worker. Pictures of "Rosies" building planes or constructing ships graced magazine covers and posters. For the first time, married women joined the paid labor force in droves, and public opinion supported them. During the Depression, 80 percent of Americans had objected to wives working outside the home; by 1942 only 13 percent still objected. However, mothers of young children found very little help. In 1943, the federal government finally responded to the needs of working mothers by funding some day-care centers. But meager to begin with and conceived as an emergency measure, government funding for child care would end after the war.

New opportunities for women also opened up in the armed services. Along with the 10 million men aged 21 to 35 who were drafted into the armed services and the 6 million who enlisted, 140,000 women volunteered for the Women's Army Corps (WACs) and 100,000 for the Navy WAVES (Women Accepted for Voluntary Emergency Service).

Most female enlistees and war workers enjoyed their work and wanted to continue after the war. The extra pay, independence, camaraderie, and satisfaction that their jobs provided had opened their eyes to new possibilities. Edith Speert, like many others, was never again content as a full-time housewife and mother. In a letter dated November 9, 1945, she wrote to her husband who was still overseas:

> *Sweetie, I want to make sure I make myself clear about how I've changed. I want you to know now that you are not married to a girl that's interested solely in a home—I shall definitely have to work all my life—I get emotional satisfaction out of working; and I don't doubt that many a night you will cook the supper while I'm at a meeting. Also, dearest—I shall never wash and iron—there are laundries for that! Do you think you'll be able to bear living with me? . . . I love you, Edith*

Wartime upheaval sent the sexual order topsy-turvy. For many young women, moving to a new city or taking a wartime job opened up new possibilities for independence, excitement, and sexual adventure. Some young women, known as "victory girls," believed that it was an act of patriotism to have a fling with a man in uniform before

Rosie the Riveter
A heroic symbol of women workers on the homefront during World War II.

he went overseas. The independence of these women raised fears of female sexuality as a dangerous, ungoverned force. The worry extended beyond the traditional concern about prostitutes and "loose women" to include "good girls" whose sexual standards might relax during wartime. Public health campaigns warned enlisted men that "victory girls" would have their fun with a soldier and then leave him with a venereal disease, incapable of fighting for his country.

Wartime also intensified concerns about homosexuality. Urban centers and the military provided new opportunities for gay men and lesbians to form relationships and build communities. Although the military officially banned homosexuals from the forces, many served by keeping their orientation secret. If discovered, gay men faced severe punishment, including confinement in cages called "queer stockades" or in psychiatric wards. Lesbians faced similar sanctions, although the women's corps, in an effort to assure the civilian world of their recruits' femininity, often looked the other way.

23.3.3 Racial Tensions at Home and the "Double V" Campaign

Along with new possibilities for women and gay people, the war opened up opportunities for people of color. The movement for racial equality gained momentum as the nation fought against racist regimes abroad. The Holocaust, Nazi Germany's campaign to exterminate European Jews, demonstrated the horrors of racial hatred taken to its ultimate extreme. The U.S. government did little to help Jewish refugees or to stem the slaughter of Jews in Europe. Official indifference and widespread antisemitism prevailed throughout the war. Nevertheless, Nazi policies against the Jews discredited racial and ethnic prejudice, forcing Americans to confront the reality of racism in their own country. Anthropologist Ruth Benedict, in her 1943 book *The Races of Mankind*, urged the United States to "clean its own house" and "stand unashamed before Nazis and condemn, without confusion, their doctrines of a Master Race." As African American leader W. E. B. Du Bois noted, World War II was a "War for Racial Equality" and a struggle for "democracy not only for white folks but for yellow, brown, and black."

Throughout the war years, racial tensions within the United States persisted. Black workers, who were excluded from the best-paying jobs in the defense industry, mobilized against workplace discrimination. Their most powerful advocate was African American civil rights leader A. Philip Randolph, who had organized the overwhelmingly black Brotherhood of Sleeping Car Porters and won the union a contract with the railroads in 1937. In 1941, Randolph pressured FDR to ban discrimination in defense industries. He threatened to organize a massive march on Washington if Roosevelt did not respond. Roosevelt issued Executive Order 8802, which created the Fair Employment Practices Commission (FEPC) to ensure that blacks and women received the same pay as white men for doing the same job. The FEPC narrowed pay gaps somewhat, but it did not solve the problem.

Sometimes the presence of racial minorities in previously all-white work settings led to hostilities. In 1943, in Detroit, white workers at the Packard auto plant walked off the job when three black employees were promoted. With increasing numbers of white and black Southerners arriving to work in the city's war industries, overcrowding strained the boundaries of traditionally segregated neighborhoods. Clashes at a new housing complex escalated into several days of rioting, resulting in 34 deaths and 1,800 arrests.

In Los Angeles, the death of a Mexican American youth, José Diaz, sparked sensational news coverage and whipped up anti-Mexican fervor. Although police never determined the cause of Diaz's injuries, they filed first-degree murder charges against 22 Mexican American boys from the neighborhood. The jury found the young men

pachucos
Young Mexican American men who expressed attitudes of youthful rebellion in the 1940s. Many wore the zoot suit, also fashionable among urban African Americans.

zoot suits
Distinctive clothing in the 1940s worn largely by Mexican American and African American men, characterized by flared pants, long coats, and wide-brimmed hats.

guilty, but an appeals court overturned the convictions. Nevertheless, hostility continued to mount against Mexican American youths, particularly *pachucos* who sported **zoot suits**, distinctive attire with flared pants, long coats, and wide-brimmed hats. Pachucos wore the zoot suit as an expression of ethnic pride and rebelliousness.

For eight days in June 1943, scores of soldiers hunted zoot-suiters in Los Angeles bars, theaters, dance halls, and even in their homes, pulling off their clothes and beating them. Soon the attacks expanded to all Mexican Americans, and then to African Americans as well, some of whom also wore the zoot-suit style. The Los Angeles police sided with the rioters. They stood by during the beatings and then arrested the naked and bleeding youths and charged them with disturbing the peace. The rioting raged until the War Department placed the entire city of Los Angeles off limits to military personnel.

In spite of discrimination at home, members of minority groups responded enthusiastically to the war effort. The numbers of blacks in the U.S. army soared from 5,000 in 1940 to 700,000 by 1944, with an additional 187,000 in the U.S. Navy, Coast Guard, and Marine Corps. Four thousand black women joined the WACs. Almost all soldiers

© Bettmann/CORBIS

John F. Kennedy Presidential Library and Museum

Lyndon Baines Johnson LBJ Library and Museum

Richard Nixon Library [A10-024.16.5.3A]

Gerald R. Ford Library/UPI/Newscom

Courtesy Jimmy Carter Library

Courtesy Ronald Reagan Library

George Bush Presidential Library and Museum

EIGHT AMERICAN PRESIDENTS AS VETERANS Eight American presidents elected consecutively following World War II were veterans of that war. Pictured in wartime service, from top left, are Dwight D. Eisenhower, John F. Kennedy, Lyndon Johnson, Richard Nixon, Gerald Ford, Jimmy Carter, Ronald Reagan, and George H. W. Bush.

In what ways did the wartime and coming-home experiences of elite white men—like the future presidents pictured above—differ from those of men of color, particularly African American, American Indian, and Japanese American enlistees?

fought in segregated units, despite protests by the NAACP that "a Jim Crow army cannot fight for a free world." African Americans fought for the "Double V"—victory over fascism abroad and racial discrimination at home.

American Indians all over the country declared their willingness to fight for the cause. Fully 25,000 Native Americans, including 800 women, served in the military during the war. By 1945, nearly one-third of all able-bodied Native American men between 18 and 50 had served. Five percent of them were killed or wounded in action. Native Americans enlisted at a higher rate than the general population, prompting the *Saturday Evening Post* to editorialize, "We would not need the Selective Service if all volunteered like the Indians."

In addition to those who enlisted, half of all able-bodied Native American men not in the service and one-fifth of women left reservations for war-industry jobs. At the beginning of the war, men on reservations earned a median annual income of $500, less than one-fourth the national average. One-third of all Native American men living off reservations were unemployed. Worse, the average life expectancy for Native Americans in 1940 was just 35 years, compared with 64 years for the population at large. Like others who found new opportunities during the conflict, Native Americans hoped that their wartime economic progress would be permanent. But the boom would end for them when the war ended. Fewer than 10 percent of American Indians who relocated to cities found long-term employment after the war.

23.4 The End of the War

What alternatives were available for ending the war in Europe and in the Pacific, and why did the United States choose the strategies it employed to end the war?

While life on the home front continued to change, Allied leaders met to plan for the postwar era. Roosevelt hoped to ensure American dominance and to limit Soviet power. At a conference in Teheran, Iran, in 1943, Roosevelt insisted that the eastern European states of Poland, Latvia, Lithuania, and Estonia should be independent after the war. As the war wound down, Churchill, Stalin, and Roosevelt met again at Yalta, in Ukraine, in February 1945. They agreed to demand Germany's unconditional surrender and to divide the conquered nation into four zones to be occupied by Britain, the Soviet Union, the United States, and France. It became obvious at Yalta that separate spheres of influence would prevail after the war. Poland was a source of contention. Although Stalin nominally agreed to allow free elections in Eastern Europe, he intended to make sure that the countries bordering the Soviet Union would be under his control. He also pledged to enter the war against Japan and received assurances that the Soviet Union would regain the lands lost to Japan in the 1904–1905 Russo-Japanese War.

In July 1945, the newly sworn-in American president, Harry Truman, joined Stalin and Churchill (replaced by Clement Attlee after Churchill's election loss) at Potsdam, near Berlin. The three leaders issued a statement demanding "unconditional surrender" from Japan while privately agreeing to let Japan retain its emperor. The rest of the conference focused on postwar Europe.

As the war ended in Europe, Allied troops liberated the Nazi concentration camps. At that moment, the world finally learned the extent of Hitler's "Final Solution." Several Japanese Americans were among the first Allied soldiers to enter the camps. Ichiro Imamura described the sight at Dachau: "When the gates swung open, we got our first good look at the prisoners. . . . They were like skeletons—all skin and bones. . . . They were sick, starving and dying." Some of the survivors saw the Japanese American soldiers and feared that they were Japanese allies of the Germans. A *Nisei* soldier reassured them, "I am an American soldier, and you are free."

The atomic bomb offered Truman a new means to end the war in the Pacific. In 1942, Roosevelt had authorized the Manhattan Project, the research program to develop

Interpreting History

Zelda Webb Anderson

"In this life, you've got to speak up for yourself"

Zelda Webb Anderson became one of the first black women to enter military service during World War II. She served as an officer in the Women's Army Auxiliary Corps (WAAC), renamed the Women's Army Corps (WAC) in 1943. After the war she earned a doctorate in education at the University of California, Berkeley. Her 42-year career in education included a stint teaching at the University of East Africa in Dar-es-Salaam, Tanzania. She related her wartime experiences to the University of Nevada Oral History Program in 1995.

I reported for duty in January 1942. . . . This was so exciting to me. We had black officers, and our basic training was the same as for men. They would simply tell us, "You wanted to be in a man's army, so now you got to do what the men do." We learned military courtesy, history, how to shoot an M-1, go on bivouac, bathe in a teacup of water, eat hardtack rations. . . .

Every evening troops of male soldiers would march by our barracks en route to the mess hall. I told the commanding officer that we would like to have some shades at the windows. "Oh, no. You wanted to be in the man's army. Fine—you have to do what the men do." I told all the girls, "Listen, they won't give us any shades. So I want you to get right in front of the windows buck naked." The next day we had shades at all the windows. . . .

They pulled me out of basic training the third week and sent me to officer training in Des Moines. All of the instructors were white, but white and black officers were being trained in the same facility, in the same classes, and we slept in the same barracks. After OCS I was assigned to a laundry unit.

A black enlisted WAAC could either be in the laundry unit or she could be in the hospital unit. In the laundry unit, if she had a college degree, she could work at the front counter. . . . If she had less than that, then she did the laundry—very demeaning. And in the hospital unit they let her wash walls, empty basins, wash windows—all that menial work. . . .

I was assigned to duty at Fort Breckenridge, Kentucky. The post commander's name was Colonel Throckmorton. In a pronounced southern accent he told me, "You're going over to that colored WAC company, and you're going to be the mess officer."

I said, "Sir, I have not had any mess training."

"All you nigras know how to cook."

ZELDA WEBB ANDERSON Zelda Webb Anderson, in her service uniform.
University of Nevada Oral History Program

According to Zelda Webb Anderson, what were the opportunities, as well as the limitations, facing women who enlisted during World War II, especially for women of color?

I said, "You just met one who does not know how to cook; but if you send me to Fort Eustis, Virginia, for training I will come back and be the best mess officer you have on this post."

"I ain't sending you to no school, and you're going over there to be a mess officer." When I about-faced, I kept on going. I didn't even salute him. . . .

[Much later, after developing a more cordial relationship with Colonel Throckmorton,] I told him that segregation has not allowed white people to know black people: "We know you very intimately, but you don't know how we think, how we react, and so you just try to push your stuff on us, not giving a damn about how we feel about this. And then when we rebel, or you meet somebody like me, who decides that you can't do this to me, then you think I'm cantankerous; you think I'm an agitator. I'm just trying to give you an education. . . ."

I lived out the rest of my days very happy in the Army. If I had succumbed to the treatment that they had given other blacks before, and not spoken up for myself, my morale would have been down. . . . In this life, you've got to speak up for yourself. You can't go around shuffling your feet with your head hung down acting apologetic. If you see something you want, you must go after it. One day somebody will recognize it, and it's a victory for you, especially when it's somebody who has denigrated you because of your race. . . .

Our country has not solved all of its problems. You have to live democracy before you can preach democracy. I've got four granddaughters, and I don't want them put in a position where they don't have equal opportunities, equal chances, and then they have to fight the same old battles that I fought again.

Questions for Discussion

1. Why do you think Anderson, as a woman and an African American, would choose to enlist in the U.S. Army during World War II?

2. According to Anderson, in what ways did the segregation of the armed forces distort white officers' views of blacks?

SOURCE: Zelda Webb Anderson, "You Just Met One Who Does Not Know How to Cook," in *War Stories: Veterans Remember World War II*, ed. T. R. King (Reno, NV: University of Nevada Oral History Program, 1995), 81–85.

nuclear weapons, at a top-secret laboratory in Los Alamos, New Mexico. Building the bomb required the work of 125,000 people and cost nearly $2 billion.

When Truman learned of the successful atomic test on July 16, 1945, while at the Potsdam Conference, he determined to use it against the Japanese. He hoped that by dropping the bomb he could avoid an invasion of Japan that would have cost the lives of many American soldiers, and he wanted to send a message to the Soviet Union that the United States would be the dominant power in the postwar world. But some of the scientists who had developed the bomb urged a "demonstration" in a remote, unpopulated area that would impress the Japanese but would not cause loss of life. General George C. Marshall and other military leaders argued in favor of dropping the bomb on military or industrial targets, with ample warning ahead of time to enable civilians to leave target areas. But others agreed with Truman that dropping the bomb on a major city, without warning, would be the only way to persuade the Japanese to surrender unconditionally.

When the first bomb exploded over Hiroshima on August 6, 1945, and the second on Nagasaki three days later, the horrifying destructiveness of nuclear weapons became apparent. Even though Americans saw few images of the carnage on the ground, the huge mushroom cloud and the descriptions of cities leveled and people instantly incinerated shocked the nation and the world. In addition to the immediate devastation wreaked by the bomb, deadly radioactive fallout remained in the atmosphere, causing illness and death for months and even years after the attack. On August 14, 1945, the Japanese agreed to surrender. The official ceremony of surrender took place on September 2–V-J (Victory in Japan) Day–and World War II was over.

Conclusion

World War II left massive devastation in its wake all across the globe. Although 400,000 Americans died in the conflict, American casualties were far below those suffered by other countries. The wartime economy provided full employment and brought the nation out of the Great Depression.

The war changed life for Americans in profound ways. Although wartime forged a sense of unity as the nation came together to fight against fascism, it also highlighted fissures within American society. Members of minority groups fought in segregated units. Racial tensions and conflicts erupted at home, even as the country fought against a racist foe. Women joined the paid labor force and the armed services in unprecedented numbers; at the same time, they were bombarded by official and cultural messages reminding them that their ultimate service to the nation was as wives and mothers.

While life at home changed dramatically, so did the place of the United States in the world. The war's conclusion did not usher in the era of peace Americans expected. European empires staggered on the brink of collapse. Only the United States and the Soviet Union remained as major military powers, shifting the international balance of power from a multipolar to a bipolar system. For the next half-century, the fallout from World War II, as well as the power struggle between the United States and the Soviet Union, would shape political relationships across the globe.

Chapter Review

23.1 The United States Enters the War

Why were most Americans initially opposed to entering the war, and what changed their minds?
World War I had been an unpopular war, and during the 1930s, when Germany and Japan embarked on aggressive military efforts to conquer and colonize other nations, Americans remained overwhelmingly opposed to intervention. Eventually, when Japan attacked the United States at Pearl Harbor, Americans overwhelmingly supported entering the war.

23.2 Total War

What were the major differences for the United States between the war in Europe and the war in the Pacific?
World War II was the first "total war" in which civilians, as well as military personnel and supplies, became legitimate targets of attack. The war in the Pacific was particularly brutal, due in part to racial attitudes on both sides. In Europe, the Nazis murdered 6 million Jews, along with Romani (Gypsies), the disabled, and dissenters.

23.3 The Home Front

In what ways did World War II alter life for the Americans who remained at home?

Wartime opened up new opportunities for work in wartime industries, which drew many people into urban centers for the first time. Women entered jobs previously held only by men; African American and Native American workers migrated to cities for well-paying jobs.

23.4 The End of the War

What alternatives were available for ending the war in Europe and in the Pacific, and why did the United States choose the strategies it employed to end the war?

Throughout the war, a secret program called the Manhattan Project developed the atomic bomb. The bomb was ready as the Allies moved toward victory over Japan. Rather than risking a land invasion that might have cost thousands of American lives, President Truman chose to drop atomic bombs on two Japanese cities.

Timeline

1937	Japan invades China
1939	Germany invades Poland, and Great Britain and France declare war
1940	Germany invades Denmark, Norway, Holland, Belgium, Luxembourg, and France
1941	A. Philip Randolph's March on Washington movement
	FDR's "Four Freedoms" speech
	Japan bombs Pearl Harbor
1942	Executive Order 9066 (internment of Japanese Americans)
1943	Zoot-suit riots in Los Angeles; attacks on blacks in Detroit
1944	Normandy invasion on D-Day (June 6)
1945	Atomic bombs dropped on Hiroshima and Nagasaki
	V-E Day (May 7); V-J Day (September 2)

Glossary

fascism A form of right-wing dictatorship exalting nation and race above the individual.

Axis Pact An alliance among Germany, Italy, and Japan during World War II.

America First Committee A group that opposed Roosevelt's efforts to intervene in World War II against the Axis powers.

free trade International economic relations characterized by multinational investment and a reduction or elimination of tariffs.

braceros Mexican nationals working in the United States in low-wage jobs as part of a temporary work program between 1942 and 1964. (The bracero program was established by an executive agreement between the presidents of Mexico and the United States, providing Mexican agricultural labor in the Southwest and the Pacific Northwest.)

Holocaust The name given to the Nazi genocide against the Jews during World War II. Six million Jews were murdered.

code talkers Navajo Marines who developed a code based on the Navajo language to transmit secret information.

Rosie the Riveter A heroic symbol of women workers on the homefront during World War II.

pachucos Young Mexican American men who expressed attitudes of youthful rebellion in the 1940s. Many wore the zoot suit, also fashionable among urban African Americans.

zoot suits Distinctive clothing in the 1940s worn largely by Mexican American and African American men, characterized by flared pants, long coats, and wide-brimmed hats.

Chapter 24
Cold War and Hot War, 1945–1953

EAST MEETS WEST Soviet and American troops meet in central Germany in May 1945. At a time when smoking was extremely widespread in the United States and the Soviet Union, sharing cigarettes was standard friendly behavior among soldiers.

US Signal Corps/Time & Life Pictures/Getty Images

Apart from lighting up each other's cigarettes, how else could soldiers, who did not share a common language, acknowledge the contribution of the other in the victory over Germany?

Contents and Focus Questions

How did American soldiers encounter their Russian allies on the ground at the end of World War II?

At 11:30 a.m. on April 25, 1945, U.S. Army private Joseph Polowsky glimpsed what looked like the future. The young Chicago native was riding in the lead jeep of an American force along the Elbe River in central Germany when he spotted Russian soldiers on the far side, their medals glistening in the morning sun. Elated, he and five of his comrades found a small boat and paddled across to the eastern bank. Using Polowsky's knowledge of German to communicate, the American soldiers embraced their Soviet allies with laughs and tears. The Russians produced bottles of vodka, and toasts, pledges, singing, and dancing ensued. After years of pressing Germany from east and west, the Allies had finally linked up in the heart of Hitler's empire. A reporter wrote of the scene, "You get the feeling of exuberance, a great new world opening up."

Despite his conservative Republican background, Polowsky spent much of the rest of his life advocating American–Russian friendship. He could not forget the transforming experience of that April day along the Elbe and the hopes it engendered for a peaceful future. However, what followed the Allied victory turned out to be not a "great new world" of international peace and brotherhood, but the **Cold War** of U.S.–Soviet hostility that lasted for more than four decades. The opposing ideologies—**communism** and capitalist democracy—joined with conflicting national interests to produce this heavily armed standoff. The American effort to contain the expansion of communist influence entailed a radical reorientation of American involvement abroad in peacetime, including the nation's first peacetime military alliance, the North Atlantic Treaty Organization (NATO). At times the Cold War turned into a hot war of actual shooting, most importantly in the Korean War of 1950–1953 and the Vietnam War in the following decade.

In some ways, the Cold War encouraged efforts at social reform. America's new leading role in world affairs brought its domestic life into the spotlight of world attention. Racial discrimination and violence at home embarrassed American leaders as they spoke of leading the anticommunist "free world" abroad.

*   *   *   *   *

But in other ways, the Cold War constrained efforts to bring American life more fully into line with its democratic and egalitarian promise. Rising tensions with communist movements and governments overseas stimulated anxieties about possible subversion within the nation's own borders. Anticommunist fervor put unions on the defensive and encouraged women to shun the workplace in favor of family life and parenting, particularly in the nation's growing suburbs. This second Red Scare—the first had followed World War I in 1919—reached flood tide by 1950 with the rise to prominence of Senator Joseph McCarthy, a Republican from Wisconsin. McCarthy made a career of blaming supposedly disloyal Americans at home for setbacks to U.S. goals abroad in places such as China and Korea. He left a bitter legacy that long outlasted his political demise in 1954.

Cold War
The conflict and competition between the United States and the Soviet Union (and their respective allies) that emerged after 1945 and lasted until 1989.

communism
A totalitarian form of government, grounded in the theories of German philosopher Karl Marx and the practices of revolutionary Vladimir Lenin in Russia, that eliminated private ownership of property in supposed pursuit of complete human equality; the system of government also featured a centrally directed economy and the absolute rule of a small group of leaders.

24.1 The Uncertainties of Victory

How were the world and the United States different at the end of World War II than they had been at the beginning?

Franklin Roosevelt's death in April 1945 stunned the nation and the world. Elected four times to the presidency, he had dominated American politics like no figure before or since. Just as the unprecedented destruction of World War II was finally ending, the leadership of the nation passed into the new and less tested hands of Harry Truman. Peace brought an array of uncertainties and immediate needs. The victors had to reconstruct a world that had been damaged, physically and psychologically, almost beyond recognition. Spared the destruction visited elsewhere, the United States faced the different challenge of demobilizing its military forces and reconverting to a peace-time economy. Intense conflicts along the color line and in the workplace revealed real differences among Americans about the shape of the democracy they had fought to defend.

24.1.1 Global Destruction

World War II wrought death on a scale that defies comprehension. From England in the west to the islands of New Guinea in the east, from the Baltic Sea in the north to the Sahara Desert in the south, much of Europe and Asia was left in ruins. Soviet and American power had finally crushed the Axis, with Berlin now a "city of the dead" and Japan's urban landscape devastated by firebombing and nuclear attacks. Some of the victors were only marginally better off.

ROOSEVELT "GOING HOME" Franklin D. Roosevelt's death at his vacation home in Warm Springs, Georgia, stunned a nation and a world that had not known another U.S. president for thirteen years. Navy bandsman Graham Jackson was one of Roosevelt's favorite musicians. As the procession began to transport the president's body north for burial in Hyde Park, New York, Jackson captured the grief of millions of Americans as he played the sweet, slow strains of "Going Home."

Ed Clark//Time Life Pictures/Getty Images

Can you think of other ways in which music unites people, other than in grief?

Only one of the major combatants emerged from the war in better shape than at the beginning. The American people, one official remarked in 1945, "are in the pleasant predicament of having to learn to live 50 percent better than they have ever lived before." Many Americans suffered terribly in the war, of course; 400,000 died, leaving behind desolate families, and millions of veterans returned with traumas that colored the remainder of their lives. But such casualties paled in comparison to those of other belligerent nations. With just 6 percent of the world's population and 50 percent of its wealth, the United States enjoyed a position of staggering economic advantage.

Americans' overriding fear was that the end of the fighting might return the country to the state it had faced when the war began: economic depression. The nation's awesome industrial productivity depended on government spending, which was now to be cut back sharply. International trade might pick up much of the slack, but the war had destroyed most of the purchasing power of U.S. trading partners in Europe and Asia. Rising tensions between the two primary victors—the United States and the Soviet Union—hampered the process of postwar reconstruction.

24.1.2 Vacuums of Power and a Turn to the Left

World War II altered the world's ideological and physical landscape. Japan and Germany, the centers of prewar power in Asia and continental Europe, were vacuums waiting to be filled and reshaped by their conquerors. In addition to defeating two nations, the Allies had also discredited the right-wing ideas on which those governments had been built: fascism and militarism. Fascism's murderous character tarred those who had collaborated with the Axis during the war, primarily conservatives in countries such as France who preferred fascism to socialism.

Into many of the postwar vacuums of power flowed a newly prominent worldwide left. Socialists, communists, and other radicals espoused communal rather than individualistic values. The occupying Soviet forces installed communist governments in eastern Europe by force, and Socialist and Communist parties rose sharply in popularity in France, Italy, Belgium, and Scandinavia. Europeans across the continent established welfare states to provide a minimum standard of living for all their citizens.

This turn to the left encompassed most of the globe. Africans began organizing for eventual independence from European rule, and Asians launched the final phase of their anticolonial struggle for liberation. Indonesia fought its way free from the Dutch, and India gained its freedom from Britain. The Allies established the new United Nations (UN) in San Francisco in April 1945. Eventually housed in New York, its General Assembly gave all nations an equal voice and vote in deliberations, and its small Security Council—responsible for guiding any UN military actions—gave a permanent seat and veto power to five nations: the United States, the USSR, Britain, France, and China. The 1948 UN Human Rights Charter helped put practitioners of colonialism and racial discrimination on the defensive by declaring worldwide support for the principles of national self-determination and equal treatment for all peoples.

24.1.3 Postwar Transition to Peacetime Life

The fundamental task for Americans at home was to convert from a wartime society back to a peacetime one. They were especially eager to bring home the 12 million men in uniform serving abroad. Ready to resume civilian life, the veterans walked off ships' gangplanks into a country in transition. Wartime rationing was lifted on goods such as sugar and gasoline, and the 35-mph speed limit was withdrawn. But as orders for war materials dried up, taking jobs with them, wartime inflation persisted. Housing remained especially scarce. In the richest country in the world, one-third of the citizens still lived in poverty, with neither running water nor flush toilets.

To ease the transition home, Congress had passed the Servicemen's Readjustment Act of 1944 (the GI Bill) to extend crucial financial aid to veterans. It provided low-cost mortgages that helped create an explosion in home ownership. It created Veterans Administration hospitals to provide lifetime medical care. And it paid tuition and stipends for college and vocational training, making higher education broadly available for the first time. The 2 percent of veterans who were women also made use of these benefits. In the postwar era, when American politics generally became more conservative—shifting away from the New Deal reform spirit and toward an anticommunist emphasis—the GI Bill was the one area in which the United States expanded its own welfare state.

The postwar transition presented particular challenges to American women. Millions of them had gone to work outside the home during the war and found economic independence in doing so. Now they faced powerful pressures to leave the workforce and return to a domestic life of old and new families. Many women accepted this return to the domestic sphere, content to focus on marriage and family life. Others felt differently. "War jobs have uncovered unsuspected abilities in American women," one argued. "Why lose all these abilities?"

24.1.4 Challenging Racial Discrimination

African Americans faced a similar problem. After finding new opportunities in industrial employment during the war, they were laid off afterward in favor of returning white veterans. Like women, blacks were expected by others to retreat into deference. Black veterans spearheaded the resistance to this notion.

African American efforts to overcome discrimination met fierce white opposition in 1946 and 1947. In the South, where most black Americans still lived, a wave of beatings and lynchings greeted black veterans in uniform and their attempts to register to vote. White Northerners also used violence to preserve the segregated character of neighborhoods in Chicago, Detroit, and other cities. They destroyed the property and threatened the lives of blacks who dared to move to previously all-white blocks, effectively confining African Americans to impoverished areas.

The retreat of European colonialism and American competition with the Soviet Union nonetheless encouraged many white Americans to acknowledge the contradiction between leading the "free world" and limiting the freedoms of Americans of color. A series of Supreme Court decisions validated the long-term strategy of the National Association for the Advancement of Colored People (NAACP) for contesting segregation in the courts. Court rulings outlawed segregation in voting primaries (*Smith v. Allwright*, 1944), interstate transportation (*Morgan v. Virginia*, 1946), contracts for house sales (*Shelley v. Kraemer*, 1948), and graduate schools (*Sweatt v. Painter* and *McLaurin v. Oklahoma*, 1950).

Popular culture moved in the same direction of breaking down racial barriers. *Billboard* magazine in 1949 changed the category of "race music" to "rhythm and blues" as white record producers and radio disc jockeys such as Alan Freed began to bring the early rock 'n' roll of African American musicians to mainstream white audiences. By 1955, young white musicians such as Bill Haley and Elvis Presley joined black stars such as Chuck Berry and Little Richard in creating a wildly popular sound that transcended racial categories. Professional baseball erased its color line when Jackie Robinson, a former four-sport star at the University of California–Los Angeles and lieutenant in the U.S. Army, joined the Brooklyn Dodgers in 1947.

Native Americans and Mexican Americans faced similar discrimination in the Southwest and elsewhere. With war veterans in the fore, they also organized to contest unfair education and election practices. "If we are good enough to fight, why aren't we good enough to vote?" asked returning Navajo soldiers in New Mexico and Arizona, where the state constitutions prohibited Indian residents from voting, until successfully challenged in 1948. The League of United Latin American Citizens (LULAC) followed a strategy similar to that of the NAACP regarding educational discrimination, leading to the Ninth Circuit Court's decision in *Mendez v. Westminster* (1946) outlawing segregated

JACKIE ROBINSON SLIDING HOME The first person of color to play modern major league baseball, Jackie Robinson starred for the Brooklyn Dodgers from 1947 to 1956, helping them win six National League pennants and one world championship. His success opened the way for other black players to follow, eventually bringing the demise of the old professional Negro Leagues. Robinson credited Dodgers general manager Branch Rickey for his willingness to break the color line in the nation's favorite game.

AP Photo/Ray Howard

When baseball's color barrier finally fell, would Americans be forced to acknowledge the contradiction between leading the "free world" abroad and limiting the freedoms of Americans of color at home?

schools for Mexican Americans in California. In parallel fashion, indigenous Alaskans organized in the Alaska Native Brotherhood successfully lobbied the territorial legislature in Juneau to pass an antidiscrimination law in 1945.

24.1.5 Class Conflict between Workers and Owners

In many ways, 1946 seemed like 1919. A world war had just ended, in which corporations had made handsome profits. American workers had enjoyed nearly full employment and improving wages and had joined unions in large numbers. In 1946 one-third of the workforce held a union card, the largest portion ever. But the end of war-related orders led to job cuts and the loss of overtime wages, and by the spring of 1946, 1.8 million workers were out on strike.

Mirroring World War I, the conclusion of hostilities in 1945 revealed rising tensions between the United States and the Soviet Union. The spread of leftist revolutions abroad amplified fears of communist influence in American unions, especially because a few of the most effective Congress of Industrial Organizations (CIO) organizers were Communist party members or at least sympathetic to an emphasis on class conflict between owners and workers. As in 1919, a Red Scare began to develop, egged on by a business community that used the supposed threat of the tiny U.S. Communist party to weaken the much larger and less radical union movement. In contrast to the end of World War I, however, federal law guaranteed the right of workers to bargain collectively, and the strikes of 1946 resulted in some negotiated wage increases.

But the tide turned against unions as anticommunism intensified. The Republican party claimed a sweeping victory in the 1946 congressional elections, taking control of both the House and the Senate in a stark rejection of Truman's leadership. Republicans and conservative Democrats then passed the Taft-Hartley Act in 1947 over the president's veto, weakening unions by prohibiting secondary boycotts (against the products of a company whose workers were on strike) and requiring union officials to swear anticommunist oaths. At the same time, the expanding U.S. economy after 1947 pulled many skilled workers up into the middle class and gave them a larger stake in the status quo.

24.2 The Quest for Security

How did the meaning of "security" change for the United States after 1945?

On February 21, 1947, a British official in Washington informed the U.S. government that Britain could no longer provide financial assistance to the anticommunist governments of Greece and Turkey. This information marked a watershed in modern world history. Long the greatest imperial power and the dominant outside force in the Middle East, Britain was beginning a slow retreat. Left in its wake were vacuums of power, particularly in the Middle East, South Asia, and Africa. President Truman and his advisers believed that either Soviet or American influence would flow into these regions. The Truman administration formulated a policy to contain communism in the eastern Mediterranean that it quickly expanded to encompass the entire noncommunist world. Powerful new nuclear weapons further increased anxieties about the nation's security.

24.2.1 Redefining National Security

U.S. policymakers had ended World War II with one primary goal. They were determined to revive the global capitalist economy that had nearly dissolved in the Great Depression of the 1930s and had then been battered by the war. American prosperity and freedom, they believed, depended on a world system of free trade because Americans simply could not consume all the products of their efficient farms and factories. If they could not sell the surplus abroad, the United States would slide back into a depression.

"National security" was expanding to mean something very different from simply defending the nation's territory against invasion. For the disproportionately powerful United States, national security after 1945 came to be identified with the creation and preservation of a free-trading capitalist world order. American national security was seen to be at stake almost everywhere around the globe.

The primary threat to that security came from the Soviet Union. The danger lay in Soviet encouragement, by example and assistance, of revolutions that rejected market economies and individualist ethics. Demoralized by the war's destruction and by grim postwar economic conditions, western Europeans and others seemed to be considering the paths of socialism and communism. "Hopeless and hungry people," Secretary of State Dean Acheson warned, "often resort to desperate measures."

24.2.2 Conflict with the Soviet Union

The antifascist alliance of the Soviet Union and the United States dissolved rapidly as their conflicting interests reemerged after the war. Long skeptical of the capitalist world it wanted to replace, the Soviet government viewed expansive U.S. interests as evidence of "striving for world supremacy." Yet Moscow was just as clearly expanding its own sphere of national security, with Soviet troops remaining in areas they had occupied during the war: Manchuria, northern Korea, Iran, and especially eastern and central Europe. Each side spoke of the other's goal as "world domination."

Contrasting experiences in World War II amplified historical and ideological differences. Whereas the war brought the United States out of the global capitalist depression (which the Soviets had avoided), it brought the USSR into a depression caused by the invading Germans' destruction of the western portion of the country. With a decimated population, a battered economy, and minimal air and naval forces, the postwar Soviet Union remained a regional power based on its army. The United States was the only truly global power, with a vast naval armada and air force projecting military might onto every continent, undergirded by the most productive economy in world history.

The two nations' visions of the postwar world order reflected these relative positions. Americans sought an open world for the free flow of goods and most ideas, and proved willing to tolerate and even embrace dictatorial governments as long as they were anticommunist and open to foreign trade and investment. Meanwhile, the Soviets called for a more traditional division into separate spheres of influence for the great powers.

Conflicts over specific areas liberated from the Nazis hastened the onset of the Cold War in the first eighteen months after the end of World War II. Whereas the Soviets wanted reparations and a deindustrialized Germany that could never threaten it again, the United States considered a rebuilt industrial German state crucial for a healthy, integrated western European economy. Britain and France had gone to war in defense of an independent Poland, but for Stalin control of Poland was not negotiable because it had been "the corridor for attack on Russia." Moscow and Washington also clashed over Iran, where the Soviets briefly encouraged a leftist uprising in the northern part of the oil-rich country to counteract British and American influence in the capital city of Tehran. U.S. policymakers worried, too, about Soviet requests to Turkey for greater control of the straits leading out of the Black Sea into the Mediterranean.

24.2.3 The Policy of Containment

containment
The U.S. policy during the Cold War of trying to halt the expansion of Soviet and communist influences.

Diplomat George Kennan best articulated the policy of **containment** in an influential telegram sent from his post at the U.S. embassy in Moscow in February 1946. Kennan explained Soviet hostility as a function of traditional Russian insecurity overlaid with newer Marxist justifications. He called for "the adroit and vigilant application of counterforce" against all Soviet efforts at expanding their influence. One month later, on March 5, 1946, former British prime minister Winston Churchill warned that a Russian iron curtain had descended across Europe, imprisoning all those to the east of it. "The reins of world leadership are fast slipping from Britain's competent but now very weak hands," the State Department argued. "These reins will be picked up either by the United States or by Russia."

Picking up those reins meant a fundamental reorientation for the United States. No longer just the dominant force in the Western Hemisphere, it would have to maintain its wartime projection of military forces around the globe—permanently. In an address to Congress on March 12, 1947, asking for $400 million in aid for Greece and Turkey, Truman simplified the world system into two "ways of life," those of "free peoples" and those of "terror and oppression" under communist rule. All nations must choose between them, he declared, and the United States must support "free peoples who are resisting attempted subjugation by armed minorities or outside pressures."

Truman Doctrine
President Truman's March 1947 speech articulating the new policy of containment.

The **Truman Doctrine**, as it became known, exaggerated a real problem in order to win public support for a new international role for the United States. It funded the governments of Turkey and Greece but it framed the new policy broadly, opening the path to supporting anticommunist regimes and opposing revolutions around the world for decades to come. The most important immediate step was the reconstruction of a vibrant, reintegrated western European economy. The United States provided $13 billion between 1948 and 1952 to fund the European Recovery Program, commonly known as the Marshall Plan for its chief architect, Secretary of State George Marshall (1947–1949).

Map 24.1 EUROPE DIVIDED BY THE COLD WAR

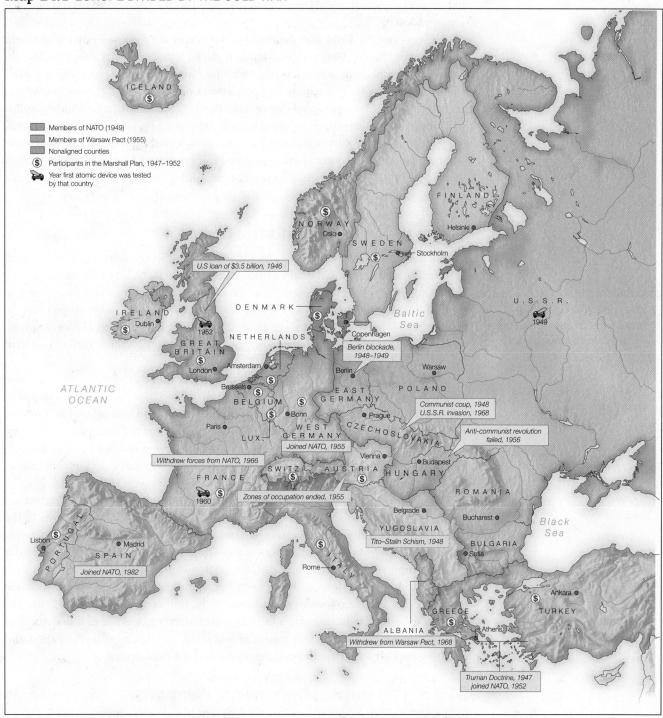

Members of NATO (1949)
Members of Warsaw Pact (1955)
Nonaligned counties
$ Participants in the Marshall Plan, 1947–1952
Year first atomic device was tested by that country

ICELAND $

NORWAY $
Oslo

SWEDEN
Stockholm $

FINLAND
Helsinki

U.S.S.R.
1949

U.S loan of $3.5 billion, 1946

Baltic Sea

DENMARK $
Copenhagen

IRELAND
Dublin $

GREAT BRITAIN 1952
London

NETHERLANDS
Amsterdam $

Berlin blockade, 1948–1949
Berlin

Warsaw

POLAND

ATLANTIC OCEAN

Brussels
BELGIUM $

EAST GERMANY

Bonn $

WEST GERMANY
Joined NATO, 1955

Prague

CZECHOSLOVAKIA

Communist coup, 1948
U.S.S.R. invasion, 1968

Paris
LUX.

Withdrew forces from NATO, 1966

SWITZ. AUSTRIA
Vienna

Anti-communist revolution failed, 1956

FRANCE $
1960

Zones of occupation ended, 1955

HUNGARY
Budapest

ROMANIA

PORTUGAL
Lisbon $

SPAIN
Madrid

Joined NATO, 1982

Belgrade

YUGOSLAVIA
Tito–Stalin Schism, 1948

Bucharest

Black Sea

BULGARIA
Sofia

Rome $
ITALY

GREECE $
ALBANIA
Athens $

TURKEY
Ankara $

Withdrew from Warsaw Pact, 1968

Truman Doctrine, 1947
joined NATO, 1952

For centuries, Europe had controlled much of the rest of the world. After 1945, Russians occupied the eastern half of the continent and Americans wielded dominant influence in the western half. This division of Europe into communist and noncommunist blocs lasted until the end of the Cold War in 1989.

Ensuring western European security against the Red Army also entailed the first U.S. military alliance in peacetime. The victors of World War II divided a defeated Germany into separate zones of occupation. The British, French, and American decision in March 1948 to create a unified state out of the western sectors of Germany led a few months later to a year-long Soviet blockade of western access to Berlin and fears of a general war. The creation of NATO in 1949 made the American military commitment to Europe permanent. The point of NATO for western Europe, its British first secretary general said, was to "keep the Americans in, the Russians out, and the Germans down."

The onset of the Cold War determined the fate of the defeated powers of World War II. Reconstructing Germany and Japan replaced initial concerns about rooting out Nazism and punishing war criminals, as at the Nuremberg trials of surviving Nazi leaders in 1945–1946. The American occupation under General Douglas MacArthur initially (1945–1947) emphasized democratization of Japanese society, including building labor unions, weakening corporate monopolies, ensuring women's political rights, and punishing war criminals. But rising U.S. tensions with the Soviets and the imminent victory of the communist forces in China's civil war prompted American officials to shift course by 1948. Henceforth, they focused on rebuilding as quickly as possible Japan's industrial economy as the hub of capitalist Asia.

24.2.4 Colonialism and the Cold War

colonialism
The centuries-old system of mostly European nations controlling and governing peoples and lands outside of Europe.

Most of the world's non-white majority still lived under European colonial control, and for them the struggle for national independence and racial equality was the great issue of the late 1940s and 1950s. In this North-South conflict of **colonialism**, as opposed to the East-West conflict of the Cold War, the United States held an awkward position. Its primary NATO partners included the greatest colonial powers: Britain, France, Belgium, the Netherlands, and Portugal. Racial segregation in the United States further undercut American leadership of the "free world."

With European rule in Asia and Africa on the way out, the Truman administration sought a gradual transfer of colonial rule into the hands of local pro-West elites. The U.S. grant of official independence to the Philippines in 1946 was offered as a model, as was the British departure from India a year later. However, the importance of Europe for America meant supporting even those imperialists who did not leave peacefully, such as the French digging in against communist-led revolutionaries in Vietnam (part of French Indochina).

The British withdrawal from Palestine in 1948 created a peculiar dilemma for the United States. Jewish settlers—primarily from Europe and often survivors of the Holocaust—proclaimed the new state of Israel against the wishes of the Arab majority. Secretary of State Marshall and others urged Truman not to recognize Israel in order to avoid imperiling U.S. relations with the Arab oil-producing states. The president sympathized with the Jewish desire for a homeland, however, and understood the importance of American Jews as constituents of the Democratic party in the 1940s. His decision to recognize Israel, which most Middle Easterners viewed as a new colonial state, set the United States on a course of enduring friendship with that nation and enduring conflict with Israel's Arab neighbors and the Palestinians.

24.2.5 The Impact of Nuclear Weapons

Scientists in the 1940s dramatically increased Americans' sense of personal safety by introducing the use of antibiotics. "Miracle drugs" such as penicillin cured common bacterial infections that had previously been debilitating or fatal. What science gave with one hand it threatened to take away with the other, however. The use of atomic weapons on Japan foreshadowed a future of utter insecurity in which instantaneous destruction of entire nations could occur without warning.

Even without being used again in war after 1945, nuclear weapons altered the American environment. Weapon tests released vast quantities of radiation into the atmosphere. Local cancer rates spiked upward for Bikini Islanders in the western Pacific, where the first tests occurred, and then for farmers and ranchers in Utah and Nevada, when tests began 65 miles northwest of Las Vegas in 1953. Navajo Indians mining uranium in the Southwest paid dearly for their intensive exposure to the poisonous material, as did thousands of workers involved in nuclear weapon production. Weapon assembly plants in Hanford, Washington, and Rocky Flats, Colorado, leaked radioactivity into the groundwater. In combination with the nuclear power industry, atomic weapon development resulted in an enormous supply of radioactive waste—deadly for 10,000 more years—that the U.S. government still does not know how to dispose of safely.

The government offered reassurances about the safety of the atom, and the Atomic Energy Commission covered up evidence of radioactivity's ill effects. But many Americans were deeply anxious about this destructive new power that loomed over their lives, especially as the Soviet–American arms race intensified. Science fiction movies painted frightening pictures of a future devastated by nuclear war and haunted by exposure to radiation. Concerns about a nuclear world escalated with the successful 1952 test of an American hydrogen bomb, a thousand times more powerful than the device that destroyed Hiroshima.

24.3 American Security and Asia

Why was Asia particularly important to the United States during the early postwar period?

Japan did not conquer independent nations in its sweep southward at the start of World War II. Instead, it defeated the forces of imperial powers: the French in Indochina, the Dutch in Indonesia, the British in Singapore and Malaya, and the Americans in the Philippines. In a single swoop, Japanese soldiers demonstrated the absurdity of white supremacy and cleared the way for the end of colonialism in Asia. Then Japan's retreat in 1945 left vacuums of power throughout the region. Into them flowed two contenders: the returning but gravely weakened European imperialists, and Asian nationalists such as Ho Chi Minh in Vietnam. Americans were not passive observers of this struggle, as they sought to establish a new free-trading order in the region. As communist forces won a civil war in China, the U.S. government bulked up its military and intelligence capacities and went to war in Korea.

24.3.1 The Chinese Civil War

Americans had long felt a special connection to China. Half of the thousands of Christian missionaries sent out by American churches in the early twentieth century had been posted there. Entrepreneurs eyed the Chinese market, home to one-fifth of the world's potential consumers. During World War II, Chinese resistance to Japan's invasion occupied millions of Tokyo's soldiers who would otherwise have been shooting at American GIs. The close U.S. alliance with the government of Jiang Jieshi seemed to confirm American hopes that Asia's largest nation would follow a pro-American path.

But the partisans of the Chinese Communist Party (CCP) under Mao Zedong's leadership fought more effectively against the Japanese than Jiang's soldiers did. Japan's withdrawal from China in 1945 initiated four years of warfare between the Communists and Jiang's anticommunist Nationalists. The Truman administration provided $3 billion in aid to Jiang. Americans watched in frustration as the CCP nonetheless defeated the Nationalists, who retreated to the island of Taiwan in 1949.

The People's Republic of China (PRC) was the first major communist government created without the presence of Soviet troops. But profound suspicions on both sides prevented any Sino-American accommodation, and the U.S. government refused to recognize the People's Republic. Faced with U.S. hostility and sharing a common ideology with the Soviet Union, Mao papered over historic Chinese-Russian tensions and signed a mutual defense pact with Moscow in February 1950. For American

STALIN AND MAO Were all communists conspiring together against the United States and its interests? New Chinese leader Mao Zedong (right) meets with Soviet ruler Josef Stalin. Two months later, the men signed a mutual defense treaty. But they shared little personal warmth. Conflicting Chinese and Russian national interests soon strained—and eventually broke—their alliance.

"The Great Friendship", Stalin and Mao, 1950 (color litho), Nalbandian, Dmitri (1906–93) / Private Collection / Archives Charmet / Bridgeman Images

What might the Sino-Soviet breakup suggest about the relationship between communist ideology and national interests?

policymakers, the so-called loss of China increased the importance of building capitalist societies in the rest of Asia, particularly Japan and—fatefully—South Korea and Vietnam. China's revolution also became a major issue in American politics. "Who lost China?" Republicans demanded rhetorically and effectively, presuming that it had once been America's to lose.

24.3.2 The Creation of the National Security State

A week before Mao's announcement that China had become a communist country, President Truman shared some equally grim news with the American public: the Soviet Union had detonated its first nuclear device. The United States had lost the atomic monopoly that for four years assured Americans of their unique position of military strength. Truman asked his advisers for a full reevaluation of the nation's foreign policy.

NSC-68

The 1950 directive of the National Security Council that called for rolling back, rather than merely containing, Soviet and communist influences.

national security state

The reorientation of the U.S. government and its budget after 1945 toward a primary focus on military and intelligence capabilities.

The result was the top-secret National Security Council document 68 (**NSC-68**), which articulated the logic of what became the **national security state**: a government focused on the imperatives of military power, global involvement, and radically increased defense spending. NSC-68 argued that the United States had entered an era of permanent crisis because of the expansion of communism and the hostile intentions of the Soviet Union. America's worldwide interests meant that it must oppose revolutions or radical change anywhere on the globe. NSC-68 went beyond the containment policy of the Truman Doctrine to call instead for fostering "a fundamental change in the nature of the Soviet system." This armed struggle necessitated secrecy and centralization of power in the hands of the federal government.

The National Security Act of 1947 and its 1949 amendments created the institutions of the new national security state. The Central Intelligence Agency (CIA) organized spying and covert operations, the Department of Defense unified the separate branches of the military, and the National Security Council (NSC) coordinated foreign policy information for the president.

24.3.3 At War in Korea

Two months after NSC-68 arrived on the president's desk, troops from communist North Korea poured across the thirty-eighth parallel into South Korea on June 25, 1950. The alarmist recommendations of NSC-68 now seemed fully justified to U.S. policymakers. But the origins of the conflict on the Korean peninsula were complicated.

Korea had been colonized by Japan since 1910. After Japan's defeat in 1945, Soviet and U.S. forces each occupied half of the peninsula. In the north, the Soviets installed a dictatorial communist regime under Kim Il Sung, who had fought with the Chinese Communists in their common struggle against Japan. In the south, the Americans established an authoritarian capitalist regime led by Syngman Rhee, who had lived in the United States most of the previous four decades. The thirty-eighth parallel was an arbitrary dividing line for a nation that had been unified for 1,300 years, and both governments sought to reunite Korea under their control. Border skirmishes intensified after the Soviets and Americans withdrew in 1948, and leftist rebellions continued across much of the south. Some 100,000 Koreans lost their lives in the fighting between 1945 and 1950.

U.S. forces arrived in late June 1950, just in time to prevent the South Korean army from being driven off the peninsula, and then slowly pushed the North Koreans backward toward the thirty-eighth parallel in hard fighting. Truman received UN approval for this "police action," along with a small number of troops from several other nations.

Americans assumed the North Korean invasion had been orchestrated by Moscow as part of a plan of worldwide communist aggression. The Truman administration considered defense of South Korea crucial to demonstrate the credibility of U.S. power. The U.S. government took preemptive actions against possible aggression elsewhere. It sent the Seventh Fleet to defend Taiwan, which it had previously assumed China would eventually conquer and reabsorb; it increased assistance to anticommunist forces in the Philippines and Vietnam; and it rearmed West Germany

KILLED IN ACTION IN KOREA Near Haktong-ni, Korea, on August 28, 1950, an Army corpsman fills out casualty tags while one American soldier comforts another who has just seen a friend killed in action. Men who fought together on the front lines in Korea, as in other wars, experienced physical and psychological traumas unparalleled in civilian life. They often developed strong friendships with each other but sometimes had difficulty making the transition back to peacetime routines at home.

Sfc. Al Chang/Defense Visual Information Center (Department of Defense), HD-SN-99-03118

In which other wars, as in Korea, have soldiers had difficulty transitioning from the battlefield back to their homes?

Interpreting History

NSC-68 (1950)

> "a defeat of free institutions anywhere is a defeat everywhere"

Concerned about the trend of international events in the wake of the Communist revolution in China and the Soviet Union's acquisition of nuclear weapons, President Truman ordered his National Security Council on January 31, 1950, to conduct "a reexamination of our objectives in peace and war and of the effect of these objectives on our strategic plans." The resulting study, known as NSC-68, called for a military buildup to counter Soviet expansionism. Some specialists on the USSR, such as George Kennan, questioned NSC-68's accuracy regarding Soviet intentions and successes. But the subsequent North Korean invasion of South Korea seemed to confirm the idea of "international communism" on the march.

From NSC-68: U.S. Objectives and Programs for National Security (April 14, 1950)

The Soviet Union, unlike previous aspirants to hegemony, is animated by a new fanatic faith, antithetical to our own, and seeks to impose its absolute authority over the rest of the world. . . .

Any substantial further extension of the area under the domination of the Kremlin would raise the possibility that no coalition adequate to confront the Kremlin with greater strength could be assembled. It is in this context that this Republic and its citizens in the ascendancy of their strength stand in their deepest peril.

The issues that face us are momentous, involving the fulfillment or destruction not only of this Republic but of civilization itself. . . . The assault on free institutions is world-wide now, and in the context of the present polarization of power a defeat of free institutions anywhere is a defeat everywhere. . . .

Our policy and actions must be such as to foster a fundamental change in the nature of the Soviet system. . . . In a shrinking world, which now faces the threat of atomic warfare, it is not an adequate objective merely to seek to check the

MISSILE ASSEMBLY, SANTA MONICA, CALIFORNIA
Workers at the Douglas Aircraft Company's Santa Monica factory assemble Nike guided missiles for the U.S. Army in 1955. Large military contracts proliferated during the Cold War and stimulated the growth of Sunbelt states like California.

Musee Bettmann/Corbis

What effect has the end of the Cold War had on defense industry contractors?

Kremlin design, for the absence of order among nations is becoming less and less tolerable. . . .

The integrity of our system will not be jeopardized by any measures, covert or overt, violent or non-violent, which serve the purposes of frustrating the Kremlin design, nor does the necessity for conducting ourselves so as to affirm our values in actions as well as words forbid such measures. . . .

The total economic strength of the U.S.S.R. compares with that of the U.S. as roughly one to four. . . . The military budget of the United States represents 6 to 7 percent of its gross national product (as against 13.8 percent for the Soviet Union). . . . This difference in emphasis between the two economies means that the readiness of the free world to support a war effort is tending to decline relative to that of the Soviet Union.

It is true that the United States armed forces are now stronger than ever before in other times of apparent peace; it is also true that there exists a sharp disparity between our actual military strength and our commitments. . . . It is clear that our military strength is becoming dangerously inadequate. . . . In summary, we must . . . [engage in] a rapid and sustained build-up of the political, economic, and military strength of the free world.

Questions for Discussion

1. What is the precise problem that the United States faces, according to NSC-68?

2. How does NSC-68's analysis of the Soviet threat in 1950 compare with American understandings today of the threat from Islamist terrorist organizations such as Al Qaeda?

SOURCE: A Report to the National Security Council by the Executive Secretary on United States Objectives and Programs for National Security, NSC-68, April 14, 1950.

as part of NATO. The U.S. annual military budget increased from $13 billion in 1950 before the war to $50 billion in 1953, setting a pattern for vast military expenditures for decades thereafter.

General Douglas MacArthur's brilliantly executed landing of fresh U.S. troops at the port of Inchon behind North Korean lines on September 15, 1950, created a turning point in the war. South Korea was retaken; containment had succeeded. Should American commanders now shift to rolling back communism by proceeding north of the thirty-eighth parallel? The opportunity was irresistible, despite Truman's determination to keep this a limited war. MacArthur ignored signals that the Chinese would not allow U.S. soldiers to come all the way to their border at the Yalu River—the equivalent for Americans of having the Soviet Red Army arrive at the Rio Grande. On November 27, 200,000 Chinese soldiers struck hard, driving American soldiers south of the thirty-eighth parallel again in the longest retreat in U.S. history.

Map 24.2 THE KOREAN WAR, 1950–1953

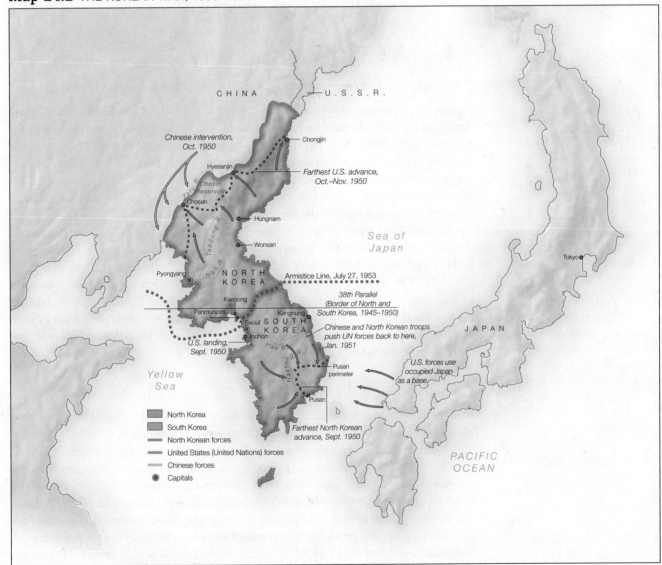

The strategic location of the Korean peninsula enhanced the importance of what had originally been a civil conflict among Koreans. Korea's close proximity to China, the Soviet Union, and U.S.-occupied Japan made the outcome of this conflict very important to all of the great powers. The Americans and Chinese wound up doing the bulk of the fighting against each other in the full-scale war that unfolded in 1950.

MacArthur wanted to take this "entirely new war" directly to the Chinese, using conventional or even nuclear bombing campaigns against the People's Republic. His growing insubordination forced Truman to fire the popular general in April 1951 because the president had no desire to start a larger war that would draw in the USSR. The bloody fighting in Korea stalemated that spring close to the original dividing line, where the front remained as the two sides negotiated for two years before signing a ceasefire in July 1953. American deaths totaled 37,000, and China lost nearly a million soldiers. Nearly 3 million Koreans on both sides died—10 percent of the population of the peninsula—and another 5 million became refugees. Containment succeeded at enormous cost, and the Korean peninsula is still divided and heavily armed today.

The Korean War shaped subsequent American politics and society in significant ways. The stalemate frustrated Americans, who agreed with MacArthur that there was "no substitute for victory." But the ominous threat of nuclear weapons meant that wars had to be limited. The fighting in Korea enabled McCarthy and the Red Scare to dominate political life in the United States. Republican presidential nominee General Dwight Eisenhower was perhaps the most popular American alive because of his leadership of the Allied victory in Europe in World War II, and he swept into the White House in 1952 over Democrat Adlai Stevenson, the governor of Illinois.

24.4 A Cold War Society

Which were the most important changes in Americans' lives in the early Cold War era?

Expanding economic opportunities and narrowing political freedoms characterized American society in the first decade of the Cold War. Anticommunist repression pushed dissident views to the margins of the nation's political life. Americans largely accepted this new conformity for two reasons: their desire to support their government during international crises, especially the Korean War, and a consumer cornucopia that surrounded them with attractive material goods. Americans in this era moved to the suburbs, and increasingly to the South and West.

By 1947, the United States was launching into an era of extraordinary economic expansion that continued for twenty-five years. Since Ben Franklin's time, Americans had been known for thrift in their pursuit of wealth. But after 1945, the long-cherished principle of delaying gratification declined steeply. "Buy now, pay later," General Motors urged as it offered an installment plan to customers. Diner's Club introduced the first credit card in 1950. In a formulation breathtaking for its distance from Puritan and immigrant traditions of saving for the future, writer William Whyte observed that "thrift is now un-American."

24.4.1 Family Lives

Many white Americans embraced the opportunity to move to the suburbs after World War II. Seeking larger homes and yards and quieter neighborhoods, they flocked to new developments such as Levittown outside New York City on Long Island. Suburbs did not welcome all, however. Even as federal courts struck down segregation laws in some spheres of American life, agencies such as the Veterans Administration and the Federal Housing Administration were encouraging residential separation by race. Private banks did the same. Other government policies, including highway construction and tax benefits for homeowners, promoted the growth of suburbs at the cost of cities. A third epoch in American residential history began by 1970 when more Americans resided in suburbs than cities, parallel to the 1920 shift from a rural majority to an urban one.

Suburban life encouraged a sharpening of gender roles among the growing middle class. Men commuted to work while women were expected to find fulfillment in marriage and motherhood, including a nearly full-time job of unpaid housework. Despite this partial retreat from wartime employment, however, fully one-third of American women continued to work for pay outside the home. The economic circumstances of most black women offered them little choice, and most wound up doing double house-work: their own and that of families employing them as domestics.

From 1946 to 1964, women giving birth at a younger age to more children created the demographic bulge known as the baby boom. Large families reinforced the domes-tic focus of most women, putting the work of child-rearing at the center of their lives. Fatherhood became increasingly a badge of masculinity.

Married mothers were celebrated, but unmarried ones were rebuked. Despite the greater freedom of the war years, the sexual double standard remained in place, with women's virtue linked directly to virginity in a way that men's was not. Birth control devices such as the diaphragm were legal only for married women and only in certain states. Women seeking to terminate unwanted pregnancies had to consider illegal abor-tions, the only kind available before 1970; millions did so, including one-fifth of all married women and a majority of single women who became pregnant. Two studies of American sexual behavior by Dr. Alfred Kinsey of Indiana University in 1948 and 1953 shocked the public with their revelation of widespread premarital and extramarital sexual intercourse as well as homosexual liaisons.

24.4.2 The Growth of the South and the West

Before World War II, American cultural, industrial, and financial power had always been centered in the urban North, but federal expenditures during the war began to change this. The U.S. Army built most of its training bases in the South, where land close to the coasts was thinly populated and inexpensive. Military bases and defense industries sprang up along the West coast to project power into the Pacific against Japan. U.S. troops built the Alcan (Alaska–Canada) Highway, and millions of GIs passed through Hawaii en route to the Pacific battlefront. Fighting against the Japanese to defend Pearl Harbor and the Aleutian Islands brought the once-distant territories of Hawaii and Alaska more fully into Americans' consciousness, setting them on the path to statehood in 1959.

The **Sunbelt** of the South, the Southwest, and California grew rapidly after the war, whereas older Rustbelt cities of the Northeast and Midwest began to lose manu-facturing jobs and population. Like the 440,000 people who moved to Los Angeles during the war, postwar migrants to California and Arizona appreciated the weather and the economic opportunities. Military spending underwrote half the jobs in Cali-fornia during the first decade of the Cold War. Migrants from south of the U.S. bor-der, meanwhile, found work primarily in California's booming agricultural sector.

Two industries particularly stimulated the growth of the Sunbelt: cars and air condi-tioning. Automobiles helped shape the economies of western states, where new cities were built out of sprawling suburbs. New car sales shot up from 70,000 in 1945 to 7.9 million in 1955. Inexpensive gasoline, refined from the abundant crude oil of Texas and Oklahoma, powered this fleet. Automobile exhaust pipes replaced industrial smokestacks as the pri-mary source of air pollution. Air conditioning also became widely available after World War II and contributed to the breakdown of the South's regional distinctiveness. From Miami and Atlanta to Houston and Washington, D.C., the new Sunbelt depended on the indoor comfort brought by controlling summertime heat and humidity.

Sunbelt
The band of states from the Southeast to the Southwest that experienced rapid economic and population growth during and after World War II.

24.4.3 Harry Truman and the Limits of Liberal Reform

On the political front, the onset of the Cold War narrowed the range of American politi-cal discourse. In seeking to consolidate the New Deal legacy, President Truman found himself boxed in by conservative Republican opponents. Allied governments in western Europe had embraced the idea that access to health care was a right of every citizen in a modern democratic state. But when Truman proposed a system of national health care, conservatives quashed his proposal in Congress.

Perhaps the most blatant omission of the New Deal had been protection against racial discrimination. Now, as the Cold War intensified, the fact that millions of Americans still lacked basic guarantees for their civil rights was an embarrassing contradiction to rhetoric about ensuring rights and liberties throughout the "free world." Truman campaigned for reelection in 1948 on a platform of support for civil rights that was unprecedented in the White House. That summer, he ordered the desegregation of the armed forces and the federal civil service.

African American voters in Chicago, Cleveland, and other northern cities played a key role in swing states; their solid support lifted Truman to a narrow and surprising victory over the heavily favored Republican candidate, New York governor Thomas Dewey. Truman's reelection was all the more impressive because of the fracturing of the Democratic party. Alienated by the civil rights plank, white Southerners walked out of the Democratic convention and ran South Carolina governor Strom Thurmond as an independent candidate. The "Dixiecrats" won four states in the Deep South, foreshadowing the abandonment by white Southerners of the party of their parents in the 1960s. Truman won as a man of the moderately liberal center, fierce against communism, usually supportive of the rights of organized labor, and opposed to discrimination.

Table 24.1 THE ELECTION OF 1948

Candidate	Political Party	Popular Vote (%)	Electoral Vote
Harry S. Truman	Democratic	49.5	304
Thomas E. Dewey	Republican	45.1	189
J. Strom Thurmond	State-Rights Democratic	2.4	38
Henry A. Wallace	Progressive	2.4	—

SOURCE: Historical Election Results, Electoral College, National Archives and Records Administration

24.4.4 Cold War Politics at Home

McCarthyism

The political campaign led by Senator Joseph McCarthy (R-Wisconsin) to blame liberals at home for setbacks to U.S. interests abroad, due to what he considered liberals' sympathies with communism.

In a pattern that became known as **McCarthyism**, mostly Republican conservatives blamed liberal Democrats in the administration for communist successes abroad—especially in China and Korea—and accused them of sympathizing with and even spying for the Soviet Union. The hunt for domestic subversives to explain international setbacks was grounded in the reality of a handful of actual Soviet spies, most notably Julius Rosenberg (executed for treason in 1953 along with his apparently innocent wife, Ethel) and nuclear scientist Klaus Fuchs. But this second Red Scare expressed primarily the frustration of being unable to translate vast U.S. power into greater control of world events. And it served, above all, to cast suspicion on the patriotism of liberals at home.

Despite his general support for civil liberties, Truman helped set the tone for pursuing suspected traitors. In an unsuccessful effort to fortify his right flank against Republican attacks, he established a federal employee loyalty program in March 1947 as the domestic equivalent of the Truman Doctrine. Attorney General Tom Clark drew up a list of supposedly subversive organizations that the FBI and state committees on "un-American activities" then hounded. In a case with sobering implications for free speech, federal courts in 1949 convicted the leaders of the U.S. Communist party of promoting the overthrow of the U.S. government. Words alone, the courts ruled, could be treasonable—the same logic as the wartime Sedition Act of 1918 (see Chapter 20).

Republicans reaped the benefits of the Red Scare. Most Americans who had sympathized in any way with the Soviet Union in the Depression years were by the late 1940s merely liberal Democrats, but the House Un-American Activities Committee (HUAC)

zeroed in on their earlier records. Investigating Hollywood, the television industry, and universities as well as the executive branch of the U.S. government, HUAC destroyed the careers of prominent figures as well as average Americans.

The era found its name in the previously obscure junior senator from Wisconsin, Republican Joseph McCarthy. With a single speech in Wheeling, West Virginia, on February 9, 1950, this ambitious politician soared to prominence. "I have here in my hand a list of 205" Communist party members working in the State Department, he declared. Over the next four years, the numbers and names changed as McCarthy stayed one step ahead of the evidence while intimidating witnesses before his Senate subcommittee. He talked about communists, but his show was about Democrats. As the war in Korea raged, he mercilessly red-baited (attacked as "soft" on communism) the Truman administration. But after the Republican electoral victory in 1952, his excesses lost their partisan utility. With the end of the war in Korea and his ill-advised attacks on the U.S. Army as supposedly infiltrated by communists (the Army-McCarthy hearings), he was at last censured by his Senate colleagues in 1954 and died an early, alcohol-related death in 1957.

Table 24.2 THE ELECTION OF 1952

Candidate	Political Party	Popular Vote (%)	Electoral Vote
Dwight D. Eisenhower	Republican	55.1	442
Adlai E. Stevenson	Democratic	44.4	89

SOURCE: Historical Election Results, Electoral College, National Archives and Records Administration

24.4.5 Who Is a Loyal American?

The Cold War politics of inclusion and exclusion established a new profile for loyal Americans. Private familial and material concerns were expected to replace public interest in social reform. Anticommunists launched a withering assault on homosexuals as "perverts" and threats to the nation's security. Church membership climbed in tandem with condemnations of "godless Communism," and Congress added the words "under God" to the Pledge of Allegiance. Discrimination against Roman Catholics and Jews, though still evident, declined as Catholics such as McCarthy proved intensely anticommunist and as pictures and stories emerged to reveal the horrors of the Nazi Holocaust against the Jews. More inclusive references to the "Judeo-Christian tradition" became common.

American leadership of the global anticommunist cause strengthened the struggle for racial equality at home, within certain limits. The NAACP and most African Americans took an anticommunist position in accord with Truman, in return for his support of civil rights. They downplayed their concern for colonial independence in Africa and Asia to support NATO. The American GI Forum (Latino veterans) and the Japanese American Citizens League also worked within the confines of Cold War politics to end discrimination.

For impoverished Native Americans, the government seemed to give with one hand and take away with the other. In 1946, Truman established the Indian Claims Commission to consider payment for lands taken and treaties broken. But Dillon S. Myer, director of the Bureau of Indian Affairs, closed reservation schools, withdrew support for traditional cultural activities, and launched an urban relocation program, all intended to move Native Americans into the mainstream and get the government "out of the Indian business."

Immigrants, too, received mixed messages. The McCarran-Walter Act (1952) ended the long-standing ban on allowing people of Asian descent not born in the United States to become U.S. citizens. But it preserved the discriminatory 1924 system of "national origins" for allocating numbers of immigrants from different countries. The bill also strengthened the attorney general's authority to deport aliens who were suspected of subversive intentions.

COLD WAR ANXIETY A comic book from 1947 dramatizes the anxiety that many Americans of the time felt over the Soviet Union and its intentions.

Advertising Archive/Courtesy Everett Collection

Were Americans soon to be enslaved by the Russians? Why were American fears so exaggerated?

THURGOOD MARSHALL In 1955, Thurgood Marshall was chief counsel for the National Association for the Advancement of Colored People (NAACP) and led the legal charge to end desegregation in the schools.

AP Images/Marty Lederhandler

Were legal challenges the best option for achieving full equality for African Americans under the law or would other remedies for advancing civil rights be more beneficial?

Conclusion

McCarthyism at home and the war in Korea ensured a generation of hostility between the United States and China. That hostility tied the People's Republic more closely to the USSR, strengthening the common belief that international communism was a unified movement. The United States committed itself to defending Taiwan from recapture by the Beijing government. The Korean War also jump-started the moribund Japanese economy as American dollars poured into Japan, where the U.S. war effort was based.

Frustrations with the course of the fighting in Korea affirmed the inward focus of American society in the 1950s.

Despite the organizing efforts of political activists such as civil rights workers, most citizens seemed to look increasingly to their personal and familial lives for satisfaction and meaning. From the powerful U.S. economy flowed an unprecedented river of consumer goods, including the new artificial materials—plastic, vinyl, nylon, polyester, Styrofoam—that have pervaded and polluted American life ever since. As peace came to Korea and U.S. soldiers returned from across the Pacific, Americans sought the good life at home.

Chapter Review

24.1 The Uncertainties of Victory

How were the world and the United States different at the end of World War II than they had been at the beginning? World War II destroyed the old multipolar international balance of power, leaving only the United States and the

Soviet Union as major powers. While much of Europe and Asia suffered great devastation from the fighting, the United States experienced enormous economic growth, leaving it far better off than most of the rest of the world in 1945.

24.2 The Quest for Security

How did the meaning of "security" change for the United States after 1945?

After World War II, the Truman administration was determined not to return to the prewar Great Depression. Instead, the U.S. government sought to establish an integrated, free-trading, capitalist world order. American national security thus expanded to encompass most of the globe, aiming to contain communism.

24.3 American Security and Asia

Why was Asia particularly important to the United States during the early postwar period?

Beyond the industrial nations of Europe and North America, the primary issue for most of the world after 1945 was ending colonialism and establishing national independence. Postwar nationalist revolutions unfolded first in Asia, raising the prospect of expanding the reach of communist rule.

24.4 A Cold War Society

Which were the most important changes in Americans' lives in the early Cold War era?

After World War II, most Americans focused on enjoying the new material affluence of an increasingly suburban, middle-class society. Modest efforts at increasing racial equality were limited by the political repression of McCarthyism, a virulent form of anticommunism.

Timeline

1945	Harry S. Truman becomes president upon death of Roosevelt
	Atomic bombs dropped on Hiroshima and Nagasaki
1946	Winston Churchill gives "Iron Curtain" speech, Fulton, Missouri
1947	Truman Doctrine of containing communism announced
1948	Truman orders U. S. armed services desegregated
1949	Establishment of People's Republic of China
	USSR acquires nuclear weapons
1950	Sen. Joseph McCarthy accuses State Department of harboring communists
	North Korean troops invade South Korea
1952	Dwight Eisenhower elected president
1953	Korean War ends

Glossary

Cold War The conflict and competition between the United States and the Soviet Union (and their respective allies) that emerged after 1945 and lasted until 1989.

communism A totalitarian form of government, grounded in the theories of German philosopher Karl Marx and the practices of revolutionary Vladimir Lenin in Russia, that eliminated private ownership of property in supposed pursuit of complete human equality; the system of government also featured a centrally directed economy and the absolute rule of a small group of leaders.

containment The U.S. policy during the Cold War of trying to halt the expansion of Soviet and communist influences.

Truman Doctrine President Truman's March 1947 speech articulating the new policy of containment.

colonialism The centuries-old system of mostly European nations controlling and governing peoples and lands outside of Europe.

NSC-68 The 1950 directive of the National Security Council that called for rolling back, rather than merely containing, Soviet and communist influences.

national security state The reorientation of the U.S. government and its budget after 1945 toward a primary focus on military and intelligence capabilities.

Sunbelt The band of states from the Southeast to the Southwest that experienced rapid economic and population growth during and after World War II.

McCarthyism The political campaign led by Senator Joseph McCarthy (R-Wisconsin) to blame liberals at home for setbacks to U.S. interests abroad, due to what he considered liberals' sympathies with communism.

Chapter 25
Domestic Dreams and Atomic Nightmares, 1953–1963

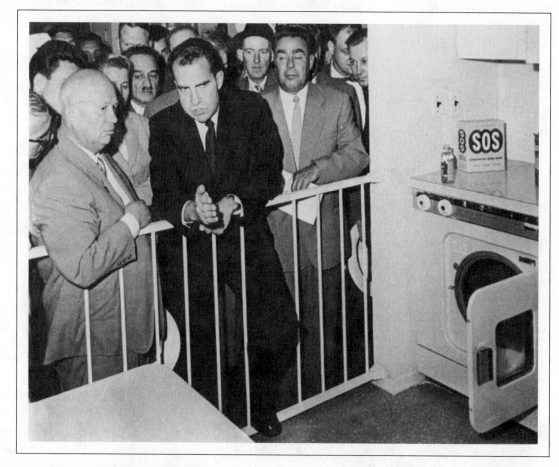

THE "KITCHEN DEBATE" Vice President Richard M. Nixon and Soviet Premier Nikita Khrushchev tour a model of a modern kitchen at the American National Exhibition in Moscow in 1959. With the international media focused on their encounter, the leaders of the two superpowers debated the merits of their respective systems in terms of consumerism and household appliances in what came to be known as the "Kitchen Debate."

AP Photo

What does the photograph of Nixon and Khrushchev suggest about the way in which the United States wished to portray itself to the Soviets and to the world?

Contents and Focus Questions

In the propaganda battle that characterized the Cold War, how did the leaders of the United States and the Soviet Union describe their nation's commitment to equality? For the United States, the idea was that capitalism provided equal opportunity. For the Soviet Union, the idea was that communism offered equal living conditions. Both visions were grounded in ideology rather than reality, but they underscored the differences in the two forms of government.

In 1959, the leaders of the superpowers articulated these ideas in a highly publicized debate. Vice President Richard M. Nixon traveled to Moscow in the Soviet Union to visit the American National Exhibition, a showcase of American consumer goods and leisure equipment. Nixon extolled the virtues of the American way of life, while Soviet Premier Nikita Khrushchev promoted the communist system.

The main attraction of the exhibition was a full-size, six-room, ranch-style house. Nixon claimed that a house like this was "within the price range of the average U.S. worker." Khrushchev responded that "all you have to do to get a house is to be born in the Soviet Union. So I have a right to a house. In America if you don't have a dollar, you have the right to sleep on the pavement." The two leaders argued over the relative merits of American and Soviet washing machines, televisions, and electric ranges in what came to be known as the "Kitchen Debate."

Each leader claimed to live in a country that promoted women's equality. "In America," Nixon said, household appliances "are designed to make things easier for our women." Khrushchev countered that the Soviets did not share that "capitalist attitude toward women." He expressed pride in productive female workers who labored side by side with men in Soviet industries.

But according to American journalists, Nixon's knock-out punch in his verbal bout with the Soviet premier was his description of the American postwar domestic dream: successful breadwinners supporting attractive homemakers in well-appointed, comfortable homes. The American National Exhibition in Moscow seemed to demonstrate the superiority of the American way of life.

*   *   *   *   *

The decade from 1953 to 1963, under the presidencies of Dwight Eisenhower and John Kennedy, was a time of expansive optimism about the future. The United States increased territorially, with the addition of Hawaii and Alaska as states in 1959. The **baby boom** demonstrated widespread faith in the future for American children. It was also a decade of growth for U.S. influence abroad, the domestic economy, consumer culture, and television. **Suburbs**, highways, and shopping malls expanded to meet the needs of increasing numbers of families with young children. Some teenagers and others rebelled against what they saw as conformity and materialism in American life. But African Americans organized in the civil rights movement to gain full access to the freedoms and comforts of this increasingly middle-class society.

baby boom
The period of increased U.S. childbirths from roughly the early 1940s to the early 1960s.

suburbs
Areas on the outskirts of a city, usually residential. Suburbs expanded dramatically after World War II.

It was also a decade of anxiety. Americans worried about the perils of the atomic age as the nuclear arsenals of both superpowers continued to grow. Science fiction films about alien invaders reflected concerns about foreign dangers. The Soviet Union's 1957 launching of **Sputnik**, the first artificial satellite to orbit the Earth, alarmed Americans and forced the nation to confront the possibility of Soviet technological superiority. The United States appeared to be at the height of its strength and power, yet at the same time, more vulnerable than ever before.

Sputnik
The first artificial satellite to orbit the earth, launched by the Soviet Union in 1957.

*GI BILL
mortgage loans to veterens. First time many Americans r homeowners Brought benefits to American housholds*

25.1 Cold War, Warm Hearth

In what ways did the suburban family home promote Cold War ideology?

The postwar era was a time of deep divisions in American society, yet in certain ways Americans behaved with remarkable conformity. This is especially evident in the overwhelming embrace of the nuclear family. The GI Bill, with its provisions for home mortgage loans, enabled veterans of modest means to purchase homes. For the first time, large numbers of working-class Americans became homeowners. Although residential segregation prevailed throughout the postwar era, limiting most suburban developments to prosperous white middle- and working-class families, many veterans of color were able to buy their first homes. Americans of all racial, ethnic, and religious groups, of all socioeconomic classes and educational levels, brought the marriage and birth rates up and the divorce rate down, producing the huge numbers of children born in the two decades following World War II, known as the "baby boom." The "American way of life" embodied in the suburban nuclear family, as a cultural ideal if not a universal reality, motivated countless postwar Americans to strive for it, to live by its codes, and—for Americans of color—to demand it.

25.1.1 Consumer Spending and the Suburban Ideal

Between 1947 and 1961, national income increased more than 60 percent. Rather than putting this money aside for a rainy day, Americans were inclined to spend it. Investing in one's home, along with the trappings that would enhance family life, seemed the best way to plan for a secure future.

Between 1950 and 1970, the suburban population more than doubled, from 36 million to 74 million. Fully 20 percent of the population remained poor during this prosperous time. But most families of ample as well as modest means exhibited a great deal of conformity in their consumer behavior, reflecting widely shared beliefs about the good life. They poured their money into homes, domestic appliances, televisions, automobiles, and family vacations.

Nuclear families who settled in the suburbs provided the foundation for new types of community life and leisure pursuits, sometimes at the expense of older ones grounded in ethnic neighborhoods and kinship networks. Family-oriented amusement parks such as Disneyland in Anaheim, California, which opened in 1955, catered to middle-class tastes, in contrast to older venues such as Coney Island, known for thrill rides, class and ethnic mixing, and romantic environments. Religious affiliation rose to an all-time high as Americans built and joined suburban churches and synagogues, complete with youth programs and summer camps. In 1949, fewer than 1 million American homes had a television. Within the next four years, the number soared to 20 million.

The Cold War made a profound contribution to suburban sprawl. Congress passed the Federal-Aid Highway Act of 1956, which provided $100 billion for building 41,000 miles of national highways. When President Dwight D. Eisenhower signed the bill into law, he stated one of the major reasons for the new highway system: "[In] case of atomic attack on our key cities, the road net must permit quick evacuation of target areas."

Many officials feared a communist takeover and the defeat of the United States in the Cold War. Pentagon strategists and foreign policy experts worried that the Soviet

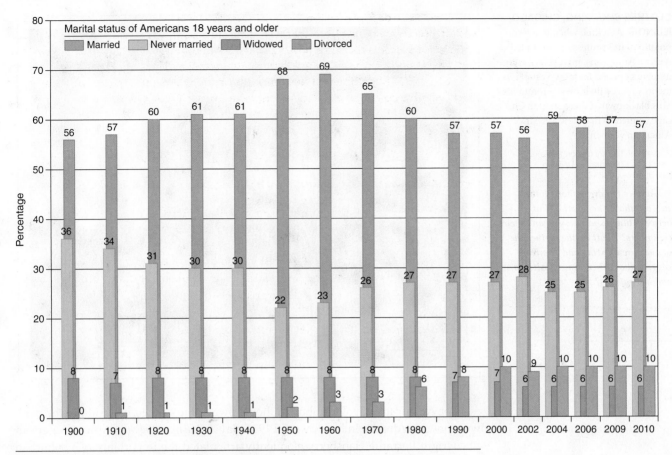

Figure 25.1 MARITAL STATUS OF THE U.S. ADULT POPULATION, 1900–2010

Following World War II, Americans married in record numbers. The high rate of marriage corresponded with a relatively low divorce rate. Beginning in the 1970s, the marriage rate plummeted and the divorce rate rose dramatically.

SOURCE: Data from *Statistical Abstract of the United States* for the years cited, compiled by Information Please, "Marital Status of the Population by Sex, 1900–2010," http://www.infoplease.com/ipa/A0193922.html.

Union might gain the military might to allow its territorial expansion and, eventually, world domination. But observers also expressed concern that the real dangers to America were internal: racial strife, emancipated women, class conflict, and family disruption. Most postwar Americans longed for security after years of economic depression and war, and they saw family stability as the best bulwark against the new dangers of the Cold War.

25.1.2 Race, Class, and Domesticity

After World War II, the nation faced a severe housing shortage. The federal government gave developers financial subsidies to build affordable single-family homes and offered Federal Housing Administration (FHA) loans and income tax deductions to homebuyers. These benefits enabled white working-class and middle-class families to purchase houses. Postwar prosperity, government subsidies, and the promise of assimilation made it possible for white-skinned Americans of immigrant background to blend into the suburbs.

Despite the expansion of the black and Latino middle class and the increase in home ownership among racial minorities, most suburban developments excluded non-whites. The FHA and lending banks maintained policies known as **red lining**, which designated certain neighborhoods off limits to racial minorities. Although Americans of color remained concentrated in urban and rural areas, some did move to the suburbs, usually into segregated communities.

red lining
Policies maintained by the Federal Housing Administration and lending banks which designated certain neighborhoods off limits to racial minorities.

CLOTHES SHOPPING, CHICAGO, ILLINOIS At a time when many corporations and professions excluded African Americans, many black entrepreneurs opened their own establishments to serve their own communities. This black-owned dress shop in Chicago catered to middle-class African American women.

Russell Lee/Library of Congress Prints and Photographs Division [LC-USF34-038683-D]

What does the dress shop photo suggest about the relationship between black shop owners and their customers? What do the clothes the women are wearing and admiring suggest about their class positions and aspirations?

For Americans of color, suburban home ownership offered inclusion in the postwar American dream. In her powerful 1959 play *A Raisin in the Sun*, African American playwright Lorraine Hansberry eloquently articulated the importance of a suburban home, not to assimilate into white America but to live as a black family with dignity and pride. Asian Americans also had good reason to celebrate home and family life. With the end of the exclusion of Chinese immigrants during World War II, wives and war brides began to enter the country, helping to build thriving family-oriented communities. After the disruptions and anguish of internment, Japanese Americans were eager to put their families and lives back together. Mexican Americans and Mexican immigrants, including *braceros*, established flourishing communities in the Southwest. Puerto Ricans migrated to New York and other eastern cities, where they could earn four times what they were making on the island.

Racial segregation did not prevail everywhere. In Shaker Heights, Ohio, a suburb of Cleveland, white residents decided, as a community, to integrate their neighborhood. Drawing on postwar liberal ideals of civil rights and racial integration, they welcomed black homeowners. Their effort succeeded by emphasizing class similarity over racial difference. White residents encouraged other white families to move into Shaker Heights, pointing out that their prosperous black neighbors were "just like us."

As residents and businesses migrated to the suburbs, slum housing and vacant factories remained in the central cities. The Housing Acts of 1949 and 1954 granted funds to municipalities for urban renewal. However, few of those federal dollars provided low-income housing. Mayors, bankers, and real estate interests used the money to bulldoze slums and build gleaming office towers, civic centers, and apartment complexes for affluent citizens, leaving the poor to fend for themselves in the remaining dilapidated corners of the cities.

Although intended to revitalize cities, urban renewal actually accelerated the decay of inner cities and worsened conditions for the urban poor. Federally funded projects often disrupted and destroyed ethnic communities. In Los Angeles, the Dodgers' stadium built in Chavez Ravine offered baseball fans access to the national pastime, but it destroyed the historically rooted Mexican American neighborhood in its path. The $5 million project displaced 7,500 people and demolished 900 homes.

Along with the urban poor, rural Americans reaped few benefits of postwar affluence. The 1950s marked the greatest out-migration from the South as the mechanization of farms—particularly the mechanical cotton picker—reduced the number of workers on the land. More than one-fourth of the population left Kentucky and West Virginia, where unemployment in some areas reached 80 percent. The harsh realities faced by America's poor demonstrate that large numbers of Americans were unable to achieve the affluent life promoted by Nixon in the Kitchen Debate.

25.1.3 Women: Back to the Future

The domestic ideal that Nixon described included not only an abundance of consumer goods, but also a full-time homemaker and a breadwinner husband. This vision of domesticity marked a giant step backward for many women, whose opportunities and experiences had expanded dramatically during World War II. The elevation of the housewife as a cultural icon contrasted sharply with the reality. The proportion of women who fit the mold of full-time homemaker was rapidly shrinking. Although most American women married, had children, and carried the lion's share of responsibility for housework and child-rearing, increasing numbers of married women also held jobs outside the home. The employment of married women began to rise during World War II and kept rising after the war, even though most of the well-paying and highly skilled jobs returned to men at the war's end.

Many women worked part-time while their children were at school, as they considered themselves homemakers, not wage earners. With few other opportunities for creative work, women embraced their domestic roles and turned homemaking into a profession. Many fulfilled their role with pride and satisfaction and extended their energies and talents into their communities, where they made important contributions as volunteers in local parent-teacher associations (PTAs) and other civic organizations. Some expanded part-time employment into full-time occupations when their children left the nest. Others felt bored and frustrated and drowned their sorrow with alcohol or tranquilizers. In 1963, author Betty Friedan described the constraints facing women as the "problem that has no name" in her feminist manifesto *The Feminine Mystique*. The

RETURN TO PINK-COLLAR WORK, INGLEWOOD, CALIFORNIA After World War II, women were forced out of most of the high-paying skilled jobs that they had occupied during wartime to make room for the returning men. The jobs available to women were mostly "pink-collar" jobs in the service industry.

Library of Congress Prints and Photographs Division [LC-USW3- 055181-C]

In the photograph above, a woman operates one of many Travelunch food carts that enabled factories to feed their workers lunch in a mere twenty minutes. What does it indicate about the workplace and working conditions of the woman pictured as well as of the male worker whom she is serving?

birth control pill, approved by the Food and Drug Administration in 1960, was initially promoted as a boon to rational, planned families. But it allowed women to control their fertility and take advantage of expanding employment and educational opportunities.

Education was one avenue available to women, as students as well as teachers. But higher education did not open its doors fully to women. Because few women gained access to graduate and professional schools and most well-paying jobs were reserved for men, college degrees for white women did not necessarily open up career opportunities or greatly improve their job and earning prospects. By 1956, one-fourth of white female students married while still in college. Many of these women dropped out of school to take jobs to support their husbands through college. But the situation was different for black women. Like their mothers and grandmothers, most black women had to work to help support their families. Job prospects for black women generally were limited to menial, low-paying occupations. Young black women knew that a college degree could mean the difference between working as a maid for a white family and working as a secretary, teacher, or nurse. Although few in number, more than 90 percent of black women who entered college completed their degrees.

Black women also aspired to the role of homemaker, but for very different reasons than white women. Although poverty still plagued large numbers of black citizens, the black middle class expanded during the 1950s. Postwar prosperity enabled some African Americans, for the first time, a family life in which the earnings of men were adequate to allow women to stay home with their own children rather than tending to the houses and children of white families. For black women, domesticity meant "freedom and independence in her own home." It is no wonder that women of color in the early 1960s bristled when white feminists such as Betty Friedan called upon women to break free from the "chains" of domesticity.

25.2 The Civil Rights Movement

What were the major goals of the civil rights movement in the 1950s?

As the civil rights movement gained momentum in the South, African American activists faced fierce opposition from local white authorities and contempt from national leaders. Persistent racial discrimination proved to be the nation's worst embarrassment throughout the Cold War. The Soviet Union pointed to American race relations as an indication of the hypocrisy and failure of the American promise of freedom for all. Yet national leaders paid only lip service to racial equality and failed to provide the strong support necessary to defeat the system of racial segregation in the South known as "Jim Crow," a legal, or *de jure*, set of institutions that prevailed throughout the South. Although the nation's leaders acknowledged the need to address Southern segregation, they did nothing to address the unofficial, or *de facto*, segregation that prevailed throughout the country.

Nevertheless, at the grassroots level, racial minorities continued to work for equal rights. For example, Mexican Americans in the Southwest pressed for desegregation of schools, residential neighborhoods, and public facilities through organizations such as the middle-class League of United Latin American Citizens (LULAC) and the Asociacion Nacional México-Americana (ANMA), a civil rights organization that emerged out of the labor movement. It was not until 1963 that the power of the civil rights movement—and the violence of white opposition in the South—finally compelled the federal government to take action.

25.2.1 *Brown v. Board of Education*

The first major success in the struggle to dismantle the Jim Crow system in the South came in the 1954 Supreme Court decision *Brown v. Board of Education*. Civil rights strategists decided to pursue their cause in the courts rather than through Congress. They knew

In what ways do the dress and demeanor of the students reflect or contradict the physical conditions of the overcrowded and segregated classroom in the photograph above?

that Democrats in Congress from the South, who held disproportionate power in the legislature, would block any civil rights legislation that came before the House or Senate. They believed that they had a better chance of success through the courts.

NAACP lawyers filed suit against the Topeka, Kansas, Board of Education on behalf of Linda Brown, a black child in a segregated school. They were targeting the 1896 *Plessy v. Ferguson* decision, which justified Jim Crow laws on the grounds that they provided "separate but equal" facilities. The case reached the U.S. Supreme Court, where NAACP general counsel Thurgood Marshall argued that separate facilities, by definition, denied African Americans their equal rights as citizens.

In 1953, during the three-year period that the Supreme Court had the *Brown* case before it, President Eisenhower appointed Earl Warren as chief justice. Warren had been state attorney general and then governor of California during World War II and had approved the internment of Japanese Americans—a decision he later deeply regretted. He now used his political and legal skills to strike a blow for justice. He knew that such a critical case needed a unanimous decision to win broad political support. One by one, he persuaded his Supreme Court colleagues of the importance of striking down segregation. On May 17, 1954, Warren delivered the historic unanimous ruling: "To separate [black children] from others of similar age and qualifications solely because of their race generates a feeling of inferiority as to their status in the community that may affect their hearts and minds in a way unlikely ever to be undone. . . . Separate educational facilities are inherently unequal."

25.2.2 White Resistance, Black Persistence

The *Brown* case was a great triumph, but it was only the first step. Desegregation would be meaningful only when it was enforced, and that was another matter entirely. At first, there seemed to be cause for optimism as many white officials in the South seemed resigned to accept the decision. However, few were willing to initiate action to implement desegregation. Even the Supreme Court delayed its decision on implementation for a full year and then simply called for the process to begin "with all deliberate speed" but specified no timetable. Political leaders did not begin to work on the task, leaving sympathetic educators and eager black Americans with no support. President Eisenhower was not enthusiastic about racial integration. He said, "I don't think you can change the hearts of men with laws or decisions."

In 1955, the year after the *Brown* decision, white Mississippians murdered fourteen-year-old Emmett Till for allegedly whistling at a white woman. Till was from Chicago but was visiting relatives in Mississippi. His mutilated body was found in the Tallahatchie River. Although Till's killers later confessed to the murder, an all-white jury found them not guilty. Eisenhower remained silent about Till's murder and the travesty of justice, even when E. Frederick Morrow, his one black adviser, beseeched him to condemn the lynching.

Eisenhower's hands-off policy emboldened segregationists to resist the Supreme Court's desegregation decision. When it became clear that the federal government would not enforce the ruling, white resistance spread across the South. State legislatures passed resolutions vowing to protect segregation, and most congressional representatives from the South signed the 1956 "Southern Manifesto," promising to oppose federal desegregation efforts.

A crisis at Central High School in Little Rock, Arkansas, finally forced Eisenhower to act. Under a federal court's order to desegregate, school officials were prepared to comply and had carefully mobilized community support. But Arkansas Governor Orville Faubus, facing reelection, instructed National Guard troops to maintain "order" by blocking the entry of black students into the school. Eisenhower initially refused to intervene in the crisis. Hoping for a compromise, he met with Faubus, who agreed to allow the school to integrate peacefully. But Faubus broke his word, withdrew the National Guard troops, and left Little Rock, leaving black students unprotected.

On September 23, 1957, as nine peaceful, dignified, and well-dressed black students attempted to enter Central High, a huge angry crowd of whites surrounded them. With international news cameras broadcasting pictures of the shrieking and menacing mob, Eisenhower was forced to federalize the Arkansas National Guard and send 1,000 paratroopers to Little Rock. Eisenhower acted to maintain federal authority rather than to support integration. But Little Rock became a turning point in the struggle for racial equality.

25.2.3 Boycotts and Sit-Ins

Under Jim Crow laws in the South, black passengers were required to sit in the back section of buses, leaving the front of the bus for whites. If the "white" section at the front of the bus filled up, black passengers were required to give up their seats for white passengers. Rosa Parks and the black community of Montgomery, Alabama, were ready to take on the system. Parks, who worked as a seamstress, was a widely respected leader in Montgomery's black community, active in her church, and secretary of the local NAACP. She had already worked successfully as an advocate for black women who had been raped by white men in the South—in a few cases sending their attackers to prison. On December 1, 1955, on her way home from work, sitting in the first row of the "colored" section of the bus when the front of the bus filled with passengers, she refused to move when a white man demanded her seat. Parks was arrested, and black Montgomery sprang into action.

Literally overnight, the Montgomery bus boycott was born. For 381 days, more than 90 percent of Montgomery's black citizens sacrificed their comfort and convenience for the sake of their rights and dignity. As one elderly black woman replied when a white reporter offered her a ride as she walked to work, "No, my feets is tired but my soul is rested."

Martin Luther King Jr., pastor of the Dexter Avenue Baptist Church, was a newcomer to Montgomery when the bus boycott began. He embraced the opportunity to become the leader of the boycott and, eventually, became the most powerful spokesperson for

Map 25.1 MAJOR EVENTS OF THE AFRICAN AMERICAN CIVIL RIGHTS MOVEMENT, 1953–1963

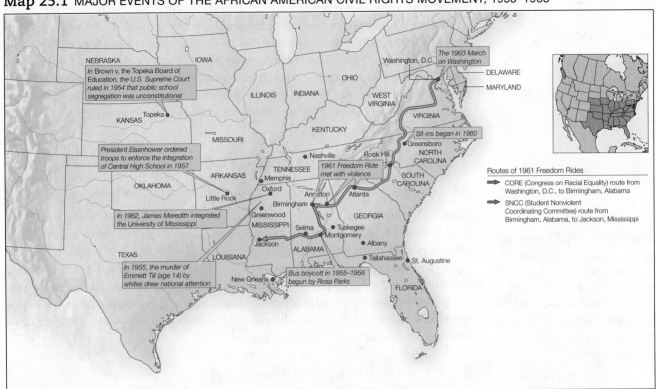

The 1963 March on Washington

In Brown v. the Topeka Board of Education, the U.S. Supreme Court ruled in 1954 that public school segregation was unconstitutional

President Eisenhower ordered troops to enforce the integration of Central High School in 1957

In 1962, James Meredith integrated the University of Mississippi

In 1955, the murder of Emmett Till (age 14) by whites drew national attention

Sit-ins began in 1960

1961 Freedom Ride met with violence

Bus boycott in 1955–1956 begun by Rosa Parks

Routes of 1961 Freedom Rides

→ CORE (Congress on Racial Equality) route from Washington, D.C., to Birmingham, Alabama

⇒ SNCC (Student Nonviolent Coordinating Committee) route from Birmingham, Alabama, to Jackson, Mississippi

Most of the major events of the early stages of the black freedom struggle took place in the South. Black southerners formed the backbone of the movement, but the grassroots protest movement drew participants from all regions of the country, all racial and ethnic groups, cities and rural areas, churches and universities, old and young, lawyers and sharecroppers.

the civil rights movement. On the first night of the boycott, 5,000 listeners gathered in the church to hear their new young leader. Dr. King stirred the crowd with an eloquent call to action, reminding them to act with courage and dignity. Their peaceful and powerful protest, he accurately predicted, would be recorded in the history books for generations to come. King continued his fight for freedom for 13 more years until his death by an assassin's bullet.

The bus boycott ended a year later when the Supreme Court ruled that Montgomery's buses must integrate, but the momentum generated by the boycott galvanized the civil rights movement. King and other leaders formed the Southern Christian Leadership Conference (SCLC), which united black ministers across the South in the cause of civil rights. The boycott tactic spread to other southern cities. As boycotts continued, a new strategy emerged: the **sit-in**.

On February 1, 1960, four African American students at North Carolina Agricultural and Technical College in Greensboro, inspired by the bus boycott, entered the local Woolworth's store and sat down at the lunch counter. When they were told "We do not serve Negroes," they refused to leave, forcing the staff at Woolworth's to physically remove the nonviolent protesters. Undaunted, they returned to the lunch counter the next day with twenty-three classmates. By the end of the week, more than a thousand students joined the protest. By this time, white gangs had gathered, waving Confederate flags and menacing the black undergraduates. But the students responded by waving American flags.

In May 1961, members of the Congress of Racial Equality (CORE) organized the Freedom Rides, in which black and white civil rights workers attempted to ride two interstate buses from Washington, D.C., to New Orleans in an effort to challenge segregation at facilities used in interstate travel. Their journey began peacefully, but when

sit-in
A form of civil disobedience in which activists sit down somewhere in violation of law or policy in order to challenge discriminatory practices or laws. The tactic originated during labor struggles in the 1930s and was used effectively in the civil rights movement in the 1960s.

they reached Rock Hill, South Carolina, a group of whites beat John Lewis, one of the young black riders, for entering a whites-only restroom. In Anniston, Alabama, a mob slashed the tires of one of the buses, threw a fire bomb through a window, and pummeled the riders with fists and pipes. After the brutal beatings, reinforcements from the Student Nonviolent Coordinating Committee (SNCC) arrived to continue the Freedom Rides. They persevered, facing beatings along the way until they reached Jackson, Mississippi, where they were immediately arrested and jailed. The spirit and strength of the civil rights workers inspired many others to join them in the movement.

25.3 The Eisenhower Years

What were the major accomplishments and limitations of Eisenhower's presidency?

military-industrial complex
The term given by President Dwight D. Eisenhower to describe the armed forces and the politically powerful defense industries that supplied arms and equipment to them.

Dwight D. Eisenhower's presidency was notable for moderation, with few major new initiatives and leadership that rested more on his personal stature than his actions. Ike, as he was known, presided during a time of great prosperity, and his policies encouraged business expansion. However, the former general did try to stem the defense buildup. In his farewell address as president, Eisenhower warned the nation against the growing power of the **military-industrial complex**, the term he coined to describe the armed forces and the politically powerful defense industries that supplied arms and equipment to them.

25.3.1 The Middle of the Road

As president, Eisenhower pursued a path down the middle of the road. His probusiness legislative agenda and appointments pleased conservatives, and he placated liberals by extending many of the policies of the welfare state enacted during the New Deal. He agreed to the expansion of Social Security and unemployment compensation and an increase in the minimum wage. He also made concerted efforts to reduce defense spending, believing that continued massive military expenditures would hinder the nation's economic growth. In December 1953, Eisenhower announced the New Look, a streamlined military that relied less on expensive conventional ground forces and more on air power and advanced nuclear capabilities.

Table 25.1 THE ELECTION OF 1956

Candidate	Political Party	Popular Vote (%)	Electoral Vote
Dwight D. Eisenhower	Republican	57.6	457
Adlai E. Stevenson	Democratic	42.1	73

SOURCE: Historical Election Results, Electoral College, National Archives and Records Administration

Eisenhower's plans to reduce defense spending derailed in 1957 when the Soviet Union launched *Sputnik*, the first artificial Earth satellite. Although *Sputnik* could not be seen with the naked eye—it was only 22 inches in diameter—it emitted a beeping noise that was broadcast by commercial radio stations in the United States, making its presence very real and causing near-hysteria among the public. The Soviet's launching of *Sputnik II* a month later confirmed widespread fears that the United States was behind in the space race and, more significantly, in the arms race. Eisenhower's popularity in the polls suddenly dropped 22 points.

Acquiescing to his critics, the president increased funds for military, scientific, and educational spending. NASA, which developed the program of space exploration, was one result. But Eisenhower believed that "the most critical problem of all" was the lack of American scientists and engineers. He led the federal government to subsidize additional science and math training for both teachers and students.

At the same time, Eisenhower continued to promote big business. His secretary of defense, former head of General Motors Charles Wilson, commented that "what's good for General Motors business is good for America." But not everyone agreed. Eisenhower's probusiness policies often harmed the nation's environment. He promoted the Submerged Land Act, which removed from federal jurisdiction more than $40 billion worth of oil-rich offshore lands. Under the control of state governments, oil companies could—and did—gain access to them. The *New York Times* called the act "one of the greatest and surely the most unjustified give-away programs" in the nation's history. The administration's willingness to allow businesses to expand with little regulation, and with virtually no concern for the environment, contributed to increasing pollution of the air, water, and land during the 1950s and helped spark the environmental movement of the 1960s and 1970s.

Eisenhower also supported the Federal-Aid Highway Act of 1956. As the largest public works project the nation had ever mounted, this centrally planned transportation system contributed to the national pastime of family road vacations and tourism. Cheap gas fueled America's car culture. Cars gave Americans increased mobility and enabled suburban dwellers to drive to work in the cities. But reliance on the automobile doomed the nation's passenger train system and led to the decline of public transportation. Cars also contributed to suburban sprawl, air pollution, and traffic jams.

25.3.2 Eisenhower's Foreign Policy

The New Look, while containing military spending, shifted American military priorities from reliance on conventional weapons to nuclear deterrence and covert operations. During Eisenhower's presidency, the United States and the Soviet Union both solidified their separate alliances. The twelve original NATO nations agreed that an attack on any one of them would be considered an attack on all, and they maintained a force to defend the West against a possible Soviet invasion. NATO expanded in 1952 to include Greece and Turkey, and West Germany joined in 1955. The Soviet Union formed a similar alliance, the Warsaw Pact, with the countries of Eastern Europe. Confrontations between the United States and the Soviet Union over the fate of Europe gave way to subtle maneuvers regarding the Third World— a term originally referring to nonaligned nations in the Middle East, Africa, Asia, and Latin America.

After Joseph Stalin died in 1953, Nikita Khrushchev became the new leader of the Soviet Union and called for peaceful coexistence with the United States. To limit military expenditures and improve relations, the superpowers arranged high-level summit meetings. In 1955, delegates from the United States, the Soviet Union, Britain, and France met in Geneva. Although the meeting achieved little of substance, it set a tone of cooperation. In 1959, Khrushchev came to the United States, met with Eisenhower, and toured the country. Despite the Soviet downing of an American U-2 spy plane in 1960, the superpowers began to discuss arms limitation. Both countries agreed to limit aboveground testing of nuclear weapons because of the health and environmental risks such tests posed. Soviet negotiations with the United States did not, however, mean greater liberty in Eastern Europe, where in 1956 Soviet forces crushed an uprising in Hungary.

The Eisenhower administration distrusted countries that maintained neutrality in the Cold War, fearing that those not aligned with the United States might turn to communism and become allies of the Soviet Union. Through covert operations, including coups and assassinations, the Central Intelligence Agency (CIA) manipulated governments around the world. In 1953, the CIA helped to overthrow the elected government in Iran—which had seized control of Western-owned oil fields in the country—and to restore the dictatorship of Shah Reza Pahlavi, whose unpopular Western-leaning regime would be overthrown by Muslim fundamentalists in 1979. The CIA helped overthrow

Map 25.2a COLD WAR SPHERES OF INFLUENCE, WESTERN HEMISPHERE, 1953–1963

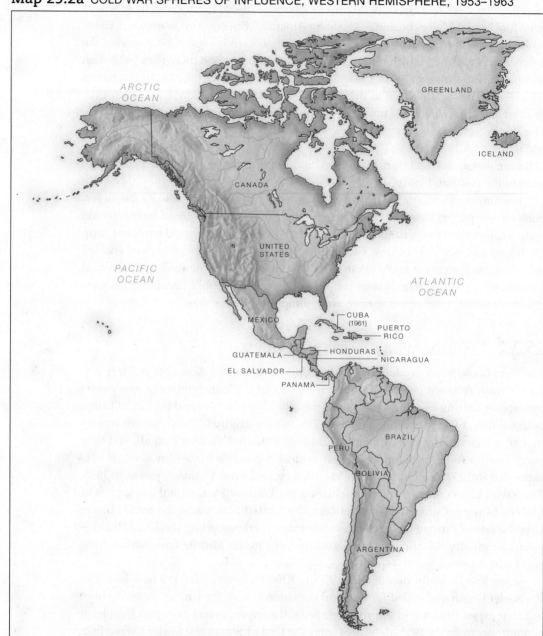

During the early years of the Cold War, the United States and the Soviet Union developed formal military alliances, most importantly NATO and the Warsaw Pact. The American and Soviet informal spheres of influence also included trading and cultural ties to other countries. Many independent nations, especially those just emerging from colonialism, remained neutral in the Cold War.

the elected government of Jacobo Arbenz in Guatemala in 1954. U.S. officials considered Arbenz a communist because he sought to redistribute large tracts of land, much of it owned by the Boston-based United Fruit Company. In 1959, revolutionary leader Fidel Castro established a regime in Cuba based on socialist principles. His government took control of foreign-owned companies, including many owned by Americans, alarming U.S. officials and investors in Cuba. Eisenhower's hostility encouraged Castro to forge an alliance with the Soviet Union. The CIA then launched a plot to overthrow Castro. In 1960–1961, the CIA also helped orchestrate the overthrow and assassination of the charismatic left-leaning Patrice Lumumba, the first minister of the Republic of the Congo in Africa, soon after its independence from Belgium.

Map 25.2b COLD WAR SPHERES OF INFLUENCE, EASTERN HEMISPHERE, 1953–1963

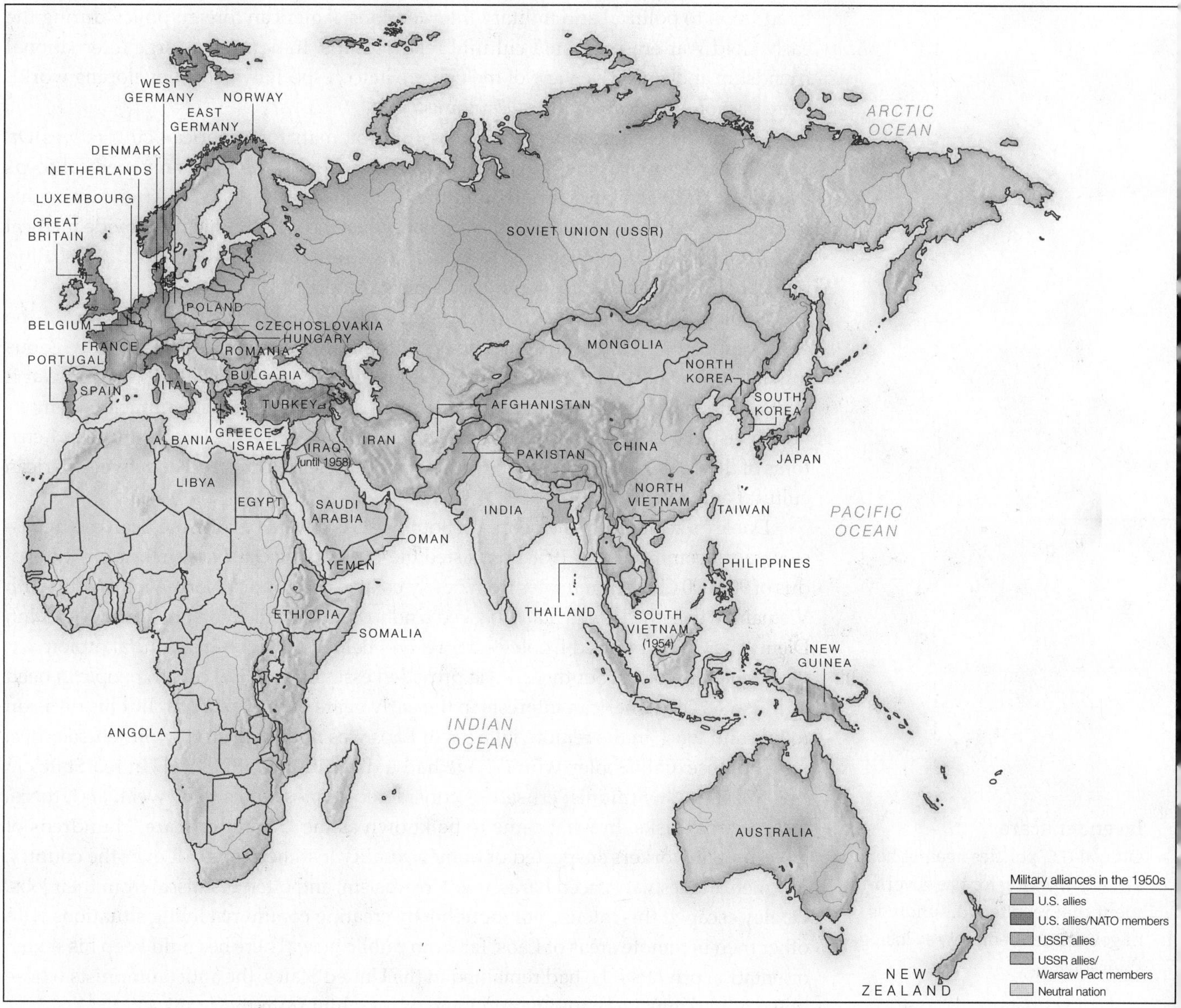

The Middle East became a focus for U.S. foreign policy under Eisenhower. When Egyptian leader Gamal Abdul Nasser nationalized the British-controlled Suez Canal in 1956, arguing that canal tolls would provide funds for a dam, the British government, with the help of France and Israel, launched an attack against Egypt to regain control of the canal. Although he distrusted Nasser, Eisenhower criticized Britain for trying to retain its imperial position in the Middle East, a move applauded by leaders in Africa and Asia. The episode weakened U.S. relations with Nasser, who forged ties with the Soviet Union. Eisenhower now feared that "Nasserism" might spread throughout the Middle East.

In the spring of 1957, Congress approved the Eisenhower Doctrine, a pledge to defend Middle Eastern countries "against overt armed aggression from any nation controlled by international communism." However, U.S. policymakers rarely distinguished between nationalist movements and designs by "international communism," which they defined as Soviet aggression. Because American leaders believed that struggles for national self-determination in Third World countries were inspired and supported by the Soviet Union, they used the Eisenhower Doctrine to provide justification for U.S. military intervention to support pro-Western governments.

25.3.3 Cultural Diplomacy

In addition to political and military interventions, American foreign policy during the early Cold War era promoted cultural relationships. Initiatives to forge international friendship and a positive view of the United States, especially in the developing world, were part of American "cultural diplomacy."

One of the earliest and most successful diplomats for American culture was Dr. Tom Dooley, known as the "jungle doctor." Dooley joined the U.S. Navy medical corps during World War II and remained in the Navy Reserve until 1950. After earning his medical degree, he moved to Southeast Asia, where he set up clinics to provide medical care for impoverished villagers. He quickly became a major celebrity. In a 1960 Gallup poll, Dooley was among the ten most admired Americans.

Dooley personified the complex legacy of U.S. cultural diplomacy during the early years of the Cold War. A practicing Catholic, he rejected the role of the religious missionary—a role tied to racism and imperialism in the anticolonial post–World War II years. Rather, Dooley promoted modernization and development, embracing an internationalist vision grounded in respect and appreciation for the local culture and customs of the people with whom he lived. As a result, he was the most effective American cultural ambassador.

Dooley's zeal to help the people of Southeast Asia went beyond medical care. A passionate anticommunist, in 1956 he assisted the CIA and the U.S. Navy in leading the exodus of 900,000 Catholic refugees from newly created communist North Vietnam to South Vietnam, where the United States backed a noncommunist dictatorship under Ngo Dinh Diem. The CIA supported Dooley's efforts and helped publicize his cultural diplomacy.

Dooley's work in Southeast Asia provided essential medical care to people in need and also served American interests in the early years of the Cold War. But his decision to live and work in the remote villages of Laos was not based simply on self-sacrifice. As a homosexual, Dooley would have had a difficult life within the United States in the 1950s. Anticommunist crusaders considered homosexuals to be weak and, therefore, security risks. In what came to be known as the "**lavender scare**," hundreds of government workers suspected of homosexuality lost their jobs. All over the country, gay men and lesbians faced harassment, ostracism, and often dismissal from their jobs. Dooley escaped this intense homophobia by creating communal living situations with other men in remote areas of Laos, far from public view. There he could keep his sexual orientation private. If he had remained in the United States, the anticommunists whose political passions he shared would have purged him from their ranks.

lavender scare
Official U.S. policies against homosexuals working for the government that resulted in hundreds of government employees losing their jobs.

25.4 Outsiders and Opposition

Beneath the surface of conformity and tranquility, what political and cultural upheavals were taking shape in the 1950s?

The 1950s often are remembered for political and cultural complacency among white Americans, with opposition to the nation's institutions emanating from people of color. But an increasing number of young whites, in the South as well as North, joined the struggle for civil rights. Others were drawn to the music and dance of black America, especially the fusion of rhythm-and-blues with country-and-western, a form of early rock 'n' roll. Distinct types of protest also emerged from the white middle class: the rebellion of the Beats who rejected staid conformity, the stirrings of discontent among women, and the antinuclear and environmental movements. Many artists rejected mainstream values, as Jackson Pollock and other abstract expressionist painters challenged artistic conventions and shifted the center of the art world from Paris to New York. Even the sexual revolution of the 1960s and 1970s had its roots in widespread defiance of the rigid sexual codes of the 1950s.

25.4.1 Rebellious Youth

One clue that all was not tranquil was the widespread panic that the nation's young were out of control. Adults worried about an epidemic of juvenile delinquency, blaming everything from parents to comic books. New celebrities such as movie stars Marlon Brando and James Dean portrayed misunderstood youth in rebellion against a corrupt and uncaring adult world. In their films, and in J. D. Salinger's now-classic novel *Catcher in the Rye*, young women and men strain against the authority and expectations of their parents and the adult world, dreaming of freedom and personal fulfillment.

Sexual mores were rigid in the 1950s—and widely violated. Single young women who became pregnant faced disgrace and ostracism unless they married quickly, which many did. Abortion, which had been illegal since the late nineteenth century but tacitly accepted until after World War II, became increasingly difficult to obtain, with hospitals placing new restrictions on legal therapeutic abortions. A double standard encouraged men to pursue sexual conquest as a mark of manhood and virility but tarnished the reputation of women who engaged in sexual intercourse prior to marriage.

In many ways, the youth of the 1950s were already undermining the constraints that toppled in the next decade. Nowhere is this more obvious than in the explosion of rock 'n' roll, with its roots in African American rhythm-and-blues, its raw sexuality, and its jubilant rebelliousness. Rock 'n' roll emerged from the fusion of musical traditions among artists from many ethnic backgrounds. Jewish songwriters Jerry Leiber and Mike Stoller wrote songs such as "Hound Dog" for black artists such as Willie Mae Thornton that were later recorded by white Southerner Elvis Presley.

JACKSON POLLOCK AT WORK Jackson Pollock shocked the art world when he began dripping paint on large canvases. Abstract expressionist painters like Pollock celebrated their break from conventional forms and representations. National leaders embraced abstract expressionism as symbolic of American artistic freedom, and thousands of Americans hung reproductions of abstract art on the walls of their suburban homes.

National Portrait Gallery, Smithsonian Institution/Art Resource, NY

What do you see in Jackson Pollock's painting, and why do you think middle-class Americans at the time would find this aesthetic form appealing?

The first Mexican American rock 'n' roll star, Ritchie Valens, sang ballads such as "Donna" along with jazzed-up versions of Mexican folk songs such as "La Bamba." Rock 'n' roll became an avenue for breaking down barriers of race and class and allowed young women to participate in the sexually charged youth culture emerging at the time.

25.4.2 Rebellious Men

Men, too, were in revolt. According to widely read studies of the time, such as William Whyte's *The Organization Man* and David Reisman's *The Lonely Crowd*, middle-class men were forced into boring, routinized jobs, groomed to be "outer-directed" at the expense of their inner lives, and saddled with the overwhelming burden of providing for ever-growing families with insatiable consumer desires.

A few highly visible American men provided alternative visions. Hugh Hefner built his Playboy empire by offering men the trappings of the "good life" without its burdensome responsibilities. The Playboy ethic encouraged men to enjoy the sexual pleasures of attractive women without the chains of marriage and to pursue the rewards of consumerism in well-appointed "bachelor flats" rather than appliance-laden homes. *Playboy* magazine celebrated this lifestyle.

Beat poets, writers, and artists offered a different type of escape. In literary works such as Allen Ginsberg's poem *Howl* and Jack Kerouac's novel *On the Road*, and in their highly publicized lives, the Beats celebrated freedom from conformity, eccentric artistic expression, playful obscenity, experimentation with drugs, open homosexuality, and male bonding. While eschewing the luxurious consumerism Hefner extolled, the Beats shared with *Playboy* a vision of male rebellion against conformity and responsibility. The mainstream men who indulged in these fantasies were more likely to enjoy them vicariously than to bolt from the breadwinner role. The dads who were honored on the new consumer holiday of Father's Day far outnumbered the freewheeling Beats and bachelors.

25.5 The Kennedy Era

How did Kennedy's foreign and domestic policies differ from those of Eisenhower?

The decade's emphasis on youthfulness seemed to be embodied in the presidency of John Fitzgerald Kennedy (JFK), the first American president born in the twentieth century and the first Roman Catholic president. In his inaugural address, he claimed that "the torch has been passed to a new generation." It was a fitting metaphor for a young man who had been reared to compete and to win, whether the contest was athletic, intellectual, or political. But at the time of his election, it was not clear that a new generation had grabbed the torch. The young candidate was largely the creation of his father, Joseph, who rose to power and wealth as a financier, Hollywood executive, and ambassador to England. Ambitious and demanding, the elder Kennedy was known for his ruthlessness in business and politics and for his blatant philandering. He groomed his oldest son, Joseph P. Kennedy Jr., for greatness, specifically for the presidency. But when young Joe was killed in World War II, the father's ambitions settled on the next in line, John.

John (Jack) Kennedy became a hero during World War II, winning military honors for rescuing his crewmates on his patrol boat, PT-109, when it was rammed by a Japanese destroyer. The rescue left him with a painful back impairment and exacerbated the symptoms of Addison's disease, which plagued him all his life and necessitated daily cortisone injections. His father coached him to bear up under the pain, hide his infirmity, and project an image of health and vitality. "Vigor" was a word Kennedy used often and an aura he projected, inspiring a national craze for physical fitness that survives to this day. Young JFK also emulated his father's brash sexual promiscuity, even after his marriage to Jacqueline Bouvier in 1953.

In 1946, Kennedy won election to the House of Representatives, and in 1952, he defeated incumbent Republican Henry Cabot Lodge to become the Democratic senator from Massachusetts. JFK's father financed all of his political campaigns, and in 1960, the elderly Kennedy bankrolled and masterminded JFK's narrowly successful run for the White House. Kennedy selected as his running mate the powerful Senate majority leader, Lyndon B. Johnson of Texas, whom he had battled for the nomination.

Table 25.2 THE ELECTION OF 1960

Candidate	Political Party	Popular Vote (%)	Electoral Vote
John F. Kennedy	Democratic	49.9	303
Richard M. Nixon	Republican	49.6	219

SOURCE: Historical Election Results, Electoral College, National Archives and Records Administration

25.5.1 Kennedy's Domestic Policy

With a thin margin of victory over Richard Nixon, who had been vice president under Eisenhower, Kennedy lacked a popular mandate for change. But he quickly established himself as an eloquent leader. In his inaugural address, the new president inspired the nation with his memorable words, "My fellow Americans, ask not what your country can do for you; ask what you can do for your country." Focusing his address on foreign policy, he declared, "Let every nation know . . . that we shall pay any price, bear any burden, meet any hardship, support any friend, oppose any foe to assure the survival and the success of liberty." He initially sought to avoid division at home and to wage the Cold War forcefully abroad. He believed that prosperity was the best way to spread the fruits of affluence, rather than government programs that would redistribute wealth. Accordingly, he supported corporate tax cuts to stimulate the economy, which grew at a rate of 5 percent each year from 1961 to 1966.

Although Democrats held strong majorities in both houses, powerful conservatives in the South often teamed up with Republicans in Congress to defeat reform legislation. Kennedy knew that it would be futile to champion the cause of civil rights in the face of that alliance. But he did support issues important to his working-class constituents and proposed a number of legislative initiatives, including increasing the minimum wage, health care for the aged, larger Social Security benefits, and the creation of the Department of Housing and Urban Development (HUD).

25.5.2 Kennedy's Foreign Policy

Kennedy was the first U.S. president to understand and recognize the legitimacy of movements for national self-determination in the Third World. He supported movements to end colonial rule while at the same time containing the spread of communism. His efforts earned him a great deal of good will among Africans and other non-Europeans. But if nationalist movements appeared friendly to the Soviet Union, Kennedy worked against them. He sharply increased military spending and nuclear arms buildup as a show of strength and preparedness against possible Soviet aggression.

One of Kennedy's most popular initiatives was the Peace Corps, a cultural diplomacy program that sent Americans, especially young people, to nations around the world to work on development projects. In 1961, Kennedy signed the Charter of Punta del Este with several Latin American countries, establishing the Alliance for Progress, a program designed to prevent the spread of anti-Americanism and communist insurgencies in Latin America. The alliance offered $20 billion in loans to Latin American countries for democratic development initiatives.

Kennedy continued the strategies of Truman and Eisenhower to fight communism in South Vietnam by supporting the corrupt regime of Ngo Dinh Diem. But the National Liberation Front (NLF), founded in 1960 and supported by Ho Chi Minh's communist regime in North Vietnam, gained the upper hand in its struggle against Diem. In response, Kennedy increased the number of military advisers there from 800 to 17,000. By 1963, it was obvious that Diem's brutal regime was about to fall to the NLF, and Kennedy allowed U.S. military advisers and diplomats to encourage Diem's dissenting generals to depose Diem.

Kennedy also faced a crisis in Cuba. Fidel Castro's revolution initially represented the sort of democratic insurgency that Kennedy wanted to support. But Castro's socialism turned the United States against him, and he established close ties with the Soviet Union. During the Eisenhower administration, the CIA began planning an invasion of Cuba with the help of Cuban exiles in Florida. Kennedy's national security advisers persuaded Kennedy to allow the invasion to proceed.

On April 17, 1961, U.S.-backed and -trained anticommunist forces, most of them Cuban exiles, landed at the Bahia de Cochinas (Bay of Pigs) on the southern coast of Cuba. Castro expected the invasion—his agents in Florida had infiltrated the Cuban exiles—so his well-prepared troops quickly surrounded and captured the invaders. No domestic uprising against Castro occurred to support the invasion. Kennedy pulled back in humiliating defeat but continued to support covert efforts that tried but failed to destabilize Cuba and assassinate Castro.

Another crisis soon erupted in Berlin. Located 200 miles deep in East Germany, with only two highways connecting it to West Germany, West Berlin was a showcase of Western material superiority and an espionage center for Western powers. In June 1961, Khrushchev threatened to end the Western presence in Berlin and unite the city with the rest of East Germany. In part, Khrushchev wanted to stop the steady stream of East Germans into West Berlin. Kennedy refused to relinquish West Berlin. On August 13, 1961, the East German government constructed a wall to separate East and West Berlin. Two years later, Kennedy stood in front of the wall and pledged to defend the West Berliners.

The most serious foreign policy crisis of Kennedy's presidency came in 1962, when the Soviet Union, at Castro's invitation, began to install nuclear missiles in Cuba. Kennedy's advisers presented several possible responses. The most dramatic and dangerous would be a full-scale military invasion of the island, which would topple Castro but would surely have prompted military retaliation by the Soviet Union. Another option was a more limited military intervention, an air strike to destroy the missiles before they became operational. Others proposed a blockade of Cuban ports to prevent the missiles from entering. Another possibility was to negotiate secretly with Castro, Soviet leaders, or both. Kennedy decided against behind-the-scenes negotiations as well as the drastic move of military intervention and instead established a "quarantine" around the island to block Soviet ships from reaching Cuba, hoping that the Soviet Union would back down and withdraw the missiles. A quarantine, unlike a blockade, was not considered an act of war; nevertheless, Kennedy put the Strategic Air Command on full alert for possible nuclear war.

It was a risky move. On national television, Kennedy warned the Soviet Union to remove the missiles or face the military might of the United States. For the next five days, tensions mounted, as Russian ships hovered in the water beyond the quarantine zone. Finally, Khrushchev proposed an agreement, offering to remove the missiles if the United States would agree not to invade Cuba. Kennedy also privately promised to remove Jupiter missiles in Turkey as soon as the crisis was over. The two leaders managed to diffuse the crisis, but they were both sobered by the experience of having come to the brink of nuclear war. In 1963, they signed a nuclear test ban treaty.

25.5.3 1963: A Year of Turning Points

While the United States faced crises abroad, there was domestic unrest as well. In 1963, the President's Commission on the Status of Women published a report that documented widespread discrimination against women in jobs, pay, education, and the professions. In response, Kennedy issued a presidential order requiring the civil service to hire people "without regard to sex," and he supported passage of the Equal Pay Act of 1963.

Also in 1963, in Birmingham, Alabama, Martin Luther King Jr. led a silent and peaceful march through the city. Chief of Police Bull Connor unleashed the police, who blasted the demonstrators with fire hoses and attacked them with vicious police dogs. Four black children were later killed when segregationists bombed an African American church. The Kennedy administration responded by bringing the full force of its authority to bear on the officials in Birmingham. But the crisis intensified. Alabama's segregationist governor, George Wallace, refused to admit two black students to the University of Alabama, threatening to stand in the doorway to block their entrance.

Finally, on June 10, 1963, Kennedy federalized the Alabama National Guard and for the first time went before the American people to declare himself forcefully on the side of the civil rights protesters and to propose a civil rights bill. A few months later, on August 28, more than 250,000 people gathered at the nation's capital in front of the Lincoln Memorial for the culmination of the March on Washington, a huge demonstration for jobs as well as freedom, where Martin Luther King Jr. delivered his inspiring "I Have a Dream" speech.

"I HAVE A DREAM" The high tide of the modern civil rights movement was the 1963 March on Washington for Jobs and Freedom, where Dr. Martin Luther King Jr. delivered his "I Have a Dream" speech. The following year, Congress passed the Civil Rights Act of 1964.

The Art Archive at Art Resource, NY

In what ways did King's call for jobs as well as freedom shift the goals of the civil rights movement?

Interpreting History

Rachel Carson: *Silent Spring* (1962)

"Can anyone believe it is possible to lay down such a barrage of poisons on the surface of the earth without making it unfit for all life?"

In 1962, Silent Spring, Rachel Carson's eloquent exposé of the chemical industry's deadly impact on the health of the planet, landed on the best-seller list, where it stayed for months. The book, which eventually sold 1.5 million copies and remains in print today, galvanized the environmental movement of the 1960s and 1970s. Carson called the chemical industry "a child of the Second World War" and creator of "elixirs of death." She reported that annual pesticide production increased from 124 million pounds in 1947 to 637 million pounds by 1960. Twenty years later it had reached 2.4 billion pounds. "In the course of developing agents of chemical warfare," she noted, "some of the chemicals created in the laboratory were found to be lethal to insects. The discovery did not come by chance: insects were widely used to test chemicals as agents of death for man."

It took hundreds of millions of years to produce the life that now inhabits the earth—eons of time in which that developing and evolving and diversifying life reached a state of adjustment and balance with its surroundings. The environment, rigorously shaping and directing the life it supported, contained elements that were hostile as well as supporting. Certain rocks gave out dangerous radiation; even within the light of the sun, from which all life draws its energy, there were short-wave radiations with power to injure. Given time—time not in years but in millennia—life adjusts, and a balance has been reached. For time is the essential ingredient; but in the modern world there is no time.

The rapidity of change and the speed with which new situations are created follow the impetuous and heedless pace of man rather than the deliberate pace of nature. Radiation is no longer merely the background radiation of rocks, the bombardment of cosmic rays, the ultraviolet rays of the sun that have existed before there was any life on earth; radiation is now the unnatural creation of man's tampering with the atom. The chemicals to which life is asked to make its adjustment are no longer merely the calcium and silica and copper and all the rest of the minerals washed out of the rocks and carried in rivers to the sea; they are the synthetic creations of man's inventive mind, brewed in his laboratories, and having no counterparts in nature.

To adjust to these chemicals would require time on the scale that is nature's; it would require not merely the years of a man's life but the life of generations. And even this, were it by some miracle possible, would be futile, for the new chemicals come from our laboratories in an endless stream; almost five hundred annually find their way into actual use in the United States alone. The figure is staggering and its implications are not easily grasped—500 new chemicals to which the bodies of men and animals are required somehow to adapt each year, chemicals totally outside the limits of biologic experience.

Among them are many that are used in man's war against nature. Since the mid-1940s over 200 basic chemicals have been created for use in killing insects, weeds, rodents, and other organisms described in the modern vernacular as "pests"; and they are sold under several thousand different brand names.

These sprays, dusts, and aerosols are now applied almost universally to farms, gardens, forests, and homes—nonselective chemicals that have the power to kill every insect, the "good" and the "bad," to still the song of the birds and the leaping of fish in the streams, to coat the leaves with a deadly film, and to linger on in the soil—all this though the intended target may be only a few weeds or insects. Can anyone believe it is possible to lay down such a barrage of poisons on the surface of the earth without making it unfit for all life? They should not be called "insecticides" but "biocides."

ENVIRONMENTALIST RACHEL CARSON
Rachel Carson, the author of *Silent Spring*, is credited with having launched the modern environmental movement.

Alfred Eisenstaedt//Time Life Pictures/Getty Images

What factors may help to explain the lasting impact of Rachel Carson's work?

Questions for Discussion

1. What connection does Carson make between time and the environment?

2. Why does Carson believe insecticides should be called biocides?

SOURCE: Rachel Carson, *Silent Spring* (Boston: Houghton Mifflin, 1962).

In the fall of 1963, a confident Kennedy began planning his reelection campaign for the next year. To mobilize support, he visited Texas. "Here we are in Dallas," he said on November 22, 1963, "and it looks like everything in Texas is going to be fine for us." Within an hour of uttering those optimistic words, the president lay dying of an assassin's bullet.

As shock and grief spread across the nation, a bizarre series of events confounded efforts to bring the assassin to justice. Police arrested Lee Harvey Oswald, who had previously lived in the Soviet Union and who had loose ties to organized crime and to political groups interested in Cuba. Oswald claimed he was innocent. But before he could be brought to trial, Oswald was murdered. Jack Ruby, a nightclub owner who also had links to organized crime, shot Oswald while he was in the custody of the Dallas police—an event witnessed by millions on live television. Ruby later died in prison. The newly sworn-in president, Lyndon B. Johnson, appointed a commission to investigate the assassination under the leadership of Supreme Court Chief Justice Earl Warren. The Warren Commission eventually concluded that Oswald and Ruby had both acted alone, although the report failed to end speculation about a possible conspiracy.

Conclusion

During the decade between the election of Dwight D. Eisenhower and the assassination of John F. Kennedy, the nation experienced unprecedented prosperity and growth. Increasing numbers of Americans moved into middle-class suburbs and enjoyed the fruits of a rapidly expanding consumer economy. Men and women rushed into marriage and childbearing, creating the baby boom and a powerful domestic ideology resting on distinct gender roles for women and men. At the same time, fears of nuclear war, intense anticommunism, and pressures to conform to mainstream political and cultural values contributed to anxieties and discontent.

Beneath the apparently tranquil surface, some Americans began to resist the limitations and exclusions of the widely touted "American way of life." African Americans in the South demanded their rightful place as full citizens, challenging the Jim Crow system and accelerating the civil rights movement through nonviolent protests, boycotts, and sit-ins. Young people created a vibrant youth culture to the pulsating rhythms of rock 'n' roll. Beats, peace activists, and environmentalists expressed incipient political and cultural dissent. The rumblings of vast social change had already begun and would explode in the years ahead, pushed along by a divisive war in Vietnam.

Chapter Review

25.1 Cold War, Warm Hearth

In what ways did the suburban family home promote Cold War ideology?
During the Cold War, an idealized image of the nuclear family came to represent the American way of life. The suburban single-family home—spacious and private, removed from the commercial centers of the city, and filled with consumer goods that reflected American abundance—symbolized the fruits of the capitalist system.

25.2 The Civil Rights Movement

What were the major goals of the civil rights movement in the 1950s?
African Americans in the South sought to dismantle the official system of segregation known as Jim Crow. Through

efforts organized in churches and by groups such as the National Association for the Advancement of Colored People (NAACP), they began to boycott public transportation, facilities, and businesses to protest against segregation.

25.3 The Eisenhower Years

What were the major accomplishments and limitations of Eisenhower's presidency?
Eisenhower is best known as a moderate president who led the country during a time of prosperity. Although not a strong advocate of the civil rights movement, he sent troops to Little Rock, Arkansas, to protect African American students entering a previously all-white school. He also warned against the increasing power of what he termed "the military-industrial complex."

25.4 Outsiders and Opposition

Beneath the surface of conformity and tranquility, what political and cultural upheavals were taking shape in the 1950s?

Many Americans chafed against the social codes of conformity. A sexually charged youth culture emerged around rock 'n' roll music. Women resisted the confines of domestic life by taking jobs and volunteering in their communities, and men vicariously protested the pressures of breadwinning by reading about sexually adventurous bachelors in *Playboy* magazine or the counterculture of the Beats.

25.5 The Kennedy Era

How did Kennedy's foreign and domestic policies differ from those of Eisenhower?

Domestically, Kennedy promoted liberal policies, including the expansion of the social safety net. While initially not a strong supporter of the civil rights movement, he quickly came to forcefully promote the struggle for racial equality. In foreign policy, Kennedy supported anticolonial struggles, especially in Africa, and promoted strong anticommunist efforts around the world.

Timeline

1954	*Brown v. Board of Education* outlaws school segregation
1955	Montgomery, Alabama, bus boycott begins
1956	Federal-Aid Highway Act
1957	USSR launches satellite *Sputnik*
1959	Cuban Revolution

1960	Oral contraceptive pill comes on the market
1961	Bay of Pigs invasion of Cuba
1962	Cuban missile crisis
1963	Betty Friedan, *The Feminine Mystique*

Glossary

baby boom The period of increased U.S. childbirths from roughly the early 1940s to the early 1960s.

suburbs Areas on the outskirts of a city, usually residential. Suburbs expanded dramatically after World War II.

Sputnik The first artificial satellite to orbit the earth, launched by the Soviet Union in 1957.

red lining Policies maintained by the Federal Housing Administration and lending banks which designated certain neighborhoods off limits to racial minorities.

sit-in A form of civil disobedience in which activists sit down somewhere in violation of law or policy in order to challenge discriminatory practices or laws. The tactic originated during labor struggles in the 1930s and was used effectively in the civil rights movement in the 1960s.

military-industrial complex The term given by President Dwight D. Eisenhower to describe the armed forces and the politically powerful defense industries that supplied arms and equipment to them.

lavender scare Official U.S. policies against homosexuals working for the government that resulted in hundreds of government employees losing their jobs.

Chapter 26
The Nation Divides: The Vietnam War and Social Conflict, 1964–1971

SNCC ACTIVIST BOB MOSES A native of New York City, Bob Moses graduated from Hamilton College in upstate New York and did graduate work at Harvard University. He was inspired by the sit-in movement that began in 1960 in the American South and soon moved south to join SNCC.

1976 George Ballis/Take Stock/The Image Works

How did the work of Bob Moses and other civil rights activists affect how other Americans thought about their society?

Contents and Focus Questions

Why did a soft-spoken black man with a strange northern accent show up in small-town McComb, Mississippi, in the summer of 1961?

Robert Parris Moses was on a mission of democracy. An organizer for the new Student Nonviolent Coordinating Committee (SNCC), he was there to encourage impoverished African Americans to register to vote. Over the next four years in the Deep South, Bob Moses paid a price for his commitments. Local police imprisoned him, and white supremacists beat him severely and murdered dozens of his fellow activists in the black freedom movement.

But Moses remained committed to nonviolence and racial integration. His quiet courage became legendary in the movement. One summer night in 1962, he returned to a deserted SNCC office in Greenwood, Mississippi, that had just been ransacked by a white mob. Three other SNCC workers had barely escaped with their lives. Moses simply looked around, made up a bed in the corner of the devastated main room, and went to sleep. He refused to be intimidated.

For all his distinctiveness, Moses did not promote himself as a charismatic leader. The women and men of SNCC worked instead to get local black communities to organize themselves and to find their leadership among their own members. During the 1960s, an extraordinary number of idealistic young people became involved in public life in an effort to make real their nation's promises of freedom, justice, and equality. The civil rights movement inspired subsequent social movements: for ending the war, for preserving the environment, and for liberating women, Latinos, Indians, and gay men and lesbians. But organizing for change inevitably brought activists up against fierce resistance from what they called "the establishment." Disillusionment and radicalization often followed. Public life became deeply contentious by 1968, as young radicals challenged more conservative citizens on issues of race, war, and gender.

*   *   *   *   *

The escalating American war in Southeast Asia loomed over all. Lyndon Johnson brought the nation to its apex of liberal reform with his extensive Great Society legislation. However, the high-flying hopes of Democratic liberals crashed to earth with the destructive war that the Johnson administration waged against seasoned Communist revolutionaries in far-off Vietnam. Out of the wreckage of 1968 emerged a Republican president, Richard Nixon, and a growing conservative backlash against the social changes advocated by people of color, the counterculture, the antiwar movement, and the rising tide of women's liberation.

By the beginning of the 1970s, American politics turned to the right, even as American culture generally remained more tolerant of different lifestyles and values than it had been before the 1960s. This libertarian combination of distrusting government while accepting greater cultural diversity has predominated in American life ever since.

26.1 Lyndon Johnson and the Apex of Liberalism

What did Johnson hope to achieve with his Great Society programs?

Wealth provided the foundation on which the **Great Society** was built. American economic expansion after World War II had created history's richest nation by 1960. From 1961 to 1966, the economy grew more than 5 percent annually with very low inflation, stimulated by large tax cuts and extensive military spending. The 41 percent increase in per capita income during the 1960s was not evenly distributed, however. And the distribution of wealth was far more skewed than that of income. The president and the Congress believed that economic expansion would continue indefinitely and the nation could therefore afford government policies to improve the welfare of less affluent Americans. Meanwhile, the Supreme Court expanded individual liberties in these same years.

Great Society
In the 1960s, President Lyndon Johnson's programs for reducing poverty, discrimination, and pollution, and for improving health care, education, and consumer protection.

26.1.1 The New President

Lyndon Baines Johnson was one of the most remarkable American characters of the twentieth century, both a giant among political leaders and a bully with those who worked for him. Johnson entered Democratic politics early as an avid supporter of Franklin Roosevelt and the New Deal and rose like a rocket through Congress to become perhaps the most powerful Senate majority leader ever (1954–1960) and then vice president (1961–1963). Kennedy's assassination catapulted him into the Oval Office as the nation's first Texan president.

Johnson retained Kennedy's cabinet and advisers and used the memory of the fallen young president to rally support for his administration. Johnson turned out to be the more liberal of the two men, in part because his early years in Texas had given him a visceral understanding of poverty and discrimination that his predecessor lacked. Johnson's focus was different, too. He retained Kennedy's anticommunist commitments abroad, but his heart remained at home, where he wanted to perfect American society.

First he had to win reelection. Less than a year remained until voters went to the polls in 1964. The Republicans nominated right-wing Senator Barry Goldwater of Arizona, a sign of the party's sharp swing away from its moderate northeastern elements toward its fiercely conservative western and southern constituencies. Goldwater believed in unrestricted markets and a minimal role for the federal government in every aspect of American life except the military. He spoke casually about using nuclear weapons against communists abroad. Goldwater declared that "extremism in the defense of liberty is no vice," but Johnson zeroed in on that extremism and swept to the largest electoral majority of any president (61 percent).

Table 26.1 THE ELECTION OF 1964

Candidate	Political Party	Popular Vote (%)	Electoral Vote
Lyndon B. Johnson	Democratic	61.1	486
Barry M. Goldwater	Republican	38.5	52

SOURCE: Historical Election Results, Electoral College, National Archives and Records Administration

26.1.2 The Great Society: Fighting Poverty and Discrimination

In pursuit of what he called the Great Society, Johnson first declared a "War on Poverty." No citizen in the richest nation on earth should live in squalor, he believed. Yet more than one out of five Americans still lived below the conservatively estimated official poverty line.

"I DO SOLEMNLY SWEAR" Lyndon Johnson took the presidential oath of office on board *Air Force One*, returning to Washington from Dallas, where John Kennedy had just been assassinated on November 22, 1963. Johnson's wife, Lady Bird, is on his right, and Jacqueline Kennedy, still in blood-stained clothes, stands on his left. Johnson adroitly channeled the public outpouring of grief for the murdered young president into support for their shared legislative goals.

World History Archive/Newscom

How did Lyndon Johnson use the image of John Kennedy as a martyred young hero to promote legislative reforms, such as his "War on Poverty"?

The president and a large congressional majority passed several measures to alleviate poverty. They sharply increased the availability of money and food stamps through the Aid to Families with Dependent Children ("welfare") program, and they raised Social Security payments to older Americans. Several programs focused on improving educational opportunities as an avenue out of poverty: Head Start offered preschool education and meals for youngsters, the Elementary and Secondary Education Act sent federal funds to the least affluent school districts, and an expanded system of student loans facilitated access to college. The Job Corps provided employment training, and Volunteers in Service to America (VISTA) served as a domestic Peace Corps, funneling people with education and skills into poor communities to serve as teachers and providers of other social services.

No barrier to opportunity in the early 1960s was higher than the color bar. Both opportunist and idealist, Johnson as president shed his segregationist voting record (necessary for election in Texas before 1960) and became the most vocal proponent of racial equality ever to occupy the Oval Office. Two factors facilitated his change in position. One, blatant inequalities for American citizens weakened the United States in its competition with the Soviets and Chinese for the loyalty of the nonwhite Third World majority. Two, the African American freedom struggle in the South had reached a boiling point. Black frustration was mounting over white brutality and the seeming indifference or even hostility of the national government.

The Civil Rights Act of 1964 fulfilled the implicit promise of the *Brown v. Board of Education* decision a decade earlier. The 1964 act made desegregation the law of the land as it outlawed discrimination in employment and in public facilities such as restaurants, theaters, and hotels. The Voting Rights Act of 1965 outlawed poll taxes and provided federal voting registrars in states that refused the ballot to African Americans. The single most important legislation of the twentieth century for bringing political democracy to the South, the Voting Rights Act increased the percentage of blacks voting in Mississippi from 7 percent to 60 percent in two years. Also in 1965, a new Immigration Act eliminated the discriminatory national-origins system, with most immigrants thereafter arriving from Asia and Latin America rather than Europe.

26.1.3 The Great Society: Improving the Quality of Life

Johnson's vision of the Great Society extended to the broader quality of life in the United States. Health care was perhaps the most fundamental issue for citizens' sense of personal security. After 1965, the new **Medicare** system paid for the medical needs of Americans age 65 and older, and **Medicaid** underwrote health care services for the poor. In 1964, when more than half of adults smoked tobacco, the surgeon general issued the first government report linking smoking to cancer. Higher federal standards for automotive safety followed a year later. Public pressures also led to the establishment of new requirements for publishing the nutritional values of packaged food. The federally funded Public Broadcasting System (PBS) was established to provide television programs that were more educational than the fare tied to advertising on the three corporate networks (NBC, CBS, and ABC). In fact, most Great Society measures targeted all Americans rather than just the disadvantaged.

Medicare
Federal program of health care insurance for all citizens age 65 and older.

Medicaid
Federal program of health care insurance for poor citizens.

Nothing more directly threatened the quality of American life than the degradation of the natural environment. The costs of the unrestrained and much-heralded economic growth since World War II showed up in the pollution of the nation's air, water, and land. Growing public awareness prompted the Clean Air Act (1963) and the Clean Water Act (1966), which set federal guidelines for reducing smog and preserving public drinking sources from bacterial pollution. Even the long dam-building tradition in the American West faced new questions, with the Wild and Scenic Rivers Act enacted in 1968. Meanwhile, Congress passed the Wilderness Act in 1964, setting aside 9 million acres of undeveloped public lands as a place "where man is a visitor who does not remain."

26.1.4 The Liberal Warren Court

The Supreme Court under the leadership of Earl Warren steadily expanded the constitutional definition of individual rights. This shift reached even those deemed to have lost many of their rights: prisoners. *Gideon v. Wainwright* (1963) established the right of impoverished prisoners to legal counsel, and *Escobedo v. Illinois* (1964) confirmed the right to counsel during interrogation, a critical hindrance to the use of torture. After *Miranda v. Arizona* (1966), police were required to inform anyone they arrested of their rights to remain silent and to speak to a lawyer.

The Warren Court bolstered other rights of individuals against potentially coercive community pressures. Decisions in 1962 and 1963 strictly limited the practice of

THE RURAL POOR, HAZARD, KENTUCKY During the 1960s, many middle-class Americans became aware of the poverty that endured across large swaths of what they thought of as their affluent society. The lives of tens of millions of Americans, from urban slums to rural mountainous communities in Appalachia, were sharply limited by indigence. Lyndon Johnson's "War on Poverty" aimed to increase economic opportunity, improve health care, and expand poorer Americans' sense of security.

AP Images

In which ways does the welfare of a nation's poorest citizens impact the quality of life for its more comfortable citizens?

requiring prayers in public schools. In 1963, the Court narrowed standards for the definition of "obscenity," allowing freer expression in the arts but also in pornography. *Griswold v. Connecticut* (1965) established the use of contraceptive devices by married people as a matter of private choice protected by the Constitution. In 1967, the Court heard the case of Mildred Jeter, a black woman, and Richard Loving, a white man, Virginians who had evaded their state's ban on interracial marriage by traveling to Washington, D.C., for their wedding and then returning home to Virginia to live. In the aptly titled *Loving v. Virginia*, the Court declared marriage one of the "basic civil rights of men" and overturned the laws of the last 16 states restricting interracial unions.

The Supreme Court's interpreting of the Constitution to expand individual rights disturbed many conservative Americans. They saw the Court as another arm of an intrusive national government that was extending its control over matters previously left to local communities. For them, the goal of integration did not justify the busing of school children. Rising crime rates worried them more than police brutality. Many Roman Catholics were troubled by the legalization of contraceptives. Incensed by the ban on requiring school prayer, Protestant fundamentalists sought redress through political involvement, which they had previously shunned, initiating a grassroots religious conservative movement that helped bring Ronald Reagan to power in 1980.

26.2 Into War in Vietnam

Why did the United States go to war in Vietnam, and why did it not win the war?

The 1960s also marked the culmination of the U.S. government's efforts to control revolutionary political and social change abroad. Johnson's accomplishments at home were forever overshadowed by the war he sent Americans to fight in the quiet rice paddies and beautiful highland forests of Southeast Asia. An aggressive U.S. anticommunist policy abroad collided with leftist revolutionaries throughout the Third World, and it was ill fortune for the Vietnamese that this collision struck them hardest of all.

26.2.1 The Vietnamese Revolution and the United States

Vietnamese nationalists, varying in ideologies but led by **Ho Chi Minh** and the Indochinese Communist party, had sought since the 1930s to liberate their country from French colonial rule. Japanese advances during World War II put the Vietminh (Vietnamese nationalists) on the same side as the Americans, and Ho worked closely with the U.S. Office of Strategic Services (OSS), precursor to the Central Intelligence Agency (CIA).

Ho Chi Minh
Communist leader of North Vietnam and nationalist hero to many dissidents in South Vietnam.

After the defeat of Germany and Japan, the French wanted to regain control of their colonies in Africa and Asia, including Vietnam. The British provided troop transport ships for French soldiers, and the United States provided most of the funds to support France in its war against the Vietminh (1946–1954). Cold War priorities won out: a weakened France had to be bolstered as the linchpin of a reintegrated, anticommunist western Europe, while the Vietminh were led by Communist party members. But the Vietnamese defeated the much more heavily armed French at the battle of Dien Bien Phu in May 1954. Two months later, the Geneva Accords divided Vietnam temporarily at the seventeenth parallel until national elections could be held within two years to reunify the country. Ho's forces solidified their control of the north, the French pulled out entirely, and the Eisenhower administration made a fateful decision to intervene directly to preserve the southern part of Vietnam from communism. The United States created a new government led by the Roman Catholic, anticommunist Ngo Dinh Diem in a new country called "South Vietnam."

The Vietnamese Revolution was only half over, however. The French colonialists withdrew, but the Saigon regime did not hold elections. In North Vietnam, the sometimes brutal internal revolution for the creation of a socialist society proceeded with an extensive program of land redistribution. In South Vietnam, Diem ruled for eight years with increasing repression of Communists and other dissenters. U.S. funding kept him in power. Southern members of the old Vietminh began a sabotage campaign against the Saigon government and formed the National Liberation Front (NLF) in 1960, with the support of North Vietnam. Diem and his American supporters called them "Viet Cong" or "VC," roughly equivalent to the derogatory American term *Commies*. As the struggle to overthrow Diem intensified, several of his own generals assassinated him in November 1963 with the tacit support of U.S. officials in South Vietnam and Washington.

26.2.2 Johnson's War

Lyndon Johnson inherited his predecessors' commitment to preserving a noncommunist South Vietnam. Bolstered by Kennedy's hawkish advisers, he believed that American credibility was at stake. But Johnson faced a swiftly deteriorating military situation. The NLF, which the administration portrayed as merely a tool of North Vietnam, was winning the political war for the South, taking control of the countryside from the demoralized Army of the Republic of Vietnam (ARVN). Faced with the choice of escalating U.S. involvement to prevent an NLF victory or withdrawing entirely from the country, Johnson escalated.

How he did so was crucially important. There was neither a national debate nor a congressional vote to declare war. Johnson did not want to distract Congress from his

Map 26.1 THE AMERICAN WAR IN VIETNAM

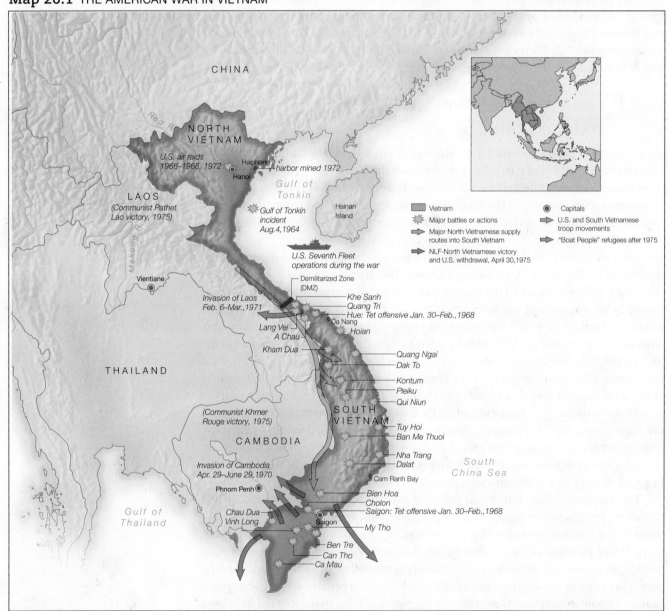

Before U.S. combat troops entered Vietnam in 1965, few Americans knew where this Southeast Asian country was. Vietnam's geography and place names quickly became familiar in the United States as hundreds of thousands of young Americans served there and some 58,000 died there. Vietnam's elongated shape, its borders with Cambodia and Laos, and its proximity to China all affected the course of the fighting between 1965 and 1973.

Great Society agenda, nor did he want to provoke the Soviet Union or China. But he believed he had to preserve a noncommunist South Vietnam or else face a debilitating backlash from Republicans, who would skewer him as McCarthy had done to Truman over the "loss" of China 15 years earlier. So the president used deception, describing offensive American actions as defensive and opening up a credibility gap between a committed government and a skeptical public.

In August 1964, North Vietnamese ships in the Gulf of Tonkin fired on the U.S. destroyer *Maddox*, which was aiding South Vietnamese sabotage operations against the North. The president portrayed the incident as one of unprovoked Communist aggression, and Congress expressed almost unanimous support through its Gulf of Tonkin Resolution. With this substitute for a declaration of war, Johnson ordered American planes to begin bombing North Vietnam, and the first American combat troops splashed ashore at Da Nang in South Vietnam on March 8, 1965. In July, the administration made the key decision to add 100,000 more soldiers, with more to follow as necessary.

American strategy had two goals: to limit the war so as not to draw in neighboring China (to avoid a repeat of the Korean War), and to force the NLF and North Vietnam to give up their struggle to reunify the country under Communist control. The problem was the political nature of the guerrilla war in the South: a contest for the loyalty of the population, in which NLF operatives mingled easily with the citizenry. This kind of war made the enemy difficult to find. The "strategic hamlet" program uprooted rural peasants and concentrated them in fortified towns, creating "free fire zones" in their wake where anything that moved was a target. The U.S. Air Force pounded the South as well as the North, dropping more bombs on this ancient land (smaller than either Germany or Japan) than had been used in all theaters on all sides in World War II. These tactics destabilized and traumatized society in South Vietnam as one-fourth of the population became refugees.

26.2.3 Americans in Southeast Asia

Who were the 3 million Americans who went to Vietnam? The initial forces contained experienced soldiers, but as the war escalated, this professional army was diluted with hundreds of thousands of young draftees. Student deferments protected more comfortable Americans, so GIs were predominantly those who lacked money and education. Very few knew anything about Vietnamese history or culture, and almost none spoke the Vietnamese language. Although 70 percent were white men, black, Hispanic, and Native American enlistees shipped out in disproportionate numbers. In sharp contrast to the motives of the NLF and the North Vietnamese army, few of these young men (along with 10,000 women who volunteered as nurses) were in Vietnam to win the war regardless of the cost or duration. They had only to survive 12 months before returning home to the safety of a peacetime society.

President Johnson spoke of the conflict in Vietnam as a case of one sovereign nation—North Vietnam—invading another—South Vietnam. However, few Vietnamese saw the war in these terms. The United States, dismissing the failure of the French before them, had intervened not so much in an international war as in an ongoing revolution that aimed to reunify the country. Few Vietnamese, whatever their opinions of communism, viewed the corrupt Saigon regime as legitimate or democratic. After all, it was kept in place by foreigners, whereas the North was ruled by people who had expelled the French foreigners.

Initial U.S. optimism reflected a grave underestimation of the NLF and the North Vietnamese. Ho Chi Minh was an extremely popular leader, and intervention from the other side of the world only strengthened his position. As the war expanded, NLF recruiting in the south snowballed, while the people of North Vietnam remained largely loyal to their authoritarian government. Communist forces proved willing to endure profound hardship and sacrifices to prevail. Their morale was much higher than that of the ARVN.

North Vietnamese regular army units came south to match the growing number of U.S. forces, and they occasionally engaged the Americans in large set battles, as at Ia Drang Valley in the fall of 1965. U.S. troops fought well in such firefights, making devastating use of their superior weapons and air power. However, the bulk of the fighting consisted of smaller engagements with deceptive enemies on their home turf who faded in and out of the civilian population with ease. Ambushes and unexpected death haunted Americans on patrol, and relentless heat and humidity wore them down.

American soldiers felt mounting frustration and rage over the nature of the war that they were ordered to fight. Lacking a clear battlefront and an understandable strategy for winning the war, they were commanded simply to kill the often mysterious enemy. Yet distinguishing civilians from combatants in a popular guerrilla war was not always easy, especially when so many civilians evidently supported the NLF and so few Americans spoke Vietnamese. Realizing that few of the people they were supposed to be defending actually wanted them there, but under orders to produce enemy bodies, many U.S. troops on the ground began to slide toward a racial war against all Vietnamese.

[handwritten margin note: war led to racist tendencies towards vietnamese since they were told to kill any asian that came their way. —My Lai 1968]

Many GIs resisted this logic, sometimes showing real kindness to Vietnamese civilians. But atrocities on both sides inevitably followed from this kind of war. The worst came in the village of My Lai on March 16, 1968, where 105 soldiers from Charlie Company—enraged by the recent deaths of several comrades in ambushes—slaughtered, often after torturing or raping, more than 400 Vietnamese women, children, and elderly men. The army covered up the massacre for a year and a half, and eventually found only Lieutenant William Calley, the leader of Charlie Company's First Platoon, guilty of murdering Vietnamese civilians.

26.2.4 1968: The Turning Point

In late 1967, the public face of the war effort remained upbeat. General William Westmoreland declared that he could now see "some light at the end of the tunnel." But hopes of an imminent victory were crushed by the startling **Tet Offensive** (named for the Vietnamese New Year) that began on January 30, 1968. NLF insurgents and North Vietnamese troops attacked U.S. strongholds throughout South Vietnam. The blow to American public confidence in Johnson and his military commanders proved irreversible. Far from being on the verge of defeat, as the administration had been claiming, the Communists had shown that they could mount simultaneous attacks around the country.

Tet Offensive
Communist military attacks across South Vietnam in January–February 1968.

The Tet Offensive coincided with two other crises in early 1968 to convince American political and business elites that U.S. international commitments had become larger than the nation could afford. First, a week before Tet began, the North Korean navy seized the U.S. intelligence ship *Pueblo* in the Sea of Japan and temporarily imprisoned its crew. U.S. commanders were left scrambling to find enough forces to respond effectively without weakening American commitments in Europe and elsewhere. Second, a British financial collapse devalued the pound and caused the London government to announce its imminent withdrawal from its historic positions east of the Suez Canal, placing new military burdens on the United States in the Middle East. These events reduced international confidence in the U.S. economy, causing a currency crisis in March 1968 as holders of dollars traded them in for gold.

black power
The slogan used by young black nationalists in the mid- and late 1960s.

The political career of Lyndon Johnson was a final casualty of these events. His support on the left withered as the antiwar and **black power** movements expanded. Meanwhile, his more centrist supporters were joining the backlash against civil rights, urban violence, and antiwar protesters, peeling off to the Republican party. On March 12, antiwar challenger Senator Eugene McCarthy of Minnesota nearly defeated the incumbent president in the New Hampshire Democratic primary. Johnson's vulnerability was clear.

Senator Robert Kennedy of New York joined the race two weeks later. In a televised speech on March 31 that caught the divided nation by surprise, Johnson announced an end to U.S. escalations in the war, the start of negotiations in Paris with North Vietnam, and an end to his own political career. He would not seek reelection.

26.3 "The Movement"

What did the protest movements of the 1960s have in common?

While national leaders were defending what they called the "frontiers of freedom" abroad, young Americans in the mid- and late 1960s organized to broaden what they considered the frontiers of freedom at home. Television for the first time tied the country together in a common culture whose shared images were transmitted simultaneously around the nation. The expanding war in Vietnam radicalized people who had initially been optimistic about reforming American society. Black power, the New Left, the counterculture, women's liberation, and other liberation movements often had quite divergent goals. But participants overlapped extensively and activists spoke of "the Movement" as if it were a unified phenomenon. At the heart of the youth movements of the decade lay a common quest for authenticity—a rejection of hypocrisy and a distrust of traditional authorities—that fused cultural and political protest.

26.3.1 From Civil Rights to Black Power

By 1966, the civil rights movement fractured as it confronted the limits of its success. It had achieved the goals of ending legal discrimination and putting southern African Americans in the voting booth, but it had not brought about a colorblind society. Racial prejudice among white conservatives remained virulent, and white liberals, such as those in the Kennedy and Johnson administrations, revealed themselves as not always trustworthy allies.

The Justice Department and the Federal Bureau of Investigation (FBI) did little to restrain the violence of the Ku Klux Klan until white organizers Michael Schwerner and Andrew Goodman and black co-worker James Chaney were murdered in the summer of 1964. Two months later, at the national Democratic party convention in Atlantic City, New Jersey, Johnson crushed the effort of the biracial Mississippi Freedom Democratic party to replace the state's regular, all-white Democratic delegates. The president was determined to avoid further alienating white southern voters as he pursued a huge victory margin in the November elections.

For centuries, the black freedom struggle had woven together elements of racial separatism with elements of integration into the larger American culture. For many younger African Americans, the pendulum now swung toward a need for greater independence from the white majority. They took inspiration from Malcolm X, the fiery and eloquent minister of the Nation of Islam (Black Muslims), who until his murder in 1965 captivated listeners with denunciations of white perfidy and demands for black self-respect. In 1966, SNCC members began to speak of the need for "black power" rather than for the integrated "beloved community" they had initially sought in 1960.

The Black Panther party formed in Oakland, California, in response to police brutality. The heavily armed Panthers engaged in several shootouts with police and were eventually decimated by an FBI campaign against them. White Americans were shocked by the uprisings and riots that swept through black urban communities during the summers of 1964–1968. Triggered by the actions of white police, the riots expressed the fierce frustrations of impoverished people whose lives remained largely untouched by the achievements of the civil rights struggle. The most destructive outbreaks occurred in the Watts district of Los Angeles in 1965 and in Detroit and Newark in 1967.

Black power thrived primarily as a cultural movement that promoted pride in African American and African history and life. The slogan "black is beautiful" captured this spirit: long degraded by their white compatriots as inferior, black Americans in the late 1960s and 1970s reversed this equation to celebrate their cultural heritage. This could be as basic as a hairstyle, the natural Afro replacing hair straightened to look like European American hair. At universities, new departments of African American studies fostered the exploration of black history. Unlearning habits of public deference to whites, most African Americans began referring to themselves as "black" rather than "Negro."

Cultural black power mixed with a different kind of political black power by the late 1960s: the election of black officials. Although militant black power advocates garnered the most media attention, most African Americans supported Lyndon Johnson and used the Voting Rights Act to pursue their goals in the realm of electoral politics. In 1966, Carl Stokes of Cleveland was elected the first black mayor of a major American city, and African Americans won local offices across the South.

26.3.2 The New Left and the Struggle Against the War

In 1962, a group of liberal college activists founded the Students for a Democratic Society (SDS). They called for a rejuvenation of American politics and society to replace the complacency that they saw pervading the country. Racial bigotry and poverty particularly troubled these optimistic young reformers, along with the overarching threat of nuclear destruction (highlighted anew by the missile crisis in Cuba). They hoped to become a kind of "white SNCC," promoting participatory democracy to redeem the promise of Cold War America.

New Left
Student-led reform movement—focused initially on poverty, racial injustice, and the threat of nuclear war—that was radicalized by the war in Vietnam.

SDS served as the central organization of the **New Left**. Communism was simply not important to these activists. Nor was conservatism, which was then at its lowest point. They focused instead on the behavior of the liberals who ran the U.S. government from 1961 to 1968. They developed a critique of "corporate liberalism" as promoting the interests of the wealthy and the business community far more than providing for the needs of the disadvantaged.

After 1965, SDS's initially broad reform agenda narrowed to stopping the Vietnam War. SDS members organized the first major antiwar protest outside the White House on April 17, 1965, bringing their organization into alliance with the small group of religious and secular pacifists already working against the war. Then mainstream Democrats began abandoning Johnson over the war as it grew. The president had alienated the powerful chair of the Senate Foreign Relations Committee, J. William Fulbright of Arkansas, by issuing misleading reports about the brief U.S. military intervention in the Dominican Republic in April 1965 to defeat a left-leaning, but not communist, coup attempt. Fulbright then held televised hearings on the American war in Southeast Asia in January 1966, raising grave doubts about its wisdom. Draft resistance increased as young men moved to Canada, as did SNCC's Bob Moses, or went to jail, as did boxing champion Muhammad Ali.

Antiwar protesters followed the same trajectory of radicalization as black power advocates. Their dismay turned to rage as the Johnson administration continued to expand a war that was destroying much of Vietnam while killing tens of thousands of American soldiers and many more Vietnamese, all for no reason its opponents considered legitimate. In combination with or in support of black militants, white radicals took over buildings on university campuses in 1968–1969: Columbia, Cornell, Harvard, San Francisco State, and many others. SDS ultimately broke apart in the confusion and exhilaration of its growing demand for revolution against the larger systemic enemies, imperialism and capitalism, not just corporate liberalism. But radical rage could not be understood apart from the ongoing destruction of Vietnam by a government acting in the name of all Americans.

26.3.3 Cultural Rebellion and the Counterculture

While the New Left moved from wanting to reform American society to wanting to overthrow it, the counterculture sought to create an alternative society. Called "hippies" by those who disliked them, these young people were alienated by the materialism, competition, and conformity of American life in the Cold War. They tried to live out alternative values of gentleness, tolerance, and inclusivity. "Do your own thing" was a common slogan.

In reaction against the conformity of mainstream society, members of the counterculture explored the limitations of consciousness to expand their self-knowledge. They went beyond the nicotine and alcohol that were the common stimulants of their parents' culture to experiment with such mind-altering drugs as marijuana, peyote, hashish, LSD, and cocaine. Spirituality was an important path into consciousness for many in the counterculture. Religious traditions associated with Asia, particularly Buddhism, gained numerous adherents, as did spiritual customs and traditional practices of Native Americans. Others rediscovered the "authentic" Jesus obscured by the institutional structures of the formal Christian church (earning themselves the nickname "Jesus freaks"); Campus Crusade for Christ, InterVarsity, and other evangelical college groups spread across the country. Music served as the most common coin of the countercultural realm, from the political folk sound of Joan Baez and Bob Dylan to the broadly popular Beatles and the more distinctly countercultural rock 'n' roll of the Grateful Dead and Jefferson Airplane.

Older Americans experienced the counterculture largely as spectacle. The mainstream media emphasized the alternative aspects of the hippie lifestyle in its coverage. Viewers were varyingly disgusted by, attracted to, and titillated by the hair, clothing, nudity, and blurred gender distinctions. Meanwhile, entrepreneurs realized that they could market the antimaterialist counterculture profitably. Young Americans eagerly bought records, clothing, jewelry, and natural foods, unintentionally revealing how consumer values pervaded American life.

One of the most visible changes of the 1960s was often called the sexual revolution. Changes in Americans' sexual behavior in the 1960s reflected in part the counterculture's goal of living an authentic, honest life in which words matched actions. The sexual revolution removed some of the penalties for the premarital and extramarital sex that had previously been fairly common but unacknowledged. The appearance of the birth control pill in 1960 underpinned the shift to more open sexual relationships by helping free women from the fear of pregnancy. Attitudes toward abortion also became more tolerant. New York passed the first state law legalizing some abortions in 1970, and three years later, the Supreme Court established a woman's constitutional right to abortion in the landmark case of *Roe v. Wade*.

26.3.4 Women's Liberation

The movement for women's liberation built on developments earlier in the decade, including Betty Friedan's *The Feminine Mystique* (1963), a widely read book that captured the frustrations of many women who had accepted the role of suburban homemaker after World War II. Friedan and other liberal feminists founded the National Organization for Women (NOW) in 1966 to lobby against sexual discrimination in the public sphere in such areas as employment, wages, education, and jury duty. These challenges had radical implications for women's and men's earnings and thus for responsibilities within families, but NOW did not yet focus on issues inside the private sphere of the home.

The shift to the view that "the personal is political" came from younger women who had been active in the civil rights and antiwar struggles. Inspired by the courage and successes of the protest movements in which they figured prominently, these female activists had also learned that traditional gender roles restricted them even in organizations dedicated to participatory democracy. Ironically, radical men could be as patronizing and disrespectful of women's abilities as mainstream men. Younger feminists in 1967 and 1968 agreed with NOW's challenge to discrimination in the public sphere, but they focused even more on the personal politics of women's daily lives, on issues such as parenting, child care, housework, and abortion.

The new wave of **feminism** that washed through American culture at the end of the 1960s triggered fierce debates about the nature of gender. Was there a uniquely feminine way of knowing, seeing, and acting, or were women in essence the same as men, distinguishable ultimately by their individuality? Was womanhood biologically or only culturally constructed? Feminists disagreed sharply in their answers. But the women's movement that emerged out of the 1960s shared a common commitment to expanding women's possibilities that permanently transformed women's lives and gender relations in American society, in areas ranging from job and educational opportunities, sexual harassment, and gender-neutral language to family roles, sexual relations, reproductive rights, and athletic facilities.

feminism
The belief that women and men are of equal value and that gender roles are, to a considerable degree, created by society rather than being simply natural.

A DIFFERENT SPIRITUAL REALITY The search by many young people in the 1960s counterculture for greater consciousness led them to a spiritual path. The young evangelists in this photograph held a Campus Crusade for Christ rally at the University of Texas at Austin in 1969. The emphasis of evangelical Christians on the person of Jesus, rather than on a particular denominational tradition, attracted many converts.

Courtesy of Cru

The sandals, long hair, and gentleness associated with Jesus made a particularly good fit with the style and values of "hippies," although most evangelicals appeared traditionally clean-cut and held conservative political views. Does this characterization of evangelicals still remain true?

EVE WAS FRAMED The new wave of organizing for women's rights that emerged in the late 1960s had many faces. Some protests against sex discrimination and disrespect of women were angry. Others were gentle, as in the scene, from 1970, captured in the photograph at left. "Raising consciousness" was a central strategy of the movement, as women and men became more aware of the gendered assumptions that had long governed—and channeled—their lives and their thoughts.

Bettmann/Corbis

To what extent do young Americans today still view being male and being female, beyond obvious physical differences, as fundamentally different ways of being in the world?

26.3.5 The Many Fronts of Liberation

Like the women's movement, the Chicano (Mexican American), pan-Indian, and gay liberation movements of the late 1960s were grounded in older organizing efforts within those communities. The struggles for "brown power," "red power," and "gay power" also reflected the newer influence of black power and its determination to take pride in what the dominant American society had denigrated for so long. Activists on college campuses successfully pressured administrations to establish interdisciplinary ethnic studies programs, such as the first Chicano studies program at California State University at Los Angeles in 1968. Ethnic cultural identity went hand in hand with the pursuit of political and economic integration into mainstream American life.

The most prominent push to organize Latinos was the effort led by César Chávez and Dolores Huerta to build a farm workers' union in California and the Southwest. These primarily Mexican American migrant workers harvested most of the hand-picked produce that Americans ate, but their hard work under severe conditions failed to lift most of them out of poverty. National consumer support for boycotts of table grapes and iceberg lettuce helped win recognition for the United Farm Workers (UFW) union and better pay by 1970.

Interpreting History

Martin Luther King Jr.: On His Opposition to the Vietnam War (1967)

> "I was increasingly compelled to see the war as an enemy of the poor and to attack it as such."

Most Americans approved of the war in Vietnam until at least 1968. Appreciative of Lyndon Johnson's commitment to reduce poverty and end racial discrimination at home, African Americans generally supported the president's policies in Southeast Asia. However, younger, more radical civil rights workers were among those who opposed the first insertion of U.S. combat troops in 1965. Within two years, the nation's most prominent black leader, Martin Luther King Jr., decided that he could no longer keep quiet about his growing unease with the American war effort. A storm of criticism greeted his public denunciation of the war, most of it suggesting that he should limit himself to domestic civil rights work. But King no longer believed that events at home and abroad could be separated. The following excerpt is from his speech at Riverside Church, New York City, April 4, 1967.

MARTIN LUTHER KING JR. His birthday now a national holiday, Martin Luther King Jr. has become widely accepted as a heroic figure in the American past.

Charles E. Kelly/Ap images

In the last few years of his life, King's increasingly sharp criticisms of injustice in American society disturbed many fellow citizens. Why?

A few years ago there was a shining moment in that struggle [against poverty and discrimination]. It seemed as if there was a real promise of hope for the poor—both black and white—through the Poverty Program. There were experiments, hopes, new beginnings. Then came the build-up in Vietnam and I watched the program broken and eviscerated as if it were some idle political plaything of a society gone mad on war. . . . I was increasingly compelled to see the war as an enemy of the poor and to attack it as such. . . .

We were taking the black young men who had been crippled by our society and sending them 8,000 miles away to guarantee liberties in Southeast Asia which they had not found in Southwest Georgia and East Harlem. So we have been repeatedly faced with the cruel irony of watching Negro and white boys on TV screens as they kill and die together for a nation that has been unable to seat them together in the same schools. . . .

As I have walked among the desperate, rejected and angry young men [in the ghettos of the North the last three summers] I have told them that Molotov cocktails and rifles would not solve their problems. I have tried to offer them my deepest compassion while maintaining my convictions that social change comes most meaningfully through non-violent action. But they asked—and rightly so—what about Vietnam? They asked if our own nation wasn't using massive doses of violence to solve its problems, to bring about the changes it wanted. Their questions hit home, and I knew that I would never again raise my voice against the violence of the oppressed in the ghettos without having first spoken clearly to the greatest purveyor of violence in the world today—my own government. . . .

[Our troops in Vietnam] must know after a short period there that none of the things we claim to be fighting for [such as freedom, justice, and peace] are really involved. Before long they must know that their government has sent them into a struggle among Vietnamese, and the more sophisticated surely realize that we are on the side of the wealthy and the secure while we create a hell for the poor.

Questions for Discussion

1. According to King, how was the U.S. war in Vietnam related to problems at home in American society?

2. What might have been the negative and positive racial aspects of the Vietnam War?

3. What, precisely, does King believe to be wrong with the U.S. war in Vietnam?

SOURCE: "Martin Luther King, Jr., and the Vietnam War" from Martin Luther King Jr., *Beyond Vietnam,* Reprinted by arrangement with the Heirs of the Estate of Martin Luther King Jr. and Writers House LLC. © 1967 Estate of Martin Luther King, Jr.

Puerto Ricans, the largest Spanish-speaking ethnic group located primarily on the East Coast, experienced a similar growth in militancy and nationalist sentiment during the late 1960s. By the 1960s, more than a million natives of the Caribbean island had moved to the East Coast, many to the New York City area. Despite being the only Latino immigrants already holding American citizenship when they arrived, Puerto Ricans experienced similar patterns of both discrimination and opportunity as Mexican Americans.

The most destitute of Americans, Indians also sought to reinvigorate their communities. On the Northwest Coast, they staged "fish-ins" in the mid-1960s to assert treaty rights. In 1968, urban activists in Minneapolis formed the American Indian Movement (AIM). On November 20, 1969, just days after the largest antiwar march in Washington, 78 Native Americans seized the island of Alcatraz in San Francisco Bay "in the name of all American Indians by right of discovery." For a year and a half, they used their occupation of the former federal prison site to publicize grievances about anti-Indian prejudice and to promote a new pan-Indian identity that reached across traditional tribal divisions. In 1973, armed members of AIM occupied buildings for two months at Wounded Knee, South Dakota, site of the infamous 1890 U.S. Army massacre of unarmed Sioux. Tribal governments sought "red power" in their own quieter way. They asserted greater tribal control of reservation schools across the country.

Although they lacked a unifying ethnic identity, gay men and lesbians also found opportunities to construct coalitions in the more open atmosphere of the late 1960s. Building on the earlier community organizing of older homosexuals in New York, San Francisco, and Los Angeles, more militant youth began to express openly their anger at the homophobic prejudice and violence prevalent in American society. The demand for tolerance and respect reached the headlines when gay patrons of the Stonewall Inn in New York fought back fiercely against a typically forceful police raid on June 27, 1969. Activists of the new Gay Liberation Front emphasized the importance of "coming out of the closet": proudly acknowledging one's sexual orientation as legitimate and decent.

26.4 The Conservative Response

What motivated the conservative revival of the late 1960s and early 1970s?

The majority of Americans had mixed feelings about the protests that roiled the nation. They were impressed by the courage of many who stood up against discrimination, and by 1968 they wanted to find a way out of the war in Southeast Asia. But they were alienated by the style and values of others who loudly demanded change in American society. Moderate and conservative citizens and generations of recent European immigrants resented what they saw as a lack of appreciation for the nation's virtues and successes. The political and social upheavals of 1968 opened the door to a Republican return to the White House, and Richard Nixon slipped through.

26.4.1 Backlashes

The backlash first developed in response to the increasing assertiveness of people of color. European Americans in every part of the United States had long been accustomed to deference from nonwhites and racial segregation, either by law in the South or by custom elsewhere. Like most white Americans, conservatives resented what they considered blacks' ingratitude at the civil rights measures enacted by the federal government, including black power's condemnation of whites as "crackers" and "honkies." Urban riots and escalating rates of violent crime, along with the Supreme Court's expansion of the rights of the accused, deepened their anger. They associated crime with urban African Americans, for although whites were still the majority of criminals, blacks (like any other population with less money) were disproportionately represented in prisons. Many European Americans were troubled by the militancy of Chicanos in the Southwest, Puerto Ricans in the Northeast, Indians on reservations and in cities, and African Americans almost everywhere.

Another backlash developed as a defense of traditional hierarchies against the cultural rebellions of the 1960s. Proud of their lives and values, conservatives rejected a whole array of challenges to American society. Raised to believe in respecting one's elders, they resented the disrespect of many youth, who warned, "Don't trust anyone over 30." A generation that had fought and sacrificed in the "good war" against the Nazis found the absence of patriotism among many protesters unfathomable. The United States remained one of the most religious of industrialized societies, and conservative churchgoers emphasized obedience to authorities. They feared the effects of illegal drugs on their children.

The backlash against the social changes of the 1960s contained elements of class antagonism as well. Working-class whites resented the often affluent campus rebels and the black and Latino poor targeted by some Great Society programs. They believed that their values of hard work, restraint, and respectability were increasingly unappreciated and even mocked. Republican leaders from Goldwater to Nixon to Reagan gave voice to these resentments and drew votes away from Democratic blue-collar strongholds.

26.4.2 The Turmoil of 1968 at Home

The traumas of 1968 brought the conservative backlash to the critical stage. First came the Tet Offensive in Vietnam, creating fears that the war might become an interminable quagmire. Then, on April 4, a gunman named James Earl Ray assassinated Martin Luther King Jr. in Memphis, where he had gone to support a strike by sanitation workers. King had become more openly radical in his final years, opposing the war and working on class-based organizing of poor people. But he remained the nation's leading apostle of nonviolence, and his murder evoked despair among millions of citizens, particularly African Americans. Police battled rioters and arsonists in black neighborhoods of 130 cities across the nation, with 46 people dying in the clashes.

Summer brought more shocking news. Charismatic senator Robert Kennedy's entry into the presidential campaign inspired renewed hopes among Democratic liberals. On the night of his victory in the June 5 California primary, Kennedy was killed by a deranged gunman. Vice President Hubert Humphrey seemed assured of the nomination at the Democratic convention in Chicago in August, despite his association with Johnson's war policies. Some 10,000 antiwar activists, including hundreds of FBI *agents provocateurs* (spies seeking to provoke violence), showed up to engage in protests outside the convention. Chicago's Democratic mayor Richard Daley unleashed thousands of police on protesters, bystanders, and photographers in an orgy of beatings that subsequent investigations called a police riot. Ninety million Americans watched on television as a deeply divided Democratic party appeared helpless before the violence.

Into the vacuum of public anger and alienation that accompanied the liberals' self-destruction in Chicago stepped two men. The spread of the conservative backlash from 1964 to 1968 gave Alabama governor George Wallace a wider constituency for his right-wing populist message of hostility to liberals, blacks, and federal officials. With the national Democratic party committed to racial integration, Wallace ran for president as an independent candidate and won 13.5 percent of the popular vote in November. Republican candidate Richard Nixon, meanwhile, campaigned as the candidate of "law and order" and promised that he had a secret plan to end the war in Vietnam. Nixon won the popular vote by less than 1 percent.

26.4.3 The Nixon Administration

A lonely, aloof man of great tenacity and ambition, Richard Nixon had worked hard to remake his public image for 1968. Widely viewed as a somewhat unscrupulous partisan since his early career in Congress, he had refashioned himself as a statesman with a broad vision for reducing international tensions between the great powers. He sounded like a conservative in the campaign against Humphrey, but once in the White House he governed as the most liberal Republican since Theodore Roosevelt, pressed by a Congress still controlled by Democrats.

Table 26.2 THE ELECTION OF 1968

Candidate	Political Party	Popular Vote (%)	Electoral Vote
Richard M. Nixon	Republican	43.4	301
Hubert H. Humphrey	Democratic	42.7	191
George C. Wallace	American Independent	13.5	46

In 1968, Republican Richard Nixon narrowly won the presidency as a law-and-order candidate. Concerned about social upheaval at home, Americans were by this time deeply unhappy about the course of the war in Vietnam. Nixon promised to end the war swiftly "with honor" and bring POWs home, including Medal of Honor recipient James Stockdale, who was the highest-ranking naval officer held in captivity during the Vietnam War.

SOURCE: Historical Election Results, Electoral College, National Archives and Records Administration below table caption

Nowhere was this clearer than on issues related to natural resources. Much had happened to the environment since Republican Theodore Roosevelt's conservation efforts, none of it for the better. A powerful movement was building to protect natural resources and human health from the effects of air and water pollution. Biologist Paul Ehrlich's best-selling *The Population Bomb* (1968) warned of the dire consequences of the globe's runaway growth in human population. In 1969, the government banned the carcinogenic pesticide DDT. That same year, a huge oil spill off Santa Barbara fouled 200 miles of pristine California beaches, and the Cuyahoga River in Cleveland, its surface coated with waste and oil, caught fire and burned for days. Environmentalists around the country proclaimed April 22, 1970, as "Earth Day."

Congress responded with legislation that mandated more careful management of the nation's natural resources. The Environmental Protection Agency was established in 1970. Amendments to the Clean Air (1970) and Clean Water (1972) acts tightened restrictions on harmful emissions from cars and factories. The Endangered Species Act (1973) created for the first time the legal right of nonhuman animals to survive, a major step toward viewing the quality of human life as inextricable from the earth's broader ecology.

What Nixon did care deeply about at home was politics, not policy. Antiwar demonstrations reached their height during Nixon's first two years in the White House (1969–1970). He and Vice President Spiro Agnew loathed the protesters, whom they saw as weakening the nation. The two men pursued what Agnew called "positive polarization": campaigning to further divide the respectable "silent majority," as the president labeled his supporters, from voluble liberal Democrats in Congress and radical activists on the streets, whom they associated with permissiveness and lawlessness. In this broad cultural battle for political supremacy, the president appealed to conservative white southern and northern ethnic Democrats.

Early in his administration, Nixon began wielding the power of the federal government to harass his political opponents. Johnson had used the FBI, the CIA, and military intelligence agencies to infiltrate and thin the ranks of antiwar demonstrators and nonwhite nationalists. Nixon continued these illegal operations. Nixon went beyond other presidents in assembling an "Enemies List" that included prominent elements of the political mainstream, especially liberals, the press, and his Democratic opponents. The president was particularly concerned about controlling secret information. The **Pentagon Papers** were a classified Defense Department history of U.S. actions in Vietnam

Pentagon Papers
Internal study by the Defense Department of the history of the U.S. war in Vietnam, detailing misleading statements by U.S. leaders.

revealing that the government had been deceiving the American public about the course of the war. When disillusioned former Pentagon official Daniel Ellsberg leaked the study to the *New York Times* for publication in 1971, Nixon was enraged. The White House created a team of covert operatives nicknamed "the Plumbers" to "plug leaks" by whatever means necessary.

26.4.4 Escalating and De-Escalating in Vietnam

Nixon and his national security adviser, Henry Kissinger, had ambitious plans for shifting the relationships of the great powers to America's advantage. To deal with China and the Soviet Union, they first had to reduce the vast U.S. engagement in the

ON THE MOON On July 20, 1969, astronauts Neil Armstrong and Edwin "Buzz" Aldrin put the first footprints on the moon. The U.S. flag they planted epitomized the sense of national accomplishment in space, even as divisions wracked American society at home. The actual flag here was made of rigid material because no lunar breeze existed to make the flag wave.

NASA Images[AS11-40-5949]

Did all Americans share the same feeling of exhilaration certainly felt by some when Apollo 11 landed on the moon?

small country of Vietnam, which had grown wildly out of proportion to actual U.S. interests there. Under the Nixon Doctrine, the United States would provide military hardware rather than U.S. soldiers to allied governments, which would have to do their own fighting against leftist insurgencies. In South Vietnam, this doctrine required "Vietnamization," or withdrawing American troops so ARVN could shoulder the bulk of the war.

The key to a successful withdrawal from Vietnam for Nixon was to preserve U.S. "credibility." The perception of power could be as important as its actual exercise, and the president wanted other nations, both friend and foe, to continue to respect and fear American military might. There was no immediate pullout but a gradual process that lasted for four years (1969–1973), during which almost half of the total U.S. casualties in Vietnam occurred. Nixon did his utmost to weaken the Communist forces during the slow withdrawal. The president ordered the secret bombing and invasion of neighboring Cambodia and Laos, an intensified aerial assault on North Vietnam, and the mining of Haiphong Harbor near Hanoi. Enormous protests rocked the country after the announcement of the Cambodian invasion on April 30, 1970. National Guard troops killed four students at a demonstration at Kent State University in Ohio and two at Jackson State College in Mississippi, deepening the sense of national division.

A majority of Americans now opposed the nation's war effort, a level of dissent unprecedented in U.S. history. Most telling of all was the criticism of some veterans returning from Vietnam. The morale of American soldiers still in Vietnam plummeted as the steady withdrawal of their comrades made clear that they were no longer expected to win the war. Drug abuse and racial conflict increased sharply among GIs. Even "fragging" (killing one's own officers) escalated before the peace accords were signed in Paris and the United States evacuated its last combat troops in 1973.

Conclusion

Between 1964 and 1971, young, nonwhite, and female Americans laid claim to greater equality. The ratification of the Twenty-Sixth Amendment in 1971 reduced the voting age from 21 to 18, in acknowledgment of the sacrifices of young people sent to fight in Vietnam. In large numbers, women challenged and began to overcome traditional limits on their personal and work lives. Racial discrimination and segregation were outlawed.

These years also witnessed striking disjunctures. The nation accomplished humanity's age-old dream of walking on the surface of the moon when Neil Armstrong stepped out of the *Apollo 11* spacecraft on July 20, 1969, while at home the country sometimes appeared to be coming apart at the seams. Poverty rates dropped to their lowest point ever, yet violence seemed to pervade the land. The slaughter of 43 people (mostly African Americans) by white state police retaking the Attica prison in upstate New York after an inmate insurrection in 1971 was one of the single most deadly confrontations between Americans since the Civil War.

The deceptive manner in which Johnson and Nixon waged the war in Vietnam eroded Americans' faith in their public officials. American life also grew more informal as the egalitarian style of the various social movements of the 1960s spread into the broader culture. But the removal of some of the most blatant distinctions of race and gender did not extend to differences of class. In the watershed cases of *San Antonio Independent School District v. Rodriguez* (1973) and *Milliken v. Bradley* (1974), the Supreme Court ruled that wealthier districts did not have to share financing with poorer ones, nor did they have to share students by means of busing. The Court found that there was no constitutional right to an education of equal quality. The ladder of social mobility remained slippery in a nation whose neighborhoods were still stratified between the affluent and the poor.

Chapter Review

26.1 Lyndon Johnson and the Apex of Liberalism

What did Johnson hope to achieve with his Great Society programs?

Johnson believed in equality of opportunity, and he sought to use the federal government to promote it. He focused on improving schools, reducing poverty, and eliminating racial discrimination. Johnson also increased citizens' personal security by creating Medicare and Medicaid to provide health insurance for the elderly and the indigent.

26.2 Into War in Vietnam

Why did the United States go to war in Vietnam, and why did it not win the war?

The U.S. government went to war in Vietnam in an effort to sustain the anticommunist but increasingly unpopular regime in South Vietnam against Communist guerillas and their North Vietnamese supporters. Despite an enormous commitment by the Americans, the corrupt and repressive South Vietnamese government proved unable to win the popular support necessary to survive.

26.3 "The Movement"

What did the protest movements of the 1960s have in common?

They all took American Cold War promises of freedom, democracy, and equality more seriously than mainstream Americans. They sought to awaken their fellow citizens to continuing injustices in American society and in U.S. foreign policy. These protest movements shared a commitment to honesty and authenticity, wanting to improve the quality of American lives and American institutions.

26.4 The Conservative Response

What motivated the conservative revival of the late 1960s and early 1970s?

Conservatives by the late 1960s were concerned about preserving U.S. strength abroad and about restoring social peace at home. They believed in sustaining traditional social hierarchies and renewing respect for authorities. Conservatives also feared the growing secularism and loosening sexual mores of American society.

Timeline

1964	Gulf of Tonkin Resolution (supporting Johnson on Vietnam)
	Civil Rights Act of 1964 (employment and accommodations)
1965	Voting Rights Act of 1965
	Watts (Los Angeles) uprising
1968	Tet Offensive (by Communist forces in Vietnam)
	Martin Luther King Jr. assassinated
	Richard Nixon elected president
1969	Huge antiwar protests in Washington, D.C.
	Astronauts Neil Armstrong and Buzz Aldrin walk on the moon
1970	National Guard troops kill four students, Kent State University in Ohio

Glossary

Great Society In the 1960s, President Lyndon Johnson's programs for reducing poverty, discrimination, and pollution, and for improving health care, education, and consumer protection.

Medicare Federal program of health care insurance for all citizens age 65 and older.

Medicaid Federal program of health care insurance for poor citizens.

Ho Chi Minh Communist leader of North Vietnam and nationalist hero to many dissidents in South Vietnam.

Tet Offensive Communist military attacks across South Vietnam in January–February 1968.

black power The slogan used by young black nationalists in the mid- and late 1960s.

New Left Student-led reform movement—focused initially on poverty, racial injustice, and the threat of nuclear war—that was radicalized by the war in Vietnam.

feminism The belief that women and men are of equal value and that gender roles are, to a considerable degree, created by society rather than being simply natural.

Pentagon Papers Internal study by the Defense Department of the history of the U.S. war in Vietnam, detailing misleading statements by U.S. leaders.

Chapter 27
Reconsidering National Priorities, 1972–1979

IN THE PILOT'S SEAT Many American women had flown airplanes before the 1970s, most famously solo flier Amelia Earhart and female pilots in World War II. But none piloted a major commercial airliner until 1973, when 34-year-old Emily Howell Warner of Denver, Colorado, was hired by Frontier Airlines.

Bill Peters/The Denver Post via Getty Images

How might passengers have reacted to the first woman in the cockpit?

Contents and Focus Questions

How could the 1970s, a decade marked in some ways by drift and failure, also be considered encouraging and progressive?

Feminism was one prominent development. ABC television news anchor Howard K. Smith began his coverage of a women's rights march in New York City in 1970 by quoting with approval the words of Vice President Spiro Agnew: "Three things have been difficult to tame. The ocean, fools, and women. We may soon be able to tame the ocean, but fools and women will take a little longer." Condescension toward women still pervaded American society, and few men even noticed it. The political upheavals of the 1960s had barely touched the relationships between most women and men by the start of the new decade. But all this changed as the 1970s unfolded.

The spread of ideas about women's liberation in the 1970s transformed the personal lives of almost every American, female and male alike. Feminism challenged the most basic and intimate assumptions about relationships, family, work, and power. It also sharply expanded women's opportunities. For example, Emily Howell Warner was born in 1939 and grew up in Colorado, wanting to be a flight attendant. Friends suggested she try flying lessons instead. On a regular commercial flight one day, a flight attendant took her up to see the cockpit. She was fascinated by "all those dials and switches" and knew she wanted to fly. After years of hard work and training, in 1973 Warner became the first woman hired as a pilot by a scheduled U.S. carrier, Frontier Airlines. Within three years, she was the first female promoted to captain, and in 1986, Warner commanded the first all-female crew on a commercial flight.

Feminism joined with other developments of the decade to force Americans to reexamine much that they had taken for granted. Elected on the promise to end the war in Southeast Asia "with honor," President Nixon escalated the fighting before eventually withdrawing U.S. forces from Vietnam. At the same time, he repaired relations with both China and the Soviet Union as those two Communist powers drew apart. Americans thus suffered their first clear defeat in war while also seeing the Cold War splinter.

* * * * *

Scandal in the White House then forced the first resignation of a U.S. president and deepened public distrust of political authorities. American economic growth—the foundation of the country's power—stumbled because of spending on the Vietnam War and oil shortages. High-paying manufacturing jobs declined as factories began to move overseas in pursuit of cheaper labor, and skilled blue-collar workers saw their status as middle-class Americans start to slip. Unemployment grew sharply. A growing environmental movement raised troubling questions about whether an expanding economy and unrestrained exploitation of natural resources should continue to top the country's list of priorities.

Journalist Tom Wolfe dubbed the 1970s the "Me Decade." The label did have some merit: many Americans turned away from the public sphere after the exhilarating but divisive politics of the 1960s and pursued self-exploration and self-fulfillment instead. Crime, divorce, premarital and extramarital sex, and drug use all increased while the nation's economic health and international status declined. But the 1970s also witnessed a rethinking of long-standing assumptions: about how democracy should work at home, what role the nation should play in international affairs, how people ought to treat the environment, and how men and women should relate to each other.

27.1 Twin Shocks: Détente and Watergate

How did détente and the Watergate scandal affect U.S. foreign relations and American politics?

Richard Nixon had long been one of the nation's leading anticommunists. No one had more fiercely opposed leftists at home and Communists in China and the Soviet Union. However, the president was more a savvy political opportunist than an ideologue. He and his national security adviser, Henry Kissinger, saw a chance to use mounting Chinese-Soviet tensions to the advantage of the United States as they withdrew American armed forces from Vietnam.

At the same time that Nixon manipulated the Cold War abroad, the Republican president initiated a campaign of illegal actions at home to weaken his political opponents in the Democratic party. This strategy backfired in the Watergate scandal, which drove him from office in 1974.

27.1.1 Triangular Diplomacy

Nixon and Kissinger prided themselves on their "realpolitik" approach to foreign policy: their pragmatic assessment of other powers' security needs, regardless of ideology, and their collaboration with those powers on issues of common concern. In 1969, China and the USSR gave Nixon and Kissinger an ideal opportunity to exercise their realpolitik skills. That year, tensions that had been building between the two Communist states erupted in brief skirmishing between Chinese and Soviet troops on their shared border. Nixon envisioned a "triangular diplomacy" that he hoped would divide the Communist world.

The president and Kissinger also shared a commitment to secrecy. Any fundamental revision of the nation's foreign policy, they believed, could happen only if they concentrated all decision-making in the White House. They set out to keep Congress, the press, and even their own State Department in the dark. Diplomatic innovation thus went hand in hand with an unprecedented extension of the secretive national security state.

Nixon's 1972 visit to China brought a host of benefits. Live television coverage showed Nixon toasting Mao Zedong, premier of the People's Republic of China, while a Chinese military band played "America the Beautiful" and "Home on the Range." Americans' impression of the People's Republic as a grim, forbidding land began to give way to a renewed interest in China as an exotic but intriguing place. Cultural exchanges soon proliferated: first ping-pong teams, and eventually legions of students. U.S. businesses also cast a covetous eye at the immense China market. Trade between the two nations rose dramatically over the next four decades.

Nixon and Kissinger now constructed the other leg of their diplomatic triangle. As they anticipated, the Soviets had taken alarm at the warming of relations between their two greatest rivals. Nixon flew to Moscow for a summit meeting with Soviet leader Leonid Brezhnev in May 1972 that initiated a policy of **détente** (relaxation of tensions). A trade pact quickly followed. The two superpowers also agreed to limit offensive nuclear weapons (the Strategic Arms Limitations Treaty, or SALT I) and to ban antiballistic missile defense systems (the ABM treaty).

détente
The lessening of military or diplomatic tensions, as between the United States and the Soviet Union.

Like the Soviet leaders, Nixon and Kissinger sought to preserve the existing international balance of power. Dealmaking with China and the USSR constituted one step in this process. In another, the two men sought to stifle socialist revolutions in Third World nations by bolstering pro-American allies there. For instance, the duo feared that the democratic election of socialist Salvador Allende in Chile in 1970 would lead to "another Cuba." A socialist leader might nationalize the investments of U.S. corporations in Chile and perhaps challenge Washington's capitalist hegemony in the Western Hemisphere. Determined to block these possibilities, the CIA secretly funded a right-wing military coup in Chile in September 1973. Allende died in the assault on the presidential palace, and the rebel forces murdered thousands of his supporters and established a brutal military dictatorship under General Augusto Pinochet. "I don't see why we need to stand by and watch a country go Communist because of the irresponsibility of its own people," Kissinger explained privately.

27.1.2 Scandal in the White House

Meanwhile, on the domestic front, Washington police caught agents of Nixon's reelection campaign breaking into the Democratic National Committee headquarters in the **Watergate** hotel and office complex on June 17, 1972. The burglars' goal was to put in place secret listening devices, or "bugs." Later, the White House tried to cover up its connections to the crime.

Watergate
The Washington, D.C., hotel-office complex where agents of President Nixon's reelection campaign broke into Democratic party headquarters in 1972. Nixon helped cover up the break-in, and the subsequent political scandal was referred to as "Watergate."

The Watergate break-in was only one part of the administration's broader campaign of illegal warfare against its political opponents. An insecure and unhappy loner, Nixon harbored an almost paranoid suspicion when he took office in early 1969. The president and his aides regularly discussed "how we can use the available federal machinery to screw our political enemies," in the words of White House counsel John Dean. They persuaded the FBI and the CIA to monitor and harass antiwar activists and pushed the Internal Revenue Service to investigate prominent Democrats. They extorted large contributions to the Republican party from corporate executives by making it clear that federal agencies would otherwise impede the pursuit of their business interests. The *New York Times*'s publication of the classified Pentagon Papers in 1971 stiffened the resolve of the Committee to Reelect the President (CREEP) to stop any further leaks. The committee assembled a group of undercover operatives (the "plumbers") to stop leaks and to engineer "dirty tricks" against the Democrats.

After the bungled Watergate break-in, the president directed the cover-up from the beginning, and then lied about it to the public. He also used the CIA to hinder the FBI's investigation into the matter. He approved payments of hush money to the burglars to keep them quiet about their ties to the White House. Nixon's abuse of power escalated as he pressured his subordinates to perjure themselves in court. For most of a year, the cover-up held, and Nixon won reelection in 1972.

Table 27.1 THE ELECTION OF 1972

Candidate	Political Party	Popular Vote (%)	Electoral Vote
Richard M. Nixon	Republican	60.7	520
George S. McGovern	Democratic	31.5	17

SOURCE: Historical Election Results, Electoral College, National Archives and Records Administration

But the persistent investigations by *Washington Post* journalists Bob Woodward and Carl Bernstein kept the heat on. In early 1973, the administration began to crack due to a grand jury probe in the federal courtroom of Judge John Sirica. The president's men lost confidence that the cover-up would hold and began looking for ways to save their own skins. Congress initiated its own televised investigations that mesmerized a national audience. The Senate Watergate committee, chaired by eloquent conservative North Carolina Democrat Sam Ervin, methodically exposed with growing bipartisan support the criminal actions in the White House. The key issue, as framed by Republican committee member Howard Baker of Tennessee, became, "What did the president know, and when did he know it?"

On July 16, 1973, White House aide Alexander Butterfield told the Senate committee that a built-in recorder taped all conversations in the Oval Office. Almost certainly, these tapes would provide answers to questions about the president's role. Both Congress and Justice Department special prosecutor Archibald Cox subpoenaed the White House tapes, but Nixon refused to hand them over. Instead, he fired Cox on October 20 in what became known as the Saturday Night Massacre. Outraged, Congress initiated impeachment proceedings against the president. In the spring of 1974, the House Judiciary Committee passed bills of impeachment for his specific abuses of power. Before the full House could vote to impeach him and the Senate decide on his guilt or innocence, the Supreme Court ruled that the White House had to turn over the subpoenaed tapes. The content of the tapes revealed the extent of the president's involvement in the cover-up and his personal crudeness, vindictiveness, and ethnic and racial prejudices. Facing a certain guilty verdict, Nixon resigned on August 9, 1974, less than halfway through his second term.

27.1.3 The Nation After Watergate

Never before had a U.S. president resigned from office. Many citizens celebrated the outcome of the Watergate investigations as evidence of democracy's resilience and power to uncover criminal activity in the White House and bring down a corrupt president. But the affair also discredited political institutions Americans had long respected. Indeed, the Nixon administration proved quite corrupt. A whole raft of senior officials, including the president's closest aides, H. R. Haldeman and John Ehrlichman, soon went to prison. Even Vice President Spiro Agnew had been forced to resign amid the Watergate investigations when a Maryland jury found him guilty of tax evasion dating back to his years as governor there. Congress swung strongly to the Democrats in the 1974 elections, slowing the Republicans' rise to the status of majority party.

The man who replaced Nixon in the White House faced a daunting situation. Gerald Ford, longtime Republican congressman and House minority leader from Grand Rapids, Michigan, had been tapped by Nixon to replace Agnew as vice president. Well liked by members of both parties, Ford seemed to embody the antidote to the extreme styles of both Nixon and Agnew. To restore decency and trust in the government, Ford saw his role as healing what he called "the wounds of the past." Within a month, he granted a "full, free, and absolute pardon" to Nixon for any crimes he may have committed as president, precluding any trial and punishment within a court of law. However, most Americans believed that Nixon should have faced justice for his actions, as had the people who carried out his orders. Ford's approval ratings plummeted overnight from 72 percent to 49 percent and never fully recovered.

If Ford inherited the fallout from Watergate at home, abroad he inherited the pending defeat in Vietnam. Military veterans returned to a nation determined to ignore or demean their sacrifices, and they quickly learned to keep their combat-induced traumas to themselves. When Saigon finally fell to the combined assaults of National Liberation Front and North Vietnamese fighters on April 30, 1975, Americans watched the televised images with both bitterness and relief. Two weeks later, Cambodian Communist forces briefly seized the U.S. container ship *Mayaguez*, provoking Ford to demonstrate that the United States was still ready and willing to flex its military muscle. But forty-one U.S. soldiers died in the rescue mission to save thirty-nine sailors whom, it turned out, Cambodia had already released. Ford and Kissinger, continuing as the new president's secretary of state, pursued détente with the Soviets at summit meetings in Vladivostok (1974) and Helsinki (1975). At the same time, they supported anticommunist forces in various Third World conflicts, such as the civil war that erupted in Angola after that country achieved its independence in 1975.

THE DANGER, THE BRAVERY, THE DESPERATION OF REFUGEES Many South Vietnamese fled the communist victory in their country in 1975, including this woman and her children crossing the Mekong River. Most of the refugees undertook extremely perilous journeys by boat to other Southeast Asian nations, and hundreds of thousands eventually made their way to the United States.

91040/picture-alliance/dpa/AP Images

Vietnamese Americans became part of a broader pattern of Asian immigration into the United States after the 1965 Immigration Act ended the discriminatory national-origins system begun in 1924. How has new Asian immigration been most visible in American society?

27.2 Discovering the Limits of the U.S. Economy

How did economic changes affect the way Americans felt about their country?

Defeat in Vietnam and corruption in the White House were soon joined by grim economic news. Generation after generation of Americans had watched their incomes rise. Since World War II had pulled the U.S. economy out of the Great Depression, median family income had doubled. But by 1973, the famous American standard of living began to decline. The three pillars of postwar prosperity—cheap energy, rising wages, and low inflation—simultaneously crumbled. The costs of the Vietnam War struck home at the same time that an oil embargo spawned by conflict in the Middle East gripped the country. Moreover, a widening environmental movement raised questions about the pursuit of endless economic growth on a planet that more and more people realized had limited natural resources.

27.2.1 The End of the Long Boom

During the 1970s, a terrible new economic scourge dubbed "**stagflation**" hit the United States. For the first time, employment and wages stagnated while prices climbed. What explained this phenomenon? Spending on the Vietnam War and on Great Society programs had pulled prices upward. The government had never raised enough taxes to cover the expense of the war, so it paid the bills by simply printing more dollars. In 1971, annual inflation stood at 4.3 percent, more than twice the pre-Vietnam rate; three years later, it reached 11 percent, and by 1980 it topped out at 13.5 percent.

These figures devastated Americans' sense of economic security. Average real wages (income adjusted for inflation) dropped by an average of 2 percent a year from 1973 to the early 1990s. Unemployment rose to 9 percent in 1975. Only the continued flow of women into the workforce, seen by most families as an economic necessity, kept the majority of U.S. families afloat financially. The portion of citizens living in poverty, which had dropped sharply through the 1960s to 11 percent in 1973, rose again, hitting 15 percent by 1982. The gap between rich and poor began widening.

This decline stemmed in part from competition from abroad, particularly West Germany and Japan. With U.S. assistance (and without the military expenditures that so burdened the United States), those countries had finally rebuilt their economies after World War II and boasted new, more efficient industrial facilities. The trade surplus that had long symbolized global U.S. economic superiority evaporated in 1971. That year,

stagflation

Unprecedented combination in the mid-1970s of a stagnant economy (with high unemployment) and price inflation.

Map 27.1 AMERICA'S RUSTBELT

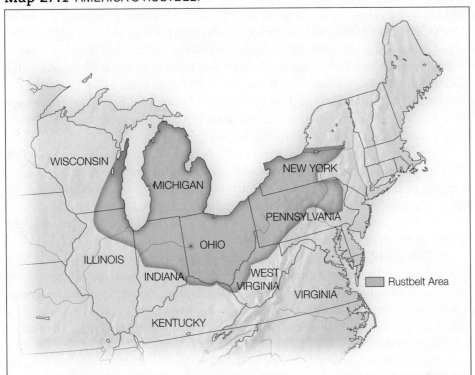

Part of the economic downturn of the 1970s included factory closings in the so-called Rustbelt, an area of the country that had previously been the center of U.S. industrial might. Increasing competition from lower-wage labor, both overseas and in the less-unionized Sunbelt of the South and Southwest, encouraged companies to move manufacturing plants out of the Great Lakes and upper Midwest region. How might potential migrants have compared their prospects in Detroit and in Phoenix, both in the 1940s and in the 1980s?

U.S. imports overtook exports for the first time in the twentieth century. Worried international investors traded in dollars for gold, forcing Nixon to end the 27-year-old Bretton Woods monetary system that had linked all other currencies to the dollar at fixed exchange rates. Freed from the fixed rate of $35 per ounce of gold, the value of the dollar dropped like a stone; by the end of the decade, it took $800 to buy an ounce of gold.

In this competitive environment, the *Wall Street Journal* reported, American companies "seek places where labor, land, electricity, and taxes are cheap." Corporations found those places in the American South and Southwest, regions characterized by few labor unions, low wage rates, minimal taxes, and negligible local government regulations. Many more such places were in neighboring Mexico, where U.S. companies established *maquiladoras*. These assembly plants, often just a few hundred yards across the Mexican–U.S. border, allowed corporations to hire primarily female workers at low wages and avoid strict U.S. environmental, labor, and safety laws. The long-term decline of the Rustbelt—the series of urban industrial centers strung across the American Northeast and Midwest—accelerated during the 1970s.

High unemployment and shrinking real wages contributed to both rising crime and growing anti-immigrant sentiment. Black Americans also faced an increasing backlash against hard-won civil rights gains. While court-ordered busing to integrate schools in segregated neighborhoods proceeded slowly but peacefully in the South, northern urban whites dug in their heels. In Boston, violence erupted in the school hallways and the streets from 1975 to 1978 as economically vulnerable working-class whites harassed African Americans attending schools in white ethnic neighborhoods of South Boston, and blacks defended themselves.

27.2.2 The Oil Embargo

Nothing revealed Americans' newfound economic vulnerability more than the 1973–1974 boycott initiated by the Organization of Arab Petroleum Exporting Countries (OAPEC), a subset of the Organization of Petroleum Exporting Countries (OPEC). The largest producers of oil were the countries around the Persian Gulf, especially Saudi Arabia. These nations had resented the creation of Israel in 1948 and the resulting displacement of the Palestinians. War broke out in 1967, and Israel seized control of the West Bank of the Jordan River and the Gaza Strip. Six years later, Egypt and Syria struck back, attacking and threatening to overrun Israel, but the United States gave the Israeli army a critical resupply of weapons that helped turn the tide of battle.

Henry Kissinger then shuttled between Tel Aviv and Cairo to negotiate a ceasefire. His diplomatic skills won him the Nobel Peace Prize and laid the groundwork for a warming of U.S. relations with Egypt (the most populous Arab nation, though not a major oil producer). However, the other Arab states expressed outrage at this demonstration of America's close links with the Israelis, and Arabs of all political persuasions were determined to voice their displeasure.

In October 1973, the OAPEC nations initiated an embargo on selling oil to the United States and to western European nations that had supported Israel in the war. Oil supplies dwindled, and prices at gas pumps skyrocketed to four times their previous levels. Even when OAPEC lifted the embargo after five months, it kept prices high by limiting production. Steeper energy costs powerfully accelerated inflation. Decades of easy access to cheap gasoline came to a sudden halt.

27.2.3 The Environmental Movement

The oil embargo encouraged many U.S. citizens to rethink the nation's cavalier use of natural resources. Environmental consciousness spread rapidly in the 1970s as evidence revealed the impact of industrial growth on the quality of life in the United States. Environmental organizations such as the Sierra Club, the National Wildlife Federation, and

"THE SOILING OF OLD GLORY" White resistance to school busing in Boston sometimes turned violent in the mid-1970s. On April 5, 1976, white high school students from South Boston and Charlestown met with a city councilwoman who supported their boycott of classes. Outside City Hall, they chanced upon lawyer Theodore Landsmark and assaulted him. Economic turmoil underlay such occasional displays of ethnic or racial tension and violence in the 1970s.

"The Soiling of Old Glory" - Pulitzer Prize 1976. www.stanleyformanphoto.com

Why do you think photographer Stanley J. Forman won the Pulitzer Prize for "The Soiling of Old Glory"?

the Audubon Society saw their memberships soar. For the first time, the media began to examine the daunting range of environmental problems plaguing the United States and the rest of the world: acid rain, groundwater contamination, smog, rainforest destruction, oil spills, nuclear waste disposal, species extinction, ozone depletion, and global warming.

Environmentalists argued that the idea of unlimited consumption of natural resources was fundamentally irresponsible, both to future human generations and to other species. They urged Congress and the Environmental Protection Agency (EPA) to require fuel-efficient engines from carmakers and to promote renewable energy sources such as water, solar, and wind power. Citizen groups such as the Clamshell Alliance in New England and the Abalone Alliance in California protested the construction of new nuclear power plants. These operations, they pointed out, had no reliable method in place for safely disposing of nuclear waste.

A broad critique of the chemical industry's impact on public health also emerged in the 1970s. As it turned out, pesticides worked their way up the food chain into people's bodies. Some artificial sweeteners proved carcinogenic, and the lead that manufacturers had added to gasoline and house paint for generations caused brain damage. Long-standing industrial dumping of toxic chemicals began to make headlines.

The crisis at **Love Canal** in upstate New York helped bring the issue of toxic waste home to Americans. The Hooker Chemical Company had buried tons of poisonous waste in a dry canal in the town of Niagara Falls between 1947 and 1952 and then

Love Canal
Upstate New York site of environmental crisis over the deleterious effects of unregulated pollution from dumping of toxic chemical wastes.

Figure 27.1 U.S. PETROLEUM CONSUMPTION, PRODUCTION, AND IMPORTS, 1950–2010

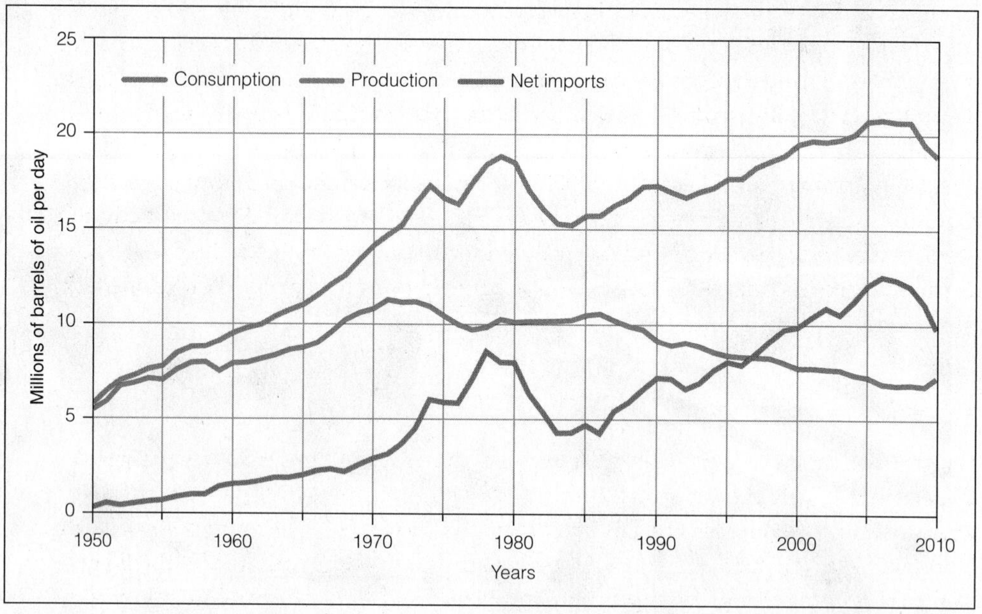

Abundant sources of coal and oil had long encouraged American feelings of national strength and autonomy, and rising economic growth after World War II hinged on rising energy consumption. By 1970, however, domestic production of oil peaked and began to decline, and the United States thereafter grew increasingly dependent on imported oil. New hydraulic fracturing ("fracking") techniques enabled drillers, by 2008, to extract previously inaccessible petroleum, and domestic oil production tipped upward. But fossil fuels remained an inherently limited natural resource—as well as a key contributor to global climate change—and the United States remained dependent on foreign sources of oil.

SOURCE: U.S. Energy Information Administration, *Monthly Energy Review*, July 2015

covered it over with dirt. The company gave the land to the town, which promptly built a school on it. A middle-class neighborhood soon grew up around the site. But the ground smelled odd and oozed mysterious substances. Sometimes it even caught on fire for no apparent reason. By the 1970s, local rates of cancer and other severe illnesses had soared. The chemical and industrial plant workers who lived in the neighborhood began to suspect that their quiet loyalty to their employers was no longer worth the risk to the health of their families. Persistent activism by community members finally overcame local, state, and company officials' efforts to keep the contents of the buried canal secret. In August 1978, New York Governor Hugh Carey at last agreed to buy out the entire neighborhood, seal it off, and move residents elsewhere.

Discovering the limits of the U.S. economy so soon after the Vietnam War and the Watergate scandal spawned a crisis of confidence. Many Americans resented the idea of limits. But others began to embrace the idea of creating a healthier lifestyle that focused less on material consumption. Exercise, especially running, began to become an increasingly common activity for middle-class adults. The wildly successful Nike athletic shoe company was founded in 1972, and the number of entrants in the New York City Marathon ballooned from 126 in 1970 to 10,000 by 1978. Interest in outdoor recreation—hiking, camping, and bicycling—grew exponentially. Recycling also started its climb from a fringe activity to common practice in a few parts of the country.

27.3 Reshuffling Politics

Which were the most significant political reforms of the 1970s?

The skepticism toward authority and tradition spawned by the counterculture, the Vietnam War, and the Watergate scandal spread through American culture in the 1970s. The use of illegal drugs, especially marijuana, was pervasive. Casual sexual relationships proliferated in a decade when contraceptive pills had become widely available and the AIDS virus had not yet appeared. Popular and critically acclaimed films featured tales of malfeasance in high places. *All the President's Men* (1976) told the story of the Nixon administration's Watergate crimes. *Apocalypse Now* (1979) revealed the madness of the American war in Vietnam. *Three Days of the Condor* (1975) portrayed the CIA as a rogue agency beyond democratic control. *Blazing Saddles* (1974) hilariously spoofed the heroic Westerns that had long served as the staple of American moviegoers' diet. *One Flew over the Cuckoo's Nest* (1975) used novelist Ken Kesey's story of an insane asylum to suggest that those in charge were more dangerous than the inmates. In this atmosphere, Congress began to reassert its authority against the "imperial presidency," and in 1976, voters put an obscure, devout Georgia peanut farmer and former one-term governor in the White House.

27.3.1 Congressional Power Reasserted

The double shock of defeat in Vietnam and the Watergate scandal reawakened a Congress that had grown accustomed to deferring to the White House in foreign affairs. Tellingly, Congress had never formally declared war on North Korea or North Vietnam, although such declaration is its constitutional duty. Angered by the illegalities and deception of both the Johnson and Nixon administrations, Congress passed the **War Powers Act** in 1973 to limit the president's capacity to wage undeclared wars. The bill required the chief executive to obtain explicit congressional approval for keeping U.S. troops in an overseas conflict longer than ninety days.

War Powers Act
1973 law requiring the U.S. president to get Congressional approval within ninety days of sending U.S. troops into a conflict abroad.

With encouragement from voters and journalists, Congress also uncovered its eyes and began to investigate the covert side of American foreign policy that had gathered momentum since 1945. After Watergate popped the cork on the bottled-up secret abuses of the executive branch, other troubling news spilled out about the nation's intelligence agencies, including CIA "dirty tricks" and the agency's Operation Chaos. The latter program of illegal domestic espionage against antiwar dissidents paralleled FBI abuses such as the Cointelpro campaigns to defame Martin Luther King Jr. and destroy the Black Panthers and the American Indian Movement. Congressional investigators documented CIA involvement in assassination attempts against leftist foreign leaders such as Fidel Castro of Cuba and Patrice Lumumba of the Congo.

These revelations stirred fierce controversy among those who took an interest in national and international politics. Many citizens decried what their government had done in their names and without their knowledge. However, officials claimed that the extreme conditions of the Cold War and the duplicity of the Soviets necessitated secrecy. At the core of this controversy were two burning questions. How transparent could a democratic society and its government afford to be when they also had global interests to protect? And when democratic openness and imperial self-interest conflicted, which should win out?

27.3.2 Jimmy Carter: "I Will Never Lie to You"

In the backwash of Watergate, two presidential candidates—both outsiders to national politics—became advocates for opposing sides in the debate about power and openness in 1976. Former California governor Ronald Reagan made a strong run at the Republican nomination, falling just short at the Kansas City convention as incumbent Gerald Ford held on to head the GOP ticket. Reagan articulated conservative Americans' anger at seeing U.S. autonomy and power abroad hemmed in. He opposed détente with the Soviets, supported anticommunists everywhere, and warned against a treaty that would return control of the Panama Canal to the Panamanians. Ford found himself burdened by the faltering economy, weakened by Reagan's criticisms from the right, and hampered by widespread resentment of his pardon for Nixon.

Interpreting History

The Church Committee: on CIA Covert Operations to Assassinate Foreign Leaders (1975–1976)

> "It may well be ourselves that we injure most if we adopt tactics 'more ruthless than the enemy.'"

In 1975–1976, the U.S. Senate Select Committee to Study Governmental Operations with Respect to Intelligence Activities engaged in the first comprehensive review by Congress of the actions of the Central Intelligence Agency. Under the leadership of Frank Church (D-Idaho), the committee investigated both intelligence gathering ("spying") and covert operations, the secret side of American foreign policy during the Cold War. One of the most controversial issues that the Church committee examined was evidence of the CIA's attempted use of assassination as a means of dealing with key figures in Cuba, the Congo, the Dominican Republic, South Vietnam, and Chile. The use of assassination raised fundamental questions about whether an egalitarian democracy could afford to engage in imperial acts of doubtful morality, without endangering that democracy's essential nature.

GET FIDEL CASTRO A star baseball pitcher who once turned down an offer to sign with the New York Giants, Fidel Castro led a leftist, anti-American revolution in Cuba in 1959. U.S. hostility and Castro's evolving politics moved him to declare Cuba a communist state in 1961. The CIA tried unsuccessfully to arrange for Castro's assassination.

Bettmann/Corbis

How ethically acceptable is it for the U.S. government—or any government—to try to assassinate a foreign leader whom it does not like?

The Committee has received evidence that ranking Government officials discussed, and may have authorized, the establishment with the CIA of a generalized assassination capability. . . .

The evidence establishes that the United States was implicated in several assassination plots. . . . Our inquiry also reveals serious problems with respect to United States involvement in coups directed against foreign governments. . . .

Once methods of coercion and violence are chosen, the probability of loss of life is always present. There is, however, a significant difference between a coldblooded, targeted, intentional killing of an individual foreign leader and other forms of intervening in the affairs of foreign nations. . . .

Non-attribution to the United States for covert operations was the original and principal purpose of the so-called doctrine of "plausible denial."

Evidence before the Committee clearly demonstrates that this concept, designed to protect the United States and its

operatives from the consequences of disclosures, has been expanded to mask decisions of the President and his senior staff members. . . .

"Plausible denial" can also lead to the use of euphemism and circumlocution, which are designed to allow the President and other senior officials to deny knowledge of an operation should it be disclosed. . . .

It is possible that there was a failure of communication between policymakers and the agency personnel who were experienced in secret, and often violent, action. Although policymakers testified that assassination was not intended by such words as "get rid of Castro," some of their subordinates in the Agency testified that they perceived that assassination was desired and that they should proceed without troubling their superiors. . . .

Running throughout the cases considered in this report was the expectation of American officials that they could control the actions of dissident groups which they were supporting in foreign countries. Events demonstrated that the United States had no such power. This point is graphically demonstrated by cables exchanged shortly before the coup in Vietnam. Ambassador Lodge cabled Washington on October 30, 1963, that he was unable to halt a coup; a cable from William Bundy in response stated that "we cannot accept conclusion that we have no power to delay or discourage a coup." The coup took place three days later. . . .

Officials of the CIA made use of persons associated with the criminal underworld in attempting to achieve the assassination of Fidel Castro. These underworld figures were relied upon because it was believed that they had expertise and contacts that were not available to law-abiding citizens. . . .

It may well be ourselves that we injure most if we adopt tactics "more ruthless than the enemy."

Jimmy Carter was the winner. The former Democratic governor of Georgia based his candidacy on moral uplift. Contrasting himself to the Nixon administration, he told audiences, "I will never lie to you." Instead, Carter promised openness, accountability, and a government "as good and decent as the American people."

Table 27.2 THE ELECTION OF 1976

Candidate	Political Party	Popular Vote (%)	Electoral Vote
Jimmy Carter	Democratic	50.0	297
Gerald R. Ford	Republican	47.9	241

SOURCE: Historical Election Results, Electoral College, National Archives and Records Administration

Carter was also a Naval Academy graduate, a former nuclear engineer, a successful peanut farmer and businessperson, and the first president from the Deep South in more than a century. A born-again Christian, he had supported civil rights during his governorship in Georgia. Carter kept his diminutive first name: Jimmy, not James nor even Jim. He wore denim, and he carried his own bags. At his inaugural parade, he and his wife Rosalynn chose to walk down Pennsylvania Avenue rather than ride in a limousine.

The new president entered the White House at a time of unusual resistance to executive authority. He encountered an assertive and suspicious Congress. And he faced an economy still mired in stagflation as unemployment and prices kept rising and interest rates reached 21 percent.

Politics and ideology also hamstrung the new president, limiting his ability to lead his own party in governing the nation. The Georgian was the first Democratic president since the 1930s who did not fully subscribe to the New Deal principle of governmental regulation of the economy. As a social moderate but an economic conservative, Carter had a strong desire to balance the federal budget. This vision placed him closer to the Republicans than to many in his own party. Carter's tendency to take moralistic stands did not mesh well with the horse-trading style of compromise that characterized Congress. The president and his aides tried to govern as outsiders to the federal government. They viewed insiders as selfish and narrow-minded. They failed to cultivate relationships with Democratic leaders in Congress such as powerful House Speaker Thomas ("Tip") O'Neill of Massachusetts. Meanwhile, seasoned legislators of both parties looked down on the new administration as inexperienced and naive.

27.3.3 Rise of a Peacemaker

Carter's idealism proved more effective, at least during his first two years, in refashioning U.S. foreign policy. The president started the national healing process with his first official act in office: he granted a "full, complete, and unconditional pardon" to those who had evaded the draft during the Vietnam War. He also tried to replace indiscriminate anticommunism with the promotion of human rights as the main theme in international affairs. "We are now free of that inordinate fear of Communism which once led us to embrace any dictator who joined us in that fear," he told an audience at the University of Notre Dame.

All presidents since 1945 had loudly supported human rights in the Soviet bloc. But Carter defended dissidents in authoritarian countries friendly to the United States as well. His commitment to ending racial discrimination at home and his promotion of human rights abroad led to his administration's strong support for an end to white minority rule in southern Africa. This included the establishment of Zimbabwe out of the old white-ruled Rhodesia in 1980.

Carter encouraged Americans to shift their attention from the East–West Cold War to the burgeoning problems between industrialized nations of the Northern Hemisphere and mostly poor countries of the Southern Hemisphere. The president made control over the Panama Canal a test case for this reorientation. The canal symbolized U.S. dominance of the hemisphere and served as a focus of resentment among many Latin Americans. Since 1903, the United States had ruled the 10-mile-wide Canal Zone as its own colony. Acknowledging this colonialist past, Carter signed treaties on September 7, 1977, to return sovereignty of the canal to Panama.

Camp David accords
Agreements between Israel and Egypt, brokered by the United States, that gave Israel its first diplomatic recognition by an Arab state, and implied future autonomy for the Palestinian occupied territories.

The Carter administration's other great diplomatic achievement came with the **Camp David accords**, an agreement between Egypt's president Anwar Sadat and Israel's prime minister Menachem Begin. The Arab–Israeli conflict had remained one of the most intractable problems in modern diplomacy. Sadat created an opening for diplomacy in 1977 by becoming the first Arab leader to visit Israel. Carter then invited Sadat and Begin to Camp David, the presidential retreat in rural western Maryland. There his persistence, plus promises of American aid to all parties, kept the marathon negotiations on track. In March 1979, the Egyptian and Israeli leaders signed two accords. Egypt became the first Arab state to grant official recognition to Israel. In turn, Israel agreed to withdraw its troops from the Sinai peninsula and apparently to stop building additional settlements on the Palestinian West Bank of the Jordan River. The framework for peace implied eventual autonomy for the Palestinians in the West Bank and Gaza.

Though promising, the Camp David accords failed to bring peace to the Middle East. Israeli settlements in the West Bank continued to proliferate, and anti-Israeli terrorism by Palestinians persisted. But Carter had persuaded two major players in the region to take a big step back from open hostility. The world rightly proclaimed him a peacemaker.

27.3.4 The War on Waste

Within three months of taking office, Carter called for the "moral equivalent of war" to meet the deepening national energy crisis. He exhorted his fellow citizens to stop being "the most wasteful nation on Earth." Conserve energy, he implored them. Switch off lights and turn down thermostats. Reducing American dependence on foreign oil would bolster national security.

The administration created the Department of Energy and granted tax incentives to promote development of alternative sources such as solar energy. The EPA required U.S. automakers to meet stricter fuel efficiency standards for their engines. High prices also encouraged a renewed search for domestic sources of oil. In 1977, workers completed the 800-mile-long, 48-inch-wide Trans-Alaska Pipeline System. The system linked the state's northern oil fields at Prudhoe Bay on the Arctic Ocean with a tanker terminal in Valdez, on Alaska's ice-free southern coast on the Pacific

Ocean. With new oil now flowing freely, Carter worked with Congress to pass the 1980 Alaska National Interest Lands Conservation Act. This legislation created the single largest addition ever to the nation's wilderness system, 47 million acres, and the new Wrangell–St. Elias National Park.

The most controversial power alternative came in the form of nuclear energy. Obtained by harnessing the force of splitting atoms, nuclear energy seemed to promise unlimited pollution-free power. But it entailed the use of a deadly radioactive fuel, uranium. In March 1979, the partial meltdown of the nuclear core of the Three Mile Island reactor near Harrisburg, Pennsylvania, leaked radiation and forced a major evacuation of the area. Nevertheless, existing nuclear power plants continued to generate 11 percent of the nation's electricity in 1979, a figure that climbed to 22 percent by 1992 as other plants under construction came on line. However, because of negative public opinion and the high cost per unit of nuclear power, no new plants ordered by utility companies after 1974 were ever completed. In 2010, nuclear power was producing 20% of U.S. electricity.

DENALI NATIONAL PARK, ALASKA Denali (formerly Mt. McKinley) in Alaska's Denali National Park rises to 20,320 feet above sea level, the tallest peak in North America. Its scale and beauty inspired many supporters of the Alaska National Interest Lands Conservation Act of 1980, which dramatically expanded the nation's parklands and wilderness areas. The Alaska Lands Act and the new Trans-Alaska oil pipeline, completed three years earlier, helped residents of the lower forty-eight states learn more about the nation's largest and most remote state.

Danny Lehman/Corbis

Why should a nation preserve some parks and wilderness areas?

Map 27.2 NUCLEAR POWER

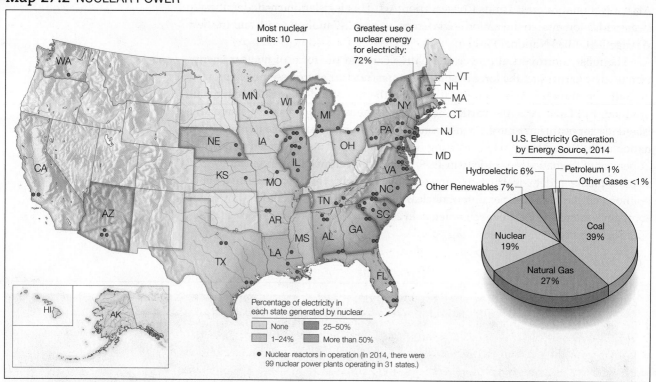

Between 1969 and 1980, all of the nation's 104 commercial nuclear power reactors either came on line (56) or were in the process of being planned or built (48). The United States has roughly one-quarter of the 435 commercial nuclear power reactors in the world. Despite nuclear energy's important role in U.S. electricity production, there is still no system in place for the permanent disposal of vast quantities of radioactive waste.

SOURCES: U.S. Energy Information Administration, "What Is U.S. Electricity Generation by Energy Source? March 31, 2015; Nuclear Regulatory Commission, Power Reactor Sites, February 18, 2015; Nuclear Regulatory Commission, State Electricity Generation Fuel Shares, May 2015.

27.4 Diffusing the Women's Movement

How successful were feminists in their struggle for gender equality?

"Good morning, boys and girls!" This standard classroom greeting suggests the central place of gender in how Americans identify people from a young age. Few people consider the phrase offensive, even though they probably would protest if a teacher addressed class members as "blacks and whites" or "tall people and short people." Should one's sex (a biological characteristic) or gender (the social assumptions associated with sex) constitute the fundamental dividing line among human beings? The spread of feminism through U.S. society from the 1970s onward raised this question.

27.4.1 Pressing for Equality

In a decade marked by hard rethinking of major issues, feminists provided one of the most profound challenges of all. Few American households avoided at least some reconsideration of the roles of men and women. Just as the nation reimagined its foreign policy in less assertive terms and with greater concern for human rights, feminists called for equality between the sexes while honoring their differences. The new title "Ms."— like Mr.—symbolized a desire not to have one's marital status revealed through the title "Miss" or "Mrs." Thousands of consciousness-raising meetings also made women aware that their own experiences with discrimination were part of a broader pattern of injustice toward women.

The millions of American women who found their lives changing in the 1970s did not agree on all issues. Female African Americans and Latinas balanced identities as women with identities as people of color, which aligned them closely with men of their communities. Working-class women of all colors often focused on issues common to all workers, including wages, workplace conditions, and union representation. Community organizers such as Lois Gibbs of Love Canal zeroed in on neighborhoods and families. The educated white women who formed the most visible part of the movement for equality differed among themselves on such issues as pornography: some found it inherently exploitive of women, while others considered it primarily a matter of free expression.

However, all women shared certain concerns. Even as many female Americans remained wary of the label *feminist*—fearing associations with anger, militancy, and dislike of men—they nonetheless tended to side with feminist positions on issues from equal pay for equal work to abortion rights and more egalitarian distribution of household chores within families. The women's movement also sought to unmask the violence constraining all women's lives: sexual harassment, domestic abuse, and rape.

27.4.2 New Opportunities in Education, the Workplace, and Family Life

In the 1970s, educated women gained access to a host of new opportunities in the workplace. Young women in college, unlike their mothers, expected to choose and develop a career after graduation even more than they anticipated getting married. The number of women entering graduate and professional schools soared. The percentage of female students in law school shot up from 5 percent to 40 percent between 1970 and 1980. In addition, most single-sex private colleges went coeducational. Many dormitories housed both men and women, allowing young people from the middle and upper classes to live in close physical proximity for the first time.

A similar process unfolded in the workplace. Employment in the United States, formerly divided into "men's" and "women's" work, saw a blurring of those lines. Help-wanted advertisements stopped categorizing jobs as male or female, and women joined the ranks of police officers and truck drivers. In 1980, more than half of women with children under six years old had paying jobs outside the home.

Not surprisingly, family life also changed shape in these years. In the 1950s, more than 70 percent of American families with children had a father who worked outside the home and a mother who stayed at home. By 1980, only 15 percent of families were configured that way. Yet society's growing acceptance of mothers in the workforce did not necessarily mean that these women enjoyed a lighter domestic load. Most working mothers still bore the brunt of the "second shift": child-rearing and housework, in addition to a full-time paid job.

Changing roles brought new marital stresses, and divorce rates climbed in this decade. In 1970, one-third as many divorces as marriages occurred annually; in 1980, the figure was one-half. No-fault divorce laws, beginning with California's in 1970, eased the process and the stigma attached to divorce, although its emotional impact on adults and children remained difficult to measure. Men tended to benefit financially when marriages split up. Their average living standard rose sharply, whereas that of women and their children plummeted.

27.4.3 Equality Under the Law

Paralleling the logic of the black civil rights movement, the modern women's movement pressured lawmakers to eliminate the legal underpinnings of sex-based discrimination. Title IX of the Educational Amendments of 1972 required schools to spend comparable amounts on women's and men's sports programs.

This critical step symbolized women's shift away from spectatorship and cheer-leading to the female athleticism that helped define American popular culture by the end of the twentieth century.

After languishing for decades among failed proposals in Congress, the proposed Equal Rights Amendment to the Constitution finally rode to an overwhelming victory among senators and representatives in 1972. The legislature then sent it to the states for possible ratification by 1980. Simple in its language, the ERA declared: "Equality of rights under law shall not be denied or abridged by the United States or by any State on account of sex."

Roe v. Wade
1973 U.S. Supreme Court decision establishing the constitutionality of a woman's right to choose an abortion in the first six months of pregnancy.

On January 22, 1973, in the landmark case of *Roe v. Wade*, the Supreme Court ruled (by a 7–2 vote) that constitutional privacy rights were "broad enough to encompass a woman's decision whether or not to terminate her pregnancy" in its first six months. This decision established women's constitutional right to determine the course of their own pregnancies.

27.4.4 Backlash

Even as the majority of Americans accepted most of the fundamental tenets of feminism, some fiercely defended existing gender roles. The mainstream media often painted women's rights activists as angry man-haters. Indeed, the media at first tended to associate feminism with "bra-burning," a titillating way to blend women's rights with the sexual revolution and thus sidestep the serious issues that women were raising. One Chicana worker involved in a strike against the Farah slacks company in Texas responded, "I don't believe in burning your bra, but I do believe in having our rights."

The women's movement posed a daunting challenge to traditional ideas about masculinity. Men wondered what equality for women really meant and how it might change their personal as well as professional relationships with women. Should men still open doors for women? Should they begin to do half (or more) of housework and parenting? Should they not comment on a female colleague's appearance? Women's growing economic independence and educational opportunities often altered the dynamics of power in male–female relationships. Many men from all classes and ethnicities, feeling defensive about assumptions and behaviors that were increasingly labeled sexist, resisted these changes. Some found the increasingly open acknowledgment of lesbianism threatening because it implied their potential irrelevance to women.

That men would have mixed feelings about women's liberation surprised no one. But some of the stiffest resistance came from women who had built their identities on motherhood and homemaking and now strongly defended that tradition. They sought to uphold an established family structure that they believed divorce, gay rights, abortion, and daycare would destroy. In their view, femininity meant service to one's family. "Feminists praise self-centeredness," antifeminist Phyllis Schlafly declared, "and call it liberation." In addition to defending their own choices, female antifeminists worried about the impact of dual-career families on children.

Opponents of women's liberation made two major legislative gains in the late 1970s. First, Congress passed the Hyde Amendment in 1976, which forbade the use of Medicaid funds for abortions. In practice, the amendment limited access to abortion to those women who could afford to pay for it themselves. Second, Schlafly's Stop-ERA campaign helped defeat the Equal Rights Amendment by limiting its ratification to only thirty-five of the required thirty-eight states. Schlafly claimed that the amendment would "destroy the family, foster homosexuality, and hurt women." ERA opponents argued that it would also draw out the worst in men, letting husbands opt out of supporting their wives and freeing divorced men from paying alimony. Antifeminists also resented the disrespect for motherhood that they believed they felt from some feminists.

ROOTS: THE SAGA OF AN AMERICAN FAMILY The 1977 miniseries version of Alex Haley's *Roots* captured the largest television audience ever up to that time. The powerful drama about Haley's ancestors offered tens of millions of Americans an intimate and sympathetic understanding of the horrific story of black slavery and survival. *Roots* also represented the post-1960s emphasis on preserving and respecting group histories and identities rather than emphasizing only individual success and assimilation into the mainstream.

ABC Photo Archives/Disney ABC Television Group/Getty Images

How is slavery portrayed today in American popular culture, such as in films and novels?

Still, they agreed with feminists that tens of millions of American women were just one man removed from welfare. The two sides differed on the best way to protect women's interests: should women's economic independence be enhanced, or instead should men be tied more tightly to their families?

Though discouraging for some, the narrow defeat of the ERA could not mask feminism's growing influence throughout American culture. The "first woman" stories that began showing up in the media during the 1970s marked the entrance of women into previously all-male roles. Like physicians, lawyers, and other figures of cultural authority, religious leaders now increasingly consisted of women, including the first Lutheran pastor (1970), the first Jewish rabbi (1972), and the first Episcopal priest (1974). In 1981, Sandra Day O'Connor became the first female Supreme Court justice. And mainstream organizations such as churches and municipalities ran feminist-created community institutions, including rape crisis centers, women's health clinics, and battered women's shelters.

Conclusion

In 1978, a divided U.S. Supreme Court handed down a ruling on the contentious policy of **affirmative action**.

affirmative action
Policies designed to improve the educational and employment opportunities of historically underrepresented groups such as women and African Americans.

The justices decided by a 5–4 vote in the *Bakke* case that strict racial quotas were unconstitutional, but that universities could consider race as one of several factors in determining a candidate's qualifications for admission. Diversity on campus, the majority argued, benefited all students. The Court, like the American public, was wrestling with the broader 1970s problem of how to reform American society in ways that would preserve its historic strengths while removing the ills that the previous decade's political activism had laid bare. One specific problem was the tension between the ideal of colorblind integration and new expressions of pride in distinctive racial and ethnic identities. Many white ethnic Americans in these years leavened their long-standing cultural assimilation into the mainstream with renewed attention to their roots in particular European countries, especially Ireland and Italy.

Americans' self-confidence and pride as a nation had been deeply shaken by the combination of the Vietnam War, the Watergate scandal, and the economic downturn after 1973. Disillusioned by the corruptions of public life, many citizens turned inward and heeded the advice of Robert J. Ringer in his 1977 bestseller, *Looking Out for Number One*. But others found motivation in the decade's events—especially the revelation that presidents, corporate executives, and other authorities had lied to them. They learned what earlier Americans had discovered in the 1760s and 1770s about imperious British officials and the corrupting effects of managing a global empire. Like the revolutionaries of George Washington's generation, they sought to strengthen representative government.

Chapter Review

27.1 Twin Shocks: Détente and Watergate

How did détente and the Watergate scandal affect U.S. foreign relations and American politics?
Détente reduced the likelihood of nuclear war, but it also raised questions about whether the extreme anticommunism of the Cold War had been necessary. The Watergate scandal, in combination with the U.S. defeat in Vietnam, gravely shook Americans' confidence in their government and in other traditional authority figures.

27.2 Discovering the Limits of the U.S. Economy

How did the economic changes affect the way Americans felt about their country?
National economic strength had long underpinned Americans' optimism about the future and confidence in their country. The "stagflation" of the 1970s marked the end of steady growth of the American middle class. Ever since, the gap between rich and poor has grown.

27.3 Reshuffling Politics

Which were the most significant political reforms of the 1970s?

Congress asserted its authority anew, particularly in foreign affairs, in order to balance the power of the presidency under Richard Nixon. Under Jimmy Carter, the U.S. government promoted energy conservation and new energy sources. Carter also signed major peace treaties with Panama and with Israel and Egypt.

27.4 Diffusing the Women's Movement

How successful were feminists in their struggle for gender equality?

The pursuit of women's equality had a long history before the 1970s, and it continues today. But these years saw a dramatic desegregation by sex of the public spheres of education and work, as women won new opportunities in American society. Along with their male supporters, women began a serious recalculation of gender roles in the United States, both in the private sphere of family and in the public sphere.

Timeline

1972   Watergate break-in
Nixon visits China

1973   American troops withdraw from Vietnam
Roe v. Wade legalizes abortion
Arab oil embargo

1974   Nixon resigns; Gerald R. Ford becomes president

1977   Carter issues general amnesty for draft evaders

1978   *Bakke* Supreme Court decision on affirmative action

1979   Camp David peace accords

Glossary

détente The lessening of military or diplomatic tensions, as between the United States and the Soviet Union.

Watergate The Washington, D.C., hotel-office complex where agents of President Nixon's reelection campaign broke into Democratic party headquarters in 1972. Nixon helped cover up the break-in, and the subsequent political scandal was referred to as "Watergate."

stagflation Unprecedented combination in the mid-1970s of a stagnant economy (with high unemployment) and price inflation.

Love Canal Upstate New York site of environmental crisis over the deleterious effects of unregulated pollution from dumping of toxic chemical wastes.

War Powers Act 1973 law requiring the U.S. president to get Congressional approval within ninety days of sending U.S. troops into a conflict abroad.

Camp David accords Agreements between Israel and Egypt, brokered by the United States, that gave Israel its first diplomatic recognition by an Arab state, and implied future autonomy for the Palestinian occupied territories.

Roe v. Wade 1973 U.S. Supreme Court decision establishing the constitutionality of a woman's right to choose an abortion in the first six months of pregnancy.

affirmative action Policies designed to improve the educational and employment opportunities of historically underrepresented groups such as women and African Americans.

Chapter 28
The Cold War Returns—and Ends, 1979–1991

RONALD REAGAN ON HORSE-BACK As President, Ronald Reagan loved spending time outdoors at his ranch near Santa Barbara, California.

National Archives and Records Administration

How might Ronald Reagan's appearance and style, as well as his acting career, have affected his subsequent political career?

Contents and Focus Questions

What would result from the spill of 94 million gallons of radioactive water into the Rio Puerco and the Rio Grande? And how would it impact Native Americans in the area?

The spill occurred on July 16, 1979, just west of Albuquerque, New Mexico, when a dam holding wastewater and residue from America's largest uranium mine broke. The Anaconda Copper Company operated this mine, producing fuel for nuclear power. The mine closed in the early 1980s. At public hearings in 1986 concerning the future of the mine and its small mountain of poisonous tailings, Anaconda's scientists argued that the mine did not threaten human health in the area. Thus, they said, the tailing piles and the polluted ponds did not need to be cleaned up.

Herman García, a Laguna Indian who lived in the adjoining village of Paguate, listened carefully but remained unconvinced. As he explained, they "lost five people from cancer" last year in tiny Paguate alone. "I'm no expert," he concluded. "I'd like for some of these experts to go out there and swim in those ponds. Then when I see them swim, then maybe I feel more secure."

The Native American West and the nuclear West have overlapped to a remarkable extent ever since participants in the Manhattan Project began building the first atomic bomb in 1942. Repeatedly, the U.S. government constructed major nuclear sites in the West on lands surrounded by Indian settlements. Some of this overlap resulted from geological coincidence: almost 90 percent of the nation's uranium lay on or adjacent to Indian lands. Some of it stemmed from politics. The sparse populations of Pueblo, Western Shoshone, and Yakima lacked the political clout to prevent their lands from becoming what the National Academy of Science called "national sacrifice areas."

*   *   *   *   *

In the 1980s, nuclear weapons and waste sparked controversy in the United States. President Ronald Reagan expanded the nation's nuclear arsenal, and his administration publicly discussed fighting and winning a nuclear war against the Soviet Union. A major accident in 1986 at the Chernobyl nuclear power plant outside the Soviet city of Kiev only heightened public concerns. Frightened by rising U.S.–Soviet tensions, citizens in western Europe and the United States organized an international movement to freeze further development of nuclear weapons.

In 1979, two international incidents raised questions about U.S. military effectiveness. A revolution in Iran led to the taking of American hostages and a dramatic rejection of American influence, and the Soviet Union sent troops into Afghanistan to prop up a Soviet-allied but weakening government. Angered, Americans put tough-talking Republicans in the White House for twelve years. The emphasis of these leaders on military might challenged the Soviet leadership, while changes in eastern Europe and the USSR brought an end to the Cold War and the breakup of the Soviet Union.

The Reagan administration also avidly promoted free markets. Its policies produced great wealth at the top of the socioeconomic ladder, increasing the distance between the daily experiences of the rich and the poor. These policies also catalyzed bitter struggles over natural resources, particularly those on western public lands.

Finally, the newly organized religious right clashed with liberal opponents over such issues as abortion and homosexuality. In these years, Christian fundamentalists and evangelicals and their allies sought to reverse cultural liberties that had emerged since the late 1960s.

28.1 Anticommunism Revived

Why did Cold War tensions increase after 1979?

"We're going down!" cried U.S. political officer Elizabeth Swift on the phone to the State Department. These were her last words as a crowd of young Iranians poured into the U.S. embassy in Tehran on the morning of November 4, 1979, and cut telephone lines. In a move that shocked Americans, Islamist militants seized fifty-two embassy personnel and held them hostage for over a year.

In the late 1970s, revolutionaries of a different political bent—socialist and leftist—took the offensive against authoritarian regimes in Central America. Indeed, the Third World seemed to be turning away from U.S. leadership in the wake of the American defeat in Vietnam. To make matters worse, the Soviet Union stepped up its support for leftists abroad. In December 1979, the Red Army invaded Afghanistan. Fed up with these humiliating events overseas and with relentless inflation at home, American voters elected Ronald Reagan as president—the most conservative chief executive since Calvin Coolidge. Reagan promised to resurrect the Cold War, and he delivered.

theocracy
A government by officials who are regarded as divinely guided.

28.1.1 Iran and Afghanistan

In January 1979, the Iranian people overthrew the longtime authoritarian government of Shah Reza Pahlavi. Under the shah's rule, the nation's enormous oil wealth had flowed into the hands of a small elite. Meanwhile, the impoverished majority of devout Shia Muslims had grown increasingly resentful of the shah's closeness with his American allies. His secret police had detained 50,000 political prisoners. The revolution found its leader in the austere religious figure Ruhollah Khomeini, who shouldered aside more moderate opposition groups. Returning from exile in Iraq and then Paris, Khomeini created a popular **theocracy** grounded in a strict interpretation of Islamic law.

Hunted by the rebels, the shah took his money and fled Iran. Several months later, the Carter administration let him fly to New York to seek treatment for cancer. Enraged that the United States now harbored their nation's most wanted criminal, Iranians demanded the shah's extradition to Tehran to stand trial. Washington refused. Within a month, militants stormed the U.S. embassy—"that nest of spies," Khomeini called it, referring to the CIA's considerable presence in Iran.

AYATOLLAH RUHOLLAH KHOMEINI Ruhollah Khomeini led the 1979 revolution in Iran that established the modern world's first Islamic theocratic state. The events in Iran encouraged Islamist revolutionaries across the Middle East, Asia, and North Africa. For Americans, the closest analogy was the Bolshevik revolution of 1917 in Russia, which provided a model for other communist revolutions abroad.

Bettmann/Corbis

Despite often fierce conflicts between Iranian Shia Muslims and the Muslim world's Sunni majority, how might Osama bin Laden, al Qaeda, ISIS, and other anti-Western Sunni Islamists have, nonetheless, been inspired by events in Iran in 1979?

The hostages' captors paraded them before television cameras in an effort to pressure Washington to return the shah. Carter refused to give in. In April 1980, he finally approved a military rescue effort. But mechanical failures forced the mission to abort, and the collision of two helicopters during the attempt killed several U.S. soldiers. Not until after the shah's death in 1980 did the two governments finally negotiate the hostages' release in January 1981.

Khomeini and his followers despised the values they associated with modern U.S. culture: secularism, materialism, gender equality, alcohol consumption, and sexual titillation. They sought to export the cleansing power of a puritanical Islamic faith throughout the Middle East and beyond. Indeed, the revolutionaries condemned the atheistic Soviets as fiercely as they did the materialistic Americans.

Just seven weeks after the seizure of hostages in Tehran, the first of 110,000 Soviet troops rolled south across the USSR's border into neighboring Afghanistan. Their goal: to stabilize the pro-Soviet government there

Map 28.1 TROUBLE SPOTS IN THE MIDDLE EAST, 1979–1993

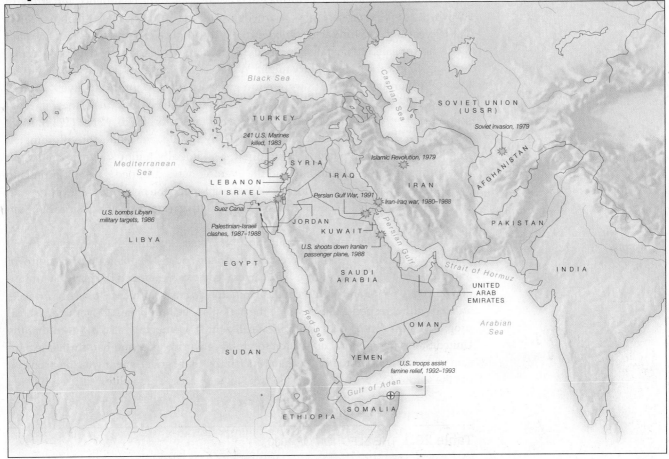

Oil production around the Persian Gulf and the close American relationship with Israel made political instability in the Middle East a central concern of the U.S. government. American leaders particularly feared the spread of either Soviet influence or Islamic revolution, both of which opposed American cultural values and U.S. strategic interests.

against anticommunist Islamist guerrilla fighters. Moscow had resolved to prevent the spread of **Islamist** revolution into the heavily Muslim central Asian regions of the southern USSR.

But few Americans saw this invasion as a defensive operation. Rather, they feared a push toward vulnerable Iran as Red Army troops marched beyond eastern Europe for the first time. The Carter administration halted most trade with the Soviets and withdrew the nuclear Strategic Arms Limitation Treaty (SALT II) from Senate consideration. In addition, the president organized a Western boycott of the 1980 summer Olympic Games in Moscow and increased military spending. The **Carter Doctrine** proclaimed the U.S. commitment to preserve the status quo in the Persian Gulf region, even if it meant the use of military force. And the CIA began funding the Afghan guerrillas.

Islamist
Pertaining to an ideology promoting the creation of governments based on a fundamentalist interpretation of Islamic law.

Carter Doctrine
A presidential assertion, during the Carter administration, that the U.S. would defend the status quo in the Persian Gulf.

28.1.2 The Conservative Victory of 1980

By mid-1980, Carter's public approval rating had dropped to the lowest level of any preceding modern president. Inflation reached 13.5 percent. Even the president acknowledged that the nation was at a "crisis stage."

Onto this stage strode Ronald Reagan. Long considered too conservative to win the presidency, the former California governor projected the confidence and strength for which many Americans now yearned, even if they did not share all of his views. The 69-year-old one-time actor sailed through the Republican primaries. For his main tactic, he appealed to nostalgia, particularly among whites, for a rosier past—a time of rising wages and U.S. military might. While Carter spoke of learning to live within limits, Reagan insisted that "we are too great a nation to limit ourselves to small dreams." The media loved Reagan. Indeed, his presidency fit with the new emphasis on constant entertainment, as cable television, VCRs (1976), ESPN (1979), MTV (1981), and CDs (1983) swept the culture. Daily newspaper readership plummeted from 73 percent to 50 percent during the 1980s. Equally telling, the average length of an uninterrupted "sound bite" on the evening news dropped from 42 seconds in 1968 to fewer than 10 seconds in 1988. Anything longer, the networks believed, would bore viewers. And no one projected simplicity with greater warmth or sincerity than Reagan.

Yet the 1980 election was about more than just Reagan's likable personality. It revealed the nation's renewed interest in conservative ideas. Republicans won control of the Senate for the first time since 1952. Several basic values united the party: an unhindered private sector and entrepreneurial initiative to create affluence, plus free markets and individual responsibility to solve the nation's social problems. Government social programs were condemned. Republicans, like most Democrats, also believed that the United States had a moral obligation to preserve world order and halt further expansion of communist influence. Reagan proclaimed that "government was the problem, not the solution."

Table 28.1 THE ELECTION OF 1980

Candidate	Political Party	Popular Vote (%)	Electoral Vote
Ronald Reagan	Republican	50.7	489
Jimmy Carter	Democratic	41.0	49
John B. Anderson	Independent	6.6	

SOURCE: Historical Election Results, Electoral College, National Archives and Records Administration

28.1.3 Renewing the Cold War

"Sometimes in our administration," Reagan once joked, "the right hand doesn't know what the far-right hand is doing." But all hands in the White House agreed on the importance of restoring confidence in the nation's engagements abroad, particularly in the Third World. In the 1970s, leftist insurgencies in Asia, Africa, and Latin America had suggested the retreat of U.S. power.

Reagan blamed the Soviet Union for "all the unrest that is going on." He rejected the 1970s policy of détente that had emerged during the Nixon administration and had taken further shape under Ford and Carter. Often, Reagan spoke as though the Chinese Soviet split had never happened. His was "a kind of 1952 world," one aide recalled. "He sees the world in black and white terms." Pointing to the Soviet occupation of Afghanistan and its 1983 shoot-down of a Korean Air Lines civilian jet that had strayed into Soviet airspace, the president denounced the USSR as "an evil empire."

The Reagan administration backed up the president's words by launching the largest peacetime military buildup in American history. The Pentagon's budget increased 40 percent between 1980 and 1984. The new president also revived covert

LEADING MAN RONALD REAGAN
Ronald Reagan's first successful career came in Hollywood films, after he moved to southern California from his home state of Illinois. His first of two marriages was to Jane Wyman, another successful Hollywood actor. Reagan frequently played the role of the handsome, tough leading man, particularly in traditional western movies.

AF archive/Alamy

How might Ronald Reagan's work as an actor have influenced his later career as president of the United States?

operations. He gave CIA director William Casey the green light to provide secret assistance to anticommunist governments and insurgencies throughout the Third World.

In Central America, extreme inequalities between landowning elites and vast peasant majorities had fueled insurgencies against the authoritarian governments of El Salvador, Guatemala, and Nicaragua. Moreover, some small assistance from Cuba and the Soviet Union had found its way to the rebels. Reagan passionately opposed these insurgents. He authorized the CIA to work hand-in-hand with the regimes, even though they used death squads to torture and murder dissidents and sometimes slaughtered whole villages and towns to wipe out possible resistance.

Contras

Counterrevolutionary guerrilla force organized by the CIA to try to overthrow the left-wing Sandinista government in Nicaragua.

Boland Amendments

Acts of Congress passed to restrain Reagan's efforts to overthrow the Nicaraguan government.

In Nicaragua, the Sandinista rebels managed to overthrow the pro-American dictatorship of Antonio Somoza in 1979. The Sandinistas set about building a more egalitarian and socialistic state while still preserving 60 percent of the nation's wealth in private hands. Carter had adopted a wait-and-see attitude. But after Reagan took office in 1981, the CIA created the counterrevolutionary **Contras**, recruited primarily from Somoza's brutal former National Guard. The Contras waged an undeclared war on the new government in the Nicaraguan capital of Managua. By 1987, 40,000 Nicaraguans had died in the fighting, most of them civilians. Reagan called the Contras "freedom fighters" and declared them "the moral equal of our Founding Fathers."

Nevertheless, several European and Latin American allies considered the Contras an illegitimate force of terrorists. A large coalition of church and university groups in the United States agreed. Christian activists formed the "Sanctuary" movement to aid refugees from the right-wing dictatorships in Central America that sympathized with the Contras. The Pentagon, for its part, had no interest in sending troops to fight a popular government abroad. The opposition finally prevailed; Congress passed the **Boland Amendments** of 1982 and 1984 to restrict U.S. assistance to the Contras.

28.2 Republican Rule at Home

What did the Reagan administration want to change about American society?

While reasserting U.S. power abroad, Reagan also aimed to reorient domestic policies toward the free market. Writer Barbara Ehrenreich told the story of a neighbor in New York City representative of welfare recipients: a single white mother with one child. Lori was what the president called a "welfare cheat." Lori had been married for two years to a man who beat her and once chased her around the house with a gun. Welfare had made it possible for her to leave him, a move she described as like being born again, "as a human being this time." Lori sometimes earned close to $100 a week from cleaning houses and waiting tables—not enough to support herself and her daughter, but a useful supplement to the small government payments. She chose not to report this to the welfare office, spending it instead on little things deemed inessential by welfare regulations: deodorant, hand lotion, and an occasional commercial haircut.

Lori's story helps illuminate some of the major trends of the 1980s. Inflation finally eased and the stock market perked up. Congress and the White House slashed taxes. However, annual budget deficits and the national debt (the accumulation of previous deficits) soon soared as tax revenues declined and military spending increased. The administration shrank government programs for the poor and portrayed welfare recipients like Lori as lazy and irresponsible. Washington was unsympathetic to concerns about the environment and opened public lands in the West to new commercial uses. By the 1990s, the gap between rich and poor widened noticeably and the vaunted American middle class worried about its declining economic security.

28.2.1 "Reaganomics"

Taxes played a crucial role in the Reagan administration's efforts to reduce government involvement in the economy. In 1981, the president proposed a new tax law to lower federal income tax rates by 25 percent over three years. Congress passed the legislation, and the top individual rate—paid only by the wealthiest Americans—dropped from 70 percent to 28 percent. Congress also slashed taxes on corporations, capital gains, and inheritances, further benefiting the most affluent Americans.

While taxes shrank, federal spending on the military soared. The Pentagon bolstered its conventional and nuclear arsenals and gave service personnel a morale-boosting salary increase. After 1983, billions of dollars poured from the U.S. Treasury into the president's proposed Strategic Defense Initiative (SDI) for a missile defense system.

Since taxes were going down, funds for the weapons buildup could come from only one source: social programs at home. However, most domestic spending went to popular programs, such as Social Security and Medicare, which primarily benefited the middle class. Leaving those in place, Reagan instead reduced funding for welfare programs, including food stamps, school lunches, job training, and low-income housing.

The assault on welfare had links to racial issues as well. The Reagan administration opposed any form of affirmative action, calling instead for the "colorblind" application of law. The president and his supporters argued that prejudice no longer had any significant effect on the decisions that employers and others made. Ironically, Reagan's own Justice Department demonstrated the opposite: it sought unsuccessfully to win tax-free status for Bob Jones University in Greenville, South Carolina, and other schools and colleges that discriminated against people of color.

'SURELY,' SAYS I . 'NOT THE JAMES WATT, FOLK-HERO AND FAMOUS WILDERNESS RAPIST!' 'THAT'S ME.' SAYS HE. AND I SAYS, 'NOT THE RENOWNED DESPOILER OF OUR PRECIOUS NATIONAL HERITAGE!' 'RIGHT.' SAYS HE. SO I ATE HIM.'

JAMES "BALDYLOCKS" WATT AND THE THREE BEARS James Watt, Reagan's first secretary of the Interior Department, became one of the most polarizing figures in a polarized decade. He made clear that he considered environmentalists to be his opponents as he worked to promote the interests of mining and timbering companies as well as ranchers. The Interior Department manages the national parks, monuments, and wildlife refuges, as well as the Bureau of Land Management's extensive lands (national forests fall under the Department of Agriculture's jurisdiction).

On which issues has the management of natural resources remained an important question in U.S. politics since the 1980s?

Reducing welfare spending did not close the budgetary gaps that lower taxes and higher military outlays had opened. To close these gaps, the government resorted to borrowing money. Formerly the world's largest creditor nation, the United States now became its largest debtor nation. Between 1981 and 1989, the national debt ballooned to almost $3 trillion. Moreover, during the twelve years of Republican rule ending in 1993, annual budget deficits jumped from $59 billion to $300 billion.

Despite these problems, "Reaganomics" did help the national economy recover somewhat from the traumas of the 1970s. The tight money policies of the Federal Reserve Board after 1979 eventually tamed inflation, which dropped from 13.5 percent in 1980 to 3 percent in 1983. The Fed's high interest rates also choked off the nation's cash flow and provoked a severe recession in 1981–1982, with unemployment reaching above 10 percent. However, the economy revived again in 1983 and was growing at a robust annual rate of 6.8 percent by 1984. In that year, rising confidence in the economy helped Reagan soundly win reelection over his opponent, Carter's former vice president Walter Mondale.

Table 28.2 THE ELECTION OF 1984

Candidate	Political Party	Popular Vote (%)	Electoral Vote
Ronald Reagan	Republican	59.0	525
Walter Mondale	Democratic	41.0	13

SOURCE: Historical Election Results, Electoral College, National Archives and Records Administration

28.2.2 The Environment Contested

The 1980 election marked the sharpest turn ever in American environmental policy. The new administration reversed two decades of growing bipartisan consensus on the need for greater protection of the environment. Reagan instead supported corporations' demands for fewer environmental regulations and easier access to natural resources on public lands. The president ridiculed the idea of preserving wilderness for its own sake. He even claimed that "trees cause more pollution than automobiles do."

The officials Reagan appointed to oversee these lands and assume responsibility for protecting them had little respect for the agencies they ran. Critics described the situation as "foxes guarding the chicken house." The officials openly disdained environmentalists, including those in the moderate wing of the Republican party, and explicitly rewrote regulations to favor private enterprise. They sold grazing, logging, and mining rights on public lands at prices far below market value, despite their stated commitment to market economics.

James Watt, the new Secretary of the Interior, declared that only two kinds of people lived in the United States: "liberals and Americans." Watt was also a Christian fundamentalist. In his Senate confirmation hearings, he suggested that the nation had little need for long-term public land management because Christ would soon be returning and the known world would pass away—an interpretation of stewardship that not even all fundamentalists shared, much less the broader American public. Watt's abrasive personal style eventually alienated even the White House, and he resigned in 1983.

The administration's reversal of federal environmental policies alarmed a wide range of citizens and stimulated a green backlash. Membership in environmental organizations soared, in such traditional groups as the Sierra Club and the Audubon Society, as well as in more radical ones, such as Greenpeace. Most Americans wanted to breathe cleaner air, drink safe water, and make recreational use of national parks and national forests. In much of the rural West, jobs in the recreation industry outnumbered those in the logging, mining, and ranching businesses. In 1989, concerns intensified when the

James Watt
Reagan's controversial first Secretary of the Interior, whose anti-environmental views and abrasive personality made him a lightning rod for criticism.

oil tanker *Exxon Valdez* ran aground in Prince William Sound in Alaska, coating 1,000 miles of pristine coastline with crude oil.

28.2.3 The Affluence Gap

As the Reagan administration eased corporate access to the nation's natural resources, the disparity between rich and poor expanded further. Whereas most Americans' real wages (wages after inflation) declined, the professional classes fared well, and the wealthiest citizens gained enormously. For example, the salary of an average corporate chief executive officer was forty times greater than that of a typical factory worker in 1980; by 1989, it was ninety-three times greater. The top 1 percent of American families now possessed more assets than the bottom 90 percent—a ratio typical of Third World nations.

A series of corporate mergers and consolidations further enriched well-off Americans, as did financial speculation and manipulation on Wall Street. *Business Week* wrote of a "casino economy" in which insider trading and leveraged buyouts (business takeovers financed by debt) created paper wealth rather than actual products. This explosion of wealth at the top fueled an emerging culture of extravagance, reminiscent of similar trends in the late nineteenth century and in the 1920s. Newly identified "yuppies" (young urban professionals) embodied the drive for material acquisition, in contrast to the anticonsumerist inclinations of the late 1960s and early 1970s. Jerry Rubin, a member of the anarchist "Yippies" in the 1960s, once dropped dollar bills onto the floor of the New York Stock Exchange—which traders scurried madly to grab—to dramatize the stock market's single-minded pursuit of profit. By the 1980s, however, Rubin was working as an investment banker. Ronald and Nancy Reagan were older but shared similar values. They relished lavish amenities like those made popular on the television shows *Dynasty*, *Dallas*, and *Lifestyles of the Rich and Famous*.

As the affluence gap widened, the broad middle class watched its job security slip. Early in the decade, the recession had prompted factory shutdowns and mass layoffs. More than a million industrial jobs disappeared in 1982 alone. Manufacturers' decisions to keep moving plants abroad for cheaper labor only worsened the situation. Although the 1980s saw the creation of 20 million new jobs, most of these were in the nonunionized service sector and offered low pay and few benefits.

The poorest Americans did not fare well in the 1980s. The bottom tenth saw their already meager incomes decline by another 10 percent. In 1986, a full-time worker at minimum wage earned $6,700 per year—almost $4,000 short of the poverty level for a family of four. Homelessness worsened in cities as the government cut funding for welfare and institutional care for the mentally ill, while housing costs rose. More than 1 million people lived on the streets, one-fifth of them still employed. One out of eight children went hungry, and 20 percent lived in poverty, including 50 percent of black children. These Americans received minimal sympathy from the nation's political leaders. By contrast, Congress and the White House provided large federal subsidies to "needy" businesses such as the Chrysler Corporation and the savings and loan industry.

Despite Reagan's record, 40 percent of union household members and 50 percent of all blue-collar workers cast their ballots for this staunch opponent of unions. Why? Part of the explanation lies in the decline of working-class voting during the 1970s. Disillusioned with a political process they saw as corrupt, numerous workers neglected to go to the polls on voting day. Many of those who did vote decided that the Democratic party had become increasingly co-opted by cultural liberalism and no longer spoke for the working class. Reagan's charisma and appeal to patriotism also attracted many citizens who might once have voted for their economic interests instead. Finally, white Americans increasingly defined their political loyalties on the basis of social and cultural issues—such as opposition to abortion, homosexuality, and affirmative action—rather than economic interests. Conservative Christians, in particular, strongly supported the Republican cause.

Exxon Valdez

Oil tanker that ran aground in Alaska's Prince William Sound in March 1989, creating the second largest oil spill in American history.

DONALD TRUMP REVELLING IN HIS WEALTH In the 1980s, Donald Trump was the very model of conspicuous wealth and was derided by many for displaying a distinct preference for money over all other things. Here Trump and his wife sit in front of their household serving staff.

Ted Thai/Time Life Pictures/Getty Images

Might many nonelite Americans in the 1980s have both admired Donald Trump's affluence and also resented it to some degree? What of Americans today?

28.3 Cultural Conflict

About which cultural issues did Americans seem to disagree most?

One of the nation's foremost religious figures of the period, Reverend Pat Robertson, controlled the Christian Broadcasting Network and ran unsuccessfully for the 1988 Republican presidential nomination. Like other social conservatives of his era, he promoted what he called "family values" and traditional gender roles. Robertson went so far as to declare that feminism "encourages women to leave their husbands, kill their children [and] practice witchcraft." In contrast, author Susan Faludi wrote the 1991 bestseller *Backlash* about opposition to the women's movement. She became an important critic of gender roles in American society and how they limit people's life experiences and possibilities. In contrast to Robertson, Faludi concluded, "All women are feminists. It's just a matter of time and encouragement."

As Robertson and Faludi demonstrate, Americans embroiled themselves throughout the 1980s in a contentious debate about values. Their society had changed in the previous generation in ways that some citizens disdained but others applauded. Americans argued primarily about issues that had come to the fore during the social movements of the 1960s and 1970s: sexuality, gender roles, the place of religion in public life, and multiculturalism. These often bitter "culture wars" dominated talk shows and newspaper editorial pages throughout much of the last two decades of the twentieth century.

28.3.1 The Rise of the Religious Right

Some of the Americans most troubled by the state of American society were conservative white Protestants, disproportionately from the South. Along with conservative

Catholics, they criticized the post-1960s shift in mainstream values away from respect for traditional authorities—the church, political leaders, and the military—and toward freer sexual expression and general self-indulgence. What the nation needed, they believed, was a return to reverence for God. The growth of Christian fundamentalism paralleled rising religious fundamentalism around the globe, whether among Jews in Israel, Hindus in India, or Muslims in Iran and the Arab Middle East. For all their differences, religious people in these cultures shared a common quest: preserving spiritual purity and cultural traditions in an increasingly secular, integrated world.

Conservative Christians were not a fringe group. As many as 45 million Americans—20 percent of the population—identified themselves as fundamentalist Christians in 1980. In combination with a similar number of Catholics, they represented a vast potential force in American politics. And their ranks were growing, while membership in the more liberal mainline Protestant denominations, such as Presbyterians and Episcopalians, declined steadily after the 1960s.

Conservative Christians mobilized in the 1980 campaign to support Reagan's candidacy. Critics noted that Reagan himself attended church only occasionally and seemed an indifferent father. They contrasted the divorced candidate with his born-again, Sunday-school–teaching opponent, Jimmy Carter. But Reagan's conservative views on abortion and gay rights and his support for school prayer resonated with fundamentalists and evangelicals. They flocked to the Republican party and to new conservative religious organizations, such as the **Moral Majority**, founded in 1979 in Lynchburg, Virginia, by Reverend Jerry Falwell. More than 60 million people each week watched—and many sent money to—televangelists, including Falwell, Robertson, and Jim Bakker.

Moral Majority
Conservative political organization of fundamentalist Christians organized in 1979 under Jerry Falwell's leadership.

Suffusing the GOP with a distinctly southern, grassroots flavor, the religious right also highlighted a major faultline in the modern Republican party: the tension between social conservatives, who emphasized community and tradition, and free marketeers, who promoted entrepreneurial capitalism. In its quest for profits, unrestrained capitalism had no inherent respect for tradition. Indeed, it could bring unwelcome changes, as Rustbelt industrial workers had discovered when their employers moved south and overseas. Marrying Jesus to the market proved difficult: should the state play a minimal role in the economy and society, as free-market libertarians believed, or should it monitor personal behavior, as social conservatives implied?

Gender and sexuality issues particularly aroused the ire of religious conservatives. They blamed feminism for weakening male authority in the family and for increasing divorce rates. A growing antiabortion movement gained national visibility by 1980, and religious conservatives opposed Americans' slowly increasing acceptance of gays and lesbians. Dismayed by the prevalence of casual sexual relationships in the 1970s, church conservatives urged abstinence on young Americans.

The heyday of the sexual revolution ended in the early 1980s, when researchers identified the human immunodeficiency virus (HIV), which causes acquired immunodeficiency syndrome (AIDS). The deadly epidemic spread swiftly through the gay male communities of San Francisco and New York as a result of unprotected sex. AIDS continued to spread during the 1990s and beyond, among gays and heterosexuals, both in the United States and abroad—especially in such places as China, southern Africa, and Russia. New drugs slowed the onset of actual AIDS in many HIV-infected Americans while scientists continued the frustrating quest for a cure.

Yet another epidemic swept through the United States during the 1980s, striking impoverished urban neighborhoods especially hard. The culprit was crack cocaine. Powerfully addictive, it contributed to gang violence and record homicide rates in several cities. Drug-related convictions skyrocketed, stimulating a boom in prison building, a doubling of the nation's inmate population, and new police special weapons and tactics (SWAT) teams to deal with heavily armed drug operators.

Interpreting History

Jerry Falwell versus Robert McAfee Brown: On Religion and Politics (1980, 1982)

> "The hope of reversing the trends of decay in our republic now lies with the Christian public in America."

In 1979, Baptist minister Jerry Falwell founded the Moral Majority in Lynchburg, Virginia. The organization represented the growing engagement of conservative fundamentalist and evangelical Christians in American politics, and Falwell emerged as the most prominent figure of the new religious right. However, not all Christians were conservative. Robert McAfee Brown, a Presbyterian minister and theologian, represented more liberal elements of the church that understood both the Bible and the problems of American society differently than Falwell.

The Goals of the Moral Majority (1980)
by Jerry Falwell

We must reverse the trend America finds herself in today. Young people . . . have learned to disrespect the family as God established it. They have been educated in a public-school system that is permeated with secular humanism. They have been taught that the Bible is just another book of literature. They have been taught that there are no absolutes in our world today. . . . These same young people have been reared under the influence of a government that has taught them socialism and welfarism. . . .

I personally feel that the home and the family are still held in reverence by the vast majority of the American public. I believe there is still a vast number of Americans who love their country, are patriotic, and are willing to sacrifice for her. I remember that time when it was positive to be patriotic. . . . I remember as a boy . . . when the band struck up "The Stars and Stripes Forever," we stood and goose pimples would run all over me. . . .

It is now time to take a stand on certain moral issues. . . . We must stand against the Equal Rights Amendment, the feminist revolution, and the homosexual revolution. . . .

Americans have been silent much too long. We have stood by and watched as American power and influence have been systematically weakened in every sphere of the world. . . .

The hope of reversing the trends of decay in our republic now lies with the Christian public in America. We cannot expect help from the liberals. They certainly are not going to call our nation back to righteousness and neither are the pornographers, the smut peddlers, and those who are corrupting our youth.

The Politics of the Bible (1982)
by Robert Mcafee Brown

In Christian terms, and I think in terms with which all Jews could also agree, my real complaint about the Moral Majority's intrusion of the Bible into American politics, is that they are not biblical enough. . . .

The Moral Majority's biblically inspired political agenda involves a very selective, very partial, and therefore very distorted use of the Bible. They have isolated a set of concerns that they say get to the heart of what is wrong with America— homosexuality, abortion, and pornography. . . .

Take the issue of homosexuality. If one turns to the scriptures as a whole, to try to come up with their central concerns, homosexuality is going to be very low on such a list even if indeed it makes the list at all. There are perhaps seven very ambiguous verses in the whole biblical canon that even allude to it. . . . [But there are] hundreds and hundreds of places where the scriptures are dealing over and over again with question of social justice, the tendency of the rich to exploit the poor, the need for all of us to have a commitment to the hungry, . . . [and] the dangers of national idolatry, that is to say, making the nation into God, accepting uncritically whatever we have to do as a nation against other nations. . . .

EVANGELIST JERRY FALWELL Before he became involved in politics, Jerry Falwell had already made a name for himself in his hometown of Lynchburg, Virginia, as the senior minister of the large Thomas Road Baptist Church and the founder of Liberty University. His organization, the Moral Majority, became the most well-known conservative evangelical Christian organization of the 1980s.

William E. Sauro/The New York Times/Redux

How does the influence of the Christian right of today compare with the Christian right when it first coalesced in the late 1970s and early 1980s under the leadership of Jerry Falwell?

When one looks over the agenda of the Moral Majority there is absolutely no mention of such things. . . . We seem to be living in two different worlds, reading two different books.

Questions for Discussion

1. Which specific issues in American society most trouble Jerry Falwell? What specifically about "liberals" seems to dismay him most?

2. What does Robert McAfee Brown find most unpersuasive about Jerry Falwell's use of the Bible to understand American society and its problems?

3. Can you imagine any common ground between the views represented by Falwell and Brown?

SOURCE: Irwin Unger and Robert R. Tomes, *American Issues*, 2nd ed. (Prentice-Hall, 1999), 2: 362–364, 375–377.

28.3.2 Dissenters Push Back

The liberal and radical reform energies that had percolated in the late 1960s and early 1970s did not evaporate entirely in the conservative 1980s. Nuclear threats engaged activists from both the peace and environmental movements. The accidents at Three Mile Island (1979) and Chernobyl (1986) intensified public anxieties about the dangers of nuclear energy. The sharp increases in both Soviet and U.S. nuclear arsenals alarmed residents in those countries and across Europe, where many of the missiles were located. The broad-based nuclear freeze movement that emerged in the United States and western Europe in the early 1980s encouraged arms control negotiations that would bear fruit a few years later.

Racial justice remained a primary concern for Americans of color and liberal and leftist activists, particularly in light of the Republican administration's opposition to affirmative action. Determined to honor the foremost leader of the civil rights movement, antiracists convinced Congress in 1983 to designate Martin Luther King Jr.'s birthday a national holiday. By 1985, a robust antiapartheid movement successfully campaigned to reduce U.S. investments in racially segregated South Africa. Perhaps the most prominent face of left-leaning politics in the decade was that of Jesse Jackson, a former aide to King. Jackson sought the Democratic nomination for president in 1984 and 1988, winning a handful of primaries in 1988 with his multiracial Rainbow Coalition. Jackson's candidacy encouraged several million African Americans to register to vote for the first time.

Gay rights advocates also raised their voices in the 1980s. Faced with the twin scourges of AIDS and homophobic violence, homosexuals and their heterosexual supporters lobbied for the inclusion of sexual orientation as a category of discrimination in civil rights laws. Others took to the streets. In October 1987, nearly half a million Americans marched in Washington in support of gay rights. A few widely admired figures, such as tennis champion Martina Navratilova, publicly acknowledged their homosexuality, helping others to imagine this sexual orientation as acceptable rather than deviant. By the end of the 1980s, the record was mixed. Gays and lesbians remained the only Americans against whom tens of millions of their fellow citizens openly believed it acceptable to discriminate, but the rights of homosexuals, nonetheless, had much wider support than ever before.

28.3.3 The New Immigrants

For two decades after the restrictive immigration law of 1924, the flow of newcomers from abroad slowed to a trickle. The trickle became a stream again after World War II, and then legislation in 1965 opened the gates even wider. As a result, a wave of new immigrants, 3.3 million in the 1960s and 4.5 million in the 1970s, hit the United States. In the 1980s, 7.3 million people entered the country legally, along with a similar number without documentation.

NBA ICONS JORDAN AND JOHNSON While immigrants brought their own distinctive cultures to the United States, American popular culture spread abroad. The broadcast of National Basketball Association (NBA) games in dozens of other countries helped basketball become the world's second most popular game (after soccer). Charismatic stars like Earvin "Magic" Johnson of the Los Angeles Lakers and particularly Michael Jordan of the Chicago Bulls became popular icons around the world.

Jim Ruymen UPI Photo Service/Newscom

What impact do sports seem to have on American culture?

These newcomers brought an unprecedented cultural and ethnic diversity. Only 10 percent of the most recent arrivals in the United States were Europeans. Forty percent came instead from Asia—particularly China, the Philippines, and South Korea—and 50 percent from Latin America and the Caribbean, particularly Mexico. From 1965 to 1995, 7 million Latinos and 5 million Asians moved to the United States.

The new immigrants came for the same reasons their predecessors had. Many were fleeing political and religious persecution in their home countries, but most sought new economic opportunity. A small number, primarily from South Korea and Hong Kong, arrived with some assets that helped them get started in business. However, most came with few resources and took what work they could find in garment sweatshops, on farms, as domestic servants and janitors, and as gardeners. These immigrants willingly endured profound hardship in order to build better lives for their families. They also rekindled the nation's long-standing cultural diversity, especially in Sunbelt cities from Miami, Florida, to San Diego, California. In 1981, citizens of San Antonio elected Henry

Cisneros as the first Mexican American mayor of a major U.S. city. In Los Angeles, one-third of residents were foreign-born by 1990.

Most Americans had foreign-born ancestors who had come to the United States with the same dreams that motivated the newest arrivals. Still, the non-European origins of the latest immigrants troubled some white citizens. Conservatives, in particular, worried about the growing diversity of American society and feared a decline of the Eurocentric culture with which they had grown up. They were also anxious that poor immigrants might drain taxpayers' dollars by winding up on welfare. The Immigration and Naturalization Service (INS) stepped up patrols of the 2,000-mile U.S. border with Mexico to limit the rising number of undocumented Mexican workers heading north. By the early 1990s, the INS was apprehending and expelling 1.7 million undocumented workers every year.

28.4 The End of the Cold War

After forty-five years, why did the Cold War end?

For Americans, the greatest surprise of the 1980s was the warming of U.S.–Soviet relations after 1985. Few had imagined such a scenario during Reagan's first two years in office, when his administration became the first in four decades not to collaborate on nuclear arms control with the USSR. But in the Soviet Union, the rise to power of Communist party reformer **Mikhail Gorbachev** permanently changed the face of international politics. The American president finally agreed to work toward the common goal of reducing tensions between the two superpowers. Reagan eventually traveled to Moscow, embraced Gorbachev in front of Lenin's tomb, and announced that the Soviets had changed.

Mikhail Gorbachev
Reformist leader of the Soviet Union from 1985 to 1991.

At the same time, the Reagan administration stumbled badly at home when a scandal involving Iran and the Nicaraguan counterrevolutionaries (Contras) came to light in 1986. The disaster revealed a secret foreign policy apparatus and a president out of touch with the daily governance process. Dramatic events in Europe then unfolded independent of the administrations of either Reagan or George H. W. Bush, his successor in the White House. In 1989, eastern Europeans tore down the Berlin Wall and ended communist rule in their countries. Two years later, the Soviet Union unraveled into its separate components, Russia being the largest. The end of the Cold War enabled Bush to focus on the Middle East, where an international force under his leadership drove Iraq out of occupied Kuwait and reestablished the status quo in that oil-rich region.

28.4.1 From Cold War to Détente

By the 1980s, the USSR's state-run economy was creaking to a halt. It simply could not provide the consumer products that Soviet citizens had learned about from the world beyond their borders. Events further weakened the authority of the Soviet government. The USSR's occupation of Afghanistan became a quagmire resembling the disastrous U.S. involvement in Vietnam, and the last Soviet troops finally withdrew in 1989. Initial government efforts to cover up the nuclear accident at Chernobyl only worsened matters, revealing the costs of corrupt Communist rule. Nationalist movements for independence in the Baltic states, the Caucasus region, and Central Asia gathered momentum. In his six years in power (1985–1991), Gorbachev tried to preserve the Soviet system by reforming it through *glasnost* (greater political liberty) and *perestroika* (economic restructuring allowing some private enterprise). However, his government proved unable to control the forces for change that it had helped unleash.

Reagan's primary role in ending the Cold War was to support Gorbachev's quest for change within the Soviet Union. To that end, Reagan moved from confrontational rhetoric to pursuing a policy of détente. Gorbachev became head of the Soviet Communist party in 1985, at the start of Reagan's second term. The American president had already built up the U.S. military and was now thinking about his place in history. He wanted to leave office having earned a reputation as a peacemaker.

Beneath Reagan's strident rhetoric about national military strength ran a streak of radical idealism, including a desire to eliminate the threat of nuclear warfare. Once he felt convinced that Gorbachev was serious about internal reform and rapprochement with the United States, Reagan worked closely with him in a series of summit meetings. In 1987, the two leaders signed the Intermediate-Range Nuclear Force (INF) treaty. The agreement removed short-range and intermediate-range missiles from Europe and enabled each side to conduct on-site verification of the other side's compliance. The INF treaty marked the first actual reduction in the total number of nuclear weapons stored in the two nations' arsenals.

28.4.2 The Iran–Contra Scandal

Failures elsewhere offset Reagan's success with the Russians. His administration suffered its worst damage when it tried through illegal means to solve two foreign policy challenges with one stroke. Its main strategy consisted of linking a problem in the Middle East with one in Central America.

Revolutionary fervor intensified in the Middle East after the 1979 Iranian revolution, and hostage-taking and terrorism—the "poor man's nuclear bomb"—proliferated. In 1986, Americans bombed the Libyan capital of Tripoli in retaliation for apparent Libyan involvement in the killing of two U.S. soldiers in Germany. Things took an even nastier turn in 1988 when an American warship in the Persian Gulf killed 290 civilians by shooting down an Iranian airliner, apparently by mistake. In revenge, pro-Iranian agents from Libya exploded a bomb on Pan Am Flight 109 over Lockerbie, Scotland, before the end of the year, killing eleven on the ground and 259 aboard the plane, including thirty-five students from Syracuse University.

Islamist revolutionaries also threatened moderate Arab leaders and assassinated Egyptian president Anwar Sadat in 1981. Lebanon became the center of a radical anti-Israeli campaign that seized Americans as hostages, especially after the 1983 engagement of U.S. troops against Muslim forces in the civil war there in 1983. Despite a campaign promise never to negotiate with terrorists, Reagan approved the illegal sale of U.S. arms to Iran in return for the freeing of a handful of hostages held by pro-Iranian radicals in Lebanon.

Events were heating up in Central America as well. The CIA-created Contras failed to overturn the new Sandinista government in Nicaragua. Even though the Contras lacked public support in Nicaragua and the United States, the president and his advisers were determined to keep them afloat. But they had a problem: how to fund the effort. Most Americans did not share Reagan's enthusiasm for the Contras and feared greater U.S. military involvement in Central America. Beginning in 1982, Congress's Boland Amendments restricted aid to the Nicaraguan counterrevolutionaries. Faced with their chief's expressed desire to shore up the Contra cause, the president's men found an alternative solution.

The National Security Council (NSC) established a secret operation run by staff member Lieutenant Colonel Oliver North. Free from public or congressional oversight, North worked closely with CIA director William Casey. North and his colleagues solicited funds for the Contras from wealthy, conservative Americans and from sympathetic foreign governments, including Saudi Arabia and Taiwan. Then North hit on what he called the "neat idea" of "using the Ayatollah Khomeini's money to support the Nicaraguan freedom fighters." Iran desperately needed weapons for its war against neighboring Iraq (1980–1988), so North and his colleagues started diverting profits to the Contras from new sales of U.S. Army property to Tehran.

The NSC's action was illegal: it sold U.S. government property without authorization from the Pentagon, and it broke U.S. laws banning aid to the Contras. When news of the operation finally leaked out in November 1986, it shocked the nation. What did the president know, and when did he know it? The old Watergate question about Richard Nixon came to the fore again. Reagan called North a "national hero" but claimed ignorance of any illegal activities, including the diversion of funds from Iranian arms sales to the Nicaraguan rebels.

But in early 1987, 90 percent of Americans did not believe Reagan was telling all he knew. His job approval ratings dropped from 67 percent to 46 percent. The first round of memoirs by former aides also appeared in the final years of his administration, revealing an isolated president out of touch with the government he nominally headed. For example, the former actor breezily admitted that he was happiest when "each morning I get a piece of paper that tells me what I do all day long."

28.4.3 A Global Police Force?

Despite running a bruising presidential campaign in 1988, Reagan's vice president, George H. W. Bush, proved cautious once in office. Hemmed in by a Democratic-controlled Congress, he had what his chief of staff admitted was a "limited agenda" at home. His most enduring domestic action came with his 1991 appointment of archconservative Clarence Thomas, an African American lawyer from Georgia, to fill the seat of retiring Supreme Court justice Thurgood Marshall. Only forty-three and with little experience as a judge, Thomas was chosen because of his conservative views and his race. The Senate narrowly confirmed him, 52–48, after contentious hearings in which a former aide, Anita Hill, accused Thomas of sexual harassment.

Table 28.3 THE ELECTION OF 1988

Candidate	Political Party	Popular Vote (%)	Electoral Vote
George H. W. Bush	Republican	53.4	426
Michael S. Dukakis	Democratic	45.6	111

SOURCE: Historical Election Results, Electoral College, National Archives and Records Administration

"I much prefer foreign affairs," the president once confided in his diary. And some of the most dramatic events of the twentieth century indeed unfolded during his presidency. Poles, Czechs, and Hungarians—encouraged by Gorbachev's promise not to intervene militarily in other Warsaw Pact nations—peacefully overthrew their Communist rulers in 1989. East Germans did the same. The Berlin Wall—the 28-year-old symbol of Cold War tensions—finally toppled on November 8. Three months later and 6,000 miles to the south, antiapartheid leader Nelson Mandela walked out of the South African prison where he had been held for twenty-seven years. The white supremacist government there agreed to hold the first elections in which all South Africans could vote. Then the Baltic states of Lithuania, Latvia, and Estonia seceded from the USSR in 1990 and 1991. After a failed coup attempt by Communist hard-liners in August 1991, the Soviet Union broke apart into its sixteen constituent states. Communist totalitarianism and racial totalitarianism both fell, huge steps toward democracy.

The Bush administration acted more boldly in its own hemisphere. In Panama, under the brutal leadership of Manuel Noriega, tensions grew between the Panamanian Defense Forces (PDF) and U.S. soldiers based in the Canal Zone. Noriega deepened his lucrative role as an intermediary in smuggling Colombian cocaine into the United States. Meanwhile, the crack cocaine epidemic tightened its grip in poor American neighborhoods. Rising popular concern about crack-related violence increased Americans' willingness to take action against Noriega. When the dictator overturned Panamanian election results that went against him and further confrontations erupted between American and Panamanian soldiers, Bush decided to step in.

In December 1989, 24,000 U.S. troops invaded the small Central American nation. They crushed the PDF, and thousands of civilians died in the crossfire. Noriega eventually surrendered and was brought to Miami, where he was convicted of drug trafficking and imprisoned.

Developments in the Middle East provoked the most important move of the George H. W. Bush administration: the initiation of the Persian Gulf War of 1991. In 1990, Iraq invaded tiny, neighboring, oil-rich Kuwait, annexing it as Iraq's "nineteenth province." With Americans and their Japanese and European allies dependent on Middle Eastern oil, Bush declared the invasion unacceptable. He rushed more than 200,000 troops to Saudi Arabia in "Operation Desert Shield" to discourage further aggression by Iraqi leader Saddam Hussein. At the same time, the United Nations slapped economic sanctions on Iraq.

Within three months, Bush shifted his attention to liberating Kuwait. He doubled the number of U.S. troops in the region to 430,000. He also gained the support of the United Nations, which demanded Iraqi withdrawal by January 15, 1991. The U.S. Congress backed him as well, voting to support any actions necessary to drive Iraq out of Kuwait. Bush went on the offensive because he faced a shrinking window of opportunity. He had wide international support, including troops from several Arab nations, but growing clashes in Jerusalem between Israelis and Palestinians threatened to break up this alliance by rekindling Arab anger at Israel, a close U.S. ally.

On January 16, 1991, U.S.-led coalition forces began five and a half weeks of bombing against Iraq. Then, on February 25, coalition forces poured across the border from Saudi Arabia in **Operation Desert Storm**. The offensive freed Kuwait and sent Iraqi troops in headlong retreat toward Baghdad. The Iraqis burned oil wells as they fell back, blanketing the battlefield in smoke. Four days later, Bush halted the U.S. advance, having restored Kuwaiti sovereignty. Saddam Hussein remained in power and later crushed uprisings by Iraqi dissidents. The politics of coalition warfare helped prohibit further U.S. action, for few Arabs wanted Americans ruling Iraq.

Operation Desert Storm
Successful 1991 effort by U.S.-led international military coalition to drive Iraqi forces out of Kuwait.

The Gulf War's outcome seemed to validate two strategic lessons that U.S. commanders had learned during the Vietnam War. The first was the importance of preserving absolute control of the media. During the Persian Gulf conflict, the Pentagon kept journalists away from most of the action, in order to control the images that Americans saw of the fighting. The public viewed endless videos of "smart" bombs hitting their targets in Baghdad but none of the tens of thousands of Iraqi soldiers being slaughtered during their retreat from Kuwait. The second lesson, advocated by General Colin Powell, the African American chair of the Joint Chiefs of Staff who emerged from the war as a national hero, was to marshal overwhelmingly superior forces before going into battle, thus ensuring the success of the operation.

The Gulf War seemed to demonstrate a U.S. willingness to act as a global police force in the post–Cold War era. But the war also stimulated the further growth of anti-Americanism among Islamist revolutionaries, including Saudi-born Osama bin Laden, who considered it a sacrilege for non-Muslim American soldiers to operate bases in Saudi Arabia, home to Mecca, Islam's holiest site. Finally, the war foreshadowed Bush's defiant claim at a 1992 international environmental conference that, when it came to oil, "the American lifestyle is not negotiable."

Map 28.2 THE SOVIET BLOC DISSOLVES

No change in world politics since World War II was greater than the collapse of the Soviet Union and its satellite states in eastern Europe. Eastern European countries soon sought membership in NATO, and post-Communist Russia at first built closer relations with the United States and western Europe. The transition from socialist to capitalist economies was difficult, however, and many poorer citizens found daily life little easier than it had been before.

Conclusion

The Republican era of Ronald Reagan and George H. W. Bush reshaped American relations with the rest of the world, as well as politics and economics in the United States. Both sets of changes hinged on the elevation of individualism and market forces above communal values and government planning. The collectivist dreams represented by the Soviet experiment evaporated into history in these years, leaving capitalism unchallenged as a system of economic organization across most of the globe. U.S. military power stepped into the vacuum left by the Soviet demise, most visibly in the 1991 Persian Gulf War. But that military revival came at the cost of vast deficit spending and a sharp recession in 1991–1992, which paved the way for Bill Clinton's victory over George H. W. Bush in the 1992 presidential campaign.

Chapter Review

28.1 Anticommunism Revived

Why did Cold War tensions increase after 1979?
The seizure of American hostages during the revolution in Iran angered Americans. The Nicaraguan revolutionaries deposed a pro-U.S. authoritarian government, and the Soviet Union invaded and occupied Afghanistan. On many fronts, communism seemed to be on the advance.

28.2 Republican Rule at Home

What did the Reagan administration want to change about American society?
Reagan and his advisers sought to bolster the flagging U.S. economy, assert American military and political influence abroad, and promote the interests of U.S. businesses. They appealed to Americans' desire to be proud again of U.S. ideals and U.S. government actions.

28.3 Cultural Conflict

About which cultural issues did Americans seem to disagree most?
Social and religious conservatives aimed to roll back the influence of the movements for multiculturalism, feminism, gay rights, environmentalism, and greater sexual freedom, all products of the late 1960s and 1970s.

28.4 The End of the Cold War

After forty-five years, why did the Cold War end?
The failures of the Soviet command economy underlay Mikhail Gorbachev's attempted reforms, which then unleashed much larger demands for an end to the injustices of communist rule in the Soviet Union and eastern Europe. Americans were mostly observers on the sidelines during the dissolution of communism, but Reagan also provided important support for Gorbachev's reform efforts.

Timeline

1979	Iranian revolution; militants take American hostages
	Soviet Union invades Afghanistan
1980	Ronald Reagan elected president
1981	United States funds Contras to try to overthrow new leftist Nicaraguan government
1983	HIV identified as virus that causes AIDS
1986	Chernobyl nuclear power plant disaster (Ukraine)
	Iran–Contra scandal revealed
1989	Berlin Wall falls
1991	Persian Gulf War against Iraq after its invasion and occupation of Kuwait
	Soviet Union dissolves into Russia and other component states

Glossary

theocracy A government by officials who are regarded as divinely guided.

Islamist Pertaining to an ideology promoting the creation of governments based on a fundamentalist interpretation of Islamic law.

Carter Doctrine A presidential assertion, during the Carter administration, that the U.S. would defend the status quo in the Persian Gulf.

Contras Counterrevolutionary guerrilla force organized by the CIA to try to overthrow the left-wing Sandinista government in Nicaragua.

Boland Amendments Acts of Congress passed to restrain Reagan's efforts to overthrow the Nicaraguan government.

James Watt Reagan's controversial first Secretary of the Interior, whose anti-environmental views and abrasive personality made him a lightning rod for criticism.

Exxon Valdez Oil tanker that ran aground in Alaska's Prince William Sound in March 1989, creating the second largest oil spill in American history.

Moral Majority Conservative political organization of fundamentalist Christians organized in 1979 under Jerry Falwell's leadership.

Mikhail Gorbachev Reformist leader of the Soviet Union from 1985 to 1991.

Operation Desert Storm Successful 1991 effort by U.S.-led international military coalition to drive Iraqi forces out of Kuwait.

Chapter 29
Post–Cold War America, 1991–2000

BILLIONAIRE JACK WELCH ON LEADERSHIP Former chief executive officer of General Electric Jack Welch, who retired in 2001 after 20 years in that position, speaks at the World Business Forum in New York in October 2012. The theme of the conference—Leadership in Action—is something for which Welch, a tireless champion of cutting costs to boost profits, has been nearly universally praised. During the prosperous 1990s, billionaires like Welch added to their riches, and the gap between the rich and the poor widened dramatically. Prosperity did not benefit everyone during the 1990s—it went disproportionately to those who were already wealthy.

Peter Foley/Bloomberg/Getty Images

What does the photograph of Jack Welch suggest about his personality—especially his drive, confidence, and power?

Contents and Focus Questions

As the Cold War came to an end, marking the triumph of capitalism over communism, what did Americans gain? Certainly there was wealth—prosperity marked the 1990s. But the strong economy did not benefit all citizens equally. The end of the twentieth century marked a growing gap between the wealthy and the poor. A very small number of people, most of them corporate executives, became extremely wealthy while the majority of Americans saw their real incomes decline.

Jack Welch was one such executive. He retired as chief executive officer of General Electric in 2001. The previous year, his income had been $123 million, mostly in stock and stock options. When he left the company, he was granted the use of a Manhattan apartment for the rest of his life, including food, wine, and laundry services. He was also given access to corporate jets and other benefits worth more than $2 million per year. Welch's enormous income and retirement package reflected the upward redistribution of wealth that occurred throughout the 1990s.

As the gap between the wealthy and the poor grew, so did the U.S. economy, which expanded throughout the decade. Increasing numbers of Americans invested in the soaring stock market, many for the first time. The crime rate declined. Moreover, the strong economy emboldened consumers to buy and use products and resources, such as huge gas-guzzling sport utility vehicles, with little concern for the environmental impact. As the new millennium dawned, the economy began to falter. The stock market fell, and there were signs of an impending recession.

The 2000 U.S. Census revealed a number of striking changes in the nation's population during the 1990s. Among the most dramatic was the growth in the Latino population, from 22.4 million to 35.3 million, making the number of Latinos—most of them Mexican American—nearly equal to that of African Americans. Immigrants from Asia and Latin America also added increasing linguistic diversity, fueling controversies over bilingual education and "English-only" political initiatives.

* * * * *

In national politics, the rifts between liberals and conservatives that had opened up in the 1960s persisted. Struggles over cultural issues such as abortion and gay rights polarized the political climate. In 1992, Democrats took back the White House, but in 1994, Republicans swept into control of Congress with a conservative agenda, hemming in President Bill Clinton, a centrist Democrat who presided over the final destruction of the Aid to Families with Dependent Children (AFDC) program, the central feature of the national welfare system since the New Deal of the 1930s. In 2000, the Supreme Court decided one of the closest and most divisive elections in the nation's history, handing the White House to the Republican candidate, George W. Bush, son of the former president.

In addition to these increasing divisions within American society, the post-Cold War era raised new questions about the role of the United States in the world. Americans no longer considered Russia to be a threat, but new international foes emerged, especially terrorist networks operating outside the authority of particular countries. Within the nation, episodes of domestic terrorism, such as the bombing of a federal building in Oklahoma City and a series of school shootings by children, made Americans aware that dangers lurked within their previously safe havens.

29.1 The Economy: Global and Domestic

How did the expanding economy affect those at the top and bottom of the income ladder?

After the sharp recession of 1991–1992, by nearly all measures, the economy expanded in the 1990s. The stock market boomed, unemployment declined, and most Americans appeared to be better off financially at the end of the decade than at the beginning. But the overall growth of the economy did not benefit everyone, and many actually lost ground—especially those who lost jobs to automation, nonunionized workers who toiled for low wages under grim working conditions, and the nation's most vulnerable workers: poor single mothers, new immigrants, and unskilled people of color.

29.1.1 The Post–Cold War Economy

The end of the Cold War had a profound effect on the nation's economy. The demise of the Soviet Union finally ended the arms race against a superpower foe and made cutting the defense budget politically acceptable. But closing defense-related plants in southern California devastated the regional economy. By the mid-1990s, half the workers in the southern California aerospace industry had been laid off.

While defense industries shrank, the technology sector of the economy expanded, opening up new opportunities for young computer experts and entrepreneurs and generating fortunes for corporate executives. At the same time, mergers of giant multinational companies concentrated wealth and power in an ever-smaller number of ever-larger corporations. In the last three years of the decade, mergers totaled $5 trillion. Media giants America Online and Time-Warner merged in 2000. In 2001, Nestlé bought Ralston-Purina for $10 billion. Many of the largest mergers crossed national boundaries, such as German automobile maker Daimler-Benz and U.S. Chrysler.

Corporations expanded and consolidated, while some faced challenges to their power. Microsoft initially lost an antitrust suit that ordered the computer software giant to be split into two companies. Microsoft appealed the ruling in 2001, and ultimately the Justice Department settled the suit with minor sanctions against the company. In several states, civil suits against huge tobacco companies limited cigarette advertising and marketing and levied fines on tobacco companies totaling in the billions of dollars.

The nation's elite were not the only ones to capitalize on new entrepreneurial opportunities. The 1988 Indian Gaming Regulatory Act enabled Native Americans to build lucrative casinos on tribal lands, bringing new jobs and an estimated $4 billion a year to formerly impoverished communities. The Mashantucket Pequot east of Hartford, Connecticut, opened Foxwoods in 1992, and it quickly became the largest casino in the Western Hemisphere. The Oneida followed suit a few years later with the Turning Stone casino near Utica, New York. In Arizona, casinos brought in $830 million a year. Some Indian casinos failed, however, and gambling took a largely hidden toll in the losses of already poor local residents. Native Americans remained divided about the wisdom of trying to profit from America's growing inclination to take risks in hopes of winning big.

29.1.2 The Widening Gap Between Rich and Poor

In the last decade of the century, the bottom 60 percent of the population saw their real income decline, even as the economy boomed. Accumulated wealth—property and investments—was an even better measure of security and influence, and the top 1 percent of Americans owned more wealth than the bottom 90 percent combined.

Microsoft chair Bill Gates alone was wealthier than the bottom 45 percent of all U.S. households together. A century earlier, famed capitalist J. P. Morgan said that no corporate chieftain should earn more than twenty times what his workers were paid, but by 1980, a typical chief executive of a large U.S. company took home forty times the earnings of an average factory worker; by 1990, the ratio had grown to 85 times, and by 2004, it reached 431 times.

Although one-third of the nation's African Americans were part of the middle class, black families had fewer assets and resources, making their hold on middle-class status more precarious than that of their white peers. The poorest African Americans were concentrated in low-paying jobs, lacking the quality health care and education that would make social and economic mobility possible. Full-time employment did not necessarily mean an escape from poverty. Among fully employed black heads of households without a high school education, 40 percent of the women and 25 percent of the men did not earn enough to achieve economic self-sufficiency. Almost 50 percent of all black children lived in households below the poverty line, compared to 16 percent of white children. The rate of unemployment was more than twice as high for blacks as for whites.

Recent immigrants from Asia, Africa, and Latin America joined African Americans in jobs at the bottom of the economy. Despite the controversy over illegal immigration, a quarter of a million undocumented workers toiled in the fields of agribusiness. At the same time, 2 percent of able-bodied citizens were in jail, nearly half of them black, because of the increasingly strict arrest and incarceration policies resulting from federal and state drug laws that hit minority communities particularly hard. Prisoners were often required to work while incarcerated. Convicts entered data, packed golf balls, and filled a wide array of jobs for less than minimum wage, and most of their earnings went back to the government. These and other workers at the bottom of the labor force gained little or nothing from the economic boom of the 1990s.

29.1.3 Service Workers and Labor Unions

Low-wage workers in the service industries have one advantage over laborers working for multinational corporations: their jobs cannot be exported. Some service workers organized successfully, in the 1990s, for better wages and working conditions. In 2000, for example, striking janitors of Service Employees International Union Local 1877 in Los Angeles achieved a wage increase of 26 percent, raising their hourly pay from less than $8 to more than $10. This was a tremendous triumph for a union whose membership was 98 percent immigrant: 80 percent Central Americans, more than half women, and all of them poor.

Other service workers also won improved contracts. Unionized hotel workers in San Francisco negotiated a five-year contract that increased pay for the lowest-paid workers, room cleaners and dishwashers, by 25 percent, from $12 to $15 an hour. In Las Vegas, African American hotel worker Hattie Canty helped organize 40,000 employees of large casino hotels. In the summer of 1997, 185,000 Teamsters went on strike against the United Parcel Service and won an improved contract with higher wages and benefits for part-time as well as full-time workers.

In spite of these successes, union membership declined. Moreover, strikes did little to benefit nonunionized workers, especially undocumented immigrants and sweatshop laborers both inside and outside the United States. There were some attempts to improve working conditions for those most exploited by the global economy. In April 1997, representatives from clothing manufacturers, human rights groups, and labor organizations drafted an agreement that tried to improve conditions for garment workers around the world. Companies that agreed to the voluntary pact would limit work weeks to sixty hours, with a maximum of twelve hours of overtime. The companies had to pay "at least the minimum wage required by local law or the prevailing industry

Map 29.1 STATES WITH LARGE NUMBERS OF UNDOCUMENTED IMMIGRANTS, 1995

Undocumented immigrants, 1995

- 1,000,000 – 2,500,000
- 500,000 – 999,999
- 100,000 – 499,999
- 25,000 – 99,999
- Less than 25,000

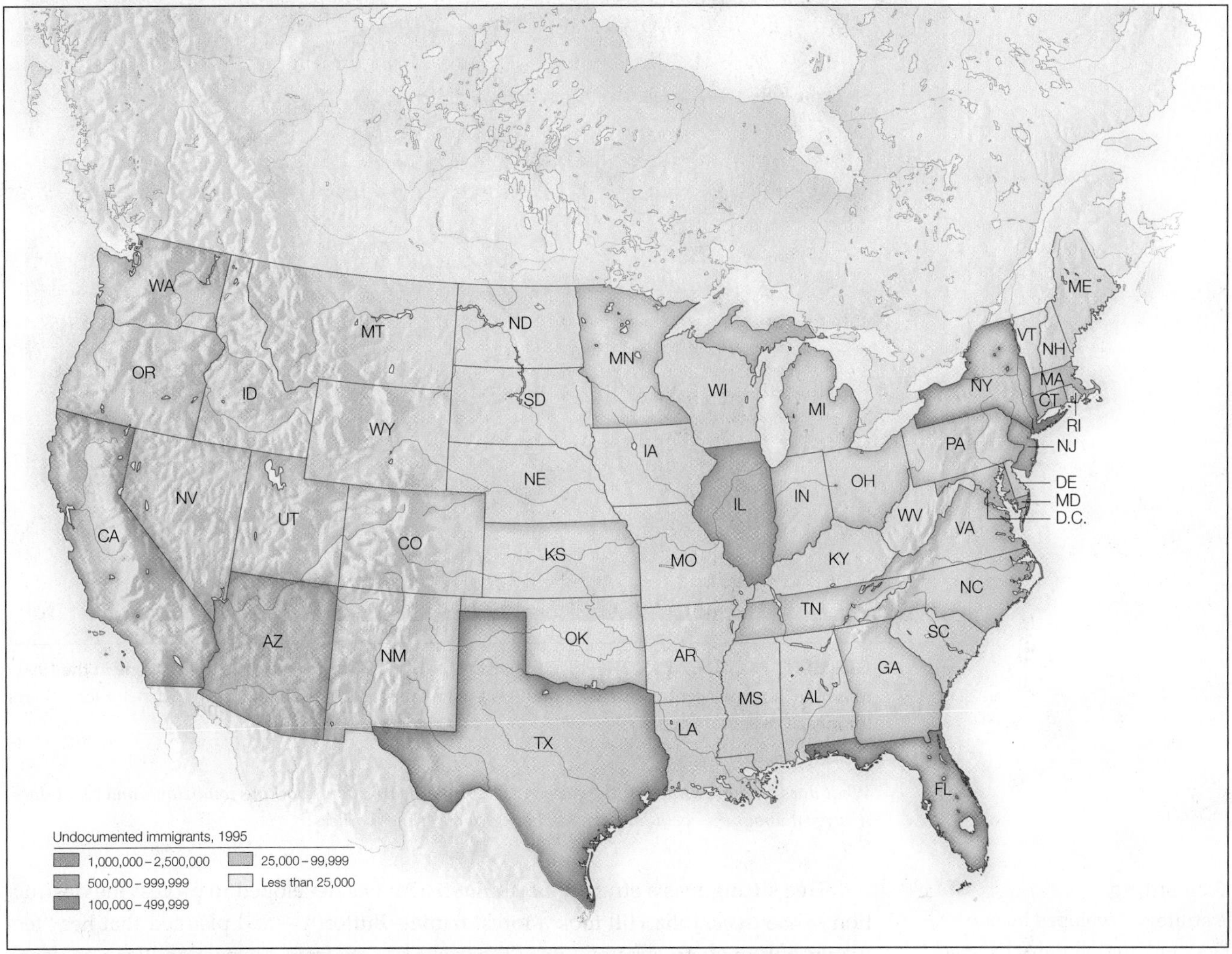

In the 1990s, fully 77 percent of all undocumented immigrants entered the country legally, with visas in hand. During the decade (1991 to 2000), the total proportion of the foreign-born population in the United States, including those with and without legal status, increased from 9 to 11 percent, still less than the proportion of foreign- to native-born population in 1900, when it was 15 percent. During the 1990s, immigrants paid $133 billion dollars annually in local, state, and federal taxes, and generated an annual contribution to the American economy in the range of $25 to $30 billion.

SOURCE: Pew Research Center, "Unauthorized Immigrant Population Trends for States, Birth Countries and Regions," December 11, 2014

wage, whichever is higher." The pact forbade children under fifteen to work and con-tained policies protecting workers from harassment and unsafe working environments. But all of these efforts were voluntary and not legally enforceable.

29.1.4 Industry Versus the Environment

The global economy also affected the natural world. Environmental activists mobilized in response, with new forms of civil disobedience. Julia Butterfly Hill was one such activist. On a cold December night in 1997, the 23-year-old environmentalist climbed onto a small platform 180 feet above ground in a giant redwood tree in Humboldt County, California. She remained there for two years, trespassing on the property of the Pacific Lumber Company, which was threatening to cut down the 1,000-year-old tree as part of its logging operations.

GARMENT FACTORY LABORERS, BROOKLYN, NEW YORK Sweatshops like this one in the 1990s resemble those of a century earlier. Immigrant women labor in garment factories, working long hours for meager wages.

Michael Sofronski Photography

What does the photograph of the garment factory indicate about working conditions, and what does it suggest about the racial or national background of the workers?

Tree sitting
A strategy developed by Earth First! environmental activists in which individuals climb into trees that are threatened by the lumber industry in order to prevent the trees from being cut down for lumber.

Tree sitting was a strategy Earth First! activists developed to protest the destruction of the trees. Julia Hill took a forest name—Butterfly—and pledged that her "feet would not touch the ground" until the tree was safe from destruction. For two years, Hill endured rain and hail storms, ninety-mile-per-hour winds, bone-chilling cold, and harassment from the logging company. Finally, the president of Pacific Lumber, John Campbell, agreed never to cut down the tree or other trees in a 2.9-acre buffer zone, and Hill agreed to come down. For her civil disobedience, she paid a $50,000 fine, contributed by supporters, which the court designated to Humboldt State University for forestry research. Although her success was modest in terms of saving endangered forests, her actions raised environmental awareness across the globe and called attention to the impact of economic expansion on the natural world.

29.2 Tolerance and Its Limits

In what ways did Americans demonstrate increasing tolerance for those different from themselves?

Racial discrimination had eased over the course of the twentieth century, but persistent inequalities of power and economic opportunity continued to disadvantage Americans of color, who remained disproportionately poor, in prison, and on welfare. The economic downturn of the early 1990s widened the chasm between affluent white and poor nonwhite Americans. Highly publicized incidents of police brutality directed against Americans of color generated protests and, occasionally, violence. Nevertheless, there were signs that Americans were becoming more tolerant of one another and more willing to accept and even appreciate their diversity.

29.2.1 The Los Angeles Riots: "Can We All Get Along"

On March 3, 1991, police pulled over Rodney King, an African American motorist, after a high-speed chase on a Los Angeles freeway. The four officers dragged the unarmed black man from his car and kicked and beat him with their batons for fifteen minutes. A bystander recorded the beating on videotape, which was broadcast repeatedly on national television, sparking outrage among Americans of all races.

At the highly publicized trial in April 1992, defense lawyers for the police officers argued that King, who was clearly cowering on the videotape, was resisting arrest and that the police responded appropriately. The jury of ten whites, one Asian, and one Latino acquitted the officers. The acquittal ignited five days of rioting in the African American community of South Central Los Angeles, leaving fifty-eight people dead and $1 billion in property destroyed. Community leaders called for calm; even Rodney King implored the public: "We can all get along. We've just got to." Months later, a federal court in Los Angeles convicted two of the officers involved in the beating of violating King's civil rights—too late to avert the violence that erupted after the initial verdict.

Of the fifty-eight people who died in the violence, eighteen were Latino, twenty-six were black, ten were white, and two were Asian. Of the 4,000 businesses that were destroyed, most belonged to Latinos and Koreans. Perpetrators of the violence, as well as the victims, came from all racial groups. Antonia Hernandez, president of the Mexican American Legal Defense and Educational Fund, noted, "The hardest part is rebuilding the spirit of the city—what holds us together as Angelinos. It's the rebuilding of trust. . . . It's connecting communities that have never been connected." Several community groups came together in an effort to ease tensions, including the Japanese American Citizens League, Chinese for Affirmative Action, and the League of United Latin American Citizens.

29.2.2 Values in Conflict

In the wake of the Los Angeles riots, many citizens worried that the bonds holding Americans together might be fraying. In 1991, former University of Colorado football coach Bill McCartney formed the Promise Keepers, a fundamentalist Christian group dedicated to restoring the traditional privileges and responsibilities of husbands and fathers in the home. The Promise Keepers held evangelical revivals that drew tens of thousands of mostly working-class white and some black men to rallies across the country. They believed that men should be good providers for their families, strong role models for their children, and committed spouses.

Although white men continued to control nearly all the major economic and political institutions in the nation, a 1993 poll found that a majority of white men believed that their advantage in terms of jobs and income, along with their influence over American culture, was declining. African American men also felt the need to bolster manhood and fatherhood. Efforts geared specifically toward African American men included the 1995 **Million Man March**, organized by Nation of Islam Reverend Louis Farrakhan, which drew hundreds of thousands of black men to demonstrate their solidarity at a rally in Washington, D.C.

At the same time, gay men and lesbians mobilized to gain acceptance and legitimacy for the families that they formed. A 1994 poll showed that 52 percent of respondents "claimed to consider gay lifestyle acceptable." But 64 percent were opposed to legalizing gay marriage or allowing gay couples to adopt children. In 2000, Vermont became the first state to grant legal status to **civil unions** between same-sex couples, although a fierce backlash threatened to overturn the legislation.

Values also collided around the rights and traditions of Native Americans as tribal communities came into conflict with non-Native environmentalists, sports enthusiasts,

Million Man March
A demonstration organized by Nation of Islam Reverend Louis Farrakhan, which drew hundreds of thousands of black men to express their pride in manhood and fatherhood at a rally in Washington, D.C.

civil unions
Relationships recognized by the state granting legitimacy and legal privileges to same-sex couples who are prohibited from legal marriage.

COMING TOGETHER AFTER THE LOS ANGELES RIOTS, 1992 In the aftermath of the violent uprising that followed the acquittal of police officers in the beating of motorist Rodney King, Koreans and African Americans in Los Angeles express their solidarity, hoping to heal the wounds and divisions that had torn apart their city.

Lee Celano

Why do you think the marchers in the photograph carry an American flag, and what does their posture and demeanor suggest about efforts to ease tensions across racial and ethnic lines?

and scientists. In the upper Midwest, treaties with the government in 1837 and 1842 granted the Chippewa hunting, fishing, and gathering rights in the territories ceded to the United States. Federal courts consistently upheld these treaties, which include rights to take up to half of the fish and game allowed by state conservation requirements and to use methods such as spear fishing that are illegal for non-Indians. In the 1980s and 1990s, non-Indians challenged these policies and accosted Native Americans in fishing boats with rocks and insults. Native American cultural practices also clashed with environmentalist sensibilities over religious rituals involving the gathering and sacrificing of golden eaglets.

29.2.3 Courtroom Dramas: Clarence Thomas and O. J. Simpson

A few dramatic cases riveted the nation and highlighted the fraught issues of race, class, and sex. Two of the most controversial legal clashes of the decade centered on accusations against successful black men. The first of these episodes was the Senate hearing of October 1991 to confirm the appointment of conservative Judge Clarence Thomas to the U.S. Supreme Court. When University of Oklahoma law professor Anita Hill accused Thomas of sexual harassment when she had worked for him at the Equal Opportunity Employment Commission in the early 1980s, the question of Thomas's professional qualifications faded to the background and the hearings focused exclusively on Hill's accusations.

In live televised hearings, the African American law professor testified that Thomas had made crude remarks to her as well as unwanted sexual overtures. Several of the all-white-male panel of senators questioned Hill's credibility, wondering why she continued to work for Thomas after the alleged harassment. Thomas drew on the long history of black men being falsely accused of sexual aggression to counter the charge of sexual harassment, accusing his Democratic opponents of conducting a "high-tech lynching." In the end, Thomas was confirmed. But Hill's testimony, and the insensitive behavior of the senators, brought the issue of sexual harassment to a high level of national consciousness. The hearings also highlighted the fact that Congress was overwhelmingly white and male, motivating female candidates and their supporters to alter that reality. After the 1992 elections, the number of female senators tripled from two to six, including the first black female senator, Carol Moseley Braun, Democrat from Illinois. The number of congresswomen rose from twenty-eight to forty-seven.

In 1994, television viewers were again riveted by a media spectacle, this time a sensational murder case in Los Angeles involving a former football star and film actor. The victims were the white ex-wife of black celebrity O. J. Simpson, and her male companion. Simpson's blood was found at the scene, hair and other forensic and DNA evidence linked him to the crime, he had no reliable alibi, and a motive was evident in his pattern of jealous rage and brutality against the murdered woman. No other suspects in the case were ever identified. But Simpson's team of lawyers unearthed evidence that, before the Simpson case, white police detective Mark Fuhrman had boasted of planting evidence and had made racist comments. The mostly black and female jury was sympathetic to the possibility that Fuhrman had framed Simpson. In Los Angeles, in the wake of the Rodney King beatings, African Americans had good reason to distrust the police.

In early October 1996, after a trial that lasted nearly a year, it took the jury only two hours to acquit Simpson of all charges. But he was later held responsible for the murders in a "wrongful death" civil suit. Pundits focused on the racial divide: blacks were more inclined to believe Simpson was innocent, and whites more likely to consider him guilty.

29.2.4 The Changing Face of Diversity

These highly charged events illuminated racial tensions, but there was also evidence that Americans were accepting the nation's diversity and adopting a more inclusive vision. Immigrants comprised 10 percent of the population, the highest proportion of foreign-born residents since the 1930s. The numbers of Asians and Pacific Islanders increased by 45.9 percent, with those of Chinese ancestry comprising the largest group, followed by those with origins in the Philippines. The Latino population grew by 39.7 percent. Among the nation's Latinos, nearly two-thirds were of Mexican ancestry.

Not everyone celebrated these trends. In California, with one-third of the nation's Latino population, voters responded with Proposition 187 to deny public education and most other public social services to undocumented immigrants, and Proposition 227 to end bilingual education. Large numbers of Latino voters opposed these measures. In subsequent elections, many young Latinos and new citizens marshaled their political power and voted for the first time. By 2000, whites no longer constituted a majority of California's multiethnic population, dropping from 57 percent in 1990 to 47 percent in 2000.

At the same time, politics and ideas based on distinct and rigid racial lines gave way to a growing recognition of intermixing. In the world of sports, young golfer Tiger Woods, son of a black Vietnam-veteran father and a Thai mother, became the reigning superstar of the sport most closely identified with the world of the white elite. Pop star Prince was one of many artists who crafted a persona that highlighted both racial and gender ambiguity. On job and college application forms, a growing number of mixed-race Americans refused to be identified as belonging to one particular racial group. Reflecting this development, the U.S. Census of 2000 allowed people to check more than one box to indicate their racial identity.

Interpreting History

Vermont Civil Union Law (2000)

"The state has a strong interest in promoting stable and lasting families"

On April 26, 2000, Vermont became the first state to grant legal recognition to same-sex couples, affording them all the legal protections, privileges, and responsibilities of married couples. The law unleashed a storm of controversy and raised questions about the legal status in other states of civil unions contracted in Vermont. Nevertheless, in the first year after its enactment, 2,479 same-sex couples forged civil unions in Vermont, 478 of them among Vermonters, and the rest from other states. Two-thirds were lesbian unions. Several states began to consider similar bills, but others moved to prohibit such unions. Nebraska amended its state constitution to outlaw same-sex marriage and civil unions. On the national level, conservative lawmakers endeavored to introduce a constitutional amendment that would ban civil unions and restrict marriage to heterosexual couples. Among other provisions, the Vermont Civil Union Law stipulated that

1. Civil marriage under Vermont's marriage statutes consists of a union between a man and a woman. . . .

2. Vermont's history as an independent republic and as a state is one of equal treatment and respect for all Vermonters. . . .

3. The state's interest in civil marriage is to encourage close and caring families, and to protect all family members from the economic and social consequences of abandonment and divorce, focusing on those who have been especially at risk.

4. Legal recognition of civil marriage by the state is the primary and, in a number of instances, the exclusive source of numerous benefits, responsibilities and protections under the laws of the state for married persons and their children.

5. Based on the state's tradition of equality under the law and strong families, for at least 25 years, Vermont Probate

FIRST GAY CIVIL UNION SERVICE, BATTLEBORO, VERMONT Kathleen Peterson and Carolyn Conrad exchange vows in front of Justice of the Peace T. Hunter Wilson. The ceremony in Brattleboro, Vermont, on July 1, 2000, marked the first legal union under Vermont's Civil Union Law. Vermont was the first state to provide recognition and legal status to gay and lesbian couples.

AP Photo/Toby Talbot

What did the official recognition of their relationship provide Peterson and Conrad, and what was still lacking because they could not legally marry?

Courts have qualified gay and lesbian individuals as adoptive parents.

6. Vermont was one of the first states to adopt comprehensive legislation prohibiting discrimination on the basis of sexual orientation. . . .

7. The state has a strong interest in promoting stable and lasting families, including families based upon a same-sex couple.

8. Without the legal protections, benefits and responsibilities associated with civil marriage, same-sex couples suffer numerous obstacles and hardships.

9. Despite long-standing social and economic discrimination, many gay and lesbian Vermonters have formed lasting, committed, caring and faithful relationships with persons of their same sex. These couples live together, participate in their communities together, and some raise children and care for family members together, just as do couples who are married under Vermont law.

10. While a system of civil unions does not bestow the status of civil marriage, it does satisfy the requirements of the Common Benefits Clause. Changes in the way significant legal relationships are established under the constitution should be approached carefully, combining respect for the community and cultural institutions most affected with a commitment to the constitutional rights involved. Granting benefits and protections to same-sex couples through a system of civil unions will provide due respect for tradition and long-standing social institutions, and will permit adjustment as unanticipated consequences or unmet needs arise.

11. The constitutional principle of equality embodied in the Common Benefits Clause is compatible with the freedom of religious belief and worship guaranteed in

Chapter I, Article 3rd of the state constitution. Extending the benefits and protections of marriage to same-sex couples through a system of civil unions preserves the fundamental constitutional right of each of the multitude of religious faiths in Vermont to choose freely and without state interference to whom to grant the religious status, sacrament or blessing of marriage under the rules, practices or traditions of such faith.

Questions for Discussion

1. What political principles and values provided the foundation for Vermont's civil union law?

2. In what ways does the Vermont civil union law distinguish between civil marriages and civil unions?

SOURCE: Vermont General Assembly, An Act Relating to Civil Unions, No. 91, H. 847 (June 26, 2000).

29.3 The Clinton Years

What was the impact of the "Republican revolution" during Clinton's presidency?

William Jefferson Clinton was the first American president born after World War II. Raised in Arkansas in a working-class family, Clinton attended Georgetown University and studied at Oxford University in England as a Rhodes Scholar. Like many college students of his generation, he opposed the Vietnam War and avoided the draft. He attended Yale Law School, where he met Hillary Rodham from Illinois, whom he married in 1975. In 1978, at the young age of 33, he was elected governor of Arkansas. After one term, he was defeated in his bid for reelection. He made a comeback by defining himself as a **New Democrat** with centrist political inclinations and reclaimed his job as governor. When he ran for president in 1992, Clinton received the support of the Democratic Leadership Council, a group of New Democrats who shifted the national party to the right of its previous New Deal liberal position.

New Democrat
Member of the Democratic party, many of them organized in the Democratic Leadership Council, who espouse center to center-right policies.

29.3.1 Clinton: The New Democrat

In 1992, the incumbent president, George H. W. Bush, faced an uphill battle. The recession of 1991–1992 hit white-collar as well as blue-collar workers as unemployment climbed above 8 percent. During twelve years of Republican presidents, the national debt had more than quadrupled to $4.4 trillion. Reflecting pressures from the right wing of the party, Republicans attacked permissiveness in American society, opposed abortion and gay rights, and called for a smaller government. The Democrats nominated the 46-year-old Clinton. A wildcard in the election was the Reform party candidacy of H. Ross Perot, a Texas billionaire who financed his own campaign and used the national media to tap into voter discontent with the two major parties.

Much of the campaign reflected the culture wars, pitting what many saw as the socially permissive legacy of the 1960s against conservative efforts to restore traditional "family values" to American public life. Many Americans worried that the prevalence of single-parent families, the high rate of divorce, and the pervasiveness of sex and violence in the popular culture all reflected a decline in moral standards and an erosion of American society.

Clinton won the election by a comfortable margin, but Perot garnered 19 percent of the popular vote, the largest showing for a third-party candidate since Theodore Roosevelt ran on the Progressive party ticket in 1912. Clinton began his term with a

Table 29.1 THE ELECTION OF 1992

Candidate	Political Party	Popular Vote (%)	Electoral Vote
William J. Clinton	Democratic	43.1	370
George H. W. Bush	Republican	37.4	168
H. Ross Perot	Independent	18.8	—

SOURCE: Historical Election Results, Electoral College, National Archives and Records Administration

solidly Democratic House and Senate, which included a new infusion of women, along with the nation's first senator of American Indian descent, Ben Nighthorse Campbell of Colorado. Saying that he wanted his advisers to "look like America," Clinton appointed two Latinos, three blacks, and three women to the fourteen-member cabinet.

29.3.2 Clinton's Domestic Agenda and the "Republican Revolution"

Clinton ran into trouble early in his administration when he tried to fulfill his campaign promise to allow gays and lesbians to serve openly in the military, reversing a policy that dated back half a century. Top military officials, already unhappy with having a new commander in chief who had avoided military service during the Vietnam War, vehemently opposed lifting the ban against gays. Ultimately, Clinton compromised and established a new policy of "**don't ask, don't tell**," which allowed homosexuals to serve as long as they did not make their sexual orientation known.

Clinton's effort to reform the health care system was equally unsuccessful. With rising health care costs and millions of uninsured citizens, efforts to provide national health insurance and reduce the cost of health care had wide public support but fierce opposition from the medical establishment and the pharmaceutical industry. Clinton appointed his wife, Hillary Rodham Clinton, an attorney and longtime advocate on behalf of children and families, to head a task force to develop a plan. But the task force, deliberating behind closed doors, failed to come up with a workable strategy acceptable to all sides. The Clintons abandoned the effort after a year of hearings and no action in Congress.

Clinton succeeded in passing a budget that raised taxes on the wealthiest Americans, cut spending to reduce the deficit, and expanded tax credits for low-income families. In the next three years, the economy markedly improved. Other legislative successes included the Family and Medical Leave Act, which required employers to grant unpaid medical leave for up to twelve weeks. Clinton appointed two relatively liberal new Supreme Court Justices, Ruth Bader Ginsburg in 1993 and Stephen Breyer in 1994.

The 1994 congressional elections hurt Clinton's legislative agenda. In the midst of the campaign, about 300 Republican congressional candidates, under the leadership of Speaker of the House Newt Gingrich, endorsed a "**Contract with America**," calling for **welfare reform**, a balanced budget, more prisons and longer sentences, increased defense spending, an end to legal abortion, and other conservative measures. Although only 39 percent of eligible voters turned out to vote, the Republicans declared a "Republican Revolution" as they took control of both the House and Senate for the first time in forty years and pushed Congress to the right of center.

The new Congress passed a large tax cut and a tough anticrime bill, increased military spending, and reduced federal regulatory power over the environment. Clinton used his veto power to limit the Republican agenda, but he also took on some conservative issues as his own, such as free trade and welfare reform. In his 1996 State of the Union address, Clinton announced that the "era of big government is over," and he signed the Welfare Reform Act, abolishing the 60-year-old program Aid to Families with Dependent Children (AFDC). Clinton won reelection easily in 1996 while Republicans stayed in control of both houses of Congress.

"don't ask, don't tell"
A policy established by the Clinton administration allowing gays and lesbians to serve in the military so long as they do not disclose their sexual orientation.

Contract with America
A platform developed by Speaker of the House Newt Gingrich during the 1994 elections that outlined a series of conservative legislative goals endorsed by about 300 Republican congressional candidates.

welfare reform
Policies enacted that limited government aid to the poor, and dismantled the program of Aid to Families with Dependent Children, which had been in effect since 1935.

Table 29.2 THE ELECTION OF 1996

Candidate	Political Party	Popular Vote (%)	Electoral Vote
William J. Clinton	Democratic	49.24	379
Robert Dole	Republican	40.71	159
H. Ross Perot	Reform	8.4	—

SOURCE: Historical Election Results, Electoral College, National Archives and Records Administration

29.3.3 The Impeachment Crisis

Clinton's personal behavior left him vulnerable to political enemies, who took full advantage of every opportunity to discredit him. Clinton's sexual behavior became an issue well before he entered the White House. During the 1992 campaign, Gennifer Flowers, a former nightclub singer, told a tabloid that she and Clinton had an affair when he was governor. Early in his presidency, Paula Jones, a former Arkansas state employee, filed a sexual harassment suit against Clinton, claiming that he had propositioned her when he was governor of Arkansas. The case was eventually dismissed, but it returned to haunt him. In 1998, Independent Council Kenneth Starr reported that he had evidence that Clinton had an extramarital affair with a young White House intern, Monica Lewinsky. Starr claimed that Clinton had broken the law in an effort to cover up the affair. Lewinsky and Clinton had both testified in the Paula Jones case, and both denied having had a sexual relationship. Starr claimed that Clinton had lied under oath and had instructed his close adviser and friend, Vernon Jordan, to find Lewinsky a job to keep her quiet. Starr charged Clinton with perjury, witness tampering, and obstruction of justice. Clinton vehemently denied the charges, but Lewinsky had saved a dress with a stain containing the president's DNA, providing the investigation with the "smoking gun" it needed.

As Starr and congressional Republicans pressed the investigation with relentless determination, the media saturated the nation and the world with sordid and graphic details of the president's sexual encounters with the young intern. Polls showed that Americans disapproved of Clinton's personal behavior, but they did not want him removed from office. With the economy booming, Clinton garnered high job performance ratings, rising to 79 percent at the height of the scandal. Negative sentiment against Kenneth Starr and congressional Republicans mounted as the investigation dragged on for four years at a cost to taxpayers of $40 million.

Public opinion notwithstanding, the House of Representatives did **impeach**—that is, brought charges against—Clinton on December 19, 1998, accusing him of perjury and obstruction of justice. But the majority of senators determined that Clinton's misdeeds did not meet the standard for "high crimes and misdemeanors" required to remove a president from office, and acquitted him.

29.3.4 Trade, Peacemaking, and Military Intervention

Stymied in Congress by Republican opposition, the president turned his attention to foreign policy. In 1993, with the president's strong encouragement, Congress approved the North American Free Trade Agreement (NAFTA), eliminating tariffs and trade barriers among the United States, Mexico, and Canada and thus creating the largest free trade zone in the world. In 1994, Congress approved the General Agreement on Tariffs and Trade (GATT), which reduced tariffs on thousands of goods and phased out import quotas imposed by the United States and other industrialized nations. Supporters argued that these measures would increase global competition and improve the U.S. economy. Businesses would benefit from the easing of trade barriers, and consumers would have access to lower-priced goods.

NAFTA and GATT barely passed Congress. Clinton faced strong opposition from liberal Democrats in industrial areas and from labor unions, who feared that these measures would result in jobs going abroad, declining American wages, and a relaxation of environmental controls over companies moving outside U.S. borders. In the first few years of NAFTA and GATT, these fears seemed justified. Some jobs went abroad, and threats of moving gave employers a negotiating edge over workers. In Mexico, the impact of NAFTA was even worse. The peso collapsed as money and goods flowed across the border, and the average wages for workers fell from $1.45 to $.78 per hour.

Equally controversial were Clinton's efforts to grant China **most-favored-nation** status, which would designate China as a full trading partner with the United States. Human rights activists argued that China's dismal record of violent suppression and imprisonment of political dissenters should preclude favorable trading terms. But with

impeach
A formal process by which an official is accused of unlawful activity. The House of Representatives has the authority to bring such charges, and the Senate is required to place the official on trial and either convict or acquit.

most-favored-nation
A designation allowing countries to export their products to the United States with tariffs no greater than those levied against most other nations.

an eye to China's huge potential market for American goods and favorable site for U.S.-owned factories, Congress approved Clinton's proposal.

Cold War politics did not entirely disappear from foreign policy. The tiny communist nation of Cuba, suffering severe economic hardship since the collapse of its benefactor, the Soviet Union, remained off limits to U.S. trade and tourism. Cuban Americans in southern Florida, who had fled Cuba after Fidel Castro's successful revolution, blocked any efforts to ease relations between the two countries. Democrats as well as Republicans were reluctant to alienate these voters; their numbers and political clout in the nation's fourth largest state gave them considerable power.

Relations between the United States and Cuba were strained anew in November 1999 by an incident that began when a small boat carrying fourteen Cubans trying to escape to Florida sank. The three survivors, who clung to inner tubes, included a six-year-old boy, Elian Gonzales. Elian's relatives in Miami argued that the boy should stay in the United States, where he could grow up in a democratic society—a goal his mother died trying to achieve. However, his father wanted him back in Cuba, and a court decided that the boy should be returned to his remaining parent. After months of intense media coverage in both countries and futile efforts at negotiation, U.S. government agents stormed the small house where Elian was staying and seized the boy, who eventually returned to Cuba with his father.

While relations with Cuba remained uneasy, most of Clinton's diplomatic efforts focused on peacekeeping and peacemaking. But some situations became violent. The legacy of the war in Vietnam and the end of the Cold War raised new questions about how and when to use American military force. Most of the overseas crises during Clinton's presidency stemmed from problems of national disintegration, ethnic conflict, and humanitarian disasters resulting from political chaos and civil wars.

In 1992, President Bush had sent U.S. marines to Somalia in east Africa as part of a UN effort to provide famine relief and to restore peace in the war-torn nation. After Clinton took office, Somali warlord Mohammed Farah Aidid killed fifty Pakistani UN peacekeepers. The U.S. forces then mobilized against Aidid, shifting the peacekeeping mission to military engagement. As part of the effort to hunt down Aidid, U.S. soldiers killed hundreds of Somali citizens, creating intense anti-American sentiment among the population. In September 1993, Aidid's forces killed eighteen American soldiers in a firefight and dragged the body of one victim through the streets. The outraged American public viewed the grim spectacle on TV, and the experience left Clinton with no clear guidelines on humanitarian intervention abroad. Largely as a result of the disaster in Somalia, when ethnic conflict led to genocide in Rwanda in central Africa in 1994, the United States and other western nations refused to intervene.

Nevertheless, Clinton endeavored to ease hostilities in some of the world's most conflict-ridden areas. Northern Ireland had been fraught with violence for thirty years, and the United States, with political and diplomatic connections to London as well as strong ties to the Irish, wanted to help resolve the crisis. Clinton made several trips to Ireland to promote peace between Irish Catholic nationalists who wanted to break ties with England and join the Republic of Ireland and Protestants loyal to Great Britain. Despite dissent and violence by extremists on both sides, by the time Clinton left office, an agreement had been reached that established a shared coalition government.

Ethnic conflict was also the cause of trouble in the Balkans. From 1945 to 1980, Marshal Josip Broz Tito ruled over a unified communist Yugoslavia, maintaining stability by suppressing ethnic rivalries. But after Tito's death in 1980 and the end of the Cold War in 1989, ethnic nationalism pulled Yugoslavia apart, with Slovenia and Croatia breaking away in 1991–1992. The region erupted in bloody conflicts. After sustained Serbian attacks on Muslims in Bosnia between 1992 and 1995, Clinton reluctantly agreed to air strikes against the Serbs, leading to the 1995 Dayton Accords, which brought an end to the war. When Serbian president Slobodan Milosevic embarked on a murderous campaign to drive the majority Muslim ethnic Albanians out of Serbia's southern province of Kosovo, Clinton finally ordered air strikes that forced the Serbs to retreat. Milosevic was voted out of office in 2000.

Map 29.2 THE BREAKUP OF THE FORMER YUGOSLAVIA

Created in 1919 as a multiethnic nation, Yugoslavia split apart in 1991–1992. After Slovenia and Croatia gained their independence swiftly, Bosnia deteriorated into fierce ethnic fighting dominated by Serb atrocities and encouraged by the Serbian government of Slobodan Milosevic. A brief U.S. bombing campaign in 1995 finally brought the Serbs to peace negotiations. Similar ethnic fighting in the province of Kosovo in 1999 led to another U.S. bombing campaign and Kosovo's current quasi-independence under NATO guidance. In 2006, Montenegro's citizens voted narrowly to establish their full independence from Serbia.

The following year, Serbian authorities arrested Milosevic and turned him over to the War Crimes Tribunal in The Hague, which had indicted Milosevic for crimes against humanity.

In the Middle East, Clinton brought Yasser Arafat, leader of the Palestine Liberation Organization (PLO), and Yitzak Rabin, Israeli prime minister, to Washington for talks that led to a historic 1993 handshake and pledges to pursue a peace agreement. Those efforts were hampered by violent extremists on both sides. Rabin was assassinated by a fanatical right-wing Israeli, leading to the election of a hawkish new prime minister, Benjamin Netanyahu. Large-scale violence between Palestinians and Israelis erupted again in the summer of 2000, and Clinton left office with no agreement in sight.

In the final weeks of Clinton's presidency in 2000, he made a historic visit to Vietnam—the first by an American president since the war. His administration was the first to reopen formal relations with the Vietnamese government. Although the United States lost the war, westernization had taken hold in Vietnam, with investment beginning to flow in from Europe, the United States, and Japan, as well as American popular culture and technology. Cheering crowds welcomed the president of the superpower that Vietnam had defeated twenty-five years earlier.

29.3.5 Terrorism and Danger at Home and Abroad

While the Clinton administration carved out a new role for the United States in the post–Cold War world, several international terrorist attacks against the United States killed hundreds of people in the 1990s and highlighted the strength of extremist groups

Why did President Clinton go to Vietnam, and why did he receive such a warm welcome from the country that fought against the United States in a long and bloody war? Had the political disaster of his impeachment battle with the U.S. Congress sufficiently receded by this time, or was that political fight unlikely to be an issue for the people of Vietnam?

whose members were deeply hostile to the United States and its interventions around the world.

International terrorism proved to be one of the most difficult issues to confront. In June 1996, a truck bomb killed 19 U.S. airmen in Dhahran, Saudi Arabia. Two years later, bombs exploded at two U.S. embassies in east Africa, killing 224 people in Nairobi, Kenya, and Dar es Salaam, Tanzania. Four men were convicted of conspiracy in the terrorist attacks. They were identified as followers of Islamist militant Osama bin Laden, a guerrilla who had been funded by the CIA in the 1980s to resist the Soviet invasion of Afghanistan. Bin Laden, originally from Saudi Arabia, was living in Afghanistan under the protection of the fundamentalist Taliban regime. He was known to be the leader of the al Qaeda terrorist network operating in several countries throughout the Middle East. On October 12, 2000, a small boat carrying a bomb pulled up next to the destroyer USS *Cole* in Yemen's port of Aden and exploded, ripping a hole in the hull and killing seventeen Americans and wounding thirty-nine others. Two suicide bombers carried out the attack. U.S. officials believed that they, too, were associated with Osama bin Laden.

Islamist radicals also struck in New York City. On February 26, 1993, a bomb exploded in the parking garage underneath the World Trade Center, the skyscrapers dominating the New York skyline in Lower Manhattan. Six people were killed and more than a thousand were injured. Eight years later, the same twin towers were attacked again, with far more devastating consequences.

Not all terrorists came from abroad. On the morning of April 19, 1995, a two-ton homemade bomb exploded at the Alfred P. Murrah Federal Building in Oklahoma City. The huge building crumbled, killing 168 people, including nineteen children. The attack was the worst act of terrorism in the nation's history to that date. Initial news reports speculated that the terrorists were Arabs, but it turned out that the attack was carried out by American citizens with a hatred for the government. Timothy McVeigh, a veteran of the 1991 Persian Gulf War, and his accomplice, Terry Nichols, were found guilty of the bombing.

Antigovernment individuals and groups had long operated within the United States, and during the 1990s their activities—as well as FBI efforts to curtail them—intensified. Investigations throughout the decade uncovered networks of antigovernment militias, tax resisters, and white supremacist groups, many of them heavily armed and isolated in remote rural areas. Some antigovernment extremists acted alone, like Theodore Kaczynski, known as the "Unabomber," who for two decades sent bombs through the mail, killing three people and injuring twenty-nine. His demand to have his antigovernment manifesto published in major national newspapers led to his identification and arrest.

The FBI tried to prevent these extremists from causing harm, but some of their efforts went awry. In 1992, during a standoff in Idaho, an FBI agent shot and killed the wife and son of Randall Weaver, a former Green Beret and antigovernment militia supporter who had failed to appear for trial on weapons charges. The following year in Waco, Texas, the FBI stormed the heavily armed compound of an antigovernment religious sect known as the Branch Davidians. The leader of the group, David Koresh, had barricaded the compound. The FBI, acting on reports of abuse of members, particularly women and children, tried to force Koresh and his group out of the building. But a fire broke out, killing eighty men, women, and children inside. The FBI came under intense criticism for its aggressive tactics in these cases. For antigovernment extremists, these actions prompted revenge. The Oklahoma City bombing apparently was intended in part as retaliation for the FBI assault against the Branch Davidians precisely two years

ALFRED P. MURRAH FEDERAL BUILDING, OKLAHOMA CITY, AFTER THE BOMBING On the day following the 1995 bombing of the federal building in Oklahoma City, Los Angeles County firefighters survey the wreckage in an attempt to find clues or survivors.

Musee des Arts d'Afrique et d'Oceanie, Paris, France/Lauros/Giraudon/The Bridgeman Art Library

What did the bombing in Oklahoma City reveal about the goals and motives of domestic terrorists?

earlier. Timothy McVeigh was sentenced to death for the Oklahoma City bombing and was executed by lethal injection on June 11, 2001.

The McVeigh case revived a debate about the death penalty, particularly in light of recent evidence of many botched legal defenses in capital cases. Opponents pointed to the preponderance of convicts of color on death row, representation by incompetent attorneys, and the execution of mentally retarded offenders, to argue that the death penalty should be abolished. The governor of Illinois declared a moratorium on executions when a study revealed that many death row inmates were cleared of charges as a result of new DNA evidence. Public opinion began to shift, but the majority—including the U.S. presidents from both parties throughout the decade—continued to support the death penalty.

The Oklahoma City bombing was the worst but not the only example of domestic terrorist attacks. After the Supreme Court's 1973 decision in *Roe v. Wade* legalized abortion, antiabortion activists worked to have the decision reversed. Most antiabortion protesters were peaceful and law-abiding. But a small militant fringe of antiabortion crusaders switched their targets of protest from elected officials to abortion providers and turned to violence. In 1993, half of all abortion clinics reported hostile actions, including death threats, fires, bombs, invasions, blockades, and shootings. In 1993 and 1994, vigilantes shot and killed one abortion provider, tried to kill another, and shot employees at two clinics in Brookline, Massachusetts.

The violence spurred Congress to pass the Freedom of Access to Clinic Entrances Act in 1994, making it a federal crime to block access to clinics. But the intimidation and violence were effective. Although abortion remained legal, the procedure became

OPPOSITE SIDES OF THE ABORTION DEBATE Abortion remained one of the most controversial political issues throughout the 1990s. Here abortion rights advocate Inga Coulter of Harrisburg, Pennsylvania, and antiabortion crusader Elizabeth McGee of Washington, D.C., take opposing sides in a demonstration outside the Supreme Court building on December 8, 1993.

Joe Marquette/AP Images

What does this photo suggest about the arguments on both sides of the abortion issue, and why the women on both sides chose to demonstrate in front of the Supreme Court building?

increasing difficult to obtain. Few medical residency programs in obstetrics and gyne-cology routinely taught the procedure, and considering the dangers posed by anti-abortion terrorists, few physicians were willing to perform abortions. By the end of the decade, there were no abortion providers in 86 percent of largely rural counties in the country. Abortions continued to be available in cities, mostly in specialized abor-tion clinics. Between 1990 and 1997, the number of abortions declined by 17.4 percent. But the political battles continued. After years of controversy and debate, the abortion pill RU-486 received FDA approval for use in the United States, making it possible for individual doctors to prescribe the pill and for women to avoid surgery.

29.3.6 Weapons and Health

In spite of episodes of domestic terrorism, violent crime declined throughout the decade, especially crimes committed by youths. But a spate of school shootings in which children murdered other children sparked national soul searching and finger pointing as Ameri-cans wondered whom and what to blame. The murderers were mostly white middle-class boys who appeared to be "normal kids." The worst of these shootings occurred on April 20, 1999, at Columbine High School in a suburb of Denver, Colorado, where two boys opened fire and killed twelve of their schoolmates and a teacher before killing themselves.

The common factors in all of these killings were that the children used guns and that they got the weapons easily, often from their own homes. Gun control advocates noted that easy access to firearms in the United States was unique among Western industrial nations. In 1992, 367 people were killed by handguns in Great Britain, Swe-den, Switzerland, Japan, Australia, and Canada combined. The total population of those countries equaled that of the United States, where in that same year, handguns killed 13,220 people. Public opinion polls showed that most Americans favored gun control, but the powerful gun lobby and the National Rifle Association argued that the Second Amendment to the Constitution guaranteed individuals the unlimited right to bear arms. Congress enacted the Brady Bill, a gun control measure named for James Brady, the White House press secretary who was gravely wounded in the 1981 assassination attempt on President Ronald W. Reagan. The bill required a waiting period for handgun purchases and banned assault rifles. Nevertheless, access to firearms remained easy.

Americans in the 1990s also harmed themselves in less violent ways. Despite the nation's near obsession with fitness, both the wealthy and the poor suffered from many afflictions. Eating disorders plagued millions of Americans. Among the affluent, ano-rexia nervosa (self-starvation) and bulimia (frequent binging and purging) affected an estimated 5 million Americans, especially young women, who were influenced in part by a fashion fad that glamorized emaciated bodies. Men also strove for a fashion-able body, sometimes with the aid of drugs to enhance athletic performance or mus-cle buildup. In 2000, the Mayo Clinic reported a 30 percent annual increase in eating disorders, mostly among young women, but in a growing number of men as well. The opposite problem plagued the lower end of the economic ladder, where obesity increased dramatically, especially among children. With popular fast-food chains offer-ing inexpensive "supersized" high-fat meals, the proportion of overweight children jumped from 5 percent in 1964 to 20 percent in 2000.

Illegal drugs, including marijuana, cocaine, and heroin, remained popular in spite of official efforts to curb the trade. However, illegal drugs represented only one dimension of Americans' desire to solve their problems through the use of chemical substances. Some mind-altering drugs, such as Prozac and other antidepressants, were legal and available by prescription. While these medications proved very effective in treating mental illness, some mental health experts worried that these drugs were being over-prescribed, especially for children, as life's normal ups and downs were increasingly diagnosed as maladies such as depression and attention deficit disorder. Aging baby boomers also boosted the profits of pharmaceutical companies. Women turned to hor-mone replacement therapies to offset the effects of menopause. Skyrocketing sales of

Figure 29.1 Childhood Overweight Rates for Boys and Girls Age 6–17, 1960s and 1990s

During the last half-century, obesity rates among children rose dramatically, especially in the 1990s. Childhood obesity is associated with a wide range of medical problems that can affect the health of overweight children throughout their lives. In the 1960s, boys and girls were equally likely to be more than 20 percent overweight. But by the 1990s, obesity had become more prevalent among boys.

SOURCE: Youfa Wan and May A. Beydoun, "The Obesity Epidemic in the United States–Gender, Age, Socioeconomic, Racial/Ethnic, and Geographic Characteristics: A Systematic Review and Meta-Regression Analysis," *Epidemiologic Reviews* 29, no. 1 (2007): 6–28.

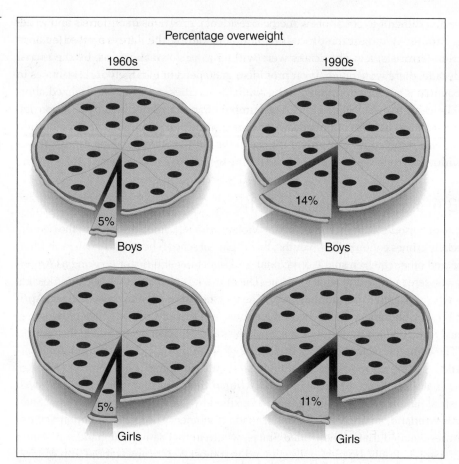

Viagra, a drug for treating male impotence, reflected middle-aged men's concerns about waning sexual potency.

Medical developments brought new cures and new worries. Antibiotics were so widely prescribed that forms of drug-resistant bacteria began to proliferate. Tuberculosis appeared in new deadly forms that did not respond to treatment with available antibiotics. In 1997, researchers in Scotland cloned a sheep, raising hopes that cloning could lead to new medical breakthroughs and fears that human cloning might be next. In 2000, scientists charted the entire human genome, or genetic code, offering the possibility of finding causes and cures for genetically linked diseases. As the century came to an end, scientific breakthroughs raised hopes as well as questions.

29.4 The Contested Election of 2000

What flaws in the American electoral system did the 2000 election reveal?

The first presidential election of the new millennium was the most bitterly contested in more than a century. The Democratic candidate won the national popular vote, but with ballot counts disputed in Florida, a Supreme Court decision ultimately made the Republican candidate the victor. The election exposed defects in the election process, from faulty ballots and voting machines to the role of the media, and raised serious questions about the value of the electoral college. The election also revealed that flaws in the system disfranchised large numbers of poor and minority voters.

29.4.1 The Campaign, the Vote, and the Courts

The campaign pitted Vice President Al Gore, the Democratic party's candidate who hoped to benefit from Clinton's high approval rating and the healthy economy, against Republican George W. Bush, governor of Texas and son of the former president. Only half of the nation's eligible voters turned out to vote. As the media reported the results state by state, it became clear that whoever took Florida, where Bush's brother Jeb Bush was governor, would win the election. By the next day, Gore had won the national popular vote by half a million votes, but Bush was ahead in Florida. Bush's lead was so narrow that it triggered an automatic recount.

With all eyes on Florida, a number of serious irregularities surfaced. Some Florida voters were given confusing ballots while others were turned away at the polls because of inaccurate and incomplete voter registration lists. Most of the disfranchised voters were African American, who usually voted Democratic. For weeks after the election, the outcome was still unknown as Democrats and Republicans argued over how to recount ballots in contested counties. Florida's secretary of state, Katherine Harris, a Republican who headed Florida's campaign for George W. Bush, refused to extend the deadline to allow the recounts to take place and declared Bush the winner by 537 votes out of 6 million cast statewide.

Gore contested the results, and the Florida Supreme Court ordered that the recount proceed. Bush then appealed to the U.S. Supreme Court to reverse the decision of the Florida Supreme Court. After thirty-six days of partial vote counting and court battles, in a sharply divided five-to-four decision, the U.S. Supreme Court stopped any further vote counting, with the most conservative judges voting in support of the Bush request. The four dissenting judges issued a stinging rebuke of their five colleagues responsible for the decision. In his dissenting opinion, Justice Stephen Breyer wrote that the majority ruling "can only lend confidence to the most cynical appraisal of the work of judges throughout the land."

Table 29.3 THE ELECTION OF 2000

Candidate	Political Party	Popular Vote (%)	Electoral Vote
George W. Bush	Republican	47.87	271
Al Gore	Democratic	48.38	266*
Ralph Nader	Green	2.72	—

*One District of Columbia Gore elector abstained.

SOURCE: Historical Election Results, Electoral College, National Archives and Records Administration

29.4.2 The Aftermath

What became clear in the months after the 2000 election were the widespread flaws in the election system in Florida and elsewhere. Across the country, outdated voting machines yielded inaccurate vote counts, and long lines at polling places prevented voters from casting ballots. Low-income and minority voters were more likely to be disfranchised because they lived in precincts with faulty voting machines or overcrowded polling places.

In addition to those whose votes did not count, many others were prevented from voting altogether. In Florida, "suspected felons" were removed from voter registration lists without being informed and without the opportunity to demonstrate that they were law-abiding citizens eligible to vote. Hundreds of African American citizens with no criminal record arrived at the polls only to discover that they had been disfranchised. According to the U.S. Civil Rights Commission, "Perhaps the most dramatic undercount in Florida's election was the nonexistent ballots of countless unknown eligible voters, who were turned away, or wrongfully purged from the voter registration rolls . . . and were prevented from exercising the franchise."

Policymakers and media moguls debated the role of the media in reporting election returns. Some argued for a blackout on early returns until all polls across the country were closed, to avoid the possibility that early results might influence voters who had not yet voted. Others proposed that only official results be announced, to avoid the problem of erroneous reporting that occurred on election night 2000. But media representatives countered that a free press should be able to report the news as it happens, although they agreed on the need to ensure accuracy.

29.4.3 Legacies of Election 2000

In addition to the unprecedented Supreme Court decision, the 2000 election was remarkable in other ways. For the first time, a First Lady was elected to public office: Hillary Rodham Clinton became a Democratic senator from New York. Third-party politics also critically influenced the outcome of the presidential election. Several third-party candidates achieved national visibility during the 1990s and won elections at the state and local levels, including professional wrestler Jesse Ventura, elected governor of Minnesota in 1998 on the Reform party ticket. In 2000, Green party presidential candidate Ralph Nader gained fewer than 3 percent of the votes, but his candidacy drew off some of the left-leaning elements of the Democratic party—enough votes to cost Al Gore the election.

President George W. Bush immediately reversed several Clinton-era policies, including a number of environmental protections. His first major legislative success was the passage of a major tax cut. During his first year in office, the economy went from boom to bust and headed into a recession. Nevertheless, as the new millennium dawned, the United States remained the wealthiest and most powerful nation in the world. Bush retreated from international treaties on issues ranging from global warming to nuclear test ban agreements, and he revived the Reagan-era proposal for a nuclear missile shield. But the place of the nation in the global community was yet to be defined. Soon, monumental events shattered the nation's sense of security and forced Bush to engage in the world in unprecedented ways.

Conclusion

In the 1990s, a half-century of political certainties evaporated, and the role of the nation in the world shifted. With the Cold War over, conflicts around the globe, many of them grounded in ancient ethnic hostilities, posed challenges for the world's most powerful nation. The United States focused on markets and trade, the nation's supply of oil, the need for political order to maintain international stability, and the danger of "rogue nations." President Clinton tried to be a peacemaker in hot spots around the world while attempting to respond to violent episodes of international terrorism.

At home, Americans demonstrated increasing tolerance for people who looked and acted differently from themselves. Polls showed declining levels of racial, ethnic, and religious hostility and greater acceptance of homosexuality, single parenthood, and family arrangements that deviated from the nuclear family model. But episodes of racial discrimination—by police, courts, and voting officials—continued. Politics remained an arena in which culture wars flared over abortion, gun control, and welfare reform. A Democratic president faced impeachment by his Republican foes in Congress while maintaining high approval ratings from the public.

At the dawn of the new century, several crises challenged Americans' sense of security. A deeply flawed presidential election revealed profound problems in the nation's voting system. A sharp and sudden downturn in the economy shattered the optimism many middle-class people felt during the booming Clinton years and forced many of the working poor into desperate circumstances. Already reeling from these disturbing developments, the nation was soon shaken to its core by a terrorist attack that forced a new reckoning at home and abroad.

Chapter Review

29.1 The Economy: Global and Domestic

How did the expanding economy affect those at the top and bottom of the income ladder?

During the 1990s, as the economy boomed, the rich got richer and the poor got poorer. The real income of the bottom 60 percent of the population declined, while those at the top accumulated huge wealth. The top 1 percent of Americans owned more wealth than the bottom 90 percent combined.

29.2 Tolerance and Its Limits

In what ways did Americans demonstrate increasing tolerance for those different from themselves?

Although inequalities persisted, there were signs of increasing tolerance and appreciation of the nation's diversity. Following devastating riots in Los Angeles, the community came together across racial lines to express cooperation. Increasing numbers of immigrants, along with official recognition of mixed-race identity in the 2000

U.S. census, reflected the changing face of diversity in the nation.

29.3 The Clinton Years

What was the impact of the "Republican revolution" during Clinton's presidency?

In the 1994 elections, Republicans took control of both the House and Senate for the first time in forty years, pushing Congress to the right of center. In response, Clinton used his veto power to limit Republican achievements, while taking on some conservative issues as his own, such as free trade and welfare reform.

29.4 The Contested Election of 2000

What flaws in the American electoral system did the 2000 election reveal?

The 2000 election revealed serious problems with the election system, such as confusing ballots, outdated voting machines that yielded incorrect vote counts, inaccurate voting registration lists that prevented eligible citizens from voting, and long lines at the polls that made it impossible for some voters to get into their polling places in time to vote.

Timeline

1991	Los Angeles police beat and arrest Rodney King	**1996**	Welfare Reform Act
1992	FBI shootout at Ruby Ridge, Idaho	**1998**	Clinton impeached by House of Representatives
1993	Congress approves North American Free Trade Agreement (NAFTA)	**1999**	Senate acquits Clinton of impeachment charges
	Arab–Israeli peace talks		U.S. bombing campaign frees province of Kosovo from Serbian rule
1994	House leadership announces "Contract with America"	**2000**	Supreme Court decides contested election; George W. Bush becomes president
1995	Truck bomb destroys federal building in Oklahoma City		
	United States intervenes against Serbs in war in Bosnia		

Glossary

Tree sitting A strategy developed by Earth First! environmental activists in which individuals climb into trees that are threatened by the lumber industry in order to prevent the trees from being cut down for lumber.

Million Man March A demonstration organized by Nation of Islam Reverend Louis Farrakhan, which drew hundreds of thousands of black men to express their pride in manhood and fatherhood at a rally in Washington, D.C.

civil unions Relationships recognized by the state granting legitimacy and legal privileges to same-sex couples who are prohibited from legal marriage.

New Democrat Member of the Democratic party, many of them organized in the Democratic Leadership Council, who espouse center to center-right policies.

"don't ask, don't tell" A policy established by the Clinton administration allowing gays and lesbians to serve in the military so long as they do not disclose their sexual orientation.

Contract with America A platform developed by Speaker of the House Newt Gingrich during the 1994 elections that outlined a series of conservative legislative goals endorsed by about 300 Republican congressional candidates.

welfare reform Policies enacted that limited government aid to the poor, and dismantled the program of Aid to Families with Dependent Children, which had been in effect since 1935.

impeach A formal process by which an official is accused of unlawful activity. The House of Representatives has the authority to bring such charges, and the Senate is required to place the official on trial and either convict or acquit.

most-favored-nation A designation allowing countries to export their products to the United States with tariffs no greater than those levied against most other nations.

Chapter 30
A Global Nation in the New Millennium

UA FLIGHT 93, NEAR SHANKSVILLE, PENNSYLVANIA Smoke rises from the crash of United Airlines Flight 93 near Shanksville, Pennsylvania. For almost all Americans, the hijackings and destruction of September 11, 2001, came out of a clear blue sky. Anti-American actions of the previous decade by Islamist terrorists had created little anxiety in a powerful nation that had imagined itself safe from major attack.

Jason Cohn/ZUMA Press/Newscom

How concerned do Americans seem to be today about terrorist threats from abroad?

Contents and Focus Questions

What did globalization mean for Americans?

At the beginning of the third millennium, the United States was more closely connected than ever to other parts of the world. The processes of **globalization**—increasing trade, communication, travel, and migration—linked the nation to places that often seemed to be torn by ethnic and religious strife.

Strife from abroad impinged on Americans in a shocking new way on September 11, 2001. On that sunny Tuesday morning, nineteen hijackers—four of them trained as pilots—seized control simultaneously of four large commercial jets and turned them into suicide missiles. At 8:48 A.M., one flew into the 110-story north tower of New York City's World Trade Center, igniting an enormous fireball. Fifteen minutes later, the second plane flew into the south tower. In less than two hours, both towers collapsed, killing thousands of people still inside. Among the dead were hundreds of firefighters, police officers, and other rescue workers who had raced into the towers to evacuate the occupants. The third plane flew into the Pentagon. The fourth was also being directed toward Washington, apparently to destroy the White House or the Capitol Building, until it crashed in a field 75 miles southeast of Pittsburgh after some of the passengers attempted to wrest control of the aircraft away from the hijackers.

The nineteen perpetrators were self-styled holy warriors of a secretive, extremist Islamist organization known as **al Qaeda**, organized by wealthy, charismatic Saudi Arabian expatriate **Osama bin Laden**. Al Qaeda worked out of Afghanistan, at odds with moderate Islamic mainstream thought. The rage of bin Laden and other Islamist terrorists against the United States had been building throughout the 1990s, fueled by the presence of "infidel" American troops in Saudi Arabia since the 1991 Persian Gulf War, by American support for Israel, and by the worldwide spread of American popular culture.

At the heart of American society remained a common assumption: that the United States was a democratic country. The events on United Airlines Flight 93, one of the four doomed planes on September 11, 2001, revealed the tenacity of the belief in majority rule. After the hijackers seized control and herded the passengers into the rear of the cabin, a dozen passengers and crew members were able to communicate by phone with people on the ground. They learned that two other planes had already crashed into the World Trade Center towers. They realized that these hijackers—unlike previous ones who sought concrete gains and an escape—planned only destruction for them all. Face to face with imminent death and the certainty that many others would perish if they failed to act, the passengers discussed what to do.

They made a plan to rush the hijackers. Should they proceed? Quintessential Americans, they took a vote. GTE Airfone operator Lisa Jefferson heard the rest: "Are you guys ready?" asked Todd Beamer, a tall father of two from Cranbury, New Jersey. Screams and a sustained scuffle

globalization
The long-term process that continues to tie the world's regions more closely together economically and culturally through more unified systems of trade, travel, and communication.

al Qaeda
A secret extremist organization established in the early 1990s that used terrorist tactics in pursuit of a backward-looking, absolutist form of Islamist government.

Osama bin Laden
A wealthy, charismatic exile from Saudi Arabia who created al Qaeda, masterminded the September 11, 2001, attacks, and was eventually killed by U.S. Navy Seals in Pakistan in 2011.

followed before the line went dead. The plane, headed for the heart of Washington, crashed in an unpopulated part of western Pennsylvania, with no casualties on the ground.

*   *   *   *   *

The September 11 attacks jolted the country's political course. President George W. Bush chose to invade not only Afghanistan but also Iraq as part of a global "war on terror." The September 11 attacks and their aftermath also highlighted how access to oil determined much of daily life and the country's foreign policy. Furthermore, the attacks demonstrated how widely American popular culture had spread around the globe and how culturally diverse American society had become. The United States, still a nation of immigrants and their descendants, embodied the new global era.

30.1 Politics in the New Millennium

What were the Bush administration's priorities, and how were they affected by the attacks on September 11, 2001?

The attacks of September 11, 2001, constituted perhaps the most significant event in American life since Japan's surrender in 1945. The economy, already sliding into recession, accelerated its downward course. Just seven months in office, the administration of President George W. Bush responded by leading the nation into a "war on terrorism" abroad and at home. Within two years, U.S.-led efforts succeeded in overthrowing the governments of Afghanistan and Iraq. Complicated, long-term military occupations ensued, with U.S. forces continuing to engage in bloody battles against insurgents in both countries. And a sharp economic recession began in late 2007, undercutting the tentative financial status of many American households.

30.1.1 The President and the War on Terrorism

George W. Bush did not have an auspicious record of achievement before his election as governor of Texas in 1994 and as president of the United States six years later. He grew up primarily in Midland, Texas, the grandson of a U.S. senator from Connecticut and the eldest son of a wealthy oilman, diplomat, and eventual U.S. president, George H. W. Bush. "W.," as he was sometimes called to distinguish him from his father, attended the elite Phillips Academy in Andover, Massachusetts, and he earned degrees from Yale and Harvard Business School, though his modest academic achievements hinted at the benefits of unofficial forms of affirmative action for the scions of wealthy and powerful families. His sociability and charisma earned him many friends. He avoided going to Vietnam when he was of draft age by serving in the Air National Guard, though he apparently failed to show up for much of a year of that service in 1972.

After a mixed career in business and a strong taste for the partying life, Bush gave up drinking at age 40 and became a devout, conservative Christian. This ambitious and now more serious man made his way up in Republican political circles, benefiting from family connections as well as a warm, "regular guy" personality that appealed to many working-class Americans. Before his presidency, Bush had traveled to few places other than Mexico. "I'm not going to play like a person who has spent hours involved with foreign policy," he admitted during the 2000 campaign. Once president, he took a unilateralist and almost isolationist stance, to the dismay of close U.S. allies. The United States rejected or withdrew from international agreements limiting global warming, weapons testing, and war crime prosecutions.

The events of September 11 stunned all Americans and gave the president a new focus. Finding and destroying al Qaeda and its allies was now "the purpose of this administration," Bush told his cabinet. Four weeks after the attacks on New York and Washington, U.S. planes initiated the "war on terrorism" by bombing Taliban and al Qaeda positions in Afghanistan. By October 19, U.S. special operations forces were working on the ground with anti-Taliban Afghan insurgents. Several European nations provided troops and other military assistance. By December, the Taliban had been driven from power throughout the country, and U.S. and allied forces had killed and captured hundreds of Taliban and al Qaeda fighters. Many of the prisoners were transferred to the U.S. naval base at Guantanamo Bay, Cuba, to be held indefinitely and interrogated as enemy combatants.

30.1.2 Security and Politics at Home

The war on terrorism was not only a foreign affair. Just as the onset of the Cold War in the late 1940s had incorporated a hunt for domestic traitors, the war on terrorism in the early 2000s included a search for potential al Qaeda sympathizers at home. Like the Cold War, the war on terrorism was framed as a long-term struggle against a maniacal, evil enemy who would not be easily defeated. Also as in the Cold War, American leaders announced that some civil liberties would have to be curtailed in order to protect the nation. The USA Patriot Act of October 2001 increased the U.S. Justice Department's range of options for spying on and detaining citizens and non-citizens suspected of pro-terrorist activities. Determined to prevent another major terrorist attack, Attorney General John Ashcroft oversaw the arrest of hundreds of illegal immigrants and their imprisonment in what the Justice Department later admitted were often unduly harsh conditions—not unlike Guantanamo, observers noted. Congress created the Department of Homeland Security (DHS) in an effort to better coordinate intelligence, police, and military authorities for defending the nation from future attacks.

Beyond terrorism, George W. Bush sought to move the nation in the direction of what he called "compassionate conservatism." One conservative activist noted that the new administration turned out to be "more Reaganite than the Reagan administration." In the economic realm, this meant promoting the private sector and reducing federal spending on social programs for the poor. It meant reducing the government's role in regulating health and safety issues in the workplace. And it meant pushing large tax cuts through Congress in 2001 and 2003 to the disproportionate benefit of the wealthiest 1 percent of Americans, including a doubling of the number of billionaires between 2003 and 2007. The budget surpluses of Bill Clinton's last years disappeared, as the Bush administration ran enormous annual deficits by retaining the tax cuts while sharply increasing military spending. Under Bush, the nation built the largest deficit in its history.

Bush's conservatism did not include conserving natural resources. Bush and Vice President Dick Cheney, both former oil executives, were strongly supported by corporate interests, particularly in the energy business, that sought easier access to public resources. The administration promoted oil drilling offshore and sought unsuccessfully to open Alaska's Arctic National Wildlife Refuge to oil production, encouraged mining and timber clear-cutting across western federal lands, and refused to regulate carbon dioxide emissions despite powerful evidence of **global warming**. The administration also loosened federal regulations on industrial air pollution, on water pollution by the coal industry, and on arsenic levels in drinking water.

global warming
The accelerating process of climate change, driven in large part by human population growth and the burning of fossil fuels such as coal and oil.

Sexual issues remained flashpoints of political controversy. Explicit and suggestive sexuality pervaded popular culture, including two-thirds of television shows, causing particular concern among parents of young children. At the same time, Americans were increasingly accepting of homosexual couples. In *Lawrence v. Texas* (2003), the U.S. Supreme Court overturned state laws banning private homosexual behavior between consenting adults. A year later, Massachusetts legalized gay marriage, followed by 37 other states by early 2015. Later that year, on June 26, 2015, the U.S. Supreme Court struck down marriage bans in all remaining states, in a 5-to-4 decision in *Obergefell v. Hodges*. Marriage and family remained social institutions in transition, for better or worse: only half of adults were now married, compared with 75 percent thirty years earlier. And in 2011, only 20 percent of American households consisted of a married couple with children.

30.1.3 Into War in Iraq

President Bush's most momentous decision was to invade and occupy Iraq in the spring of 2003. This was a very different proposition from the attack on Afghanistan. The effort to destroy al Qaeda and its Taliban hosts in Afghanistan had widespread support in the United States and across much of the world. By contrast, invading a sovereign nation that had not attacked nor even threatened the United States divided Americans and alienated most of the rest of the world. The United Nations refused to support the invasion. America's western European allies were dismayed. Among America's major allies, only the British government of Prime Minister Tony Blair provided enthusiastic political support and a significant number of troops. Given this lack of support, why did the Bush administration invade Iraq?

Some observers pointed to personal reasons. Bush would be "finishing" the Persian Gulf War of 1991, when his father oversaw the liberation of Kuwait from Saddam Hussein's invading Iraqi forces but did not send troops to Baghdad to overthrow Saddam.

Map 30.1 IRAQ AND AFGHANISTAN

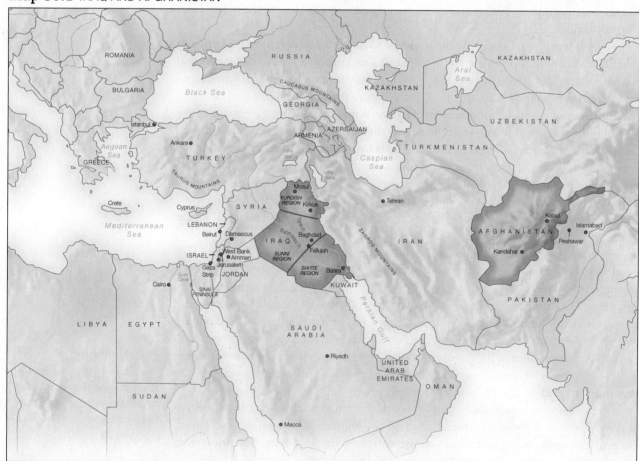

The U.S. occupation of Iraq that began in 2003 placed more than 100,000 American soldiers in the center of the volatile Middle East. A multisided insurgency against those forces grew in strength, with Iraq increasingly divided ethnically into three parts, dominated respectively by Kurds in the north, Sunnis in the center, and Shia in the south. By 2007, civil war between Sunnis and Shia had convinced a majority of Americans that the United States should withdraw its troops from a situation growing only more perilous. The last U.S. troops left Iraq in 2011.

Bush would also be avenging Saddam's effort to assassinate the elder Bush on a later visit to Kuwait. Other observers emphasized the centrality of Iraq's oil reserves, the fourth largest in the world. "If the Gulf produced kumquats, would we be doing this?" asked one administration official rhetorically. The president himself claimed two primary reasons for the invasion: that Saddam possessed "weapons of mass destruction"—chemical, biological, or nuclear—and could attack the United States or its allies "on any given day," and that Iraq had ties to al Qaeda "and was equally as bad, equally as evil and equally as destructive." But after U.S. forces occupied Iraq, these two official reasons for the war evaporated. U.S. troops found no weapons of mass destruction (though Saddam had indeed used chemical weapons on dissident Iraqi civilians fifteen years earlier), and Secretary of State Colin Powell admitted there was no "smoking gun" proof of a link between al Qaeda's religious zealots and Saddam's fiercely secular dictatorship. The bipartisan reports of both the 9/11 Commission and the Senate Intelligence Committee in 2004 found that the primary reasons the president gave for invading Iraq were not true.

A deeper reason for the U.S. invasion of Iraq appeared to be the administration's view of September 11 as an opportunity to preemptively reshape the Middle East into a region less hostile to the United States and its ally Israel. A liberated Iraq, right in the center of the Middle East, might have a "demonstration effect" of pro-American capitalist democracy that would turn the rest of the region away from authoritarianism and Islamist revolution. Bush spoke of the overthrow of Saddam as "a watershed event in the global democratic revolution." In the war on terrorism, the president declared in 2002, "we must take the battle to the enemy and confront the worst threats before they emerge."

The U.S.-led offensive in Iraq that began on March 19, 2003, was a successful military action. Some 200,000 U.S. and British troops, with a few other allied forces, overran Saddam's defenses and occupied the nation of 25 million people within four weeks. Most Iraqis celebrated their liberation from Saddam's brutal regime, and many seemed to welcome the American soldiers. Seven months later, U.S. soldiers captured Saddam himself, and the new Iraqi authorities executed him.

But military occupations rarely age well, especially without sufficient troops for the task. Widespread looting ravaged Baghdad, and essential services and personal security deteriorated in the aftermath of the old government's defeat. "Baghdad," one gasoline station owner observed, "is like the Wild West now." Saddam loyalists, Iraqi nationalists of various stripes, and arriving foreign Islamist revolutionaries initiated a multisided insurgency against the American occupiers. The number of U.S. and Iraqi deaths shot upward. The U.S. invasion of Iraq seemed to be increasing rather than reducing the threat of terrorism to Americans and others. Sunnis and Shia also faced off against each other in what began to look like civil war. The Bush administration turned over official sovereignty to a new Iraqi government on June 28, 2004, with 130,000 U.S. troops remaining in the country in an effort to provide security against insurgents. "We don't do empire," insisted Secretary of Defense Donald Rumsfeld. But two months earlier, photographs and eyewitness reports were made public of U.S. troops abusing, torturing, and sexually humiliating Iraqi detainees at the Abu Ghraib prison outside Baghdad—a similar story to that at the U.S. prison in Guantanamo Bay. After a week's delay, the president finally apologized for Abu Ghraib. For most Middle Easterners and for Muslims around the world, however, this was compelling evidence that Bush's rhetoric about liberating Iraq was merely a fig leaf covering what they saw as fundamental American disdain for Muslims.

30.1.4 From Bush to Obama

President Bush entered his campaign for reelection in 2004 with solid support in his own party but mixed reviews from others. Most other nations considered the U.S. attack on Iraq unjustified and unwise. Western Europeans resented Bush's lack of interest in their concerns, making him probably the least-popular American president ever in

POSTERS OF ABU GHRAIB ABUSES Nothing undercut the U.S. effort to extend its influence in the Middle East more than the photographs that emerged in the spring of 2004 of U.S. troops abusing Iraqi detainees at Abu Ghraib prison outside Baghdad. Here, two of these photographs are displayed as posters on a street in neighboring Iran. The Abu Ghraib scandal dismayed America's allies, enraged Muslims everywhere, and almost certainly enhanced al Qaeda recruiting. One Iraqi American observed that the Bush administration had "done a good job of occupying the land of Iraq, but a horrible job of occupying the hearts of the Iraqi people."

Behrouz Mehri/AFP/Getty Images

How did this compare with the U.S. occupations of Japan and western Germany after World War II?

Europe. The Democratic party hoped to exploit Bush's vulnerability by nominating Senator John Kerry of Massachusetts, a decorated Vietnam War hero with a moderately liberal legislative record. It did not quite work. The president prevailed in a narrow popular-vote victory. The electoral college outcome hinged on Ohio, where a difference of 136,000 votes put Bush over the top. Christian conservatives were particularly important in getting Republican voters to the polls, and being at war made other voters wary of changing leadership.

Table 30.1 THE ELECTION OF 2004

Candidate	Political Party	Popular Vote (%)	Electoral Vote
George W. Bush	Republican	50.7	286
John Kerry	Democratic	48.3	251
Ralph Nader	Independent	<1	—

SOURCE: Historical Election Results, Electoral College, National Archives and Records Administration

Hurricane Katrina
The ferocious storm that swept on to the Gulf Coast in August 2005, killing over 1,800 people, primarily in Louisiana and Mississippi, and leaving much of New Orleans under water. The storm prompted a slow and ineffective response by the federal government under President George W. Bush.

The president's political fortunes declined swiftly after his reelection. At home, financial and sexual scandals brought down several prominent Republicans in Congress, including the once-powerful House majority leader, Tom DeLay of Texas. On August 29, 2005, **Hurricane Katrina** flooded New Orleans, causing hundreds of deaths and a massive evacuation of nearly the entire city. Republican Senator John McCain of Arizona joined a bipartisan and international chorus of voices that denounced the Bush administration's slow response to Katrina for "the terrible and disgraceful way that it was handled." In the November 2006 elections, the Republicans lost their majorities in both the House and the Senate.

Violence continued to ravage Iraq, rooted in deep ethnic and religious divisions that undermined American efforts to reconstruct a stable and orderly society. More than 4,000 U.S. military personnel had died in Iraq by the end of Bush's second term. In Afghanistan, a renewed Taliban insurgency increasingly challenged a deeply corrupt government backed by Washington. Osama bin Laden remained at large. Further details of the administration's abuse and torture of detainees continued to leak out, including what even conservative Republican Senator Lindsey Graham of South Carolina called "a pretty aggressive, bordering on bizarre, theory of inherent authority that had no boundaries."

Then the bottom dropped out of the economy. A largely unregulated bubble in the real estate market popped in 2007, revealing an entire array of irresponsible banking and investment practices that began to unravel in a major recession. The flow of credit in the United States slowed to a trickle. The stock market lost more than half its value from October 2007 to March 2009, traumatizing investors and hollowing out citizens' retirement accounts. Consumers cut back sharply on purchasing. Vulnerable industries such as automobile manufacturing teetered on the verge of bankruptcy. The global economy followed the U.S. economy into a downward spiral, with manufacturing and trade everywhere declining and unemployment rising. By 2008, Bush's approval ratings reached a record presidential low, below even those of Richard Nixon on the eve of his resignation after the Watergate scandal. Bush's former speechwriter, David Frum, declared that the president "had led his party to the brink of disaster."

A young U.S. senator from Illinois, Barack Obama, emerged victorious from the 2008 Democratic presidential primary, having bested the much better known senator from New York and former First Lady, Hillary Clinton. The son of a Kenyan father and a white Kansas mother who divorced when he was young, Obama grew up in Hawaii and Indonesia with his anthropologist mother and her parents. He graduated from Columbia University and Harvard Law School, worked as a community organizer and law professor, and won seats in the Illinois state legislature and the U.S. Senate. Obama's opponent in the 2008 general election was Senator John McCain, who campaigned with the burden of a Republican party associated at that moment with failure in governing abroad and at home, from diplomacy to the economy. Obama revealed himself to be a charismatic and inspiring campaigner, as well as a politician of unusually calm and deliberate demeanor. Obama defeated McCain soundly, 53 percent to 46 percent in the popular vote, and in January 2009 became the nation's first African American president.

Table 30.2 THE ELECTION OF 2008

Candidate	Political Party	Popular Vote (%)	Electoral Vote
Barack Obama	Democratic	52.9	365
John McCain	Republican	45.7	173

SOURCE: Historical Election Results, Electoral College, National Archives and Records Administration

No president since Franklin Roosevelt had entered the White House facing such enormous challenges. *The Onion,* a satirical website, wryly announced: "Black man given nation's worst job." Obama set a new tone for a new administration, departing markedly from his predecessor: he opened previously closed government records, appointed distinguished scientists to deal with global warming, ordered the closing of overseas CIA secret prisons, and warmed relations with traditional European allies of the United States. He was even awarded the Nobel Peace Prize in 2009, and a few years later initiated the process of reopening diplomatic relations with Cuba. Obama declared that the United States "is not, and will never be, at war with Islam." Under his direction, U.S. Navy Seals in 2011 finally found and killed Osama bin Laden, who had been hiding in Pakistan. Six months later, in December 2011, the last U.S. combat troops left Iraq. However, a multi-sided civil war next door in Syria soon spread into Iraq, introducing into the region a brutal new organization that called itself the Islamic State (also called ISIS).

At home, Obama got a vast new stimulus bill passed by Congress in an effort to restart the ailing economy. The new president appeared pragmatic and levelheaded to most observers. Conservative columnist David Brooks called the president's personnel appointments "admired professionals" who were "not excessively partisan" and "not ideological." Conservative columnist Peggy Noonan noted Obama's "bearing and dignity" and the feeling he gave Americans that "now I know someone's in charge, finally someone's taken ownership of the mess" left in U.S. foreign policy and the American economy. Stimulus spending helped stave off financial disaster and rescued the U.S. automobile manufacturing industry. Unemployment peaked at 10 percent in 2010 and then steadily declined to 5.5 percent by 2015, as the economy and the stock market both recovered their strength.

However, the challenges to the president and the nation remained stiff, particularly in the face of solid opposition from Republicans to nearly all White House initiatives. The Democrats narrowly succeeded in their primary goal of reforming the U.S. health

BARACK OBAMA, AS A YOUNG BOY, WITH HIS MOTHER The son of a visiting Kenyan student and an American mother, future president Barack Obama is shown here as a young child with his mother, Ann Dunham. Obama was born and mostly raised in Hawaii, and spent four years in Indonesia with his mother, an anthropologist. He was very close to his maternal grandparents, who were from Kansas. His grandfather, Stanley Dunham, was a World War II veteran. Obama later attended Occidental College, Columbia University, and Harvard Law School, where he served as president of the *Harvard Law Review*. A scholarship student who was raised mostly by a single mother, Obama was familiar with the struggles of average Americans.

AP Photo/Obama Presidential Campaign

How does Obama's background compare to that of other presidents?

care system—to provide insurance coverage for more Americans through the **Affordable Care Act (ACA)**, popularly known as Obamacare—in 2010. The party of an incumbent president typically does poorly in off-year congressional elections, and Republicans took back control of the U.S. House of Representatives in November 2010. Particular enthusiasm for the Republican cause came from a loose coalition of small-government conservatives who referred to themselves as the "Tea Party," in reference to the American colonists in Boston in 1773 who had also been unhappy with their government at the time. Voters reelected Obama to a second term in 2012 but gave control of the U.S. Senate to Republicans in the 2014 midyear elections, which further hardened the sense of national political gridlock.

Affordable Care Act (ACA)
Also known as Obamacare, this legislation, signed into law in 2010, was the largest overhaul of the U.S. health care system since the creation of Medicare and Medicaid in 1965. It sharply reduced the number of uninsured Americans and ended the previous practice of insurance companies charging higher premiums on the basis of preexisting conditions.

30.2 The American Place in a Global Economy

How did globalization affect Americans' lives?

While the new president navigated difficult political waters, average Americans struggled to keep their footing in a changing world economy. Mollie Brown James, for example, grew up in a small Virginia town west of Richmond. In 1950, at age 19, she moved to Paterson, New Jersey, joining the broad river of black Southerners who sought better economic opportunities and greater personal freedom in the North. She took a job in 1955 with the Universal Manufacturing Company in Paterson, with decent wages and benefits, unlike what had been available to her in Virginia. She stayed with Universal for thirty-four years. With union-negotiated wages, overtime work, and company-paid health insurance, she helped pull her family into the middle-class world of owning their own home and car and saving for retirement. But the peace of mind that came from a secure job vanished in 1989 when Universal closed the Paterson plant and moved its manufacturing operations to Matamoros, Mexico, just across the Rio Grande River from Brownsville, Texas.

James's job did not disappear. It moved and was inherited by 20-year-old Balbina Duque Granados. She, too, had grown up in a small town located in an agricultural area, in the Mexican province of San Luis Potosí, and she, too, had moved 400 miles north to find better-paying work in a booming manufacturing city. She was thrilled to land the difficult, repetitive job—her "answered prayer"—at a *maquiladora*, one of the foreign-owned assembly plants along Mexico's border with the United States that wed First World engineering with Third World working conditions. Her employer was also satisfied, paying her $0.65 an hour to do that for which James had been paid $7.91 an hour. But Granados's job was no more secure than James's had been. The beginnings of successful worker organizing in Matamoros encouraged the company to shift many of its operations 60 miles upriver to Reynosa, where the union movement was weaker. A journalist asked whether she would move there if her job did. "And what if they were to move again?" she replied. "Maybe to Juarez or Tijuana? What then? Do I have to chase my job all over the world?"

30.2.1 The Logic and Technology of Globalization

Like many other workers in the United States and abroad, Mollie James and Balbina Duque Granados learned firsthand the relentlessly international logic of the economic system known as capitalism. Those who have capital—extra money—invest it in corporations, whose purpose is to produce a profit for their shareholders. A corporation's profitability depends on containing costs—labor and materials—and expanding into new markets. Just as the telegraph and telephone had helped create a nation unified by rapid communication, the spread of personal computers and the **Internet** linked Americans even more closely to other nations.

Internet
A worldwide system of computer networks, established in the early 1990s, that allows for rapid global information transmission.

"On the Internet, nobody knows you're a dog."

"ON THE INTERNET, NOBODY KNOWS YOU'RE A DOG" The Internet provided both immediate connections with other people around the world and the safety of personal anonymity. Internet users could not be judged by their appearance or material possessions, only by the words they typed. Americans debated whether the popularity of the Internet represented a new kind of virtual community that would strengthen their connections to each other, or merely another way for citizens to remain isolated in their own homes rather than engage with each other in civic organizations and other face-to-face interactions.

Peter Steiner/The New Yorker Collection/www.cartoonbank.com

What evidence is there so far of the Internet's impact on Americans' daily lives and sense of community?

At the start of the twenty-first century, engineering breakthroughs sped up the process of globalization. The integration of computers into every aspect of commerce and private life increased the efficiency with which businesses could operate. Computers boosted American productivity (the amount of work performed by a person in a given time period), which had declined between 1973 and 1996. Cable News Network (CNN) offered a standardized package of world news available twenty-four hours a day around the globe. CNN was so international in its aims that it banned the word *foreign* from its broadcasts.

Americans were also speeding up their daily routines in the new millennium. The desire for immediate gratification and efficiency that had nurtured fast food and microwave ovens encouraged the spread of smartphones, overnight package delivery, and constant news headlines scrolling across TV screens. Computers processed more information faster on ever-smaller silicon chips. Increased international air travel helped tourism compete with oil as the world's largest industry. The spread of the Internet—especially such popular sites as YouTube and Facebook—and the use of texting and e-mail epitomized the shift toward instant global communication.

30.2.2 Free Trade and the Global Assembly Line

The ideology of **free trade** underpinned the tighter meshing of Americans' lives with the world economy. Advocates of free trade argued that global markets unhindered by national tariffs benefited consumers everywhere by giving them access to the best goods at the lowest prices. America's NAFTA treaty with Canada and Mexico reflected this belief (see Chapter 29), as did the European Union with its newly unified currency, the euro. In the United States, by the start of the new millennium, most leaders of both major political parties, corporate executives, bankers, and most other elites supported free trade.

But others objected to this internationalist economic ideology. Environmentalists warned of the pollution costs to the world's environment of U.S. factories relocating to poorer and less regulated nations, such as Mexico and China. Labor organizers decried the flight of American jobs as manufacturers sought less expensive and more compliant—often desperate—workers abroad. Human rights activists spotlighted the grim working conditions in many overseas plants, including the prevalence of child labor.

A "race to the bottom" for labor and environmental standards resulted from the development of a global assembly line. With capital able to move swiftly around the world and take its factories with it, nations and localities believed that they had little choice but to compete in offering multinational corporations the most advantageous terms possible. Such terms meant minimal government regulation, little protection for workers, nonexistent pollution standards, and local subsidies in place of corporate taxes. Corporate income taxes, which had been dropping since the 1950s, shrank by another third between 1986 and 2000. The *maquiladoras* on the Mexican border were part of a broader pattern of the corporate search for efficiency and profit, as companies, like Mollie James's Universal Manufacturing Company, took their production lines first to the American South and then abroad.

As a result, corporations and their products became less identifiable by nationality. Boeing Aircraft had long been the largest employer in the Seattle area, but was its new Boeing 777, manufactured piece by piece in twelve different countries, an "American" airplane? Japanese companies also moved many manufacturing plants overseas, including to the United States, to be closer to important markets. Was a Toyota made by American workers in Georgetown, Kentucky, a "foreign" car?

30.2.3 Who Benefits from Globalization?

The increasing globalization of the U.S. economy in the early twenty-first century created enormous wealth while sharpening class inequalities. The stock market skyrocketed. The Dow Jones average of the value of thirty top companies' stocks rose steadily from 500 in 1956, to 1,000 in 1972, to 3,000 in 1991. Then it more than quadrupled in value in just sixteen years, surpassing 14,000 in 2007 and reaching 18,000 in 2014. Wealthy Americans who owned the bulk of corporate stock reaped the greatest gains, but middle- and even working-class Americans with retirement funds invested in the market also benefited handsomely. The process of globalization and the steady expansion of the U.S. economy after 1992 also encouraged a growing belief among Americans, especially affluent ones, that markets alone offered the best solution to social problems. But markets and their strict dependence on the profit motive proved unable to preserve the quality of the environment, to pull the 45 million officially poor Americans above the poverty line ($24,418 for a family of four in 2014), or to preserve the security of the vast middle class that had stabilized American politics since World War II.

free trade
A system of economic relations characterized by the buying and selling of goods and services between nations with few or no taxes or tariffs to hinder that exchange.

American consumers enjoyed many of the fruits of the more integrated world economy. At least in industries not dominated by monopolies, the corporate quest for lower production costs, along with fierce international competition and technological innovation, reduced prices of many goods and services. Computers, airline travel, and gasoline were all significantly less expensive in real dollars (adjusted for inflation) than they had been a generation earlier. Competition abounded in the retail sector of the U.S. economy, including catalog and Internet shopping. Wal-Mart represented the epitome of how the globalized economy could benefit consumers. By 2000, the discount store surpassed General Motors as the largest American company, responsible for 6 percent of all U.S. retail sales. By 2007, Wal-Mart was also Latin America's largest retailer. Wal-Mart's success resulted from relentlessly cutting costs through sharp management, using cheaper imported goods and employing a nonunion workforce, and passing some of its savings along to customers in the form of lower prices.

The benefits that Americans experienced as consumers in the global economy were balanced by their declining status as workers. As manufacturers moved to the Sunbelt and then overseas, high-wage, unionized jobs providing health insurance and pension benefits disappeared. Average real wages declined for more than two decades after 1973 and increased only slightly after that. Union membership shrank from one-third of the workforce in the early 1950s to one-tenth in 2000. Family incomes were maintained only

Figure 30.1 TOP TEN U.S. TRADING PARTNERS, 2014 (total value of imports and exports in billions of dollars)

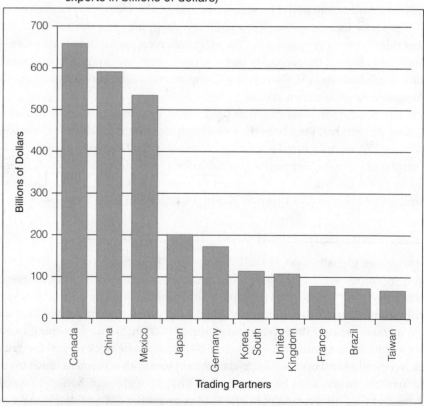

America's largest trading partner is Canada. China, second in rank, has recently overtaken Mexico, which now ranks third. After Canada, China, and Mexico, Americans do the most business with countries in eastern Asia and in western Europe. Brazil is an exception. U.S. economic vitality has always depended to some extent on foreign trade, but that dependence has grown steadily over the past generation. What are some aspects of daily American life where this robust trade pattern shows up most readily?

SOURCE: U.S. Bureau of the Census, "Top Trading Partners" December 2014.

"*Meritocracy worked for my grandfather, it worked for my father, and it's working for me.*"

MERITOCRACY AT WORK An important tension in American history is the conflict between the ideal of equal opportunity for all and the reality of inherited wealth and privilege. The unsuccessful efforts of the George W. Bush administration to eliminate the federal estate tax, which affected the inheritances of less than 1 percent of U.S. citizens, represented the latest round in the debate about the relationship between political democracy and inherited economic inequality. In a pure meritocracy, all citizens would be rewarded for their personal achievements rather than those of their parents or ancestors.

Barbara Smaller/The New Yorker Collection/www.cartoonbank.com

How does the commitment to individual property rights serve to limit equality of opportunity among the poorest Americans?

by the addition of second and third wage earners, especially women. Americans spent more than they earned. At the start of the new millennium, the average household had thirteen credit cards and carried $8,000 in debt on them, in addition to owing car and home mortgage payments. In 2005, the average personal savings rate even dropped below zero for a time.

Already wider in the United States than in any other industrialized nation, the distance between rich and poor continued to grow, whittling away at Americans' self-image as a middle-class society. The share of the national income going to the richest 1 percent nearly doubled in the last quarter of the twentieth century, while the share going to the bottom 80 percent shrank. More than 3 million Americans lived in gated communities in extremely affluent suburbs, while more than one in five American children grew up in poverty. In 2011, 43 million citizens sought emergency food assistance, and half of U.S. citizens fell into the official census categories of "poor" or "low-income."

The political system, which helps determine how wealth and opportunity are distributed in a society, seemed to offer little respite from the widening gap between haves and have-nots. The fraction of eligible citizens who made the effort to vote in presidential elections declined to just over half in 2004 and in off-year congressional elections to just over a third, with the likelihood of voting closely correlated to a person's affluence. The fierce partisanship, personal attacks, and culture of scandal that dominated American politics alienated many. Independents now outnumbered members of either major party. Citizens were also disillusioned by the blatant manner in which money came to dominate the political process. The average cost by 2010 of a successful Senate campaign at $10 million and a House campaign at $1.4 million meant that few but the wealthy could campaign for Congress. The U.S. Supreme Court, in the *Citizens United* decision (2010), then opened the floodgates still wider for private money to influence public elections, ruling that the government could not restrict political expenditures by corporations or unions.

30.3 The Stewardship of Natural Resources

What are the most important ways in which the environment is changing, and how might these affect American society?

No issue in the early twenty-first century was more global or more significant than the environment. Winds and waters do not respect political boundaries, nor do the materials borne on them. The condition of the natural environment affects all living creatures, yet the prevailing calculus of the market and private ownership does not apportion responsibility for its care. The free market system has no mechanism for offsetting, or even measuring, the costs of depleted natural resources. More than a generation ago, biologist Garrett Hardin warned of "the tragedy of the commons": that individuals' incentives to preserve the quality of their own property do not carry over to resources held in common. Litter is an obvious example, and air, water, and ground pollution are the more serious cases. Global warming—or climate change—is the issue looming over all others.

American culture had long celebrated human domination of the natural world and the benefits it brought, especially the growth in productivity that permitted living standards to improve dramatically across decades and centuries. At the same time, the rise of environmentalism and ecological understanding since 1960 offered a different way of imagining people's place on the earth.

30.3.1 Ecological Transformation Since 1900

Ecosystems are always dynamic, and changes in weather and Native American land use had reshaped the North American environment long before the followers of Christopher Columbus arrived on the continent. But European settlement and industrialization altered the face of the land in ways that would dumbfound a time traveler from the 1500s. Even a visitor from 1900 would be astonished by the intensity of human development of the land: vast cities with their sprawling suburbs and roads and highways everywhere. The key factor was population growth. Just as the number of people in the world quadrupled from 1.5 billion to 6 billion during the twentieth century, the population of the United States quadrupled from 75 million in 1900 to 321 million by 2015. Immigration and natural reproduction accounted for much of this, as did the much-longer average lifespan ushered in by antibiotics and antiviral vaccines.

The most dramatic changes in the land in the twentieth century resulted from the exploitation of wood, minerals, and water, particularly in the greater part of the country lying west of the Mississippi River where the population grew fifteen times larger. Commercial logging eliminated all but 3 percent of the old-growth forests of the fifty states. The clearcuts scarring the mountainsides and hillsides of the Pacific Northwest and Alaska told the tale, as did the erosion caused by the overgrazing by cattle on public lands managed by the Interior Department's Bureau of Land Management in Utah, New Mexico, and other western states. The Mining Act of 1872 still granted to private corporations the rights to such valuable minerals as gold and copper on public land for the remarkable nineteenth-century price of $2.50 per acre. Mining companies took full advantage of the opportunity, resulting in rock and chemical wastes piled in vast slagheaps and dumped in toxic holding ponds from Arizona to Montana. In the arid, but increasingly populated, western states, water was the most critical resource for population growth. Increasing diversions of the Rio Grande left that now misnamed river so dry that, by 2001, it failed to reach the Gulf of Mexico, trickling to a halt 50 feet short. Similarly, groundwater pumping for agricultural irrigation in the plains states and on the eastern slope of the Rocky Mountains was draining the vast underground Ogallala Aquifer at a rate that threatens to empty it within a few more decades.

American prosperity came at a price. The prodigious growth of the U.S. economy in the twentieth century depended on the consumption of ever-increasing amounts of energy, most of it from coal, oil, and natural gas. Though making up less than 5 percent of the world's population, Americans accounted for a quarter of the globe's energy consumption. They depended on other countries to provide much of it for them: in the early 2000s, the United States imported a quarter of its total energy needs and a half of its oil, primarily from Canada, Mexico, Saudi Arabia, and Venezuela. Hydraulic fracturing ("fracking") techniques provided a boost in domestic oil production beginning in 2008. But fossil fuels, such as coal and oil, could not be renewed; once burned, they were gone, and the world had a finite supply of such fuels. Americans were constructing a lifestyle that appeared unsustainable in the long run.

SOURCES OF CLEAN ENERGY, PALM SPRINGS, CALIFORNIA

The burning of fossil fuels for energy production has been identified as the largest human contributor to global warming, and the United States uses more energy than any other nation. In the twenty-first century, research and development have begun making clean, nonpolluting energy sources increasingly accessible and cost-efficient. Two of the most prominent clean energy sources, solar and wind, are on display in this installation of solar panels and windmills near Palm Springs, California.

© Nik Wheeler/Corbis

Are there other reasons, besides cost and accessibility, why Americans should or should not turn to cleaner sources of energy to meet their needs for power?

30.3.2 Pollution

The world's growing population was consuming five times as much fossil fuel in the early 2000s as in 1950, helping stimulate a steady rise in the earth's average temperatures. Americans caused 25 percent of carbon dioxide emissions, the largest contribution to the foremost environmental problem, global warming. In the summer of 2000, startled scientists found open water at the North Pole, a sight humans had never before seen. Greenhouse gases also contributed to a thinning of the ozone layer in the atmosphere, which enabled more of the sun's ultraviolet rays to reach the earth's surface and caused skin cancer rates to soar.

The internal combustion engine had long since surpassed coal burning as the leading cause of pollution. The United States produced and used more cars and trucks than any other nation. With minimal public transportation outside a handful of major cities, Americans were deeply committed to a car-dependent lifestyle. The highway infrastructure strained under the pressure of a 60 percent rise in the number of licensed drivers from 1970 to 2000, but only a 6 percent growth in total miles of roads. Negotiating traffic jams became a standard part of the daily lives of the majority of Americans who lived in the suburbs created by urban sprawl, especially around such cities as Los Angeles and Atlanta. Smog increasingly obscured the once-spectacular vistas of Arizona's Grand Canyon.

Daily life in the United States came to depend in countless ways on the use of synthetic chemicals, production of which was hundreds of times greater than it had been before World War II. More than 50,000 known toxic waste dumps in the United States leached poisonous chemicals and heavy metals into the soil and water. No synthetic product was more pervasive in the United States than plastic, a post-1945 material made from petroleum. But the most deadly and durable pollutants remained the radioactive wastes created by seven decades of nuclear development. No one yet knew how to dispose safely of millions of tons of materials impregnated with plutonium and other human-made radioactive elements. The U.S. nuclear weapons complex of some 3,000 sites put its often fatal touch on the lives of millions of Americans: uranium miners, military workers, soldiers used to observe test explosions at close range, and citizens living downwind from the Nevada Test Site in Nevada and Utah. The National Academy of Sciences concluded in 2000 that many of these sites would be permanent national sacrifice zones, toxic to humans for at least tens of thousands of years.

30.3.3 Environmentalism and Its Limitations

The ideas of most Americans about how to manage natural resources changed in the twentieth century. Environmental consciousness blossomed since the 1960s. Awareness of humans' connections with their broader ecological context led to significant reforms, such as the banning of carcinogenic pesticides and leaded gasoline, the cleaning up of polluted water in the Great Lakes, and the introduction of catalytic converters to reduce harmful emissions from automobile exhaust pipes and factory smokestacks. Recycling became common, and some dams were dismantled, freeing long-constricted rivers, such as the Penobscot in Maine and the Elwha in Washington State. Yet issues of public land management and pollution control remained among the most controversial problems in American public life.

The relationship of Americans to their natural environment continued to be paradoxical. By large majorities in public opinion polls, Americans supported strong antipollution laws and the preservation of public lands from economic development. They also told pollsters that they supported strong action against global warming. But in their daily lives, Americans consumed natural resources, especially gasoline, electricity, and water, at a rate unmatched by other societies. Measures that had reduced some of the nation's energy consumption since the 1970s were soon reversed: Congress revoked the national 55-mph speed limit in 1995, and ever larger cars, trucks, and especially sport utility vehicles reduced the average gas mileage of passenger vehicles thereafter.

30.4 The Expansion of American Popular Culture Abroad

Why is American culture attractive to many peoples elsewhere?

Just as the U.S. economy and American environmental problems could not be separated from the outside world, the nation's cultural life grew more closely tied to that of other nations at the dawn of the new millennium. American popular culture rather than armed strength seemed to have emerged as the leading edge of U.S. influence around the world. American themes and products stood out in an increasingly global society, although they were resisted by some abroad who preferred more local identities and traditions, often rooted in ethnicity or religious conviction.

30.4.1 A Culture of Diversity and Entertainment

Known for its informality and diversity, American culture proved powerfully attractive to peoples all over the world, partly because racial and ethnic diversity was more pronounced in the United States than in any other major nation. African Americans, Hispanic Americans, and Asian Americans all figured prominently in the popular realms of sports, music, and films. The Internet and television were the leading media for this culture of entertainment, beaming CNN, MTV, ESPN, and "reality" shows around the world. From jazz to rock 'n' roll to rap, American popular music spread across the globe, as did American jeans and sneakers, symbols of informality and comfort. Hollywood's movies dominated cinemas and DVD players everywhere, providing 85 percent of films screened in Europe.

Advertising grew in prominence as the central link between popular culture and the selling of products. Sports became steadily more commercialized. Postseason college football games began in 1985 to include the names of their corporate sponsors, creating such events as the Chick-fil-A Peach Bowl and the Weed Eater Independence Bowl. By the early 2000s, newspapers ranked bowl games—once hallowed for their own distinctive traditions—by the simple criterion of how much money sponsors paid to participating teams. In the 1990s and 2000s, "hoops" joined baseball as a popular U.S. export. National Basketball Association (NBA) games were telecast to more than 190 countries in more than forty languages. Sports also brought foreigners to the United States, as professional baseball and basketball teams began recruiting Latin American, European, African, and Asian athletes.

30.4.2 U.S. Influence Abroad Since the Cold War

Cultural influences flowed both ways for Americans, with immigrants in particular bringing with them traditions and perspectives that refreshed the cultural mix of life in the United States. Japanese comics, Thai cuisine, Cuban salsa music, and soccer helped shape daily routines for many Americans. But increased trade and communication since the end of the Cold War above all enabled the further spread of American popular culture. American-accented English straddled the globe, the language of international commerce and of a large majority of postings on the Internet. The informality and individualism of the Internet made it seem quintessentially American in style. The U.S. dollar remained one of the world's two primary trading currencies, along with the euro, and the dollar served as the de facto and even the de jure currency of several other nations.

America's most popular eatery served 69 million customers a day at its 36,000 franchises across the globe. McDonald's Golden Arches appeared everywhere, from Japan and France to Russia and China. Even Mecca in Saudi Arabia, Islam's holiest site and the destination of millions of Muslim pilgrims, had a McDonald's. The company generated half of its revenues from non-U.S. operations.

America's cultural influence went beyond material interests. American religious missionaries worked in poor countries around the world, combining their spiritual mission with a commitment to improving daily life in concrete ways involving health care, education, and agriculture. Pentecostalists gained millions of converts in Latin America since the 1970s, and mainstream denominations, such as Lutherans, Epis-copalians, and Roman Catholics, saw their numbers rise sharply in Africa. The most fully home-grown American religion was especially active in proselytizing abroad: the Church of Jesus Christ of Latter Day Saints (Mormons), headquartered in Salt Lake City. The Mormons had at least 5 million members in the United States and another 5 million worldwide.

Another channel for American influence abroad was the U.S. military. The United States retained its military superiority, with a defense budget as large as that of the next ten biggest military powers combined. When provoked, as by the September 11 attacks, American forces could wield extraordinary power and quickly reshape the histories of other nations, as demonstrated in Afghanistan and Iraq. But occupying other nations and charting the long-term future of other societies proved difficult. Instead, the expansion of American culture abroad seemed a safer and more effective way to influence other nations.

30.4.3 Resistance to American Popular Culture

Like Christian, Jewish, and Hindu fundamentalists, all of whom grew prominent in the final decades of the twentieth century, Muslim fundamentalists rejected the radical egalitarianism and the unbridled pursuit of pleasure so prevalent in American popular culture. The relative equality of women and the lack of respect for traditional social and religious hierarchies seemed to them emblems of American decadence, as the Islamist rulers of Afghanistan—the Taliban—demonstrated in the 1990s in their brutal repression of women's rights. During the 1991 Persian Gulf War, Saudi Arabian officials tried to isolate U.S. troops from Saudi citizens, fearing the effects of contact with such diverse forces as female soldiers, bawdiness, Christianity, and American music and television.

The demise of communist regimes in Russia and eastern Europe opened the gates to a flood of Western influences and brought the opportunities and inequalities of a suddenly privatized economy. State-provided safety nets disappeared, class differences widened, women's economic status declined, and the old Communist parties regained some popularity among voters frightened by the instabilities of American-style capitalism. Western Europeans also remained ambivalent about the spread of American values and lifestyles. Although many of them, especially among the young, found American culture attractive and learned English in record numbers, traditionalists who were proud of their own national culture took a dim view of such innovations as fast food.

Other nations sometimes found the U.S. government overbearing and resented its unparalleled military power. Rapidly modernizing China, the world's most populous country, was a growing and ambitious rival to the United States in Asia, even as the two nations became major trading partners.

Two opposing trends characterized world affairs. One consisted of the unifying forces of economic internationalism and globalization, carrying with them a tide of American-dominated cultural styles. The other was made up of the resisting forces of political and ethnic nationalism. A world more tightly integrated in economic ways was at the same time divided by ethnic conflicts. As people around the world felt themselves increasingly sucked into the vortex of a powerful global economy that they could not control, many responded by renewing their allegiances to older, more local traditions. Ethnic, religious, and national identities often offered more meaningful alternatives to a purely economic identity as consumers.

30.5 Identity in Contemporary America

Which are the most important kinds of identity in the United States?

The 2000 and 2010 U.S. Censuses revealed a society in the midst of change. Americans have long been known as a particularly restless and mobile people, and one out of five changed residences every year. The post-1965 wave of immigrants continued to rise (and foreign adoptions rose dramatically), bringing in millions of new Americans of Asian heritage. Latinos surpassed African Americans as the nation's largest minority. This latest surge in immigration boosted the number of Roman Catholics and Buddhists as American society remained the most openly religious—still primarily Protestant—of the industrialized nations. Geographically, Americans lived farther south and west than earlier generations, as none of the twenty fastest-growing states were in the Northeast or Midwest. And more than half of Americans lived in suburbs.

30.5.1 Social Change and Abiding Discrimination

One of the most striking changes in American society over the past five decades has been the desegregation of public life. Latinos and Asian Americans became much more numerous in the United States, and African Americans emerged from the enforced separation of Jim Crow into greater prominence. Roughly one-third of blacks were middle-class, and thousands won election to local, state, and national political offices. Black Americans became central in the nation's cultural life in music, literature, theater, and sports. By 2001, even a new president from the Republican party—known since 1964 for its lack of support from black voters—appointed two African Americans to direct the nation's foreign relations: Secretary of State Colin Powell and National Security Adviser (and later Secretary of State) Condoleezza Rice. In 2008, voters elected the first black president, Barack Obama, and reelected him four years later. Workplaces were racially integrated to an extent that would have been hard to imagine in 1950, and interracial marriages became significantly more common by the first decades of the twenty-first century.

Table 30.3 THE ELECTION OF 2012

Candidate	Political Party	Popular Vote (%)	Electoral Vote
Barack Obama	Democratic	51.1	332
Mitt Romney	Republican	47.2	206

SOURCE: Historical Election Results, Electoral College, National Archives and Records Administration

The lives of women in the United States also changed dramatically during the last half of the twentieth century. Most worked outside the home, from jobs in the service and manufacturing sectors to careers in the professions and politics. By the early 2000s, women made up one-half of the students in the nation's medical schools and law schools. Their presence in leading political positions ranged from local officials to more than a dozen U.S. senators, three U.S. Supreme Court justices, a U.S. attorney general, and three U.S. secretaries of state. The passage of Title IX in 1972,

Figure 30.2 SELF-DESCRIBED RELIGIOUS AFFILIATION IN THE UNITED STATES, 2014

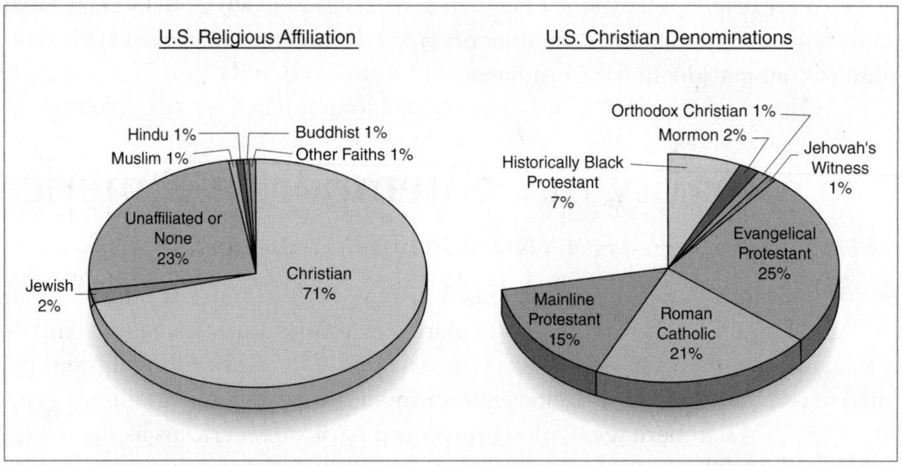

The most noticeable change in American religious life since 2000 has been the growth both of the unaffiliated religious and the religious "nones" and the shrinking proportion of mainline Protestants and Roman Catholics among U.S. Christian demoninations.

NOTE: Data in chart at left do not not sum to 71 owing to rounding.

SOURCE: Pew Research Center, "Religious Landscape Study," 2014.

prohibiting gender discrimination in school programs that received federal money, created a tidal wave of social change for American girls. In 1971, one in twenty-seven girls played high school sports; by 1998, the ratio was one in three. Sports programs and teams for girls comparable to those for boys nourished a new generation of American women for whom athletic competition and achievement were the norm rather than the exception.

In similar fashion, many gays and lesbians experienced rapid change in their social, political, and cultural status in American life. While decisions about making one's sexual orientation public remained complicated and deeply personal, homosexuals in the 2000s and 2010s found a much more accepting society than that of a generation earlier. Public expressions of homophobia, long common, now produced swift and widespread condemnation. The U.S. Supreme Court decriminalized gay sexuality in 2003 and, in its decision in *Obergefell v. Hodges* (2015), ruled that marriage was a fundamental right of all Americans, regardless of their sexual orientation. Gays and lesbians now served openly in the U.S. military. Young Americans, in particular, tended to find the anti-gay prejudices of previous generations mysterious and even ridiculous.

These improvements for the majority of Americans who were not heterosexual white men jostled against abiding forms of discrimination and inequality. Violence and the threat of violence against homosexuals, people of color, and particularly women (primarily domestic violence at the hands of husbands and partners) remained very real, but most prejudices found more subtle avenues of expression. Working women continued to average about three-quarters of the wages of working men. Many employers, police officers, store owners, bank loan officers, and others in positions of authority treated African Americans and Latinos with greater suspicion than they did other citizens, a practice that became known as racial profiling. Poverty and unemployment disproportionately affected black communities and families. Residential neighborhoods and public schools remained largely segregated by race, and the deeply symbolic Confederate flag still occupied a place of public honor in some southern states.

Native Americans shared this combination of improving status and continuing discrimination. Their numbers were reviving, from a mere 250,000 in 1900 to 2 million in 2000. A series of federal court decisions in the 1970s and 1980s strengthened Indians' "unique and limited" sovereignty over the tribal reservations, which constituted 2 percent of U.S. land. Starting with the Iroquois of upstate New York in 1970, several eastern Indian nations successfully sued state and federal governments for the return of parts of lands that had been illegally seized from them in the past, or for compensation. Beginning in the 1990s, casino revenues brought much-needed resources to a number of Indian nations. At the same time, the process of assimilation continued as a majority of Indians lived in urban areas and were married to non-Indians. Reservations suffered from severe unemployment rates and remained some of the poorest communities in the country, dependent on federal assistance for food and other basic necessities. Anti-Indian sentiments continued to surface at times in states as diverse as Montana, Wisconsin, Arizona, and New York.

30.5.2 Still an Immigrant Society

Economic opportunity and individual liberty still lured millions of people from other nations to the United States at the start of the new millennium. In 2009, about a million arrived legally each year, and another 300,000 entered without official papers. For the first time since the 1930s, one in seven Americans had been born abroad; in New York City the ratio was one in four. In 2004, 15 percent came from Europe, 33 percent from Asia, and 43 percent from Latin America and the Caribbean. Like Italy in 1900, Mexico became, in 2000, the most important single source of new Americans. The demographic transition of California from a white majority in 2000 to a more diverse ethnic and racial mix like that of Hawaii symbolized the nation's turn to the south and west, even as the aspirations and work habits of the newcomers remained very much the same as those of their European predecessors. Only the hardiest and most motivated people made the difficult, emotionally wrenching, and often dangerous move to the United States.

Map 30.2 STATE OF SAME-SEX MARRIAGE IN THE STATES

Homosexual rights progressed swiftly after the first gay rights march in 1970 and after the American Psychiatric Association's 1973 decision to drop homosexuality from its list of mental disorders. Since Vermont passed the first state civil union law in 1999, the U.S. Supreme Court has handed down two landmark decisions affecting the status of gay and lesbian Americans. In 2003 the Court overturned remaining state laws against sexual relations between consenting same-sex adults, and in 2015 the Court ruled that marriage was a fundamental right of all Americans, regardless of their sexual orientation. Massachusetts became the first state to allow same-sex couples to marry, in 2004, and, in 2011, the U.S. military enacted a new policy of allowing gays and lesbians to serve openly in the armed forces, just like their heterosexual peers.

The influence of younger Americans, who are much less inclined than older Americans to discriminate against gays and lesbians, has likely been instrumental in the rapid shift in the legalization of marriage equality over the last few years.

SOURCE: Pew Research Center, "Same-Sex Marriage by State," June 26, 2015.

Interpreting History

National Academies of Sciences, Engineering, and Medicine: Immigration in Contemporary America (2015)

> "There are 41 million immigrants and 37.1 million U.S.-born children of immigrants in the United States today."

One of the most prominent and sometimes controversial features of contemporary American society is the presence of large numbers of recent immigrants, particularly people arriving from Latin America and Asia. In the twenty-first century, Mexico has been the source of the greatest number of people coming to the United States. The U.S.–Mexican border represents one of the world's starkest divides in terms of wealth, which explains much of the motivation for migration. Roughly three-quarters of Mexican immigrants arrive legally, but the other quarter arrives by more difficult routes and without legal status, leaving them in precarious circumstances. For a variety of reasons, immigration from Mexico has slowed in recent years. Researchers project that the most important sources of future migration to the United States may be nations in Asia.

Immigration and human population movement have always been part of U.S. history. Although many Americans welcome and even admire new arrivals, others take a more skeptical view. At the heart of recurring political debates about U.S. immigration policy has been the issue of integration, or assimilation. How well do immigrants fit into American society?

Recent scholarly evidence on this issue comes from the National Academies of Sciences, Engineering, and Medicine. The National Academies finds that recent immigrants seem to integrate into American life just as previous immigrants had but doing so, ironically, does not always leave them better off.

As immigrants and their descendants become integrated into U.S. society, many aspects of their lives improve, including measurable outcomes such as educational attainment, occupational distribution, income, and language ability, but their well-being declines in the areas of health, crime, and family patterns, says a new report

from the National Academies of Sciences, Engineering, and Medicine. . . .

There are 41 million immigrants and 37.1 million U.S.-born children of immigrants in the United States today. Together, the first and second generations account for one-quarter of the U.S. population. . . .

In comparison with native-born Americans, the report says, immigrants are less likely to die from cardiovascular disease and all cancers, and they experience fewer chronic health conditions, have lower infant mortality and obesity rates, and have a longer life expectancy. However, over time and generations, these advantages decline as their health status converges with that of the native-born population.

Other measures of individual and community well-being show the same pattern, the committee found. Neighborhoods with greater concentrations of immigrants have much lower rates of crime and violence than comparable nonimmigrant neighborhoods. Foreign-born men age 18–39 are incarcerated at one-fourth the rate of native-born American men of the same age. However, in the second and third generations, crime rates increase and resemble that of the general population of native-born Americans.

Similarly, immigrant divorce rates and out-of-wedlock birth rates start off much lower than native-born Americans, but over time and generations, they rise toward those for native-born families. This indicates that immigrant and second-generation children across all major ethnic and racial groups are more likely to live in families with two parents than are third-generation children. . . .

Despite large differences in starting points among first-generation immigrant groups, their children meet or exceed the schooling level of typical third-generation and higher native-born Americans. . . .

Available evidence indicates that today's immigrants are learning English at the same rate or faster than earlier waves of

GROWTH WITHOUT IMMIGRANTS? More than 50 million citizens and residents of the United States come from Hispanic backgrounds. They include a vast diversity of socioeconomic circumstances, from poor agricultural laborers to middle-class suburbanites to wealthy elites. Fourteen percent of U.S. military personnel are Latino, as are two U.S. governors, Susana Martinez (R-NM) and Brian Sandoval (R-NV).

ZUMA Wire Service/Alamy

What kinds of concerns does a large influx of immigrants create for current citizens, and what kinds of benefits do immigrants bring?

immigrants. However, the U.S. education system is currently not equipped to handle the nearly 5 million English-language learners in the K-12 system—9 percent of all students—and this may stymie the integration prospects of many immigrants. . . .

Immigrants are more likely to be poor than the native-born, even though their labor force participation rates are higher and, on average, they work longer hours. The poverty rate for the foreign-born was 18.4 percent in 2013, compared with 13.8 percent for the native-born. Among adults, the poverty rate overall declines over generations, from over 18 percent in the first generation to 13.6 percent in the second generation and 11.5 percent in the third. . . .

Over time, most immigrants and their descendants gradually become less segregated from native-born whites and more dispersed across regions, cities, and neighborhoods. . . .

Questions for Discussion

1. In which ways is the impact of moving to the United States positive for foreigners, and in which ways is it negative?

2. How might the National Academies findings help to inform public discussions of U.S. policy toward immigrants?

SOURCE: "Report Finds Immigrants Come to Resemble Native-Born Americans Over Time, But Integration Not Always Linked to Greater Well-Being for Immigrants" (News press release, National Academies of Sciences, Engineering, and Medicine, September 21, 2015).

Americans responded to the wave of newcomers with an ambivalence common in previous periods of high immigration. Many in the working class feared competition from highly motivated laborers accustomed to much lower wages. Many elites worried whether cultural diversity might weaken national unity. Conservative political leaders promoted new restrictions and stronger border patrols, particularly in Arizona with its high number of immigrants from neighboring Mexico.

Mostly, Americans got used to having more immigrants around. Americans cheered for the one in four major league baseball players who were born in Latin America or had parents from there, and they became accustomed to the high number of Asian Americans in college classrooms. Many churches worked to help new arrivals adjust to life in the United States. Above all, American employers depended on immigrant workers to keep the nation's powerful economy afloat—to pick its fruits and vegetables, tend its young children, construct its new buildings, and work in its factories.

Conclusion

What held Americans together as they set off into the twenty-first century was a common loyalty to a set of ideas about economic opportunities and individual liberties. Unlike such nations as Germany and Israel, where citizenship was extended automatically only to people of a certain ethnicity, the United States awarded citizenship to all those who were born within its borders, regardless of ethnicity or race. Those born elsewhere became citizens on the basis not of their past lineage but of their future commitments—of their newly sworn loyalty to the U.S. Constitution, with its guarantees of freedom and its responsibilities of citizenship. In a vast society of multiple political and cultural beliefs, the scope of specific freedoms and the nature of individual responsibilities inevitably remained matters of ongoing tension and conflict. Nonetheless, the United States continued to address most of its problems through an orderly legal system, in contrast to the ethnic and religious strife marking so many of the world's nations.

Americans will face some basic challenges in the near future. Will the currently increasing inequality in American society—in terms of income, wealth, and power—weaken the bonds that hold the nation together? Policies regarding taxes, Social Security, health care, and welfare will help determine if most Americans will continue to see themselves as middle-class members of a mostly middle-class society. The process of globalization will not make this any easier. The tighter integration of the U.S. economy and the world economy has thus far helped create great wealth, but that wealth has been distributed very unevenly among Americans. Who has how much wealth and influence will remain a crucial determinant of the nation's future.

Another challenge will be the use and distribution of natural resources, which will almost certainly become more contentious issues. As national and world populations continue to increase, so will the demand for oil, water, and timber. How will crowding and greater competition affect the quality of American life? How long can American society remain centered on the automobile and its emphasis on individual mobility? Behind all environmental issues looms the largest issue of all: global warming and how it may reshape societies around the world.

The expansion of American influence abroad will continue to create challenges as well as benefits for Americans. U.S. military, economic, political, and cultural leadership is clear. But the enormous reservoir of goodwill toward the United States that was evident around the world through much of the twentieth century has been draining rapidly in recent years. U.S. military operations in Afghanistan and Iraq convinced millions of peoples in those regions and elsewhere, rightly or wrongly, that the United States is an aggressive nation bent on dominating the world in general and humbling Islamic nations in particular. Whether the United States will gain more than it loses by its military engagements abroad remains an open question.

And finally, how well will Americans respond to the greater complexity of their society as their ranks come to include larger numbers of immigrants, non-Christians, people of color, open homosexuals, and people of other identities not previously considered mainstream? In comparison to most other cultures, American society has been unusually inclusive of people of diverse backgrounds and beliefs. Whether it will continue to be so will shape, as much as any other factor, the future of the United States.

Chapter Review

30.1 Politics in the New Millennium

What were the Bush administration's priorities, and how were they affected by the attacks on September 11, 2001?
President George W. Bush enacted large tax cuts in 2001 and 2003, whose primary effect was to benefit wealthy Americans. He focused on the private sector of the U.S. economy, particularly the oil and gas industry, not the public sector. The September 11 attacks turned his administration from almost isolationist to aggressive in its posture of response to Afghanistan and in waging preemptive war in Iraq.

30.2 The American Place in a Global Economy

How did globalization affect Americans' lives?
Globalization was a two-edged sword for most working Americans. As consumers, they enjoyed greater competition among producers and cheaper prices. As workers, they suffered from the same competitive forces and the lower wages it brought. Business owners also found both greater opportunity and greater competition. Better-educated citizens tended to benefit the most from globalization.

30.3 The Stewardship of Natural Resources

What are the most important ways in which the environment is changing, and how might these affect American society?
National and global population growth drive greater demand for the use of natural resources, depleting nonrenewables. Industrialization in formerly agrarian societies, such as China and India, also create new demand for water, oil, and other resources, while also increasing pollution. Climate change is the largest threat of all. The sprawling cities of the American Southwest are likely to experience the first serious shortage of a natural resource—water.

30.4 The Expansion of American Popular Culture Abroad

Why is American culture attractive to many peoples elsewhere?
American popular culture tends to be multicultural, inclusive, and democratic in style. It also tends to promote the value of economic success. The prevalence of U.S. movies and television and the prominence of U.S. culture on the Internet make American life and values readily accessible to most of the world.

30.5 Identity in Contemporary America

Which are the most important kinds of identity in the United States?
Americans base their personal identity on many factors, including class, religion, region, sex, race, sexual orientation, and politics. These factors blend together in a wide variety of ways. What Americans tend to have in common is a commitment to personal liberty, democratic politics, a diverse and inclusive society, and an optimism about the future.

Timeline

2001	Al Qaeda terrorists attack World Trade Center and Pentagon	**2007**	Economic recession begins
		2008	Barack H. Obama elected president
	U.S. forces attack Afghanistan and overthrow Taliban regime	**2009**	Sonia Sotomayor becomes first Hispanic justice of the U.S. Supreme Court
2003	U.S. and allied forces invade and occupy Iraq	**2011**	Last U.S. combat troops leave Iraq
	Supreme Court legalizes gay sexual conduct in *Lawrence v. Texas*		U.S. Navy Seals kill Osama bin Laden in Pakistan
2005	Hurricane Katrina devastates New Orleans		

Glossary

globalization The long-term process that continues to tie the world's regions more closely together economically and culturally through more unified systems of trade, travel, and communication.

al Qaeda A secret extremist organization established in the early 1990s that used terrorist tactics in pursuit of a backward-looking, absolutist form of Islamist government.

Osama bin Laden A wealthy, charismatic exile from Saudi Arabia who created al Qaeda, masterminded the September 11, 2001, attacks, and was eventually killed by U.S. Navy Seals in Pakistan in 2011.

global warming The accelerating process of climate change, driven in large part by human population growth and the burning of fossil fuels such as coal and oil.

Hurricane Katrina The ferocious storm that swept on to the Gulf Coast in August 2005, killing over 1,800 people, primarily in Louisiana and Mississippi, and leaving much of New Orleans under water. The storm prompted a slow and ineffective response by the federal government under President George W. Bush.

Affordable Care Act (ACA) Also known as Obamacare, this legislation, signed into law in 2010, was the largest overhaul of the U.S. health care system since the creation of Medicare and Medicaid in 1965. It sharply reduced the number of uninsured Americans and ended the previous practice of insurance companies charging higher premiums on the basis of preexisting conditions.

Internet A worldwide system of computer networks, established in the early 1990s, that allows for rapid global information transmission.

free trade A system of economic relations characterized by the buying and selling of goods and services between nations with few or no taxes or tariffs to hinder that exchange.

References: Essential Documents and Data

The Declaration of Independence

In Congress, July 4, 1776

The Unanimous Declaration of the Thirteen United States of America

When, in the course of human events, it becomes necessary for one people to dissolve the political bonds which have connected them with another, and to assume, among the powers of the earth, the separate and equal station to which the laws of nature and of nature's God entitle them, a decent respect to the opinions of mankind requires that they should declare the causes which impel them to the separation.

We hold these truths to be self-evident: That all men are created equal; that they are endowed by their Creator with certain unalienable rights; that among these are life, liberty, and the pursuit of happiness; that, to secure these rights, governments are instituted among men, deriving their just powers from the consent of the governed; that whenever any form of government becomes destructive of these ends, it is the right of the people to alter or to abolish it, and to institute new government, laying its foundation on such principles, and organizing its powers in such form, as to them shall seem most likely to effect their safety and happiness. Prudence, indeed, will dictate that governments long established should not be changed for light and transient causes; and accordingly all experience hath shown that mankind are more disposed to suffer, while evils are sufferable, than to right themselves by abolishing the forms to which they are accustomed. But when a long train of abuses and usurpations, pursuing invariably the same object, evinces a design to reduce them under absolute despotism, it is their right, it is their duty, to throw off such government, and to provide new guards for their future security. Such has been the patient sufferance of these colonies; and such is now the necessity which constrains them to alter their former systems of government. The history of the present King of Great Britain is a history of repeated injuries and usurpations, all having in direct object the establishment of an absolute tyranny over these states. To prove this, let facts be submitted to a candid world.

He has refused his assent to laws, the most wholesome and necessary for the public good.

He has forbidden his governors to pass laws of immediate and pressing importance, unless suspended in their operation till his assent should be obtained; and, when so suspended, he has utterly neglected to attend to them.

He has refused to pass other laws for the accommodation of large districts of people, unless those people would relinquish the right of representation in the legislature, a right inestimable to them, and formidable to tyrants only.

He has called together legislative bodies at places unusual, uncomfortable, and distant from the depository of their public records, for the sole purpose of fatiguing them into compliance with his measures.

He has dissolved representative houses repeatedly, for opposing, with manly firmness, his invasions on the rights of the people.

He has refused for a long time, after such dissolutions, to cause others to be elected; whereby the legislative powers, incapable of annihilation, have returned to the people at large for their exercise; the state remaining, in the mean time, exposed to all the dangers of invasions from without and convulsions within.

He has endeavored to prevent the population of these states; for that purpose obstructing the laws for naturalization of foreigners; refusing to pass others to encourage their migration hither, and raising the conditions of new appropriations of lands.

He has obstructed the administration of justice, by refusing his assent to laws for establishing judiciary powers.

He has made judges dependent on his will alone, for the tenure of their offices, and the amount and payment of their salaries.

He has erected a multitude of new offices, and sent hither swarms of officers to harass our people and eat out their substance.

He has kept among us, in times of peace, standing armies, without the consent of our legislatures.

He has affected to render the military independent of, and superior to, the civil power.

He has combined with others to subject us to a jurisdiction foreign to our constitution, and unacknowledged by our laws, giving his assent to their acts of pretended legislation:

For quartering large bodies of armed troops among us;

For protecting them, by a mock trial, from punishment for any murder which they should commit on the inhabitants of these states;

For cutting off our trade with all parts of the world;

For imposing taxes on us without our consent;

For depriving us, in many cases, of the benefits of trial by jury;

For transporting us beyond seas, to be tried for pretended offenses;

For abolishing the free system of English laws in a neighboring province, establishing therein an arbitrary government, and enlarging its boundaries, so as to render it at once an example and fit instrument for introducing the same absolute rule into these colonies;

For taking away our charters, abolishing our most valuable laws, and altering fundamentally the forms of our governments;

For suspending our own legislatures, and declaring themselves invested with power to legislate for us in all cases whatsoever.

He has abdicated government here, by declaring us out of his protection and waging war against us.

He has plundered our seas, ravaged our coasts, burned our towns, and destroyed the lives of our people.

He is at this time transporting large armies of foreign mercenaries to complete the works of death, desolation, and tyranny already begun with circumstances of cruelty and perfidy scarcely paralleled in the most barbarous ages, and totally unworthy the head of a civilized nation.

He has constrained our fellow-citizens, taken captive on the high seas, to bear arms against their country, to become the executioners of their friends and brethren, or to fall themselves by their hands.

He has excited domestic insurrection among us, and has endeavored to bring on the inhabitants of our frontiers the merciless Indian savages, whose known rule of warfare is an undistinguished destruction of all ages, sexes, and conditions.

In every stage of these oppressions we have petitioned for redress in the most humble terms; our repeated petitions have been answered only by repeated injury. A prince, whose character is thus marked by every act which may define a tyrant, is unfit to be the ruler of a free people.

Nor have we been wanting in our attentions to our British brethren. We have warned them, from time to time, of attempts by their legislature to extend an unwarrantable jurisdiction over us. We have reminded them of the circumstances of our emigration and settlement here. We have appealed to their native justice and magnanimity; and we have conjured them, by the ties of our common kindred, to disavow these usurpations, which would inevitably interrupt our connections and correspondence. They, too, have been deaf to the voice of justice and of consanguinity. We must, therefore, acquiesce in the necessity which denounces our separation, and hold them, as we hold the rest of mankind, enemies in war, in peace friends.

We, therefore, the representatives of the United States of America, in General Congress assembled, appealing to the Supreme Judge of the world for the rectitude of our intentions, do, in the name and by the authority of the good people of these colonies, solemnly publish and declare, that these United Colonies are, and of right ought to be, FREE AND INDEPENDENT STATES; that they are absolved from all allegiance to the British crown, and that all political connection between them and the state of Great Britain is, and ought to be, totally dissolved; and that, as free and independent states, they have full power to levy war, conclude peace, contract alliances, establish commerce, and do all other acts and things which independent states may of right do. And for the support of this declaration, with a firm reliance on the protection of Divine Providence, we mutually pledge to each other our lives, our fortunes, and our sacred honor.

John Hancock

New Hampshire	*New Jersey*	*Maryland*	*South Carolina*
Josiah Bartlett	Richard Stockton	Samuel Chase	Edward Rutledge
William Whipple	John Witherspoon	William Paca	Thomas Heyward Jr.
Matthew Thornton	Francis Hopkinson	Thomas Stone	Thomas Lynch Jr.
	John Hart	Charles Carroll of Carrollton	Arthur Middleton
Massachusetts	Abraham Clark		
John Adams		*North Carolina*	*Connecticut*
Samuel Adams	*Pennsylvania*	William Hooper	Roger Sherman
Robert Treat Paine	Robert Morris	Joseph Hewes	Samuel Huntington
Elbridge Gerry	Benjamin Rush	John Penn	William Williams
	Benjamin Franklin		Oliver Wolcott
New York	John Morton	*Virginia*	
William Floyd	George Clymer	George Wythe	*Georgia*
Philip Livingston	James Smith	Richard Henry Lee	Button Gwinnett
Francis Lewis	George Taylor	Thomas Jefferson	Lyman Hall
Lewis Morris	James Wilson	Benjamin Harrison	George Walton
	George Ross	Thomas Nelson Jr.	
Rhode Island		Francis Lightfoot Lee	
Stephen Hopkins	*Delaware*	Carter Braxton	
William Ellery	Caeser Rodney		
	George Read		
	Thomas McKean		

SOURCE: Records of the Continental and Confederation Congresses and the Constitutional Convention, 1774–1789, Record Group 360, National Archives and Records Administration

The Articles of Confederation

Between the States of New Hampshire, Massachusetts Bay, Rhode Island and Providence Plantations, Connecticut, New York, New Jersey, Pennsylvania, Delaware, Maryland, Virginia, North Carolina, South Carolina, Georgia

Article 1

The stile of this confederacy shall be "The United States of America."

Article 2

Each State retains its sovereignty, freedom and independence, and every power, jurisdiction, and right, which is not by this confederation expressly delegated to the United States, in Congress assembled.

Article 3

The said states hereby severally enter into a firm league of friendship with each other for their common defence, the security of their liberties and their mutual and general welfare; binding themselves to assist each other against all force offered to, or attacks made upon them, or any of them, on account of religion, sovereignty, trade, or any other pretence whatever.

Article 4

The better to secure and perpetuate mutual friendship and intercourse among the people of the different states in this union, the free inhabitants of each of these states, paupers, vagabonds, and fugitives from justice excepted, shall be entitled to all privileges and immunities of free citizens in the several states; and the people of each State shall have free ingress and regress to and from any other State, and shall enjoy therein all the privileges of trade and commerce, subject to the same duties, impositions, and restrictions, as the inhabitants thereof respectively; provided, that such restrictions shall not extend so far as to prevent the removal of property, imported into any State, to any other State of which the owner is an inhabitant; provided also, that no imposition, duties, or restriction, shall be laid by any State on the property of the United States, or either of them.

If any person guilty of, or charged with treason, felony, or other high misdemeanor in any State, shall flee from justice and be found in any of the United States, he shall, upon demand of the governor or executive power of the State from which he fled, be delivered up and removed to the State having jurisdiction of his offence.

Full faith and credit shall be given in each of these states to the records, acts, and judicial proceedings of the courts and magistrates of every other State.

Article 5

For the more convenient management of the general interests of the United States, delegates shall be annually appointed, in such manner as the legislature of each State shall direct, to meet in Congress, on the 1st Monday in November in every year, with a power reserved to each State to recall its delegates, or any of them, at any time within the year, and to send others in their stead for the remainder of the year.

No State shall be represented in Congress by less than two, nor by more than seven members; and no person shall be capable of being a delegate for more than three years in any term of six years; nor shall any person, being a delegate, be capable of holding any office under the United States, for which he, or any other for his benefit, receives any salary, fees, or emolument of any kind.

Each State shall maintain its own delegates in a meeting of the states, and while they act as members of the committee of the states.

In determining questions in the United States, in Congress assembled, each State shall have one vote.

Freedom of speech and debate in Congress shall not be impeached or questioned in any court or place out of Congress: and the members of Congress shall be protected in their persons from arrests and imprisonments, during the time of their going to and from, and attendance on Congress, except for treason, felony, or breach of the peace.

Article 6

No State, without the consent of the United States, in Congress assembled, shall send any embassy to, or receive any embassy from, or enter into any conference, agreement, alliance, or treaty with any king, prince, or state; nor shall any person, holding any office of profit or trust under the United States, or any of them, accept of any present, emolument, office or title, of any kind whatever, from any king, prince, or foreign state; nor shall the United States, in Congress assembled, or any of them, grant any title of nobility.

No two or more states shall enter into any treaty, confederation, or alliance, whatever, between them, without the consent of the United States, in Congress assembled, specifying accurately the purposes for which the same is to be entered into, and how long it shall continue.

No State shall lay any imposts or duties which may interfere with any stipulations in treaties entered into by the United States, in Congress assembled, with any king, prince, or state, in pursuance of any treaties already proposed by Congress to the courts of France and Spain.

No vessels of war shall be kept up in time of peace by any State, except such number only as shall be deemed necessary by the United States, in Congress assembled, for the defence of such State or its trade; nor shall any body of forces be kept up by any State, in time of peace, except such number only as, in the judgment of the United States, in Congress assembled, shall be deemed requisite to garrison the forts necessary for the defence of such State; but every State shall always keep up a well regulated and disciplined militia, sufficiently armed and accoutred, and shall provide, and constantly have ready for use, in public stores, a due number of field pieces and tents, and a proper quantity of arms, ammunition and camp equipage.

No State shall engage in any war without the consent of the United States, in Congress assembled, unless such State be actually invaded by enemies, or shall have received certain advice of a resolution being formed by some nation of Indians to invade such State, and the danger is so imminent as not to admit of a delay till the United States, in Congress assembled, can be consulted; nor shall any State grant commissions to any ships or vessels of war, nor letters of marque or reprisal, except it be after a declaration of war by the United States, in Congress assembled, and then only against the kingdom or state, and the subjects thereof, against which war has been so declared, and under such regulations as shall be established by the United States, in Congress assembled, unless such States be infested by pirates, in which case vessels of war may be fitted out for that occasion, and kept so long as the danger shall continue, or until the United States, in Congress assembled, shall determine otherwise.

Article 7

When land forces are raised by any State for the common defence, all officers of or under the rank of colonel, shall be appointed by the legislature of each State respectively, by whom such forces shall be raised, or in such manner as such State shall direct; and all vacancies shall be filled up by the State which first made the appointment.

Article 8

All charges of war and all other expences, that shall be incurred for the common defence or general welfare, and allowed by the United States, in Congress assembled, shall be defrayed out of a common treasury, which shall be supplied by the several states, in proportion to the value of all land within each State, granted to or surveyed for any person, as such land and the buildings and improvements thereon shall be estimated according to such mode as the United States, in Congress assembled, shall, from time to time, direct and appoint.

The taxes for paying that proportion shall be laid and levied by the authority and direction of the legislatures of the several states, within the time agreed upon by the United States, in Congress assembled.

Article 9

The United States, in Congress assembled, shall have the sole and exclusive right and power of determining on peace and war, except in the cases mentioned in the 6th article; of sending and receiving ambassadors; entering into treaties and alliances, provided that no treaty of commerce shall be made, whereby the legislative power of the respective states shall be restrained from imposing such imposts and duties on foreigners as their own people are subjected to, or from prohibiting the exportation or importation of any species of goods or commodities whatsoever; of establishing rules for deciding, in all cases, what captures on land or water shall be legal, and in what manner prizes, taken by land or naval forces in the service of the United States, shall be divided or appropriated; of granting letters of marque and reprisal in times of peace; appointing courts for the trial of piracies and felonies committed on the high seas, and establishing courts for receiving and determining, finally, appeals in all cases of captures; provided, that no member of Congress shall be appointed a judge of any of the said courts.

The United States, in Congress assembled, shall also be the last resort on appeal in all disputes and differences now subsisting, or that hereafter may arise between two or more states concerning boundary, jurisdiction or any other cause whatever; which authority shall always be exercised in the manner following: whenever the legislative or executive authority, or lawful agent of any State, in controversy with another, shall present a petition to Congress, stating the matter in question, and praying for a hearing, notice thereof shall be given, by order of Congress, to the legislative or executive authority of the other State in controversy, and a day assigned for the appearance of the parties by their lawful agents, who shall then be directed to appoint, by joint consent, commissioners or judges to constitute a court for hearing and determining the matter in question; but, if they cannot agree, Congress shall name three persons out of each of the United States, and from the list of such persons each party shall alternately strike out one, in the petitioners beginning, until the number shall be reduced to thirteen; and from that number not less than seven, nor more than nine names, as Congress shall direct, shall, in the presence of Congress, be drawn out by lot; and the persons whose names shall be drawn, or any five of them, shall be commissioners or judges to hear and finally determine the controversy, so always as a major part of the judges who shall hear the cause shall agree in the determination; and if either party shall neglect to attend at the day appointed, without shewing reasons which Congress shall judge sufficient, or, being present, shall refuse to strike, the Congress shall proceed to nominate three persons out of each State, and the secretary of Congress shall strike in behalf of such party absent or refusing; and the judgment and sentence of the court to be appointed, in the manner before prescribed, shall be final and conclusive; and if any of the parties shall refuse to submit to the authority of such court, or to appear or defend their claim or cause, the court shall nevertheless proceed to pronounce sentence or judgment, which shall, in like manner, be final and decisive, the judgment or sentence and other proceedings being, in either case, transmitted to Congress, and lodged among the acts of Congress for the security of the parties concerned: provided, that every commissioner, before he sits in judgment, shall take an oath, to be administered by one of the judges of the supreme or superior court of the State where the cause shall be tried, "well and truly to hear and determine the matter in question, according to the best of his judgment, without favour, affection, or hope of reward": provided, also, that no State shall be deprived of territory for the benefit of the United States.

All controversies concerning the private right of soil, claimed under different grants of two or more states, whose jurisdictions, as they may respect such lands and the states which passed such grants, are adjusted, the said grants, or either of them, being at the same time claimed to have originated antecedent to such settlement of jurisdiction, shall, on the petition of either party to the Congress of the United States, be finally determined, as near as may be, in the same manner as is before prescribed for deciding disputes respecting territorial jurisdiction between different states.

The United States, in Congress assembled, shall also have the sole and exclusive right and power of regulating the alloy and value of coin struck by their own authority, or by that of the respective states; fixing the standard of weights and measures throughout the United States; regulating the trade and managing all affairs with the Indians not members of any of the states; provided that the legislative right of any State within its own limits be not infringed or violated; establishing and regulating post offices from one State to another throughout all the United States, and exacting such postage on the papers passing through the same as may be requisite to defray the expences of the said office; appointing all officers of the land forces in the service of the United States, excepting regimental officers; appointing all the officers of the naval forces, and commissioning all officers whatever in the service of the United States; making rules for the government and regulation of the said land and naval forces, and directing their operations.

The United States, in Congress assembled, shall have authority to appoint a committee to sit in the recess of Congress, to be denominated "a Committee of the States," and to consist of one delegate from each State, and to appoint such other committees and civil officers as may be necessary for managing the general affairs of the United States, under their direction; to appoint one of their number to preside; provided that no person be allowed to serve in the office of president more than one year in any term of three years; to ascertain the necessary sums of money to be raised for the service of the United States, and to appropriate and apply the same for defraying the public expences; to borrow money or emit bills on the credit of the United States, transmitting, every half year, to the respective states, an account of the sums of money so borrowed or emitted; to build and equip a navy; to agree upon the number of land forces, and to make requisitions from each State for its quota, in proportion to the number of white inhabitants in such State; which requisitions shall be binding; and, thereupon, the legislature of each State shall appoint the regimental officers, raise the men, and cloathe, arm, and equip them in a soldier-like manner, at the expence of the United States; and the officers and men so cloathed, armed, and equipped, shall march to the place appointed and within the time agreed on by the United States, in Congress assembled; but if the United States, in Congress assembled, shall, on consideration of circumstances, judge proper that any State should not raise men, or should raise a smaller number than its quota, and that any other State should raise a greater number of men than the quota thereof, such extra number shall be raised, officered, cloathed, armed, and equipped in the same manner as the quota of such State, unless the legislature of such State shall judge that such extra number cannot be safely spared out of the same, in which case they shall raise, officer, cloathe, arm, and equip as many of such extra number as they judge can be safely spared. And the officers and men so cloathed, armed, and equipped, shall march to the place appointed and within the time agreed on by the United States, in Congress assembled.

The United States, in Congress assembled, shall never engage in a war, nor grant letters of marque and reprisal in time of peace, nor enter into any treaties or alliances, nor coin money, nor regulate the value thereof, nor ascertain the sums and expences necessary for the defence and welfare of the United States, or any of them: nor emit bills, nor borrow money on the credit of the United States, nor appropriate money, nor agree upon the number of vessels of war to be built or purchased, or the number of land or sea forces to be raised, nor appoint a commander in chief of the army or navy, unless nine states assent to the same; nor shall a question on any other point, except for adjourning from day to day, be determined, unless by the votes of a majority of the United States, in Congress assembled.

The Congress of the United States shall have power to adjourn to any time within the year, and to any place within the United States, so that no period of adjournment be for a longer duration than the space of six months, and shall publish the journal of their proceedings monthly, except such parts thereof, relating to treaties, alliances or military operations, as, in their judgment, require secrecy; and the yeas and nays of the delegates of each State on any question shall be entered on the journal, when it is desired by any delegate; and the delegates of a State, or any of them, at his, or their request, shall be furnished with a transcript of the said journal, except such parts as are above excepted, to lay before the legislatures of the several states.

Article 10

The committee of the states, or any nine of them, shall be authorized to execute, in the recess of Congress, such of the powers of Congress as the United States, in Congress assembled, by the consent of nine states, shall, from time to time, think expedient to vest them with; provided, that no power be delegated to the said committee for the exercise of which, by the articles of confederation, the voice of nine states, in the Congress of the United States assembled, is requisite.

Article 11

Canada acceding to this confederation, and joining in the measures of the United States, shall be admitted into and entitled to all the advantages of this union; but no other colony shall be admitted into the same, unless such admission be agreed to by nine states.

Article 12

All bills of credit emitted, monies borrowed and debts contracted by, or under the authority of Congress before the assembling of the United States, in pursuance of the present confederation, shall be deemed and considered as a charge against the United States, for payment and satisfaction whereof the said United States and the public faith are hereby solemnly pledged.

Article 13

Every State shall abide by the determinations of the United States, in Congress assembled, on all questions which, by this confederation, are submitted to them. And the articles of this confederation shall be inviolably observed by every State, and the union shall be perpetual; nor shall any alteration at any time hereafter be made in any of them, unless such alteration be agreed to in a Congress of the United States, and be afterwards confirmed by the legislatures of every State.

These articles shall be proposed to the legislatures of all the United States, to be considered, and if approved of by them, they are advised to authorize their delegates to ratify the same in the Congress of the United States; which being done, the same shall become conclusive.

SOURCE: Records of the Continental and Confederation Congresses and the Constitutional Convention, 1774–1789, Record Group 360, National Archives and Records Administration

The Constitution of the United States of America

The Constitution was submitted on September 17, 1787, by the Constitutional convention, was ratified by conventions of the several states at various dates up to May 29, 1790, and became effective on March 4, 1789.

Note: Passages no longer in effect are printed in italic type.

Preamble

We the People of the United States, in Order to form a more perfect Union, establish Justice, insure domestic Tranquility, provide for the common defence, promote the general Welfare, and secure the Blessings of Liberty to ourselves and our Posterity, do ordain and establish this Constitution for the United States of America.

Article I

Section 1

All legislative Powers herein granted shall be vested in a Congress of the United States, which shall consist of a Senate and House of Representatives.

Section 2

The House of Representatives shall be composed of Members chosen every second Year by the People of the several States, and the Electors in each State shall have the Qualifications requisite for Electors of the most numerous Branch of the State Legislature.

No Person shall be a Representative who shall not have attained to the Age of twenty five Years, and been seven Years a Citizen of the United States, and who shall not, when elected, be an inhabitant of that State in which he shall be chosen.

Representatives and direct Taxes shall be apportioned among the several States which may be included within this Union, according to their respective Numbers, *which shall be determined by adding to the whole Number of free Persons, including those bound to Service for a Term of Years, and excluding Indians not taxed, three fifths of all other Persons.* The actual Enumeration shall be made within three Years after the first Meeting of the Congress of the United States, and within every subsequent Term of ten Years, in such Manner as they shall by Law direct. The Number of Representatives shall not exceed one for every thirty Thousand, but each State shall have at Least one Representative; *and until such enumeration shall be made, the State of New Hampshire shall be entitled to chuse three, Massachusetts eight, Rhode-Island and Providence Plantations one, Connecticut five, New York six, New Jersey four, Pennsylvania eight, Delaware one, Maryland six, Virginia ten, North Carolina five, South Carolina five, and Georgia three.*

When vacancies happen in the Representation from any State, the Executive Authority thereof shall issue Writs of Election to fill such Vacancies.

The House of Representatives shall chuse their Speaker and other Officers; and shall have the sole Power of Impeachment.

Section 3

The Senate of the United States shall be composed of two Senators from each State, *chosen by the Legislature thereof,* for six Years; and each Senator shall have one Vote.

Immediately after they shall be assembled in Consequence of the first Election, they shall be divided as equally as may be into three Classes. The Seats of the Senators of the first Class shall be vacated at the Expiration of the second Year, of the second Class at the Expiration of the fourth Year, and of the third Class at the Expiration of the sixth Year so that one third may be chosen every second Year; and if Vacancies happen by Resignation, or otherwise, during the Recess of the Legislature of any state, the Executive thereof may make temporary Appointments until the next Meeting of the Legislature, which shall then fill such Vacancies.

No Person shall be a Senator who shall not have attained to the Age of thirty Years, and been nine Years a Citizen of the United States, and who shall not, when elected, be an Inhabitant of that State for which he shall be chosen.

The Vice President of the United States shall be President of the Senate, but shall have no Vote, unless they be equally divided.

The Senate shall chuse their other Officers, and also a President *pro tempore,* in the Absence of the Vice President, or when he shall exercise the Office of President of the United States.

The Senate shall have the sole Power to try all Impeachments. When sitting for that Purpose, they shall be on Oath or Affirmation. When the President of the United States is tried the Chief Justice shall preside: And no Person shall

be convicted without the Concurrence of two thirds of the Members present.

Judgment in Cases of Impeachment shall not extend further than to removal from Office, and disqualification to hold and enjoy any Office of honor, Trust or Profit under the United States: but the Party convicted shall nevertheless be liable and subject to Indictment, Trial, Judgment and Punishment, according to Law.

Section 4

The Times, Places and Manner of holding Elections for Senators and Representatives, shall be prescribed in each State by the Legislature thereof; but the Congress may at any time by Law make or alter such Regulations, except as to the Places of chusing Senators.

The Congress shall assemble at least once in every Year, *and such Meeting shall be on the first Monday in December, unless they shall by Law appoint a different Day.*

Section 5

Each House shall be the Judge of the Elections, Returns and Qualifications of its own Members, and a Majority of each shall constitute a Quorum to do Business; but a smaller Number may adjourn from day to day, and may be authorized to compel the Attendance of absent Members, in such Manner, and under such Penalties as each House may provide.

Each House may determine the Rules of its Proceedings, punish its Members for disorderly Behaviour, and, with the Concurrence of two thirds, expel a Member.

Each House shall keep a Journal of its Proceedings, and from time to time publish the same, excepting such Parts as may in their Judgment require Secrecy; and the Yeas and Nays of the Members of either House on any question shall, at the Desire of one fifth of those Present, be entered on the Journal.

Neither House, during the Session of Congress, shall, without the Consent of the other, adjourn for more than three days, nor to any other Place than that in which the two Houses shall be sitting.

Section 6

The Senators and Representatives shall receive a Compensation for their Services, to be ascertained by Law, and paid out of the Treasury of the United States. They shall in all Cases, except Treason, Felony and Breach of the Peace, be privileged from Arrest during their Attendance at the Session of their respective Houses, and in going to and returning from the same; and for any Speech or Debate in either House, they shall not be questioned in any other Place.

No Senator or Representative shall, during the Time for which he was elected, be appointed to any civil Office under the Authority of the United States, which shall have been created, or the Emoluments whereof shall have been encreased during such time, and no Person holding any Office under the United States, shall be a Member of either House during his Continuance in Office.

Section 7

All Bills for raising Revenue shall originate in the House of Representatives; but the Senate may propose or concur with Amendments as on other Bills.

Every Bill which shall have passed the House of Representatives and the Senate, shall, before it become a Law, be presented to the President of the United States; If he approve he shall sign it, but if not he shall return it, with his Objections to the House in which it shall have originated, who shall enter the Objections at large on their Journal, and proceed to reconsider it. If after such Reconsideration two thirds of that House shall agree to pass the Bill, it shall be sent, together with the Objections, to the other House, by which it shall likewise be reconsidered, and if approved by two thirds of that House, it shall become a Law. But in all such Cases the Votes of both Houses shall be determined by yeas and Nays, and the Names of the Persons voting for and against the Bill shall be entered on the Journal of each House respectively. If any Bill shall not be returned by the President within ten Days (Sundays excepted) after it shall have been presented to him, the Same shall be a Law, in like Manner as if he had signed it, unless the Congress by their Adjournment prevent its Return, in which Case it shall not be a Law.

Every Order, Resolution, or Vote to which the Concurrence of the Senate and House of Representatives may be necessary (except on a question of Adjournment) shall be presented to the President of the United States; and before the Same shall take Effect, shall be approved by him, or being disapproved by him, shall be repassed by two thirds of the Senate and House of Representatives, according to the Rules and Limitations prescribed in the Case of a Bill.

Section 8

The Congress shall have Power To lay and collect Taxes, Duties, Imposts and Excises, to pay the Debts and provide for the common Defence and general Welfare of the United States; but all Duties, Imposts and Excises shall be uniform throughout the United States;

To borrow Money on the credit of the United States;

To regulate Commerce with foreign Nations, and among the several States, and with the Indian Tribes;

To establish an uniform Rule of Naturalization, and uniform Laws on the subject of Bankruptcies throughout the United States;

To coin Money, regulate the Value thereof, and of foreign Coin, and fix the Standard of Weights and Measures;

To provide for the Punishment of counterfeiting the Securities and current Coin of the United States;

To establish Post Offices and post Roads;

To promote the Progress of Science and useful Arts, by securing for limited Times to Authors and Inventors the exclusive Right to their respective Writings and Discoveries;

To constitute Tribunals inferior to the supreme Court;

To define and punish Piracies and Felonies committed on the high Seas, and Offences against the Law of Nations;

To declare War, grant Letters of Marque and Reprisal, and make Rules concerning Captures on Land and Water;

To raise and support Armies, but no Appropriation of Money to that Use shall be for a longer Term than two Years;

To provide and maintain a Navy;

To make Rules for the Government and Regulation of the land and naval Forces;

To provide for calling forth the Militia to execute the Laws of the Union, suppress Insurrections and repel Invasions;

To provide for organizing, arming, and disciplining, the Militia, and for governing such Part of them as may be employed in the Service of the United States, reserving to the States respectively, the Appointment of the Officers, and the Authority of training the Militia according to the discipline

prescribed by Congress;

To exercise exclusive Legislation in all Cases whatsoever, over such District (not exceeding ten Miles square) as may, by Cession of particular States, and the Acceptance of Congress, become the Seat of the Government of the United States, and to exercise like Authority over all Places purchased by the Consent of the Legislature of the State in which the Same shall be, for the Erection of Forts, Magazines, Arsenals, dock-Yards, and other needful Buildings;—And

To make all Laws which shall be necessary and proper for carrying into Execution the foregoing Powers, and all other Powers vested by this Constitution in the Government of the United States, or in any Department of Officer thereof.

Section 9

The Migration or Importation of such Persons as any of the States now existing shall think proper to admit, shall not be prohibited by the Congress prior to the Year one thousand eight hundred and eight, but a Tax or duty may be imposed on such Importation, not exceeding ten dollars for each Person.

The Privilege of the Writ of Habeas Corpus shall not be suspended, unless when in Cases of Rebellion or Invasion the public Safety may require it.

No Bill of Attainder or ex post facto Law shall be passed.

No Capitation, or other direct, Tax shall be laid, unless in Proportion to the Census or Enumeration herein before directed to be taken.

No Tax or Duty shall be laid on Articles exported from any State.

No Preference shall be given by any Regulation of Commerce or Revenue to the Ports of one State over those of another: nor shall Vessels bound to, or from, one State, be obliged to enter, clear, or pay Duties in another.

No Money shall be drawn from the Treasury, but in Consequence of Appropriations made by Law; and a regular Statement and Account of the Receipts and Expenditures of all public Money shall be published from time to time.

No Title of Nobility shall be granted by the United States: And no Person holding any Office of Profit or Trust under them, shall, without the Consent of the Congress, accept of any present, Emolument, Office, or Title, of any kind whatever, from any King, Prince, or foreign State.

Section 10

No State shall enter into any Treaty, Alliance, or Confederation; grant Letters of Marque and Reprisal; coin Money; emit Bills of Credit; make any Thing but gold and silver Coin a Tender in Payment of Debts; pass any Bill of Attainder, ex post facto Law, or Law impairing the obligation of Contracts, or grant any Title of Nobility.

No State shall, without the Consent of the Congress, lay any Imposts or Duties on Imports or Exports, except what may be absolutely necessary for executing its inspection Laws: and the net Produce of all Duties and Imposts, laid by any State on Imports or Exports, shall be for the Use of the Treasury of the United States; and all such Laws shall be subject to the Revision and Controul of the Congress.

No State shall, without the Consent of Congress, lay any Duty of Tonnage, keep Troops, or Ships of War in time of Peace, enter into any Agreement or Compact with another State, or with a foreign Power, or engage in War, unless actually invaded, or in such imminent Danger as will not admit of delay.

Article II

Section 1

The executive Power shall be vested in a President of the United States of America. He shall hold his Office during the Term of four Years, and, together with the Vice President, chosen for the same Term, be elected, as follows:

Each State shall appoint, in such Manner as the Legislature thereof may direct, a Number of Electors, equal to the whole Number of Senators and Representatives to which the State may be entitled in the Congress: but no Senator or Representative, or Person holding an Office of Trust or Profit under the United States, shall be appointed an Elector.

The Electors shall meet in their respective States, and vote by Ballot for two Persons, of whom one at least shall not be an Inhabitant of the same State with themselves. And they shall make a List of all the Persons voted for, and of the Number of Votes for each; which List they shall sign and certify, and transmit sealed to the Seat of the Government of the United States, directed to the President of the Senate. The President of the Senate shall, in the Presence of the Senate and House of Representatives, open all the Certificates, and the Votes shall then be counted. The Person having the greatest Number of Votes shall be the President, if such Number be a Majority of the whole number of Electors appointed; and if there be more than one who have such Majority, and have an equal Number of Votes, then the House of Representatives shall immediately chuse by Ballot one of them for President; and if no Person have a Majority, then from the five highest on the List the said House shall in like Manner chuse the President. But in chusing the President, the Votes shall be taken by States, the Representation from each State having one Vote; A quorum for this Purpose shall consist of a Member or Members from two thirds of the States, and a Majority of all the States shall be necessary to a Choice. In every Case, after the Choice of the President, the Person having the greatest Number of Votes of the Electors shall be the Vice President. But if there should remain two or more who have equal Votes, the Senate shall chuse from them by Ballot the Vice President.

The Congress may determine the time of chusing the Electors, and the Day on which they shall give their Votes; which Day shall be the same throughout the United States.

No person except a natural born Citizen, *or a Citizen of the United States, at the time of the Adoption of this Constitution,* shall be eligible to the Office of President; neither shall any Person be eligible to that Office who shall not have attained to the Age of thirty five Years, and been fourteen Years a Resident within the United States.

In Case of the Removal of the President from Office, or of his Death, Resignation, or Inability to discharge the Powers and Duties of the said Office, the Same shall devolve on the Vice President, and the Congress may by Law provide for the Case of Removal, Death, Resignation or Inability, both of the President and Vice President, declaring what Officer shall then act as President, and such Officer shall act accordingly, until the Disability be removed, or a President shall be elected.

The President shall, at stated Times, receive for his Services, a Compensation, which shall neither be encreased nor diminished during the Period for which he shall have been elected, and he shall not receive within that period any other Emolument from the United States, or any of them.

Before he enter on the Execution of his Office, he shall take the following Oath or Affirmation:—"I do solemnly swear (or affirm) that I will faithfully execute the Office of President of the United States, and will to the best of my Ability, preserve, protect and defend the Constitution of the United States."

Section 2

The President shall be Commander in Chief of the Army and Navy of the United States, and of the Militia of the several States, when called into the actual Service of the United States; he may require the Opinion, in writing, of the principal Officer in each of the executive Departments, upon any Subject relating to the Duties of their respective Offices, and he shall have Power to grant Reprieves and Pardons for Offences against the United States, except in Cases of Impeachment.

He shall have Power, by and with the Advice and Consent of the Senate, to make Treaties, provided two thirds of the Senators present concur; and he shall nominate, and by and with the Advice and Consent of the Senate, shall appoint Ambassadors, other public Ministers and Consuls, Judges of the supreme Court, and all other Officers of the United States, whose Appointments are not herein otherwise provided for, and which shall be established by Law: but the Congress may by Law vest the Appointment of such inferior Officers, as they think proper in the President alone, in the Courts of Law, or in the Heads of Departments.

The President shall have Power to fill up all Vacancies that may happen during the Recess of the Senate, by granting Commissions which shall expire at the End of their next Session.

Section 3

He shall from time to time give to the Congress Information of the State of the Union, and recommend to their Consideration such Measures as he shall judge necessary and expedient; he may, on extraordinary Occasions, convene both Houses, or either of them, and in Case of disagreement between them, with Respect to the Time of Adjournment, he may adjourn them to such Time as he shall think proper; he shall receive Ambassadors and other public Ministers; he shall take Care that the Laws be faithfully executed, and shall Commission all the officers of the United States.

Section 4

The President, Vice President and all civil Officers of the United States, shall be removed from Office on Impeachment for, and Conviction of, Treason, Bribery or other high Crimes and Misdemeanors.

Article III

Section 1

The judicial Power of the United States, shall be vested in one supreme Court, and in such inferior Courts as the Congress may from time to time ordain and establish. The Judges, both of the supreme and inferior Courts, shall hold their offices during good Behaviour, and shall, at stated Times, receive for their Services, a Compensation, which shall not be diminished during their Continuance in Office.

Section 2

The judicial Power shall extend to all Cases, in Law and Equity, arising under this Constitution, the Laws of the United States, and Treaties made, or which shall be made, under their Authority;—to all Cases affecting Ambassadors, other public Ministers and Consuls;—to all Cases of admiralty and maritime Jurisdiction;—to Controversies to which the United States shall be a Party;—to Controversies between two or more States;—*between a State and Citizens of another State;*—between Citizens of different States;—between Citizens of the same State claiming Lands under Grants of different States, and between a State, or the Citizens thereof, and foreign States, Citizens or Subjects.

In all Cases affecting Ambassadors, other public Ministers and Consuls, and those in which a State shall be Party, the supreme Court shall have original Jurisdiction. In all the other Cases before mentioned, the supreme Court shall have appellate Jurisdiction, both as to Law and Fact, with such Exceptions, and under such Regulations as the Congress shall make.

The Trial of all Crimes, except in Cases of Impeachment, shall be by Jury; and such Trial shall be held in the State where the said Crimes shall have been committed, but when not committed within any State, the Trial shall be at such Place or Places as the Congress may by Law have directed.

Section 3

Treason against the United States, shall consist only in levying War against them, or in adhering to their Enemies, giving them Aid and Comfort. No person shall be convicted of Treason unless on the Testimony of two Witnesses to the same overt Act, or on Confession in open Court.

The Congress shall have Power to declare the Punishment of Treason, but no Attainder of Treason shall work Corruption of Blood, or Forfeiture except during the Life of the Person attainted.

Article IV

Section 1

Full Faith and Credit shall be given in each State to the public Acts, Records, and judicial Proceedings of every other State. And the Congress may by general Laws prescribe the Manner in which such Acts, Records and Proceedings shall be proved, and the Effect thereof.

Section 2

The Citizens of each State shall be entitled to all Privileges and Immunities of Citizens in the several States.

A Person charged in any State with Treason, Felony, or other Crime, who shall flee from Justice, and be found in another State, shall on Demand of the executive Authority of the State from which he fled, be delivered up, to be removed to the State having Jurisdiction of the Crime.

No Person held to Service or Labour in one State, under the Laws thereof, escaping into another, shall, in Consequence of any Law or Regulation therein, be discharged from such Service or Labour, but shall be delivered up on Claim of the Party to whom such Service or Labour may be due.

Section 3

New States may be admitted by the Congress into this Union; but no new State shall be formed or erected within the Jurisdiction of any other State; nor any State be formed by the Junction of two or more States, or Parts of States, without the Consent of the Legislatures of the States concerned as well as of the Congress.

The Congress shall have Power to dispose of and make all needful Rules and Regulations respecting the Territory or other Property belonging to the United States; and nothing in this Constitution shall be so construed as to Prejudice any Claims of the United States, or of any particular States.

Section 4

The United States shall guarantee to every State in this Union a Republican Form of Government, and shall protect each of them against Invasion; and on Application of the Legislature, or of the Executive (when the Legislature cannot be convened) against domestic violence.

Article- V

The Congress, whenever two thirds of both Houses shall deem it necessary, shall propose Amendments to this Constitution, or, on the Application of the Legislatures of two thirds of the several States, shall call a Convention for proposing Amendments, which, in either Case, shall be valid to all Intents and Purposes, as Part of this Constitution, when ratified by the Legislatures of three fourths of the several States, or by Conventions in three fourths thereof, as the one or the other Mode of Ratification may be proposed by the Congress; Provided *that no Amendment which may be made prior to the Year One thousand eight hundred and eight shall in any Manner affect the first and fourth Clauses in the Ninth Section of the first Article;* and that no State, without its Consent, shall be deprived of its equal Suffrage in the Senate.

Article VI

All Debts contracted and Engagements entered into, before the Adoption of this Constitution, shall be as valid against the United States under this Constitution, as under the Confederation.

This Constitution, and Laws of the United States which shall be made in Pursuance thereof; and all Treaties made, or which shall be made, under the Authority of the United States, shall be the supreme Law of the Land; and the Judges in every State shall be bound thereby, any Thing in the Constitution or Laws of any State to the Contrary notwithstanding.

The Senators and Representatives before mentioned, and the Members of the several State Legislatures, and all executive and Judicial Officers, both of the United States and of the several States, shall be bound by Oath or Affirmation, to support this Constitution; but no religious Test shall ever be required as a Qualification to any Office of public Trust under the United States.

Article VII

The Ratification of the Conventions of nine States, shall be sufficient for the Establishment of this Constitution between the States so ratifying the Same.

Done in Convention by the Unanimous Consent of the States present the Seventeenth Day of September in the Year of our Lord one thousand seven hundred and Eighty seven and of the Independence of the United States of America the Twelfth IN WITNESS whereof We have hereunto subscribed our Names,

George Washington
President and Deputy from Virginia

Delaware
George Read
Gunning Bedford Jr.
John Dickinson
Richard Bassett
Jacob Broom

Maryland
James McHenry
Daniel of St. Thomas Jenifer
Daniel Carroll

Virginia
John Blair
James Madison Jr.

North Carolina
William Blount
Richard Dobbs Spraight
Hugh Williamson

South Carolina
John Rutledge
Charles Cotesworth Pinckney
Charles Pinckney
Pierce Butler

Georgia
William Few
Abraham Baldwin

New Hampshire
John Langdon
Nicholas Gilman

Massachusetts
Nathaniel Gorham
Rufus King

Connecticut
William Samuel Johnson
Roger Sherman

New York
Alexander Hamilton
New Jersey
William Livingston
David Brearley
William Paterson
Jonathan Dayton

Pennsylvania
Benjamin Franklin
Thomas Mifflin
Robert Morris
George Clymer
Thomas FitzSimons
Jared Ingersoll
James Wilson
Gouverneur Morris

SOURCE: Records of the Continental and Confederation Congresses and the Constitutional Convention, 1774–1789, Record Group 360, National Archives and Records Administration

Amendments to the Constitution

Note: The first ten amendments (the Bill of Rights) were ratified and their adoption was certified on December 15, 1791.

Amendment I

Congress shall make no law respecting an establishment of religion, or prohibiting the free exercise thereof; or abridging the freedom of speech, or of the press; or the right of the people peaceably to assemble, and to petition the Government for a redress of grievances.

Amendment II

A well regulated Militia being necessary to the security of a free State, the right of the people to keep and bear Arms, shall not be infringed.

Amendment III

No Soldier shall, in time of peace be quartered in any house, without the consent of the Owner, nor in time of war, but in a manner to be prescribed by law.

Amendment IV

The right of the people to be secure in their persons, houses, papers, and effects, against unreasonable searches and seizures, shall not be violated, and no Warrants shall issue, but upon probable cause, supported by Oath or affirmation, and particularly describing the place to be searched, and the persons or things to be seized.

Amendment V

No person shall be held to answer for a capital, or otherwise infamous crime, unless on a presentment or indictment of a Grand Jury, except in cases arising in the land or naval forces, or in the Militia, when in actual service in time of War or public danger; nor shall any person be subject for the same offense to be twice put in jeopardy of life or limb; nor shall be compelled in any criminal case to be a witness against himself, nor be deprived of life, liberty, or property, without due process of law; nor shall private property be taken for public use, without just compensation.

Amendment VI

In all criminal prosecutions, the accused shall enjoy the right to a speedy and public trial, by an impartial jury of the State and district wherein the crime shall have been committed, which district shall have been previously ascertained by law, and to be informed of the nature and cause of the accusation; to be confronted with the witnesses against him; to have compulsory process for obtaining witnesses in his favor, and to have the Assistance of Counsel for his defence.

Amendment VII

In Suits at common law, where the value in controversy shall exceed twenty dollars, the right of trial by jury shall be preserved, and no fact tried by a jury, shall be otherwise re-examined in any Court of the United States, than according to the rules of the common law.

Amendment VIII

Excessive bail shall not be required, nor excessive fines imposed, nor cruel and unusual punishments inflicted.

Amendment IX

The enumeration in the Constitution, of certain rights, shall not be construed to deny or disparage others retained by the people.

Amendment X

The powers not delegated to the United States by the Constitution, nor prohibited by it to the States, are reserved to the States respectively, or to the people.

Amendment XI [Adopted 1798]

The Judicial power of the United States shall not be construed to extend to any suit in law or equity, commenced or prosecuted against one of the United States by Citizens of another State, or by Citizens or Subjects of any Foreign State.

Amendment XII [Adopted 1804]

The Electors shall meet in their respective states, and vote by ballot for President and Vice President, one of whom, at least, shall not be an inhabitant of the same state with themselves; they shall name in their ballots the person voted for as President, and in distinct ballots the person voted for as Vice President, and they shall make distinct lists of all persons voted for as President, and of all persons voted for as Vice President, and of the number of votes for each, which lists they shall sign and certify, and transmit sealed to the seat of the government of the United States, directed to the President of the Senate;—President of the Senate shall, in the presence of the Senate and House of Representatives, open all the certificates and the votes shall then be counted;—The person having the greatest number of votes for President, shall be the President, if such number be a majority of the whole number of Electors appointed; and if no person have such majority, then from the persons having the highest numbers not exceeding three on the list of those voted for as President, the House of Representatives shall choose immediately, by ballot, the President. But in choosing the President, the votes shall be taken by states, the representation from each state having one vote; a quorum for this purpose shall consist of a member or members from two-thirds of the states, and a majority of all the states shall be necessary to a choice. And if the House of Representatives shall not choose a President whenever the right of choice shall devolve upon them, before *the fourth day of March* next following, then the Vice President shall act as President, as in the case of the death or other constitutional disability of the President.—The person having the greatest number of votes as Vice President, shall be the Vice President, if such number be a majority of the whole number of Electors appointed, and if no person have a majority, then from the two highest numbers on the list, the Senate shall choose the Vice President; a quorum for the purpose shall consist of two-thirds of the whole number of Senators, and a majority of the whole number shall be necessary to a choice. But no person constitutionally ineligible to the office of President shall be eligible to that of Vice President of the United States.

Amendment XIII [Adopted 1865]

Section 1

Neither slavery nor involuntary servitude, except as a punishment for crime whereof the party shall have been duly convicted, shall exist within the United States, or any place subject to their jurisdiction.

Section 2

Congress shall have power to enforce this article by appropriate legislation.

Amendment XIV [Adopted 1868]

Section 1

All persons born or naturalized in the United States, and subject to the jurisdiction thereof, are citizens of the United States and of the State wherein they reside. No State shall make or enforce any law which shall abridge the privileges or immunities of citizens of the United States; nor shall any State deprive any person of life, liberty, or property, without due process of law; nor deny to any person within its jurisdiction the equal protection of the laws.

Section 2

Representatives shall be apportioned among the several States according to their respective numbers, counting the whole number of persons in each State, excluding Indians not taxed. But when the right to vote at any election for the choice of electors for President and Vice President of the United States, Representatives in Congress, the Executive and Judicial officers of a State, or the members of the Legislature thereof, is denied to any of the male inhabitants of such State, being twenty-one years of age, and citizens of the United States, or in any way abridged, except for participation in rebellion, or other crime, the basis of representation therein shall be reduced in the proportion which the number of such male citizens shall bear to the whole number of male citizens twenty-one years of age in such State.

Section 3

No person shall be a Senator or Representative in Congress, or elector of President and Vice President, or hold any office, civil or military, under the United States, or under any State, who, having previously taken an oath, as a member of Congress, or as an officer of the United States, or as a member of any State legislature, or as an executive or judicial officer of any State, to support the Constitution of the United States, shall have engaged in insurrection or rebellion against the same, or given aid or comfort to the enemies thereof. But Congress may by a vote of two-thirds of each House, remove such disability.

Section 4

The validity of the public debt of the United States, authorized by law, including debts incurred for payment of pensions and bounties for services in suppressing insurrection or rebellion, shall not be questioned. But neither the United States nor any State shall assume or pay any debt or obligation incurred in aid of insurrection or rebellion against the United States, or any claim for the loss or emancipation of any slave; but all such debts, obligations and claims shall be held illegal and void.

Section 5

The Congress shall have power to enforce, by appropriate legislation, the provisions of this article.

Amendment XV [Adopted 1870]

Section 1

The right of citizens of the United States to vote shall not be denied or abridged by the United States or by any State on account of race, color, or previous condition of servitude.

Section 2

The Congress shall have power to enforce this article by appropriate legislation.

Amendment XVI [Adopted 1913]

The Congress shall have power to lay and collect taxes on incomes, from whatever source derived, without apportionment among the several States, and without regard to any census or enumeration.

Amendment XVII [Adopted 1913]

The Senate of the United States shall be composed of two Senators from each State, elected by the people thereof, for six years; and each Senator shall have one vote. The electors in each State shall have the qualifications requisite for electors of the most numerous branch of the State legislatures.

When vacancies happen in the representation of any State in the Senate, the executive authority of such State shall issue writs of election to fill such vacancies: *Provided*, That the legislature of any State may empower the executive thereof to make temporary appointments until the people fill the vacancies by election as the legislature may direct.

This amendment shall not be so construed as to affect the election or term of any Senator chosen before it becomes valid as part of the Constitution.

Amendment XVIII [Adopted 1919, repealed 1933]

Section 1

After one year from the ratification of this article the manufacture, sale, or transportation of intoxicating liquors within, the importation thereof into, or the exportation thereof from the United States and all territory subject to the jurisdiction thereof for beverage purposes is hereby prohibited.

Section 2

The Congress and the several States shall have concurrent power to enforce this article by appropriate legislation.

Section 3

This article shall be inoperative unless it shall have been ratified as an amendment to the Constitution by the legislatures of the several States, as provided in the Constitution, within seven years from the date of the submission hereof to the States by the Congress.

Amendment XIX [Adopted 1920]

The right of citizens of the United States to vote shall not be denied or abridged by the United States or by any State on account of sex.

Congress shall have power to enforce this article by appropriate legislation.

Amendment XX [Adopted 1933]

Section 1

The terms of the President and Vice President shall end at noon on the 20th day of January, and the terms of Senators and Representatives at noon on the 3d day of January, of the years in which such terms would have ended if this article had not been ratified and the terms of their successors shall then begin.

Section 2

The Congress shall assemble at least once in every year, and such meeting shall begin at noon on the 3d day of January, unless they shall by law appoint a different day.

Section 3

If, at the time fixed for the beginning of the term of the President, the President elect shall have died, the Vice President elect shall become President. If a President shall not have been chosen before the time fixed for the beginning of his term, or if the President elect shall have failed to qualify, then the Vice President elect shall act as President until a President shall have qualified; and the Congress may by law provide for the case wherein neither a President elect nor a Vice President elect shall have qualified, declaring who shall then act as President, or the manner in which one who is to act shall be selected, and such person shall act accordingly until a President or Vice President shall have qualified.

Section 4

The Congress may by law provide for the case of the death of any of the persons from whom the House of Representatives may choose a President whenever the right of choice shall have devolved upon them, and for the case of the death of any of the persons from whom the Senate may choose a Vice President whenever the right of choice shall have devolved upon them.

Section 5

Sections 1 and 2 shall take effect on the 15th day of October following the ratification of this article.

Section 6

This article shall be inoperative unless it shall have been ratified as an amendment to the Constitution by the legislatures of three fourths of the several States within seven years from the date of its submission.

Amendment XXI [Adopted 1933]

Section 1

The eighteenth article of amendment to the Constitution of the United States is hereby repealed.

Section 2

The transportation or importation into any State, Territory, or possession of the United States for delivery or use therein of intoxicating liquors in violation of the laws thereof, is hereby prohibited.

Section 3

This article shall be inoperative unless it shall have been ratified as an amendment to the Constitution by conventions in the several States, as provided in the Constitution, within seven years from the date of the submission hereof to the States by the Congress.

Amendment XXII [Adopted 1951]

Section 1

No person shall be elected to the office of the President more than twice, and no person who has held the office of President, or acted as President, for more than two years of a term to which some other person was elected President shall be elected to the office of the President more than once. But this Article shall not apply to any person holding the office of President when this Article was proposed by the Congress, and shall not prevent any person who may be holding the office of President, or acting as President, during the term within which this Article becomes operative from holding the office of President or acting as President during the remainder of such term.

Section 2

This article shall be inoperative unless it shall have been ratified as an amendment to the Constitution by the legislatures of three-fourths of the several States within seven years from the date of its submission to the States by the Congress.

Amendment XXIII [Adopted 1961]

Section 1

The District constituting the seat of Government of the United States shall appoint in such manner as the Congress shall direct:

A number of electors of President and Vice President equal to the whole number of Senators and Representatives in Congress to which the District would be entitled if it were a State, but in no event more than the least populous State; they shall be in addition to those appointed by the States, but they shall be considered, for the purposes of the election of President and Vice President, to be electors appointed by a State; and they shall meet in the District and perform such duties as provided by the twelfth article of amendment.

Section 2

The Congress shall have power to enforce this article by appropriate legislation.

Amendment XXIV [Adopted 1964]

Section 1

The right of citizens of the United States to vote in any primary or other election for President or Vice President, for electors for President or Vice President, or for Senator or Representative in Congress, shall not be denied or abridged by the United States or any state by reason of failure to pay any poll tax or other tax.

Section 2

The Congress shall have the power to enforce this article by appropriate legislation.

Amendment XXV [Adopted 1967]

Section 1

In case of the removal of the President from office or his death or resignation, the Vice President shall become President.

Section 2

Whenever there is a vacancy in the office of the Vice President, the President shall nominate a Vice President who shall take the office upon confirmation by a majority vote of both houses of Congress.

Section 3

Whenever the President transmits to the President pro tempore of the Senate and the Speaker of the House of Representatives his written declaration that he is unable to discharge the powers and duties of his office, and until he transmits to them a written declaration to the contrary, such powers and duties shall be discharged by the Vice President as Acting President.

Section 4

Whenever the Vice President and a majority of either the principal officers of the executive departments or of such other body as Congress may by law provide, transmit to the President pro tempore of the Senate and the Speaker of the House of Representatives their written declaration that the President is unable to discharge the powers and duties of his office, the Vice President shall immediately assume the powers and duties of the office as Acting President.

Thereafter, when the President transmits to the President pro tempore of the Senate and the Speaker of the House of Representatives his written declaration that no inability exists, he shall resume the powers and duties of his office unless the Vice President and a majority of either the principal officers of the executive department or of such other body as Congress may by law provide, transmit within four days to the President pro tempore of the Senate and the Speaker of the House of Representatives their written declaration that the President is unable to discharge the powers and duties of his office. Thereupon Congress shall decide the issue, assembling within 48 hours for that purpose if not in session. If the Congress, within 21 days after receipt of the latter written declaration, or, if Congress is not in session, within 21 days after Congress is required to assemble, determines by two-thirds vote of both houses that the President is unable to discharge the powers and duties of his office, the Vice President shall continue to discharge the same as Acting President; otherwise, the President shall resume the powers and duties of his office.

Amendment XXVI [Adopted 1971]

Section 1

The right of citizens of the United States, who are 18 years of age or older, to vote shall not be denied or abridged by the United States or any state on account of age.

Section 2

The Congress shall have the power to enforce this article by -appropriate legislation.

Amendment XXVII [Adopted 1992]

No law, varying the compensation for the services of the Senators and Representatives shall take effect, until an election of Representatives shall have intervened.

SOURCE: Constitution of the United States of America: Analysis, and Interpretation, Congressional Research Service, Library of Congress

PRESIDENTIAL ELECTIONS

Year	Candidates	Parties	Popular Vote	Electoral Vote	Voter Participation
1789	**George Washington**		a	69	
	John Adams			34	
	Others			35	
1792	**George Washington**		a	132	
	John Adams			77	
	George Clinton			50	
	Others			5	
1796	**John Adams**	Federalist	a	71	
	Thomas Jefferson	Democratic-Republican		68	
	Thomas Pinckney	Federalist		59	
	Aaron Burr	Dem.-Rep.		30	
	Others			48	
1800	**Thomas Jefferson**	Dem.-Rep.	a	73	
	Aaron Burr	Dem.-Rep.		73	
	John Adams	Federalist		65	
	C. C. Pinckney	Federalist		64	
	John Jay	Federalist		1	
1804	**Thomas Jefferson**	Dem.-Rep.	a	162	
	C. C. Pinckney	Federalist		14	
1808	**James Madison**	Dem.-Rep.	a	122	
	C. C. Pinckney	Federalist		47	
	George Clinton	Dem.-Rep.		6	
1812	**James Madison**	Dem.-Rep.	a	128	
	De Witt Clinton	Federalist		89	
1816	**James Monroe**	Dem.-Rep.	a	183	
	Rufus King	Federalist		34	
1820	**James Monroe**	Dem.-Rep.	a	231	
	John Quincy Adams	Dem.-Rep.		1	
1824	**John Quincy Adams**	Dem.-Rep.	108,740 (30.5%)	84	26.9%
	Andrew Jackson	Dem.-Rep.	153,544 (43.1%)	99	
	William H. Crawford	Dem.-Rep.	46,618 (13.1%)	41	
	Henry Clay	Dem.-Rep.	47,136 (13.2%)	37	
1828	**Andrew Jackson**	Democratic	647,286 (56.0%)	178	57.6%
	John Quincy Adams	National Republican	508,064 (44.0%)	83	
1832	**Andrew Jackson**	Democratic	687,502 (55.0%)	219	55.4%
	Henry Clay	National Republican	530,189 (42.4%)	49	
	John Floyd	Independent		11	
	William Wirt	Anti-Mason	33,108 (2.6%)	7	
1836	**Martin Van Buren**	Democratic	765,483 (50.9%)	170	57.8%
	William Henry Harrison	Whig		73	
	Hugh L. White	Whig	739,795 (49.1%)	26	
	Daniel Webster	Whig		14	
	W. P. Magnum	Independent		11	
1840	**William Henry Harrison**	Whig	1,274,624 (53.1%)	234	80.2%
	Martin Van Buren	Democratic	1,127,781 (46.9%)	60	
	J. G. Birney	Liberty	7,069	—	
1844	**James K. Polk**	Democratic	1,338,464 (49.6%)	170	78.9%
	Henry Clay	Whig	1,300,097 (48.1%)	105	
	J. G. Birney	Liberty	62,300 (2.3%)	—	
1848	**Zachary Taylor**	Whig	1,360,967 (47.4%)	163	72.7%
	Lewis Cass	Democratic	1,222,342 (42.5%)	127	
	Martin Van Buren	Free-Soil	291,263 (10.1%)	—	
1852	**Franklin Pierce**	Democratic	1,601,117 (50.9%)	254	69.6%
	Winfield Scott	Whig	1,385,453 (44.1%)	42	
	John P. Hale	Free-Soil	155,825 (5.0%)	—	

[a]Electors selected by state legislatures.

PRESIDENTIAL ELECTIONS (CONTINUED)

Year	Candidates	Parties	Popular Vote	Electoral Vote	Voter Participation
1856	**James Buchanan**	Democratic	1,832,955 (45.3%)	174	78.9%
	John C. Frémont	Republican	1,339,932 (33.1%)	114	
	Millard Fillmore	American	871,731 (21.6%)	8	
1860	**Abraham Lincoln**	Republican	1,865,593 (39.8%)	180	81.2%
	Stephen A. Douglas	Democratic	1,382,713 (29.5%)	12	
	John C. Breckinridge	Democratic	848,356 (18.1%)	72	
	John Bell	Union	592,906 (12.6%)	39	
1864	**Abraham Lincoln**	Republican	2,213,655 (55.0%)	212[b]	73.8%
	George B. McClellan	Democratic	1,805,237 (45.0%)	21	
1868	**Ulysses S. Grant**	Republican	3,012,833 (52.7%)	214	78.1%
	Horatio Seymour	Democratic	2,703,249 (47.3%)	80	
1872	**Ulysses S. Grant**	Republican	3,597,132 (55.6%)	286	71.3%
	Horace Greeley	Dem.; Liberal Republican	2,834,125 (43.9%)	66[c]	
1876	**Rutherford B. Hayes**[d]	Republican	4,036,298 (48.0%)	185	81.8%
	Samuel J. Tilden	Democratic	4,300,590 (51.0%)	184	
1880	**James A. Garfield**	Republican	4,454,416 (48.5%)	214	79.4%
	Winfield S. Hancock	Democratic	4,444,952 (48.1%)	155	
1884	**Grover Cleveland**	Democratic	4,874,986 (48.5%)	219	77.5%
	James G. Blaine	Republican	4,851,981 (48.2%)	182	
1888	**Benjamin Harrison**	Republican	5,439,853 (47.9%)	233	79.3%
	Grover Cleveland	Democratic	5,540,309 (48.6%)	168	
1892	**Grover Cleveland**	Democratic	5,556,918 (46.1%)	277	74.7%
	Benjamin Harrison	Republican	5,176,108 (43.0%)	145	
	James B. Weaver	People's	1,041,028 (8.5%)	22	
1896	**William McKinley**	Republican	7,104,779 (51.1%)	271	79.3%
	William Jennings Bryan	Democratic People's	6,502,925 (47.7%)	176	
1900	**William McKinley**	Republican	7,207,923 (51.7%)	292	73.2%
	William Jennings Bryan	Dem.-Populist	6,358,133 (45.5%)	155	
1904	**Theodore Roosevelt**	Republican	7,623,486 (57.9%)	336	65.2%
	Alton B. Parker	Democratic	5,077,911 (37.6%)	140	
	Eugene V. Debs	Socialist	402,283 (3.0%)	—	
1908	**William H. Taft**	Republican	7,678,908 (51.6%)	321	65.4%
	William Jennings Bryan	Democratic	6,409,104 (43.1%)	162	
	Eugene V. Debs	Socialist	420,793 (2.8%)	—	
1912	**Woodrow Wilson**	Democratic	6,293,454 (41.9%)	435	58.8%
	Theodore Roosevelt	Progressive	4,119,538 (27.4%)	88	
	William H. Taft	Republican	3,484,980 (23.2%)	8	
	Eugene V. Debs	Socialist	900,672 (6.0%)	—	
1916	**Woodrow Wilson**	Democratic	9,129,606 (49.4%)	277	61.6%
	Charles E. Hughes	Republican	8,538,221 (46.2%)	254	
	A. L. Benson	Socialist	585,113 (3.2%)	—	
1920	**Warren G. Harding**	Republican	16,152,200 (60.4%)	404	49.2%
	James M. Cox	Democratic	9,147,353 (34.2%)	127	
	Eugene V. Debs	Socialist	919,799 (3.4%)	—	
1924	**Calvin Coolidge**	Republican	15,725,016 (54.0%)	382	48.9%
	John W. Davis	Democratic	8,386,503 (28.8%)	136	
	Robert M. La Follette	Progressive	4,822,856 (16.6%)	13	
1928	**Herbert Hoover**	Republican	21,391,381 (58.2%)	444	56.9%
	Alfred E. Smith	Democratic	15,016,443 (40.9%)	87	
	Norman Thomas	Socialist	267,835 (0.7%)	—	
1932	**Franklin D. Roosevelt**	Democratic	22,821,857 (57.4%)	472	56.9%
	Herbert Hoover	Republican	15,761,841 (39.7%)	59	
	Norman Thomas	Socialist	881,951 (2.2%)	—	
1936	**Franklin D. Roosevelt**	Democratic	27,751,597 (60.8%)	523	61.0%
	Alfred M. Landon	Republican	16,679,583 (36.5%)	8	
	William Lemke	Union	882,479 (1.9%)	—	

[b]Eleven secessionist states did not participate.
[c]Greeley died before the electoral college met. His electoral votes were divided among the four minor candidates.
[d]Contested result settled by special election.

PRESIDENTIAL ELECTIONS (CONTINUED)

Year	Candidates	Parties	Popular Vote	Electoral Vote	Voter Participation
1940	**Franklin D. Roosevelt**	Democratic	27,244,160 (54.8%)	449	62.5%
	Wendell L. Willkie	Republican	22,305,198 (44.8%)	82	
1944	**Franklin D. Roosevelt**	Democratic	25,602,504 (53.5%)	432	55.9%
	Thomas E. Dewey	Republican	22,006,285 (46.0%)	99	
1948	**Harry S. Truman**	Democratic	24,105,695 (49.5%)	304	53.0%
	Thomas E. Dewey	Republican	21,969,170 (45.1%)	189	
	J. Strom Thurmond	State-Rights Democratic	1,169,021 (2.4%)	38	
	Henry A. Wallace	Progressive	1,156,103 (2.4%)	—	
1952	**Dwight D. Eisenhower**	Republican	33,936,252 (55.1%)	442	63.3%
	Adlai E. Stevenson	Democratic	27,314,992 (44.4%)	89	
1956	**Dwight D. Eisenhower**	Republican	35,575,420 (57.6%)	457	60.6%
	Adlai E. Stevenson	Democratic	26,033,066 (42.1%)	73	
	Other	—	—	1	
1960	**John F. Kennedy**	Democratic	34,227,096 (49.9%)	303	62.8%
	Richard M. Nixon	Republican	34,108,546 (49.6%)	219	
	Other	—	—	15	
1964	**Lyndon B. Johnson**	Democratic	43,126,506 (61.1%)	486	61.7%
	Barry M. Goldwater	Republican	27,176,799 (38.5%)	52	
1968	**Richard M. Nixon**	Republican	31,770,237 (43.4%)	301	60.6%
	Hubert H. Humphrey	Democratic	31,270,533 (42.7%)	191	
	George Wallace	American Indep.	9,906,141 (13.5%)	46	
1972	**Richard M. Nixon**	Republican	47,169,911 (60.7%)	520	55.2%
	George S. McGovern	Democratic	29,170,383 (37.5%)	17	
	Other	—	—	1	
1976	**Jimmy Carter**	Democratic	40,828,587 (50.0%)	297	53.5%
	Gerald R. Ford	Republican	39,147,613 (47.9%)	241	
	Other	—	1,575,459 (2.1%)	—	
1980	**Ronald Reagan**	Republican	43,901,812 (50.7%)	489	52.6%
	Jimmy Carter	Democratic	35,483,820 (41.0%)	49	
	John B. Anderson	Independent	5,719,722 (6.6%)	—	
	Ed Clark	Libertarian	921,188 (1.1%)	—	
1984	**Ronald Reagan**	Republican	54,455,075 (59.0%)	525	53.3%
	Walter Mondale	Democratic	37,577,185 (41.0%)	13	
1988	**George H. W. Bush**	Republican	48,886,000 (53.4%)	426	57.4%
	Michael S. Dukakis	Democratic	41,809,000 (45.6%)	111	
1992	**William J. Clinton**	Democratic	43,728,375 (43.0%)	370	55.0%
	George H. W. Bush	Republican	38,167,416 (38.0%)	168	
	H. Ross Perot	Independent	19,237,247 (19.0%)	—	
1996	**William J. Clinton**	Democratic	47,401,185 (49.2%)	379	48.8%
	Robert Dole	Republican	39,197,469 (40.7%)	159	
	H. Ross Perot	Reform	8,085,294 (8.4%)	—	
	Ralph Nader	Green	684,871 (<1%)	—	
2000	**George W. Bush**	Republican	50,456,002 (47.9%)	271	51.2%
	Al Gore	Democratic	50,999,897 (48.4%)	266[e]	
	Ralph Nader	Green	2,882,955 (2.7%)	—	
	Other	—	834,774 (<1%)	—	
2004	**George W. Bush**	Republican	62,040,610 (50.7%)	286	55.3%
	John Kerry	Democratic	59,028,444 (48.3%)	251	
	Ralph Nader	Independent	465,650 (<1%)	—	
2008	**Barack Obama**	Democratic	69,456,897 (52.9%)	365	
	John McCain	Republican	59,934,814 (45.7%)	173	
2012	**Barack Obama**	Democratic	65,446,032 (51.0%)	332	57.5%
	Mitt Romney	Republican	60,589,084 (47.4%)	206	
	Gary Johnson	Libertarian	1,273,168 (<1.0%)		
	Jill Stein	Green	464,510 (<1.0%)		

[e]One District of Columbia Gore elector abstained.

SOURCE: Historical Election Results, Electoral College, National Archives and Records Administration

Glossary

affirmative action Policies designed to improve the educational and employment opportunities of historically underrepresented groups such as women and African Americans.

Affordable Care Act (ACA) Also known as Obamacare, this legislation, signed into law in 2010, was the largest overhaul of the U.S. health care system since the creation of Medicare and Medicaid in 1965. It sharply reduced the number of uninsured Americans and ended the previous practice of insurance companies charging higher premiums on the basis of preexisting conditions.

aliens Foreign-born residents of the United States who have not been naturalized as U.S. citizens.

al Qaeda A secret extremist organization established in the early 1990s that used terrorist tactics in pursuit of a backward-looking, absolutist form of Islamist government.

America First Committee A group that opposed Roosevelt's efforts to intervene in World War II against the Axis powers.

anarchists Persons who reject all forms of government as inherently oppressive and undesirable.

anti-semitism Prejudice against Jews.

assembly line A form of industrial production popularized by the Ford Motor Company in which workers perform one task repeatedly as the products they are jointly assembling move along a conveyor.

Axis Pact An alliance among Germany, Italy, and Japan during World War II.

baby boom The period of increased U.S. childbirths from roughly the early 1940s to the early 1960s.

"birds of passage" A term applied to immigrants who came to the United States for a brief period of time, and then returned to their home countries.

Black Codes Southern state laws passed after the Civil War to limit the rights and actions of newly liberated African Americans.

black power The slogan used by young black nationalists in the mid- and late 1960s.

bloody shirt A partisan rallying cry used to stir up or revive sectional or party animosity after the American Civil War; for example, post–Civil War Republicans "waved the bloody shirt," associating some Democrats with a treasonous acceptance of secession during the war, while opponents had spilled their blood for the Union.

Boland Amendments Acts of Congress passed to restrain Reagan's efforts to overthrow the Nicaraguan government.

Bolsheviks The Communist revolutionaries who seized power in Russia in 1917 and established the Union of Soviet Socialist Republics (USSR).

Boston marriages Unions of two women based on long-term emotional bonds in which the women live together as if married to each other.

braceros Mexican nationals working in the United States in low-wage jobs as part of a temporary work program between 1942 and 1964. (The bracero program was established by an executive agreement between the presidents of Mexico and the United States, providing Mexican agricultural labor in the Southwest and the Pacific Northwest.)

Bull Moosers Supporters of Theodore Roosevelt in the 1912 presidential election when he broke from the Republican party and ran as a third-party candidate on the ticket of the Progressive (or Bull Moose) party.

Camp David accords Agreements between Israel and Egypt, brokered by the United States, that gave Israel its first diplomatic recognition by an Arab state, and implied future autonomy for the Palestinian occupied territories.

capitalism The now almost worldwide economic system of private ownership of property and profit-seeking corporations.

carpetbaggers A negative term applied by Southerners to Northerners who moved to the South after the Civil War to pursue political or economic opportunities.

Carter Doctrine A presidential assertion, during the Carter administration, that the U.S. would defend the status quo in the Persian Gulf.

Chinese Exclusion Act Legislation passed by Congress in 1882 to deny any additional Chinese laborers entry into the country while allowing some Chinese merchants and students to immigrate.

Civil Rights Act of 1875 Congressional legislation that guaranteed black people access to public accommodations and transportation; the Supreme Court declared the measure unconstitutional in 1883.

civil service reform Measures designed to eliminate the spoils system in government hiring, in favor of maintaining professional standards in public service.

civil unions Relationships recognized by the state granting legitimacy and legal privileges to same-sex couples who are prohibited from legal marriage.

code talkers Navajo Marines who developed a code based on the Navajo language to transmit secret information.

Cold War The conflict and competition between the United States and the Soviet Union (and their respective allies) that emerged after 1945 and lasted until 1989.

colonialism The centuries-old system of mostly European nations controlling and governing peoples and lands outside of Europe.

communism A totalitarian form of government, grounded in the theories of German philosopher Karl Marx and the practices of revolutionary Vladimir Lenin in Russia, that eliminated private ownership of property in supposed pursuit of complete human equality; the system of government also featured a centrally directed economy and the absolute rule of a small group of leaders.

conservationists Advocates of conserving and protecting the natural world through the use of renewable natural resources.

conspicuous consumption A term coined by the American social theorist Thorstein Veblen to describe the behavior of wealthy persons who flaunt their status through their purchase of fine clothes, large houses, fancy cars, and other highly visible material goods.

consumer economy An economic system in which most people work for wages, which they use to purchase manufactured goods and foodstuffs.

containment The U.S. policy during the Cold War of trying to halt the expansion of Soviet and communist influences.

Contract with America A platform developed by Speaker of the House Newt Gingrich during the 1994 elections that outlined a series of conservative legislative goals endorsed by about 300 Republican congressional candidates.

Contras Counterrevolutionary guerrilla force organized by the CIA to try to overthrow the left-wing Sandinista government in Nicaragua.

Coxey's Army A mass protest march, numbering an estimated 5,000 persons, organized by Ohioan Jacob Coxey, who led his followers to Washington, D.C., to demand that the federal government enact relief measures in response to the depression that began in 1893.

détente The lessening of military or diplomatic tensions, as between the United States and the Soviet Union.

"Dollar Diplomacy" President William Howard Taft coined the term to refer to a policy that encouraged economic investment in foreign countries.

"don't ask, don't tell" A policy established by the Clinton administration allowing gays and lesbians to serve in the military so long as they do not disclose their sexual orientation.

Dust Bowl The plains regions of Oklahoma, Texas, Colorado, New Mexico, and Kansas affected by severe drought in the 1930s.

Edmunds Act Congressional legislation passed in 1882 and aimed at Utah Mormons; it outlawed polygamy, stripped polygamists of the right to vote, and provided for a five-member commission to oversee Utah's elections.

Eighteenth Amendment Allowed Congress to prohibit the production of alcoholic beverages, creating the period of Prohibition that lasted until 1933.

Entente The alliance of Britain, France, and Russia, later joined by Italy and the United States, during World War I.

Equal Rights Amendment (ERA) A proposed amendment to the U.S. Constitution that would have guaranteed equal rights for women.

Espionage and Sedition Acts Banned written and verbal dissent against U.S. participation in World War I, imperiling freedom of speech.

Exxon Valdez Oil tanker that ran aground in Alaska's Prince William Sound in March 1989, creating the second largest oil spill in American history.

family wage A level of income sufficient for an individual worker, usually a man, to support a spouse and family through a single salary.

fascism A form of right-wing dictatorship exalting nation and race above the individual.

feminism The belief that women and men are of equal value and that gender roles are, to a considerable degree, created by society rather than being simply natural.

fireside chats The broadcasts by President Franklin Delano Roosevelt during which he spoke directly to American families, often gathered around a radio in their living room.

flapper Young woman in the 1910s and 1920s who rebelled against the gender conventions of the era with respect to fashion and behavior.

foundling home A residence for orphaned children.

"Fourteen Points" speech Wilson's address to the world outlining U.S. aims for the postwar order.

Freedmen's Bureau Federal agency created by Congress in March 1865 and disbanded in 1869. Its purposes were to provide relief for Southerners who had remained loyal to the Union during the Civil War, to support black elementary schools, and to oversee annual labor contracts between landowners and field hands.

Free Silver The idea, popular among some groups in the late nineteenth century, that the United States should adopt an inflationary monetary policy by using both silver and gold as the nation's official currency.

free trade A system of economic relations characterized by the buying and selling of goods and services between nations with few or no taxes or tariffs to hinder that exchange. International economic relations characterized by multinational investment and a reduction or elimination of tariffs.

Ghost Dance A dance performed as part of a mystical vision of the future, a time free of disease and armed conflict, as offered by an Indian named Wovoka in 1889. Many of the Plains Indians who performed the dance fell into a trance-like state.

globalization The long-term process that continues to tie the world's regions more closely together economically and culturally through more unified systems of trade, travel, and communication.

global warming The accelerating process of climate change, driven in large part by human population growth and the burning of fossil fuels such as coal and oil.

gold standard A monetary system in which the standard of currency is tied to a fixed weight of gold; favored by creditors who support a "hard money" policy.

Grange An organization founded by Oliver H. Kelly in 1867 to represent the interests of farmers by pressing for agricultural cooperatives, an end to railroad freight discrimination against small farmers, and other initiatives. Its full name was National Grange of the Patrons of Husbandry.

Great Migration The movement of African Americans out of the South to northern cities, which accelerated during World War I.

Great Society In the 1960s, President Lyndon Johnson's programs for reducing poverty, discrimination, and pollution, and for improving health care, education, and consumer protection.

Harlem Renaissance A period in American history immediately following World War I (c. 1918–37) characterized by a surge of creativity in the literary, theatrical, musical, and visual arts among African Americans.

hayseeds A derogatory term applied to rural people deemed uneducated and naïve/(in contrast to self-proclaimed sophisticated city dwellers).

hobos Migrant workers or poor and homeless vagrants who traveled on trains from location to location, usually in search of employment.

Ho Chi Minh Communist leader of North Vietnam and nationalist hero to many dissidents in South Vietnam.

Holocaust The name given to the Nazi genocide against the Jews during World War II. Six million Jews were murdered.

Hoovervilles Shantytowns, named for President Hoover and occupied largely by people who lost their homes and farms during the Great Depression.

Hurricane Katrina The ferocious storm that swept on to the Gulf Coast in August 2005, killing over 1,800 people, primarily in Louisiana and Mississippi, and leaving much of New Orleans under water. The storm prompted a slow and ineffective response by the federal government under President George W. Bush.

impeach A formal process by which an official is accused of unlawful activity. The House of Representatives has the authority to bring such charges, and the Senate is required to place the official on trial and either convict or acquit.

imperialism The policy of extending a nation's authority by territorial acquisition (through negotiation or conquest) or by the establishment of political or economic control over other nations.

installment buying A system in which a consumer could make a down payment to purchase a product and then pay the remaining installments over time.

Internet A worldwide system of computer networks, established in the early 1990s, that allows for rapid global information transmission.

Islamist Pertaining to an ideology promoting the creation of governments based on a fundamentalist interpretation of Islamic law.

James Watt Reagan's controversial first Secretary of the Interior, whose anti-environmental views and abrasive personality made him a lightning rod for criticism.

Jim Crow The name given to the set of legal institutions that ensured the segregation of nonwhite people in the South.

Knights of Labor A secret fraternal order founded in 1869. Terence V. Powderly was the most influential leader of the Knights, which sponsored local labor-organizing drives among all kinds of workers, black and white and skilled and unskilled. Their motto was "an injury to one is an injury to all."

kickbacks Money paid illegally in return for favors (for example, to a politician by a person or business that has received government contracts).

laissez-faire A belief in little or no government interference in the economy.

lavender scare Official U.S. policies against homosexuals working for the government that resulted in hundreds of government employees losing their jobs.

League of Nations Created by the Treaty of Versailles as a forum for peaceful resolution of international problems in the future.

Love Canal Upstate New York site of environmental crisis over the deleterious effects of unregulated pollution from dumping of toxic chemical wastes.

mass consumption society The term refers to a shift in the early twentieth century from a society focused on frugality and production to one that embraced and celebrated consumer goods and leisure pursuits.

McCarthyism The political campaign led by Senator Joseph McCarthy (R-Wisconsin) to blame liberals at home for setbacks to U.S. interests abroad, due to what he considered liberals' sympathies with communism.

Medicaid Federal program of health care insurance for poor citizens.

Medicare Federal program of health care insurance for all citizens age 65 and older.

Mikhail Gorbachev Reformist leader of the Soviet Union from 1985 to 1991.

military-industrial complex The term given by President Dwight D. Eisenhower to describe the armed forces and the politically powerful defense industries that supplied arms and equipment to them.

Million Man March A demonstration organized by Nation of Islam Reverend Louis Farrakhan, which drew hundreds of thousands of black men to express their pride in manhood and fatherhood at a rally in Washington, D.C.

Moral Majority Conservative political organization of fundamentalist Christians organized in 1979 under Jerry Falwell's leadership.

most-favored-nation A designation allowing countries to export their products to the United States with tariffs no greater than those levied against most other nations.

muckrakers The name given to a group of investigative journalists in the early twentieth century whose exposés often challenged corporate and government power.

national security state The reorientation of the U.S. government and its budget after 1945 toward a primary focus on military and intelligence capabilities.

New Democrat Member of the Democratic party, many of them organized in the Democratic Leadership Council, who espouse center to center-right policies.

New Left Student-led reform movement—focused initially on poverty, racial injustice, and the threat of nuclear war—that was radicalized by the war in Vietnam.

New Nationalism Theodore Roosevelt's plan for a far-reaching expansion of the federal government to stabilize the economy and institute social reforms.

New South A term coined by Atlanta journalist Henry Grady in 1886 to suggest that the former Confederate states were now willing to embrace industrialization and modernization.

NSC-68 The 1950 directive of the National Security Council that called for rolling back, rather than merely containing, Soviet and communist influences.

Okie Migrant from Oklahoma who left the state during the Dust Bowl period in search of work.

Operation Desert Storm Successful 1991 effort by U.S.-led international military coalition to drive Iraqi forces out of Kuwait.

Osama bin Laden A wealthy, charismatic exile from Saudi Arabia who created al Qaeda, masterminded the September 11, 2001, attacks, and was eventually killed by U.S. Navy Seals in Pakistan in 2011.

pachucos Young Mexican American men who expressed attitudes of youthful rebellion in the 1940s. Many wore the zoot suit, also fashionable among urban African Americans.

Pendleton Act Congressional legislation passed in 1883; established a merit system for federal job applicants and created the Civil Service Commission, which administered competitive examinations to candidates in certain job classifications.

Pentagon Papers Internal study by the Defense Department of the history of the U.S. war in Vietnam, detailing misleading statements by U.S. leaders.

planned obsolescence A concept whereby producers intend for their products to eventually become obsolete or outdated and require replacement, thus perpetuating a cycle of production and consumption.

Platt Amendment A measure (1901) stipulating the conditions for the withdrawal of U.S. troops from Cuba at the end of the War of 1898. Ensured continued U.S. involvement in Cuban affairs, and affirmed U.S. claims to certain parts of the island, including Guantanamo Bay Naval Base.

Plessy v. Ferguson The 1896 case in which the Supreme Court decided that states could segregate public accommodations by race.

pocket veto An indirect veto of a legislative bill made when an executive (such as a president or governor) simply leaves the bill unsigned, so that it dies after the adjournment of the legislature.

political machines Groups that effectively exercise control over a political party, usually at the local level and organized around precincts and patronage.

Populists Agrarian reformers who formed the Populist, or People's party, a major (third) political party that emerged mostly in the Midwest and South in the late 1880s to address the needs of workers and farmers in opposition to government monetary policies and big business. The party faltered after its presidential candidate, William Jennings Bryan, lost in the 1896 election.

Progressivism A belief in the potential for progress through social reform that found expression in the Progressive Era, when political leaders and urban reformers sought to solve local and national problems through political and civic means.

race suicide A fear articulated by Theodore Roosevelt and others that the low birthrate of Anglo-Saxon Americans, along with the high birthrate of immigrants from southern and eastern Europe and elsewhere, would result in a population in which "inferior" peoples would outnumber the "American racial stock."

Reconstruction Act of 1867 An act that prevented the former Confederate states from entering the Union until they had ratified the Fourteenth Amendment and written new constitutions that guaranteed black men the right to vote. It also divided the South (with the exception of Tennessee, which had ratified the Fourteenth Amendment) into five military districts and stationed federal troops throughout the region.

Reconstruction era The twelve years after the Civil War when the U.S. government took steps to integrate the eleven states of the Confederacy back into the Union.

red lining Policies maintained by the Federal Housing Administration and lending banks which designated certain neighborhoods off limits to racial minorities.

Red Scare Post–World War I repression of socialists, communists, and other left-wing radicals ("Reds").

Roe v. Wade 1973 U.S. Supreme Court decision establishing the constitutionality of a woman's right to choose an abortion in the first six months of pregnancy.

Rosie the Riveter A heroic symbol of women workers on the homefront during World War II.

scakawags A negative term applied by southern Democrats after the Civil War to any white Southerner who allied with the Republican party.

Second New Deal The agenda of policies and programs initiated by President Franklin Delano Roosevelt beginning in 1935 that was intended to improve the lot of American workers while simultaneously preserving the capitalist system.

Sherman Anti-Trust Act Congressional legislation passed in 1890 outlawing trusts and large business combinations.

sit-down strike A strategy employed by workers agitating for better wages and working conditions in which they stop working and simply sit down, thus ceasing production and preventing strikebreakers from entering a facility to assume their jobs.

sit-in A form of civil disobedience in which activists sit down somewhere in violation of law or policy in order to challenge discriminatory practices or laws. The tactic originated during labor struggles in the 1930s and was used effectively in the civil rights movement in the 1960s.

Social Darwinism A late-nineteenth-century variation on the theories of British naturalist Charles Darwin, promoting the idea that only the "fittest" individuals will, or deserve to, survive (i.e., the idea that society operates on principles of evolutionary biology).

Social Gospel A reform movement around the end of the twentieth century that stressed the responsibility of religious organizations to remedy a wide range of social ills related to urban life.

social settlement house An institution (most but not all were located in cities) that offered various services to local impoverished populations, usually immigrants, as a means of assimilating them. Many settlement houses also served as meeting places for intellectuals, policy-makers, writers, and labor leaders who debated the relative worth of various kinds of social reform.

speakeasies Establishments where alcohol was illegally sold during the Prohibition era.

Sputnik The first artificial satellite to orbit the earth, launched by the Soviet Union in 1957.

stagflation Unprecedented combination in the mid-1970s of a stagnant economy (with high unemployment) and price inflation.

suburbs Areas on the outskirts of a city, usually residential. Suburbs expanded dramatically after World War II.

Sunbelt The band of states from the Southeast to the Southwest that experienced rapid economic and population growth during and after World War II.

Tet Offensive Communist military attacks across South Vietnam in January–February 1968.

theocracy A government by officials who are regarded as divinely guided.

Townsend Plan A proposal by Dr. Francis Townsend in 1934 for a 2 percent national sales tax that would fund a guaranteed pension of $200 per month for Americans older than age 60.

Tree sitting A strategy developed by Earth First! environmental activists in which individuals climb into trees that are threatened by the lumber industry in order to prevent the trees from being cut down for lumber.

Truman Doctrine President Truman's March 1947 speech articulating the new policy of containment.

trust A combination of firms or corporations created for the purpose of reducing competition and controlling prices throughout an industry.

U-boats German submarines in World War I that attacked civilian and officially neutral ships, helping bring the United States into the war.

vocational training Instruction, usually in manual or skilled trades, to prepare a student for future gainful employment.

War Powers Act 1973 law requiring the U.S. president to get Congressional approval within ninety days of sending U.S. troops into a conflict abroad.

Watergate The Washington, D.C., hotel-office complex where agents of President Nixon's reelection campaign broke into Democratic party headquarters in 1972. Nixon helped cover up the break-in, and the subsequent political scandal was referred to as "Watergate."

welfare reform Policies enacted that limited government aid to the poor, and dismantled the program of Aid to Families with Dependent Children, which had been in effect since 1935.

welfare state A nation in which the government provides a "safety net" of entitlements and benefits for citizens unable to economically provide for themselves.

Wobblies Members of the Industrial Workers of the World (IWW), a radical labor union formed in 1905.

women's suffrage The right of women citizens to vote, and the movement to win that right.

Wounded Knee Creek The site of a massacre of 150–250 South Dakota Indians by U.S. troops in 1890. This was the last violent encounter between Plains Indians and U.S. Cavalry forces.

yellow journalism Newspaper articles, images, and editorials that exploit, distort, or exaggerate the news in order to inflame public opinion.

zoot suits Distinctive clothing in the 1940s worn largely by Mexican American and African American men, characterized by flared pants, long coats, and wide-brimmed hats.

Text Credits

Chapter 15   page 384: M. C. Fulton to Brig. Gen. Davis Tillson, 17 April 1866, Unregistered Letters; **page 388:** Walt Whitman, Complete Prose Works: Specimen Days and Collect, November Boughs and Goodbye My Fancy. Library of Alexandria, 1901; **page 393:** John Muir, July 27, 1869; **page 394:** Frederick Douglass, 1871; **page 395, para 1:** Eunice Beecher; **page 395, para 3:** Frederick Douglass, 1868.

Chapter 16   page 406: Dodge City Times; **page 419:** Grover Cleveland, Message to the House of Representatives (16 February 1887); **page 420:** William Graham Sumner. What Social Classes Owe To Each Other, 1883, Harper; **page 421:** Taming the savage, New York Times (15 April 1875), 6.

Chapter 17   page 426: 1869, Labour Slogan; **page 430:** Frances Ellen Watkins Harper, speech, in Rachel F. Avery, ed., Transactions of the National Council of Women of the United States, assembled in Washington, D.C. on Feb. 22–25, 1891 (Philadelphia: J. B. Lippincott, 1891), 86–91. Reprinted in Gerda Lerner, The Female Experience: An American Documentary (Indianapolis: The Bobbs-Merrill Company, Inc., 1977), 355–357; **page 431:** E. B. Reynolds. Special United States Indian Agent, 1890; **page 432:** James Creelman. On the Great Highway. The Wanderings and Adventures of a Special Correspondent. Boston: Lothrop Publishing Co., 1901. 299-302; **page 436:** The Knights of Labor, 1896; **page 442-443:** L. L. Dalton, 1876.

Chapter 18   page 448: Frederick Jackson Turner's "Frontier Thesis". July 12, 1893; **page 451:** Ida B Wells-Barnett; Alfreda Duster. Crusade for justice: the autobiography of Ida B. Wells; **page 453:** John Hope, 1896; **page 456:** Frick to Carnegie, Oct. 31, 1892, quoted in David Brody, Steelworkers in America, The Nonunion Era (N.Y.: Harper & Row, Torchbooks ed., 1969), p. 53; **page 458:** Official Proceedings of the Democratic National Convention Held in Chicago, Illinois, July 7, 8, 9, 10, and 11, 1896, (Logansport, Indiana, 1896), 226–234. Reprinted in The Annals of America, Vol. 12, 1895–1904: Populism, Imperialism, and Reform (Chicago: Encyclopedia Britannica, Inc., 1968), 100–105; **page 461:** Theodore Roosevelt, The Winning of the West (1889–1896).

Chapter 19   page 474: Theodore Roosevelt; **page 475:** Theodore Roosevelt, 1904; **page 479:** Upton Sinclair, The Jungle (1905), Chapter Nine; **page 480:** "Leads her sisters out of bondage: chinese woman begins a crusade against social conditions in her country", San Francisco Chronicle, November 3, 1902 p. 7; **page 490:** "Biography: Clara Lemlich". Triangle Fire. PBS. Retrieved 11 May 2014.

Chapter 20   page 495, para 2, first quote: W.E.B. Du Bois. The Crisis. 1981; **page 495, para 2, second quote:** W.E.B. Du Bois. The Crisis. 1981; **page 504, para 1:** Eugene Debs, 1914; **page 504, para 4:** Secretary of State Robert Lansing; **page 508:** President Woodrow Wilson, Paris, March 1919; **page 513, Conclusion, first quote:** Warren G. Harding, The White House; **page 513, Conclusion, second quote:** Woodrow Wilson, 1920.

Chapter 21   page 517, para 2: President Calvin Coolidge, 1924; **page 517, para 4:** Equal Rights Amendment (ERA); **page 521:** Marcus Garvey, Amy Jacques Garvey. The Philosophy and Opinions of Marcus Garvey, Or, Africa for the Africans, Volume 1. The Majority Press, 1923; **page 522:** Herbert Hoover, 1928; **page 523:** President Herbert Hoover; **page 525:** Quoted in Valerie J. Matsumoto, Blake Allmendinger, William Andrews Clark. Over the Edge: Remapping the American West. University of California Press, 1999; **page 528:** Quoted in Daniel J. Kevles. In the Name of Eugenics: Genetics and the Uses of Human Heredity. University of California Press, 1985; **page 532:** Harry Crews. Classic Crews: A Harry Crews Reader. Simon and Schuster, 08-Oct-1993.

Chapter 22   page 540: Erminia Pablita Ruiz Mercer; **page 541:** Interview with Julia Luna Mount, November 17, 1983; **page 543:** John Steinbeck; Herman Finkelstein Collection (Library of Congress). The Grapes of Wrath, New York: The Viking Press, 1939; **page 547:** First inauguration of Franklin D. Roosevelt, 1933. **Page 548:** Quoted in Robert S. McElvaine, Down and Out in the Great Depression: Letters from the Forgotten Man, University of North Carolina Press, 2009.

Chapter 23   page 570: Howard Conner; **page 571:** Quoted in May, L. (2000). The big tomorrow: Hollywood and the politics of the American way. Chicago: University of Chicago Press. P.177; **page 572:** Quoted in Judy Barrett Litoff and David C. Smith. Since You Went Away. (New York: Oxford University Press, 1991) 157; **page 573:** W.E.B. Du Bois; **page 575:** Ichiro Imamura.

Chapter 24   page 585: Dean Acheson; **page 586, para 4:** U.S. State Department; **page 586, para 5:** Harry Truman. Friday, February 21, 1947, http://www.trumanlibrary.org/teacher/doctrine.htm; **page 594:** Quoted in Joshua Yates, James Davison Hunter, Thrift and Thriving in America: Capitalism and Moral Order from the Puritans to the Present, Oxford University Press, USA, 29-Jul-2011. p. 267.

Chapter 25   page 601, para 3, first quote: Richard M. Nixon. The Kitchen Debate. 24 July 1959. Vice President Richard Nixon and Soviet Premier Nikita Khrushchev, U.S. Embassy, Moscow, Soviet Union. CIA; **page 601, para 3, second quote:** Richard M. Nixon. The Kitchen Debate. 24 July 1959. Vice President Richard Nixon and Soviet Premier Nikita Khrushchev, U.S. Embassy, Moscow, Soviet Union. CIA; **page 603:** Dwight D. Eisenhower. Quoted in Crabgrass Frontier: The Suburbanization of the United States. Oxford University Press, 10-Oct-1985; **page 607:** Brown v. Board of Education of Topeka (1954); **page 608:** President Eisenhower; **page 611:** Charles Wilson. Quoted in John Mack Faragher. Out of many: a history of the American people. Prentice Hall, 1997; **page 616:** John Fitzgerald Kennedy; **page 617:** Inauguration of John F. Kennedy, January 20, 1961; **page 621:** John Fitzgerald Kennedy.

Chapter 26   page 625: Barry Goldwater, 1964.

Chapter 27   page 646, para 2: Spiro Agnew; **page 646, para 3:** Emily Howell Warner; **page 648:** Henry Kissinger, June 27, 1970; **page 658:** Jimmy Carter, University of Notre Dame-Address at Commencement Exercises at the University May 22, 1977; **page 662, para 2:** Equal Rights Amendment; **page 662, para 6:** Phyllis Schlafly.

Chapter 28   page 667: Herman García; **page 670, para 1:** Ronald Reagan; **page 670, para 2:** Ronald Reagan. Quoted in William Minter. King Solomon's Mines Revisited: Western Interests and the Burdened History of Southern Africa. William Minter, 01-May-1988; **page 670, para 3:** Ronald Reagan. Quoted in William Minter. King Solomon's Mines Revisited: Western Interests and the Burdened History of Southern Africa. William Minter, 01-May-1988; **page 676:** Robertson, Faludi. Quoted in

Edward R. Beauchamp. Comparative Education Reader. Psychology Press.

Chapter 29   page 693: Antonia Hernandez; **page 707, para 3:** Stephen Breyer; **page 707, para 5:** U.S. Civil Rights Commission.

Chapter 30   page 712: George W. Bush. April 2000: Bush Characterizes His Foreign Policy Experience; **page 715:** President Bush Delivers Graduation Speech at West Point United States Military Academy West Point, New York; **page 717, para 2:** Republican Senator Lindsey Graham; **page 717, para 3:** David Frum; **page 718:** Quoted in Barack Obama in Turkey: US 'will never be at war with Islam'. The Telegraph.

Source for all Maps unless otherwise noted: © Pearson Education, Inc.

Index